AN INTRODUCTION TO SOCIAL PSYCHOLOGY

AN INTRODUCTION TO SOCIAL PSYCHOLOGY

HENRY CLAY LINDGREN
SAN FRANCISCO STATE COLLEGE

JOHN WILEY AND SONS, INC. NEW YORK LONDON SYDNEY

The photograph on the front and back covers and the photograph on the title page are by Erich Hartmann, Magnum.

This book is dedicated to the memory of

GORDON S. IERARDI

Preface

The purpose of this book is twofold: first, to introduce the student to the field of social psychology; and second, to present him with some perspectives whereby he may develop a better understanding both of his social environment and its relationship to him and his behavior.

The first of these objectives is obvious. Introductory textbooks are expected to introduce students to whatever their special area happens to be. A casual perusal of such textbooks, however reveals a variety of approaches. This is true among introductory texts in social psychology, as well as in any number of fields. Such variety in approaches is a reflection of the diversity that exists among authors with respect to their philosophies of teaching as well as to the material they believe is important.

What an author hopes a book will do for students determines what material he chooses to cover, and this leads to the second of my objectives: that of trying to help students understand their relationship to their social environment. An author who writes a book for a course that is a rigorous proving ground for would-be research workers in behavioral-science laboratories will select material that is heavily oriented toward research. The author who hopes that students will go on to become well-organized social theoreticians will select somewhat different material. For my part, I am concerned with providing something for both types of students, but I am also aware that taken all together such students constitute a minority of those who enroll in introductory courses in social psychology. Some students, to be sure, have their sights already set on the PhD in social psychology, but their number is matched or even exceeded by those who are not sure whether this field or some other is the one they will want to specialize in. Probably the greater number of the students enrolled in introductory social psychology in most colleges and universities do not, for the moment at least, have any intention of doing graduate work in any field, and are enrolled in the course because it sounds interesting and relevant. In my opinion, most introductory textbooks in most fields treat this latter type of student as a kind of second-class citizen and are instead preoccupied with meeting the needs of the potential graduate student. I come to this conclusion not so much because of the detailed coverage introductory textbooks give to research and theory, but rather because they generally omit discussion of the relevance of either research or theory for life outside the laboratory. In so doing they overlook the fact that for most students, whatever they study has relevance primarily in terms of their own experience.

It is because of my interest in helping students of all types perceive this relevance that I have oriented my approach to social psychology in the direction of the kinds of experiences and interests they are likely to have.

I have drawn upon research studies that have more than the usual amount of relevance for students, have included anecdotal material, and have introduced comments and even speculations about the possible meaning of psychological research findings, especially where several studies present contradictory findings. I have attempted to do this while still giving judicious coverage to the topics that are included in most introductory social psychology textbooks. Showing proper appreciation for the work of my colleagues in social psychology as well as respect for the interests and background of students is an admittedly difficult task, and the reader will have to decide for himself how successful I have been.

For myself, the writing of this book has been an interesting and stimulating experience. Working and living in a variety of cultures and contexts in and out of the United States, as well as in and out of the academic world, have given me a special appreciation how theories and research findings of social psychologists can aid our understanding of the problems and issues in everyday life. This appreciation has led me to specialize in social psychology both as a researcher and as a teacher. Teaching in particular has given me an opportunity to share some of my interest and enthusiasm for the field, and my quest for better ways of understanding and presenting material led me to write this book.

Some of this excitement has also involved my wife, Fredi, who has worked with me as a colleague in the thinking and research that has gone into this book. I am particularly indebted to her for her work in preparing the manuscript. I would also like to express my appreciation for the suggestions of David S. Dustin, of the State University of New York at Plattsburgh, who read and commented on the manuscript during its development. The critical comments and encouragement of Daniel Katz, of the University of Michigan were especially helpful. Among my own colleagues at San Francisco State College, I have been aided and stimulated by interchange of ideas with Joseph Luft, Daniel Adler, Marcelle Kardush, Herbert Naboisek, Dorothy Westby-Gibson, Philburn Ratoosh, Shepard Insel, and Walcott H. Beatty.

Henry Clay Lindgren

San Francisco State College

Contents

tudes. Types of measures. *The Authoritarian Personality:* The Berkeley Study. Further research on authoritarian attitudes. *Social Motives Considered as Needs:* The achievement motive. Crossvalidation of n Ach research. N Ach is entrepreneurial work. Task-orientation and n Ach. Childhood experiences and n Ach. Crosscultural studies of n Ach. Historical developments and n Ach. The significance of n Ach as a social motive. *Summary. Suggested Readings.*

gressiveness. Interest in social interaction. Instinct. Culture. Biological determinants. Interaction between social learning and biology. Status. The merging of sex roles. *Conflicts in Roles:* Conflicts for men. Conflicts for women. Role conflicts in organizations. Role conflict for the "hasher." Compartmentalization. *Summary. Suggested Readings.*

responsibility. The irrelevancy of external factors. *Social Climate:* Perceptual set. The leader's effect on climate. Roles and expectations. *Types of Groups:* Primary and secondary groups. Formal and informal groups. Exclusive and inclusive groups. In-groups and out-groups. Membership groups and reference groups. The measurement and analysis of group interaction. *Summary. Suggested Readings.*

Groups vs. individuals in problem solving. Improving the functioning of groups through democratic leadership. Improving the functioning of groups through structure. *Centralized and Decentralized Group Structure. Cooperation and Competition:* Formalized cooperation. Cooperation in problem-solving groups. Cooperation, competition, and group feeling. *Cooperation and Competition in Two-Person Games:* The "trucking game." *Summary. Suggested Readings.*

Functions of Leaders: Definitions of leadership. Leadership and the power to influence. Power and prestige. The transferability of leadership. *Types of Leaders and Categories of Leadership:* The administrator. The bureaucrat. The policy-maker. The expert. The ideologist. The charismatic leader. The political leader. The symbolic leader. The parent figure. The leader as a target for hostility. *Characteristics of Leaders:* Salience. Intelligence. Adjustment. Deviancy. Social distance. *Structure Initiation versus Consideration in Leaders:* The Hawthorne study. The International Harvester study. Leaders' attitudes toward their "least preferred co-workers." *Leaders as Facilitators of Social Learning:* The leader as a model. The leader as a participant. The leader's effect on self-regarding attitudes. Effect of the group on the leader. *Summary. Suggested Readings.*

Organizational Structure: Characteristics of organizations. Bureaucracies. Types of organizations. *Psychological Needs Met through Organizations:* Satisfactions in employment. Managerial satisfactions. Styles of orientation toward group life. *Organizations as Systems of Communication:* Communication as a function of status. Communication and organization size. Communication and influence. Integrating subgroups into the organization. Autonomy, productivity, and job satisfaction. *Organizational Change:* The persistence of traditional patterns. Improvement in human relations. Group decisions method. T-groups, sensitivity training, and therapy groups. *Summary. Suggested Readings.*

Movement toward, away from, or against others. Hostility and aggression. Hostility and outsiders. Biological bases of aggression. The perception of threat. The stimulus value of violence and aggression. The effect of the culture on hostility and aggression. Institutionalized and personal forms of aggression. *Prejudice and Intergroup Hostility:* The nature of prejudice. Perceived difference as the basis for prejudice. Vulnerability as the basis for aggression. The prejudice of the passive observer. Prejudice, hostility, and aggression as "normal" behavior. *Intergroup Conflict:* The perception of external threat. Coping with hostility through catharsis. Coping with hostility through social learning. Social norms and the control of aggression. Norms for international behavior. *Summary. Suggested Readings.*

CHAPTER ONE

The Problems and Methods of Social Psychology

Psychology and Social Problems. The most perplexing problems faced by man today are *social*[1] problems. This statement appears to be valid no matter which of man's many problems we choose to deal with.

Let us test this proposition by assuming that biological survival is the chief problem facing man. We have solved the technological problems of producing and distributing food, shelter, and clothing, but have not worked out the social problems well enough to satisfy the reasonable needs of more than a third or so of the world's population. One difficulty is that the rate of population increase among the most deprived groups keeps well ahead of the world's ability to supply their reasonable needs. This is a social problem. Survival is also conditional on man's ability to restrain his aggressive impulses, and some people believe that the abolition of war is man's major unresolved problem. The prevention of war and the waging of peace are also social problems.

Perhaps man's chief problem is not biological survival, but the more philosophical and existential one of learning to live with himself. Man does not exist, however, as an isolate in time and space, because he is a product of his relations with others and must be understood in those terms if he is to be understood at all. Hence, living with oneself is also a social problem.

There are many other ways of stating man's most pressing problems, but no matter which statement we prefer, its main dimensions will turn out to be social in nature: the causes and the results of individuals and groups interacting with one another. The fact that the behavior of individuals is involved makes these problems of interest to psychologists, and the particular branch of psychology concerned with the relationship between social interaction and the behavior of individuals is social psychology.

If such problems are to be resolved, or if they are to be coped with at all, it follows that strategies based on an understanding of the factors concerned will be more successful than strategies based on guesswork, impulse, or irrelevancy. An understanding of any problem would obviously be useful to the extent that it is relevant, accurate, and complete. Accuracy and completeness describe the kind of knowledge and understanding that scientists strive for. Evidence of the value of scientists' contributions can be seen all around us, especially in the products of modern technology. Man today is the master of his physical environment to an extent that few in past ages thought would be possible, and this mastery has come about through the understanding provided by the physical and natural sciences.

The work of the physical and natural scientists is, unfortunately, only indirectly relevant to the understanding of the social aspects of man's problems. There are significant gaps between our biochemical understanding of man's behavior and the understanding required to explain his social behavior. Social psychologists are working to bridge this gap, but they work only occasionally with physiological psychologists on the same research problems. On the other hand, there is relatively good communication and a sharing of information between the two branches of psychology, and techniques developed in experimental psychology are used extensively by social psychologists.

Information regarding the interaction between social forces and man's behavior has accumulated rapidly, particularly since World War II. Unfortunately, this growing body of information has had little effect on the policies or practices of those

[1] The term *social*, as used by psychologists and other behavioral scientists, refers to interaction among individuals and/or groups, as well as to the influence of individuals and/or groups on one another.

3

who play leading roles in the task of coping with the major problems of mankind. This gap between information and practice is due partly to the fact that many explanations are at present incomplete or limited in scope, making it difficult for people to determine how they may be applied to social problems. There are, however, other sources of reluctance on the part of the general public and its leaders.

Common Sense and the Conventional Wisdom. Generally speaking, people prefer to deal with human problems on the basis of what is ordinarily called "common sense" or what John Kenneth Galbraith (1958) has termed "the conventional wisdom."

In this textbook we shall use these two terms interchangeably to refer to the beliefs about human behavior that people ordinarily turn to when they have to make decisions or predictions involving others. "Common sense" usually refers to a body of information derived from mature experience and carries implications of hardheadedness and objectivity. The term can, however, be used by anyone or any group to justify a wide range of actions, some of them quite irrational. Common sense is used, for example, to justify the execution of murderers, because it predicts that this will discourage crime. Data show, however, that such is not the case. There is little difference in the murder rate in states that execute murderers and those that do not; hence the "common sense" of those who support capital punishment must be based on some consideration other than objective evidence. What this other consideration might be is of course a major concern in this book, but the point here is that "common sense" is hardly an infallible basis for making decisions and predictions about human behavior and may actually serve to conceal the decision maker's real motives from himself.

Galbraith uses the term "conventional wisdom" to apply to widely accepted beliefs that may have represented an advance in thinking some time in the past but are no longer valid and appropriate.

The fact that such beliefs lack current validity has no bearing on the degree to which they are accepted. The conventional wisdom of the eighteenth century held that a nation's wealth is represented by its store of gold bullion, although traders in England and the Low Countries had demonstrated that the way to wealth lay through freedom in trade. Adam Smith formulated the principles of free trade in his treatise, *The wealth of nations,* a book that was rejected and ridiculed at the time as being contrary to what everyone "knew"—that is, the conventional wisdom. In due time Smith's ideas about free trade were accepted by economists and assumed the status of a kind of conventional wisdom of their own. As Galbraith points out, conventional wisdom tends to outlive the events that made it valid and becomes cherished and defended by the multitude at the very moment when events call for an entirely new approach.

Galbraith's examples are drawn from the field of economics, but similar examples could be found in other areas of human behavior as well. Psychologists and the other behavioral scientists are continually testing premises based on common sense and the conventional wisdom. Often they are found to be valid, but sometimes the evidence disproves them and new principles are propounded. When this occurs, there is a long lag between the discovery of the new principle and its acceptance as part of the conventional wisdom. An example of this may be found in the research conducted in the Western Electric plant at Hawthorne, Illinois, during the late 1920's and early 1930's. The conventional wisdom of that day held that employees were motivated almost solely by the prospect of monetary gain. The Hawthorne studies showed, on the contrary, that social motives were at least as significant as economic ones, and perhaps even more so. It has taken more than thirty years for these findings to become accepted as part of the conventional wisdom of employers, and the process of assimilation is still incomplete.

Galbraith suggests that "the conventional wisdom" becomes a kind of rallying point for those who resist advanced ideas in the area of social behavior. Making decisions that involve other people can be, and often is, rather stressful and anxiety provoking. When we are anxious, we prefer to use "tried and true" methods and to have clear-cut, uncomplicated reasons for doing what we have decided to do. "Common sense" and "the conventional wisdom" have the virtues of being familiar, comfortable, and formulated in relatively simple terms. Inasmuch as the beliefs incorporated into what we know as "common sense" represent our understanding of human behavior, we feel committed to it and even defensive about it. People have, as Galbraith says, such a vested interest in this understanding that they react with something like a religious passion whenever it happens to be challenged. It is partly for this reason that scientists have come to mistrust the validity of "common sense" and prefer instead theories, formulations, principles, and information based on the result of inquiries conducted along scientific lines.

An example of a study disproving common-sense predictions is one conducted by Ewart E. Smith (1961) for the Quartermaster of the United States Army, who was interested in getting some ideas about methods of changing the attitudes of Army personnel toward various foods. Smith developed an experimental situation in which Army reservists were asked to eat fried grasshoppers. Some were asked by an affable, agreeable instructor and some by an instructor who was formal, cool, and official in his manner. Common sense would have predicted that the friendly instructor would be able to induce more attitude change toward the strange food, but actually the greatest amount of attitude change was obtained by the formal, cool instructor, a finding that had been predicted by the experimenter on the basis of cognitive dissonance theory (discussed in Chapter 7). The point we wish to make is that psychological theory provided a better basis for

production in this situation than did common sense.

Social Psychology as a Science. Social psychology today is a science, in the sense that it represents the results of inquiries carried out according to methods accepted by scientists, as well as the ongoing process of making such inquiries. It is a science by virtue of the fact that it accepts the discipline of science—that is, data must be gathered precisely, objectively, and under carefully controlled conditions, to the end that they produce results similar to those that would be obtained by other scientists using the same approach and the same methods.

Research in social psychology begins, as does research in other scientific disciplines, with questions that become testable hypotheses, and, if investigation shows hypotheses to be valid, the resultant findings become the bases for making predictions. The specific ways in which social psychologists carry out research will be taken up later in this chapter. Here we only show how the procedure of social psychologists differs from that of people who use common sense or the conventional wisdom as bases for making predictions about behavior.

It follows from this discussion that although social psychologists are concerned with the same phenomena—behavior—that laymen are, they approach them in a much different way and may make predictions that are at variance with the predictions of laymen. This does not mean that all lay interpretations and predictions are invalid, but it does mean that such predictions are suspect, as far as the social psychologist is concerned, until they have been put to the scientific test. The prediction that people who have similar values will associate with one another is consistent with common sense and appears in the old saw "Birds of a feather flock together." This prediction can be and actually has been verified experimentally, as we show in Chapter 3. Common sense, however, would probably *not* predict that people would find similarity in values a more significant basis for attraction than racial similarities; yet research shows that even highly prejudiced whites find Negroes whose values are similar to theirs more attractive than whites whose values are markedly different (Byrne & Wong, 1962). This is only one of many instances in the book where psychological research disconfirms the predictions of common sense and the conventional wisdom.

The Price of Ignoring Social Factors: the Green Bank Episode. Perhaps one of the most common errors made by people who use common sense as a basis for predictions is that of ignoring social factors altogether. In 1956 a committee of radio astronomers, working under the auspices of the National Science Foundation, an agency of the Federal government, decided to locate the National Radio Astronomy Observatory near the village of Green Bank, West Virginia. This decision was made on the basis of atmospheric conditions, freedom from radio broadcast interference, and other physical criteria relative to the successful operation of a radio observatory. The observatory was built as planned, and a small colony of some 90 resident scientists and technicians was recruited and settled, with their families, in special housing near the observatory.

It soon became evident that the planning committee had overlooked some important social psychological factors in selecting Green Bank as the location for the observatory. Green Bank is high in the Appalachian Mountains near the Virginia–West Virginia border. Its population is about 250, and the nearest approximation to an urban center is the county seat of Marlington, population 1500, located thirty miles away. Elkins, a town of 8000, is fifty miles away; Charlottesville, Virginia, is 100 miles away; Charlestown, West Virginia, is 170 miles; and Washington, D.C., is more than 200 miles away. These mileages do not tell the whole story, because the mountainous terrain makes driving difficult. It takes about $2\frac{1}{2}$ hours to drive to Char-

lottesville, the nearest airport, and a trip to Washington takes five to six hours.

Several problems developed, but the major one was the attitudes of the scientists and their families toward the community. They found, first of all, that they had no one to socialize with but themselves, and that going to Charlottesville, which has a population of only 29,000, was like escaping to the outside world. Not only did the men miss contacts with people outside their field, but the women missed shopping and complained about the limited educational facilities for their children. As reports of life in Green Bank spread among scientists in other parts of the country, it became increasingly difficult to recruit personnel for the observatory, and the decision was finally made to move the majority of the staff to Charlottesville (Langer, 1965).

Although hindsight is easier than foresight, it does appear that at least some of the problems encountered by the observatory staff and their families could have been anticipated by social psychologists. A considerable amount of data has been accumulated by psychologists and other behavioral scientists showing that man is an integrated part of his social environment. Common sense tends to overlook or to minimize the importance of this relationship. Decisions made daily by administrators in government and business assume that Mr. A will have the same capacity to produce for his employer irrespective of whether he is permitted to stay in Salt Lake City, where he had worked for the last five years, or whether he is transferred to Washington, Key West, or Coos Bay, Oregon. There is a common tendency to overlook the fact that Mr. A's competence on the job is to a large extent affected by his attitudes toward it and toward his employers. These attitudes, in turn, are influenced by all segments of his social environment, and particularly by the attitudes and feelings of Mrs. A. Mr. A may or may not perform as adequately in Key West as he did in Salt Lake City, but it is a mistake to assume that his feelings toward his job, his employer, his future, and his everyday experiences will be the same in both places. The more unfamiliar the new environment, the greater the dislocation will be.

In the Green Bank episode it is quite likely that many of the scientist-administrators believed that astronomers would do an even *better* job in Green Bank, because there would be less interference in the form of the "outside disturbances" ordinarily found in an urban area. The common-sense idea that "the fewer the distractions, the better the job" has some short-range validity, but it overlooks the fact that once the day's (or night's) work is over, even dedicated scientists find distractions pleasantly stimulating.

Social Psychology and General Psychology. All psychology is concerned directly or indirectly with the behavior of the individual organism, and it is this focus on the individual that puts the "psychology" into "social psychology." Social psychology differs from other branches of psychology in its emphasis as well as the scope of its investigation and theory building. There is admittedly some overlap between social psychology and other specialties in the general field of psychology. Robert J. Zajonc (1966) points out that psychologists interested in problems of learning study behavior as influenced by practice and reinforcement; psychologists interested in perception study behavior as modified by changes in physical stimuli; whereas psychologists interested in motivation are concerned with antecedent states of deprivation or arousal in the organism. Although these psychologists are all in different fields, they may nevertheless study the same set of responses. A rat's turning left in a T-maze, for instance, may be studied in terms of the number of reinforced trials (learning), the physical properties of the maze's left or right arm (perception), or the animal's hunger level (motivation). But if all these variables are held constant, and we observe the rat turning left when there is a

second rat in the right arm of the maze, we become, as Zajonc puts it, social psychologists.

Social psychology is concerned with the behavioral processes, causal factors, and results of interaction* among persons and groups. Interaction may be investigated either as an on-going event or in terms of antecedent or subsequent events. Any or all of these types of events may be studied on three different levels or dimensions: individual behavior, interpersonal behavior, and group behavior. It is not always clear which level or dimension is being studied. When we say that a certain group rates high in responsibility, we may be talking about the value system of the individuals (first level) who comprise the group. If this value system is reflected in the social behavior of the members, as it is likely to be, it will very probably appear in some form characteristic of the group members as they interact with one another and with people who are nonmembers (second level). If such behavior is indeed characteristic of the group, it will be what is termed a "social norm." It is also quite possible that when this group interacts as a group with other groups (third level) its behavior is still characterized by a high level of responsibility. Hence, to say that a group's behavior is marked by a high degree of responsibility (or any other behavioral trait) is to suggest something about behavior at all three levels.

Levels of Social Behavior

Individual Behavior. The behavior of individuals may be studied in terms of the attitudes, values, beliefs, and habits characteristic of certain individuals or of individuals-in-general. Social psychologists are likely to be more interested in individuals-in-general, because they are inter-

---

* The term *interaction* is used in social psychology to refer to the mutual or reciprocal way in which individuals and/or groups influence one another's behavior, whereby the behavior of an individual or group becomes a stimulus that evokes responses from others.

ested in human behavior in general. An understanding of the general principles of human behavior enables us to make better predictions about individuals, whereas an analysis of the behavior of a single individual may yield data relevant only to that individual. Slight differences or changes in behavior on the part of one or two individuals may have little value, as far as developing any general theories of behavior are concerned, but small variations may assume a high degree of significance if displayed by all or most people in a rather large sample. Social psychologists, like other behavioral scientists, are continually on the alert for indications of basic trends and consistencies in human behavior, and such trends are usually revealed more accurately or reliably by observing sizable samples of individuals rather than a few isolated individuals.

Let us say that we are interested in what happens to the attitudes of students who attend college and decide to focus on changes in bigotry. For the purpose of our study, we select samples of 100 members of each freshman class entering a university for five successive years. Nine years later, when we terminate our data gathering, we find that the students made a mean score of 50 on our bigotry scale when they were freshmen, and 45 when they were seniors. If instead of reporting our results for the combined group of students we had reported the results for each student separately, the result would be somewhat confusing, for we would have a random list of 500 paired scores. In some instances the scores made as seniors would be higher than those made as freshmen, in some instances lower, and in other instances the same. The mean or average score for the combined group is really a composite score of the individuals who comprise the group. Furthermore, a mean drop of five points might be overlooked if all scores for individuals were reported separately, but computing a pair of statistics that represents the composite attitudinal status of the groups at two points in time enables us to recognize that a change has probably taken place among most of the individuals in the group. By computing the necessary statistics, we can even determine the statistical significance of the observed difference. In any event, we should recognize that our scores primarily reflect changes in behavior at the first or individual level and are only indirectly related to interpersonal or intergroup behavior.

It is common practice in social psychology, as well as in other branches of psychology, to report findings based on samples consisting of a number of subjects, rather than on separate individuals. In the example given, social psychologists are likely to be more interested in the fact that the bigotry scores of, say, half the students declined, rather than the fact that a third actually increased. The students showing increases might be useful as subjects in another kind of study— one undertaken to determine, for example, the characteristics of students who show countertrend changes and become more bigoted during their stay in college. But even such research would be concerned with the discovery of general principles rather than with the highly individual or unique experiences of a series of students, because the object of such a study would be that of finding out what general conditions (for example, child-rearing experiences) are related to the behavior of students who become more bigoted when exposed to the kinds of forces that cause most students to become less bigoted.

We should also note that the prediction of behavior for an individual is more hazardous than prediction for a group, even when we have data based on normative trends. Again referring to the foregoing example, we would predict that another freshman class going through the same university would become less bigoted during the four-year period. If conditions had not changed very much (same faculty, same curriculum, and a relatively stable political environment), the results should be somewhat the same. Suppose the original study actually had shown that one-third of the freshman class increased their bigotry scores. This would lead us to predict that a sizable minority of the new freshman class would also show an increase in scores. Richard Whitmore is a freshman in an incoming class. If his class has approximately the same experience as the classes that took part in the study, we might rate his chances of becoming less bigoted as 50 per cent, becoming more bigoted as 33 per cent, and showing no change as 17 per cent. But unless further research has turned up data to suggest why some students resist the antibigotry trend, we cannot really say with very much confidence into which of the three groups he will fall. However, we can predict with a great deal more assurance that the members of this year's freshman class will show a decline in bigotry.

None of this should prevent us from using the data of social psychology to understand, explain, and predict the behavior of individuals. Predicting the behavior of individuals is a necessary part of everyday experience, and the better understanding we have of the principles that affect behavior, the better our chances are of making correct predictions. When we write a letter to a hotel, requesting a reservation, we predict that our letter will be answered. Knowing something about the attitudes and values of hotel managers, we enhance the validity of that prediction by typing a neat letter and phrasing it in a businesslike tone. If we are making reservations at small provincial French hotels, we draw on our intercultural fund of information and decide to write our letters in French, because we can predict that letters in English might be ignored. To return to our bigotry study, if we are talking to a freshman and a senior in the university in question, we might expect the senior to be more "open" in talking about matters relating to religious and racial minorities. There is a good chance that our predictions are valid, but we should nevertheless be alert to the possibility that either or both of the two students we are addressing may not be representative of the main trend in their classes.

Another way of stating this is to say that the individual about whom we are supplied with data by the research of social psychologists is not a real person. Instead he is a fictitious "everyman" —the "person" who represents the collection of individuals described in the research in question. The "person" may also be "everyman" in a much broader sense, when social psychologists construct theories relating to general behavioral trends.

A similar generalization holds true with respect to "the self." The "self as a psychological construct" certainly refers to the individual, but it refers again to "everyman." What we know about "everyman" is nevertheless useful in developing self-understanding. Each of us is like all others, like some others, and like no others (Kluckhohn, Murray, and Schneider, 1953). It is to the extent that a given individual resembles all others and some others that theory and research in social psychology can aid in understanding his behavior.

Interpersonal Behavior. It is within the interaction between ourselves and other individuals that the most significant events of our lives are likely to occur. These are the events that bring us joy or sorrow, that shape our behavior and help make us the persons we are today, and that give life most of whatever meaning it has for us. As we shall show, groups (societies, cultures, nations, organizations) also have a significant effect on our lives, but this influence is usually expressed in the form of an interpersonal event. The beliefs and values that determine individual behavior are to a large degree derived from the culture, but they must all be learned. The process of learning them from agents of the culture (parents, friends, authority figures) takes place in every instance in the form of interpersonal events. Even the impersonal tone of a form letter from the draft board does not keep it from being an interpersonal event—an interpersonal transaction, to be exact. It is, after all, from a real person who represents a real group of people, and it is addressed to another real person.

Social influence is two-way process. Just as groups influence individuals through interpersonal transactions, the influence that individuals exert on groups also takes place interpersonally. Groups are, after all, composed of individuals, and changes in the belief systems of individuals are likely to reflect themselves in changes in group behavior.

Social psychologists are interested in studying all aspects of interpersonal events: antecedents and results, as well as the attitudes and other motivational states of the actors in the event; and the results may also be reflected in attitudes and feelings that lead to further interpersonal actions. Interpersonal events may also be studied in terms of the kinds of action taken: acceptance, rejection, aggression, love, avoidance, or whatever. Interpersonal events may also be viewed in terms of categories of behavior, for example, as communication processes, as indications of social learning, or from the standpoint of cooperation or competition.

Group Behavior. The smallest type of group, a dyad, consists of two persons. At this level of analysis, behavior is rather obviously at the interpersonal level. The dyad may nevertheless be studied in terms of its rather special characteristics as a group. Two people acting together are likely to behave in different ways than the same two people separately. If we study their behavior in terms of each individual's relationship to the other, we are likely to consider it from the standpoint of interpersonal behavior, but if we are concerned with the particular characteristics of dyads, we have moved to another level of social interaction and are considering their actions as a form of group behavior.

People seem to have an overriding need to associate with others, and this need can be met most efficiently within the context of groups. We can identify certain patterns of behavior that function to enable groups to maintain themselves and to satisfy the needs of their members. Among these patterns are social norms that govern the behavior of group members; conformity to such norms is the price that members must pay in order to enjoy the advantages of associating with others in groups. Social psychologists study norms in terms of how they develop, how they influence the behavior of individual members, and how they affect interpersonal behavior.

There are many different levels of group interaction, each of which sets special conditions for behavior. The degree of personal involvement felt by individual members also affects behavior and may vary with the size of the group, as well as with its character. Active participation is generally easier in smaller groups than in larger ones; hence there is often a tendency for people to become involved in groups in which they can interact on a face-to-face basis. This does not always hold true, because contrary patterns may be learned in some cultures. In more traditional cultures, people are likely to feel the highest degree of commitment to their family, which is a face-to-face or primary group. This commitment may be higher than their commitment to their nation, as is indicated by the fact that members of their family have more influence on their behavior than do officials of their government. In more industrialized cultures the individual's commitment is likely to be more diffuse; employers, various levels of government, and voluntary organizations tend to absorb more of the commitment that individuals in more primitive cultures feel toward their families, and in certain instances the demands of the larger group may be given a higher degree of priority than family demands. A personnel officer in a Mediterranean or Latin American bank would feel duty-bound to give his brother a job, even though the latter rated fifth or sixth in a list of applicants, whereas a person occupying a similar position in Northern Europe or in North America would be more inclined to hire the best man.

History of Social Psychology

Early Beginnings. It is difficult to set any beginning point for social psychology. It can perhaps be said to have begun when man first developed symbolic terms to deal with his relations with others, which undoubtedly occurred in prehistoric times. The word "social" itself comes from the Latin *socialis*, which has roots that go back as far as linguistic history can take us—to Sanskrit, in which the word *sacati* means "he follows or accompanies." *Sacati* is, in turn, related to words in Greek and the Romance languages that have to do with association, following, sharing, and similar concepts.

The appearance of civilization, as indicated by the construction of cities, is said to have taken place in the valley of the Tigris and Euphrates Rivers. The stability and success of these early settlements was undoubtedly assured by the fact that their people had developed a written language enabling them to record social norms in the form of laws and regulations. These laws were codified about 2000 B.C. and issued by the reigning king, Hammurabi, in what is probably the first social document. The Code of Hammurabi is particularly notable in that it promulgated a social order based on the rights of the individual, as protected by the authority of the state. It doubtless influenced the formulation of laws included in the first five books of the Bible, which appeared about the first millenium before the present era. The relationship between the individual and society also interested the Greeks, especially the Athenians. The chief figures here are Solon, whose code of laws was a marked step in the direction of democracy, and Plato and Aristotle, who both wrote on political matters.

Concern about man's relation to man appears in the writings of many philosophers and theologians during the centuries that followed. The eloquent statement of John Donne (1572–1631) about man's social identity is only one example. The British philosophers of the seventeenth and eighteenth centuries speculated about the motives of social behavior: Thomas Hobbes about power, Adam Smith about self-interest, and Jeremy Bentham about pleasure.

The Appearance of Sociology. All this, however, was preliminary to the appearance of social psychology as a field. Auguste Comte, the French mathematician and philosopher, writing about the middle of the nineteenth century, stated that he was going to write a treatise on social psychology (*Le système de morale positive*), but he died before he could carry out this intention. He is also credited with being the founder of sociology; his *Système de politique positive* expounds the view that man is both the cause and the consequence of society. Later in the century, other scholars began to subject social behavior to a scientific scrutiny. Charles Darwin included social forms of behavior in his *Descent of man* (1871), and in 1893, Herbert Spencer published his *Study of sociology*. The next few decades saw a great deal of activity on the part of sociologists. Gustave Le Bon published his classic book on crowds and their behavior in 1895. Both he and Emile Durkheim maintained that human behavior is dominated by a "group mind." Charles Horton Cooley and George Herbert Mead, both American sociologists, disputed this idea and developed theories with respect to the development of "the self," which in turn contributed to the self-theories that personality psychologists proposed during the 1940's and 1950's.

Contributions of Psychologists. We have given particular emphasis to the work of sociologists, inasmuch as psychologists played only a minor part in the early development of social psychology. The first psychologists to show an interest in social behavior were Heymann Steinthal and Moritz Lazarus who were active in developing "folk psychology" in Germany during the 1860's. They founded a journal that reported folklore, but their work was directed toward mysticism and philosophy, as they speculated about the thought processes of primitive people. Wilhelm Wundt, the father of experimental psychology, also wrote extensively on folk psychology and the evolution of culture.

William McDougall, a British psychologist, published his *Introduction to social psychology* in 1908, the same year that an American sociologist, Edward A. Ross, also published a *Social psychology.* McDougall's social psychology was focused on the individual, in contrast to the development of social psychological thought up to that point, but it proposed that social behavior could be explained largely in terms of instincts. Although McDougall's approach was welcomed at first, within a couple of decades it had been largely discarded by social psychologists. The publication of Floyd H. Allport's *Social psychology* in 1924 marked the beginning of what might be called the "modern era" in social psychology. Allport accepted the individual approach to social behavior proposed by McDougall and rejected the "group mind" idea that had been a recurring theme in the writings of European sociologists and psychologists, but he refused to accept the instinctual theories of McDougall, preferring to view social behavior as the result of what he called "prepotent reflexes," which are modified through conditioning. This contribution not only made his work consistent with the behavioristic psychology of the day, but also stimulated a line of research found today in studies of social learning. The publication of Allport's book also marked a turning point in social psychology, because it was the first social treatise to be based on results of experimentation rather than on observation, theorizing, and speculation. It thus initiated a trend that has become a major approach in social psychology today.

Scientific experimentation in social psychology first began in 1898, when Norman Triplett found that children winding up reels of string to which flags had been attached worked faster when they were with others than when they were alone. This "group effect" on individual behavior was also observed by Walther Moede, a German psychologist, who noted that hand-grip strength and pain endurance were greater when subjects were with others than when they were alone. However, it was Allport's report of experiments measuring the influence of the group on individual behavior that attracted the interest of experimentally minded psychologists and led to what we recog-

nize today as experimental social psychology. Two classic studies during the 1930's are mileposts in this developmental trend. One is the study of the development of social norms conducted by Muzafer Sherif (1935), and the other is the study of social climates by Kurt Lewin and his associates (1939).

Recent Events. Social psychology has gone through a number of major changes in the last thirty or forty years. The most noticeable trend has been the growing importance of the experimental approach since its beginnings in the 1920's. Another trend has been the development of personality psychology, an area of interest shared by both clinical and social psychologists. The growing interest in both personality and social psychology led Morton Prince in 1921 to change the title of his *Journal of abnormal psychology* to the *Journal of abnormal psychology and social psychology,* later shortened to the *Journal of abnormal and social psychology.* Under the latter title, the journal played a leading role in the field of social psychology until 1965, when it once again became the *Journal of abnormal psychology* and the American Psychological Association started the *Journal of personality and social psychology* to serve as the major vehicle for research in these overlapping fields. The *Journal of social psychology* was founded by Carl Murchison and John Dewey in 1929 to serve as an additional resource for this growing area of research interest. The years since World War II have seen an increase in the number of journals devoted to various aspects of social psychology. *Human relations,* the *Journal of experimental social psychology,* and the *Journal of conflict resolution* are three examples.

Social psychology has also branched out into applied fields. In 1935 George Gallup began sampling public opinion by polling stratified samples of the public. The same year saw the founding of the Society for the Psychological Study of Social Issues, now a division of the American Psychological Association. There has also been an increasing amount of "cross-fertilization" between social psychology and industrial psychology. The classic study of production and morale at the Hawthorne plant of the Western Electric Company in the late 1920's and early 1930's was essentially a field study of social behavior, and much of the work and the research conducted by industrial psychologists today can be called "applied social psychology." Educational psychology has also moved from an earlier preoccupation with problems of measurement, coupled with attempts to apply rather narrowly defined principles of learning as developed in psychological laboratories, to a concept of the classroom and the school as social situations. Developmental, clinical, and counseling psychologists are also making more extensive use of data derived from research in social psychology.

Although the majority of studies in social psychology today are carried out by psychologists, sociologists continue to play an active role in the field. Their major contributions have been in the form of theory building. We have mentioned the self theories of Mead and Cooley. More recently there have been the contributions of Robert K. Merton (1957) to role theory, as well as the concepts of position, status, and role that were particularly emphasized in the work of Talcott Parsons and Edward Shils (1951). Sociologists have also done some important field research with results of considerable psychological importance. Perhaps the most significant of these are the studies of social class conducted by Lloyd Warner and his associates (1941, 1949) in the 1930's and 1940's.

Studies of social status showed that people in different social classes have different beliefs, attitudes, values, and patterns of behavior and that each social class is, in effect, a kind of subculture within the larger national culture. The importance of culture as a social variable was largely revealed by cultural anthropologists, who were studying primitive peoples long before sociology or social psychology became academic disciplines. Most of the early research was descriptive, but after World War I anthropologists began to write about topics of psychological interest. Bronislaw Malinowski (1929) observed behavioral trends among tribes in the Western Pacific that raised questions about the general applicability of Freud's theories of personality development. Ruth Benedict (1934) and Margaret Mead (1928, 1930) drew conclusions from their studies of primitive societies that challenged assumptions about human behavior based on American and European norms. A number of cultural anthropologists, including Margaret Mead (1949), have also turned their attention to psychological aspects of the cultures of technically advanced nations. Ralph Linton (1945) has synthesized much of the work of cultural anthropologists and psychologists in his work on the cultural aspects of personality.

The Methods of Social Psychology

Social psychologists make use of a wide variety of methods in gathering data and in testing hypotheses about social behavior. There are some shades of difference with respect to the methods preferred by social psychologists trained in psychology and those trained as sociologists. The experimental method is generally but not exclusively used by psychologically trained personnel, whereas nonexperimental methods are generally but not exclusively used by sociologically trained personnel. These different emphases tend to be in keeping with the experimental orientation received by psychologists in their training and the more descriptive orientation received by sociologists. In experiments, furthermore, the focus is on the behavior of the individual, whereas in nonexperimental methods it is more likely to be on groups.

Experimental Methods. Experiments conducted by social psychologists follow the procedure that is standard practice in all sciences. The researcher observes what he thinks may be certain regular (or "lawful") consistencies in a field of behavior that interests him and formulates a hypothesis that might serve to explain or to describe his observations. He then sets up an experiment under carefully controlled conditions to test his hypothesis. Controls can include such measures as selecting experimental and comparison (control) groups of subjects that are matched (made comparable) on any variable that might possibly affect the results. If the experiment deals with an hypothesized improvement in problem solving which might result from an experimental treatment, the experimenter would presumably make sure that the experimental and control groups were matched in intelligence, since the latter is a variable which has been shown to be related to success in problem-solving. He also sees to it that the two groups use similar materials, that they work in the same environment, and that they work under the direction of the same personnel. The only difference in the conditions experienced by the two groups will be the difference between the control treatment (which usually approximates "normal" conditions) and the experimental treatment. The differences in the "before" and "after" performance of the two groups are then analyzed and statistically compared.

In actuality, a number of variations on this standard procedure may occur without the experimenter feeling that he has violated any major canons of research practice. For example, he may begin his research by wondering: "What will happen if I try . . . ?" However, even this approach is not as hypothesis-free as it seems, because the researcher usually has a vague or unformulated hunch as to what might happen, and the choice of an experimental approach in such a situation is not likely to be a random one. This kind of "fooling around" with research techniques is probably much more common than the carefully reasoned and detailed planning of which research supposedly consists. In such instances, however, it is common practice to do a "dry run" with a method that seems to have possi-

bilities, and, if positive results are obtained, the researcher takes steps to planning a more meticulously worked-out study of the type that usually gets published.

Another variation is the research that does not actually involve a treatment but that looks primarily for relationships among variables. In such a study, the experimenter may be looking for clues to causal factors in certain observed phenomena. He may, for example, be testing the hypothesis that successful leaders are less authoritarian than less successful ones. In such research his task is first to find or develop reliable and valid measures of successful leadership and authoritarianism, whereupon he would administer the measures under conditions that are as controlled as possible. The results obtained for the two groups of leaders are then analyzed and statistically compared.

Example of an Experiment: Effects of Severity of Initiation. Let us review an example of research undertaken to test a hypothesis that developed partly out of the common observation that people tend to value goals in terms of the difficulty they have experienced in attaining them. The experimenting psychologists, Elliot Aronson and Judson Mills (1959), were interested in studying the effect of initiations on group members' perception of the group they joined. Using the cognitive dissonance theory developed by Leon Festinger (1957), which we discuss at length in Chapter 7, they predicted that people who joined groups with a more severe initiation would show a greater liking for the group than would people who joined groups with a less severe form of initiation. They predicted, furthermore, that if the severely initiated subjects came to prefer their group, it would be because they had ignored or minimized certain of its unpleasant features and had exaggerated its more positive ones.

The experiment was conducted with sixty-three college women, who had volunteered to participate in group discussions on the psychology of sex. The subjects were directed to report one at a time to the experimental room, where each girl was met by the experimenter. He said that he was interested in investigating the "dynamics of the group discussion process" and explained that sex had been chosen as the topic for the groups in view of its potential interest. If the subject was one of those who had been chosen (unbeknownst to her, of course) for the severe initiation treatment, she was told that some of the discussants had difficulty in discussing sexual matters and that it had been found necessary to screen applicants before letting them join groups. The screening device was described as an "embarrassment test," which consisted of the subject reading sexually oriented material aloud in the presence of the experimenter. The subject was also told that the experimenter would be judging her degree of embarrassment and would be basing his decision as to whether she would be permitted to join the group on the amount of blushing and hesitation that she displayed. The subject was then asked to read aloud twelve obscene words from 3 x 5 cards and two passages from contemporary novels vividly describing sexual activity. One-third of the subjects underwent the "severe initiation" treatment, and another third underwent a "mild initiation" treatment, in which they read five words that were related to sex but not obscene. Subjects assigned to the control treatment were not asked to read anything.

Subjects were then told that the group discussion was to take place among four participants seated in booths and communicating over microphones about a book, *Sexual behavior in animals*. The subject was then asked if she had read the book; invariably she had not. The experimenter then suggested that inasmuch as she had not read the book, perhaps she should merely listen during this session and not try to enter into the discussion in any way. He then went through the motions of introducing the subject by microphone to the other members of the group, who were presumably waiting in their cubicles, and then handed the earphones to the subject. What the subject heard was actually a prerecorded discussion by three undergraduate women students. It was a discussion that was deliberately designed to be as dull and as boring as possible. The students spoke haltingly and in technical terms of secondary sex behavior in the lower animals, "accidentally" contradicting themselves and one another, mumbling non sequiturs, starting sentences they never finished, hemming and hawing, and generally conducting one of the most uninteresting and worthless discussions imaginable.

When the discussion was concluded the experimenter then asked each subject to rate the discussion she had heard on a number of scales —dull-interesting, intelligent-unintelligent, and so forth. Nine of the scales dealt with the subject's reaction to the discussion; the other scales elicited her reaction to the participants. When this task had been completed, the experimenter explained the nature of the experiment to the subjects, none of whom expressed any annoyance or resentment at having been misled. In fact, the majority were very much interested and several returned at the end of the school term to learn the results of the experiment.

As predicted, the results showed that subjects who had experienced the severe initiation valued both the discussion and the discussants higher than did subjects in the other two treatments, and those who experienced the mild initiation rated it slightly higher (but not significantly so) than had the control group.

Aronson and Mills' experiment demonstrates the value of exercising adequate controls. Their subjects were all randomly drawn from the same pool of available subjects: women attending the same university who were interested in participating in discussions dealing with the psychology of sex. Each of the three groups of subjects received the same treatment, except for the two types of initiation procedures. Analysis of the results showed that statistically significant results were obtained between the major independent variable (the severity of initiation) and the two dependent variables: liking for the discussion and the discussants.

If an experiment has been properly conducted, it should be possible for another researcher to replicate it and obtain the same results. Indeed, its replicability can be considered as a test of the validity of the findings. Aronson and Mills' approach has been used in a somewhat different study, in which confirmation of their results was obtained (Schopler & Bateson, 1962).

Nonexperimental Methods. One of the shortcomings of laboratory experiments is the artificiality of the situations they create. The advantage of being able to control the relevant variables and to exclude the influence of intervening variables makes for highly precise and reliable results, but the question always remains whether the same results would be obtained in a "real life" situation. Hence there are those who maintain that the true test of social psychological theories can only be made in the field, where social behavior is actually lived and experienced.

Nonexperimental techniques take many forms. Researchers carry out some studies by actually remaining for long periods within the physical context of the group being studied, while they observe and take notes as inobtrusively as possible. The study of social class in Newburyport, Massachusetts, by Lloyd Warner and P. S. Lunt (1941) was of that nature. Opinion polls are another form of field study. These polls are usually structured interviews (interviews that follow a definite schedule of questions), but may also consist of unstructured or "open-ended" questions, with the interviewer saying only enough to get the respondent to say what is on his mind. The latter type of interview is harder to analyze, but it does have the advantage of not giving respondents cues as to what the interviewer is seeking and thus leaves them free to express concerns and interests that are really theirs and not the interviewer's.

Example of Nonexperimental Research: a Study of Suicide. One example of a survey is Warren Breed's (1966) study of suicide in New Orleans. Breed, a sociologist at Tulane University, was interested in the influence of migration, sex, and race on suicide rates. Inasmuch as suicide is presumably related to the amount of social and psychological stress people sustain, he hypothesized that migrants would be characterized by a higher suicide rate than would established residents of the city. He was also interested in determining whether there were any other discernable patterns in the causes of suicide.

Breed's method was to conduct interviews with the relatives, friends, neighbors, employers, co-workers, and physicians of all suicide victims between the ages of 18 and 60 who died in New Orleans over a several-year span in the 1950's and 1960's. When he classified the female victims in terms of the amount of time they had been living in New Orleans, he found that those suicides who had been living there less than ten years tended to be young, lower class, with little education, and without family in the nearby area. All of them had borne children. Their chief problems appeared to revolve around their inability to find and hold men either in marriage or in a common-law relationship. The background of women suicides who had been living in New Orleans longer than ten years was quite different. These women were older and were more likely to be married, middle class, and childless. They were also more inclined to have relatives in the area. Their suicides were due to a variety of causes, except that about 60 per cent of them had poor relationships with their spouses. The background of the women native to New Orleans was similar to that of nonnatives who had lived there ten years or more, and family problems were the chief cause of their suicide.

The pattern was both similar and different for male victims. They were less likely to have come to the city at an early age, but many of them had no relatives in the area. Their overall family situation was poor, as it was for the female suicides. The chief difference between men and women, however, lay in the fact that more of the men were occupational failures. They had suffered a decline in occupational status, and, when compared to a control group of males who had not committed suicide, they were more likely to be unemployed.

The Negro suicide rate in New Orleans was quite low, although the suicide for middle-class Negroes was higher than that for lower-class Negroes. Breed offers several explanations for the differences between Negroes and whites. One possibility is that social and particularly familial ties are stronger among Negroes and that members of the Negro community are more likely to show personal concern for one another. This interpretation receives some support in statistics on Negro suicide rates in northern cities, which are considerably higher than those in New Orleans and other southern cities. Another interpretation is that occupational failure is less of a blow to the Negro male ego in southern cities, where he is not expected to compete with whites and consequently is less likely to develop "status anxiety." The higher suicide rates for northern Negroes may be a partial result of exposure to different standards for job performance and success, coupled with adjustment problems resulting from migration.

Inasmuch as a disproportionate number of relatively recent arrivals of both sexes had committed suicide, Breed's hypothesis that immigrants would be more prone to suicide was supported.

Breed's study differs from the experiment by Aronson and Mills in that it is descriptive, makes use of interviews, presents case studies, and produces conclusions that are more general and at the same time more tentative and speculative. Both types of studies are needed if social psychology is to help us develop a better understanding of human behavior. Nonexperimental studies can explore a wider variety of variables than experimental studies and can suggest a greater range of alternative interpretations for findings.

Experimental studies are needed for their accuracy and precision and their ability to focus on a specific bit of behavior, whereas nonexperimental studies are needed for their breadth and their ability to encompass wider ranges of social behavior.

Experimentation in the Field. Sometimes the two approaches can be combined, as they were in the series of studies of conflict and cooperation in small groups undertaken by Muzafer Sherif and his associates (1953, 1961, 1963). Sherif integrated both field and laboratory psychology in a single research design by establishing controls over a social situation and by manipulating conditions to produce conditions found in real life. His first step was a survey of research findings dealing with friendship, hostility, cooperation, and competition. He then selected groups of boys who were relatively homogeneous according to a number of significant variables, such as age and social class. A summer camp was chosen as ideal for the site of the experiment because its isolation enabled the experimenters to control variables that might intervene. When the subjects assembled at the experimental area, the experimenters presented them with a series of tasks that would enable groups to organize and to develop structures, status systems, and norms. When the structure of the groups had satisfied certain predetermined criteria, the groups were then involved in a number of interactions designed to arouse intergroup hostility, whereupon they were faced with situations that required collaboration in dealing with joint problems, with a resulting diminution of hostility.

Throughout the study, elaborate precautions were taken to keep the boys from knowing that they were being observed and rated. Every effort was made to make the assessment techniques a natural part of the camp situation by presenting them in the form of appropriate activities. The experimenters' control over the arrangements gave them ample opportunity to manipulate and to maneuver situations and subjects in ways that made it possible to test hypotheses about group formation and intergroup relations. Finally, the findings were subjected to a system of cross-checking and cross-validation, using a number of different measures and independent ratings. The success that Sherif had with this series of studies shows that laboratory and field methods can be used to supplement one another. This combination of techniques has been also undertaken by others. One such study is that of Theodore M. Newcomb (1961), which we introduce in our discussion of acquaintanceship processes.

The Rationale of This Book

We begin in Chapter 2 with the problem basic to all forms of social interaction: why people seek to associate with one another. In this chapter we also introduce some basic concepts that are referred to from time to time throughout the book: the inverted-U hypothesis, dealing with the relationship between social stimulation, stress, and performance; the search for meaning in the social context; and the use of social interaction as a basis for personal identity and definition. Chapter 3 carries on with the theme of association, but with particular reference to the processes of social attraction. Chapter 4 deals with the result of interacting with others: social learning. Chapter 5 is concerned with the motivational aspect of what is learned. Chapter 6 takes note of the fact that the privilege of associating with others has its price: susceptibility to influence. Chapter 7 focuses on another motivational aspect in attitude formation, decision making, and interpersonal attractiveness: the tendency to prefer consonance and to avoid dissonance.

These six chapters focus principally on the individual as he develops and exists in a social context. The next group of chapters is likewise concerned with the relationship between the individual and his social environment, but the material here is more concerned with the environment as a source of forces which impinge on the individual and shape his behavior. It is recognized,

of course, that the individual plays an active part in the process by helping to determine both the kinds of forces and the kinds of groups that serve as his social environment. Chapter 8 deals with status as it is derived from the individual's position in social structures, whereas Chapter 9 is concerned with the roles that are related both to status and position. Chapter 10 discusses personality, which is determined to a large degree by the roles played by the individual. Personality and roles, as Chapter 11 attempts to show, are also strongly influenced by the individual's culture, which sets the pattern for the social matrix in which the individual is embedded.

Chapters 12 to 16 are concerned with group processes and structure. Chapter 12 deals with communication, the basis of all social interaction. Chapter 13 discusses some of the general aspects of group behavior; Chapter 14 is concerned with the ways in which groups deal with problems. Chapter 15 moves into a discussion of leaders and their influence on the behavior of others. This theme is continued in Chapter 16, where the chief topic is organizational behavior.

The final chapter, Chapter 17, deals with a major social problem: the management and control of aggression.

SUMMARY

The most pressing problems faced by man today are not problems relating to biological survival, but social problems. The particular branch of psychology concerned with the relationship between social interaction and the behavior of individuals is social psychology. The work of social psychologists may aid our understanding of the factors involved in social problems and thus our ability to cope with them. Most people, however, prefer to deal with problems in terms of what is ordinarily termed "common sense," and what Galbraith calls "the conventional wisdom." Although common sense implies the use of mature experience and objectivity, it is also invoked as a way of justifying a wide range of decisions and policies, including some that are quite irrational. Both conventional wisdom and common sense include beliefs which may have been valid in the past, but which have outlived their usefulness.

Social psychologists make use of scientific techniques and accept the disciplines of the scientific method in gathering and interpreting data. Hence their conclusions and predictions regarding behavior often run contrary to those derived from common sense or the conventional wisdom. An example cited of the problems that result when social factors are ignored is the experience of radio astronomers who located an observatory in a remote area of West Virginia. Astronomers and their families reacted unfavorably to being isolated from their usual contacts, and a morale problem developed. Inasmuch as people become integrated with their social environment, bringing about drastic changes in that environment creates many types of problems.

All psychology is to some extent concerned with the study of individual behavior, and social psychology deals with the areas of behavior that involve interaction and relationships between the individual and others. The focus is not on any specific individual, however, but on individuals-in-general. General principles that apply to behavior and may be used as bases for predicting behavior are derived from the study of behavior samples or collections of subjects. The principles so derived have a statistically better chance of proving to be valid when applied to numbers of individuals similar to those on whom the study was based than they would be if applied to the behavior of a single individual. Each of us is like all others, like some others, and like no others. It is to the extent that we are like some others and all others that research in social psychology can aid in understanding and predicting our behavior.

The behavior studied by social psychologists may take place on interpersonal levels where the events of our lives that have the most immediate significance are likely to occur, or on the level of the larger group, where forces are generated that have a significant, long-range effect on our lives.

Social psychology may be said to have begun with the first codes of laws regulating social behavior. British philosophers of the seventeenth and eighteenth centuries speculated about the motives of social behavior, but it was not until the nineteenth century that scholars directed serious study to sociology and cultural anthropology, precursors of modern social psychology. The first formal works in social psychology appeared early in this century and were largely of a speculative and theoretical nature. Scientific experimentation in social psychology began in 1898, but the first book in the field was not published until 1924. Since that date social psychology has undergone a rapid expansion and now has become a source area for a number of fields in the behavioral sciences, including public opinion sampling, educational psychology, industrial psychology, and personality. The majority of social psychologists today are psychologists, although sociologists were the early leaders in the field and continue to be active. There is considerable cross-fertilization among the fields of social psychology, sociology, and cultural anthropology.

Social psychologists use both experimental and nonexperimental methods. Experiments yield more precise results, but the need for precision and control restricts the applicability of findings. Nonexperimental methods are less precise but have the advantage of dealing directly with "life situations." Some studies consist of experiments in field settings and thus combine the best features of the two approaches.

SUGGESTED READINGS

Berelson, B. (Ed.), *The behavioral sciences today.* New York: Basic Books, 1963.

Deutsch, M. & Kraus, R. M., *Theories in social psychology.* New York: Basic Books, 1965.

Klineberg, O. & Christie, R. (Eds.), *Perspectives in social psychology.* New York: Holt, Rinehart, and Winston, 1965.

Lindgren, H. C. (Ed.), *Contemporary research in social psychology.* New York: Wiley, 1969. See papers by Katz, Smith, and Breed in Section 1.

CHAPTER TWO

Jim Jowers, Nancy Palmer

Ken Heyman

Wayne Miller, Magnum

Why We Associate with Others

It can be argued that the basic fact in social psychology is that individuals both seek and avoid one another. This fact lies at the center of a whole complex of intriguing questions: Why are people attracted or repelled? Why do they seek some, but not others? What effect does attraction or avoidance have on the persons concerned? How are attraction and avoidance expressed?

These questions are fundamental to all the research and theory building that constitutes the special area of scientific endeavor we call "social psychology."

In this chapter we are principally concerned with social attraction. For one thing, attraction is generally a more important factor than avoidance; for another, avoidance is likely to derive its significance from the fact that social attraction is the more prevalent form of behavior. When others avoid us, we are upset because we expect or seek a relationship characterized by mutual attraction. Conversely, we may use the same technique on people who have incurred our displeasure. We can be reasonably sure that our avoidance will upset them, because we know that association with others has some kind of positive value for everyone. The need to associate with others is universal and overriding and may be considered as a basic human need or motive.

Social Attraction: Classic Explanations. The universality of social attraction can be explained in terms of the fact that the human infant must spend years in a state of dependency, during which period his needs can be satisfied only through others. The infant thus learns to associate the presence of others with the satisfaction of physical needs—with satiation, warmth, comfort, and security.

This theory has a great deal to recommend it. For one thing, it is consistent with psychological learning theory in the sense that the infant's turning to others produces rewards which serve to reinforce social responses on his part. These responses thus possess a degree of instrumental value in that they accomplish something the infant needs to have done. The process continues beyond infancy as well, for the child gets into the habit of associating with others, even though such behavior is not always rewarded or reinforced. The fact that the reinforcement is on an intermittent schedule does not impair the strength of the social response. Research with various schedules of reinforcement shows that partial reinforcement is more likely to evoke sustained response patterns than is complete or 100 per cent reinforcement (Jenkins & Stanley, 1950).

Social Attraction: Instrumental Explanations. In addition to learning to associate with others, we are also likely to learn, as children, that by cooperating with others and complying with their wishes we can enlist their aid in helping us satisfy many of our needs. This learning pattern continues into adulthood, for we are continually reminded that we need the help of others in maintaining and protecting ourselves. Food gathering is more efficient if there is cooperation, collaboration, and division of labor; shelters are more substantial if others who are expert, skilled, and well-organized plan and build them; individuals are also more effective in their ability to withstand attacks and disasters if they participate in social arrangements than if they try to cope alone.

It is obvious, however, that such explanations of social attraction leave a great deal of social interaction unexplained. They do not explain why people get together when there is no practical advantage to be gained or when practical considerations would suggest independent rather than group interaction. Probably most social interaction has little, if anything, to do with matters of survival, and we must look elsewhere for sources of motivation.

Another variation of this explanation might be the proposition that people associate with each other in order to learn how to deal with their environment more effectively. Social interaction undoubtedly facilitates some kinds of learning of this type and may indeed be fundamental to most of it. For example, the zoologist Alison Jolly (1964) presents arguments, based on his own research and the research of others, that the social organization of monkeys and other primates (including man), preceded the development of the ability to invent and to manipulate tools. Joly found that lemurs, a primitive type of primate, have complex social organizations and display behavior that results from social learning. Through imitation, lemurs learn what foods to eat and what to avoid, how to protect themselves against predators, and how to behave toward one another. They do not, however, possess the skill and ingenuity in solving mechanical problems that characterize the laboratory performance of, say, rhesus monkeys, who are higher on the phylogenetic scale. A primate who can invent and use tools is obviously better able to cope with his environment than one who cannot, and we might reason that the need to cope more effectively with the environment should be in itself sufficient incentive for developing the ability. But Jolly's work puts a different light on the matter, because it suggests that the ability to manipulate the physical environment may be acquired at least partly because of its social value. Learning to use a tool may be rewarding because it enables one to accomplish a needed task, but the process of imitation itself may be a source of satisfaction. It can be observed that humans, as well as monkeys, learn many techniques because they provide a basis for interaction with others, that is, the techniques are learned primarily because of the social value they possess, rather than because of their long-range or short-range utilitarian value.

We learn to read because other children are reading and because we want to please adults who are interested in having us read, and this occurs long before we have any practical need for the information contained in books.

It thus appears that the need to associate with others may have some basis other than the instrumental one of getting others to help us meet survival needs. This is not to deny the importance of instrumental goals in our learning to seek the company of others, but the fact that association with others seems to have a reward value independent of survival considerations suggests that other factors may be involved. For example, social attraction might derive from what could be termed a "social instinct."

Explanations Based on Theories of Instinct. Although behavioral scientists in this country have come to prefer theories of behavior that do not include the concept of instinct, or that at least relegate it to a minor role, many European scientists still find it an attractive and useful idea. In effect, the instinct theory holds that people associate with others because they are biologically organized in such a way that seeking the company of others becomes universal and inescapable. There may be a considerable degree of validity in this idea, for organisms at all levels of the phylogenetic scale seek out and associate with others of their kind. For example, white-footed mice that had been confined alone sought out and remained in each other's company when they were brought together in like-sexed pairs. Although the members of the pairs had markedly different patterns of behavior when alone, their behavior changed, becoming more like that of the other, when they were brought together (Kavanau, 1967).

Theories of instinct, however, appear to explain more than they actually do. To say that associating with others is instinctive merely says that it occurs universally, and does not account for the great range and variety of behavior displayed by individual members of any given species in their associations with one another. Man's social behavior shows the widest degree of variation, resulting in part from his greater capacity to learn, a subject we examine in Chapter 4.

Even if organisms are biologically organized to socialize, however, the social psychologist finds it more fruitful to study the conditions under which socialization is more likely to take place, what stimulates and inhibits it, and so forth. Although the main interest of the social psychologist is focused on social interaction, this does not mean that he is not interested in biological causes and effects. The latter can, in fact, be quite fascinating, yet there is the problem of where to draw the line, where to delimit the area of study. As a matter of general practice, the circle of interest is usually drawn wide enough to include biological phenomena that seem to be directly or obviously related to social behavior.

In that connection, research in recent years has turned up some findings that point to a relationship between cognitive and social behavior on the one hand, and the chemistry and structure of the brain on the other. We shall touch on some of this research in the course of our third explanation of social attraction: the need for stimulation.

The Need for Stimulation. We have raised questions about our first two explanations of social attraction, largely because they do not explain enough behavior. What we needed, then, is a theory which accounts for social behavior that has no obvious survival value, either in infancy or adulthood, and that is nevertheless a factor in all social interaction.

Let us start with the proposition that all organisms are to some degree stimulus seeking. At the very simplest level, the search is for stimuli that enable the organism to maintain and reproduce itself. As we go up the phylogenetic scale, organisms show an increasing tendency to seek and expose themselves to stimuli that are less obviously related to maintenance and that seem to have no utilitarian aim. After learning the shortest route through the maze to the feed-box, rats will take the longer route and explore blind alleys; a hungry rat, before settling down to eat, will explore novel features of his surroundings (Chance & Mead, 1955). Infants prefer to look at complex visual presentations, rather than simple ones, and the degree of complexity preferred is positively correlated with age (Berlyne, 1966; Brennan, Ames, & Moore, 1966).

Experiments with rats raised in "stimulus-enriched" environments, when contrasted with those raised in "impoverished" conditions, show that they develop greater thickness of cortical tissue (the "thinking" area of the brain). This development is accompanied by increases in cholinesterase and acetylcholinesterase, chemicals essential to neural activity. In other words, the research shows not only that growing up in a stimulating environment improves competence in problem solving, but also that such improvement is reflected in differences in the structure and chemistry of the brain (Bennett, Diamond, Krech, & Rosenzweig, 1964).

Stimuli have the effect of stress on the organism. Mild stress evokes a barely noticeable level of arousal whereas strong stress increases tension to painful levels and beyond. Organisms must maintain tension within a certain range in order to function at an optimal level. Environmental stimuli play an important role in producing tension, particularly with lower organisms. Animals higher on the phylogenetic scale are capable of generating and maintaining tensions more or less independently of the external environment, although the environment is an ever-ready source of tension-producing stimuli. Thus the hungry rat who postpones eating to explore an unfamiliar environment and the infant who turns his gaze toward complex patterns in preference to simple ones, are both seeking stimulus-rich environments to experience arousal and maintain tension at more satisfying levels. Stimulation, arousal, and tension are reduced when the rat stops exploring and goes to his food and the infant looks at a pattern simpler than the more complex pattern

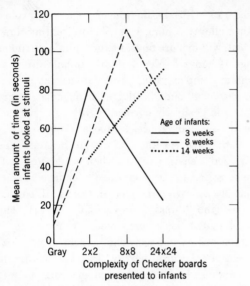

Figure 2-1. Attractiveness of stimuli of varying degrees of complexity for infants at different ages (Brennan, Ames, & Moore, 1966).

that has been presented to him. As Figure 2-1 shows, infants tend not only to prefer more complex stimuli with each increment in age, but to look at them longer. Data presented in this figure are from an experiment in which 30 infants, 3, 8, and 14 weeks old, were presented with four stimuli of four levels of complexity: a 2 x 2 checkerboard, an 8 x 8 checkerboard, a 24 x 24 checkerboard (the most complex), and a plain gray card (the simplest). The infants were more attracted to the greater complexity of checkerboards than to the gray card, and older infants found the more complex designs more interesting than the simpler ones (Brennan, Ames, & Moore, 1966).

This trend continues throughout the years of growth and development into adulthood. In general, adults seek out and enjoy more complex arrangements of stimuli and enjoy them for longer periods than do children and adolescents. To be sure, children and adolescents seek out some kinds of situations, like body-contact sports and surfing, which are highly stressful and pro-

duce a great deal of arousal and tension, but such arrangements of stimuli are relatively simple as compared, say, to playing bridge, and are interspersed with periods in which the individual avoids stimulation as much as possible to achieve complete relaxation and rest. In contrast with children and adolescents, adults are likely to seek complex arrangements of stimuli that produce moderate degrees of stress and tend to maintain their contact with these stimuli over relatively long periods.

The study by Bennett and others with rats raised in stimulus-enriched environments suggests that exposing higher forms of living organisms to increased levels of stimulation during the formative period of life prepares them to cope with higher levels of arousal and greater degrees of environmental complexity. Although it is difficult, if not impossible, to conduct similar studies of environmental enrichment with humans, such studies as we do have seem to point in that direction. Elizabeth A. Borum and Norman Livson (1965), for example, selected two samples of children from those participating in a longitudinal study conducted by the Institute of Human Development at the University of California in Berkeley and whose intelligence had been tested annually since infancy. One group of children attended kindergarten; the other had not. What is of interest here is that on entering the first grade the intelligence test scores of children who had attended kindergarten showed a small but significant increase over those who had not. The fact that there was no significant difference in the educational level attained by each set of parents, plus the fact that the two groups of children had shown no marked differences in earlier testing, suggests that the kindergarten experience played a significant part in the increase. One explanation of the difference (consistent with a considerable body of research with children in other contexts) is that the child who attends kindergarten has experienced an environment considerably richer in terms of novel stimuli than

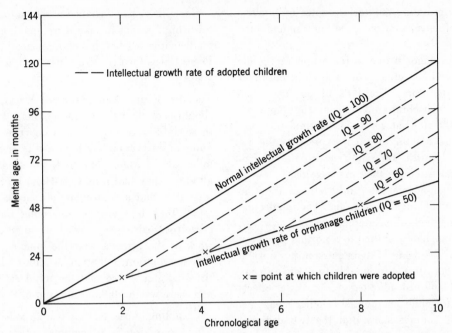

Figure **2-2.** A schematic representation of the hypothetical intellectual growth pattern of adopted and nonadopted orphans in Beirut, Lebanon* (Dennis, 1967).

have children who have remained at home, in the sense that he has had to cope with a greater variety of both pleasant and stressful situations, as well as with an environment that is considerably more complex than the more familiar home situation. He has had to cope, furthermore, with two different kinds of environment—school and home—whereas the child who does not attend kindergarten deals with only one. If intelligence test scores can be considered as an index to the ability to cope with problems of ever-increasing complexity, it would appear that the kindergarten children, like the rats in the enriched environment, were stimulated to greater effectiveness.

Some research by Wayne Dennis (1967) also shows the importance of stimulation in the development of children's intelligence. Dennis con-

ducted a longitudinal study of the intellectual development of orphans who as infants and young children were adopted from an orphanage in Beirut, Lebanon, over a period of years. As long as the children remained in the orphanage, their IQ remained at approximately 50, which is about the lowest ever reported for any group of institutionalized but otherwise normal children. What a mean IQ of 50 signifies is that the intelligence of children in this orphanage was developing at an extremely slow rate, as compared to the pace at which the intelligence of normal children develops. Dennis found, however, that when children were adopted, their intelligence began to develop at a normal rate. Children adopted during the first year of life, therefore, had IQ's within the normal range, whereas those who were adopted later improved their IQ's over 50, but were unable to overcome the handicap incurred during the years they had spent in the orphanage. Figure 2-2 shows schematically the hypothetical

* The statistics reported in this diagram are estimates and approximations and represent extrapolations of the findings and conclusions of Dennis, who has seen and approved the diagram.

relationship among the various rates of intellectual development for adopted and nonadopted children.

The top diagonal line in the graph represents the average intellectual growth of children under normal conditions. The IQ's of an unselected group of such children should average approximately 100 at whatever point in time they are tested. The bottom diagonal represents the intellectual growth of children in the Beirut orphanage. Although they made gains, it was at a slower-than-normal rate, and averaged about 50 irrespective of when it was tested. The intellectual growth rate of children adopted at age 2, however, almost immediately shifted to a normal pace, but because of the delay of their entry into a normal environment, they were unable to attain a mean IQ of 100, and instead tested at 90. Similar effects obtained for children adopted at other ages.

Dennis' findings show that the two different social environments, the orphanage and the adoptive home, had quite different effects on the intellectual development of children. One strong probability is that the differences were due to the differing amounts of social stimulation and attention received by the children. The children in the orphanage numbered about 100 and were in the charge of five nuns, who did their best to care for the children. Their interest in and concern for the children is shown by the fact that the program of adoption which they initiated is unique among Middle East orphanages. However, a ratio of one adult to twenty children is quite different from the adult-to-child ratio that exists even in large families. Therefore the most obvious difference between the orphanage and adoptive homes is the greater · amount of attention and social stimulation available in the latter environment.

A question may well be put at this point in our discussion: This is all very well for children and rats, but how does it apply to adults? As a starting point for an answer to this question, let us consider these vignettes from everyday life:

Gary Fister had a chance to return to his hometown high school to take a well-paying job as a mathematics teacher, but chose instead to join the Peace Corps for two poorly paid but adventurous years.

Pedro Fontes told his wife, Maria, that she should pack their things and get herself and their three children ready, because tomorrow they were going to start off on foot for Brasília, five hundred miles away. Maria objected, pointing out that although they had little to eat and no money, at least they had a roof over their heads. Furthermore, they had always got along on the few cruzeiros Pedro had earned through occasional work at the fazenda near the village, and there was no guarantee that he would find work in Brasília. But Pedro had his mind set on going and there was no talking him out of it.

Gambling houses employ people called "shills," whose only job is to gamble with the house's money at tables where there is no "action."

These examples may be multiplied many times. Many people who find themselves free to choose among various kinds of jobs make their decision on the basis of opportunities for interesting work and adventure. In effect, Gary Fister is choosing a novel, potentially stimulating situation in favor of one that is more familiar and therefore less challenging. Pedro Fontes is joining the millions of migrants who, in almost every country of the world, are turning away from the slow, monotonous life of rural communities and seeking the more unstable and hazardous, but at the same time more exciting and more stimulating, life in the city. And gambling halls use shills to attract people to empty tables because they know that most people do not like to gamble alone, but enjoy the stimulation and tension generated when people cluster around a gaming table.

These tendencies are not universal in the sense that everyone who has a job choice will pick an exciting job in favor of a secure, well-paying one. Nor do all the residents of Pedro Fontes' village want to go to Brasília. But virtually everyone whose level of tension is relatively low is in some way or other attracted by situations that have some degree of novelty and that provide more stimulation and hence a higher degree of tension.

Social Situations as Sources of Stimulation and Tension. One of the most dependable sources of stimulation, stress, arousal, and tension are situations in which individuals interact with others—social situations. There is a degree of unpredictability and novelty about even the most conventional encounter. The presence of another person arouses us: we must cope with him and respond to him. Even the decision not to respond to another is one which must be made and which occasions a degree of arousal and tension. Charles H. Cooley (1902) commented on the negative aspects of the presence of others, how the "sense of other persons" and the awareness that one is being observed may evoke a feeling of vague discomfort, tension, and self-doubt. What he was describing, of course, are the conditions under which tension begins to become uncomfortable. These can be matched by other experiences in which we are bored at being alone and hence deliberately seek the kinds of stresses and tensions that are inevitably a part of interacting with others. The many studies and reports of psychological disorganization resulting from social isolation show how dependent we are on the presence of others (Brownfield, 1965). Social interaction may be stressful, but it is infinitely more welcome than prolonged or even temporary isolation.

The Control of Stress and Tension. Although novelty and complexity are attractive because they are stimulating, it is obvious that there are limits to the amount of stimulation we can tolerate comfortably. Nor is stimulation always welcome. Everyday observation shows that stimulation is enjoyed to the extent we can control it. When this control is out of our hands, stimulation becomes less enjoyable. We might enjoy the stimulation of picking up and reading a play by

Shakespeare or browsing through Rousseau, but when Shakespeare and Rousseau are made the subjects of class assignments, and the decision to read them is taken out of our control, they are not as interesting. It is fun to play tennis with someone who is our equal in skill, or who is somewhat inferior, because we can predict and to some extent anticipate the course of the game and thus maintain some degree of control. Playing tennis with an expert is a totally different matter, since it is he, not we, who determines where the ball will go and how far and how fast we will have to run to hit it or, more likely, miss it. The pace of the game and the resulting degree of stress is his choice, not ours.

One of the reasons we prefer social situations that have some degree of familiarity is that this familiarity enables us to predict, anticipate, and thus control somewhat the course of events and the social stimulation we will experience. The amount of desired social stimulation will of course vary from time to time. When we are bored, we may deliberately seek the company of people who are quite different from us, as did Gary Fister and Pedro Fontes, but when we have been put under severe stress, we are likely to want less rather than more stimulation. After a grueling final examination in chemistry, students will often gather for a few minutes of "post mortem," during which time they talk over the questions they missed or did particularly well on. What they are seeking is not stimulation but reassurance and relaxation. They have been highly stimulated and operating under some stress of anxiety or tension, and what they want to do is to reduce it. The post-mortem group consists of acquaintances, or at least of people who have been through the same experience, and there is a degree of acceptance and mutual understanding that one would not find in just *any* group.

Paul McReynolds (1956) has theorized that we have "an innate tendency to seek novel perceptual experience," and that we normally accommodate these new perceptions by incorporating them into our experience. During situations of stress, however, we become keyed up, more sensitive to novel stimuli, and hence perceive and try to respond to a greater range and variety of perceptions than we usually do. On such occasions, however, we may become saturated with perceptions to the point where we find ourselves trying to cope with more data than we can handle effectively. As the situation gets out of hand, we may experience a feeling of panic or feel less than adequate to deal with problems. To put this in other words, a surfeit of percepts leads to a feeling of anxiety. Hence it is quite understandable that we tend at such times to seek some less stressful and more familiar situation which enables us to deal with the accumulated percepts at a slower rate.

The relationship between stress-induced tension (or anxiety) and individual performance has been a subject of considerable study on the part of psychologists in recent years, although it was originally propounded by Robert M. Yerkes and J. D. Dodson (1908) over sixty years ago. The relationship may be described as an inverted U (Hebb, 1955a). As Figure 2-3 shows, performance

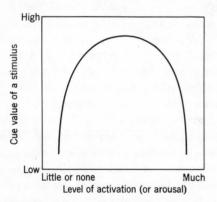

Figure **2-3.** The relationship between level of arousal and performance (Hebb, 1955a).

"Level of arousal" can be interpreted as the tension, anxiety, or stress experienced by the individual, whereas "cue value of a stimulus" is an indicator of the level of performance that has been elicited by the situation he faces.

reaches its peak when tension or arousal is in the middle ranges. When the degree of tension is minimal, performance is likely to suffer. The organism is relaxed, feels no need to act or to cope with the environment, and is generally passive. As the environment becomes more stimulating, presents more problems, more unexpected events, and thus becomes more stressful, the organism becomes more attentive, is aroused, becomes somewhat more tense or anxious, and becomes organized to cope with things. But as stress, tension, and anxiety increase even more, and as the organism becomes still further aroused, it becomes increasingly less able to deal with the situation. This relationship between tension and performance seems to hold whether we are speaking of problem solving, learning, interpersonal relations or any other kind of situation that calls for coping behavior.

In the foregoing examples the amount of tension varies with changes taking place in the environment. It should also be noted that individuals may also vary in the amount of tension they generate. One individual may have a generally relaxed or apathetic reaction to events that others find highly stressful, whereas another may live in a chronic anxiety state in an environment that others find calm and placid. In either event, performance will obviously suffer. Social psychologists are not generally concerned, however, with individual variations in tension except as they are related to generalized classes of variables, such as culture, social class, and group climate.

Tension can also be reduced by withdrawing from social contacts or by avoiding them altogether. In the situation described earlier in which students had taken a stiff chemistry examination, some might actually prefer to be alone afterward, although the more usual tendency, at least in the American culture, is for students to prefer to interact for a little while after an examination before going their separate ways. Perhaps such interaction enables them to avoid reducing stress too rapidly. And students all over the world often "throw a party" when examinations are over. This is, of course, a way of celebrating the end of a stressful period, but we should recognize that parties also are "stimulus-rich" situations, in which the tension level is likely to be moderately high. However, participants in a party are in relative control of the amount of stimulation they expose themselves to. They can participate actively, moderately, or minimally and are free to leave when they are satiated.

In general, we avoid others for the opposite reason that we are attracted to them. In other words, we avoid them when they cannot satisfy our needs or drives. One reason, which we have already given, is that we are satiated with stimulation. Another reason that we have also proposed is that certain individuals are able to exercise more control over our input of stimulation than we can. As an example, when we are in the mood to socialize we are generally less likely to seek out persons in authority over us because they have more power than we have to control the social situation. We have to defer to them, laugh at their jokes, and act in various ways to maintain the senior-junior relationship. We have to be more than usually careful of what we are saying and are not as free to leave and thus terminate the interaction. Nor do we usually seek out the company of people who are hostile to us or who hold views that are antithetical to our values, for the necessity to be ready to attack and defend leaves us less free to "be ourselves." Perhaps these individuals do have something we want in the way of providing social interaction, but they also have something that interferes with our ability to see that our own interests are served.

In actuality, of course, no social situation is a completely free one. There are, as we shall point out in subsequent chapters, social forces that limit and predetermine our behavior to a much greater degree than we are generally aware. When we are interacting with our peers, however, these pressures are more likely to be equalized for all participants, whereas when we react with

people of significantly higher status or who are hostile to us, the situation becomes unbalanced, and we must continually work to adapt ourselves to the unequal power ratio, or, in the case of hostile persons, to adjust the balance in our favor.

We should not terminate this discussion of attraction and repulsion without noting that we may be attracted to others for negative or hostile reasons; that is, we may wish to injure, embarrass, or humiliate them because we perceive them as a threat or because we see them as symbolizing something that runs contrary to our values. Such behavior may be, however, a special case of attraction because of the need for stimulation. Altercations are almost always accompanied by a state of arousal, and the person who is "looking for a fight" is likely to welcome such arousal. The point is that interaction with others is potentially stimulating and this is what makes them attractive, irrespective of whether we are attracted to them for friendly or for hostile reasons.

The Need for Attention. Some theories of personality—that of Abraham Maslow (1954), for example—state that the human organism has a need to be loved or to receive attention. Proponents of such theories hold that if the need for love or attention is not met in some way, the organism may develop pathological symptoms and may even die. This idea runs through much psychoanalytic thinking about mental health. The need for love or attention may actually be a variant of the general need for stimulation we discussed in the previous section. On the other hand, it may actually be of a somewhat different order, because it specifies a particular *kind* of stimulation.

It can be argued that a basic need for human beings is that of being aware of one's own reality. The fact that others interact with us and direct attention toward us is an indication that we do exist. Every touch, every word or glance directed toward us is an affirmation of our reality, as well as an indicator of the kind of reality we represent.

If this line of reasoning has any validity, it

may provide yet another clue as to why we find association with others rewarding: it enables us to receive attention and reaffirms our reality. It also helps explain why attention directed toward others, instead of toward ourselves, may be disconcerting at times and arouse feelings of hostility (jealousy) within us. Such attention may be interpreted as a kind of denial of our own reality and an indication that others are more real (more important) than we are.

Although such ideas are speculative and in fact infringe on territory claimed by philosophy and metaphysics, we put them forth here because they may serve as an additional and possible explanation of why the drive to associate with others is both persistent and pervasive.

The Need for Structure and Meaning

Structure and Relationship. The need to have some degree of order and predictability in life is far more complex and has more potential for influence than we are ordinarily aware of. The underlying motive may be described as a need for *meaning*, a term that seems obvious but that calls for interpretation and definition.

Uncertainty may have a profoundly disorganizing and upsetting effect on the individual. Man's attempts to resolve uncertainty and to bring order to his world has led to his preoccupation with a "search for meaning" (Bartlett, 1932; Cantril, 1950; Krech & Crutchfield, 1948; Newcomb, 1950).

"Meaning," as used in this sense, refers to the perceived relationships among events—that is, among objects, persons, institutions, occurrences, and so forth. The particular kind of relationship that is of greatest interest to us is of course the relationship between events and ourselves. Any event possesses meaning for us in terms of the relationship we perceive between it and our needs. Meaning may also result from the perception of the relationship between two or more objects or events, but what gives such a relationship its meaning is the fact that it is perceived. Thus the perceiver always plays a part in meaning. The perception of an event whose meaning has not been ascertained induces feelings of doubt, insecurity, and anxiety, because we do not know whether the event is potentially threatening, benign, or neutral, nor do we know whether it calls for us to modify our behavior, continue what we are doing, or become inactive. We are awakened at three in the morning by a thumping noise and a crash in another part of the house. We have a sensation of anxiety, even panic, because we do not know what the sound means. What does the sound have to do with us? Is it a burglar? Is it a strange animal? None of these answers seem reasonable, yet our anxiety remains unabated until we get up to see what it is. It turns out to be a vase, upset by a sudden gust of wind coming through an open window. Gazing on the mess of broken glass, water, and flowers on the floor, we feel annoyed, but nevertheless there is a sense of relief, because we now know the meaning of the sound.

The process of giving an ambiguous situation order or structure gives it meaning by clarifying the relationship among the various events or objects, including ourselves, that make up the situation. Once this order has been established, the situation assumes a certain degree of predictability because we know what to anticipate and how we should behave.

The experience of attending college for the first time is a good example of how a confusing, ambiguous situation may generate feelings of inadequacy and anxiety, and how these feelings diminish as we discover the relationship among objects and events and the meaning they have for us. George Stern, a new student, enters the administration building of Megaloid University. He wants to begin the process of registration for the fall term, but he does not know where to go. He sees a sign over a door that says "Office of Admissions," but does not know whether it applies to him or not. This is the office that admitted him to the university, and he wonders if he should pick up some documents or papers there. At any rate, he might find the answer to his questions. He enters the door, only to find a long line of students patiently waiting to see a clerk behind a window. The line does not seem to be moving, and George has a slightly panicky feeling while he tries to decide whether he should join it, or commit the unforgivable sin of going to the head of the line to ask his question, or what. He asks one of the people in line why they are waiting and learns that they are persons who applied for admission after the deadline and who petitioned for special consideration. Since George applied long before the deadline and has received a letter to the effect that he has been admitted, he realizes that he does not belong in the line. What was an ambiguous, relatively meaningless situation now has assumed a degree of order and structure, and he now knows what his action should be; namely, leave the room and seek his answer elsewhere.

During the first few days George has this type of experience repeatedly. By trial and error, coupled with shrewd guesswork, he discovers which lines he should be standing in and what actions he should initiate. The campus itself, at first a confused conglomeration of buildings, begins to make sense. One of the buildings is the student union, which will occupy a central position in his life, for it is there that he finds refreshment, information, and people with whom he can socialize. In the process of identifying the other buildings, he also determines their relationship to him. The low edifice near the gymnasiums is the student health center. George learned this when he was directed there for his physical examination and he made a note of its location. As a person with chronic upper respiratory infections, this building has special meaning for him. By the afternoon of George's first day, the campus has assumed sufficient structure and meaning for him to direct other new students to the post office and the men's residence halls.

Although situations encountered by George Stern during the first days of registration and in-

struction rapidly took on meaning, there were many times when he experienced feelings of apprehension, inadequacy, irritation, and anxiety. These feelings were strongest when he was not sure what he should do next; when he found himself doing something without knowing why, such as standing in a line or filling out a form; or when he found that he had inadvertently done something that either was not necessary or might even cause future difficulties. The next term, however, things went much more smoothly. By this time, George had a fairly good understanding of the system, knew what he was supposed to do, which lines to join and which to ignore, and how to proceed efficiently toward his objective of registering for classes. The registration situation had taken on more meaning for him, for he had a good understanding of how the events and objects in the situation were related to one another and to him.

Let us now turn to the question of how George happened to be involved in the confusion of registration in the first place. He grew up in Micro City, a small town some fifty miles from the nearest major urban area. On graduating from high school, some of his friends elected to attend the local junior college, and others went to distant schools which their parents had attended or which offered training in special fields of interest. Like many high school graduates, George had no specific occupational goals; hence he was not interested in schools that offered special training. He was under no pressure from his parents to attend one college or another, since they themselves were not college graduates. They did suggest he attend Micro Junior College so that he could live at home, but George felt strongly motivated to leave the town where he had grown up and to live away from home. He chose a large university, well-known throughout the region, and located in the suburbs of a metropolis. Like Pedro Fontes, in the brief vignette we presented earlier in this chapter, George left the even-paced, relatively quiet environment of the small town for the stimulating environment of a university located in an urban area. For George such a move might appear to be a step toward uncertainty and meaninglessness, but it was a move that solved a number of problems for him. For one thing, it determined what he would be doing for the next four years, and thus resolved his indecision as to what to do after high school. The greater freedom George would experience living away from home would create ambiguities for him, but ambiguities can be ordered and structured, and such ordering and structuring can also be sources of satisfaction. His home town had lost its attraction for 'him. Like Gary Fister, who joined the Peace Corps, he sought a situation that had both novelty and stress, but which also had an order and a stability of its own.

Meaning through Identity. There are two basic ways in which interaction with others can provide meaning. One is through identity and the other through definition. Identity tells us who we are, in a positive sense—whom we resemble, in particular. Definition also tells us who we are, but in a more negative sense, by indicating *differences* between ourselves and others, and between those we resemble and those we do not resemble. Definition sets limits to identity.

The kind of meaning represented by identity, as Daniel R. Miller (1963) points out, is universally recognized and viewed in every society as having social value. He also notes that identity is so basic to all social relationships that it has to be taken into account in research dealing with such fundamental topics as the relationship between social structure and personality, the socialization of children, the dynamics of social motives, and the resolution of inner conflict.

Our association with others thus enables us to find identities. By noting similarities between ourselves and various individuals or groups, we are able to resolve a considerable degree of ambiguity as to "who we are," that is, what we mean to ourselves as persons and what we mean to others. This process will be discussed further in

succeeding chapters, when more detail is given about how membership in groups shapes behavior, attitudes, and self-concepts, but for the moment we are concerned with how association with others comes to be attractive. What we are saying, then, is that we take advantage of the opportunity to associate with others because it is through such association that we find similarities between us and them and that these similarities give us clues as to our identity or meaning.

What people perceive or do not perceive is also affected by the degree to which individuals are able to identify themselves with the object to be perceived. James W. Bagby (1957) presented American and Mexican subjects with pairs of photographs, one depicting people in the North American culture and the other, the Mexican culture. The photographs were exposed stereoptically, so that one eye was focused on the North American scene, the other on the Mexican, and both were seen simultaneously. Each pair of photographs was presented for a one-minute period, during which time the subject told the experimenter what he was seeing. There was a marked tendency for American subjects to report the details of American pictures and to ignore the Mexican ones, whereas Mexican subjects tended to ignore the American photographs and reported on the Mexican ones. Both American and Mexican subjects, therefore, were so strongly conditioned by the cultural groups with which they identified themselves that they tended to notice or to ignore visual stimuli in terms of this identification. One's social group thus becomes a source of meaning which serves as a frame of reference through which the environment is viewed. This is a subject that will be discussed further in the chapter on culture, society, and the individual.

Meaning through Definition. As noted previously, it is as important for us to know what we are not as it is to know what we are. The groups in which our identities are anchored are limited by their boundaries, the line that divides the in-group member from the out-group member. George Stern is an American by virtue of the fact that he is a member of the very large national and cultural group called "Americans." When we say that George is an American, we not only identify him, but we also define, that is, set limits to, what he is. Identifying and defining are ways of ordering events. By attaching labels to them (identifying) and determining what they are not (defining), we not only give them more meaning, but we can make some decisions as how to treat them. If we are Peace Corpsmen in the mountains of Turkey and we hear that there is an American named George Stern in the area, we probably will decide to seek him out to welcome him to this remote area and to socialize with him. In a more usual context, knowing that George Stern is an American leads us to expect that George will exhibit some of the patterns of behavior that are more characteristically American than those that are not. We do not expect him to relax in the storklike, Nilotic stance, with the right foot braced on the left knee, as people do in the Sudan; we will not expect him to squat on the ground, in the position used by people in most parts of the world outside Europe and North America; and we will not expect him to chew betel nuts or coca leaves.

It usually is not enough to know that George Stern is an American, because this fact does not generally give us enough data on which to make judgments and to behave toward him. Knowing that he is a male, is 18 years old, attends Megaloid University, is an Episcopalian, a member of De Molay, and an Eagle Scout helps us further to identify and define him. This may indeed be enough information for us to decide whether we want to socialize with him or whether we wish to seek further in order to find someone with whom we perceive a greater degree of similarity. Such memberships and affiliations also have a significant value for George, because without them he literally would not know who he is.

The drive to be identified with a group and

thus to be defined is so strong that it can sometimes lead to distortions in cognitive functioning. Eric Hoffer (1951), in his book *The True Believer,* describes the behavior of people who are so hungry for identity and so eager to be defined that they lose much of their ability to make rational decisions, as well as their individuality, by submerging themselves in mass movements.

Group Membership as a Reference Point. Just as groups enable us to identify ourselves through the discovery or development of similarities, even so do they serve as a basis for finding differences. Persons affiliated with a group have certain similarities that give them identity and make them functioning members of the group, but each member of the group has certain characteristics not shared with the other members. Each person's participation in the group is marked by some degree of difference. Even the rituals and ceremonies that are part of the activity of many groups are performed in slightly different ways by different individuals. These differences are as much a part of the individual as are the similarities he shares with others. However, the group also figures in the definition of differences, just as it does in the definition of similarities. Identifying and defining differences also brings up the question: Different from what? The answers to this question often show that the group provides the reference point from which differences are determined. When George arrived at Megaloid University he was assigned to Held Hall, and when he paid his board and lodging bill, he automatically paid his dues to the Held Hall Association. Being a member of the Association further identifies and defines him on the university campus. It may, for example, determine the role he will play in student politics, and some girls may decide to go out with him, or not, because he is a "Held Hall man."

There are, however, differences between George and the other residents at Held Hall. He is, for example, the only person in the hall from his county and he is the only one who can play the flute. Yet these differences achieve whatever significance they have only because the rest of the members in the group are from elsewhere and are not flute players. Without a group to differ from, there would be no difference, or, to borrow a concept from Gestalt psychology, without the ground there would be no figure. The fact that the ground provides a contrast enables us to see the figure. In George's flute class, his flute playing does not make him appear different. What makes the difference there is that he is the only male student in a group of six. His masculinity stands out against a background of femininity.

Thus we find in groups not only cues as to who we are, but also cues as to who we are not.

The Need to Affiliate with Others in Stress Situations. In times of stress, when the level of arousal is high, there is a common tendency for people to seek some kind of reassurance. But even this general behavioral trend does not affect everyone in the same way. Much depends on the situation, as well as on the individual's past experience. The past few years have seen a number of studies dealing with this phenomenon, beginning with the work of Stanley Schachter (1959), who conducted research on the psychology of affiliation. In one experiment, Lawrence S. Wrightsman, Jr. (1960) resorted to a clever bit of stage business to raise the anxiety of his subjects. As each subject entered the room set aside for the experiment, he was ushered by a nurse into another room where hypodermic needles, syringes, cotton, alcohol, and other injection equipment were prominently displayed. He was then told that he would be participating in an experiment in which it would be necessary to inject either glucose or a depressant drug directly into the blood stream, and that the injections might be painful. The subject then indicated on a form-sheet how at ease or ill at ease he felt about participating in the experiment and was then sent to a waiting room, where one of three conditions prevailed: (1) other subjects were in the room,

and talking was permitted; (2) other subjects were in the room, and no talking was permitted; and (3) the subject waited alone. After the waiting period, a second questionnaire was administered. Subjects who waited with others showed more of a drop in anxiety than those who waited alone, but the difference was not statistically significant. However, the decline was significant for those subjects who were first-born or only children in their family. For such subjects it did not seem to matter much whether they were allowed to talk or not, for merely being with others reduced their anxiety considerably. As for subjects who were later-born in their families, it made little difference as far as the reduction in apprehensiveness was concerned whether they waited alone or with others. Somewhat similar results were reported in a later study by Robert L. Helmreich and Barry E. Collins (1967).

Wrightsman did not attempt to account for the difference between the later-borns and the first-born and only children, although he did point out that it must be due to childhood experiences. He suggested that the fact that both first-born and only children receive more parental attention than later-born children may be a factor. It would also appear that first-born children are often given supervisory roles and authority that serves to alienate them at times from their siblings, and only children are more likely to have the experience of being alone and isolated from other children. These factors might perhaps lead to an overvaluing of the opportunity to be with others in times of stress.

Wrightsman did, however, note one effect that occurred when subjects waited with others and were permitted to talk. Such interaction tended to produce a degree of uniformity in the anxiety level of the participants. The participants seemed to use one another's experience as a reference point to determine for themselves how much anxiety they should feel. We shall have more to say about this phenomenon when we discuss the development of group norms, but for the present we will merely point out that this is an example of how people use groups as a way of giving structure and meaning to ambiguous situations. This use of group interaction as a way of resolving ambiguity in one's feelings not only contributes to a feeling of security, but also helps clear the way for deciding what steps one has to take next. In other words, a person who is under stress and who feels unsure of what to do next can use his participation in a group as a basis for coming to a decision as to what his attitudes should be with regard to the matter in question and what his consequent action should be. In this way, social interaction may be seen as a facilitator of individual activity of one kind or another.

Whether this actually facilitates positive forms of behavior, such as improved production or reality-based problem solving, depends, of course, on the kinds of attitudes and values the group has toward production and problem solving. Still another factor is how the individual group member perceives the group. As the research just described shows, it apparently makes a difference whether the group member was a first-born or a later-born child. Hence it is difficult to formulate general principles relating to the effect of social interaction or the presence of others on individual behavior. In general, however, it does appear that association with others does have some kind of impact on the individual and that this impact tends to have some degree of positive value, although it is granted that the degree of attraction varies widely from individual to individual, from culture to culture, and from situation to situation. Association with others may also facilitate individual functioning, although the conditions under which facilitation occurs have to be specified for different individuals. What people receive from their association with others appears to be a reduction of ambiguity in the situations with which they are faced. There are many exceptions

to this conclusion as well, but the use of the group as a source of meaning is so widespread and so pervasive that it must be recognized as a recurring factor in the relationships between the individual and the group. It may indeed be a fundamental consideration in all forms of social interaction.

SUMMARY

The overriding tendency of people to seek the company of others is basic to all research and theory in social psychology. The universality of this drive can be explained in terms of the learning that takes place during infancy, when dependency on others is reinforced and rewarded; the need for others' help in accomplishing tasks and coping with the environment; instinctual drives; and a need for stimulation. Each of these explanations has something to recommend it, although most American psychologists prefer explanations that stress learning more than instinct.

The need for stimulation is a drive that exists to some degree in all organisms. The presence of this need is shown in a variety of behavioral forms, including infants' preferences for complex (rather than simple) visual presentations. The need also appears to have a relationship to effectiveness in functioning: rats raised in a stimulus-enriched environment not only have superior problem-solving ability, but also develop a thicker cerebral cortex. Environments that are stimulating also appear to enhance development of intellectual functioning on the part of children.

Situations involving social interaction have a high stimulation potential and hence are sources of stress, although the degree of stress may range from mild and almost imperceptible to painful. Social stimulation is more likely to be pleasurable when we are able to control the amount of stress and thus protect ourselves from saturation. Anxiety is one outcome of stimulus saturation. The inverted-U hypothesis may be used to describe the relationship between stress (or anxiety) and performance, or effectiveness. Very low and very high levels of stress are associated with reduced levels of effectiveness, whereas a moderate degree of stress is associated with superior performance.

The drive to interact with others can also be explained in terms of a need for attention which in turn relates to the need to be aware of one's own reality. We also derive a sense of meaning from our association with others. Knowing what events mean enables us to resolve puzzling and disconcerting ambiguities, which otherwise would cause anxiety. Through associating with others we learn to impart a degree of structure or meaning to our experiences, and this in turn enables us to learn whom we resemble (identity) and whom we do not resemble (definition). One of the chief sources for this type of meaning comes from our association and affiliation with groups. The inducement of emotional stress can heighten the need to associate with others, but it does not have the same effect on everyone. Research has shown that individuals who were first-born in their family, for example, have a greater need to associate with others under stress than do individuals who were later born.

SUGGESTED READINGS

Berlyne, D. E., *Conflict, arousal, and curiosity*. New York: McGraw-Hill, 1960.

Brownfield, C. A., *Isolation: clinical and experimental approaches*. New York: Random, 1965.

Haggard, E. A., Isolation and personality. In Worchel and Byrne (Eds.), *Personality change*. New York: Wiley, 1964.

Harvey, O. J. (Ed.), *Experience, structure, and adaptibility*. New York: Springer, 1966.

Hebb, D. O., Drives and C. N. S. (conceptual nervous system). *Psychological Review*, 1955, **62**, 243–254.

Hebb, D. O., The mammal and his environment. *American journal of psychiatry*, 1955, **111**, 826–831.

Schachter, S., *The psychology of affiliation*. Stanford: Stanford University Press, 1959.

Solomon, P. et al. (Eds.), *Sensory deprivation*. Cambridge: Harvard University Press, 1961.

CHAPTER THREE

Henry Clay Lindgren

Raimondo Borea

Burt Glinn, Magnum

Social Attraction

Chapter 2 discussed at some length the social drive or motive that is present in us all. To review some of the points made in that chapter, it was said that this drive or motive leads to our becoming involved with others when there is no practical reason for doing so—no reason, that is, that can be explained in terms of biological survival. Associating with others seems to have a stimulating or arousal effect on us, an effect that generally has positive value although a saturation level may be reached, at which point less stimulation becomes rewarding. Furthermore, association with others provides us with a basis for determining the nature and meaning of our immediate environment and the world in general, as well as our position therein. In other words, our association with others enables us to identify and define ourselves and our relationships with the social and physical world.

In this chapter we are concerned with much the same material but the focus is on the specific kinds of interaction that enable us to establish relationships with others. The desire to establish relationships implies some degree of attraction, that is, it implies that we are attracted to others and are interested in attracting them to us. This chapter is concerned with such matters as what is communicated, why it is communicated, and what kinds of effects our communication has on others.

Attraction through Appearance

Common sense tells us that appearance is the main basis for attraction between strangers and, indeed, that it is necessary to maintain appearances if attraction is to result in any kind of lasting positive relationship. In fact, in everyday language the term "attractiveness" has reference to the surface aspects of a person or object.

The idea that the appearance is the sole or even the main basis of attraction is somewhat repugnant to psychologists, partly because it does not take into account the readiness of the audience to be attracted, the standards the audience has, and the relationship between the surface aspects of the person and his underlying personal qualities or personality. It also tends to overlook the idea that attraction is likely to be a mutual process. Psychologists are made uneasy also by the implication that surface aspects can be put on, taken off, or changed at will, without reference to the "real self." In research, therefore, the search is for more "significant" variables. This research has been largely successful, but before reviewing the evidence that supports the psychological approach it may be well to see whether common-sense ideas about attraction have any validity.

The strongest evidence for the common-sense view comes from an ingenious study conducted at the University of Minnesota with 752 freshmen men and women who paid one dollar each to attend a "Computer Dance" during preregistration orientation week. Participants filled out questionnaires under the assumption that the information would be processed by a computer and matched with the personal qualities of a person of the opposite sex who would then become the "date" for the evening. As participants registered for the dance and filled out the questionnaires, their physical appearance was, unbeknownst to them, quickly rated by four judges, who were assistants of the experimenters. The questionnaire yielded information relating to the self-acceptance and self-esteem of the participant. The University's student personnel files also provided information regarding each participant's high school grades, his academic aptitude (intelligence), and other personality test data. The dance took place two days after the initial data had been collected. Although the participants thought they were being

Table 3.1. Various measures of university freshmen's liking for their dates and their desire to date their partners again (Walster, Aronson, Abrahams, & Rottmann, 1966)

	Judges' ratings of physical attractiveness of date		
	Ugly	Average	Attractive
1. Percentages of subjects saying they wanted to date partner again:			
According to ugly males	41	53	80
According to average males	30	50	78
According to attractive males	04	37	58
According to ugly females	53	56	92
According to average females	35	69	71
According to attractive females	27	27	68
2. Percentages of subjects actually asking date out:			
According to ugly males	16	21	40
According to average males	12	25	22
According to attractive males	00	26	29
3. Mean number of subsequent dates the couples actually had:			
Ugly males	.09	1.23	.73
Average males	.30	.94	.17
Attractive males	.00	2.08	.53
4. How much subjects say they liked their dates:			
According to ugly males	.06[a]	.57	.90
According to average males	−.10	.58	1.56
According to attractive males	−.62	.16	.82
According to ugly females	.03	.71	.96
According to average females	−.10	.61	1.50
According to attractive females	−.13	.21	.89
5. How much subjects say they think their date likes them:			
Guesses by ugly males	.47[b]	.52	.43
Guesses by average males	.55	.64	.65
Guesses by attractive males	.77	.53	.58
Guesses by ugly females	.41	.41	.35
Guesses by average females	.38	.58	.55
Guesses by attractive females	.63	.65	.61
6. Numbers of subjects in each category:			
Ugly males	(32)	(43)	(30)
Average males	(43)	(36)	(41)
Attractive males	(26)	(38)	(38)

[a] The higher the positive number, the more the subjects said they liked their dates. The higher the negative number, the more the date was disliked.

[b] The higher the number, the more the subjects thought their dates liked them.

paired by computer, they were actually paired randomly, except that no man was paired with a girl taller than himself.

Participants had been told that there would be a drawing for a $50 prize during the intermission and that they would get a chance to tell the organizing committee how successful the computer matching had been. This gave the researchers an opportunity to administer another short questionnaire, which asked how much the participant liked his (or her) date, how physically attractive the date seemed to be, how comfortable or uncomfortable he (she) was with his (her) date, how similar to himself (herself) the date seemed to be, and whether the participant would like to date his (her) partner again. In a follow-up survey, conducted four to six months after the dance, participants were asked whether they had attempted to date their "computer date" after the dance at any time.

The results, as shown in Table 3-1, demonstrate clearly that physical attractiveness is a very significant variable. Attractive partners were more sought after than were ugly or average partners. As might also have been predicted from common sense, ugly and average partners were more impressed by their dates' attractiveness than were physically attractive participants, even when the partners of the latter were themselves attractive. Attractive partners tended to be somewhat "choosy."

The significant finding of this research is that none of the other measures—intelligence, self-acceptance, extroversion, etc.—proved to have any relationship to liking or to subsequent dating. Physical attractiveness was the only really significant variable. (Walsten, Aronson, Abrahams, & Rottman, 1966).

It can be argued, of course, that the kind of dating situation contrived by the researchers is highly artificial. In real life, people do not pair off at random but are likely to have some expectations about the kind of dating partner who will please them. It is possible, too, that different people might have different kinds of expectations. This possibility was explored by Robert H. Coombs and William F. Kenkel (1966) in another computer dating study, in which partners were actually matched according to their hopes and expectations. The questionnaire that the participants filled out before they were paired showed that men were much more interested in the physical attractiveness of their partner, whereas women were more concerned with getting a partner who had high status, intelligence, and was of the same race and religion. Women tended to set higher standards than the men and also were less likely to be satisfied with their date. Actually, the matching added very little to their satisfaction. When asked how much they would enjoy further dates with their computer partner, 39 per cent of the men and 26 per cent of the girls said "A great deal" or "Quite a bit." This compares with approximately 50 per cent of the men and 56 per cent of the women who said they wanted to date their partners again in the University of Minnesota study we described, in which partners were paired randomly.

Attraction Resulting from Similarity

Research dealing with physical appearance tends to be somewhat inconclusive as an explanation of social attraction. Perhaps the most that can be said in respect to this attribute is that the cultural or subcultural group of which one is a member defines certain standards of appearance that take on a certain normative value. The closer a person approaches this normative standard in his appearance, the more attractive he becomes to those who use the norm as a basis for their judgments. Physical appearance is, however, only one basis for social attraction. Studies with a number of different variables show that shared similarities may be equally important, if not more important. The similarities that are shared do not necessarily have to be positive in nature. We would expect, for example, that losers in a tennis tournament might, for a while at least, seek the company of other losers rather than that of the individuals who defeated them. It is well known that "misery loves company," but, as Stanley Schachter (1959) puts it, "misery does not love just any kind of company, it loves only miserable company." The fact that an individual has undergone disappointment may lead him to perceive similarities between himself and others who have had a similar experience. If so, he is likely to be attracted to them and to recognize them as a potential source of sympathy.

Similarity in Attitudes as a Basis for Attraction. In recent years, much research has been done on measuring the relationship between attractiveness and shared similarities in attitudes and values. Theodore M. Newcomb (1956, 1961, 1963) has played a leading role in such research and has used it as a way of testing a general theory of interpersonal attraction dealing with the attempts of individuals involved in interpersonal situations to develop affectional relationships that are harmonious or, as Newcomb puts it, "symmetrical." Newcomb's theory of symmetry is discussed in the chapter devoted to theories of consonance and balance, but for the present we are concerned specifically with his findings with respect to social attraction.

Newcomb studied the acquaintanceship process in two sets of seventeen male university students who lived together in a house provided by the experimenter for a sixteen-week period. The students had all been strangers before the study. Acquaintanceship patterns were studied by asking students each week to fill out questionnaires revealing friendship choices and attitudes. Newcomb found that roommates tended to be attracted to each other from the first, irrespective of similarity in attitudes and values, but as the weeks wore on, and residents of the house got to know one another, mutual liking grew stronger among individuals with similar attitudes and beliefs. This liking was especially strong when two students shared similar attitudes about other members of the group. Attitudes toward oneself were

also crucial: an individual tended to be attracted to members whose attitudes toward him were similar to those he held about himself.

In another type of study, subjects listened to a tape recording of a problem posed by a hypothetical emotionally disturbed individual. At the end of the recording, they were asked to determine which of two alternative courses the individual should choose. After they had made their selection, they heard what sounded like another subject who was also selecting one of the alternatives. What they actually heard was one of a pair of recordings that had been programmed by the experimenter in such a way that half the subjects heard a statement that agreed with the choice they had made and the other half heard a statement that disagreed. Subjects were then asked what they thought of the person whose choice they had heard. Results showed that subjects were more inclined to be attracted to the individual whose choice agreed with theirs (Worchel & McCormick, 1963).

The importance of similarity as a basis for attractiveness in dating was shown by a survey conducted by Ira L. Reiss (1965) of high- and low-status fraternities and sororities. Reiss found that the fathers of members of fraternities and sororities that had high status on the campus were more likely to have high-status occupations than were the fathers of lower-ranking fraternity and sorority members. The fathers of students who were not members of fraternities and sororities, in turn, ranked still lower in occupational status. In other words, there was a positive correlation between the social status of students (as derived from the social status of their fathers) and the status of the campus organizations of which they were members. Reiss also found that dating practices tended to be restrictive. As Table 3-2 shows, there was a marked tendency for fraternity and sorority members to select their serious dating partners from groups whose social status was similar to their own. Evidently similarity in social status has a considerable degree of reinforcement value, as far as learning to like a dating partner is concerned.

Some research by Donn Byrne and William Griffitt (1966) has also produced results consistent with the foregoing studies. Byrne and Griffitt asked elementary and secondary school students to fill out brief questionnaires dealing with topics in which children their age are likely to be interested. Each student was later given a similar questionnaire which presumably had been filled out by another student of the same sex, but which had actually been filled out by the experimenters in such a way that the percentage of agreement with the student's own questionnaire could be controlled. They were then asked to indicate the extent to which they thought they would like the other person and their willingness to accept him (or her) as a work partner. Both of these replies were taken as an index of the degree to which the student would be attracted to the fictitious individual. The experimenters varied the amount of similarity over the full range from complete agreement to no agreement at all. As Figure 3-1 shows, there was almost a straight-line relationship between the amount of similarity between subjects' responses and those of the fictitious individuals, with respect to the degree to which they felt attracted to them. Indeed, the relationship was quite consistent with that observed in other studies of this type. An analysis

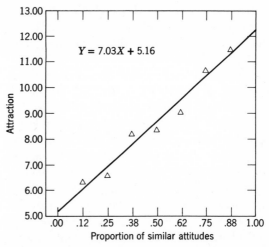

Figure **3-1.** Degree of attraction expressed by elementary and secondary students toward a fictitious stranger, represented in terms of a linear function of the proportion of attitudes similar to theirs as stated by him (Byrne & Griffitt, 1966).

The triangular points represent the mean of the attractiveness scores for students who rated a fictitious stranger whose questionnaire contained the indicated proportion of responses that were similar to their own. Students who rated a stranger who was only 12 per cent similar to them, for example, gave him an attractiveness score of about 6.3. The line represents the smoothed-out relationship suggested by the seven scores. The formula is the algebraic formula for a line with the indicated slope.

Table **3-2.** Status and membership of serious dating partners of members of high- and low-ranking fraternities and sororities ("Greeks") (Reiss, 1965)

Status of group	Percentage of each type of partner			
	High-ranking "Greeks"	Low-ranking "Greeks"	Independent group members	Off-campus residents
High-ranking fraternity members	63	12	8	17
Low-ranking fraternity members	14	19	44	23
High-ranking sorority members	44	8	0	48
Low-ranking sorority members	15	21	19	45

of the results also showed that children in grades 4 to 8 tended to be generally more accepting of the fictitious other than did secondary school students. One explanation of this finding is that as children grow older, they become more selective and more critical in making friends. It becomes more important to them to associate with others who express some degree of agreement with them, or, as Byrne and Griffitt put it, "as soon as a child acquires a sufficient mastery of the language to hold and to express opinions, beliefs, and attitudes, he responds to agreement by others as positively reinforcing and [to] disagreement by others as negatively reinforcing."

Similarity and Race Prejudice. Similar results were obtained with a study comparing the reactions of subjects rating high and low in race prejudice. In this instance, university students were given standard attitude measures to determine their degree of race prejudice, and those scoring high or low were selected for the study. These two groups were given an attitude scale of 26 items, much like the one given the elementary and secondary school students in the study just cited. Then, for each member of the group, the experimenter filled out a scale which was presented to the students as being that of a Negro stranger whom they were to rate as a possible work partner. As in the previous study, questionnaires had been filled out in such a way as to present varying amounts of agreement with their own questionnaires, ranging from zero to 100 per cent. Figure 3-2 shows there was an increase in the attractiveness of the fictitious stranger, depending on the extent to which his attitudes were in agreement with those previously expressed by the subjects. This relationship was almost a straight-line function for the less-prejudiced subjects, but was less regular for the highly prejudiced subjects. It is important to note that even the highly prejudiced students found the Negro stranger more attractive as a work partner when his opinions agreed with theirs (Byrne & McGraw, 1964). In still another study, conducted along the

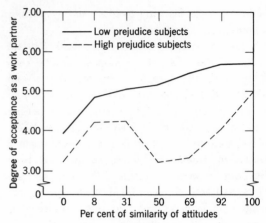

Figure **3-2.** The relationship between similarity of attitudes and willingness to accept a Negro stranger as a work partner, as expressed by subjects of high or low prejudice (Byrne & McGraw, 1964).

same lines, white segregationists reported themselves as more attracted to Negro segregationists than they were to white integrationists (Byrne & Wong, 1962).

Making Friends and Acquaintances. The research on similarity as a basis for interpersonal attraction makes a great deal of sense, both from the standpoint of common sense and from the standpoint of behavioral scientists. Suppose we are at a large party where we know no one—a party, say, given for newcomers at a school or a place of employment. The host introduces us to a number of people, but this is done so rapidly as to seem almost meaningless. Eventually we find ourselves talking to a number of people. We are perhaps pleased to learn that they share many of our beliefs and attitudes and find this mildly surprising, inasmuch as the encounter seemed to be a random one—we just happened to speak to them. It is possible that such encounters are not as random as they seem and that they are actually initiated after either or both of the two parties have made judgments of the other's similarity, using a number of cues—mode of speech, tone of voice, dress, stance, manner of responding to others, and the like. Since we are likely to prefer the company of people who are similar to us, it follows that we learn to judge others according to the evidence provided by such cues, and the similarity we discover may lead to and reinforce friendship.

The question of whether friends actually are similar has been explored by a number of researchers, with somewhat equivocal results. Carroll E. Izard (1960) found that personality test patterns of mutual friends were more similar than those of randomly selected pairs. In a later study, however, Izard (1963) was able to find such similarity among friends who were college freshmen but not among seniors. Howard M. Rosenfeld and Jay Jackson (1965) studied the friendship patterns of women white-collar workers in two large offices and found that mutual friends who had been employed a year or less were indeed similar with respect to scores on personality tests, but those who had been employed longer than a year were similar in one office but not in the other.

In an analytical review of research dealing with social relations, Daniel R. Miller (1963) noted that similarity alone is not a basis for mutual liking. Generally speaking, strength in a dimension of behavior is more conducive to attraction than is a deficit. He notes, for example, that people are more likely to get together if they are skilled artists than if they lack artistic ability. Miller identifies four subtypes of the kind of similarity likely to lead to mutual attraction: similarity of personality, similarity of traits that facilitate endeavors leading to a common goal, similarity in the ability of individuals to gratify the same needs in each other, and the possession of mutually valued emotional commodities. As an example of the latter, Miller cites a study by P. T. Beisser and others (1953) of disorganized families in which ineffectual, detached individuals were drawn together because the ineffectuality of one spouse did not threaten the detachment of the other.

Complementarity as a Basis for Attraction

Much of the research on attraction through similarity confirms the old saying, "Birds of a feather flock together." There is, however, another saying that goes, "Politics make strange bedfellows." The two sayings do not exactly contradict each other, because the first says that likes attract, and the second says that expediency often forces unlikes to work together. The second saying also finds its equivalent in a psychological theory of attraction: the complementarity hypothesis. This explanation of attraction is expressed in the work of Robert F. Winch (1958), who proposed that members of dyads (two-person groups) are attracted to each other, not because their particular patterns of needs are similar, but because they are different, although in complementary ways. In other words, an individual who rates high in trait A and low in trait B, is attracted to an individual who is low in trait A and high in trait B, and vice versa. Winch found some support for this proposition in a study of the psychological needs and emotional traits of twenty-five married couples. A statistical analysis of scores made on psychological measures showed that assertive individuals tended to marry receptive ones, and vice versa, and that dominant individuals tended to marry submissive ones. Similar complementary patterns were found for other traits.

Other attempts to validate Winch's proposal have generally failed to find much in the way of supporting evidence. For example, Thomas J. Banta and Mavis Hetherington (1963) found more similarity than complementarity among mutually attracted persons. They administered the questionnaire measuring psychological needs (the Edwards Personal Preference Schedule) to twenty-nine groups of six subjects each, each group consisting of an engaged couple and a male and a female friend of each fiancé. The engaged couples were similar on eight out of the fifteen needs measured by the questionnaire. The female friendship pairs were also similar to each other, the male pairs, less so, although even in the latter instance there was little evidence of complementarity.

In spite of this negative evidence, however, everyday observation will turn up any number of instances in which two or more individuals are mutually attracted because they find matching strengths and weaknesses in each other. An engaging conversationalist and a taciturn individual may become good friends. The conversationalist needs an audience, and the taciturn person needs to be entertained. A tax lawyer and an accountant develop a good working relationship; each has skills that the other lacks, and they are more effective working together than they would be separately. The problem is that these are rather specific instances, and it is difficult to develop and test general theories for special cases.

The main body of research dealing with interpersonal attraction does, as has been pointed out, support the idea that individuals are attracted to those similar to them and that a perceived similarity tends to attract. To return to some ideas proposed earlier in this chapter, it would appear that the perception of similarities in another person aids in the process of identity in that the traits one perceives in oneself are reaffirmed when they are perceived in another. Interpersonal similarities also facilitate social interaction, as we shall see in succeeding chapters, because they can serve as the basis for communication, empathy, the development of group norms, and cultural patterns of behavior.

Attraction Resulting from Propinquity

The sociologist George C. Homans (1950) writes: "If the frequency of interaction between two or more persons increases, the degree of their liking for one another will increase, and vice versa." The "vice versa" portion of this statement is especially consistent with common sense: the more we like people, the more we will try to find opportunities to see them. However, we tend to be somewhat less aware of the validity of

Homans' main proposition, namely, that merely seeing people frequently results in our finding them attractive. As a matter of fact, some common sayings contradict this principle: "Familiarity breeds contempt," and, "Absence makes the heart grow fonder," but then the latter is contradicted by the saying, "Out of sight, out of mind."

The validity of Homans' statement can be tested by observing the behavior of people who are brought together by chance and determining whom they find attractive. In the previously cited study by Newcomb, students who were roommates tended to express preferences for each other from the very start of their stay in the house. A somewhat earlier study that also illustrates Homans' point was conducted by Festinger, Schachter, and Back (1950) shortly after World War II, when young veterans and their families were housed in "veterans' housing" at colleges and universities throughout the United States. One such housing area was a complex of seventeen buildings arranged around a court, each building consisting of ten apartments, five to a floor. The researchers observed and charted spontaneous group formation among the families and found that propinquity (of residence) was the major factor in determining who became friends with whom. "Functional distance" was more important than actual physical distance between apartments. People who used the same stairs and the same utility rooms were more likely to socialize with one another and become friends than were persons who lived in another apartment house or even in another part of the same house. The usage of common areas resulted in their seeing one another more often and thus meant that they were functionally closer than they were to other residents, even those who lived next to them, but whom they saw less often because they used a different entrance.

William H. Whyte, Jr. (1956) studied the social notes appearing in a newspaper published in a suburban area near Chicago and noted the families who participated together in various social gatherings. He found that the overwhelming percentage of co-participants were neighbors, particularly those who lived next door to one another or across the street. Families whose children played together also were drawn into interaction by that fact—not through any initiative of their own.

Another study showing the effect of propinquity consisted of a survey conducted by Robert F. Priest and Jack Sawyer (1965) of attraction patterns in a new, 320-man dormitory at a university. They found that students were more likely to choose their friends from those who lived near them, although being members of the same class in college (peership) was also an important factor. The longer the students lived in the dormitory, however, the less important propinquity became, and they made an increasing number of friendships with students living at some distance from the dormitory.

It appears that propinquity is an important factor in attraction, partly because it provides more opportunity to interact, and partly because it gives people something in common—that is, they feel a degree of similarity because they share the same residence area and probably have quite similar homes. In all the studies cited, the groups are quite homogeneous in age, education, economic standing, and interests. This gave them a kind of "built-in" similarity that made it easier for them to find common topics of common interest and frames of reference than it would have been had their background been more heterogeneous.

Sociometry: The Measurement of Attraction

Like any other psychological variable, attraction can be measured, irrespective of whether it derives from similarity, complementarity, or propinquity. The simplest and most obvious way of assessing the relative attractiveness of members in a group is by asking each individual whom he prefers as companions and/or work partners. The number of choices an individual

receives is a measure of his attractiveness. Similar information may be secured on the extent to which members are disliked. This method of gathering data, called *sociometry* by its inventor, J. L. Moreno (1953), has been used extensively in studying the social structure of work groups, play groups, and classrooms, as well as for measuring the interpersonal attractiveness of individual group members.

Sociometric data can be reported in terms of the number of choices (or rejections) received by a given group member, or they can serve as the basis for a diagram, or *sociogram*, like Figure 3-3. Sociograms have the added advantage of providing the observer with a bird's-eye view of a group's social structure, and at the same time indicating the degree of social attraction possessed by members of the group. Figure 3-3 shows the choices made by children in a play group who were asked to name the three children in the neighborhood they would most like to play with. This group is highly cohesive, all the more remarkably so because of the considerable age span between the oldest and the youngest. There is a tendency for the older members in the group to choose one another, but there are a number of mutual choices that span several years of age. The fact that there are no exclusive cliques (caused by a few members choosing one another and no one else) is an indication of cohesiveness, easy interaction, and mutual acceptance. Although there is a tendency for choices to run along sex lines, there is enough crossing of the line to suggest that relationships among the children are generally positive. Nan, Linette, and Doris are the "stars of attraction" among the girls. They are the "natural leaders" in their sex group. Larry and Bill are the leaders among the boys, with Little Mark filling a status position for girls. The two "isolates" among the girls, Cathy and Lee, are only five years of age, which may account in part for their not being chosen. Little Laura, aged four, also comes close to being an isolate, being chosen only by Lee, another and very young isolate. Age seems to be less important in

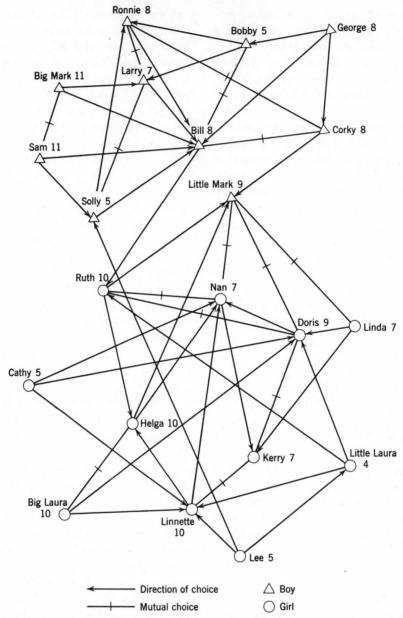

Figure **3-3.** Sociogram of a neighborhood play group. Numbers refer to age
of children (Holmes, 1963).

attraction among boys in this neighborhood, because both five-year-olds have two choices each,
and the only isolate, George, is eight.

J. G. Jenkins (1948) used sociometric methods
to evaluate the morale of naval air squadrons
during World War II. Squadron A, which had

high morale, had no cliques, and only two of its officers expressed negative feelings toward group members. Furthermore, the commanding officer and the executive officer were the two best liked members in the group. Squadron B, which had poor morale, presented quite a different picture. There were two cliques of four officers each, and only three of the remaining nine officers expressed any positive regard for each other. All officers in Squadron B expressed negative feelings about one or more of their colleagues, and nine officers said that they disliked the executive officer.

Sociometric methods are widely used in psychological research and have been employed in most of the studies cited in this chapter. Sociometric methods can also be used to measure any personal dimension on which group members are likely to have an opinion: leadership potential, tendencies to be disruptive, personal warmth, ambition, dominance, political conservatism. Indeed, any factor in any way related to interpersonal attraction can be measured sociometrically.

SUMMARY

Although research has confirmed the commonsense idea that physical appearance is a basis for social attraction, other factors are also important, the most notable being similarity in attitudes and values. Some studies have shown that similarity of opinions can, to some degree, even counteract resistance in the form of race prejudice. Research findings are somewhat equivocal on the extent to which similarity functions in friendships. But the opposite hypothesis, complementarity—the idea that people are attracted because of differences in their needs and emotional traits—also lacks firm support. Although people may be attracted to one another because of complementarity in needs and traits, a survey of the full range of evidence shows that similarity is probably a more significant factor than complementarity.

The accessibility of others, propinquity, is also an important factor in acquaintanceship patterns, and many friendships are generated merely because people happen to see one another frequently.

The measurement of social attraction is called *sociometry,* and diagrams showing the interpersonal preference patterns in groups are termed *sociograms.* A number of group characteristics, such as cohesiveness and morale, are reflected in patterns of interpersonal attraction, which can in turn be measured by sociometric techniques.

SUGGESTED READINGS

Byrne, D., & Clore, G. L., Jr., Effectance arousal and attraction. *Journal of personality and social psychology,* 1967, **6,** No. 4 (August), Part 2 (Monograph).

Festinger, L., Schachter, S., & Back, K., *Social pressures in informal groups: a study of human factors in housing.* New York: Harper, 1950.

Jennings, H. H., *Leadership and isolation.* New York: Longmans, Green, 1950.

Lindgren, H. C. (Ed.), *Contemporary research in social psychology.* New York: Wiley, 1969. See Section 2, "Social attraction."

Miller, N., Campbell, D. T., Twedt, H., & O'Connell, E. J., Similarity, contrast, and complementarity in friendship choices. *Journal of personality and social psychology.* 1966, **3,** 3–12.

Moreno, J. L., *Who shall survive?* New York: Beacon House, 1953.

Newcomb, T. M., *The acquaintance process.* New York: Holt, Rinehart, and Winston, 1961.

Winch, R. F., *Mate selection: a study of complementary needs.* New York: Harper and Row, 1958.

CHAPTER FOUR

Henry Clay Lindgren

Suzanne Szasz

Suzanne Szasz

Social Learning

Learning is a term used by psychologists to designate relatively permanent changes in an organism's behavior that result from its experience. The term can also refer to the processes within the organism involved in producing such a change. Changes due to maturation, sensory adaptation, injury, surgery, drugs, fatigue, or disease are of course specifically excluded from this definition.

Chapters 2 and 3 discussed the overriding, general tendency of man to associate with others in order to ensure his own survival and to seek stimulation, meaning, identity and definition. In the language of learning theorists, associating with others can be considered as a goal, and success in attaining this goal serves to reinforce behavior that is oriented toward being with others. Those people who are able to reward us through their willingness to attend to us or interact socially with us are thus in a position to be selective about the kind of behavior they wish to reinforce, and we, in turn, will find ways to secure and hold their attention. In this chapter we are concerned with some of the ways in which others may reward us and what effect such rewards have on our behavior. Whereas Chapters 2 and 3 were largely concerned with why and how we are attracted to others, this chapter deals with social learning—the process that is set in motion because of this association.

Attention as a Facilitator of Learning. One of the ways in which others can reward us is by attending to us. Getting the attention of another person is generally rewarding; being ignored is generally nonrewarding and may even be disturbing. There are many specific exceptions, of course; for example, the unprepared student who hopes the teacher will call on another. But the principle still holds as a general rule.

If attention is rewarding, one would predict that individuals who are trying to bring about changes in the behavior of others would succeed if they gave them more attention than if they gave them no more than the routine amount. This prediction has been confirmed by the research of Ellis Batten Page (1958), who conducted an experiment concerned with behavioral changes of high school and junior high school students taking quizzes under normal classroom conditions. Page asked seventy-four randomly selected teachers to give one of three kinds of treatment to whatever objective examination they were using in their classes at the time of the experiment. After the teachers had scored the examination papers, they were asked to divide the papers randomly into three groups. One group was returned to the students without written comment, and with only the score and the letter grade. A second group received comments that were standardized as to the grade received. For example, all "C" papers received the comment, "Perhaps try to do still better?" The remaining third of the papers received the "free comment" treatment, in which teachers were asked to write whatever they deemed appropriate on the papers. The three treatments thus represented three levels of attention, ranging from the "no comment" treatment, representing the least amount of attention, to the "free comment" treatment which represented the greatest amount of attention.

Grades on the very next examination given by the teachers to the same students were used as a dependent variable, that is, as a measure of the effect of the three kinds of treatment on student behavior. Results showed that students whose papers had been given the "free comment" treatment (maximum attention) scored significantly higher on the second examination. Students whose papers had received the "standardized comment" (moderate amount of attention) showed some gain, but not as much as those whose papers had received the "free comment" treatment. Those students who were in the "no comment" (no attention) group showed no gain at all.

It is interesting to note that the teachers had no idea of how influential their comments would be. When Page asked them, before the experiment began, to predict the effect their comments would have on the performance of students, they said that better students would respond favorably, but that poorer students would be inclined to do the opposite of the teachers' recommendations. The results showed, however, that those who received the most attention, in the form of free comments on their papers, improved irrespective of whether they were "A" or "F" students.

Page's research demonstrates two things: that attention has reward value, and that changes in behavior can be brought about as a function of the extent to which attention is increased. It can be said, of course, that Page's study represents a special case: after all, it *did* take place within the context of a classroom, where students are *supposed* to respond favorably to the efforts of teachers to get them to improve. It can also be argued that the attention received from an authority figure, like a teacher, has a greater impact than the attention received from peers.

Let us therefore turn to a second study, one which was undertaken in a setting less obviously oriented to academic improvement and in which changes in behavior were induced by persons who were not authority figures. Allen D. Calvin (1962) asked the students of his psychology class at a women's college to play the role of experimenters and to compliment all girls wearing blue during the lunch hour in the college dining hall. The day before the complimenting began, 25 per cent of the girls were wearing blue. After five days of compliments, the percentage wearing blue rose to 37 per cent. When the special treatment stopped, the percentage dropped to 27 per cent. The experimenters then switched to praising girls wearing red. An average of 12 per cent of the student

body wore red during the days prior to the special treatment, but during the period of the experiment, the percentage increased to 22 per cent and leveled off to 18 per cent.

Both Page's study and Calvin's study show that individuals can be induced to change their behavior (learn) when they become the object of favorable attention on the part of another person. Still other research shows that similar effects obtain when the reward comes from a group, rather than another individual. William Abbott Scott (1957) conducted an experiment in which pairs of subjects participated in debates about issues on which they had previously committed themselves: universal military training, university policies regarding night check-in time for women's residence halls, and de-emphasis of football at the university. Each debater was required to speak against the position he had already expressed. After the debates were concluded, the experimenter went through the motions of polling the audience to determine who had won the debate. In actuality, subjects were assigned to the "winner" or the "loser" category on a random basis. After the results of the "balloting" were announced, debaters were asked how they now stood on the issues. Results showed that "winners" were much more likely to report a change in their opinions, and "losers" were more likely to maintain their previous position. Expressions of opinion that were "accepted" by the audience (i.e., that resulted in "winning") had evidently become more attractive to the subjects, and this in turn led to changes in their behavior. In other words, they *learned* a different point of view on the issues.

If attention and approval have any positive value for the individual, it should follow that withdrawing or withholding them should have negative value. There is a suggestion of this in the studies we have reviewed in this chapter. The students in Page's study who received no special attention did not improve; the girls in Calvin's experiment reduced their wearing of blue or red when they were no longer complimented; and the debaters reaffirmed their original point of view when they were declared "losers."

Deprivation of Attention. It should also follow that persons who have not been the objects of attention for some time—deprived of attention—would be more responsive than those who have had considerable attention—satiated with attention. One study designed to test this possibility used first-grade boys as subjects. At this age, adult attention has even more impact than it does during later years of development when the individual normally has other sources of satisfaction. Subjects involved in this study underwent two kinds of treatment before they entered the room in which the experimental trials were to take place. The socially "satiated" group were first told by their teacher that they would be playing a "fun" game in which no one could fail or do poorly. The experimenter was introduced to the class in a pleasant and warm manner, and as he took each child to the experimental room, he chatted with him, addressed him by name, and inquired after his interests. Subjects in the socially "deprived" group got no attention. The teacher simply asked the child to "Go with this man," when the experimenter appeared in the classroom. On the way to the experimental room, the experimenter conversed with the child only when necessary, and then briefly.

The dependent variable in this study was performance at a learning task. Each subject was seated before a box that had a right and a left switch lever and was told that he was to press one of them every time a buzzer sounded. "Right" and "wrong" responses to the signal were programmed in such a way that 70 per cent of the time a left response was right, whereas a right response was correct 30 per cent of the time. Thus the subject's best chance of being correct was through pressing the left lever each time the buzzer sounded. In the experimental situation, two methods were used to inform subjects of the correctness of their response. In the "social re-

inforcement" condition, the experimenter would say "Good" or "Fine," whenever the subject made a correct response, whereas in the "nonsocial reinforcement" condition, a red light would come on to indicate a correct response. Thus there were four possible combinations of treatment: socially satiated subjects could be socially or nonsocially reinforced, and socially deprived subjects could be socially or nonsocially reinforced. Figure 4-1 presents the results. All groups increased the percentage of left responses during the 150 trials, but subjects who had not received special attention prior to the learning trials (socially deprived) were more responsive to the learning situation than were the socially satiated subjects. This advantage held true, however, only when the experimenter reported their success to them personally (social reinforcement) (Dowart et al., 1965). It was as though their appetite or readiness for social approval had been built up by the brief period of social deprivation (about three minutes) they had undergone prior to the learning trials. Inasmuch as the approval of the experimenter was more important to them than it was to the satiated group, they worked harder to get it and learned more efficiently and effectively.

Reinforcement and Social Learning. The term "reinforcement," introduced in the discussion of Dowart's study, is a term that some psychologists, notably B. F. Skinner, prefer instead of the term "reward" when discussing learning, maintaining that the latter term implies too much. In the studies reported so far in this chapter, the reinforcing event would ordinarily seem to have reward value for the learner, in that expressions of approval are generally considered to be pleasant and welcome. Not all rewarding events are reinforcing, however. In the study just cited, being told "Good" or "Fine" by the experimenter was much more reinforcing for the socially deprived group, but was no better as a reinforcer than a flashing light for the socially satiated group. Furthermore, the comments written on papers by teachers in the study by Page were not all in the nature of praise and yet they facilitated learning.

Reinforcement is the central idea in the concept of learning proposed by B. F. Skinner (1963) of Harvard University, a leading figure in research dealing with operant or instrumental conditioning. One of the attractive features of his approach is its simplicity, as revealed by his explanation of how reinforcement affects learning.

"By arranging a reinforcing consequence, we increase the rate at which a response occurs; by eliminating the consequence, we decrease the rate. These are the processes of operant conditioning and extinction."

To apply these principles to the study by Calvin (1962), compliments directed at girls wearing blue came as a consequence of wearing blue. The wearing of blue was thus reinforced. When the compliments stopped, the rate of wearing blue dropped off. The processes of operant learning or conditioning were reversed, and an extinction of the learned response took place.

Social Learning through Imitation. Although principles of operant learning have proved to be very useful in the psychological laboratory, they fall short when it comes to explaining many, if not most, changes in the behavior that appear outside the laboratory. Albert Bandura and Richard H. Walters (1963) acknowledge the validity of operant theory in explaining the appearance of behavior that is already in the repertoire of the learner, but state that it fails to explain adequately the appearance of *novel* behavior, behavior that the learner has never before displayed. Skinner (1953) explains the appearance of new responses in terms of "shaping," or the reinforcement of successive approximations of the new behavior. In the laboratory, pigeons can be taught to play table tennis or guide military missiles, provided the experimenter reinforces any behavior that is in any way related to the behav-

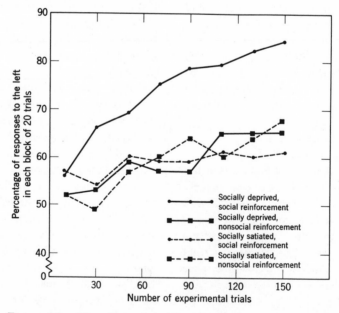

Figure 4-1. The effect of social reinforcement and nonsocial reinforcement on socially deprived and socially satiated subjects (Dowart, et al., 1965).

ior he eventually wants performed. As Bandura and Walters point out, however, very little social behavior would ever be learned if we had to depend on someone going through the detailed, demanding, and tedious process of conditioning successive approximations to the desired behavior. The process used by the higher animals, and particularly by man, is *imitation*. Through observing and imitating the behavior of others, learners can bypass much wasteful random behavior and come close to reproducing the behavior desired. The learning of language is a good example. Young children learn to express themselves in words and sentences not so much because adults reinforce certain sounds that are embedded in infant gurgles, but rather generally through a process of imitating the speech of others.

Bandura and Walters nevertheless consider reinforcement to be a very important part of the learning process. For one thing, individuals (usually parents) who serve as the models for children's behavior often reinforce approximations of their behavior through praise or some more concrete form of reward. Moreover, the child's attempts to imitate the behavior of others enables him to accomplish certain desired goals: he gets the food into his mouth more efficiently, and people respond to him with some kind of desired action, instead of with confusion or not at all. In other words, the child learns to imitate behavior that gets results.

Albert Bandura and Frederick J. McDonald (1963) conducted an ingenious experiment designed to determine the relative effectiveness of reinforcement of imitation in children's learning. The experiment used several pairs of brief stories of a type used by Jean Piaget (1948) in his research with the development of moral judgment in children. Piaget has found that children go through at least two easily recognizable developmental stages in their attitudes toward misbehavior. In the earlier stage, which Piaget calls the stage of "objective responsibility," children are

inclined to evaluate misbehavior or mishaps in terms of the gross amount of damage done, without reference to the intentions of the individual involved. In the later stage, which he calls the stage of "subjective responsibility," children evaluate behavior in terms of the individual's intent, rather than its material consequences. Thus when someone tells them two stories, one in which a boy accidentally breaks fifteen cups that were on a tray located unseen on the opposite side of a door he was opening on the way to dinner, and the other in which a boy breaks one cup in the course of robbing the cookie jar, children who are still in the stage of objective responsibility will say that the boy who broke fifteen cups did the naughtier thing, whereas children whose development has reached the stage of subjective responsibility will say that the boy who broke the single cup in pursuit of the illicit cookies was the more culpable.

Bandura and McDonald tested a group of children between the ages of 5 and 11 on pairs of stories like those used by Piaget and divided them into two groups, one consisting of children more likely to make moral judgments along the lines of objective responsibility, and the other consisting of those more likely to make judgments characterized by subjective responsibility. These two groups were further subdivided to form six groups, each of which was treated differently in the experiment that followed. Twelve pairs of stories like the one described were read to all the children, one child at a time. In one treatment, the stories were read to the child in the presence of an adult model, who was asked to give his (or her) judgment before the child was asked. The model had been instructed to make judgments contrary to the kind the child had made in an initial testing situation. The model's judgments were reinforced by the experimenter's saying "Very good," "That's fine," or "That's good," and when the child gave similar responses, he, too, was reinforced. The second treatment was like the first, except that the model was reinforced but the child was not. No model was present in the treatment received by the third group, but the child was reinforced for giving responses contrary to the type he had given in the initial testing session. In all treatments, the experimenters attempted, either through reinforcement, or by reinforcing a model, or both, to get the child to make judgments that were in the opposite direction to those he had made in the initial testing session. After the experimental treatment, the child was given another set of similar pairs of stories and asked to make judgments without a model being present and without reinforcement. The experiment thus enabled the researchers to determine whether reinforcement or modeling is a more important force in inducing learning.

The results, as shown in Figure 4-2, show conclusively that the behavior of the model was a more powerful influence in the behavior of children than was the reinforcement they received. As a matter of fact, reinforcement proved to be a negligible factor, as is indicated by the lack of

any significant difference in the performance of the children in the model-present condition who were reinforced and those who were not. There was relatively less change in the behavior of children who did not have a model and who were reinforced only and, in the case of children who had originally given objective judgments, there was no permanent effect, for after the reinforcing session was over, they reverted to their original position.

The impact of the model's behavior on the children can be explained partly in terms of the fact that they were able to "identify" with him, that is, the children were able to perceive a relationship or degree of similarity between themselves and him. The experimental situation, is, after all, a relatively artificial and unfamiliar one to the children. They are, in effect, "put on the spot" and asked to give their opinions about the moral aspects of two examples of misbehavior. Perhaps the fact that the stories are about children who are misbehaving or are in trouble is enough to

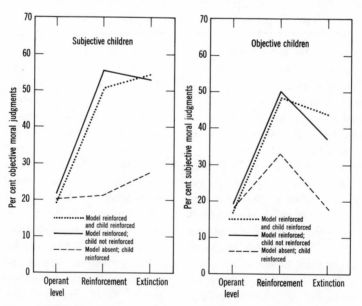

Figure 4-2. The effect of models' responses and reinforcement on children's moral judgments (Zajonc, 1966, after Bandura & McDonald, 1963).

arouse anxieties. In any event, the forthright statement of the model who is then reinforced by the experimenter provides the child with an anchoring point of security in this ambiguous situation, thus making it easy for the child to claim some degree of identity with him by imitating his reply. Indeed, Bandura and Walters (1963) state that there is really no difference between imitation and identification. They maintain that the fact that one person observes and imitates another is evidence that he identifies with him.

It can also be argued that imitation is a special case of reinforcement, in that the person who successfully imitates can be said to be self-reinforcing. Such a formulation does not simplify the problem for the psychological researcher who wishes to study the effects of reinforcement on behavior, because results of research are much more clear cut if reinforcement is controlled by the experimenter. If the decision as to what is reinforcing is left in the hands of the subject, the experimenter can never be sure what is producing the effects he is observing, because individuals vary widely in their perceptions of what is reinforcing. No doubt techniques will eventually be developed to control this source of variability, but at present it is difficult to determine the relative extent to which reinforcement and imitation operate to shape human behavior. It hardly seems likely that all the variations in human behavior can be accounted for by the chance appearance of reinforcing agents; hence imitation seems a very plausible explanation, particularly for behavior that appears after infancy.

Early Reinforcement. Social learning is the basis of identity: we learn to become the persons we are. This learning begins at birth and possibly before, since it has been shown that the fetus can be conditioned to various sounds (Spelt, 1948). During the first few months of life, the infant learns to do those things that bring physical satisfaction: warmth, contact with soft-textured materials, a full stomach, an empty bladder, and so forth. Some of this learning is simple and re-

flexive, but not all of it is. Consider the matter of sleeping. Adults sometimes forget that being put to bed is a form of social isolation. Before hand, the infant has been the object of attention for an extended period: he has been cuddled, talked to, played with, fed, and diapered. Then suddenly he is put into a dark room. Many a child complains about this treatment and does so bitterly. Parents in our culture rather characteristically try to ignore the child's crying for several minutes and then begin to worry about whether something is wrong with him. Perhaps he has gas on his stomach; perhaps his diaper needs changing. And so they go in to investigate. The crying stops during the period of attention, but begins again once the parent is out of the room. What the parent unwittingly has done is to reinforce the crying, say the learning theorists. They point out, furthermore, that much of our child care operates to reinforce obstreperous, noisy, demanding, behavior, and consequently extinguishes quiet, happy, constructive behavior. Inasmuch as attention is a reinforcer, and we have shown that it is a powerful one, we are in the position of reinforcing misbehavior rather than positive behavior. What parents should do, they say, is to pay attention to a child when he is engaging in the kind of behavior of which they approve and to ignore him when he misbehaves. Most parents, however, for practical reasons or otherwise, are unable to administer schedules of reinforcement that require them to ignore crying babies. Perhaps the solution would be to have the baby's crib in the family room so that he would not be put to bed when the family is still up and around, but such a solution would be out of place in a culture that requires that children have a bedtime and that it be enforced, and in which parents are inclined to value and look forward to "some time to themselves."

Culturally Determined Expectations. Some of the variability in human behavior can be accounted for by differences in the biological makeup of infants—some are energetic, some passive, some hypersensitive and querulous, some wakeful, and some always sleepy. Families begin to modify this behavior from the very beginning. For one thing, they have certain expectations for children which are derived from the culture, as filtered through their more personalized views of the world in general and infants in particular. Clyde Kluckhohn (1949) reported that certain proportions of white and Zuñi babies born at a New Mexico hospital could be classified as unusually active, average, or quiet. When the same children were observed two years later, the white babies who were unusually active still displayed a high degree of restlessness, but the Zuñi babies who were unusually active at birth were much more subdued. Such a baby may have been more active than other Zuñi children his age, but he was markedly less active than the white children who were hyperactive at birth. The reason for the difference may be found in the different ways of life that characterize the cultures of Anglo-Americans and Zuñis. Whereas vigorousness and forthright self-expressiveness are valued, imitated, and reinforced in the dominant middle-class Anglo-American culture, Zuñis tend to be mild-mannered, relaxed, and nonaggressive. Their disapproval of people who show initiative and drive runs so high that in former times such people were branded as witches and hung up by their thumbs (Benedict, 1934). As Kluckhohn says, "culture channels biological processes." Culture does not replace or eliminate a biologically determined behavior pattern, such as hyperactivity, but it shapes it, puts its stamp on it, and attempts to make it compatible and consistent with the values and norms of the society into which the child is born.

Kluckhohn's observations regarding the activity level of Anglo-American children have, incidentally, been corroborated more recently by a study comparing the reactions of junior high school children in Austin, Texas, with a comparable group in Mexico City. When asked what their probable response would be to a number of different situations, children in the United States were much more likely to select active alternatives, whereas Mexican children were more likely to select passive alternatives (Hereford, Selz, Stenning, & Natalicio, 1967).

Much of what is called "national character" consists of patterns of behavior that are learned during the formative years of childhood, when parental expectations have the maximum effect on children's behavior, first through direct reinforcement of behavior parents believe is appropriate, and later through imitation, when children adopt parental expectations as their own. We shall have more to say about this process when we discuss the effect of culture on behavior, but are introducing the idea here because the acquisition of culturally determined behavior is an example of social learning.

Values and Expectations. It is important to note that parents are often not immediately aware of the kinds of expectations they are expressing

"There, there, honey... "Why DON'T they?" Boys don't cry."

in their treatment of children. In fact, there is often a gap or a disparity between the parents' "official position" (the culturally determined values they subscribe to publicly) and the kind of social behavior they display. This type of disparity occurs when people try to live in accordance with a number of different sets of values, and is characteristic of cultures that are in periods of change. Pluralistic cultures, like ours, which are made up of values and attitudes that immigrants have brought with them from their parent cultures are likely to create problems because they create situations in which conflicting ideologies exist side by side. The ideas that boys should be boisterous and aggressive, and that they should not disturb or annoy others, are examples of two sets of mutually inconsistent values that exist side by side in our culture.

As a result of such conflicts in values, parents may say one thing and do another. Rajput mothers in Khalapur, India, claim that they praise their children when they do things that meet with parental approval. The observation of anthropologists disconfirms this self-image, however, because the mothers actually seldom praise their children and instead use adversive methods of control: scolding, cursing, threatening, and the like. Incidentally, one threat commonly used by mothers is that of telling children that Americans will come and give them injections, take them away, beat them, or even eat them (Minturn & Hitchcock, 1963).

Parallel examples of disparity between public statements and private actions are not difficult to find in other cultures. Although American mothers and fathers would heatedly deny that they are interested in encouraging their adolescent children to engage in sexual intercourse, the fact that they actively encourage dating when children are barely into puberty, tolerate kissing and hugging, and condone "going steady" would suggest to any detached, objective observer that the parents may be working at cross purposes to their official position. Indeed, some behavioral

scientists believe that increases in heterosexual activity among teenagers in recent years may be attributed in part to corresponding increases in parental permissiveness, which in turn reflect changing cultural norms and values (Bandura & Walters, 1963). This is another example of how biologically determined behavior can be shaped by cultural influences. In some primitive cultures, children are expected to engage in heterosexual activity quite early, but the general pattern in industrialized cultures is for them to postpone such behavior. As a result, parents in the primitive cultures in question believe that the sex drive appears very early, but parents in industrialized cultures believe that it does not occur until middle or late adolescence. Just to be on the safe side, however, secondary school authorities in most Western countries segregate students by sex beginning with the pubertal years, the schools in the United States and Canada being notable exceptions.

The existence of mutually incompatible systems of values may create problems for children who are striving to learn appropriate patterns of behavior. It is confusing when parents and other authority figures state that adolescents should under no circumstances engage in sexual intercourse, backing up their position with severe penalties, and at the same time permit, encourage, and actually arrange social affairs in such a way that both sexes spend a great deal of time together, much of it alone. When sexual intercourse does occur, as it often does, there is a sense of outrage on the part of adults and of guilt on the part of the participants. Everyone is distressed and confused. One of the things learned, therefore, is that sexual relations are distressing and confusing, outrageous and guilt producing: a natural outcome when people are trying to subscribe to two sets of values and are strongly committed to both.

The situation with respect to sex is further complicated by the fact that the mass media present an image of sex that is associated with fun and games. Children and teenagers thus have three sets of values to sort out: (1) Judeo-Christian attitudes condemning premarital or extramarital sex; (2) the parental idea that it is permissible, if not desirable, for teenagers (and even "preteens") to date and to "go steady"; and (3) the values of the mass media, which maintain that premarital or extramarital sex is fun and that everyone is doing it.

The Choice of Models. There are sets of models available for each of these points of view. The first group consists of most middle-class parents, teachers, clergymen, and other authority figures; the second is composed of teenagers who take advantage of parental permissiveness, are sexually active, and encourage their adventurous peers to do likewise; and the third is made up of people in the entertainment world whose real adventures are broadcast in the public press, and whose fictional adventures form the content of film and television romances. Adults today spend much time speculating why so many teenagers prefer and often imitate the second and third type of model. The answer seems to be that these models are the individuals whose behavior is setting the trend of the times: the emerging norms and values of our pluralistic culture. They are, furthermore, somewhat younger, livelier, and more visible than the first group of models, and teenagers find it easier to identify with them.

Reference Groups. These models also constitute what is termed a *reference group* for a great many teenagers. Reference groups are ". . . groups to which an individual relates himself or aspires to relate himself as a part psychologically . . ." (Sherif, 1963). Reference groups may serve as sources of attitudes and values, which are imitated and which serve as bases for further social learning. In effect, persons making use of reference groups *refer* to the attitudes and behavior of such groups in determining their own attitudes and behavior. A person does not have to be a member of a reference group to have it affect his behavior. Popular musicians are refer-

ence groups for many teenagers who are not themselves musicians and never will be. On the other hand, the group of which the teenager is actually a member may also be a reference group for him in the sense that he uses it as a basis for learning attitudes and patterns of behavior. Inasmuch as we reveal "who we are" by our attitudes and behavior, the reference groups which we use as models help us learn our identity.

Parents serve as reference groups for children under ordinary circumstances, particularly during the years when children are first beginning to imitate. As the child approaches school age, he begins to identify with and imitate other reference groups, some of them rather remote, like television cowboys of the Old West or comic strip characters, but others quite real, like kindergarten teachers or older brothers.

Reference Groups and Complexity of Behavior. Children's behavior becomes increasingly complex and varied with each year of development. The highest degree of similarity and the least variability is to be found in the behavior of infants. Although there are differences in temperament and activity, as noted earlier, new-born infants are more similar at this stage of development than they are at any future time. They all require a great deal of sleep, they can ingest only soft foods, they have no inhibitory control over the evacuation of body wastes, and so forth. As they begin to develop and acquire new behaviors, however, variations begin to appear. Jimmy, who was born at the same time as Johnny, began to smile at three weeks of age, but Johnny did not smile until he was over a month old. On the other hand, Johnny learned to crawl a month sooner than Jimmy did. At one year of age, Jimmy could say three or four words, but Johnny was still making baby sounds. At one year of age there are many more differences between Jimmy and Johnny than there were at birth. As their behavior is being shaped by two different sets of parents and as they come to imitate some of the behavior of their parents, they will develop still more differences. By the time they are in school, the number of differences is still further increased by the fact that each refers his behavior to a different set of reference groups. Jimmy goes to mass every Sunday, and his chief ambition is to be an altar boy. His father is a plumber and is also active in the local Democratic organization. Jimmy likes to sit in the corner of the kitchen after supper and listen to his father talk politics with his friends. Johnny's reference groups include Superbatman, a television character; a group of older boys who spend all their spare time sailing; and two older brothers who are amateur scientists. By the time Jimmy and Johnny are teenagers, the number of different reference groups with which they identify, and from which they learn, will be further increased, thus promoting even additional differences in their behavior.

As children become adolescents and adults in a complex, urbanized, and industrialized society like ours, the number of reference groups that are available continues to increase. The more reference groups that figure in an individual's life, the more complex his behavior will become, and this complexity furnishes a further basis for behavioral differences.

If we are to map out a useful scheme for understanding an individual's social learning, we must determine what reference groups he is using, what importance he attaches to each of them, and what he is learning from them. A person obviously cannot imitate all the behavior of even one reference group; he must select out certain characteristics or aspects of the great range that the group presents. Presumably he will select aspects that are more central than others, but this does not always hold true. A teenager who uses folk musicians as his reference group may not even try to imitate their most central characteristic— playing guitars and singing folk songs—but instead may imitate their dress. This, for him, symbolizes the group. Another teenager whose reference group is a gang of motorcyclists is also a member of the group. Central to this group is owning and riding a motorcycle. This he does, but he also copies the dress, mannerisms, attitudes, and values of the group.

Attitudes and values may be the most psychologically significant things that are learned from a reference group, because they serve as the basis for a vast complex of social behaviors. Like the other kinds of individual differences we have discussed, values and attitudes are learned, that is, we learn to value or prefer one type of event, course of action, or object over the others that are possible or available to us. Because values and attitudes are such an important part of social behavior, the following chapter is devoted to a discussion of this topic.

Perceptual Factors in Social Learning. Attitudes and values are determined by how people perceive, which in turn tends to be determined by preexisting patterns of attitudes and values. There is a circular, mutually reinforcing relationship between attitudes and values, on the one hand, and perceptual styles on the other. We learn as children what is important and what is to be ignored, and this learning forms one of the bases for the structure of attitudes and values that will develop. The Japanese child learns to be intolerant of dirt on his person, but to be tolerant of it in public places. Dirt that comes in contact with the skin is perceived as a kind of threat, but dirt and clutter that accumulate in railroad stations and in the streets is likely to be overlooked. The Japanese child is also likely to learn the values inherent in a fairly authoritarian social structure which stresses differences in status and even incorporates them into the grammar of the language. These values lead him to perceive relations between himself and others in terms of sharply stratified positions, and his perception of the behavior of others tends to confirm the validity of these values.

The American child also learns a value system that reflects a degree of social stratification, together with appropriate grammatical forms of address—very formal, moderately formal, and familiar. However, this value system is in conflict with another set of cultural values that stress personal equality as a social virtue. As a consequence, social differences are likely to be blurred and somewhat confused for American children. A three-year-old American child is, for example, more likely to use the first-name form of address in speaking to an adult than is a European or an Oriental child. Although some American adults will correct a child who uses this form of address, a great many of them will tolerate it. The fact that the adult continues to treat the child in an accepting way may reinforce the child's belief that the social distance between him and the adult is small or that it is of little importance. As a consequence, American children tend to adopt a direct, open approach to adults, an approach that may be friendly or aggressive, but that is quite different from the apprehensive, subdued air that European and Oriental children generally have when they are approached by adults.

Reward Differences among Models. As American children grow older, they become more aware of the status differential that exists between children and adults. For one thing, they learn that it is appropriate for adults to address children by their given names, but that adults expect to be addressed as "Mr. Jones," "Miss Smith," or "Mrs. James." With this learning comes an awareness that in spite of the ambiguities and pretensions that characterize the social relations between adults and children, differences in status and power are very real and important. For one thing, the adult's higher status means that he has considerable control over the reward system that applies to children.

Joan Grusec and Walter Mischel (1966) studied the learning that takes place in children as they interact with adults with varying potentialities for reward. In their experiment, one of two kinds of persons (who were to serve as behavior models in the experiment) introduced themselves to individual four-year-old children. One type of model told the child she was his new nursery school teacher and spent some time with him playing with a number of very attractive toys and displaying much warmth and affection. The idea was for her to establish herself as an unconditionally rewarding person, having attractive resources at her disposal. The other type of model introduced the child to some wornout toys, seated herself at a desk, saying she had some work to do, and made no attempt to initiate interaction with the child. The idea here was to present herself as a low-reward person, with few resources at her disposal. After this initial period of orientation, each model played a game with the child involving a series of ritualistic and irrelevant acts—marching, counting, posing with a hat on her head, and the like. After the model left, a confederate, who had been in the room during the game, asked the child how many of the actions of the model he could remember and could imitate. Results showed that children could remember more of the actions of the first type of model than the second. In other words, the model who said she was the children's teacher, and who thus indicated that she had some future power to reward them, was the model from whom the children learned most readily.

What Grusec and Mischel found in this study applies to older children and adults as well: we are more likely to imitate those individuals who have some power to reward or reinforce us in the future. Our learning is in effect "payment in advance" for rewards yet to be received. We prefer such models to those who are more psychologically remote and who lack the power to reward.

A great deal of learning in social contexts is concerned with determining who our models shall be. If the power of models to reinforce us directly is relatively equal, we are inclined to prefer models that are highly visible, who appear to represent the major trend in the groups of which we are members, and who represent values that are not too dissimilar to the ones we subscribe to.

As we interact with other members of our

groups, including the models themselves, we imitate behavior that is reinforced and is reinforcing. Indeed, every social situation is one in which we are reinforcing the behavior of others and are ourselves reinforced in return. In one sense, the entire field of social psychology may be viewed as being concerned with the conditions, processes, and products of social reinforcement. This is not the only way, of course, in which social phenomena may be perceived or studied, but it constitutes a significant dimension of social behavior and opens up many avenues for research and investigation.

SUMMARY

Inasmuch as association with others has a reward value, we learn patterns of interaction and social behavior in order to secure these rewards and enhance their continuance. Performance can be facilitated by the amount of attention paid us by others, as well as the degree to which the attention is favorable. Individuals who have previously received relatively less attention are more responsive to social rewards than are those who have received more attention.

Reward and reinforcement explain only part of the behavior that is learned in social contexts.

Bandura and Walters have shown that many forms of behavior are learned through a process of imitating the behavior of models, and that imitation may be more of an inducement in learning than reinforcement.

Social learning begins in infancy; even cultural styles and patterns of behavior make themselves felt at this age. Cultural value systems are learned during the childhood years, but cultures are often equivocal and may teach mutually inconsistent patterns. Attitudes toward sex in Western societies are an example. The situation is further complicated by the availability of different models for each set of value systems. These models generally constitute reference groups, which serve as sources of behavior and value patterns that are imitated by young people. The fact that a variety of reference groups is available leads to the development of complex patterns of behavior. Values and attitudes learned by young people help determine their perceptual styles: their way of perceiving their environment, as well as their own behavior.

One factor that determines the attractiveness of models is their ability to reward. Given a choice of models, we are likely to prefer those that have a higher reward potential.

SUGGESTED READINGS

Bandura, A. & Walters, R. H., *Social learning and personality development.* New York: Holt, Rinehart, and Winston, 1963.

Lindgren, H. C. (Ed.), *Contemporary research in social psychology.* New York: Wiley, 1969. See Section 3, "Social learning."

Whiting, B. B. (Ed.), *Six cultures: studies of child rearing.* New York: Wiley, 1963.

CHAPTER FIVE

Suzanne Szasz

Raymond Nania, Nancy Palmer

Elizabeth Wilcox

Social Attitudes and Motives

Social Motives and Behavior. In Chapters 2, 3, and 4 we pointed out that interaction with others has positive value for us, enables us to identify and define ourselves, and has the effect of reinforcing certain aspects of our behavior, thus bringing about the phenomenon we have termed social learning. In this chapter we explore some of the characteristics of the identities and definitions that we learn and that in turn lead us to select certain models and reinforcements and to avoid others. We are particularly interested in the kinds of motives generally overlooked by the casual observer, motives that are likely to be implicit and subtle, rather than explicit and obvious.

As Donald T. Campbell (1963) points out, a number of terms with overlapping meanings are used by psychologists to describe social motives and related motivational states. Campbell lists seventy-six of them, running alphabetically from "acquired drive" to "value," and including such terms as "attitude," "frame of reference," "belief," "idea," and "set." Each of these terms describes a somewhat different aspect of the individual's predisposition to behave in one way or another, but all of them are affected by or result from social learning.

In our discussion we use the term "social motive" as the general term that includes all the others. Motives, of course, produce behavior, and some of the terms listed by Campbell, like "attitude" and "set," may not necessarily lead to any kind of action. It can be argued, however, that if they exist at all they will reveal themselves in some way in the individual's behavior; otherwise their existence may be questioned. Indeed it is through the behavior of the individual, be it in some direct and obvious form, verbally, or in some indirect way, that we are able to deduce that he does in fact have such-and-such a motive.

Campbell (1963) prefers to use the term "acquired behavioral dispositions," instead of "social motives." His general idea is consistent, however, with the direction we have taken, in that both learning and behavior are implied. He notes that as behavior is modified by experience, there is a certain residue of experience that serves to "guide, bias, or otherwise influence later behavior." It is this residue that concerns us in this chapter.

The Nature of Attitudes. Attitudes are of greater interest to the social psychologist than are the other subvarieties of social motives, probably because of their key role in social behavior. This interest is indicated by the large number of research studies that have been conducted on the measurement and manipulation of attitudes. Daniel Katz and Ezra Stotland (1959) define an attitude as "an individual's tendency or predisposition to evaluate an object or a symbol of that object in a certain way." They conceive of attitudes as having affective, cognitive, and behavioral components, that is, as involving feelings and emotions, beliefs, and action. More of one component than another may be present in a given attitude. Some attitudes are heavily loaded with affective components and do not require any action beyond the expression of feelings. Other attitudes are heavily intellectualized to the point where they cannot be used as valid predictors of the course the individual will take in a social situation. Action-oriented attitudes may involve a minimum of feeling and belief and may emerge when a need can be satisfied simply and directly.

Katz and Stotland maintain that each attitude has a single referent, but that attitudes may be organized into consistent and coherent structures known as *value systems*. The term *ideology* is used to designate integrated sets of beliefs and values that justify the policies of a group or an institution.

Social attitudes, according to Campbell (1963), are characterized by consistency in response to social objects. This consistency facilitates the development of integrated systems of attitudes and values which we use in determining what kind of action to take when faced with any of a wide array of possible situations. These systems enable us to interpret and evaluate events around us and within us; without such a source of cues for interpretation and action, events would seem ambiguous and confused. Value systems determine how we shall perceive and are in themselves ways of perceiving; in fact, it is difficult and often impossible to distinguish between the motive to perceive in a certain way and the perceptual act itself.

A system of attitudes and values may also be conceived as a learned perceptual style that we come to depend on for the apprehension of "reality." The kind of style we learn and the kind of reality we perceive depends to a large extent on our models. We may occasionally get a glimpse of the insubstantial nature of our "reality" when our predictions of people's future behavior are disconfirmed, or when we find that our interpretations of an event differ markedly from those of people who have been subjected to a different set of learning experiences. Americans view the Hindu custom of permitting cows to wander about the streets, leading a parisitical existence in a land that cannot find enough food for its people, as completely unrealistic and irrational. Hindus, on the other hand, take the stand that cows are really living representations of the mother goddess Kamadhenu, and that to kill them off would be a form of murder. Hindus also maintain that the execution of criminals, which is legal in most of the United States, is actually murder, an allegation that is denied by most Americans, who are certain that they do not become murderers when they execute a criminal. Both the Hindu and the American are generally unaware, in these examples, of the extent to which their "reality" is determined by their culture, as expressed in the attitudes and values of the persons with whom they associate.

Conflicts between Attitudinal Systems. We noted previously that intellectualized attitudes may serve as poor predictors of the kind of social behavior that actually emerges. People may develop attitudes that are wholly or partially intellectualized out of a need to satisfy two or more conflicting systems of beliefs and or values. Let us consider the case of Abu Marques, a lawyer and legislator in one of the new, developing countries that was until recently a colonial possession of a European power. Mr. Marques is publicly committed to democracy, for he participates in and openly supports a government based on a democratic constitution. However, Mr. Marques grew up in a tribal village in the back country that is still dominated by traditional and highly authoritarian patterns of behavior. In his village, power and influence are held in direct proportion to the individual's age and position in the tribal organization. Furthermore, status can only be inherited; it cannot be earned. Women there are treated as second-class citizens, although they received the right to vote when the country gained its independence.

Although Mr. Marques' legislative behavior is exemplary according to democratic standards, his wife and children must defer to him at home. He makes all decisions in his family; his wife has a money allowance on which to run the household, and she must account for every penny. His law office runs along similar lines: his clerks and assistants are expected to treat him with a deference that borders on obsequiousness. Mr. Marques also displays much the same kind of deference to the prime minister and the members of the cabinet. It is clear that his open support of democratic ideals and his political behavior are rather inconsistent with his private behavior and his behavior toward high government officials. Hence it is not clear what system of values Mr. Marques subscribes to. Some of his behavior is consistent with democratic attitudes, but other aspects are consistent with more authoritarian and traditional patterns. It is also quite possible that Mr. Marques is unaware of the discrepancy between his public statements regarding democracy and his behavior outside the legislative halls.

The classic study of this discrepancy between publicly avowed attitudes and observed behavior was conducted by Richard T. LaPiere (1934) who journeyed across the United States with a Chinese couple many years ago. Only one out of the 184 restaurants they attempted to eat in refused to serve them, but when LaPiere wrote them later to ask if they served Chinese, 91 percent of the 128 who replied stated they did not do so. Obviously, the questionnaires evoked a different reaction (and obviously a different kind of attitude) on the part of restaurant personnel than was evoked by the appearance of guests expecting to be served. Experiences of Negroes seeking apartments suggests that a similar study conducted today would produce the opposite effect, namely, a questionnaire polling of landlords would probably elicit the response that they do not practice segregation, but the Negro who appears in person and asks to see an apartment is told by the manager that it has been rented. Again, the questionnaire evokes a different response than does the person on whose behalf it is sent.

Although these examples are notable for the marked degree of inconsistency between stated motives and observed behavior, the persons in each of the situations may be somewhat more consistent than they appear. As we pointed out in Chapter 4, when we discussed the difference between society's official position on sex and the behavior it seems to encourage, people in complex social situations are often faced with the need to respond to a variety of value systems. It would make their problem easier and their behavior more consistent if they would reorient their values and make them mutually compatible, but such an undertaking is hardly feasible in a pluralistic society that tolerates and supports a number of competing ideologies. Some values are likely to have more significance for an individual than are others. Hence he is inclined to give lip service to certain values that he thinks are widely accepted, but when faced by a critical situation in which there is a high degree of stress he may react according to a different set of values altogether. To the observer, the behavior seems inconsistent; to the individual involved there is no inconsistency, because the differences in the two situations simply call for the application of different sets of principles or values.

One task here is that of determining what processes enable individuals to view their apparently inconsistent behavior as consistent. Such investigation may lead to the discovery of underlying attitude and value structures that would enable us to predict behavior in a wider variety of situations. The basic assumption in such research is that there will be a thread of consistency running through attitudes, values, and the social behavior they govern. Indeed, the fact that people generally behave consistently underlies much of the research concerned with the measurement of attitudes.

The Measurement of Attitudes

Attitudes cannot be directly observed, but must be inferred from behavior, either from observation of an individual's responses to objects, persons, and other events or from his evaluative statements and other verbal expressions. It is difficult to observe the actions of an individual in any direct, systematic way, although sometimes this approach is the only way of determining the significance an attitude has for a person. It is usually easier and more efficient to base such judgments on the individual's verbal—written or spoken—statements. This can be done through interview, but the task can be accomplished even more efficiently and precisely with paper-and-pencil scales and questionnaires. There are some disadvantages to the paper-and-pencil method, but because this technique permits the collection of a great deal of information in a short time, and because instruments can be refined and elaborated to a high degree, social psychologists have used this approach more than others. Results obtained from paper-and-pencil instruments also have the added advantage of being easier to analyze statistically.

Dimensions of Attitudes. Attitude measures are concerned first of all with the *direction* of the attitude being assessed: is it for or against the object, person, or event that is the target or focus of the attitude? On a typical attitude scale, direction may be indicated on a "like-dislike" dimension, by checking "yes" or "no," or one of similar pairs of options.

The *intensity* or strength of an attitude is also important. Does the respondent feel strongly about the target of the attitude, or are his feelings weak or ambivalent? Intensity can be measured in various ways: by indicating one's position on a graduated scale of values, by selecting a statement from an array whose intensity ranges from "strong" to "weak," or checking a greater or lesser number of options weighted in a given direction. Both direction and intensity are heavily loaded with the affective component of attitudes mentioned earlier. Direction indicates feeling for or against, and intensity indicates the strength of feelings involved in the attitude being expressed.

Measurers of attitudes are sometimes concerned about the *centrality* of an attitude. Is it close to the center of a system of attitudes and values that are highly significant to the welfare and goals of the individual? Does it occupy a key position? Or is it a peripheral and marginal attitude? Implications for affective, cognitive, and behavioral aspects are all involved. Attitudes that are strongly held are likely to be central, are likely to be supported by a set of beliefs, and are also likely to provide motives for action. An example of centrality is those attitudes held with reference to the self. People tend to feel more strongly about themselves than about any other object. Their beliefs about themselves and their relations with their environment are likely to be strongly

held, to the point where they are quite ready to go on the defensive if either attitudes or supporting beliefs are attacked or questioned. Self-regarding attitudes also serve as guidelines for actions of all kinds and hence can be considered as important motivators for behavior.

Related to centrality and intensity is *salience*— the degree to which an attitude is given prominence by its holder—its visibility, so to speak. Not all central attitudes are salient. Henry Long's attitudes toward himself are, like most people's, both central and intense, but he does not give them any particular prominence in his everyday interaction with others. He does, however, work very hard trying to recruit members for the religious sect to which he belongs, even bringing religion into every conversation. Anyone who knows Henry thinks of him in terms of the sect he represents, and his attitudes on religion therefore have a high degree of salience.

Attitudes may also be measured in terms of their *consistency*—the extent to which various attitudes and attitude systems fit together and are related. We would expect that because Henry Long is such a devout and loyal member of his particular religious sect, he also has a high regard for other members of that sect. Such an attitude would be consistent with the attitudes whose salience he has revealed by his industrious attempts to proselytize. If we discover that he actually has a *low* opinion of his fellow church members, we are surprised, because such an attitude is inconsistent with his attitudes toward his religion. The attitudes that an individual has toward an institution, such as a church, are ordinarily consistent with his attitudes toward persons associated with the institution. There tends to be a degree of consistency among all the attitudes held by a person, but inconsistencies are common. In the example cited earlier of Abu Marques and the study by LaPiere (1934), the inconsistencies were due to attempts to cope with two different value systems. The individuals concerned resolved their dilemma by perceiving the two situations as essentially different and thus calling for the application of different rules of conduct, but the inconsistencies in their behavior are nonetheless readily apparent to the objective observer.

Types of Measures. Early attempts to measure attitudes consisted of fairly loose, ad hoc lists of statements presumably related to the attitude at issue. L. L. Thurstone, with the help of E. J. Chave (1929), developed a more refined method of scaling statements which he called "the method of subjectively appearing equal intervals" (Thurstone, 1931). The "Thurstone equal appearing interval scale" is a more common term today. The Thurstone method consists of making a collection of opinions, ranging from very positive to very negative, about a certain object, person, or institution. The statements are then given to a group of individuals who are asked to judge the opinions on an eleven-point scale, on which 1 represents the least favorable, and 11 the most favorable. The judges are asked to try to arrange the statements in such a way that they are distributed over the full range from 1 to 11. The median rating that judges assign any given statement is then taken as an index to the strength and direction of the attitude expressed by the statement. Table 5-1 presents a sampling of items drawn from the Desegregation Scale, a twenty-six-item scale that has been used in a study of attitudes toward Negroes in the South (Kelly, Ferson, & Holtzman, 1958). The researchers began with a pool of 200 statements, from which they selected seventy-six that they considered to be better than the others. The seventy-six statements were then submitted to a panel of 102 college students, who rated them on Thurstone's eleven-point scale. The twenty-six items on which the judges showed the most agreement were then selected to form the Desegregation Scale. The values to the left of each item in Table 5-1 represent their original scale values. These values were converted to a five-point scale for simplicity in scoring. In other words, a respondent who agrees

Table **5-1.** A sampling of Thurstone-type items drawn from the Desegregation Scale and ranked from the least favorable (10.4) to the most favorable (1.1) (Kelly, Ferson, & Holtzman, 1958)

10.4   The Negro will remain ignorant and superstitious despite equal educational opportunities.

8.9   Negroes living in white neighborhoods lower the standards of cleanliness.

7.7   Admitting Negroes to white schools would not work because most Negroes do not have the necessary background to keep up with white students.

4.3   The Negro race will eventually reach the cultural and intellectual level of white people.

3.4   I would not object to participating in school athletics with Negroes.

2.1   I would not object to dancing with a good Negro dancer.

1.1   The best way to solve the race problem is to encourage intermarriage so that there will eventually be only one race.

with the first item in the sample would receive a "4" for that response, whereas a respondent who agrees with the last item would receive a "0." The highest possible score on the scale would therefore be 104 and the lowest possible would be 0. The higher the score, the more negative the attitude toward Negroes.

A different method of measuring attitudes has been developed by Rensis Likert (1932). Like the Thurstone questionnaire, the respondent is confronted with a series of statements, but instead of indicating mere agreement or disagreement, he is able to choose one of five alternatives: strongly agree (1), agree (2), undecided (3), disagree (4), and strongly disagree (5). The statements are then submitted to a group of respondents who make their responses to each item. The results are then analyzed statistically; items that have the highest intercorrelation with the total score on all the items are retained and the others eliminated. The purpose of this procedure is to obtain a group of items which measure the same attitude or complex of attitudes. Such a test thus possesses a high degree of internal consistency and shows significant differences between those who are positively oriented to the matter in question and those who are negatively inclined.

Another method, introduced by Louis Guttman (1950) ranks groups of statements in such a way that an affirmative answer to any one of them assumes an affirmative answer to all the others ranking below it on the scale. Questions have to be meticulously phrased and carefully pretested to meet this criterion, but the resulting instrument is said to be highly reliable and consistent.

Still another type of scale is the semantic differential, which requires the respondent to rate an object, person, or event on a number of bipolar scales (e.g., good-bad, hot-cold). This method has been used to measure the affective aspects of the meaning of words, and we shall give it more extended treatment in the chapter on communication.

There are also various kinds of free-response techniques, some of which are verbal and others which use paper and pencil. They have the advantage of enabling respondents to mention salient attitudes that might otherwise escape the attention of researchers, but have the disadvantage of being difficult to score, and results generally do not possess a high degree of statistical precision. Free-response methods are also useful in gathering information on highly significant attitudes that respondents would conceal if more direct forms of questions were used. For example, when respondents in one study were asked, in an hour-long interview, what they worried about, only one mentioned sex or "love life." But when respondents were shown a cartoon of a person being asked what kind of problem was bothering him, they were much more likely to suggest that his problem was his "love life" (Sanford, 1951).

The Authoritarian Personality

We are using authoritarian attitudes as our main example of the way in which attitude research is conducted because of the prominent place that such research has occupied during the past twenty years. More studies have appeared dealing with this attitude than with any other. Furthermore, authoritarian attitudes have important implications for many different kinds of social behavior, such as child-rearing practices, leadership, group problem solving, and ethnic prejudice.

Authoritarian attitudes are expressed in behavior variously described as dogmatic, rigid, strongly supportive of traditional values, and highly status-oriented—behavior, in other words, that is submissive toward individuals possessing higher status and domineering where lower-status individuals are concerned. Also consistent with authoritarian attitudes are tendencies to endorse the use of power tactics, toughness in dealing with failure and noncooperativeness, arbitrariness in decision making, and willingness to use drastic methods in dealing with deviant behavior. The activities of Nazis and other fascist groups are often cited as prime examples of authoritarianism, but any individual who uses or endorses harsh, punitive, or violent methods is motivated by authoritarian attitudes.

The word "authoritarian" is roughly equivalent to "autocratic," and its opposite, "equalitarian," is approximately equivalent to "democratic." Authoritarian attitudes are characteristic of relations among people who regard themselves and one another as basically unequal in value, whereas democratic attitudes imply equal-value relationships. We are not referring here to inequality or equality in wealth, skill, or physical strength, but rather to the way in which people regard one another. The more people regard themselves and each other as worthy of equal consideration, merely by virtue of their existence as human beings, the more their relationships will take place on a democratic basis. The more the mutually perceived personal value departs from equality, the more the relationship is likely to be characterized by authoritarian attitudes and behavior.

Striving to maintain equal-status relationships

precludes the use of power, inasmuch as recourse to power tactics would imply an inequality in status. Maintaining democratic or equalitarian relationships thus means that problems must be resolved on the basis of a desire to understand and consider the interests of all concerned. Inasmuch as such an approach is time consuming and may lead to lengthy negotiation, it follows that patience, restraint, and self-control are needed to keep matters from regressing to the kind of drastic and arbitrary tactics characteristic of authoritarian modes of behavior.

Although social psychologists often refer to the "authoritarian personality" as though it were a distinct type, they recognize that in actuality there is a scale of behavior that ranges from "extremely authoritarian" to "extremely democratic." Social behavior and attitudes can be referred to positions on such a scale to determine whether they are more or less authoritarian. Similarly, individuals can be rated on such a scale in terms of the kind of behavior they usually or most characteristically display, keeping in mind that people may vary somewhat from one social situation to another, but also recognizing that there tends to be a mode or a norm that most of us conform to in our relations with others. The point is that both "authoritarian" and "democratic" represent extreme polar positions and that most people would be grouped around the middle of such a scale.

The Berkeley Study. The classic study of authoritarian traits was conducted at the University of California in Berkeley during the 1940's and published in 1950. The study was subsidized by the research department of the American Jewish Committee, and the motivation to conduct the investigation seems to have been, at least as far as the Committee was concerned, the fear that fascism might become as much of a menace in the United States as it did in Germany. The researchers designed a number of special questionnaires, collected large quantities of data over a period of several years, and published their re-

port, *The authoritarian personality,* in 1950 (Adorno, Frenkel-Brunswik, Levinson, & Sanford, 1950). The appearance of *The authoritarian personality* was a signal event in the history of social psychology for a number of reasons. It represented the first large-scale study of attitudes and personality using a combination of personality tests and attitude scales, together with clinical interviews and projective techniques. The study further focused on a topic that was of immediate and long-range importance from the standpoint of national and international politics, as well as from the standpoint of personal interest. The values and attitudes probed by the researchers lay at the very center of interpersonal and intergroup behavior.

The researchers proceeded by surveying opinions of the total membership of a number of different groups. Subjects included students from universities, public school teachers, prison inmates, psychiatric clinics, veterans' groups, labor unions, and service clubs. Over 2000 subjects were studied in one way or another. Four basic types of questionnaires were developed for the study: measures of anti-Semitism, political and economic conservatism, ethnocentrism, and antidemocratic trends. The latter two variables were measured by the E scale (for ethnocentrism) and the F scale (for fascism), instruments that have attracted a great deal of attention from psychologists, and it is these two scales that shall concern us primarily as we discuss authoritarian attitudes in this textbook. Here are representative items from the scales:

"America may not be perfect, but the American Way has brought us about as close as human beings can get to a perfect society." (E scale)
"Negroes have their rights, but it is best to keep them in their own districts and schools and to prevent too much contact with whites." (E scale)
"Homosexuality is a particularly rotten form of delinquency and ought to be severely punished." (F scale)

"To a greater extent than most people realize our lives are governed by plots hatched in secret by politicians." (F scale)

As data from questionnaires, personality tests, and interviews were accumulated and analyzed by the researchers, a number of trends emerged. For one thing, the correlations among the four scales were quite high and positive. The anti-Semitic scale, for example, correlated .80 with the E scale, and the E scale correlated .73 with the F scale. Persons scoring high on any of these scales also seemed to differ in a number of significant ways from those scoring low. There was a tendency, for example, for low scorers to be more "intraceptive" than high scorers—that is, the low scorers were more inclined to be introspective and self-analytical and to question their own values and behavior, whereas the high scorers resisted any idea of self-appraisal and based their life decisions on a reality that they perceived as being ordered by hard-and-fast rules. Persons scoring high on the scales were inclined to see a multitude of dangers in ambiguous situations, to deal with deviant behavior in drastic ways, to insist on obedience and deference on the part of low-status individuals, and to accord obedience and deference to those of higher status. High scorers tended to react to sex with guilt and anxiety, but also to see it as the means for achieving status and dominance, whereas low scorers saw sex as implying warmth, companionship, and mutual affection. Low-scoring subjects were more accepting of themselves and more ambivalent toward their parents and authority figures; they also showed more tolerance of ambiguous situations, were less inclined to be rigid or to excuse their own hostile or disturbing feelings by blaming them on the actions or intentions of others.

The Berkeley study has received considerable criticism, largely because the researchers were not as meticulous as they should have been in maintaining the usual scientific controls. For example, determination of subjects' ratings on authoritarianism was made by interviewers who had access before the interview to each subject's completed questionnaire. It was thus possible for preconceptions to color the percepts of interviewers. Furthermore, each interview record was scored by only one judge, thus making it impossible to determine the amount of bias that had entered into the scoring.

Further Research on Authoritarian Attitudes. Much of the research on authoritarian attitudes that has been published since the appearance of *The authoritarian personality* has been concerned with the validity of the F scale. Inasmuch as the correlations between the F scale and the other three scales used in the Berkeley study were so high, it is usually considered to be a measure not only of authoritarianism, but an indirect measure of anti-Semitism, ethnocentrism, and economic conservatism as well.

Validity studies conducted with the F scale have turned up some additional unresolved problems growing out of the Berkeley study. People who are rigid, who demand absolute and unquestioning obedience to persons in higher authority, who are intolerant of ambiguity, and who believe in drastic solutions to social problems ought to score high on the F scale. The work done by the Berkeley group and the researchers who have followed them shows that such people do, in fact, score high, but only if they are politically conservative or reactionary. People with *leftish* political views who are rigid, demand absolute obedience, etc., do *not* score high, but score in the middle and low ranges. In other words, the F scale appears to be a test of right-wing, traditional authoritarianism only, and not of left-wing radical authoritarianism (Christie, 1956).

Another problem relates to the question of whether the F scale measures authoritarian tendencies or merely acquiescence. The F-scale items, like most of the items in the four scales developed by the researchers, are stated in a positive form, so that agreement with an item results in increases in scores on the authoritarian side of the ledger, and disagreement leads to decreases. It is obvious, therefore, that persons who characteristically and uncritically agree with printed statements will score high on the F scale, irrespective of the extent to which they possess other characteristics associated with authoritarianism. It is also quite possible, of course, that highly authoritarian people are more inclined to mark statements "agree" than are persons with strong democratic leanings, but the original researchers on the authoritarian personality did not explore this possibility.

The question of whether the F scale measures authoritarian tendencies or acquiescence or both has stimulated a great deal of research. Bernard Bass (1955), for example, maintained that the F scale is so contaminated with response set (a tendency to react to *any* questionnaire item in a certain way) as to render it almost useless as a measure of authoritarian tendencies. Bass based his conclusion on the fact that scores made on a "reversed" F scale (one composed entirely of negative statements) bore almost no relationship with scores obtained on the original F-scale items. Further analysis by other researchers, however, has shown that F-scale items are not easily reversible, that is, reversing them does not necessarily give a meaning that is the direct opposite of the original. A later study by Couch and Keniston (1960), however, found that it was possible to construct F-scale-type items that could be scored negatively and that were not mere reversals of the original positive F scale. Here are two items:

"People tend to place too much emphasis on respect for authority."

"It may well be that children who talk back to their parents actually respect them more in the long run."

Couch and Keniston devised a 360-item test for measuring tendencies to agree with questionnaire items. Persons scoring high on this test they termed "yeasayers," and those scoring low "naysayers." When they studied yeasayers more intensively, using other measures and clinical interviews, they found that they appeared to be impulsive, anxious, dependent, and easily upset—persons who are described by clinical psychologists as having "weak ego controls." Naysayers, on the other hand, tended to be more mature and independent, with good impulse control. The important outcome of this research, as far as our present discussion is concerned, was the finding that there was only moderate agreement between yeasaying and authoritarianism as measured by the revised positive F scale. The correlation was .37, which, though statistically significant, meant that acquiescence was involved in only about 14 per cent of what the F scale measures. The correlation of acquiescence with a *balanced* F scale (one composed of both positive and negative items) was only .09, which suggests that the best way to eliminate acquiescence as a factor when measuring authoritarian tendencies is to use a balanced scale.

In spite of methodological flaws, and in spite of questions raised about the validity of the F scale, *The authoritarian personality* still remains an impressive work. Its main theses—that authoritarianism is a significant variable in social behavior, that it can be measured with a fair degree of accuracy, and that it is related to a large number of personality variables—have stood the test of much painstaking research. Table 5-2 presents in brief form the findings of a few of these studies. A quick review shows that whatever its shortcomings, the F scale does distinguish between persons whose behavior shows authoritarian tendencies and those whose behavior does not. The net effect is a rather firm endorsement of the general conclusions of the Berkeley study.

Social Motives Considered as Needs

The Concept of Needs. The concept of psychological needs is both different from and similar to the concepts we have already discussed in this book. "Need" is a term borrowed from physiology by way of clinical psychology and personality research. A need is, basically, a lack of some-

Table **5-2.** Brief summaries of the findings of research studies using the F scale as a measure of authoritarianism.

Tendencies to express hostility toward low-status persons.

1. High scorers on the F scale were more likely to respond with personal hostility to low-status frustrators, but with only indirect hostility to high-status frustrators (Roberts & Jessor, 1958).

2. In an experiment in which subjects thought they were administering electric shocks, high F scorers were more aggressive and punitive than low F scorers, particularly toward low-status individuals (Epstein, 1965, 1966).

Tendencies to attribute hostile and derogatory motives to others (projection).

3. When asked to rate the photographs of strangers on personality traits, high F scorers tended to display more suspicion, fear, and moral condemnation in rating the strangers. At the same time, they gave themselves high ratings on the same scales on which they had rated the strangers low (DeSoto. Kuethe, & Wunderlich, 1960).

4. High F scorers had more dreams in which aggression was directed at out-group members and more dreams with friendly content about in-group members (Meer, 1955).

Tendencies to endorse conventional and traditional values.

5. There was a high correlation (+ .61) between the F scale and a scale measuring agreement with traditional attitudes about family relationships (between children and parents, between husbands and wives, etc.) (Byrne, 1965).

Tendencies to be rigid and dogmatic.

6. When placed in an ego-involving situation, high F scorers were more likely to display rigid patterns of behavior, which in turn interfered with their ability to solve complex problems (Brown, 1953).

7. A measure of tendencies to be rigid in personal matters correlated + .62 with the F scale. (Meresko, Rubin, Shontz, & Morrow, 1954).

8. The F scale was found to be significantly correlated with a measure of intolerance of ambiguity (Kelman & Barclay, 1963).

Validation of F scale by pooled ratings of peers.

9. F scores of the members of college fraternities were found to correspond to the fraternities' reputations for being authoritarian or nonauthoritarian (Wells, Chiaravallo, & Goldman, 1957).

thing vital or important to the organism—a deficit. We all have needs for water, nourishment, oxygen, and warmth. We also have needs to be active, to rest, and to void wastes. The use of the word "need" is sometimes criticized because it actually explains nothing: it merely seems to be a label tacked on to the fact that everyone does these things. It does more than merely designate goals or behaviors, however; it also implies that a given goal or behavior is vital, and that without it life would cease or normal growth would be compromised or impeded.

Psychological needs are an extension of this basic idea, except that we do not generally think of psychological needs as being crucial to human existence in an immediate sense, although they may have long-range implications with respect to the ability to survive. They are, instead, categories of goals and/or behaviors that vary considerably from person to person, but that function to a greater or lesser extent in all of us. Another way to look at psychological needs is to think of them as motives rooted in systems or complexes of attitudes or values that are more or less consistent with one another and that function to generate certain kinds of behavior.

Although there is considerable interpersonal variation in the strength of physiological needs, there tends to be even greater variation in psychological needs. Even the universal need to associate with others, discussed in Chapter 2, is highly variable in persistence and intensity. Although physiological needs can be modified in their intensity by social learning, psychological needs are even more responsive to such modification, and indeed some needs, like the need for achievement and the need for power, are principally the result of social learning.

Personality theorists use a number of different systems of classifying needs. Abraham Maslow (1954) uses a rather simple, five-fold structure, as follows:

1. *Physiological needs*—needs involved in maintaining bodily processes.

2. *Safety needs*—needs to avoid external dangers or anything that may harm the individual.

3. *Belongingness and love needs*—the need to be given love, affection, and nurturance by another person or persons.

4. *Esteem needs*—needs to be valued, accepted, and appreciated as a person; to achieve and be adequate; to acquire status, recognition, and attention.

5. *Self-actualization*—the need for self-fulfillment.

Maslow makes a number of points about his list of needs. First, they are ordered in a developmental sequence, from those that are lower in their biological development, to those that are higher. Second, the order represents a kind of priority. Biological needs must be satisfied before an individual can turn his attention to higher needs. Furthermore, although higher needs can be postponed and are less urgent, living at the level of higher needs leads to greater biological efficiency.

It can be seen from Maslow's list that socialized needs are largely at the third and fourth levels, although social learning affects attitudes and behavior at all five levels.

A more complex array of needs has been proposed by Henry A. Murray (1938). There are twenty needs in Murray's list, ranging alphabetically from the "need for abasement" to the "need for understanding." Murray's needs are counterbalanced by "presses," which were defined in terms of what an object may do to the individual or for the individual, that is, in terms of its power to affect the well-being of the individual in one way or another. The strength of needs and presses in an individual's life may be determined by a number of clinical techniques, but the method most favored by Murray is the Thematic Apperception Test (TAT), a series of photographs and drawings that psychologists use to elicit stories from subjects. These stories can be analyzed and scored in terms of the degree to which they reflect the presence of various needs and presses.

The Achievement Motive. Although all of Murray's needs have been incorporated in one way or another in personality research, the need that has attracted the greatest amount of attention in recent years has been the need to achieve (for which we will use the common abbreviation "n Ach"). As the term implies, n Ach relates to accomplishment: mastering, manipulating, and organizing the physical and social environment; overcoming obstacles and maintaining high standards of work; competing through striving to excel one's previous performance, as well as rivaling and surpassing others; and the like. It is often contrasted with n Aff (need to affiliate), a need that relates to socializing: interacting with others, particularly with peers; pleasing others and winning their affection; expressing and maintaining attitudes of loyalty to family and to friends. Obviously, although n Ach and n Aff are not exact opposites, they imply different things. Under the goad of n Ach we tend to avoid others so as to concentrate on getting our work finished and are attracted to others only to the extent that they can help us accomplish our self-assigned tasks. Under the influence of n Aff, we are likely to place socializing and maintaining good relationships with others ahead of getting our work done. If personal accomplishment makes our friends' efforts appear inferior, we are likely to conceal our successes or even stop making efforts to succeed. It is difficult to maintain a balance between n Ach and n Aff; most of us try to accomplish this end by "compartmentalizing" our lives—by reserving some time and some activities for personal accomplishment and some for socializing.

Also contrasted with n Ach is n Power, the need to dominate and control. At first glance, n Ach and n Power seem similar, because people who are driven by a need to achieve often seek power to further their own ends, and people with power appear to be in a position to achieve many goals that are beyond the reach of those who lack the means. However, people who are dominated by n Power are more likely to be conservative and to use their power to keep things as they are, whereas people in whom n Ach is strong are more tolerant of change, inasmuch as achievement and progress are possible only in an atmosphere that tolerates changes. Later in this chapter a study is cited that shows this difference between n Ach and n Power.

The psychologists who have taken the lead in much of the research relating to n Ach are David C. McClelland of Harvard University and John W. Atkinson of the University of Michigan. McClelland and Atkinson (1948) first observed the effects that varying degrees of food deprivation have on stories written in response to the presentation of a selection of TAT pictures. They found that subjects who had been deprived of food for 16 hours tended to introduce more food-deprivation themes into their stories than had subjects who had been deprived for only 4 hours, and the latter used more such themes than did subjects who had been deprived only one hour. The experiment thus established the fact that differences in a motivational state—hunger—will appear in fantasy material.

McClelland and Atkinson then turned to research in which n Ach was manipulated and the results measured by selected TAT cards. In the "relaxed" condition, male students at Wesleyan University took some mental ability tests under the direction of an experimenter who was introduced to them as a graduate student trying out some psychological measures still in a developmental state. In the "aroused" condition, the tests were administered to subjects without their being given any advance information as to why they were taking them. At the end of an initial test period they were shown how to correct the tests and calculate their own scores. They were then directed to put their names on their booklets, together with information about secondary schools and colleges they had attended and an estimate of the level of their intelligence. The subjects were

then told that the tests they had taken were measures of intelligence, administrative ability, and leadership potential and that they were given as part of a Navy research program designed to identify colleges that were most successful in producing graduates qualified to enter administrative work. The experimenter also noted that Wesleyan University students excelled on this test and then cited (fictitious) averages achieved by "typical" Wesleyan students. The norms quoted were so high that it became obvious to all subjects that they had failed badly. Additional tests were then given, and once again norms were announced that showed the subjects had failed again. The purpose of this treatment was thus to deprive the subjects of achievement, in the same way that subjects in the earlier experiment had been deprived of food.

After this phase of the experiment had been completed, subjects were asked to write brief 5-minute stories suggested by pictures that were flashed on a screen for a few seconds. All the pictures represented work situations and represented visual samples of the kinds of things the experimenters believed people would think about when the need to achieve has been aroused. Results showed that the stories written by subjects in the "aroused" condition showed significantly more achievement-oriented themes than did stories by subjects in the "relaxed" condition. A "neutral" condition, in which the mental ability tests were given after the stories were written, produced fantasy material that was intermediate in the amount of achievement imagery displayed (McClelland, Atkinson, Clark, & Lowell, 1953). Results thus showed that achievement motivation could be manipulated experimentally and that it could be measured by fantasy material.

A more detailed discussion of the method used in the n Ach research subsequently carried out by McClelland, Atkinson, and their associates may be in order. A typical picture used to elicit fantasy material depicts a boy sitting at a desk with an open book in front of him. A subject low in n Ach may write a story something like this:

"A boy in a classroom who is daydreaming about something. He is recalling a previously experienced incident that struck his mind to be more appealing than being in the classroom. He is thinking about the experience and is now imagining himself in the situation. He hopes to be there. He will probably get called on by the instructor to recite and will be embarrassed" (McClelland, 1961).

There is nothing in this story that indicates anything in the way of n Ach. In fact, there is much that is antithetical. The following story written by another subject for the same picture is quite different:

"The boy is taking an hour written. He and the others are high-school students. The test is about two-thirds over and he is doing his best to think it through. He was supposed to study for the test and did so. But because it is factual, there were items he saw but did not learn. He knows that he has studied the answers he can't remember and is trying to summon up the images and related ideas to remind him of them. He may remember one or two, but he will miss most of the items he can't remember. He will try hard until five minutes are left, then give up, go back over his paper and be disgusted for reading but not learning the answers" (McClelland, 1961).

A number of themes in this story suggest a high level of n Ach. The boy keeps trying to do his best, in spite of repeated failures to remember. He takes responsibility for his performance and blames himself for his failure. The fact that the boy fails in the end is not, according to McClelland (1961), an indication that the subject was lacking in n Ach. Actually, there is no difference in the outcomes of stories written by persons who are high or low in this motive. The difference lies in the greater number of achievement themes that appear in their stories.

McClelland's method of measuring n Ach is more cumbersome than the questionnaire approach used in other studies of social motives, but it has a number of points to recommend it. One of the problems with questionnaires is the possibility that the respondent will become aware or even suspicious of the intentions of the experimenter and as a consequence will consciously or unconsciously slant his responses accordingly. Such response bias is less likely to occur with a free-response or projective technique like the one employed by McClelland and his associates, inasmuch as the content of the picture is quite ambiguous and the subject has few clues, if any, as to what the experimenter is measuring. Another advantage of the McClelland method is that it is well suited to cross-cultural research: pictures translate more readily with less distortion of meaning than do questionnaire items. One of the significant features of the approach used by McClelland and Atkinson has been the amount of cross-cultural research it has inspired.

Cross-Validation of n Ach Research. We have shown that the McClelland-Atkinson-TAT method produces valid results in laboratory experiments. The question now is whether the technique can be used to measure differences in n Ach that occur outside the laboratory. It is common knowledge that some people characteristically achieve more than others. Can the TAT approach produce scores that actually differentiate between achievers and nonachievers? Results indicate they do. For example, when 400 adults in upstate New York were divided at the median into high and low n Ach groups, those whose n Ach was high were more likely to have risen in social status during their lives, that is, they were more likely to be white-collar employees who had grown up in blue-collar families. On the other hand, persons with low n Ach were more likely to have remained at the same status level or to have dropped from white-collar to blue-collar status. Figure 5-1 shows the contrast between men rating high and low in

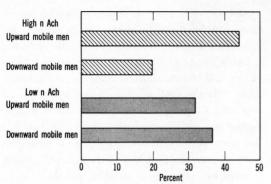

Figure **5-1.** Relationship between n Ach and ambition as indicated by upward mobility (Littig &
Yeracaris, 1965).

n Ach with respect to their status mobility. The
figure compares men with high n Ach with those
with low n Ach and should be read as follows:
44 per cent of the men with high n Ach, whose
fathers were in blue-collar occupations, now are
white-collar, whereas 20 per cent of men with high
n Ach, whose fathers were in white-collar occupations, are now blue-collar. This contrasts with 32
per cent of the men with low n Ach, whose fathers
were in blue-collar occupations, who are now
white-collar, and 37 per cent of low n Ach men,
whose fathers were in white-collar occupations,
who are now blue-collar (Littig and Yeracaris,
1965).

If ambition to move up in the social order may
be taken as one way to express n Ach, this study
shows that the McClelland method of scoring
TAT cards is a reasonably valid indicator of n
Ach differences that occur in the general population.

N Ach in Entrepreneurial Work. The need to
achieve is obviously more important in some
white-collar occupations than in others. Entrepreneurial occupations should be more likely to
attract persons rating high in n Ach. These occupations involve:

1. More responsibility for *initiating* decisions,
rather than for merely making decisions when
presented by problems.

2. More *personal* responsibility for decisions
and their results.

3. More objective feedback of data showing
success in decision making. Such data may take
the form of commissions, sales volume, production figures, and the like, rather than the subjective evaluation of success by peers or by
superiors.

4. Some degree of risk or challenge, that is,
some chance of failure if a wrong decision is
made (Meyer, Walker, & Litwin, 1961).

Entrepreneurial jobs are found in sales (ex-
cepting sales clerks), real estate and insurance,
business ownership and management, management consulting, fund raising, officership in large
corporations, and production management. Nonentrepreneurial jobs in business would include
credit managers, traffic managers, office managers, appraisers, data processers, and lower-level
jobs in money management. One study made of
business specialists in nonentrepreneurial jobs
and production managers showed that managers
had significantly higher scores on a TAT-type
measure of n Ach. Furthermore, when managers
were asked to indicate what kinds of risks they
preferred, they expressed a preference for intermediate or moderate risks, whereas persons in
nonentrepreneurial jobs tended to prefer very low
or very high risks (Meyer, Walker, & Litwin,
1961). The point here is that moderate risks represent a challenge to a person's ability, whereas
low risks are not much of a challenge and very
high risks are so chancy that the individual's
ability is a minor factor in success.

If n Ach has any stability as a personality
variable, it should persist over a period of time,
and if the TAT method of measuring n Ach is
valid, it should therefore be possible to predict
the kinds of jobs college students will find. A test
of these two propositions was made by McClelland (1965), whose associates had administered
n Ach tests to students at Wesleyan University in
1947. The students were followed up in 1961,
eleven years after they had graduated. The re-

sults of this follow-up study were striking: 83 per cent of those who had gone into entrepreneurial work had scored high in n Ach fourteen years earlier, as contrasted with only 21 per cent of those who had not gone into that kind of work.

Task Orientation and n Ach. There is a tendency for persons high in n Ach to be very task oriented. When they undertake a task that challenges them, they are reluctant to put it down or leave it before they are finished. Initial failures only make the task more attractive for them, whereas persons low in n Ach are also more easily discouraged (Weiner, 1965). Persons high in n Ach are more likely to be concerned with the time factor in getting tasks done (Meade, 1966). On the other hand they are more willing to postpone rewards if they are promised a better reward for waiting (Mischel, 1961).

Childhood Experiences and n Ach. Childhood experiences are likely to have a significant effect on n Ach. Rosen and D'Andrade (1959) studied child-parent interaction in a very interesting way. Dissatisfied with the usual method of eliciting reports on questionnaires, they visited the homes of twenty boys aged 9 to 11 who scored high in n Ach and twenty who scored low. The boys were told to build towers of irregularly shaped blocks, blindfolded, with one hand only. Parents were permitted to watch the process and asked to estimate the number of blocks their son would be able to pile without the tower toppling over. Mothers of boys with high n Ach tended to be both dominant and full of advice but also warmly enthusiastic about their sons' successes. Fathers of these boys tended to be less authoritarian than the mothers and were more likely to offer encouragement than advice. However, fathers of boys who were low in n Ach tended to be authoritarian, dominant, and interfering. It appears that fathers' authoritarianism interferes with the development of n Ach, but that mothers' authoritarianism does not, at least as far as boys are concerned.

Cross-Cultural Studies of n Ach. Authoritarian behavior is a marked and rather consistent characteristic of fathers in many traditional societies. In less advanced countries sons may not make decisions of their own, even when they are grown. If the research by Rosen and D'Andrade has any wider relevance, we would suppose that the n Ach of men growing up in such societies might rate very low and that it might also vary with the extent to which fathers are in a position to dominate the lives of their sons. These propositions were tested by Norman M. Bradburn (1963), who had the opportunity to administer TAT cards to groups of Turkish and American junior executives taking a course in schools of business administration in their respective countries. The difference between the two cultures is shown by the fact that the American subjects had a median n Ach score of 11, whereas the median for their Turkist counterparts was 6.5. Three times as many American executives as Turkish scored above the combined median. Even so, there was considerable variation among the Turkish executives. Some of them had left their families at the age of 14 to live in "village institutes," which are schools founded by the Turkish government to train teachers for the more remote areas of the country. When Turkish educational administrators were compared on n ach, it was found that those who had left home to live in village institutes at the age of 14 were twice as likely to score high on n Ach as those who had continued to live with their parents. Somewhat similar results were obtained for business executives; those who had lost their father or had lived away from their parents before they were 18 years old were three times as likely to score high on n Ach.

We noted earlier that n Ach tends to be antithetical to n Aff and n Power. John D. W. Andrews (1967) used the McClelland-Atkinson-TAT approach with executives from two business firms located in Mexico. Firm A was an American subsidiary that had shown great progress in recent years, as indicated by higher levels of production and increases in profits. Most of its employees were Mexicans. Their opportunities for advancement were quite good because the company's operations were expanding and its policy was to fill executive positions by promoting Mexican employees, even to the extent of moving out Americans. Company P was an all-Mexican firm which was on the decline. Its head ran his firm like a feudal empire, was unpredictable, and treated his employees capriciously. Whereas promotion in Firm A was based on competence and general effectiveness, top executives in Firm P tended to promote people who would be less likely to challenge their positions. The emphasis in Firm A was on doing one's job well and on increasing production, whereas in Firm P the emphasis was on keeping one's job.

When the stories written by the two groups of executives were compared, top-level executives in Firm A scored significantly higher in n Ach than did comparable executives in Firm P, whereas the latter scored significantly higher in n Power. Differences between lower-level executives in the two firms were the opposite, but statistically these differences were small and barely significant. Andrews surmised that the difference between top-level and lower-level executives within the same company could be explained in terms of the climate in Firm A being favorable to achievement-oriented employees, and the climate in Firm P being favorable to power-oriented employees. This hypothesis was borne out by his finding that n Ach scores correlated positively and significantly with job level and promotion in Firm A, but that n Power correlated negatively. In Firm P, n Power correlated significantly with job level and promotion, but n Ach correlated negatively. In other words, n Ach, but not n Power, was rewarded in Firm A, and n Power, but not n Ach, was rewarded in Firm P.

The effect of differing levels of n Ach on economic production and the course of history was studied by McClelland (1961), who undertook a survey of recent and past achievement in a number of different countries. As a measure of n Ach he used the extent to which achievement themes

have appeared in children's story books in the countries studied. Criteria used to measure the level of achievement of a country included per capita income (corrected for differences in foreign exchange prices) and electrical production in kilowatt hours per capita (corrected for the availability of natural resources, such as water power and coal deposits). Growth in achievement was calculated over a twenty-five year period, from the mid-1920's to 1950. Some countries, as might be expected, showed more than the expected amount of growth, and some showed less. When the n Ach as revealed by an analysis of the stories was compared with deviations from the expected growth rate, the resulting correlation was a highly significant .43. In other words, in countries where children's stories showed a high degree of achievement imagery, the growth rate tended to be higher than expected, and in those countries whose story books rated low in n Ach, growth rate tended to be less than would ordinarily be expected.

Historical Developments and n Ach. Not content with showing a relationship between n Ach and economic productvity in modern times, McClelland turned his analysis to the rise and fall of Ancient Greece, Pre-Columbian Peru, sixteenth-century Spain, and England from Tudor times to the Industrial Revolution. His measures of n Ach consisted of the number of achievement themes that appeared in the literature of ancient Athens, medieval Spain, and England (1550 to 1800). As measures of actual (economic) achievement, he used the extent of the Athenian trade area (550 to 300 B.C.), shipping volume for Spain, and coal import figures for London. Achievement imagery for ancient Peru was scored according to themes appearing on funerary urns. McClelland's general finding was that high levels of n Ach tended to appear fifty to one hundred years before increases in economic activity took place. Figure 5-2, for example, shows how changes in levels of n Ach, as shown by the number of achievement themes in English literature, antici-

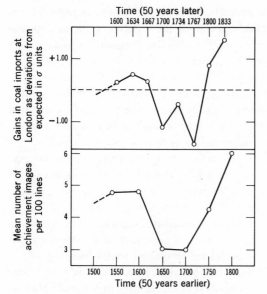

Figure 5-2. Relationship between n Ach and economic activity in England between 1500 and 1833 (McClelland, 1961).

pated changes in levels of economic production by about fifty years. The bottom graph line represents the amount of achievement imagery appearing in samples of English writing at various points between 1500 and 1800. The top line represents deviations (plus or minus) from the norm of coal imports received at London during the indicated years.

The Significance of n Ach as a Social Motive. We have engaged in this extended discussion of n Ach for a number of reasons. First, it provides an example of how attitudes and values can serve as sources of motivation for the way in which people interact with their environment. Persons rating high on n Ach tend to look for problems and to try harder when they encounter frustrations and difficulties. They enjoy problem solving and are task oriented. Persons rating low in n Ach try to avoid problems and are easily discouraged by difficulties. They tend to regard problems primarily as annoyances and as sources of anxiety and irritation. They are likely to rate

higher in n Aff (the affiliation motive) than are those who score high in n Ach.

Second, the degree to which a person's attitudes and values are characterized by n Ach has a great deal to do with his interpersonal behavior. Persons scoring high on n Ach are more likely to perceive socializing as interfering with "getting the job done." Such a person is more likely to react to others in terms of the extent to which he sees them as helping or interfering with his achievement. In working with others he is more likely to prefer to be independent and to avoid dependency relationships.

Third, n Ach is a culturally determined variable—that is, some societies or cultures foster personal achievement and place it in a central position within a complex of interrelated attitudes and values, whereas others may regard high achievement persons with suspicion and as threats to group solidarity and loyalty. The degree to which the values of a culture are characterized by n Ach or n Aff will of course have an important effect on how the members of the culture perceive themselves and their environment. There is an almost infinite range of variables on which cultures differ. N Ach may not even be the most important source of variation, but in a world composed of societies that are achieving and affluent and those that are economically deprived, of industrialized nations and nations trying to emerge from the the restraining bonds of traditionalism, national variations in n Ach may prove to be more significantly related to progress and economic survival than almost any other kind of difference.

SUMMARY

The individual's predisposition to behave in one way or another is likely to be reflected in his attitudes and other socially acquired motives. Attitudes have varying amounts of affective, cognitive, and behavioral components and may be organized into value systems. Integrated sets of beliefs and values that justify the policies of a group or institution are termed *ideologies*. Attitudes also determine how reality is perceived. Intellectualized attitudes which do not visibly affect social behavior may be the result of a need to satisfy two or more conflicting sets of beliefs or values.

Inasmuch as attitudes cannot be directly observed, they must be inferred from behavior of some type, for example, from social behavior or from the responses to the items in a questionnaire or rating scale. The latter devices can be used to measure the direction, intensity, centrality, salience, and consistency of the attitudes in question. Attitude measures may consist of Thurstone-type scales of equal-appearing intervals, constructed of items evaluated on an eleven-point scale and then converted to a conventional "yes-no" format. Responses are then scored in accordance with the weight the judges give each item. With the Likert-type scale, respondents indicate the degree to which they agree or disagree with sets of statements which have previously been analyzed in order to ensure internal consistency. Of the several other approaches to the measurement of attitudes, the free-response type has the advantage of being less biased, but is harder to score.

The cluster of attitudes related to authoritarian patterns of belief and behavior has been subjected to intensive and extensive analysis for the last two decades. Authoritarian or autocratic attitudes are characterized by preferences for the use of power in human relationships, whereas equalitarian or democratic attitudes are more likely to emphasize the use of understanding and patience. Much of the research dealing with authoritarian attitudes has been initiated by a series of studies conducted at the University of California in Berkeley and published in 1950 under the title of *The authoritarian personality*. Researchers found that authoritarian attitudes tended to be associated with race prejudice, rigidity, punitiveness, and guilt and anxiety about sex. Although this research has been criticized on methodological grounds, its basic findings have proved to be valid, and one of the questionnaires used in the study, the F scale, has become the most widely used instrument for measuring authoritarian attitudes. The F scale, too, has been subjected to extensive scrutiny and criticism, but the repeated finding that its scores are positively correlated with other measures and indications of authoritarianism indicates that the scale is valid.

Social motives may also be considered as psychological needs. The system of needs developed by Maslow posits five levels, ranging from the most basically biological "maintenance" needs, to the need for self-actualization. The needs relating to belongingness, love, and esteem are the most socialized, although social learning affects attitudes and behavior at all levels. Murray's system of needs is more complex than that of Maslow and includes a list of twenty specific needs that may motivate people in various ways and in various situations. Needs are counterbalanced by "presses," which represent environmental forces affecting the behavior of the individual. Both needs and presses may be identified and measured by a subject's responses to a series of pictures which constitute the Thematic Apperception Test, or TAT. Of all the needs proposed by Murray, the need for achievement, or n Ach, has been given the greatest amount of attention by researchers. McClelland and Atkinson have used a series of pictures similar to the TAT as a way of measuring n Ach and have found that this measure discriminates between persons who have high levels of ambition and aspiration and those who do not. People with high n Ach are more likely to be found in sales work, in business administration posts, and in production, whereas people with low n Ach are likely to have jobs where the following established procedures and routines is an important factor.

There appears to be a significant relationship between n Ach and early childhood experiences. Authoritarian attitudes on the part of fathers appear to interfere with the development of n Ach in their sons. Values in traditionally oriented cultures also tend to foster the need for affiliation (n Aff) and the need for power (n Power), rather than n Ach, as cross-cultural research with the McClelland-Atkinson methods of appraisal shows. McClelland has also analyzed achievement themes in the literature of ancient Greece, medieval Spain, and England between 1500 and 1800, and has found that the amount of such themes is correlated with increases in economic activity fifty to one hundred years later. The general finding of research studies dealing with n Ach is that it is a personality variable characteristic of people who enjoy problem solving and "getting the job done" and is likely to be fostered more by some cultures than by others.

SUGGESTED READINGS

Adorno, T. W., Frenkel-Brunswik, E., Levinson, D. J., & Sanford, R. N., *The authoritarian personality.* New York: Harper, 1950.

Atkinson, J. W. & Feather, N. T., *A theory of achievement motivation.* New York: Wiley, 1966.

Bechtel, R. B. & Rosenfeld, H. M., Expectations of social acceptance and compatibility as related to status discrepancy and social motive. *Journal of personality and social psychology,* 1966, **3**, 344–349.

Christie, R. & Jahoda, M. (Eds.), *Studies in the scope and method of "the authoritarian personality."* Glencoe, Ill.: Free Press, 1954.

Lindgren, H. C. (Ed.), *Contemporary research in social psychology.* New York: Wiley, 1969. See Section 5, "Social motives, attitudes, and their measurement."

McClelland, D. C., *The achieving society.* Princeton: Van Nostrand, 1961.

McClelland, D. C., Atkinson, J. W., Clark, R. A., & Lowell, E. L., *The achievement motive.* New York: Appleton-Century-Crofts, 1953.

Moulton, R. W., Effects of success and failure on levels of aspiration as related to achievement motives. *Journal of personality and social psychology,* 1965, **1**, 399–406.

CHAPTER SIX

Cornell Capa, Magnum

Sybil Shackman, Monkmeyer

Elliott Erwitt, Magnum

Social Influence

In Chapters 2-5 we have considered social behavior largely from the standpoint of the individual: why he seeks the company of others and the learning that results because of this interaction. In this chapter we turn our attention to the social environment and the forces it brings to bear on the individual in order to influence his behavior. We shall not lose sight of the individual in this discussion because we shall think of him as the focal point of these forces, but we shall be interested in considering the processes that result in social learning and that guide and direct his behavior.

Social Facilitation of Performance

We begin our discussion by observing what occurs when people perform tasks in the presence of others. The point in the studies to be described is that the mere presence of other people is a source of influence. This influence may be the result, as we suggest in Chapter 2, of the fact that other people are a source of stimulation or even stress. Very likely the inverted-U hypothesis holds here, in that mild stress or stimulation is helpful, but that stress beyond a certain level results in a deterioration of performance. As the research reviewed by Robert B. Zajonc (1965) shows, stress can be a factor of the task as well as of the social situation. The more complex and potentially stressful the task, the less helpful the presence of others is likely to be; the simpler and less stressful the task, the more the presence of others is likely to aid performance.

Familiar and Unfamiliar Tasks. The first group of studies reviewed by Zajonc deals with the facilitation of performance. In one of these studies, National Guard trainees were required to spend $2\frac{1}{4}$ hours monitoring a circle of twenty red lamps that were lighted serially in a clockwise sequence, twelve sequences per minute. On the average of once every $2\frac{1}{2}$ minutes, one of the lights failed to come on in its proper sequence. The subject's task was to signal when this occurred. Subjects in the control group carried out this monotonous task alone, whereas subjects in the experimental group were told that from time to time a lieutenant colonel or a master sergeant would enter their booth to observe their performance. These visits actually took place at approximately half-hour intervals. Results showed that subjects who were visited by a superior were far more accurate than those who worked alone. During the latter part of the experiment, the supervised subjects missed noting only 20 per cent of the times a lamp failed to light, whereas those who were never visited missed 64 per cent of the lamp failures (Bergum & Lehr, 1963).

Other studies reviewed by Zajonc, however, showed that the presence of others did not facilitate responses, but instead led to a deterioration of performance. In another experiment, subjects were seated in a chair, attached to electrodes, told not to smoke or vocalize in any way, and left alone. They then received a half second of electric shock every 10 seconds. On the table before them was a red button. Most subjects discovered that pressing the button delayed the onset of a shock by 10 seconds; hence pressing the button at frequent intervals effectively eliminated the possibility of shock. It took the average subject about $11\frac{1}{2}$ minutes to learn this. When subjects were tested in pairs, however, only two pairs out of the twelve tested were able to learn the relationship between button pressing and relief from being shocked, and those two required 47 minutes and 69 minutes, respectively. The other pairs never did learn (Ader & Tatum, 1963).

Zajonc's explanation for the two different kinds of effects—facilitation of and interference with performance—is that the presence of others tends to facilitate performance if responses are part of a well-learned repertoire, whereas it interferes if the responses are novel and have to be learned. To relate this explanation to our previous discussion, it is as though the stress produced in the individual by the presence of others is welcomed as long as the task has been well learned and requires minimal attention. The National Guardsmen probably looked forward to the visits of a superior officer in the course of their extremely dull task of monitoring the circle of lamps. But the presence of others when we are coping with an unfamiliar, complex task produces a new and unwelcome element. Not only do we have to cope with the task of determining the meaning of the more or less ambiguous situation with which we are faced, but we must respond to the stress, however mild it may be, of attending to the other persons.

Brainstorming Experiments. A number of experiments involving brainstorming and problem solving bear out this point. "Brainstorming" is the name given by Alex F. Osborn (1957), an advertising man, to the activity of a group of individuals who, charged with solving a problem, get together and invent as many solutions as they can. Participants are told "the wilder the better," are instructed to refrain from criticizing others' solutions, and are urged to build and improvise on the solutions proposed by others. The situation is therefore calculated to produce a high degree of social interaction. Osborn claims that "the average person can think up twice as many ideas when working with a group than when working alone." However, if Zajonc's analysis of the conditions under which the presence of others facilitates or inhibits performance is valid, we would expect participants in brainstorming to be more productive when working alone, because the invention of new solutions is a fairly unfamiliar task, and the presence of others would hamper, rather than facilitate learning. At least two research studies, one by Taylor, Berry, and Block (1958), and the other by Dunnette, Campbell, and Jaastad (1963), arrived at results consistent with

Zajonc's conclusions. The latter study, however, produced an additional finding that may be of interest here. In this study, half the group worked alone before they participated in brainstorming, and the other half brainstormed before they worked alone. In both instances working alone was a more productive condition than was brainstorming, but those who worked alone *after* they had brainstormed were more productive than those who worked alone beforehand. The results thus suggest that brainstorming may have had some kind of facilitative aftereffect on innovation.

This possibility was investigated by Lindgren and Lindgren (1965a,b), who found that the performance of persons writing cartoon captions improved after they had participated in a brainstorming session. The improvement was particularly noticeable in the degree of creativity shown by the captions. Subjects who were given the task of writing captions were told to write as many as they could and to make them as interesting or humorous as possible. They were then assigned to brainstorming groups of four or five individuals and told to develop captions for a second cartoon as a group, not to criticize one another's ideas, and to use one another's ideas as much as possible. After brainstorming, they were given a third cartoon, with instructions as during the first trial. Subjects in a control group worked alone during all three phases of the experiment. The effect of brainstorming was measured by comparing the number of responses and the level of creativity attained during the third phase of the experiment (after brainstorming) with that attained during the first phase. As the graph in Figure 6-1 shows, the performance of the experimental group improved during the third phase, whereas that of the control group did not.

It should be noted that producing captions is a task that has some degree of familiarity, that is, it involves expressing oneself in writing, a type of behavior that the subjects tested (all college students) had mastered to some degree. When a similar experiment was attempted with drawing

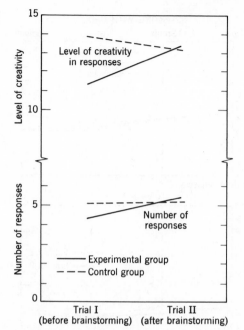

Figure **6-1.** The effect of social interaction on performance (Lindgren & Lindgren, 1965b).

or sketching, a mode of expression that most students have not mastered, somewhat different results obtained. There was a gain in the level of creativity expressed by drawings after brainstorming, but it was not significantly different from that shown by a control group who had filled out a questionnaire instead of participating in brainstorming (Lindgren, 1967).

Social Influences on Perception and Cognition

In the foregoing chapters we have stated in various ways that the individual looks to others for cues that enable him to structure and organize his environment and give it meaning. It is from these cues that he learns the attitudes, beliefs, and values that he uses as a guide for future action. Although this process is more active during the so-called "formative years," it continues throughout the life span. Members of a group faced by a new and ambiguous situation almost automatically turn to one another for help in determining the meaning of the array of stimuli they collectively face. At such times, the more dominant member who speaks up first may set the pattern for the group's behavior. This is the experimental situation in the research conducted by Muzafer Sherif to be examined in the first part of this section.

Suppose, however, that the stimulus is not at all ambiguous and that most of the group members are confederates of the investigator, who has coached them to give wrong answers. In this instance, two kinds of learning are in conflict: the perceptual patterns we have learned through a lifetime of experience and our equally lifelong habit of using the percepts of others as guides to the apprehension of reality. The question now is, which will take priority: the individual member's own perception of reality, or the patently incorrect and indefensible position taken by the group majority? This is the question examined by the studies reviewed in the second part of this section. Both types of study are important, because each sheds light on the process whereby attitudes, beliefs, and values are developed.

The Development of Social Norms. In the study conducted by Muzafer Sherif (1936), a classic in social psychology, subjects were ushered into a room and seated at a table on which a telegraph key had been placed. They were instructed that after the room had been darkened a light would appear. They were to press the key as soon as the light started to move, whereupon they were asked to say how far it had moved from its original position. Actually, the light did not move at all, but all the subjects *perceived* movement, a phenomenon that Sherif termed "autokinetic effect." Subjects were tested individually and in groups, and it is the "group effect" that interests us here.

Figure 6-2 shows what happened when subjects were first tested alone, in contrast to when they started their testing in groups of two or three. Note that there is a considerable variation among

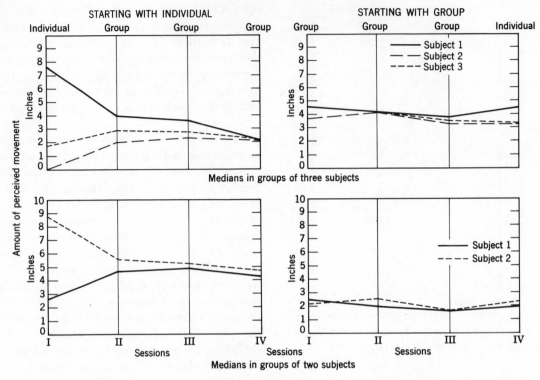

Figure 6-2. The effect of group participation on the judgments of individuals (Sherif, 1936.)

judgments made by subjects in the "alone" condition. This variation is reduced when they make judgments in the company of others. What appears is a kind of tacit agreement that the expressed judgments of members of the group should be more or less consistent, one with the other. Sherif calls this mutually dependent agreement to control behavior a "social norm." Note that subjects who start out in groups develop a norm rather quickly and that this norm continues to affect their judgment even after they leave the group and are working independently on the final set of trials. Incidentally, Sherif found that the majority of the subjects seemed to be unaware that their judgments were affected by those of the other group members—that is, they were not aware that they were reporting the consensus of the group and thought that the judgments they were making were their own.

Sherif's study illustrates a number of important principles. First, it shows that individuals faced by an ambiguous situation are inclined to depend on one another for clues or suggestions about the course of action to take. Second, it shows that group consensus has an effect that carries over to behavior outside the context of the group. Third, it suggests that this process usually goes on without our being aware of it.

Sherif's study attracted a great deal of interest from social psychologists of the day, because it offered a neat explanation of the dynamics of social norms, at least as far as ambiguous situations were concerned. The study left unanswered, however, the question of whether the same effect would obtain in less ambiguous situations. Supposing subjects were asked to judge situations that had a degree of objective reality about them —would the same effects obtain? Would individ-

uals respond to others' norms or to the evidence of their own eyes? Or, put in social learning terms: would individuals learn to make false judgments?

Studies of Yielding to Social Pressure (Asch). A second series of classic experiments was needed to provide the answers to these questions. This research was conducted by S. A. Asch (1956) during the late 1940's and early 1950's. The basic idea in the experiments was to place a naive subject in a group that had been instructed to give incorrect judgments at predetermined points in the proceedings.

In the Asch studies, subjects are seated in a rough semicircle, facing an easel on which the experimenter places a pair of large cards. The left-hand card bears a single vertical line, and the right-hand card displays three vertical lines of varying lengths, numbered "1," "2," and "3." The members of the group are asked to say which one of the three lines is equal in length to the line on the card at the left and to call out its number. The first trial presents no difficulty: the comparison line is 10 inches and lines 1, 2, and 3 are 8¾, 10, and 8 inches, respectively. One by one the members of the group call out "Number 2." Nor is there difficulty with the second trial. On the third trial, the comparison line is 3 inches, and lines 1, 2, and 3 are 3¾, 4¼, and 3 inches, respectively. Line No. 3 is obviously the correct answer, but the first person in the group says, "Number 1." So does the second person, the third, and so on down the line. Supposing you are the eighth person in a group of nine, what would you say? You can see that the correct answer is

"Number 3," but everyone so far has said "Number 1." You have the choice of agreeing with the majority and reporting an answer you can see is wrong, or standing up to the group and reporting what you know is right. The question is, Which will win out—group pressure or objectivity?

The results showed that only 26 per cent of the subjects were able to resist the false norm on every trial. The experiment consisted of eighteen trials, during which the majority gave the wrong answer twelve times. The amount of yielding to the false norm produced a trimodal distribution, with about a fourth of the subjects not yielding at all; about half yielding an average of three times each, or on 25 per cent of the trials; and a final fourth yielding an average of approximately nine times each, or on 75 per cent of the trials (See Table 6-1.).

Although the results reported in Table 6-1 are based on an experimental situation in which one naive subject is confronted by an unanimous majority of eight, Asch found that a majority of three arrayed against one is equally effective. Figure 6-3 shows that unanimous majorities of three and four produce mean agreement with false judgments of 33 and 36 per cent, respectively, and that there is nothing to be gained by increasing the majorities beyond four.

Asch also manipulated the experimental conditions in a number of different ways. In one set of experiments, one member of the group of accomplices was instructed to give the correct answer on the first half of the critical items and then join the majority on the balance. When this

Table **6-1.** Percentage of subjects in experimental and control situations giving incorrect judgments regarding the comparative length of lines (Asch, 1958)[a]

Number of critical errors[b]	Percentage of subjects making errors	
	Experimental situation	Control situation
0	26	94
1	8	3
2	10	3
3	12	0
4	6	0
5	8	0
6	2	0
7	4	0
8	10	0
9	6	0
10	6	0
11	2	0
12	0	0
	100	100

[a] Fifty experimental subjects were exposed to unanimous incorrect judgments 12 times out of a total of 18 trials; 37 control subjects made their judgments without such pressure.

[b] "Critical errors" refers to the 12 occasions when the unanimous majority made incorrect judgments.

occurred, the naive subjects' mean error rate jumped from 5.5 per cent for the first half to 28.5 per cent. The presence of a partner, in other words, was found to be extremely reassuring, but the tendency to defy the majority did not carry over after the partner had joined the majority. Under the opposite condition, when a member of the unanimous majority broke away from the group and started giving accurate judgments half-way through the experiment, the support of a confederate also had a reassuring effect so that the number of errors dropped to 8.7 per cent as contrasted with 32 per cent in experiments using a unanimous majority. In another version, the naive subjects were each given a "partner" who gave accurate judgments throughout the series. Under this condition the error percentage dropped to 5.5 per cent. In still another version, the number of naive subjects was increased to two, and the percentage of errors was 10.4, or about one-third that of the standard situation. It is clear that the presence of a partner strengthens the will to resist the majority, but does not entirely eliminate the effects of group pressure.

Interviews conducted with naive subjects after the experiment showed that those who had yielded

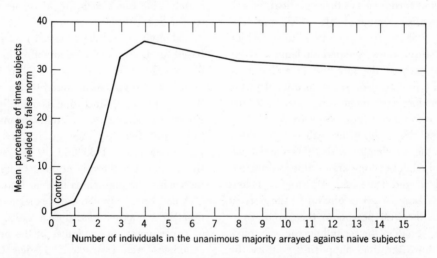

Figure **6-3.** Percentage of agreement with false norm on the part of naive subjects (Asch, 1958).

at least half the time were mostly unaware that they were being hoodwinked. Most of the yielders were aware that their perceptions were different from those of the majority but concluded that the majority was probably right. Some of the yielders were not aware that their perceptions differed from the majority—they merely perceived what the majority reported. A minority of yielders were aware that their perceptions were different, felt that the majority was wrong, but decided to go along with the group in order not to appear different.

What we have in the Asch situation is an example, on a small scale, of social learning. The behavior—in this instance, the judgment—of the subject is being altered by the group. During the period of the experiment the yielding subject learns either not to trust his own judgment or not to have any judgment at all but to take his cues from the group. The subject's behavior is reinforced or rewarded by his feeling of being "with" the group. Since this is merely an *ad hoc* group, assembled for purposes of the experiment, there is no real advantage to being accepted by the group, because deviation carries no penalty. There is no doubt, however, that other learnings intervene here: deviation is avoided because the subject has learned in other contexts that deviation will be followed in most groups by loss of acceptance and even exclusion. The fact that some subjects were able to resist group influence is beside the point. The point is that a majority of the subjects were affected by the massed group opinion at one point or another and thus learned to imitate the behavior of other members of the group. The Asch experiment thus shows, in a very succinct and effective way, how effective groups are as agents of learning and how much leverage they can exert on behavior.

A number of questions arise from a review of the Asch research. First: can subjects be made to alter their judgment on other types of material? After all, judging the length of lines is a rather artificial situation. What about opinions and attitudes? Second: how much modifying effect would the group have had on the judgment of the individual if he had known or suspected that the experiment had been rigged? Third: how lasting are the effects of the experimental treatment? If a person is led to utter a judgment contrary to his beliefs or to objective evidence, will he then hold to that opinion afterward?

Studies of Yielding to Social Pressure: The IPAR Experiments. To answer these questions we turn to a series of experiments that use somewhat different techniques in creating the same effect achieved by Asch. At the Institute for Personality Assessment and Research (IPAR) in Berkeley, Richard S. Crutchfield (1955) developed a variation of the Asch situation that eliminated the need for confederates and enabled him and his associates to test the effect of social pressure on a number of subjects simultaneously. In this variation five naive subjects are seated in adjoining booths so that none of them can be seen by any of the others but all may see slides projected on the screen in front of the group. Each booth has an array of numbered switches whereby the subject can communicate his judgment of the material on the screen. A series of lights in each booth presumably indicates the judgments being given by the other four subjects. Actually, the signal lights are instead controlled by the experimenter, who is thus able to manipulate the experimental situation and communicate any degree of consensus he wishes. Since each booth is labeled E, each subject believes he is the last to report after subjects A, B, C, and D. Crutchfield's method not only makes it possible to test a much larger group of subjects in a shorter time than would be possible with the Asch situation, but also permits the use of a wider variety of materials. The results are very much the same, however. For example, the statement "I believe we are made better by the trials and hardships of life" evoked virtually no disagreement on the part of members of a control group, but when subjects in an experimental group were informed of a group consensus in disagreement, 31 per cent of them expressed disagreement. In one control sample of males, no one agreed with the statement "I doubt whether I would make a good leader," but when members of an experimental group were told of a consensus in agreement, 37 per cent also agreed.

The ease with which attitudes could be manipulated was demonstrated by two items. Among control subjects, only 19 per cent agreed with the statement "Free speech being a privilege rather than a right, it is proper for a society to suspend free speech whenever it feels itself threatened." But when experimental subjects believed that the other members of the group were unanimous in accepting the statement, 58 per cent endorsed it as well.

The second item was in the form of a multiple-choice question: "Which one of the following do you feel is the most important problem facing our country today?" The five alternatives were:

A. Economic recession
B. Educational facilities
C. Subversive activities
D. Mental health
E. Crime and corruption

Only 12 per cent of control subjects named C, "subversive activities," as the most important problem, but under pressure of reported group consensus, 48 per cent of the experimental subjects selected this option.

Crutchfield's work does give us an answer to the first question we raised, for it shows that attitudes, even self-regarding attitudes, can be changed under group pressure.

The second question dealt with the effect of group pressure on subjects who knew or suspected that the experimental situation had been rigged in some way. In one experiment using the equipment designed by Crutchfield, thirty female subjects, out of a total of 150, indicated that they knew the apparatus was rigged. When the conformity scores of these thirty "sophisticated" subjects were compared to those of the 120 de-

ceived subjects, the latter were found to have conformed about twice as much as the former—26 per cent, as contrasted with 12 per cent. This difference is in the expected direction; we would assume that subjects who were aware that they were being manipulated would be less likely to conform more than those unaware. But why should the sophisticated subjects conform at all, if they were aware of what was being done? The answers of the subjects provide some clues to what was happening. Some were not sure of their suspicions. For example, "I fluctuated . . . between believing the people were planted and believing them simply nonprejudiced subjects like myself." Others were bothered by how their responses would appear: "Even though I was very suspicious of the experiment, I was still bothered by being different." Some found it easier to fall in line with the majority, and others felt that they were being cooperative (Allen, 1966). Whatever the reasons given, however, the realization that one's judgment is being manipulated evidently is not insurance against being persuaded against one's better judgment.

The third question we raised, and perhaps the most significant one, is whether there is any lasting effect of changes in judgment or attitude brought about by social pressure. One study of group pressure at IPAR using the Crutchfield technique showed that approximately half of the original group-pressure effect remained after a period of several weeks, although there was large individual variation (Krech, Crutchfield, & Ballachey, 1962). A study by Norman Endler (1966), using the Crutchfield situation, also showed some aftereffect. Subjects were shown thirty-six slides of multiple-choice items. They were subjected to social pressure on eight verbal items (obscure facts) and eight perceptual items (geometric figures). The mean conformity score was 6.35, which contrasts with the mean score made by a control group (not subject to pressure) of 2.3. Since the latter score was achieved by chance alone, the effect of the social pressure on the experimental group can be expressed by a net mean score of 4.05. When the groups were run through the series of slides again without any social pressure, the net score was still 1.15 higher than the control group. In other words, about one-third of the effect remained. Some subjects in the same experiment also were reinforced by the experimenter's informing them, after they had responded, which items were "right." These subjects not only conformed a great deal more than those who were only told the group norm, but they also showed significantly greater aftereffect.

Although this area has not been extensively researched, the available data suggest that there can be a lingering aftereffect. In real life, of course, the effect would vary with the significance of the attitude being placed under group pressure, the amount of pressure applied, and the value of the group to the individual. Some of these variables were included in an experiment by Robert S. Wyer, Jr. (1966), who found that subjects were more likely to conform to bogus group estimates of the number of dots on a projected slide when they were told that the task was important, but this effect did not hold when they were not attracted to other members of the group being tested or did not feel accepted by them.

Attitudes Associated with Yielding Behavior. So far we have said nothing about the kind of people who are inclined to yield or resist group influence. Crutchfield (1955) reported that the F scale correlated $+.39$ with conformity as measured by his version of the Asch situation. He also found that ratings of authoritarianism, assigned by members of his research staff who observed subjects playing roles in psychodramatic situations, correlated $+.35$ with conformity. A similar relationship was also found by Wells, Weinert, and Rubel (1956), who used an Asch-type situation in which students were asked to say which driver was at fault in a picture of an automobile collision. Sixty out of sixty-two members of a control group said that Driver A was at fault, because he had obviously gone through

a red traffic light. In an experimental group of sixty-two, however, twenty-one yielded to the false norm and blamed Driver B. The mean score per F scale item for the yielders was 4.0, whereas it was 3.1 for those who resisted. The results rather clearly show that yielding was associated with authoritarian tendencies.

Further clues as to the kinds of people who resist or yield in social pressure experiments are provided by Crutchfield (1955), whose co-workers at IPAR analyzed the two kinds of subjects without reference to their performance in the stress situation. When their evaluations were matched with the scores of subjects who were high or low yielders, the pattern reported in Table 6-2 emerged. Because the yielders also tended to have high F scale scores, it appears that both yielding and authoritarianism are associated with the kinds of behavior listed in the bottom half of the table. Both resistance to pressure and low F scores are associated with behavior described in the top half of the table.

In the preliminary statement about this section we noted that the influence studies shed light on the formation of attitudes, beliefs, and values. It should be recognized, of course, that the experiments reviewed here consisted of miniature segments of experience. It is doubtful whether any of them would lead to any permanent distortion of judgment, for as individuals who have been influenced encounter objective evidence that disproves the false information they learned under group pressure, the effects of the experience should be extinguished in time. However, if the presentation of the false norms were to occur repetitively, as an everyday experience, one result might be a set of attitudes and beliefs based on group consensus, rather than on objective reality. Many examples of normative beliefs existing in the face of objective evidence to the contrary may be found in the annals of history. One example is the Romans' belief in the divinity of the emperor, a belief that often withstood the test of the emperor's death. Such beliefs are not mere

Table **6-2.** Differences between men exhibiting extremes of independence or conformity in resisting false norms (Crutchfield, 1955)

The resisters were seen[a] as:

1. Showing effectiveness in leadership.
2. Taking an ascendant or dominant role in relations with others.
3. Being persuasive in winning others over to their point of view.
4. Used frequently by others as sources of advice and reassurance.
5. Capable and efficient.
6. Active, vigorous, and energetic.
7. Expressive and enthusiastic.
8. Seeking and enjoying aesthetic and sensuous experiences.
9. Being natural, unaffected, and free from pretense.
10. Self-reliant, able to do their own thinking, and independent in judgment.

The yielders were seen[a] as:

1. Submissive, compliant, and overly accepting of authority figures.
2. Conforming, limiting their behavior to that which has been prescribed.
3. Operating within a narrow range of interests.
4. Showing a very high degree of impulse control, inhibited, tending to delay or deny gratification needlessly.
5. Vacillating, unable to make decisions without great delay.
6. Becoming confused, disorganized, and nonadaptive under stress.
7. Lacking insight into their own motives or behavior.
8. Highly suggestible and overly responsive to the evaluations of others.

[a] Appraisals were made by staff members of the Institute for Personality Assessment and Research [IPAR] at the University of California in Berkeley.

happenstances, but grow out of some need of the group—in this instance, the need for a politically unifying symbol.

Social pressures are not as a general rule aimed at making group members believe things that are not so, but the general social process resulting in normative attitudes, beliefs, and values is much the same, irrespective of whether they are based on objective reality or not.

Attraction and Conformity

The Price of Social Attraction. The rewards we receive from our association with others have a price: we must work for them. In reinforcement theory terms, we pay for our rewards through learning modes of behavior that enable us to continue receiving reinforcement.

This point is illustrated by a study of social learning, involving two stooges and a naive subject, conducted by Jay S. Efran and Andrew Broughton (1966). When the naive subject arrived at the psychological laboratory he found another subject (actually the first stooge) already waiting. The latter engaged him in friendly conversation for a few minutes, until another subject (the second stooge) arrived, followed immediately by the experimenter. The three were then escorted into a room and seated at a conference table so that the naive subject could be observed through a one-way mirror. They were then told that each was to spend 5 minutes talking about himself and that subject "A" (who always turned out to be the naive subject) was to begin. The experimenter then left the room to observe the naive subject's behavior through the one-way mirror. Both stooges had been instructed by the experimenter to look at the naive subject during his discourse, without seeming to stare. The stooge who had been waiting for the subject was to smile on occasions, when it seemed appropriate; the other stooge was not to smile or nod, but merely to look interested. The experimenter recorded the amount of time the naive subject looked directly at each of the stooges.

Results showed that the naive subject spent about 16 per cent of the 5-minute period in looking at one or the other of the two stooges and that he spent 71 per cent of this time looking at the stooge who had originally talked to him in a friendly way. The results of this study appear to show that people are likely to look at those from whom they expect visual cues indicating approval. Looking at others is a social technique.

In this instance it also appears to be a way of communicating a desire for approval. To put this into social learning terms, the smiles of the first stooge reinforced the eye-contact behavior of the naive subject. The point is, however, that social approval is worth something to us and that we are willing to do something to receive it.

Working for social approval usually results in some degree of conformity. If we are to continue to be rewarded by others, we must maintain the favorable quality of their attitude toward us. Conforming to others' expectations is one way of encouraging them to maintain positive attitudes. If we value others' approval, but find that conformity is not possible, we usually try to avoid behavior that reveals our nonconformity, or at any rate we do not flaunt it.

Compliance and Ingratiation. In an analysis of how conformity figures in social behavior, Edward E. Jones (1965) pointed out that all interpersonal relationships involve some measure of mutual dependence, in the sense that each person involved in a social interchange has some potential influence over both the rewards available and the psychological costs to be incurred by the others. When the status of two parties is approximately equal, they tend to work out a balance of rewards and costs in a mutually agreeable fashion. When one person in a two-person relationship (a dyad) has more status than the other, however, the more dependent person is somewhat at the mercy of the more powerful one. In such instances, less powerful individuals are likely to be concerned about their situation and to attempt to take steps to improve it.

According to Jones, a number of strategies are available to dependent persons. Some of these strategies ensure the availability of rewards, but at the same time strengthen the power of the dominant person and reaffirm the dependence of the weaker one. Compliance is one example of a tactic of this sort. The more reliable a worker becomes in meeting his employer's demands, the more confident the employer becomes that his

demands are reasonable and that the employee is content with the "bargain," as represented by the differences in their power and status. This type of conformity works out to the advantage of the person of higher status, but not to that of the dependent person.

Jones suggests that techniques associated with ingratiation do not have this disadvantage. Ingratiation includes a number of maneuvers through which dependent persons make themselves more attractive in the eyes of more powerful persons. If the tactics are successful, the more powerful individual finds himself less able to exploit or punish the ingratiator, because he then risks alienating an attractive person and thus cutting off a source of reward. His power has, in effect, been reduced.

Ingratiation is a word that has somewhat sinister and Machiavellian overtones in everyday usage, yet, as Jones points out, it is something we do almost every time we interact with other people, usually without being aware that we are doing so. The fact that we are concerned about the good opinion of others leads us to be ingratiating: to be circumspect and cautious in uttering opinions, to avoid making statements that might upset others, to play up areas of agreement, and to play down matters on which we disagree. We do this every day without feeling at all guilty about it; most of us would regard such tactics as merely "good sense." Jones suggests three ways in which ingratiation can be undertaken: compliments, agreement, and presenting oneself in a favorable light.

The discomfort we feel at the use of the term "ingratiation" is due in some degree to the fact that ingratiators sometimes overdo it and appear too obvious. When this occurs, persons with higher status are likely to realize that they are being manipulated and therefore react by negative behavior. Under such circumstances, pleasing statements uttered by the lower-status persons are perceived as insincere and false and hence no longer possess any reward value. High-status persons are therefore more likely to be attracted to dependent persons who show restraint in their praise or in the degree of their agreement. Jones notes, however, that the latter are protected in some degree by the vanity of the high-status person—that is, his willingness to believe fairly extravagant compliments without suspecting that he is the target of manipulative intentions. Often a kind of autistic* conspiracy results, with both the status person and the ingratiator collaborating to represent the former as being better than he actually is. Jones believes that this autistic conspiracy can be and often is maintained by the most intricate interpersonal tactics, to the end that the ingratiator's real intentions are concealed from himself, as well as from the object of his attention. To carry out these maneuvers effectively, most of us avoid extremes of obvious flattery and sycophancy, because such extremes would give the game away and reveal the conspiracy to both parties.

Jones has tested his propositions in a number of experiments. His naval ROTC subjects received messages consisting of opinions which they believed were written by an ROTC student of higher or lower rank than their own. The messages, twelve in all, were actually simulated and were alike for each subject. Nine of the messages deviated considerably from opinion norms that had previously been established in a questionnaire administered to an equivalent sample of subjects. Subjects were to write their own opinions below the opinions received. Each subject was also told that his "partner" had expressed a preference for working with him on a leadership testing project later in the semester and he was therefore urged to make a special effort to gain the liking and respect of the prospective partner. Jones found that subjects tended to shift their

* *Autistic*—a tendency for perception and other cognitive processes to be dictated to an unreasonable degree by one's own needs, to the extent of being unreasonable, irrational, or unrealistic, with the result that the world is perceived as closer to one's wishes than it actually is.

points of view as they reacted to the deviant statements. In general, they tended to express views about halfway between their original positions and those expressed in the opinions they received. Both the high- and the low-status persons made some shift, because the subordinate wished to keep the good will of his superior, and the high-status subject wanted to show the subordinate that he was approachable.

This accommodation tended to take different directions for the high- and low-status groups. As Figure 6-4 shows, high-status subjects shifted least in reacting to deviant opinions relating to the Navy, whereas low-status persons shifted the most. High-status subjects shifted somewhat more than low-status subjects on items relating to miscellaneous matters which were of no great importance, but were somewhat more resistive on academic matters, which were considered more important, but still not as crucial to their status as naval matters. The high-status subjects were of course yielding on the less important items in order to appear flexible to their juniors, whereas the latter were conforming strictly on naval items which they knew were relevant to the status of their seniors, and were putting up a show of resistance on the less crucial items in order not to appear supine and overconforming.

Jones and his colleagues have investigated ingratiation in other experimentally contrived conditions. In one experiment the dependent subjects reduced the danger of being thought opportunistic by publicly expressing low confidence in their opinions. In another, dependent subjects avoided conformity with the views expressed by an irritable and insulting superior, but tended to agree with his supporting arguments. In still another experiment, expression of conformity was delayed until it became clear that the high-status person would appreciate agreement.

Ingratiation may also take the form of doing favors. In fact, agreement and compliance are often thought of as favors by the givers, although receivers are understandably less likely to see

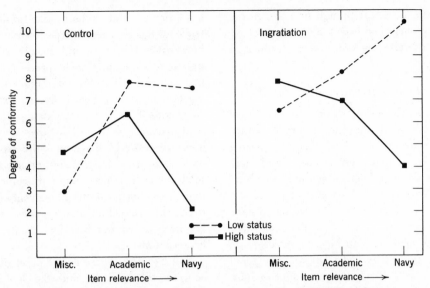

Figure **6-4.** Willingness of high- and low-ranking naval ROTC students to conform by shifting their previously expressed viewpoints on various items when confronted by opinions deviating from the norm (Jones, 1965).

them as such. An interesting point about favors, and one that is often overlooked by donors, is that they restrict the freedom of the receiver, that is, they put him under some kind of imperative to reciprocate. Favors done by a superior can presumably be repaid by continued attention, but favors performed by a subordinate serve to put the superior in a somewhat subordinate position. Superiors, therefore, prefer to maintain control of the favor situation by determining what favors are to be done and who is to do them. This is sometimes arranged by superiors taking the attitude that *they* are the only ones with the power to do favors. If *they* do something ingratiating, it is because they are kindly people who enjoy doing favors, but if *subordinates* do something ingratiating, it is not a favor (according to the superior) but is done in the line of duty and is merely what any decent subordinate should do. Superiors view it as proper, in other words, for subordinates' freedom to be restricted, since they are already dependent, but it is not proper for them to restrict the freedom of their superiors.

When one individual does a favor for a person of equal status, the relationship between them is, for the moment, out of balance until the latter can do something to bring their relationship back into balance. If the individuals are not friends, however, and if the favor is unrequested and unneeded, it may even be resented. Jack W. Brehm and Ann Himelick Cole (1966) created an experimental situation in which a naive subject and a confederate were given the task of judging each other. Prior to the judging, the confederate left the room and appeared with a soft drink for the naive subject, refusing any payment. After the judging, the confederate was given a rather dull repetitive task. Under conditions in which the judging was done rather casually and no great importance was attached to it, the naive subject almost always (fourteen times out of sixteen) volunteered to help the confederate, thus discharging the debt incurred by the favor. Under conditions in which the judging was made to sound very important, however, the naive subject almost never (only once out of fourteen times) volunteered to help. It was as though he resented the fact that an attempt had been made to restrict his freedom to exercise his own judgment through ingratiation.

Social Influence through Manipulation

Although people are often unaware that they are being influenced, they are generally aware that social influence can lead them to behave in ways not in their best interest, and they consequently develop defenses against being persuaded against their will. This everyday observation has led people who have something to gain from the compliance of others to look for ways whereby these defenses can be penetrated.

The "Foot-in-the-Door" Technique. The foot-in-the-door technique is used by door-to-door salesmen with considerable success—hence its name. It is also used by any number of people who are faced with the task of getting others to do things that they might object to doing. Politicians use this technique extensively. A country's leader asks a legislative body to authorize a small military action. The grounds for this action are good, the risk is small, and the permission is granted with a minimum of argument or question. However, the action proves to be bigger than was anticipated, and the legislative body is asked for more authority, more funds, and the commitment of more forces. Eventually, what was a decision in a small matter becomes a full-blown war. This military example can be paralleled by political maneuvering in the field of social welfare, foreign aid, civil rights, or whatever. It is furthermore an important basic technique in the repertoire of anyone who has to achieve his aims by negotiation and persuasion, whether he be politician, salesman, diplomat, teacher, or psychotherapist.

The basic idea of the foot-in-the-door technique is that the target individual is asked to grant an inconsequential favor. Granting the favor evidently leads to a lowering of defenses, because the individual then finds himself less able to resist the request to grant a larger favor that he would

have denied had it been asked initially. This tendency has been tested experimentally by asking housewives if they would answer a few simple questions about household products. After they had complied with this modest request, the experimenter then asked them if five or six men could come into their houses to catalog all the household products in use. Fifty-three per cent of the housewives surveyed agreed to this second, rather outrageous, request, after first granting the initial small favor. This percentage of acquiescence was in marked contrast to the 22 per cent of the housewives who granted the major request and who had not been asked the first favor (Freedman and Fraser, 1966).

Role Playing. There is one point of similarity between role playing and the foot-in-the-door technique. In both instances, the subject is asked to perform a task that seems harmless enough and is unaware that the performance of the task will make him more susceptible to persuasion. Furthermore, the subject does not remain passive, but becomes actively involved in a sequence of behavior under the direction of another person.

In one study of the effect of role playing, Alan C. Elms (1966) asked cigarette smokers to pretend that they were nonsmokers trying to convince other smokers that they should stop. Eighty smokers took part in the study and were assigned randomly to the task of playing the role of the nonsmoker or serving as the listener. Both role players and listeners were tested as to their beliefs about smoking before the experiment, immediately afterward, and three weeks later. Although both types of participants modified their attitudes in favor of stopping smoking, role players showed more attitude change than the listeners did. During the three weeks following the experiment, the attitudes of the listeners tended to regress in the direction of their previously held attitudes about smoking, whereas those of the role players became more favorable toward stopping. Data regarding actual smoking behavior are even more convincing: 46 per cent of the role players reduced the number of cigarettes they smoked per day, and only 11 per cent showed an increase. This is in marked contrast with the behavior of the listeners, for 27 per cent of the latter cut down on the number of cigarettes smoked, and 30 per cent actually smoked more than ever.

Presumably neither the role players nor the listeners in Elms' study had any more than the usual intention to cut down on their smoking. Yet at the end of three weeks, we find that the role players said they were more favorably disposed to stopping and were actually cutting down on the number of cigarettes smoked to a greater degree than were the listeners. All this was brought about merely because the role players *pretended* they were nonsmokers trying to persuade others and the other group merely listened. The whole experiment took only two hours, but the results in terms of measurable changes in behavior were perceptible three weeks later. The power of this simple type of manipulation would thus seem to be considerable. It is rather obvious that attitudes would have priority in determining the kind of behavior displayed, but the research done by Elms, as well as by others who have experimented with this technique, suggests that the relationship may sometimes be reversed, with behavior determining attitudes. We shall explore this puzzling relationship more fully in Chapter 7.

Influence through Fear, Shame, and Guilt

The Arousal of Fear through Propaganda. Although we have indicated that politicians, salesmen, teachers, and others who have developed some skill in influencing others make extensive use of indirect methods in achieving their goals, most people tend to prefer a more direct approach, such as that of informing the person to be influenced that his interests would be better served by a course of action different than the one he has been following or is intending to follow. These attempts to persuade commonly take the form of arguments intended to present logical reasons for following this or that course of action. Such arguments may be simple statements to the effect that this or that is true or will occur, or they may be elaborate propaganda campaigns, designed to change the attitudes and consequent behavior of large numbers of people. Sometimes these arguments take a positive form, in the sense that the persuader points out the pleasant and satisfying outcomes of taking this or that course of action, but often the negative is emphasized, and an attempt is made to arouse fear. Antismoking propaganda, for example, may stress the almost inevitable horror of lung cancer, and safe-driving propaganda may make use of traffic accident figures during the holidays to remind drivers to slow down and be careful. We have no evidence that such programs have any effect, because no adequately controlled studies have been made of them, but they are continued because of the firm belief people have in the efficacy of fear arousal as a means of persuasion.

Psychologists have, however, made studies on a small scale that are beginning to shed some light on some of the effects that fear arousal has on behavior. One of the earlier studies of this type was conducted by Irving L. Janis and Seymour Feshbach (1953), who exposed high school freshmen to one of three types of propaganda regarding care of the teeth. One group received the strong appeal, which included pictures of diseased gums and emphasized the dangers that would result from lack of proper dental hygiene. The moderate appeal described the advantages of proper care in an impersonal way and made use of photographs showing some pathology, but not as lurid or as severe as that used in the strong appeal. The minimal appeal was brief, entirely factual, and made use of X-ray photographs and pictures of healthy teeth. Results showed that the minimal appeal got the best results, as shown by changes in the behavior of the students, even though students were more interested in and reported themselves more worried by the strong appeal. When the researchers later exposed the students to a campaign of counterpropaganda, designed to counteract some of the recommendations made during the first part of the experiment, students who had conformed to the minimal appeal also showed more resistance to the counterpropaganda message, whereas those who had been exposed to the strong appeal were more impressionable. A similar study conducted with strong (high-threat) and minimal (low-threat) appeals with respect to attitudes toward smoking also secured more attitude change with less fear arousal (Janis & Terwilliger, 1962).

Although there have been a number of other studies whose results have confirmed the findings of these two studies, other researchers have reported contrary results. James M. Dabbs, Jr. and Howard Leventhal (1966) found that Yale University seniors who had been exposed to propaganda with high fear content were more likely to take tetanus shots than were those who were exposed to propaganda with less threat potential. Howard Leventhal and Patricia Niles (1964) conducted a study in which visitors at a New York City Health Exposition were exposed to a film showing the effects of lung cancer. Those under a "high arousal" condition saw a film portraying the story of a young smoker whose diseased left lung was removed because of the onset of cancer, whereas those under "mild arousal" conditions saw only the first portion of the film which took the patient as far as the operating room. As the film ended, the viewers were given questionnaires to fill out and were urged by the experimenter to take advantage of the free chest X-ray service available next door to the theater. Results showed that the high-fear appeal was most effective; not only did respondents exposed to this condition admit greater concern about the possibility of cancer, but they were also more likely to take advantage of the free X-ray service.

A subsequent experiment by Howard Leventhal and Jean C. Watts (1966) using somewhat similar techniques obtained different results, however. The researchers employed three levels of arousal, instead of two, and results were analyzed in terms of the behavior of light and heavy smokers, as well as of nonsmokers. In this experiment, the mild arousal condition was more successful in getting the light smokers to have chest X-rays taken, whereas the medium arousal level was most successful with heavy smokers. High arousal was most successful in getting smokers to say that they planned to give up or cut down on smoking, but when a follow-up was made five months later, it appeared that there was no difference in the amount of fear exposure among the proportions of those who had tried to give up smoking, but those who had tried, and who had been exposed to higher levels of fear arousal, appeared to be the most successful in carrying out their intentions.

It is difficult to find a theory that explains the complex and contradictory results obtained by these two sets of studies. William J. McGuire (1966) has proposed that the differences in results can be explained in terms of differences in the amount of anxiety involved, that is, the level of anxiety that is characteristic of the individuals concerned, the degree of initial concern, and the amount of fear or anxiety resulting from the propaganda message. The maximum attitude change, he theorized, should take place when anxiety is at a moderate level, not too high nor not too low. This theory would be in keeping with the inverted-U relationship between stress and performance proposed by Hebb (1955a) and discussed in Chapter 2. The task of determining which would be more effective, high or low fear-arousing propaganda, would then take the form of determining the anxiety level of the audience and the way in which they perceived the attitude or behavior to be manipulated.

The importance of knowing the audience for which the propaganda is intended is shown by an experiment conducted by Robert Paul Singer (1965) who used strong and weak fear appeals about dental hygiene practices in an attempt to modify the behavior of high school freshmen. He found that high fear appeals were more likely to get students to express the intention to follow the recommendations of the communicator. However, much of the effect disappeared two weeks later. Less intelligent students tended to learn more as a result of high-fear communications, whereas more intelligent students learned more when the fear appeal was either low or absent. Follow-up survey also showed that less intelligent students under all conditions were more likely to forget the content of the message. With respect to intentions to follow the recommendations, fear appeared to facilitate the behavior of only the less intelligent students, whereas information alone (without fear) was sufficient to induce acceptance in the more intelligent students.

Irrespective of the validity of McGuire's model of availability to persuasion, the research conducted in this field does show that we can no longer safely assume that raising the audience's level of fear or anxiety is a sure way of securing compliance. Enough data have now been gathered to enable us to question that assumption. Like other attempts to bring about changes in the behavior of others, the use of propaganda has turned out to be more complex than common sense and the conventional wisdom would lead us to believe, and the more understanding we gain with respect to human behavior, the less certain we become that the control of human behavior is merely a matter of learning a few techniques.

Fear as a Form of Social Control. Many of our forms of social control have as their aim the arousal of fear. This is particularly true of laws and regulations that prescribe drastic punishment, such as incarceration or death, as a penalty for transgressing against society. However, highly complex societies could not exist if they depended on fear alone as the means of social control. Their existence depends instead on the fact that all but a small proportion of their members have learned the appropriate attitudes, values, and forms of social behavior to the point that they have been internalized, that is, they have become an integrated part of the person. Social control in such societies is thus for the most part exercised through internalized norms, rather than through fear induced through threats of punishment.

There are, however, differences among cultures in the extent that internalized social norms are employed as a guide to conduct. Gerhart Piers and Milton Singer (1953) have proposed that a distinction can be made as to "guilt cultures," in which behavior is regulated by the individual's unwillingness to suffer guilt as a result of having violated an internalized norm, and "shame cultures," in which members conform to social norms only when other members are present to shame them. To elaborate somewhat on these concepts, guilt cultures emphasize self-control in the face of temptation, as well as self-initiated responsibility for one's actions if transgression occurs, whereas shame cultures exercise control through the intervention of various members of society, who in various ways coerce, threaten, or otherwise arouse fear (Grinder & McMichael, 1963). The distinction between the two kinds of cultures is of course a relative one, inasmuch as the most complex and highly urbanized society makes some use of threat as a way of persuasion, and the societies that rely heavily on external controls depend to some extent on internalized norms.

Although the distinction between shame and guilt cultures has been subject to some criticism (Spiro, 1961), there is some experimental evidence that it possesses some validity. Robert E. Grinder and Robert E. McMichael (1963) designed an interesting experiment to test the hypothesis that shame cultures would produce weak consciences and that guilt cultures would produce strong ones. They compared the behavior of Samoan (shame culture) and American Caucasian (guilt culture) sixth and seventh grade children living in rural Hawaii. Subjects operated a shooting gallery in which a ray-gun was used to shoot at a revolving target. Prearranged scores from 0 to 5 appeared in lights with each pull of the trigger. Subjects were told that they would be awarded badges for scores of 35 or more; however, the equipment was rigged in such a way that scores never exceeded 32. Each subject worked alone and recorded his own scores, whereupon he brought his score sheet to the experimenter, who was in another room in the same building. It was thus possible for subjects to falsify results under the belief that they were able to escape detection on the part of the experimenter. Two weeks after the shooting gallery phase of the experiment, subjects responded to a test consisting of a number of stories in which characters violated social norms because of their dishonesty, untrustworthiness, and lack of self-control. Each story was followed by a number of optional completions, which yielded measures of remorse, willingness to confess, and willingness to make restitution.

The results of the shooting gallery phase of the study showed that Americans were much more likely to resist temptation than Samoans. None of the nineteen Samoans resisted temptation and all reported impossible scores, whereas seven out of fifteen American subjects resisted. On the story-completion test, Americans were more likely to express remorse, willingness to confess, and willingness to make restitution. Differences in guilt measures, however, turned out to be relative ones. Samoan subjects did make choices consistent with feelings of guilt, but they did not make them as often as American children did. Nor, as the ray-gun experiment showed, were their guilt responses strong enough to keep them from cheating.

Even in industrialized and urbanized societies will there be differences in the extent to which guilt and shame operate to control behavior. Mediterranean and Latin American cultures tend to be less guilt-oriented and more shame-oriented than Northern European and North American

cultures. This explains the sense of outrage experienced by North Americans and Northern Europeans when they are forced to result to bribery for normal services from governmental agencies in other parts of the world. Bribery and corruption exist in North America and Northern Europe, of course, but they are much less widespread and are held in check by the inhibitions of guilt-oriented societies.

Navaho-Eskimo Differences. Not all primitive societies are shame-oriented. Russell Eisenman (1965) has compared Eskimo (guilt-oriented) and Navaho (shame-oriented) societies in terms of the way in which the members of each culture deal with their transgressions. In the Eskimo culture there are many ways of transgressing—failure to wear some amulet, omission of homage to some particular spirit, and the like. Hence opportunities to feel sin and guilt abound. The community's sense of guilt can be assuaged, however, when the angakok or spiritual leader accuses someone of having committed a sin. When this occurs, the sinner admits he has broken a taboo. The community's reaction is to treat him as a wayward child and to extend help and sympathy. In effect, the sinner becomes a kind of scapegoat and in turn receives a large measure of reassuring attention.

The Navaho who is accused of some transgression immediately blames it on his having been bewitched. This is accepted by the community, because it is widely believed that witches cause all kinds of suffering and may induce good Navahos to commit crimes. Hence he is treated with sympathy and understanding by his community. Eventually, however, there must be a reckoning, and this occurs when a witch is discovered. Feelings against the witch may run so strong that he (Navaho witches are male) may be physically assaulted or even killed. As a result, Navahos are more afraid of being accused of witchcraft than they are of engaging in illicit behavior. So strong is this fear that Navahos will avoid behavior that will make them appear different in any way and will not strive to become affluent or successful. Anything that might bring them to the special attention of the community increases the probability of being accused of witchcraft and being publicly shamed, humiliated, or even attacked.

SUMMARY

A number of experiments show that the presence of others appears to facilitate the performance of familiar tasks, but interferes with the performance of tasks that are less familiar. The inverted-U hypothesis regarding the relationship between stress and performance may apply here: the presence of others is a source of stress, and coping with an unfamiliar task is also a source of stress. Hence the amount of stress from two sources may interfere with the individual's effectiveness. On the other hand, a routine, well-learned task may not generate enough stress to command the subject's full attention, and the presence of others may supply the stress needed to raise the performance to a more adequate level of efficiency.

The fact that we look to others for cues that enable us to organize and structure our environment gives them a considerable leverage in guiding our behavior. Studies by Sherif of judgment in ambiguous situations show that the opinions of others set norms for behavior that are adhered to when others are no longer present. Opinions of others can also have a pronounced effect on our judgment in false-norm situations, that is, situations in which objective evidence contrary to the majority opinion is available. In the experimental situations designed by Asch, 74 per cent yielded at least once in the series of twelve trials. Extensive yielding to false norms was also obtained at the Institute of Personality Assessment and Research at the University of California in Berkeley. Even "sophisticated" subjects (those

who suspected the experiment was rigged) were not immune to such pressure. In an experiment by Crutchfield, such subjects conformed to false norms 12 per cent of the time, as contrasted with 26 per cent for "naive" subjects.

Studies comparing people most likely to yield to false norms (yielders), with those who tend to resist (independents), show that yielders tended to be more authoritarian, conforming, compliant, overcontrolled, vacillating, confused, lacking in insight, and suggestible.

Inasmuch as associating with others has reward value for us, we will go to some pains to secure this reward. The techniques we use include attempts to make eye contact with others, conformity, and ingratiation, as indicated by willingness to make statements that do not reflect our true opinions. Both high- and low-status individuals make use of ingratiation tactics, because approval and support are necessary for both.

The behavior of others can also be manipulated by such devices as asking small favors as a preliminary to requesting major ones. Playing roles appropriate to people whose points of view differ from ours also has an impact on our opinions, beliefs, and subsequent behavior.

Research dealing with attempts to manipulate attitudes and behavior through the arousal of fear presents mixed results. Earlier studies showed that the communication of information was more effective than the arousal of fear, but later studies show that fear is a strong motivator under some circumstances. It has been suggested that the greatest change is likely to take place when the level of anxiety is moderate, not too high and not too low. Cross-cultural studies show that some societies make use of shame and fear-producing tactics to secure conformity, whereas others depend more on internalized norms and guilt.

SUGGESTED READINGS

Asch, S. A., *Social psychology*. Englewood Cliffs, N.J.: Prentice-Hall, 1952. Chapter 16.

Barron, F., *Creativity and psychological health*. Princeton: Van Nostrand, 1963.

Getzels, J. W. & Jackson, P. W., *Creativity and intelligence*. New York: Wiley, 1962.

Holt, R. R., Forcible indoctrination and personality change. In Worchel & Byrne (Eds.), *Personality change*. New York: Wiley, 1964.

Lindgren, H. C. (Ed.), *Contemporary research in social psychology*. New York: Wiley, 1969. See papers on social influence in Section 4.

Peristiany, J. G. (Ed.), *Honour and shame: the values of Mediterranean society*. Chicago: University of Chicago Press, 1966.

Sherif, M., *The psychology of social norms*. New York: Harper, 1936. (Available as paperback.)

CHAPTER SEVEN

CHAPTER SEVEN

Theories of Dissonance, Consonance, and Balance

Chapter 6 dealt with changes in attitude and behavior largely in terms of pressures brought to bear by others. In this chapter we examine changes in terms of actions initiated by the individual concerned. We shall discuss theories that have as their common basis the view that people strive to maintain some degree of consistency in their views of themselves and their environment, as well as in their relations with others. Sometimes this striving for consistency leads an individual to take steps or make statements that actually appear illogical or irrational but which, when examined more closely, turn out to be quite logical in terms of the past behavior of the individual and his attempts to maintain symmetry, balance, and consonance among the various elements in his life.

Cognitive Dissonance Theory

Theoretical Background. The theory of cognitive dissonance, as propounded by Leon Festinger (1957), is one of the most important concepts in social psychology today. It is applicable to a wide variety of situations, both in the psychological laboratory and in everyday life, and has stimulated a great deal of research in the relatively brief period since its appearance.

Festinger's theory rests on the assumption that the individual attempts "to establish internal harmony, consistency, or congruity among his opinions, attitudes, knowledge, and values,"—what Festinger terms "cognitive elements." He observes that pairs of cognitive elements may exist in irrelevant, consonant, or dissonant relationships with each other. The relationship is an irrelevant one if the two elements have nothing to do with each other; is consonant if one element follows from the other; and is dissonant if, considering these two elements alone, the obverse of one element follows from the other. What Festinger means by "follows" is illustrated by this example: an event occurs that invalidates a belief that is important to members of a certain group. In this instance, the belief has led the group members to expect something other than that which actually occurred—in other words, the event does not follow logically from what they believed ("knew") to be true.

Inasmuch as the individual strives to maintain harmony or consonance among cognitive elements, the presence of dissonance leads to pressure to reduce the dissonance, the amount of pressure being consistent with the amount of dissonance that exists. Festinger points out that dissonance functions like a drive, need, or tension. Its presence leads to action to reduce it, just as the presence of hunger leads to action aimed at reducing the hunger. Dissonance can be resolved or at least reduced by changing one of the cognitive elements involved, by adding new elements, or by decreasing the importance of elements. For instance, dissonance that results when others disagree with us can be reduced by changing our opinion, by getting others to change their opinion, or by deciding that there is no basic disagreement.

Another example of dissonance and its resolution is as follows: The experimenter asks a child to rate a number of toys for their attractiveness. He selects two that the child has rated as equally attractive and asks the child to chose one for himself. He then asks the child to rate the two toys again. If the child behaves as most children do, he will rate the chosen toy as more attractive than the other one. The evaluation is obviously not consistent with his previous one. The logic of this seems to be: "Although I said that the toys were equally attractive, I must have thought the one I chose was more attractive, otherwise I would not have chosen it." This type of reasoning is not confined to children, as we shall see from the research.

In this example the dissonance is created by the child's first rating the two toys as equal in value and then selecting one. When we are free to choose between two objects, we generally make our choice on the basis of one object having higher value than the other. The fact that choices between two objects are generally made on the basis of one of the object's having a higher value suggests the way in which dissonance can be resolved, and the child therefore decides that the two objects did not have the same value after all. He modifies his initial judgment to make it agree with the choice he has made.

Other writers in the field point out that dissonance operates mainly when a person has made a choice he believes is free, in which he acts of his own volition and is not coerced (Brehm & Cohen, 1962). If the individual has no choice in following an action that is contrary to his preexisting beliefs, he does not feel any need to change his attitudes toward the action, but if he makes the choice to perform the action freely, dissonance is created and he feels some pressure to reduce it.

The Classic Experiment: Payment for Lying. In one well-known study, Festinger and Carlsmith (1959) had subjects complete a very dull and fatiguing task which lasted an hour and then asked them to tell other subjects (actually accomplices of the experimenters) that the task was interesting. Although the experimenters did not say or even imply that a lie was being requested, the subjects were all aware that the task was dull and boring. Some of the subjects were offered a dollar to tell this falsehood (and to remain on call for possible future experiments) and some were offered twenty dollars. The dissonance was produced by the disparity between the magnitude of the reward and that of the task. One dollar is a rather low price to be paid for a lie. Common sense would say that the students who had been paid one dollar would at this point be more inclined to say that they disliked the experiment and would not like to do another, but cognitive dissonance theory would predict the opposite, on the grounds that the person who had been paid only a dollar to lie would have more cognitive dissonance. He would be likely to believe that his reason for trying to convince the other subject that the experiment was fun was the fact that he did indeed enjoy it. He would have difficulty in imagining that he would tell anyone a falsehood for only a dollar—therefore, he must be telling the truth.

The results were consistent with cognitive dissonance theory: those who had been paid a dollar were more likely to tell the experimenter that they had enjoyed the experiment and would like to participate in another, whereas those who had received twenty dollars were inclined to admit that the experiment was boring, thus tacitly admitting they had not told the other subject the truth. Figure 7-1 presents the major findings.

A subsequent replication of this experiment by Carlsmith, Collins, and Helmreich (1966) found similar results: subjects who had been paid to tell another subject that the dull task had been fun and interesting and who had been paid only fifty cents expressed significantly more positive evaluation of the task afterward than did those who had received a dollar and a half, and the latter made more favorable evaluations than those who were paid five dollars. The opposite effect was obtained, however, with subjects who wrote essays saying that the task was fun and interesting. Under such conditions, the higher the pay, the higher the evaluation of the dull task. One interpretation of this difference is that Festinger and Carlsmith required their subjects to make an oral affirmation. Making such a statement before witnesses may have had more in-

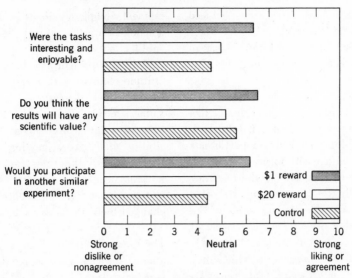

Figure **7-1.** Differences between two experimental groups and a control group in their subsequent evaluations of a dull, boring task which they had been asked to describe as "interesting and fun" and for which statement they had paid varying amounts (Festinger & Carlsmith, 1959).

fluence on subsequent behavior than did writing the essays.

This is not to say that dissonance created by writing essays is necessarily ineffectual in changing attitudes. Arthur R. Cohen took advantage of a tense situation at Yale University, following student riots occasioned by the actions of New Haven police on the campus, and asked students to write essays in support of the police. Students were generally antagonistic to the police and essays were solicited and paid for under the guise of securing arguments on both sides of the question. Attitude scales administered after the essays had been written showed that students who had been paid fifty cents (maximum dissonance) reported themselves as being more favorably disposed to the police than were students who had been paid ten dollars (minimum dissonance). The attitudes of the latter were no more favorable than were those of students who wrote no essays

but merely took the attitude scales (Brehm & Cohen, 1962). Although the Cohen experiment shows that dissonance created by writing an essay can be instrumental in bringing about attitude change, the situation is by no means comparable to that of the essay writers in the Carlsmith, Collins, and Helmreich study, inasmuch as the students in the Yale experiment very likely had more negative feelings about the police than the other subjects had about telling a small lie (Linder, Cooper, & Jones, 1967).

Role Playing and Cognitive Dissonance. In Chapter 6 we described an experiment by Elms (1966) in which smokers who made a public commitment by telling others why they should not smoke actually changed their own attitudes toward smoking, as their subsequent behavior showed. By making these statements they created dissonance between what they were saying (taking a stand against smoking) and their usual behavior (smoking). Dissonance was reduced somewhat by changing their attitudes and their actual smoking behavior to a position closer to the one they had taken when they told their listeners not to smoke.

Another experiment with role playing produced even greater attitude change when an extra element of dissonance was introduced. John Wallace (1966) asked for volunteers to participate in a debate to defend a position on capital punishment which was the opposite to the one they had taken when filling out a questionnaire prior to the experiment. After the debate, some of the subjects were told that the *intellectual content* of their speeches was superior (content reward), others were told that the *manner* in which they gave their speeches was superior (role reward), and still others were told that they did as well as their opponent, or that the group favored their opponent. Questionnaires completed after the experiment showed that members of all four groups changed their attitudes (although most of the change was restricted to those who originally favored capital punishment). The greatest amount of cognitive dissonance was created for subjects who were told that the *manner* in which their speeches were presented was superior. In effect, such a compliment says: "You were talking like a person who believes what he is saying." People are likely to be caught off guard by such an idea, and dissonance is created between what they believe and the way they were told they were behaving. The prediction of dissonance theory was confirmed by the finding that the greatest change took place in this group. One subject explained what happened to him in this way:

"I tend to think of myself as an honest and sincere person. When you told me that the others considered me 'a very good actor,' I was somewhat baffled . . . actually, a little offended. The more I thought about it, the more I became convinced that what I had said in the debate was what I truly believed."

This subject reversed his stand on capital pun-

ishment completely in order to resolve the dissonance between what he believed and how others said he behaved.

Role playing can also be used to bring about attitude changes with respect to other social issues—racial integration, for example. Frances Culbertson (1957) measured attitudes before and after role-playing experiences related to the possibility of Negroes moving into white neighborhoods. All the roles favored integration in housing. Half the subjects were role players, and the other half were observers. All subjects changed their attitudes in the expected direction, with the role players showing greater change. The most significant changes, incidentally, were among subjects who scored low (in the democratic direction) on the F scale.

"I'd Rather Be Consistent than Right." Research studies involving the manipulation of behavior through the creation of cognitive dissonance cover a wide range of behavior. Paul R. Wilson and Paul N. Russell (1966) used the administration of an inconsistent reward to induce dissonance. They paid subjects in one group a shilling for moving a 1-pound weight and a penny for moving a 7-pound weight. A second group received the shilling for lifting the heavy weight and a penny for lifting the light one. The control group received no remuneration. Basing their hypotheses on dissonance theory, the researchers predicted that subjects who had been underrewarded for moving the heavy weight would underestimate how much work they had done to move it. Results confirmed this expectation.

Physiological Changes due to Dissonance. When dissonance theory predicts and confirms a response that is contrary to common sense, the question is likely to arise as to whether the obtained results are very significant. Are they rather superficial, temporary aberrations, or do they really involve the total organism? Even though psychologists have officially abandoned the idea of the separate existence of mind and body, results somehow seem more convincing if it can be shown that physiological as well as psychological or cognitive processes are involved.

Philip G. Zimbardo and others (1966) carried out a study to determine what physiological changes, if any, accompany subjects' attempts to reduce cognitive dissonance. The experiment consisted of two phases, but subjects were not told of this beforehand. In the first phase of the experiment, they were each given two painful electric shocks per learning trial until they had learned nine words. When the subjects had completed this task, they naturally thought the experiment was over and prepared to leave, but the experimenter asked them to volunteer instead for a second phase that was to be similar to the experience they had just gone through. Low dissonance was created for one group of subjects by giving them plausible reasons for volunteering—importance to the experimenter, to science, to the subject himself, to the space program, and the like. High dissonance was created for the subjects in a second group by not giving them any justification for requesting them to volunteer.

In some respects, the dissonance thus created was similar to that created for subjects in the Festinger and Carlsmith (1959) experiment in which people uttered a falsehood for only a dollar. There was little or no dissonance for the subjects who were given elaborate reasons for asking them to volunteer. Their volunteering appeared plausible to them because it is represented to them as having social value. A much greater amount of dissonance was created for the other group of subjects, because no reasons were given for their volunteering, and in fact they probably wondered why they were volunteering. (Incidentally, there was no difference in the numbers who refused to volunteer from the two groups.)

The effect of dissonance was measured by asking subjects to indicate on a scale the degree of pain caused by the shocks they were receiving. All subjects receiving strong shocks gave similar ratings of the amount of pain they were experi-

encing, except that those in the high dissonance group reported that their pain was less intense. Many, in fact, said the shock "doesn't hurt so much." Such a perception would be consistent with dissonance theory, because it would enable them to perceive their otherwise inexplicable willingness to volunteer as somewhat more plausible.

The fact that there was a real difference in the amount of pain they felt is shown by two additional measures. Learning words while being shocked is not easy, for the pain interferes with cognitive processes and is distracting. The high dissonance group, however, actually improved their learning efficiency during the second phase of the experiment, whereas those with low dissonance actually worsened somewhat. In fact, the performance of the high dissonance group was quite similar to that of a control group who had not been given any choice about volunteering for the second phase and who had received high shock in the first phase and moderate shock in the second. In effect, therefore, the high dissonance subjects behaved as though the high level of shock they were receiving was actually only moderate.

Reactions to pain-producing stimuli can also be measured by galvanic skin response (GSR). Subjects in a control group that were given a high level of shock in both phases showed an increase in GSR during the experiment, but the high dissonance subjects showed a reduction in GSR similar to that of a second control group that received high shock in the first phase and moderate shock in the second.

The evidence thus seems quite clear and incontrovertible that the behavioral changes resulting from attempts to reduce cognitive dissonance are pervasive and involve the whole organism.

Similar results were obtained with experiments conducted by Jack W. Brehm (1962), who observed the reactions of subjects who had been deprived of food and who then were asked to volunteer to continue fasting. Subjects were asked to show up for an afternoon testing session without having eaten breakfast and lunch. Each subject was shown some sandwiches, cookies, and milk that would be his after he had finished the tests. At this point, the subject was asked to indicate on a scale how hungry he was. After a brief period of testing the subject was asked if he would continue to fast in order to participate in some experiments that evening. Although he had received some credit toward his final grade in psychology for the first phase of the experiment, he would receive no further credit for the second phase. It was made clear, however, that the decision to participate or not was his and that there was no penalty for refusing. Low dissonance subjects were told that they would receive five dollars for continuing to fast and returning for the evening session. After the subjects had committed themselves to going without dinner and were scheduled for an evening session, they were asked to fill out the hunger rating scale again.

A high level of dissonance was created for the volunteers who were not being paid, because there was really no valid reason why they should have volunteered to spend another six hours or so fasting. As dissonance theory predicted, they rated their hunger as lower after they had committed themselves to a continuation of the fast than they did when they had just arrived for the test sessions.

Applications of Dissonance Theory. We have devoted this much space to a discussion of cognitive dissonance because it has been one of the most productive concepts in social psychology. It has gone a long way in enabling behavioral scientists to free themselves from dependence on common-sense formulations and to open up new dimensions of human behavior for research. It is difficult to determine, however, just how far one should go in extending the implications of dissonance theory. As we have tried to show, there are a number of aspects of human behavior that are made clearer and more understandable when seen in terms of dissonance, but this does not

necessarily mean that all behavior is an attempt to avoid dissonance. As we pointed out at the beginning of this chapter, we tend to avoid dissonance because we seek consonance. We are more comfortable, psychologically speaking, when we can behave toward the various events in our lives as though they were consistent and interrelated.

For example, some of the research on interpersonal attractiveness can be explained in terms of cognitive dissonance, as well as in terms of mutual attraction based on similarity. We cited research in Chapter 3 to show that people who are similar tend to be attracted to one another, but it may frequently happen that people are attracted to one another for one reason or another and *then* develop similarities.

Some evidence for this is provided in a study by Dorothy M. Kipnis (1961). She asked eighty-seven male freshmen students, who had lived together in a dormitory for the first five weeks of the school year to describe themselves and the eight students who lived nearest them and to indicate which of the eight they would like as companions on a double date, as a roommate, classmate, and the like. They were also asked to name their best friend and their least-liked roommate. Six weeks later she administered the same measures and asked the same questions. At the start of the study, students tended to perceive smaller differences in personality between themselves and their best friends than between themselves and their least-liked roommate, but by the end of the study those students who had originally perceived their best friends to be relatively unlike themselves had changed their self-perceptions more than students who had originally perceived their friends to be more like themselves. Thus there was a tendency for students to change self-perceptions to harmonize with the perceptions they had of their best friends. If they originally believed that their friends had negative traits, they tended to perceive similar negative traits in themselves, and conversely, they tended to adopt the same positive traits they saw in their friends. It is interesting to note that students who attributed more negative traits to their friends than to themselves tended to break off friendships more readily than those who had perceived a preponderance of positive traits.

Kipnis' research suggests that we prefer to think that our friends are similar to us. Such perceived similarity is cognitively consonant, rather than dissonant. Whenever we perceive that our friends' characteristics are different from ours, dissonance is created which can be resolved either by our changing our values and attitudes so that they become more consonant with those of our friends or by terminating the friendship.

Still another way of resolving dissonance is to assume that greater similarity exists than is actually true. George Levinger and James Breedlove (1966) interviewed sixty middle-class couples (husbands and wives separately) and secured a considerable amount of information about family goals, communication patterns, social-emotional supportiveness, etc. They found that the couples' satisfaction with their marriage was more significantly related to their *assumed* agreement on goals than to their actual agreement. In other words, couples who were getting along best tended to assume that they had similar points of view. Whether or not they actually *were* similar appeared to be less important. Whatever dissonance existed between their attitudes and beliefs had been resolved by their tacit assumption of similarity. They were saying, in effect, "Since we like each other, we must of course have similar points of view."

Controversies Regarding Cognitive Dissonance. The interpretations that Festinger and the other cognitive dissonance researchers have made of their results have aroused some controversy among psychologists. Festinger (1961) observes that organisms learn to like and value things for which they have worked very hard or have suffered, but for which they have been inadequately rewarded. In a sense this contradicts the more conventional learning theories, which maintain that organisms learn to like things for which they have been rewarded. Festinger notes that the cognitive dissonance theory is not in direct opposition to reward-based theories, but that it proposes instead that a different kind of process may also operate.

The study by Aronson and Mills (1959), described in Chapter 1, is cited by Festinger as an example of the effectiveness of inadequate rewards. To review this experiment briefly, girls who had expressed an interest in joining a discussion group whose topic was sex experienced either an embarrassing or a nonembarrassing oral test as a prerequisite for being admitted to membership. After the subjects were presumably admitted to the group, they then heard what they thought was a discussion conducted by the other members, but what was actually a tape recording of a long, rambling, uninteresting discussion. Girls who had been through the embarrassing initiation rated the group as more desirable than those who had been through the mild one. In other words, girls who had received the least reward valued the goal higher.

Proponents of more conventional learning theories have been critical of conclusions based on dissonance studies and have attempted experiments of their own to disprove the concept. Although each of these attempts has been somewhat successful in pointing up flaws in individual dissonance studies, none of them has been able to disprove the main body of evidence. Dissonance theory is still the best single theory available to explain the findings of all the studies (McGuire, 1966).

Theories of Consonance and Balance

Coping with Cognitive Stress and Strain. Although psychologists have developed a number of systems to explain how individuals maintain consonance, balance, and organization among attitudes, we shall confine our discussion to the systems of Fritz Heider (1946, 1958) and Theodore M. Newcomb (1953, 1961), which appeared somewhat earlier than the other systems and which contributed substantially to their development. The Heider and Newcomb systems have many common features in that they both describe a kind of cognitive homeostasis, that is, a tendency for attitudes to develop or orient themselves in such a way that a state of consistency or balance is developed. This state of balance is of course theoretical, because viable systems are always somewhat out of balance—as one element in the system changes, in response to external conditions or other causes, the relationship among the other elements changes as well. Consequently, systems tend to be in a state of continual movement and adjustment. Three kinds of states can be identified in such a theory: (1) a normal state (or state of rest or balance), (2) the intrusion of certain forces or events that upset this normal state, and (3) the operation of certain mechanisms or processes that have the function of bringing the system back to the normal state.

Heider designates these three states as *balance, imbalance,* and the *stress to change in order to restore balance.* Figure 7-2 consists of diagrammatic representations of four states of balance and four of imbalance.

In the first of the balanced states, the individual (P) likes the other person (O), and both of them are favorably disposed to some object (X) to which they both have a relationship. In the second, P likes O, and they both are unfavorably disposed toward X. In the third, O behaves or feels negatively toward both P and X, but P likes X. In the fourth, O feels or behaves positively toward X, but P dislikes both of them.

The unbalanced states lack the harmony of the balanced states and generate activity to restore harmony. In the first of these states, P likes both O and X, but O dislikes X. This puts pressure on P to change his attitude toward X or to get O to change his attitude. The second unbalanced state can be resolved in similar fashion—by having either P or O change his attitude toward X. The

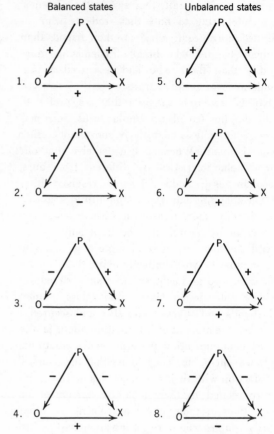

Figure **7-2.** Diagrams representing balanced and unbalanced states and depicting relations among an individual (P), another person (O), and an object (X) (after Heider, 1958).

third and the fourth unbalanced states can be balanced by P's changing his feelings about either O or X.

The balanced states are characterized by comfort and harmony among the elements, whereas the unbalanced states are characterized by discomfort, disharmony, and the generation of activity intended to restore some kind of balance. Unbalanced systems are represented in life situations by psychological conflicts in attitudes or behavior toward others. George (P) is very fond of Joe (O). They have been close friends ever since they stood together in the registration line as freshmen. They are enrolled in the same English class, and a paper is due the next day. George, who is very conscientious and task oriented, has finished his paper, whereas Joe has let things slide and is now faced with a desperate situation. He asks George if he can borrow his paper to look it over and get some ideas for his own. George is rather shocked at this proposal, because it sounds like cheating. Joe therefore appears to have positive feelings about cheating (X), whereas George has negative ones. Balance can be restored only by George changing his ideas about Joe's request (e.g., deciding that it is not really cheating, after all) or changing his feelings about Joe (deciding that Joe is not the kind of person he wants as a friend).

The fourth diagram in the unbalanced column of Figure 7-2 sometimes causes problems with students. If all relationships are negative, they ask, should not the state be balanced? An example may serve to clarify this problem. George (P) is against war or any kind of military involvement. He also dislikes his English instructor, Dr. Mayo (O), intensely. He thinks Dr. Mayo is hopelessly out of touch with today's world, is pedantic, formalistic, and hypercritical. Imagine his surprise when he turns on the television one evening and finds Dr. Mayo participating in a panel devoted to a discussion of international tensions. Contrary to George's expectations, Dr. Mayo does not defend "the establishment," but instead makes an eloquent plea for this country's immediate withdrawal from all military or quasi-military operations. This point of view coincides exactly with George's position.

George is now in a quandary about his feelings toward Dr. Mayo, and his conflict is precisely of the type depicted in the fourth diagram in the unbalanced column in Figure 7-2. He has negative feelings about both Dr. Mayo and war, but has just learned that Dr. Mayo has negative feelings about war, too. Although he would like to keep his feelings toward Dr. Mayo at a strongly nega-

tive level, he cannot help identifying with him to some degree. He finds himself thinking, "Anyone who feels that strongly about war can't be *all* bad." Thus he feels under considerable stress to change his attitude toward Dr. Mayo. Of course, the other way of resolving the dilemma and restoring harmony to the triad would be for him to change his feelings about war. He may decide that he dislikes Dr. Mayo so intensely that he must reject even his stand against war, and he finds himself finding reasons why his nation must continue to be involved in military operations. It depends on which value is the more central to him: being against war or being against Dr. Mayo.

In real life situations we do not, as a general rule, readily reverse pluses and minuses. Although our feelings toward others may be depicted in terms of triads of tension and balance, these triads are linked together in complex and multiplex systems with the various segments interrelated and interlocking. George may be tempted to change his attitude toward Dr. Mayo as a result of the latter's television performance, but in all likelihood he cannot do so without taking stock of *all* his attitudes toward middle-aged people in positions of authority. This may be more than he wants to undertake at present and hence is content for the moment with making a slight reduction in his negative feeling toward Dr. Mayo. The fact that most people, like George, do not immediately reverse signs when systems are unbalanced does not contradict Heider's theory. Heider maintains that imbalance sets up *stresses*. Whether or not we reverse attitudes (or signs) depends on the strength of the stresses. Newcomb (1961) describes stresses as a "strain toward symmetry" (he prefers to use the term "symmetry" instead of "balance"), whereby systems that lack harmony are said to be under a kind of strain that tends to move the individual in the *direction* of restoring harmony once more. Most of us, however, can tolerate a considerable degree of strain without feeling compelled to reverse our attitudes, once they have been formed.

Strain and the Complexity of the Cognitive System. The amount of strain we can tolerate also depends on the complexity of the cognitive system. People who lead fairly complex lives, who are involved in a variety of activities, are usually able to accommodate more strain than are those who lead simpler, less complex lives. An illiterate *caipira,* or peasant, who works on a coffee fazenda in the back country of Brazil has relatively few elements in his cognitive structure. He is conversant with a few events in a relatively limited area, both geographic and psychological. Any change in attitudinal relationship among the elements in his cognitive system calls for major changes which he is likely to resist; and if changes are inescapable, he may become extremely upset and disorganized.

Let us say, for example, that our *caipira* has a positive regard for the overseer, and both have positive feelings about raising coffee. However, the world market becomes glutted with coffee, and the Brazilian government finds that it no longer has the funds to buy up coffee surpluses and store them. The government recommends that growers shift to other crops, and the owner asks his overseer to plant a number of different cash crops as an experiment. Coffee now assumes a negative value for the overseer, inasmuch as the owner can no longer grow it at a profit. The overseer's cognitive system is more complex than that of the *caipira.* He is better educated, has traveled to São Paulo and to Rio, has a wider circle of friends and acquaintances, reads newspapers and other mass media, and is more widely informed. He may be very reluctant to stop growing coffee; after all, he has grown it all his life, and his father before him, and he does not know how the new types of crops will fare or what problems he will encounter with them. He may not be convinced that the coffee problem is as severe as the owner thinks it is, but he follows his orders to experiment with new crops. He worries considerably about the problems involved in changing over from coffee to a new crop, but he also has other

things on his mind. For example, he carries on an active correspondence with relatives back in Portugal he has never seen, his son is attending a technical institute in Rio Branco, and when he sits down with his wife in the evening to listen to their collection of records, he forgets his other problems.

The overseer's cognitive system is under some strain because he has positive regard for both the owner and for growing coffee, but the owner has negative feelings about coffee. But because the overseer's cognitive system, is multiplex and complex it absorbs some of the tension and enables him to shift it elsewhere.

The *caipira's* simple cognitive system does not permit this latitude. Whereas the overseer feels moderately threatened by the impending changeover to other crops, the *caipira* feels very threatened. Coffee is the only thing he knows; it is an important part of his life. He cannot imagine not working in coffee. The overseer knows that all agricultural operations are similar, no matter what crop is grown and that the *caipira* will be just as able to work on soybeans, potatoes, or cotton, as he is to work on coffee. But the *caipira* does not know that. His system has now gone out of balance. Whereas before he felt positively toward the overseer and toward coffee, and the overseer also felt positively toward coffee, the fact that the overseer is beginning to experiment with other crops is incontrovertible evidence that he will change his mind about coffee. Furthermore, the owner has already changed his mind about coffee, which is good indication that the overseer will change his mind as well.

The *caipira's* cognitive system is less able than is the overseer's to withstand imbalance or strain. He is not psychologically involved in events away from the fazenda. Opportunities for distraction are few and socially unacceptable; that is, he could get drunk every payday or beat his wife and children. The alcohol would anesthetize him so that he would not feel the tension, but the effect would be only temporary, and he would get into trouble for drinking up the money needed by his family. Beating his family would temporarily reduce tension in the sense that he could displace on them the hostility he feels toward the owner and the overseer but which he is afraid to express. He could attempt to restore balance by threatening the overseer or the owner, but he would only lose his job and perhaps be thrown into jail. In short, his cognitive system is too simple to absorb the strain and he is forced to live with his tensions, whereas the overseer is able to dissipate most of his.

The situation we have described is a real one faced by peasant populations in many one-crop countries like Brazil. Often the tensions become so severe that drastic action appears to be the only release. One popular solution is to leave the local area and escape to the city. This only creates new problems, but the escapee is for the moment only concerned about leaving a situation that has become intolerable for him. Sometimes balance is achieved by making owners and overseers the villains and by joining in a peasants' revolt. This changes the plus between P and O to a minus, and leaves unchanged the minus between O and X and the plus between P and X. It does not solve the coffee glut, but it does create a psychologically comfortable situation, at least for the present and immediate future.

The Ability to Merge Concepts. Eli Saltz and John Wickey (1965) undertook a study which shows that the more salient attitudes and beliefs are, the less tolerant an individual is of imbalance. The attitudes of political liberals toward the various explanations of President Kennedy's assassination provided an opportunity to test hypotheses derived from balance theory. Many liberals were unwilling to accept an explanation that linked Lee Harvey Oswald (a Communist, and hence an "ultra-liberal") to the assassination. The situation is that of diagram 5 in Figure 7-2 (the first one in the "unbalanced" column), in that P (the liberal person) would ordinarily find himself attracted to O, Oswald, because the latter is also

a liberal. But P is also attracted to X, President Kennedy, another liberal. If O actually hates X and kills him, a state of imbalance is created. Such a state can be avoided by deciding that O actually did not kill X. This puts pluses on all sides of the triangle and creates balanced state No. 1. Imbalance can also be avoided by deciding that Oswald was not a liberal, but was in the pay of reactionaries. This changes the plus between P and O to a minus, and produces balanced state No. 3.

There is a third possibility; namely, Oswald was the assassin, but was not alone in the crime, which was the result of a complex plot whose complete details we shall probably never know. This is an attempt to bring new cognitive elements of unknown validity into the picture and does not lend itself readily to the diagrams in Figure 7-2.

Saltz and Wickey found that the majority of the liberals (53 per cent) had no difficulty accepting Oswald as a liberal and as the assassin. The subjects were able to merge the two concepts because for them the two conceptual systems of "Oswald the liberal" and "Oswald the assassin" were relatively flexible, or, to use Salz's term, had "weak boundaries." The researchers predicted that subjects who were generally inclined to be rigid about their concepts, or who had "strong boundaries," would be less able to merge the two concepts. A concept-merging test provided evidence to support this hypothesis. There was a tendency for subjects who had more-than-average difficulty in merging concepts to reject the idea that Oswald was both liberal and an assassin. They also found that subjects who were ranked at the more conservative end of a liberal-conservative scale had the least difficulty in believing that Oswald was both a liberal and an assassin. The researchers interpreted this to mean that imbalance does not require a modification of beliefs for individuals who do not feel strongly about one of the unbalanced elements, in this instance, the liberalism of O and/or X.

Balance and the Acquaintanceship Process. Theodore M. Newcomb has developed a theoretical system similar to that of Heider's which is concerned with attitude development in the process of acquaintanceship. Newcomb (1963) states that as group members interact with one another, each individual selects and processes information about objects of common interest, about other members of the group in terms of their attitudes toward the objects, and about other members in terms of their attitudes toward one another. This information is selected and processed in order to avoid the inconsistencies and conflicts involved in imbalanced relationships.

The chief reason why imbalances are avoided is that they are painful. In another context, Newcomb and his associates note that imbalance involves the following: (1) a state of conflict between the preference for a consistent, neatly ordered world—a world that makes sense—as opposed to the confrontation of a reality that is less consistent; (2) anxiety over the possibility that such a conflict may eventuate; or (3) both (Price, Harburg, & Newcomb, 1966).

Newcomb (1963) notes further that in attempting to avoid anxiety and conflict, the individual must decide whether he will maintain "balance at all costs," because of its importance to his psychological adjustment, or whether he will accept "the truth, whatever it costs." The decision as to which of these modes will prevail depends of course on the strength of the attitudes concerned and on individual differences in personality.

As interaction with strangers begins, we inevitably start to accumulate information of the type indicated above, and changes in attitude result from the need to adapt oneself simultaneously to such information and the desire to maintain balanced relationships.

As members of dyads and larger groups interact, they tend to make changes in attitudes toward one another simultaneously. If such changes are based on realistic information, they are likely to result in satisfying mutual rela-

tionships. Realism tends to increase with acquaintanceship, and when it is combined with continuing tendencies toward balance the inevitable trend is in the direction of mutual attraction. Stable relationships tend to persist, and balanced relationships tend to be stable because they are mutually rewarding and are unlikely to be disturbed by additional information. In other words, the longer people are acquainted, the more realistic they are about each other, but such realism is more likely to strengthen the relationship than to interfere.

Newcomb's observations are largely drawn from his analysis of the behavior of two groups of seventeen male students who lived together for sixteen weeks.* When they first arrived at the residence reserved for their use, the students were all strangers. Most of the changes in mutual attraction took place during their first few weeks together. Relationships among strangers during early periods of contact tend to be characterized by imbalance. For example, Bill likes both Fred and Mark, but then learns that the two do not get along with each other. This creates an imbalanced situation on the order of unbalanced state No. 5 in Figure 7-2. Bill can restore balance by getting to know the two men better and deciding which one he prefers, by encouraging them to become friends, or by withdrawing from the situation altogether. As Newcomb points out, unbalanced relations are unstable, that is, they are likely to undergo changes. Hence relationships among strangers during early periods of contact are likely to be characterized by both imbalance and instability, which tend to diminish as relationships become more balanced and stable and as group members become better acquainted.

Newcomb predicted that individual members' estimates of the attitudes of others in the group would become increasingly accurate with continued acquaintanceship. Results confirmed this

* This research was mentioned in Chapter 3 in connection with the discussion of similarity in attitudes and beliefs as a basis for social attraction.

prediction insofar as individual estimates of the attitudes of others toward one another were concerned, but not with respect to the perception of attitudes of others toward oneself. With respect to the latter, the errors were usually in the direction of overestimating the extent to which the individual's attraction to others is reciprocated by them. In such instances the overriding need to be liked apparently interferes with the ability to perceive reality.

Results also bore out another of Newcomb's predictions, namely that sensitivity to others' responses to oneself would lead to similar levels of attraction among dyads or pairs of members. An incidental finding with interesting implications was Newcomb's discovery that persons scoring low on the F scale (low authoritarians) were more accurate than high F scale scorers in estimating the attitudes of others. Low F scorers also went about the acquaintanceship process by finding out which members of the group were in agreement with them on various topics and picked their friends accordingly. In other words, they were more skillful in making friendship alliances that minimized the possibility of imbalance. Subjects scoring high on the F scale, on the other hand, were more likely to keep as friends those persons to whom they were initially attracted and to perceive more agreement with them than actually existed with respect to matters of common interest.

In another test of balance theory, Price, Harburg, and Newcomb (1966) asked students to answer a questionnaire that presented them with eight imaginary situations, arranged according to Figure 7-2, involving combinations of one of their two best friends and one of the two persons on the campus they disliked the most. They were asked to indicate the extent to which each situation made them feel "uneasy" or "pleasant." In one situation, for example, they were asked how they would feel if they learned that their friend strongly liked one of the people they themselves disliked (diagram 6, Figure 7-2).

Balance theory would predict that such a situation would be viewed as unbalanced and hence as unpleasant. Other situations followed the other seven arrangements of acceptance and rejection listed in Figure 7-2. Predictions of the researchers were borne out quite nicely in the imagined situations where the first-named person (O, in Figure 7-2) was liked by the subject (P)—in other words, the situations represented by diagrams 1 and 2. This was shown by the fact that in situations represented by diagrams 1 and 2 in Figure 7-2, almost 90 per cent of the subjects stated that they found the imagined situations pleasant, whereas in the two unbalanced states, diagrams 5 and 6 in Figure 7-2, an almost equal percentage reported that the situations made them feel uneasy. In the four remaining situations, however, in which the subject (P) does not like the first person named (O), balance theory was less effective as a predicter, because subjects were more inclined to report themselves as ambivalent or neutral. In light of these findings, the researchers suggested that there might actually be three kinds of balance situations, instead of two: (1) states in which balance has been achieved; (2) nonbalanced states, in which the individual feels indifference; and (3) imbalanced states, in which psychological forces are mobilized to correct the imbalance.

The researchers also hypothesized that negative relations between P and O tend to be characterized by uncertainty. When we like others, we are inclined to believe that they like us, as Newcomb's (1963) research has shown. When we do not like others, however, an element of uncertainty has been introduced, perhaps stemming from the relative complexity of such situations, or perhaps from the lack of information about reciprocal attitudes. This uncertainty, according to the authors, is likely to lead to ambivalence and thus to indifference.

Comparisons between Dissonance Theory and Balance Theory. Although both dissonance theory and balance theory rest on the assumption that an individual's behavior is to some extent motivated by a drive to maintain consistency, consonance, or symmetry among cognitive elements, there are some differences between them. Balance theories are concerned with describing balance systems and how they are maintained, whereas dissonance theories attempt to predict what happens when balance is *not* maintained because some unexpected cognitive element intervenes.

Dissonance, as we noted previously, results from decisions that are freely made (or that the individual *believes* are freely made) (Brehm & Cohen, 1962). It occurs *after* the decision and leads to some kind of action. As Festinger (1957) describes it, dissonance is a drive that leads to some kind of behavior aimed at reducing it. Once the kind of situations that produce dissonance are known, it becomes possible to design studies that demonstrate its effects in a wide variety of situations. Although some studies have been concerned with sequences of behavior that superficially, at least, do not seem to be logical or rational, one of the aims of the researchers has been to show that these apparently irrational actions are actually motivated by the general drive to attain consonance. Thus the two types of theory do not negate or contradict each other, but actually serve to complement each other.

SUMMARY

The theories discussed in this chapter rest on a common base: the attempts of the individual to arrive at and maintain a certain degree of consistency in his attitudes, beliefs, and behavior. Festinger's theory of cognitive dissonance is concerned with behavior that takes place when consistency is not maintained, when one cognitive element does not "follow" from another. Dissonance may be reduced by changing one of the cognitive elements, adding new elements, or decreasing the importance of the elements. Dissonance is most likely to be created in situations in which individuals make (or believe they have made) a free choice.

In one experiment, subjects were paid either twenty dollars or one dollar to tell other subjects that a boring task was interesting and to remain on call for future experiments. Telling the lie was purely voluntary; subjects were free to refuse if they wished. Investigation showed that subjects that had been paid one dollar were more likely to believe their lie than those who had been paid twenty. The rationale seems to have been: "If I made such-and-such a statement for only one dollar it must have been true, because I would not tell a lie for such a ridiculous sum." Research in a number of other situations appears to support dissonance theory; attitude change under role-playing conditions appears to be another example of the operation of cognitive dissonance. Attitude changes under cognitive dissonance conditions appear to be profound, for some research shows that not only do subjects claim to feel less pain when they have volunteered to reexperience a shock, but that there are measurable differences in skin conductance. Dissonance theory may also explain a trend that has been noted in acquaintanceship patterns whereby individuals become friendly with others they have as roommates or neighbors and subsequently alter their self-perceptions to conform to their perceptions of their new friends.

Cognitive dissonance theory contradicts learning theories to some extent because it maintains that learning may take place in *negative* relationship to the amount of reward. Hence it is not surprising that a number of criticisms have been leveled at it. A review of cognitive dissonance studies shows that other theories would have predicted the same results in a number of instances, but that cognitive dissonance theory is nevertheless the best single theory available to account for all the evidence.

Theories have been developed by Heider and by Newcomb to describe how cognitive systems maintain balance, consistency, or symmetry. The implications of these theories have been studied with respect to friendship patterns whereby our attitudes toward an acquaintance are affected by his and our attitudes toward a third object. Some arrangements of positive and negative attitudes, as represented by the axes of this three-way relationship, lead to balanced situations; some do not. Imbalance produces what Newcomb calls a "strain toward symmetry," where the individual concerned is impelled to change some of the elements in the relationship. As the acquaintanceship process progresses, it normally generates an increase in accurate information about others, and this in turn facilitates attraction, according to Newcomb. Unbalanced relationships tend to be unstable; whereas the acquisition of information

aids stability. Research with balance systems suggests that there may actually be three kinds of situations: (1) states in which balance has been achieved; (2) nonbalanced states in which the individual feels indifference; and (3) imbalanced states in which the individual takes steps to restore balance.

Dissonance and balance theories are both concerned with individuals' attempts to maintain consistency among cognitive elements: perceptions, attitudes, beliefs, and the behavior that results from these states or motives. Balance theory attempts to explain how balance is maintained, and dissonance theory attempts to predict what happens when it is not maintained. The two types of theories are not in opposition, but complement each other to a large degree.

SUGGESTED READINGS

Adams, J. S., Toward an understanding of inequity. *Journal of abnormal and social psychology*, 1963, **67**, 422–436.

Brehm, J. W. & Cohen, A. R., *Explorations in cognitive dissonance*. New York: Wiley, 1962.

Chapanis, Natalia P. & Chapanis, A. C., Cognitive dissonance: five years later. *Psychological bulletin*, 1964, **61**, 1-22.

Festinger, L., *A theory of cognitive dissonance*. Evanston: Row, Peterson, 1957.

Festinger, L., *Conflict, decision, and dissonance*. Stanford: Stanford University Press, 1964.

Heider, F., *The psychology of interpersonal relations*. New York: Wiley, 1958.

Lindgren, H. C. (Ed.), *Contemporary research in social psychology*. New York: Wiley, 1969. See papers on dissonance and consonance in Section 4.

Newcomb, T. M., *The acquaintanceship process*. New York: Holt, Rinehart, and Winston, 1961.

Tannenbaum, P. H., Mediated generalization of attitude change via the principle of congruity. *Journal of personality and social psychology*, 1966, **3**, 493–499.

CHAPTER EIGHT

Social Status

In Chapter 7 we discussed cognitive systems used by the individual in organizing his attitudes toward and relations with others. In the present chapter and the one that follows we shall also be concerned with systems, but systems that societies and other relatively stable groups develop in order to facilitate effective interaction among their members and to provide for their own continuity. Such a system is developed by the interaction of members with one another, as well as with the system itself. As such, social systems have important implications for the development of attitudes, particularly the attitudes that others have toward us, as well as those we have toward ourselves.

Position, Status, and Role. In a review of research and theory rating to social structure, Daniel R. Miller (1963) points out that a social system can have three different dimensions: (1) organized and unorganized social units, (2) structures, and (3) a set of social positions. Examples of organized units are family, church, school, and club; examples of unorganized units are men, women, working class people. The structures of a social system may include its government, its military organizations, its banking system, etc. Any social unit can be divided into positions: a family may consist of father, mother, son, daughter, brother, sister; a school may be divided into administrators, teachers, students, clerical personnel, and so forth. Each position in a social system has both rights and obligations and can be occupied only by a person who has the requisite qualifications.

Status is ordinarily but not necessarily influenced by the position an individual holds in a social system. A father usually has high status in his family, but some fathers are insulted, exploited, or merely ignored. The point is that status is always dependent on how others perceive and value an individual—on the amount of prestige they are willing to accord him. The amount of status possessed by an individual will be determined by the extent to which he is able to influence others, to make his own decisions, and to expect deference from others. A fourth dimension consists of the relative ease or difficulty that will be experienced by those wishing to attain the status level in question. The status of a position, therefore, may be defined in terms of its power, prestige, and exclusiveness.

The fact that one occupies a position in a social system also implies that he plays certain roles, for he is expected by other members of society to behave in certain ways and to perform certain functions. His awareness of society's expectations leads him to develop similar expectations for his own behavior. Inasmuch as persons occupying the position we call "physician" are expected to perform certain prescribed roles, we sometimes refer to the "social role(s) of the physician," instead of the "position of physician."

Figure 8-1 is a graphic presentation of the relationship between position, status, and role.

Position is described here in terms of the occupations held by the individual. Each occupation may be defined by the roles assigned to it by society. Roles influence the values that tend to be held by persons occupying the position, values influence attitudes, values influence percepts, or the way in which the individual views himself and his environment, and, finally, the individual's percepts influence his roles and the way in which he plays them.

Positions are arranged in Figure 8-1 in a hierarchy according to the social status or social class of the individuals who are likely to occupy them. Social distance is also represented horizontally, to show the exclusiveness of groups of persons occupying certain positions. The zigzag vertical

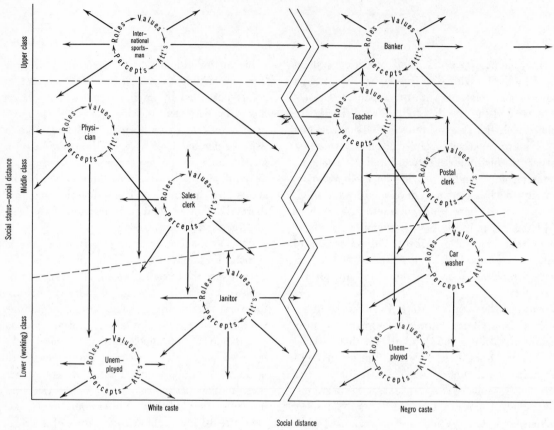

Figure 8-1. The social structure, as expressed in terms of social status, distance, position, class, caste, and influence.

break depicts the social gap between the white and the Negro caste.* Lines terminating in arrows that radiate out from the social positions indicate the degree and direction of social influence or power that individuals occupying the positions are able to bring to bear on the behavior of others. The longer the line, the more effective the influence.

---

* This is, of course, not the only caste division in the United States. There are, for instance, also caste differences between Mexicans and Anglos, whereas other minority groups (Japanese-Americans, Chinese-Americans, Amish, etc.) are regarded (or may regard themselves) in such a way that barriers are to some degree erected between them and the dominant social group or groups.

The diagram includes a number of distortions, introduced partly because of space limitations and partly because of the difficulty of representing a multidimensional situation two-dimensionally. The social distance expressed by the vertical scale (social status) is vastly understated, as is the social distance represented by the gap between the white and the Negro caste. Hence the diagram should be considered only as suggestive of the relationships existing between the variables here depicted.

Although we have used position as the anchor point for this diagram, it should be recognized that each of these aspects of social behavior influences the others. An individual's status depends in part on the position he occupies, and the status that is accorded him by other members of society which enables him to occupy the position. The individual maintains his hold on a certain position by performing the roles that go with it. It sometimes happens that people come to occupy certain positions because they play certain roles. For example, people who play leaderlike roles are likely to find themselves occupying positions of leadership, although not necessarily the ones to which they aspire.

People occupying different positions at approximately the same level of social status often have more in common with one another than they do with people in positions above and below them, even though the latter may live in the same community with them or work in the same field. To use an illustrative example, let us say that Tom Schwartz is twenty-five years old and is a junior executive with a major oil company in California. The company makes a cruise to Hawaii available at below-cost rates to employees and their families. Mr. and Mrs. Schwartz go on the cruise and after a day at sea become quite friendly with two other couples whom they have never seen before and who live in other California cities. Also on the cruise are senior executives from the same branch where Tom is employed, as well as service station attendants from his locale —all people with whom he is acquainted. Mr. and Mrs. Schwartz greet these people in a friendly way when they encounter them on board the ship, but they spend most of their time with the two couples they have just met. It comes as little surprise to us to learn that the other two men are also junior executives in their mid-twenties. The Schwartzes are also quite aware of the senior executives and are a bit envious of the more luxurious quarters they occupy, but they do not seek them out. When one of the senior executives bought the Schwartzes a drink, they felt pleased and flattered, but did not really feel at ease.

People at a given status level find themselves attracted to their peers—those equal to them in status—because with them they find themselves more socially and psychologically comfortable. This more or less spontaneous mutual attraction at certain status levels helps produce the groupings that are termed *social classes*. Figure 8-1 shows how certain positions may be arranged within the social-class limits that divide the social structure into horizontal bands or layers. Social classes in the United States are relatively permeable. It is possible, for example, for persons born into the lower classes to learn the behavior patterns of the middle class and to find ways of entering the middle class. W. Lloyd Warner and James C. Abegglen (1955) studied the backgrounds of executives in large business firms and found that the proportion coming from working-class homes increased between 1928 and 1952. It is the general availability of low-cost education coupled with a widespread tolerance of upward mobility that enables working-class members to become middle class.

Social caste boundaries are less permeable than class boundaries. Interaction among members of different castes is highly restricted, even when individuals are of the same social class and occupy similar positions. Of course, such distinctions are relative and are specific as to situation. There is relatively little differentiation between Negro and white caste in the American Army, particularly during military operations, but differentiation along color lines is more likely to appear among soldiers when they are on leave in recreation centers and even more so when they visit their home towns (Moskos, 1966). However, the Army has another caste system: military rank, which takes precedence over caste differences based on skin color. Here again there is more intimate association between officers and enlisted men during military operations, and considerably less when they are off duty. Caste differences in America are not as sharply drawn as they are in India, but even in India there are urban and rural differences in the strictness with which caste lines are observed.

The barriers that interfere with association between people occupying various positions tend to increase social distance. Within a given caste, vertical social distances tend to be the major ones. As noted earlier, it is easier for people occupying different positions within the same class to associate with one another than it is for them to associate with persons in other classes. Caste lines, however, create a horizontal social distance and make it difficult for persons at the same class level to associate with one another.

The American Social-Class Structure. Once a society has been analyzed in terms of who associates with whom on a basis that is characterized by more or less equal status, it is possible to sort out groups or clusters and arrange them in layers in terms of the amount of prestige and influence that is ascribed to them by other members and groups in the society. Those individuals who exercise the greatest power, and hence are accorded the highest prestige, are considered to be upper class, and those with the least power and prestige, the lower class.

It is relatively easy to determine who has the most and the least power and prestige in a given society. The problem of how the rest of the population should be divided up is more complex. A. B. Hollingshead (1949), a sociologist who studied "Elmtown," a small town in the American Midwest in the late 1940's, divided the social spectrum into five classes, because most of the people he interviewed in the town he was studying were able to discern five status levels. W. Lloyd Warner and Paul S. Lunt (1941), sociologists who studied "Yankee City" (Newburyport, Mass.), during the 1930's, decided on a three-fold scale—upper, middle, and lower—with each class subdivided into an upper and a lower segment. Thus they recognized two middle classes: an upper middle and a lower middle. Richard C. Centers (1949) polled a broad sampling of American

men and found that all but 2 per cent could assign themselves to one of the following classes: upper, middle, working, and lower. Most social psychologists and sociologists recognize an upper- and a lower-middle class. What Warner and Lunt would call "upper-lower class" is often referred to as "working class."

Figure 8-2 attempts to sort out the classifications used in these three sets of research studies and should be interpreted as follows:

Each column represents 100 per cent of the population sampled by the respective researchers whose names are at the heads of the column. The area in each column reflects the percentage of the sample falling in that category. Centers found that 2 per cent of his sample were unable to identify their social class or did not believe in classes; about 1 per cent of the residents of Newburyport could not be classified by Warner and Lunt. These two residuals have been excluded from the cells in the figure, which represent percentages of classifiable persons in the respective samples. It should also be noted that these studies are twenty or more years old and that changes in education and affluence have probably increased the proportion of the middle classes at the expense of the lower classes.

Only the study by Centers makes any claim to be representative of the nation as a whole; the other two studies presumably reflect local situations, although it may be argued that "Elmtown" and "Yankee City" are more or less representative of many other American communities. A cursory comparison of these two rating systems shows that they are roughly similar, and if Centers' "working class" category is redefined to read "lower class," his categories are consistent with those of Warner and Lunt.

The major social-class studies were published in the 1940's. They attracted a great deal of attention at the time, partly because many people had thought that our forebears left the idea of social class behind in Europe and that as a consequence

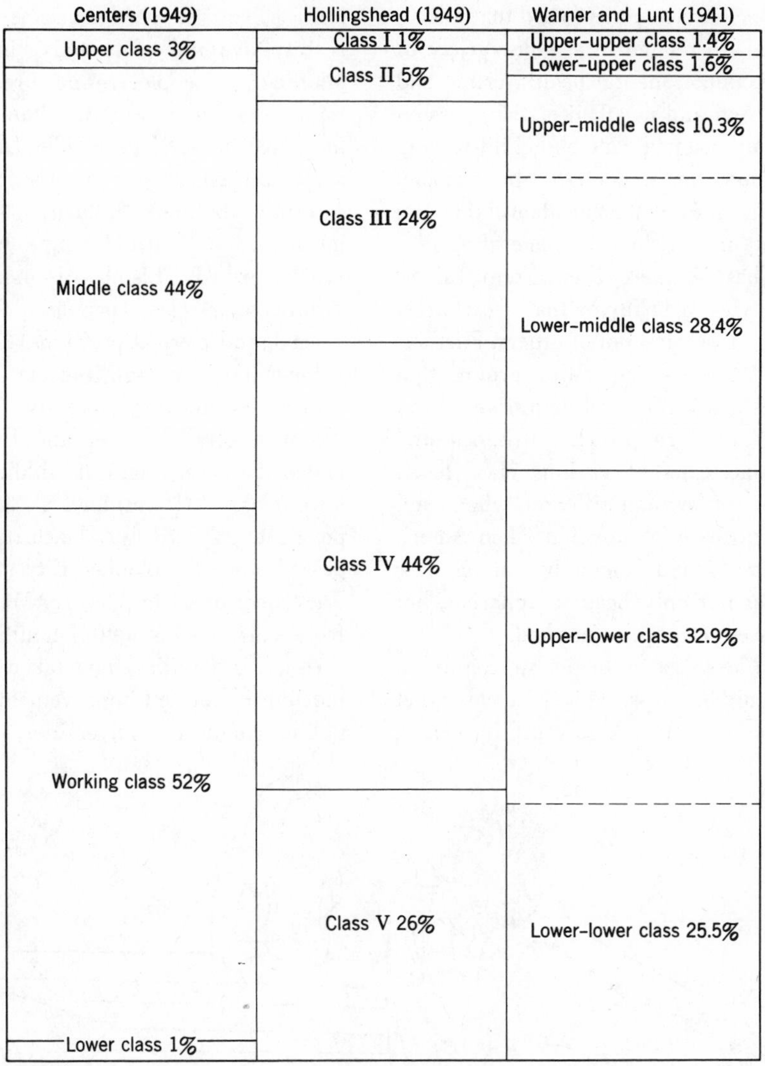

Centers (1949)	Hollingshead (1949)	Warner and Lunt (1941)
Upper class 3%	Class I 1%	Upper-upper class 1.4%
	Class II 5%	Lower-upper class 1.6%
Middle class 44%	Class III 24%	Upper-middle class 10.3%
		Lower-middle class 28.4%
	Class IV 44%	Upper-lower class 32.9%
Working class 52%	Class V 26%	Lower-lower class 25.5%
Lower class 1%		

Figure **8-2.** Social-class stratification in the United States.

the United States was relatively free of class differences. People arrived at this notion because they tended to think of social class in economic and political terms. Inasmuch as Americans had achieved a higher degree of economic and political freedom than people in most countries, it seemed to them that social class must somehow

have been eliminated. The sociologists' reports that differences in social status actually exist and that they have significant effects on many different aspects of thinking, feeling, and behaving had an unsettling effect on many people.

In the years since the appearance of these pioneering studies, psychologists, cultural anthropologists, and sociologists have found that social-class differences are related to a wide variety of variables, for example, mental health, crime and delinquency, n Ach and n Aff, life style, personality patterns, authoritarianism, and child-rearing patterns. We now know enough about social classes to say that they represent identifiable and definable subcultures within the general American culture. That is, there are certain values, attitudes, and styles of behavior that are characteristic of some classes and not of others. Furthermore, social classes are the major groups that serve as sources of identity and definition within the larger national group. The attitudes and behavior of Americans of various class levels may seem more similar than different, when compared with Mexicans or Arabs, but when Americans are compared among themselves along class lines, differences not only become apparent, but in many instances seem quite marked.

The Middle Class. Let us begin by examining the American middle class. This is a class that has received the most intense scrutiny by behav-ioral scientists, partly because it is the most readily available for study, in the sense that middle-class people are more responsive to questionnaires and interviews than are members of the other classes. The middle class today is probably the largest social class in America. It is certainly the most influential as far as social norms, values, attitudes, and behavior patterns are concerned. This class is sometimes called the "white-collar" class (people in professional, managerial, and clerical positions), in contrast to the "blue-collar" or "working class" (skilled, semiskilled, and unskilled operatives). In the study of "Yankee City" Warner and Lunt (1941) estimated the percentages of middle-class (MC) and lower-class (LC) residents at 38 per cent and 58 per cent, respectively. The thirty years that have passed since the Yankee City study have seen a great deal of social change. Many young people from working-class (WC) families or even lower-class (LC) families, have taken advantage of opportunities for self-improvement provided by the public schools and universities, training programs

"When you come right down to it, I'm hopelessly middle class."

© *Saturday Review;* Ned Hilton.

in industry, government agencies, and the armed forces, and have entered the middle class (MC).*

What we today call the middle class is a linear descendant from what has been historically the bourgeoise or burgher element in society: the residents of towns and cities who were involved in some kind of "service occupation," that is, who were not involved in the cruder forms of production. Today, most MC people are still involved in service occupations: as government employees and businessmen, as teachers and social workers, as undertakers and public relations representatives. Chief values of the MC include a high regard for education, thrift, self-improvement, cleanliness, the pleasures and the duties of family life, home ownership, responsibility for one's own actions, and respectability. In North America and Northern Europe the MC is largely future oriented in the sense that immediate pleasures and satisfactions are put aside or postponed in favor of larger future rewards. Thrift is practiced by setting aside small amounts of money for college, for setting up medical or law practices, or for a down payment on a home. The emphasis in the MC is on control and inhibition of impulses; fighting and destructiveness are discouraged, and every effort is made to channel hostility into more constructive (or at least socially acceptable) forms of behavior, such as competitiveness, sports, and games.

The MC does not seem to be as sexually restrained as it once was. Marriages are taking place at a younger age than formerly, and there is said to be more premarital sexual experience and more postmarital infidelity. It is difficult to be certain about alleged changes in morality because there are few, if any, hard statistics to use as guidelines. Widespread public interest in changes in MC standards for sexual behavior have,

however, led many to overlook the really significant differences between MC and LC practices. In contrast to the LC, the typical MC person still appears to be sexually inhibited and straightlaced, for it is in the LC that the majority of cases of unwed motherhood, prostitution, rape, and incest are to be found. It may be, of course, that the LC members look worse in this respect because they are more likely to come to the attention of the authorities, whereas MC sexual aberrations are hushed up or suppressed and are less likely to come to public attention. But even discounting liberally for this factor, social-class differences in the amount of extralegal sexual activity are considerable. The other significant ways in which MC and LC people tend to differ shall be discussed in due course.

The Upper Class. Less is known about the upper class than any of the three major social classes. For one thing, only a small percentage of a given community may be considered truly UC. Hollingshead (1949) found only four families in Elmstown that could be considered Class I, and he combined them with Class II for all his comparisons. Many communities may not actually have anyone who would qualify as genuinely UC, and people who are "upper crust" in one community would be considered "very middle class" in another. Another problem has to do with the lack of consistent patterns of UC behavior from one region or community to another. In the Southwest, UC life is organized around the ranch; in the larger urban centers it may focus on art collecting, the symphony and opera, and civic improvement. Such variability, coupled with the small number of samples, makes it difficult to generalize as to the salient characteristics of UC people. Still another problem is accessibility. Behavioral scientists are all MC and are by nature of the social system excluded from intimate contact with UC members of society. The UC people are singularly uninterested and may even be quite hostile about being subjects in scientific research. Hence descriptions of their behavior

---

* From this point on in our discussion, we will use the symbol UC to represent "upper class," MC for "middle class," UMC for "upper-middle class," LMC for "lower-middle class," WC for "working class," and LC for "lower class."

must be made by inference, based on second-hand information obtained at long range. It is hardly surprising that behavioral scientists have focused their research activities mostly on the other social classes.

In spite of these handicaps it has been possible to identify some UC characteristics. Family reputation and family ties are generally given a high degree of importance in UC circles. Whereas an MC youth expects to attain economic and social success through his own efforts, with a minimum of help from his parents, UC youths know that their economic and social future is assured. They are free to exert themselves or not; whatever they do, they will always be a Vanderbilt or a Mellon or whatever. In schools and colleges they are therefore inclined to be much less competitive and to show less n Ach than the typical MC student.

The most obvious fact about the UC is of course their affluence, but it would be a mistake to say that this is the major difference. Actually, there are many UMC families whose income and financial holdings are quite sizable, yet who would not be considered to be UC. This is particularly true of people who have made their money within their own lifetime. It takes some time—at least two generations—for a family to become established as UC. The UC affluence thus tends to be inherited. It is less likely to come from salary or professional fees as is usual with MC people, but rather is more likely to come in the form of income from securities and capital gains resulting from sales and exchanges of property. How money is spent is also important. In America it has become customary to give large sums of money to family foundations, which not only serve to carry out projects related to the donors' special interest— be it art, education, little magazines, scientific research, or social welfare—but which also serve to glorify and magnify the family name. Money is also spent in ways that have no obvious practical value or utility: in travel, entertainment on a grand scale, for elegant clothes, and for horses and yachts. The MC people are more likely to look for practical reasons to help them rationalize similar expenditures: for example a mountain cabin is justified on the basis that it is a good investment in real estate, as well as a pleasant vacation hideaway.

The kind of house one lives in and its location are also important. The UC families are more likely to prefer older houses in pleasant scenic districts—on a hill, for example, or overlooking a bay or river. Expensive new houses are bought by UMC families rather than by the UC.

A major difference between UC and wealthy MC families lies in the amount of influence they are able to demonstrate—what we have termed "prestige." Common sense and the conventional wisdom would explain prestige in terms of money and political pressure, yet UC persons are able to exert a considerable degree of influence without a major investment of either money or political activity. It is customary, for example, to appoint a member of a prestigious family as the chairman of a national or community fund drive. Such a move serves as a kind of insurance against failure. The fact that such an important person is willing to serve as the figurehead (sometimes a hardworking figurehead and sometimes not) shows that the cause is a legitimate one. It reassures people to the extent that they are willing to give more than they would otherwise contribute. When UC people try their hand at politics, their prestige gives them an extra advantage. For one thing, they do not have to invest as much time and money in publicity as their opponents, for they are already well known. Their motives are less likely to be questioned, and their family name gives them a reputation (sometimes unearned) for respectibility, honesty, and altruism.

Still another characteristic of UC families is the greater power and influence exerted by women. By and large it is the women who determine who shall be invited and included, and who shall be excluded. They are the ones who make the rules that govern the activities and relationships within the subculture, and who classify each member into a hierarchy based on precedent and prestige. Their power is somewhat in contrast with MC society, in which the influence and power of women is approximately equal to that of men.

The Working Class and the Lower Class. A major difference between WC and LC families on the one hand, and UC and MC families on the other, lies in the status of women. The WC and LC women are expected to play roles that are more subordinate than those played by women in the two upper classes. The WC and LC men have a definite edge over women when it comes to freedom and power, and a sizable number of them take advantage of this fact and abandon their families when the going becomes difficult. This is particularly common in LC families. As a consequence, the proportion of fatherless families may run as high as 30 or 40 per cent in many LC neighborhoods. The "welfare family," consisting of six or eight or more young children more or less cared for by an ailing, fatigued, distraught, and angry or apathetic woman, is the inevitable and all-too-common result of this exercise of the LC male perogative.

Before commenting on other contrasts between the two upper and the two lower classes, it may be well to note some of the differences between the WC and the LC. The designations are somewhat confusing, because some behavioral scientists refer to both classes as LC, whereas some refer to both as WC. Warner and Lunt (1941) do not refer to WC at all, and Hollingshead (1949) refers to the classes only by number. We shall try to be consistent, however, by equating WC with Warner and Lunt's "upper-lower class" and Hollingshead's Class IV. In general, WC members are more likely to have steadier employment than are members of the LC. They are also likely to be better trained, to work at higher levels of skill and responsibility, and to be better paid. They are in addition more likely to aspire to MC status. In many communities, WC and MC people live side by side in similar houses in the same neighbor-

hoods, and it is often difficult to find economic differences between them. In fact, many WC members earn more money than MC members, own their own homes, aspire to send their children to college, and in many other ways display patterns of behavior that are largely MC.

Differences between Middle Class and Working Class. As Harold L. Wilensky (1966) reported in a survey and analysis of class structure research, there are some important differences between the WC and the MC way of life. Although the WC family may enjoy an income of, say $10,000 per year, it often requires two jobs and many overtime hours to keep income at that level. Their affluence is also likely to be unsteady. Many WC members move from job to job and have to cope with lay-offs, slack seasons, and periods of unemployment. They may be *relatively* better off economically than LC people, but their situation is likely to be more precarious than that of the typical MC family. Like MC families, WC families say they want their children to go to college, but are inclined to see a college education in strictly vocational terms. Although MC parents also see college education paying off in terms of a better job, they also see it as leading to a more enjoyable life and as preparation for "getting along with other people."

Wilensky also sees similar differences in choice of housing. Both MC and WC people escape from the city to the suburbs in search of "a better way of life," but for the WC family, owning a suburban tract home is more likely to represent freedom from the landlord and avoidance of racial conflict in the central city. The MC family views a suburban home more in terms of a validation of their MC status. Wilensky believes that WC families are more inclined to do their own repairing and servicing of home appliances and automobiles, whereas MC families hire the work to be done. WC families, he says, are also more likely to take aimless Sunday drives that end in a "drive-in" with food or film, rather than a dinner in a downtown restaurant. For vacations, WC families are more inclined to remain at home or visit relatives than to travel great distances for planned adventures.

John Brooks (1966) has commented on some of the differences between white-collar and blue-collar families. He contrasts two families who live next door to each other, both in their late twenties, and both living on incomes of $8000 per year. Mr. White works for a book-publishing firm, and Mr. Blue is a garage mechanic. The Whites live in an old house they have made over; the Blues live in a small, neat house less than five years old. The Blues' lawn is immaculately trimmed; the Whites' lawn is not mowed as efficiently and is full of gray spots and weeds. The Blues drive a Chevrolet, three years old; the Whites drive a Volkswagen of unknown vintage. The Blues' conversation is liberally sprinkled with references to the television shows they watch; the Whites watch televison only occasionally and are reluctant to admit that they do so. The Whites have many, many books, which they even use as a decorating motive; the Blues do not have a book in the house.

The differences between the WC and the MC can be recognized and described, but are hard to measure. If anything, they add up to a difference in aspiration level. Mr. White hopes for advancement within the publishing industry, whereas Mr. Blue will always be a mechanic. Mr. White is striving to become something more than he is, whereas Mr. Blue is interested in security and in maintaining his status quo.

Differences between Working Class and Lower Class. According to Wilensky, the differences between life in the LMC and the upper levels of the WC are not as pronounced as the differences between the WC and the LC. The semiskilled and unskilled operatives who constitute the LC are plagued by high unemployment rates and have more chaotic work histories. They also encounter more obstacles if and when they try to escape into the upper WC levels or into the MC. They lack sophistication in making purchases, are easily vic-timized by "easy credit," and are continually in debt. Like the LC throughout the world, they receive less of every good thing that modern society has to offer: economic security, health services, personal safety, living space, opportunity for education, and interesting work. Their typical response to their inhospitable social environment is retreat. They are more likely to eat, drink, and watch television alone. Family life is more likely to be impoverished and unstable, and homes broken by divorce, death, or desertion are a commonplace. Mental illness rates are approximately three times as high as they do in any other social level.

Although these generalizations apply to the LC as a whole, we should recognize that the LC is composed of many diverse groups—probably more than can be encountered in any other social class. We have already referred to semiskilled and unskilled operatives with poor work histories. There are also migrant workers and share-croppers, white "hillbillies" in the Appalachians, and chronic welfare cases. Wilensky notes that half of the poor—those with incomes of less than $3000 per year—are over 65 years of age, are nonwhite, or are women heads of households, and that a majority of the poor, especially the chronically poor, are white, rural, Southern populations.

The Lower-Class Culture. American society is basically a MC society. Even the UC conforms to MC norms and values in much of its behavior. The people living in urban and rural slums, the lowest social class, however, do not have any strong identification with MC values, and it is for this reason that they are often described as socially deprived and as alienated from society. The abiding characteristic of LC society is its instability. Whereas the MC and UC are future oriented and invest much time and energy in planning and ordering what they expect to do for years to come, the lowest levels of the LC live on a day-to-day basis. If the future is considered at all, it is regarded with apathy, fatalism, and the belief that luck and luck alone determines the course of human events. In the face of such a prevailing attitude, the typical LC member sees little point to make an effort to prepare himself for a better job or to take any other steps to improve his chances for future success.

The unstable, chaotic quality of the slum culture has been described graphically by Samuel Tenenbaum (1963), who watched what happened when a hotel across the street from his apartment house in New York was taken over by the city government as a hostel for families on relief. The streets and sidewalks around the hotel began to swarm with children engaged in all kinds of energetic and violent play. There were fights, shouting, screaming, and friendliness, all mingled together. Automobiles parked near the hotel were occasionally torn apart and dismantled, with everyone pitching in with evident enjoyment. Adults leaned out of the window and scolded or shouted approval at the goings-on, or merely drank beer and carried on shouted conversations with their neighbors. These happenings went on far into the night, long after the MC people in Tenenbaum's apartment house had gone to bed. The whole scene was one of turbulence, violence, and instability.

Social life in the MC and WC cultures centers largely around the home, but in the LC culture it is more likely to take place elsewhere: in the street, at street corners, in bars, or at work. The relatively insignificant role played by the home is both a cause and an effect of the diffuseness of life in the LC culture. The MC and WC families work to make their homes comfortable, attractive, and "livable," and UC families do much entertaining in their homes. But LC families regard them primarily as places to eat and sleep. They are little inclined to fix them up or to take any responsibility for their maintenance. The fact that a LC person is more likely to be a renter, rather than an owner, explains some of his lack of interest in maintaining or decorating his home,

but even MC people who rent often take a high degree of responsibility in this respect—painting, installing carpeting, and making small repairs, without compensation from the owners.

Social-Class Differences in Child-Rearing Patterns

The most significant differences between cultures are found in the values to which members subscribe, because values determine attitudes, which in turn determine behavior. Values are not easy to study, however. For one thing, people take values for granted. As a general rule they do not make a practice of discussing them, and it is only when we note the choices people make or the kinds of behavior patterns in which they engage that we become aware that certain values are operating. The easiest and most effective way to approach the study of a culture's values is to study child-rearing patterns. Because people are more likely to be able to discuss how children should be brought up—it is a topic of almost universal interest, particularly in literate societies—data are readily available. Furthermore, comparisons of child-rearing practices reveal differences in implicit value patterns. If there are any real differences in UC, MC, WC, and LC subcultures, therefore, a comparative study of child-rearing practices should find them.

The Middle Class, as Contrasted with the Working Class and the Lower Class. What the studies show is that MC parents are generally more lenient and permissive, whereas WC and LC parents are more restrictive and punitive. Urie Bronfenbrenner (1958) surveyed a number of studies ranging over a twenty-five year period and found that WC and LC parents consistently favor the use of physical punishment, whereas MC parents make more use of reasoning, appeals to guilt, and other techniques involving the threat of withdrawal of love. He also found that parent-child relationships in the MC are more likely to be based on equalitarian or democratic principles, whereas those in the WC and LC are oriented more toward maintaining order and exacting obedience.

Bronfenbrenner also noted a number of trends. There seems to have been a reversal of attitudes between WC and MC mothers during the period after World War II, as contrasted with the prewar period. During the 1930's, MC mothers were less likely to breast-feed their children and to give them their bottle on some kind of a predetermined schedule, whereas WC mothers were more likely to breast-feed and to use a self-demand schedule. Since the 1930's, however, most MC mothers have turned to self-demand feeding schedules and have used breast feeding more than have WC mothers. This increased trend toward permissiveness is also reflected in toilet-training practices.

Although Bronfenbrenner speculates that the appearance of Benjamin Spock's (1957) book on infant and child care next to the Bible on the bookshelves of WC homes may have the effect of ameliorating disciplinary practices of the WC, he presents no evidence to show that such a trend is actually taking place. Instead, he cites evidence to show that WC parents, as contrasted with MC parents, are themselves consistently more aggressive, expressive, and impulsive, and are at the same time more demanding of compliance and control on the part of their children. On the other hand, WC parents emphasize what are usually regarded as traditional MC virtues of cleanliness, conformity, and control. Bronfenbrenner notes that although the methods of WC parents are less effective than those of MC parents, they are perhaps more desperate. He continues:

"Perhaps this very desperation, enhanced by early exposure to impulse and aggression, leads the working-class parent to pursue new goals with old techniques of discipline. While accepting middle-class levels of aspiration he has not yet internalized sufficiently the modes of response which make those standards readily achievable for himself or his children. He has still to learn to wait, to explain, to give and withhold his affection as the reward and price of performance."

There are several implications in Bronfenbrenner's findings. One is that the more drastic methods favored by WC and LC societies indicate that they are more shame oriented, whereas MC society tends to be more guilt oriented. Another is that WC and LC parents tend to be more authoritarian, preferring to use force and drastic means of control as a way of keeping children in a subordinate and dependent relationship to them. The MC children are expected to learn how to think for themselves and to use guilt feelings as bases for self-control, whereas the more drastic methods of control used with WC and LC children suggests that their parents believe they can only be shocked into acceptable behavior. When MC mothers were asked what they would do if they were told that their child talked in class and caused a disturbance, they were likely to say that they would try to find out why the child felt the need to behave in this way before they decided what to do about the problem. The WC mothers said that they would just give the child a good spanking (Hess, 1964).

Melvin L. Kohn (1963) says that differences between MC and WC-LC patterns of child rearing stem from the fact that MC values center on self-direction, whereas WC and LC values focus on conformity to external prescriptions. Each set of parents, therefore, are attempting to train their children to live in the world they perceive. Kohn points out that MC occupations are ones that require individuals to make many of their own decisions, without clearly laid out guidelines, whereas working-class occupations require that one follow explicit rules set down by persons in authority. Self-control is an important value to MC people; persons who lack self-control are unable to think clearly and thus to arrive at good decisions. Conversely, it is disobedience that is likely to cause trouble for WC and LC individuals. Therefore, MC children are more likely to be punished for loss of self-control, whereas WC and LC children are more likely to be punished for disobedience (Kohn, 1959).

Kohn has also worked with Eleanor E. Carroll (1960) on a research study aimed at describing differences between fathers' and mothers' roles in MC and WC families with respect to two dimensions of interaction: support and constraint. When parents and children from both social classes were interviewed about these two variables, both MC parents and children were more inclined to say that boys turn to their fathers as readily as to their mothers for encouragement and support. This was true of two-fifths of the MC families surveyed. However, no WC family agreed that sons turn to their fathers. Differences were in the same direction for daughters, although not as marked. When it came to setting limits and controls to children's behavior, a MC mother was more likely to believe that her husband was encouraging and supportive to the children when he did not play the major part in discipline. This was in contrast to the WC home, where the mother felt that the father was more supportive if he *did* play a major role in setting limits. In MC homes, fathers and mothers share roles and responsibilities in dealing with children. This is true irrespective of whether the interaction involves love or discipline. The WC homes, however, are more traditional, and parental roles are more sharply differentiated. Love, encouragement, and support are more consistent with the mother's roles, whereas punishment, control, and discipline are considered to be more consistent with the father's role. It is significant, however, that although WC mothers felt that fathers could be firmer in setting limits than they are, there was a tendency for WC fathers to withdraw from problems of child rearing, leaving the entire matter to their wives.

The authors also asked whether children (who were ten or eleven years old) tried to use their parents as models for their behavior. Results showed that MC boys were more likely to "try to act like" their fathers, whereas almost no WC boys did so. This is further evidence that WC fathers tend to play neutral, uninvolved roles in their families.

Cross-Cultural Research. A few studies have shown that the differences between MC and LC practices may be universal and not merely characteristic of American families. E. Terry Prothro (1966) used interviewers to ask Greek mothers about their child-rearing practices and about other patterns of behavior in their families. His results, some of which are presented in Table 8-1,

Table **8-1.** Differences in child-rearing practices among Greek middle-class, working-class, and peasant mothers with children 4½ to 6½ years of age (Prothro, 1966)

Interview questions on child-rearing practices	Percentages responding positively to interview questions		
	Middle class (urban)	Working class (urban)	Peasant class (rural)
Insists on immediate obedience	51	81	99
Gives affection or reward if child performs task	28	16	2
Prefers discipline by explaining and reasoning	37	12	8
Believes physical punishment is useful	42	56	71
Spanked child more than once during past 2 weeks	42	61	72
Admits she makes empty threats	35	72	85
Hopes child will attend university	89	50	13
Father helped take care of infant	54	51	25
Father helps discipline child	36	27	21
Father makes most of family decisions	30	49	81
Father does not consult mother on money matters	30	53	84

show differences and trends consistent with the findings of studies done in the United States. The MC mothers are more affectionate and more permissive than WC mothers, who are in turn more affectionate than peasant mothers. The latter, who would correspond to LC in America, are much more traditional than the city mothers. They are more likely to play subordinate roles in their families, which are dominated by their husbands. There is more sharing of responsibility for child care and family decisions in the urban families, especially in those that are MC.

In a study of Javanese families, Kurt Danziger (1960a) found that there was a direct relationship between the amount of independence expected of children and the social class of the parents. Oriental women are much more inclined, than are European or North American women, to carry their young children around with them. Such a practice would of course be inconsistent with developing feelings of independence in children, and one would predict that MC mothers would stop the practice sooner than LC mothers. Danziger's findings are consistent with that prediction. The UMC Javanese mothers said, on the average, that children should not be carried about after 18 months of age; LMC mothers set the age at two and a half; and LC mothers said that children should be carried until about three and a half. The MC mothers were more inclined to favor psychological punishment, whereas LC mothers were more likely to favor physical punishment. There were similar differences with respect to the age at which children were expected to take care of their own things and put them away in an orderly fashion. UMC mothers expected this to occur when the children were about six: LMC mothers when they were about eight and a half; and LC mothers when the children were well over ten years of age.

Danziger (1960b) also found differences in the expected direction when it comes to scheduling. The MC people in North America and Europe are rather insistent on promptness and getting things done on time. The MC society works on schedule. One goes to work or school on time; meals are served at a certain hour; bedtime must come at the proper time if one is to get enough sleep before the time comes to get up and go to school and work again. Very likely some of this expected punctuality is nonfunctional—that is, punctuality is demanded and expected for its own sake, and not because of any practical value. Most scheduling, however, is not an instance of order for its own sake, but is rather a social device to enable people to accomplish their tasks and meet their personal needs without getting into each other's way and without being let down or disappointed. When buses do not show up on time, or employers are late with pay checks, awkward situations are created, and people have to remake their plans and find some way to cope with the unexpected problems.

Nonindustrialized societies, like those of much of Asia and Latin America, have the reputation of being unconcerned about scheduling. Danziger's research suggests that much of this observed difference may be due to the fact that MC norms and values are less in evidence in those countries, for he found that UMC mothers in Java, like those of the United States thirty years before, were insistent on schedules for their children. Only 5 per cent of these mothers said they had not prescribed an eating and sleeping schedule, as contrasted with 45 per cent of the LMC mothers, and 75 to 90 per cent of the LC mothers. When they were asked when they first started to institute feeding schedules, virtually the same percentages of the mothers said "at birth."

Social Class and Social Perception. If differences in child-rearing have any significance, they should show up in the way in which children view the world. Inasmuch as LC parents show less concern for the feelings of their children than MC parents do, we would expect that LC children would show less interest and concern for the feelings of others and would make fewer attempts to try to understand the behavior of others. This hypothesis was put to the test by Eugene S. Gollin (1958), who showed UMC and LC adolescents a film in which the main character, a boy, did two good things and two bad things. Gollin was interested in determining the extent to which his subjects use "inference", that is, would think of events occurring outside the context of the situations shown in the film that might serve to explain the boy's inconsistent behavior. He also wanted to see whether his subjects would try to develop concepts that would attempt to explain the diversity of behavior themes in the same person. He found, among other things, that subjects who were sixteen years old were more inclined to do both of these things than were thirteen-year-olds, who in turn were more inclined to do so than were ten-year-olds. In other words, the willingness and the ability to use insight and imagination in analyzing the behavior of others appear to increase with age and may be considered to be characteristic of a socially mature pattern of behavior. When Gollin divided his subjects according to the occupations of their parents into an UMC and a LC group, he found that UMC children were more socially mature at all the ages tested. Among thirteen-year-olds, for example, 73 per cent of the UMC boys made use of inference in explaining the behavior of the boy in the film, as contrasted with only 20 per cent of the LC boys. At sixteen years, 84 per cent of the UMC girls attempted to develop concepts in order to explain the inconsistencies of the boy's behavior, whereas only 52 per cent of the LC girls did so.

Occupational and Educational Aspects of Social Class

Social Class and Occupational Status. The research studies cited in the last few pages have used occupational status as an index for social class. Actually, occupational status is only one criterion of social status. We have already mentioned some of the other criteria: where one lives, for instance. Communities whose populations cover a range of social classes have rather well-defined residential areas that can be considered as UMC, WC, and UC or whatever. Some communities have become homogeneous, particularly in the suburban areas of large cities, where communities that are almost entirely WC or UMC may be found.

We have also mentioned affluence and income. We noted that UC persons draw their income from investments, rents, and capital gains, whereas UMC persons use fees, salaries, and business profits as sources of income. There is a status hierarchy in the way salaries are quoted, ranging from an annual (UMC) to a weekly (LMC) basis. Members of the WC and the LC are paid by the hour.

It is fairly obvious that income and occupation are interrelated. Fees are received by physicians, lawyers, dentists, and architects, who are also members of the UMC. Skilled, semiskilled, and unskilled workers are members of the WC or the LC and are paid by the hour. Salaries are received by white-collar employees, who are members of the middle classes. Occupational status can thus be considered to be a fairly accurate index of an individual's social status.

Another index related to both social and occupational status is the number of years of schooling completed. Persons with education beyond the bachelor's degree are likely to be members of the professions and hence UMC, as are a great many people who have completed four years of college. Persons with some college work short of the bachelor's degree are mostly in the middle ranges of the MC, whereas those who have completed high school are likely to be LMC. Some WC people have completed high school, but many have not, whereas many LC people have had no high school education at all. In general, younger persons in each of these categories have had more education than the older ones. For instance, it is quite common to find successful, middle-aged businessmen who are UMC and who have had a year or two of college or have only completed high school. In the LC, most young people have had a year or so of high school (usually unsuccessful), whereas older people generally have not completed grammar school or may, in some instances, be illiterate.

Since both occupational level and the number of years of education completed are highly and positively correlated with other indices of social status, they are often used together or singly in research studies as prima facie evidence of membership in the appropriate social classes (Hollingshead & Redlich, 1958; Coopersmith, Church, & Markowitz, 1960).

Education and Social Class. We noted at the beginning of this chapter that education provides the means whereby LC and WC youth can achieve positions at the MC level. Entry into occupations over a certain level is governed by the amount of education possessed by the applicant, and, inasmuch as occupational level is a major determinant of both income and social status, movement up the social ladder can be accomplished by completing educational requirements.

Although education may offer an escape from the slum environment, it is by no means an easy one, as many observers of educational and social processes have noted (Hollingshead, 1949; McCandless, 1961; Tenenbaum, 1963; Westby-Gibson, 1965; Riessman, 1962). Schools, as these observers point out, are MC institutions run by MC people along MC lines. They teach MC values and attitudes and reward MC behavior. The LC person, adult or child, is bound to have some difficulty in adapting his behavior to the demands of the schools. Values and attitudes cannot be put on or taken off as easily as a coat. The LC person who succeeds in school is able to do so only by making some major changes in the way he sees himself and the world around him. In effect, he can succeed only by becoming a different kind of person—a MC person.

In an earlier discussion of shame and guilt cultures we described the kinds of sanctions and punishments that are visited on members of a shame culture who dare to behave differently,

particularly those who make gestures that indicate they have intentions of entering another culture. Such individuals are subject to all kinds of harrassment. The LC boy who takes school seriously is subjected to such comments as: "What's the matter with you, think you're too good for us?", or "Fred's some kind of a teacher's pet!", or "Books are for sissy kissers!" (Usually in stronger terms than these). If his need for affiliation is at all strong, and if he places any great value in keeping the good will of his playmates and peers, his interests in educational success will crumble under the impact of such ridicule.

Still another problem is the behavior that is characteristic of MC teachers, who do not realize what it takes for a LC child to make a serious attempt to succeed at school work. All things considered, the task of escaping from the LC by way of public education is one that can be accomplished only by persons of strong character who have a firm grip on reality and an unusual degree of confidence and self-assurance. In light of these considerations, it is surprising how many actually do escape.

One study that shows how educational level, child-rearing practices, and generalized attitudes toward the social environment are interrelated was conducted by Sol L. Garfield and Malcolm M. Helper (1962), who contrasted the attitudes of three groups of mothers, using the Parent Attitude Research Instrument (PARI), a schedule of questions that explore various aspects of parents' relationships with their children. One group of mothers, whom we shall designate as "lower class," had their children delivered at the University of Nebraska Hospital. To be eligible for this service they had to report an income of less than fifteen dollars per week. A majority of these mothers had not completed high school. A second group of mothers, whom we shall designate as "upper-middle-class," had children attending a nursery school. A third of these mothers were college graduates, and more than half of them had some college education. The third group, included for purposes of comparison and control, consisted of mothers of mixed educational background. As might be expected, the most marked differences in attitude were between the UMC and the LC group of mothers. In general, the LC mothers expressed more irritability and were more inclined to foster the dependency of the child. They felt it was necessary to "break the child's will," to establish adequate control over its behavior. At the same time, they expressed greater fear of harming the child. They tended to look upon themselves as martyrs. Furthermore, they strove to shelter their child from influences outside the family, and they themselves led more secluded lives than did the UMC mothers.

Attitudes toward the Social Environment. This general tendency to be fearful and apprehensive about outside influences is a significant attitude as far as the development of children's attitudes is concerned. The MC parent's emphasis on independence training rests on the assumption that the environment can be controlled and mastered. The MC children are taught social skills only partly because of the pleasure they may derive from using them. The main purpose in this training lies in the practical use that may be made of such skills. The MC people are keenly aware that finding one's way and succeeding in a complex social world depends to a large degree on mastery of a full range of social skills—skills relating to communication, negotiation, argument, agreement, compromise, anticipation of the behavior and attitudes of others, as well as the more formal skills, such as good manners and courtesy. Coping with the social environment presents a series of problems to the MC person, but they are problems that can be understood and solved, if the formulas are used intelligently.

The LC person, on the other hand, tends to approach the social environment with much more of a defeatist attitude. Whereas the MC person thinks of society as in the main good and as a potential source of security and personal rewards, the LC person thinks of it as a source of harassment, failure, and rejection. Instead of trying to understand society's complications, he tries to isolate himself and to build defenses against getting involved with it more than is minimally required. It is quite understandable, therefore, why an LC parent would teach his child to hate and fear society, which, after all, is largely run by and for MC persons.

Attitudes toward School. These attitudes toward the social environment determine the attitudes toward the school. The MC child learns to see school first as an exciting opportunity to learn more about the world around him. Then, as the excitement and newness of learning wears off, generally about the middle grades in elementary school, he comes to see school experiences as absolutely necessary to further success and happiness in life. In subtle ways he is led to realize that people who fail (usually LC) do so because they have not completed the recommended minimum of education. He may secretly admire or may occasionally openly emulate children who challenge the educational establishment in dramatic ways, but he realizes that failure in school amounts to a life sentence to failure. A small proportion of MC children do not make the grade and become high school dropouts, but we are talking here about the vast majority who resist distraction and who go on to graduate from high school and enter college, loyal to the MC way of life.

The LC child is likely to see the school as a potentially hostile, threatening institution, to which he has been sentenced to spend endless hours, months, and years. His best defense, his mother is likely to tell him, is to behave himself. If he behaves himself "they" will let him alone. This is true only in part, because if "they," the teachers, are at all dedicated and competent, they will insist that he learn the three R's, gain some understanding of science, geography, and government, and practice MC social techniques of cooperation, leadership, ease in communication, and the like. Many, if not most, LC children thwart their teachers' goals and aspirations by remaining quiet and compliant, by meticulously conforming to the details of teachers' demands, without accepting the underlying rationale and philosophy. One cannot learn what one does not believe. A few, made conspicuous by the very vehemence of their hostility, rebel openly, are disruptive and destructive, and become the "problem cases" that occupy a major part of the attention of school social workers, psychologists, attendance officers, and other personnel assigned to deal with school failures. If these aggressive children encounter weak teachers, or schools in which top or middle leadership is ineffective, they serve as foci of dissension and disorder in creating anarchic conditions in the classroom, on the playground, and in the halls and cafeterias.

School personnel, being MC, and subscribing to the attitudes and values of a different subculture, are generally unaware of or insensitive to the more basic aspects of the problem. Since they have never been LC and have little idea of how a LC person views the world, they tend to treat each child as though he were a product of a MC home, conversant with MC attitudes and placing an MC value on education. Most school people think of themselves as being democratically motivated and, indeed, set great store on teaching the attitudes and techniques of democratic living. To many of them, this means treating each child alike to the point of ignoring the differences we have been discussing. Consequently, when they encounter behavior that is quite normal from the standpoint of the LC culture, they are shocked, apalled, hostile, outraged, anxious, or frightened —whatever their characteristic reaction to social stress happens to be. Some react by tightening controls and becoming more demanding and punitive; others abandon normal controls and contribute to an anarchy that makes any kind of positive behavior impossible.

In any event, most MC teachers tend to behave in ways that confirm the rather pessimistic expectations of the typical LC student. He enters school expecting that it will be an unhappy experience—that is, he expects to fail, to have trouble with the teachers, to find out that other students do not like him, to be ignored, or to be punished. In general, school personnel fall into the trap of reinforcing behavior consistent with these expectations, to the end that the LC child's approach to school is in the nature of a "self-fulfilling prophecy." His expectations to be disappointed and to fail lead him to display the kind of behavior that causes teachers to be disappointed in him or treat him as a potential failure.

School personnel also have their self-fulfilling prophecies that are consistent with and complement the expectations of LC children. Partly because of their MC values and partly as a result of real experiences with apathetic or negative LC children, they come to anticipate failure or problem behavior or both from LC children, and, as a consequence, do not approach them with the same kind of optimism that they do MC children. What aggravates the problem still further is the tendency of many school departments to put their least experienced teachers in slum schools (Green, 1966). Positions in MC schools are considered in the nature of rewards for services loyally and obediently rendered. Hence the MC children who are already motivated to work hard at the tasks of education get the more experienced teachers, and the LC children who need special care and attention get the inexperienced ones. The various Federally sponsored and financed antipoverty campaigns have corrected this imbalance to some degree by making it possible to offer premium pay for teachers willing to work with slum children in special projects, but the seniority rule persists nevertheless in many, if not most, large cities.

Although we have gone to some lengths to show how difficult it is for LC children to use the schools to escape from LC status, we should nevertheless be aware that a considerable degree of upward mobility does take place. Some LC children discover through the schools that a different and more promising way of life exists and that it can be attained through education. Other LC children are reached through the personal interest shown them by some of their teachers. One of the characteristics of a slum home is that the ratio of children to adults is very high. This means that the average child receives considerably less attention than he would in a MC family with fewer children and a lower child-adult ratio. Many LC parents are genuinely fond of children, but the LC adult is likely to be preoccupied with coping with life's problems, and a harassed, tired, and often distraught parent has little time for positive interaction with children. The LC children quickly learn to keep out of the way and to make as little fuss as possible. In a school, things may be different, if the teacher has enough time and is sufficiently motivated to work with a child on his learning problems. Many a LC child has learned to be enthusiastic about learning through imitating the behavior and attitudes of a much-admired teacher.

A still further contribution lies in the atmosphere of the school. Although it is admittedly MC and foreign to the experience of many LC children, it may at the same time provide the only secure and dependable experience in their lives. This is particularly true of slum children who come from highly unstable homes where they are not sure whether their father is going to be living with them tomorrow, or what kind of a man their mother will bring home with her at night, or whether adults will draw knives and break bottles fighting in a drunken rage, or where there is little violence, but just a dirty, messy chaos.

What we have said about the lives and experiences of LC, slum children applies to a lesser degree to children from WC homes. The problem here seems to be largely that of a low level of intellectual stimulation. The progress that children make in school seems to be highly correlated to the number of books in the home, and it is in this respect that WC and MC homes are likely to differ. The WC homes are likely to have fewer children than LC homes, as well as fewer absent fathers, more stability and security, and a stronger support for education, at least in terms of its more practical goals. Furthermore, as we pointed out earlier, WC adults strongly and firmly support the middle-class core ideology, which is generally favorable to education, as long as it does not become too intellectual. As a result of all these factors, WC children are more responsive to school influences than LC children are. Although proportionately fewer of them are successful in school and go on to college, as compared with the proportions of MC youth, a sizable percentage do come to accept the school's goals as their own. In fact, most elementary and secondary school teachers have their origins in the working class and the lower middle class.

Upward Mobility

Self-Help and the Lower Class. In recent years a great deal of interest has developed in the possibility of finding ways to help the poor improve their lot. The traditional approach to the LC and their problems has been based on the assumption "the poor are always with us." Since poverty was considered to be the inevitable lot of most of mankind, there was nothing anyone could do about it except give an occasional financial contribution to make their conditions easier to bear. The growing political and economic democracy of the nineteenth and twentieth centuries has, however, changed much of that thinking. Making education readily available on a free or low-cost basis has enabled millions of the poor to become economically secure or even affluent MC citizens, thus showing that poverty was caused by, or at least related to, the lack of opportunity for self-improvement.

Large numbers of the poor, however, do not improve themselves even though the opportunity is within their grasp. Just how available opportunity is to the average slum youth is a matter of conjecture and controversy. It is easy to show that school prejudice against the slum child, be he white, Negro, Puerto Rican, or Indian is a reality, and it is tempting to explain lack of self-improvement solely on those grounds. The fact remains, however, that millions of people from the ranks of the poor do indeed find ways to improve their lot. To the behavioral scientist, this means that there must be some difference between those who improve and those who do not. To the social reformer, the politician, the civic leader, and the interested citizen, the problem is more likely to be seen in terms of how the residual poor may be led to undertake self-improvement. The number of failures encountered by the latter group suggests that a prerequisite to helping the poor help themselves may lie in the direction of a better understanding of their motivation.

Lower Class and n Ach. One possible explanation may be drawn from the research dealing with the need to achieve (n Ach) we described in Chapter 5. It would seem reasonable that LC people who take advantage of schools and improve themselves have a higher degree of n Ach than those who do not. It would also seem reasonable to assume that LC people who do not develop n Ach do not do so, because achieving types of behavior run counter to the norms of their subculture. There has been little research regarding differences in n Ach between LC individuals who take advantage of opportunities to move up socially and those who do not. One study by Bernard C. Rosen (1959) suggests that levels of n Ach differ from one LC ethnic group to another, although he did find that LC subjects generally have a lower level of n Ach than middle class groups. His results, which are reported in Table 8-2, show that LC members of cultural groups that are "upward mobile," such as Jews and Greeks, score higher than those who are relatively static, such as French-Canadians and Negroes. One interesting finding that emerges from his research is the sharp difference in n Ach between LMC and LC groups. It would seem that the LC individual who has decided to advance must be

Table **8-2.** Mean n Ach scores reported for various ethnic groups subdivided according to social class (Rosen, 1959, as reported by McClelland, 1961)

Ethnic group	Social class			Means for ethnic group	N
	UMC	LMC	LC		
French-Canadian	5.00[a]	5.92	3.26	3.85	61
Italian	4.43	7.94	3.75	4.78	74
White Protestant	6.85	6.00	4.03	5.19	120
Negro	6.36	4.00	2.67	3.40	65
Jew	5.06	5.41	6.00	5.53	57
Greek	4.17	7.13	4.67	5.81	47
Means for social classes	5.69	6.34	3.78	4.76	
N's	77	106	241		424

[a] One case only.

rather markedly different than the one who accepts his low status.

Emotional Problems and Upward Mobility. It is quite likely that LC individuals who strive to rise differ in other ways as well. Comparative studies of high and low school achievers in the United States and other industrialized countries routinely show that high achievers generally have fewer emotional problems, are less anxious, and have a better adjustment than low achievers. Few studies, however have included controls for social class. One study that suggests that achievement may come at some psychological cost was conducted among the LC and WC students of a school in Brazil, where findings ran contrary to expectations, for high achievers reported more psychological problems and displayed more anxiety than low achievers (Lindgren & Mello, 1965). Similarly, Sheldon and Eleanor Glueck (1950) found that boys from an LC neighborhood who did not get into trouble with the police or with school authorities had more emotional problems, were less well adjusted (as indicated by personality test scores), and presumably experienced a higher level of anxiety than those who did get in trouble. If staying out of trouble and succeeding in school is as consistent with MC patterns of behavior, it would appear that LC individuals who strive to move up the social status ladder pay some price in the form of increased anxiety.

The heightened level of anxiety may very well be due to the ambiguity of the situation faced by the upward-bound LC child. The LC child who stays at his own social level faces a much less ambiguity. He knows what he is and where he is going. He may not like what he knows, but he does know and thus does not have to face the task of learning the values of a different culture and of continually redefining himself in those terms. As contrasted with MC children, such a child has less assurance that he will succeed and is continually plagued with doubts as to whether he will attain the sought-after self-image. The encouragement he receives from his teachers when he shows progress must be balanced against the lack of support and down-right hostility he receives from his peer group. It is hardly surprising that the upward-mobile LC child is likely to experience more than his share of anxiety.

Such a child, however, will also experience anxiety if he does not make progress. The LC people are continually being admonished by society to try to improve themselves—to be good workers, good soldiers, good students, to keep sober and stay out of trouble. Such reminders would be a source of anxiety for most MC people, just as they are for the upward-mobile LC child. A great many LC people have, however, developed a number of effective defenses against such anxiety. If one's condition is perceived as being beyond one's control, then one does not need to feel guilty about one's lowly status. Such attitudes also help to "structure" the environment, so that problems are seen as consisting of sharply differentiated, simple issues, rather than as ambiguous and complex. The LC individual thus learns to view the environment in terms of good and evil, the "good guys" and the "bad guys," free of all encumbering nuances and ambiguities.

Authoritarian Attitudes and Class Structure. A number of studies show that persons rating low in social class are more likely to display attitudes than those of higher status. MacKinnon and Centers (1956), for example, interviewed respondents in downtown Los Angeles, using an abbreviated form of the F scale, and classified them according to education, occupational status, ethnic background, and social class. They found that people who identified themselves as UC and MC were much less authoritarian than those who identified themselves as WC or LC. People who identified themselves as "poor" were twice as likely to score high on the F scale than were people who said they were "wealthy" or "average plus." People who completed "some grade school" were four times as likely to score high on the F scale than were people who said they had completed college. Similar differences appeared between unskilled workers and professional men.

Seymour Martin Lipset (1959) surveyed a large number of studies relating to political attitudes and behavior in the WC and the LC and found that the evidence rather conclusively showed that, despite popular opinion, WC and LC groups tended to prefer authoritarian rather than democratic modes of behavior. Lipset attributed this preference to the tendency of low levels of social status and education to predispose individuals to prefer extremist, intolerant, and drastic forms of behavior, behavior that is more characteristic of authoritarian than democratic or equalitarian modes. He said that the historical success that Communists and Socialists have had with the WC group can be explained in terms of their espousal of direct action, rather than their endorsement of democratic and egalitarian values. He also pointed out that there is a close connection between low social status and conservative, fundamentalist religion. This class division among church membership has created a dilemma for clergy of the more liberal churches, who tend to be liberal in their politics as well as in their religion, and who have often wanted to disseminate their social gospel among members of the lower social classes. The latter, however, tend to resist the message, because they generally prefer absolutist and authoritarian ministers who preach of hell-fire and salvation and the need to make a choice between God and Satan.

Lipset attributed this orientation on the part of LC and WC members in part to the fact that they were as children exposed to environments characterized by aggressiveness, punishment, and general lack of love, environments that foster race prejudice and authoritarianism.

Mexican-American Laborers: a Static, Lower-Class Subculture. A brief summary of the results of a survey conducted by Horacio Ulibarri (1966) of the University of New Mexico, who interviewed a sample of sixty-five Spanish-speaking migrant and ex-migrant agricultural workers in the Southwestern States is relevant here. Ulibarri's study draws together a number of the concepts presented in this chapter and shows how they are interrelated. No single subcultural group in America can be considered to be wholly representative of any social class, and Ulibarri's group of respondents is no exception. Much of what they say, however, does illustrate both the values that characterize LC groups, as well as the problems they face as a consequence of these values.

This similarity to other LC groups appears most strongly with respect to the Mexican-American attitudes toward education. Although their lack of education was perhaps their greatest single handicap with regard to getting and holding worthwhile jobs, they seemed unaware that it actually was a major factor. When asked if they would attend tuition-free adult education classes if any were to be established, they said, "Yes, but we are too old to learn any more," or "I am too stupid to learn."

When it came to education for their children,

their attitudes seemed to be more positive. They said that they wanted their children to become lawyers, doctors, or "at least teachers," because, as they put it, they did not want their children to have to work as hard as they did. When pressed, the majority of the parents admitted, however, that they doubted whether their children would finish high school. These doubts were reflected by the children as well, and neither parents nor children seemed much upset by this. The parents in the group had completed an average of about five years of education, and the children tended to drop out about three or four years beyond the level completed by their parents. There seemed to be a complete lack of concern for the bleak economic future the children would face because of educational deficiencies. Instead, there was a preoccupation with immediate economic problems.

The workers expressed considerable anxiety about obtaining work. Most of them felt that they were not making enough money to sustain their families, and believed that the government should develop projects that would provide them with job opportunities. During the growing season, a worker might make as much as seventy dollars a week, but during the off season, he would be lucky to make twenty-five dollars. In spite of the fact that hard times were an annual recurrence, money earned during peak seasons was not put aside. None of the workers had any savings or any money in the bank. When they had money, they spent it impulsively on such items as television sets and encyclopedias.

Most of the Mexican-Americans had as little as possible to do with the government and were unaware of any of the types of governmental aid available. There was no interest in taking advantage of government opportunities for retraining in new skills. Each person seemed resigned to his fate of having to do the hardest kind of menial work and considered himself fortunate if any job at all were offered. Although they were willing to have their earnings supplemented by the distribution of free commodities or food stamp programs, none of them expressed a desire to become a public welfare client.

On the positive side, family relations were generally good. Families stayed together, drawn by need to share what little they had. They were, in general, closely knit units, in which all members appeared to enjoy considerable status and esteem and showed mutual concern for each other. Families appeared to be concerned entirely about the present and seemed to be content that they were together at the moment. Indeed, the self-satisfaction that families expressed may have had something to do with their unwillingness to take any action, individually or as a family, to improve their situation or solve the problems that faced them. Although the members of the family were concerned about the fact that their resources of food, clothing, and shelter were much less than satisfactory, their reaction tended to be along the lines of "I wish I could do more, but what can I do?"

The Problem of the Lower-Class Immigrant. There is also a mutually reinforcing interaction between the way in which MC people regard LC people and the way in which the latter come to regard themselves. This phenomenon is probably characteristic of MC and LC everywhere and has appeared in a number of research studies of social class attitudes. One such study was concerned with North African immigrants to Israel. These immigrants are educationally, professionally, and economically disadvantaged in comparison with the majority of the population who had come from Europe. Judith T. Shuval (1966) found that immigrants to Israel from Europe and the Middle East had negative attitudes toward North African immigrants. They were inclined, for example, to view the latter as being "aggressive," dirty, and uncultured, and as having undesirable personal traits. For their part, the North Africans agreed. Sixty per cent of both European and North African immigrants said that they would prefer to have other European immigrants as

neighbors, but only 19 per cent of North Africans said that they wanted other North Africans in the neighborhood. Shuval concluded that her data confirmed George Herbert Mead's (1947) theory that group members are likely to internalize whatever the prevalent stereotype says about them, even though that stereotype may be a negative one.

The failure of LC members to improve their lot, therefore, is partly the result of their accepting the prevailing belief that they are inferior and inadequate. This belief thus effectively blocks attempts at self-betterment; after all, there is no point in trying, if one is going to fail. This belief may also have the effect, as we have noted, of a "self-fulfilling prophecy." On those occasions when a LC person makes a gesture of self-improvement, he does so expecting to fail, and this feeling is shared by his friends and relatives. It is only when a LC person is able to turn his back on culture, family, and friends that he is able to free himself from the handicap of this negative stereotype.

SUMMARY

Social systems consist of organized and unorganized social units, which may be divided into positions having rights and obligations. An individual's status is ordinarily influenced by the position he holds but is in any event influenced by the way in which others in the social unit perceive and value him. Status is a reflection of an individual's power and prestige, and is also affected by the exclusiveness of the position he holds. Individuals who occupy certain positions are expected to play the roles appropriate to that position, and hence must be properly qualified. People occupying positions in a social system at approximately the same status level often find that they have more in common with one another than they do with people in positions above or below them. This mutual attraction within certain broad status levels results in the groupings known as social classes. The boundaries of social classes in America are relatively permeable, but the boundaries of other groups, or castes, are less so.

Although systems of labeling social classes vary, it is common practice to recognize upper, middle, working, and lower classes, here designated as UC, MC, WC, and LC. Social class differences tend to be correlated with a wide range of variables, including the prevalence of various kinds of problem behavior, n Ach, n Aff, life style, personality traits, authoritarianism, and child-rearing patterns. The various social classes may also be said to represent subcultures within the larger national culture.

The MC, also termed the white-collar class, is the largest social class in America and has the most influence in terms of norms, values, attitudes, and behavior patterns. MC individuals have a high regard for education, thrift, self-improvement, cleanliness, family life, home ownership, responsibility, and respectability. There is also a strong emphasis on future orientation, control of impulses, and the channeling of hostility into socially acceptable forms of behavior.

The UC constitutes only a small fraction of the population and consists of members of families which have inherited prestige and affluence, usually over a span of several generations. UC individuals tend to be less competitive than MC, because their family connections give them security of position. Women tend to be more influential at this level than at other class levels. The MC women have more status than WC women, who in turn have more status than LC women.

The WC individuals are likely to be better educated and more highly trained than LC members. They may live in MC neighborhoods and may actually earn more money than many MC individuals, although their employment tends to be less stable. Leisure-time activities of WC and MC people are likely to differ. There is a tendency for MC activities to be more intellectual and more active, and for WC activities to be more passive and to involve socializing with relatives and friends. In contrast to the LC, however, the WC appears to be closer to the MC pattern.

Individuals in the LC receive less of every good thing that modern society has to offer: economic security, health services, personal safety, living space, opportunity for education, and interesting work. Their usual reaction to their many problems tends to be that of apathy, retreat, and resignation, although violence and turbulence are more common in this class than in any other.

Studies of child-rearing patterns show that MC parents prefer to use reasoning and appeals to conscience in controlling their children, whereas WC and LC parents tend to be more punitive. Before World War II, MC parents tended to schedule infants when it came to feeding and toilet training, but have become more relaxed and permissive in recent years. It is the WC parents who now seem to be emphasizing the traditional MC virtues of cleanliness, conformity, and control. One factor in child-rearing patterns is that MC children are brought up to fill positions that require them to exercise a considerable degree of independence in decision making, whereas WC and LC children will eventually obtain positions in which they are expected to carry out orders. Hence it makes some sense that self-control and self-direction are emphasized in the rearing of MC children and obedience and conformity in the rearing of WC and LC children. Analyses of roles of parents show that WC fathers tend to be less involved in child rearing than do MC fathers.

Studies of child-rearing practices in other countries have produced findings similar to those in the United States, in that MC families tend to be more affectionate and permissive, less punitive, and to involve fathers in child care more than LC families.

Social-class differences are determined by a number of variables, the most significant of which appears to be occupational level, which in turn is influenced by the amount of education completed. Education is the major avenue for social mobility, but LC students can succeed in school only if they abandon or change a number of attitudes and forms of behavior characteristic of their culture. For its part, the school is an MC institution and has difficulty in adapting its procedures to the needs of LC children. The life style of the LC family does not stimulate the development of n Ach to any great extent, and the LC child who does attempt to achieve may pay a price in terms of rejection by his family and by members of his peer group. Consistent with this general pattern is a tendency for authoritarian attitudes and behavior to prevail. In some LC cultures, such as that of the Mexican-American, there are compensating rewards in the form of emotional support from a closely knit family structure. This tends to give the individual a high degree of psychological security, but makes it difficult for him to develop the achieving patterns of behavior demanded by the host culture. The mutually reinforcing patterns of rejection and self-abasement that are experienced by LC people occur whenever they come in contact with a progress-oriented society dominated by MC values, as experience with immigrants from North Africa has shown in Israel.

SUGGESTED READINGS

Empey, L-M. T. & Erickson, M. L., Hidden delinquency and social status. *Social forces*, 1966, **44**, 546-554.

Katz, F. M., The meaning of success: some differences in value systems of social classes. *Journal of social psychology*, 1964, **62**, 141-148.

Kohn, M. L., Social class and parent-child relationships: an interpretation. *American journal of sociology*, 1963, **68**, 471-480.

Lindgren, H. C. (Ed.), *Contemporary research in social psychology*. New York: Wiley, 1969. See papers on social status in Section 6.

Lipset, S. M., Democracy and working-class authoritarianism. *American sociological review*, 1959, **24**, 482-501.

Riessman, F., Cohen, J., and Pearl, A. (Eds.), *Mental health of the poor*. New York: Free Press, 1964.

Wilensky, H. L., Class, class consciousness, and American workers. In W. Haber (ed.), *Labor in a changing America*. New York: Basic Books, 1966.

CHAPTER NINE

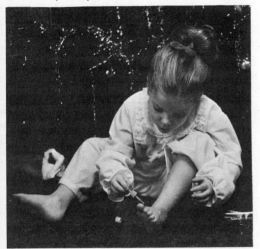

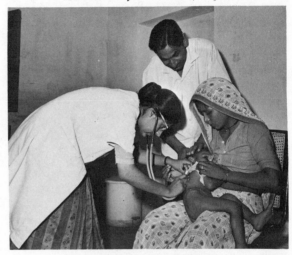

Social Roles

Characteristics of Roles. In Chapter 8 we described social systems in terms of interlocking positions, each conferring status on the occupant and defined by appropriate roles. We then discussed differences in behavior among people who occupy positions at various status levels.

In this chapter we shall take up roles: the patterns of action that indicate the position being occupied and the appropriate status. Each position carries with it certain rights and obligations, which set the norms specifing the kinds of behavior that are appropriate. Ralph Linton (1936) defines roles in terms of actions performed by an individual to validate his occupancy of a position. Daniel R. Miller (1963) also points out that roles have a certain normative effect on social behavior. He states: "The mutual responses of two people can often be explained more readily by their shared conceptions of the behavior appropriate to their two *roles* than by their psychological characteristics or the unique qualities of the social interaction." In other words, although there are wide variations among the needs, motives, and personality patterns of customers and sales clerks, we can nevertheless predict with a high degree of reliability that a customer in a supermarket will bring his purchases to the checkout stand and that the clerk will ring up the price of each item on a register, place it in a bag, tell the customer the total shown on the register tape, and accept payment, whereupon the customer will pay the amount requested. The specifics of these two reciprocating roles are set by culture and prevailing custom, and are shared by both sales clerk and customer.

As Miller also notes, social roles function to set limits to the behavior of members of a society, but these limits make sense when one realizes that roles are essential to the existence of a social structure. Roles cannot be regarded by position holders as rules of a game that they can change at will. A social structure must of necessity limit the behavior of persons who occupy positions within it, if it is to carry out its functions and serve its members adequately. This does not mean that the roles and functions of any given unit of society are totally beneficial, but rather that the total set of structures within a given society is likely to aid the functioning of the society, rather than to interfere with it, otherwise the society would not survive.

Miller continues as follows:

"The fact that structures are interlocked within the society makes constraints even greater. Thus the modern family is responsible for the care, feeding, and socialization of immature children; no other structures in the society can completely take over these functions for intact families. Consequently, a woman who has young children and wants to work full time may face the antagonism of her husband and such simple obstacles as the unavailability of baby sitters, the lack of nurseries for children under three, and the part-time schedule of most nurseries. Thus it is only by personal attention that a woman can fulfill her obligations to her children."

The way in which roles determine behavior is governed by the position the individual occupies, as we have noted previously. However, positions may shift from minute to minute in terms of the situation that prevails. Mr. Bassett occupies the overlapping positions of husband to Mrs. Bassett and father to his children. The two positions also merge into one that might be termed "head of the household." When guests arrive, however, these positions are subordinated to his position as host. When one of the children is heard crying in another room, Mrs. Bassett, who is serving the coffee at that moment, will ask Mr. Bassett to investigate, thus changing the situation momentarily into one in which the positions of husband and father are more relevant. Mr. Bassett excuses himself, goes off to quiet the child, and then returns to resume his position as host. On the other hand, if Mr. Bassett is in the middle of an involved anecdote he may refuse to have the situation restructured, preferring to continue in the position of host. His wife's request creates a conflict in roles for him, a topic we will take up later in the chapter.

Prescription of Roles. Roles that are attached to certain positions tend to be more or less standardized. The roles that are attached to the position of host and guest are highly prescriptive in the Middle East. In middle-class North America they are less so, but there are, nevertheless, certain standard forms of behavior expected of hosts even in this more permissive society. For example, it is customary to greet guests at the door in somewhat neater and more formal attire than one would wear if guests were not expected. The guests' coats and hats will be taken from them and they will be invited into the living room. They will be offered something to drink, and, if they happen to have come near mealtime, they will probably be asked to share the meal. If the guests are unexpected, and there is insufficient food, the host may suggest that they go out to eat. Interruptions and distractions are kept at a minimum. For example, if the host should be called to the telephone during the visit, he will try to make the conversation a short one, or will ask the caller to ring back later.

It is understood, of course, that there are many variations in the way these roles are played, and that some people may wittingly or unwittingly deviate from the prescribed patterns of behavior. A host may, for example, become engaged in a long telephone conversation while his wife attempts to keep a conversation going with the guests. Such behavior on the part of the host is usually considered an affront to guests, although it is good form for guests not to show that they have been affronted.

What we have described, however, is the kind of behavior prescribed for hosts that is displayed by them *most* of the time. Other kinds of behavior may be consistent with the roles prescribed for a certain position, but may be followed only by a limited number of people. Some women in UC circles may, for example, follow a ritual of serving afternoon tea, British style, whenever guests are present. The tendency is usually to engage in behavior that is consistent with the role prescriptions for the position, and to avoid those that are not. An example of inconsistent behavior would be that of telling guests that they have stayed long enough and that it is time to leave.

Certain roles become so attached to certain positions that they can be recognized whenever they are played, even out of context. A senior secretary who acts in a protective way toward the much younger secretaries and typists in her department and who sympathetically listens to their problems is said to be playing a "mother role." An elementary teacher says that she does not like "yard duty," because she does not enjoy playing the role of a policeman. An instructor who is a clinical psychologist objects to giving grades in mental hygiene courses, because he does not like the role of "playing judge," particularly where mental health is concerned.

Types of Positions. Robert Linton (1945) states that there are at least five different kinds of positions that will be found in any society, no matter how simple or primitive it may be:

1. Age-sex groupings: specifically, infant, boy, girl, young man, young woman, old man, and old woman.

2. Family, kinship, clan, or household groupings, as indicated by some generic term: John Bassett, one of the Steen family, or the Grahams' maid.

3. Prestige or status groupings, such as president, ordinary seaman, customer, chairman, and slave.

4. Occupational groupings, such as workman, dentist, or salesman.

5. Friendship and common interest groupings, such as friend, club member, chess player, and political party member.

A sixth category should be added to this list: *organizational groupings*, such as board member, receptionist, public-relations expert, and comptroller. Linton omitted this category; he was concerned with primitive societies and therefore did not include the organizations that have become essential to the functioning of industrialized and urbanized modern societies.

The term "groupings" is used in the foregoing context to show that persons who hold any of these positions may be thought of collectively, because certain standardized roles, functions, percepts, values, and attitudes apply to all of them to a greater or lesser degree. Each of the individuals who occupy the kind of position known as "accountant" tends to perform certain prescribed roles and functions, to subscribe to certain common values, to hold certain shared attitudes, and to perceive certain kinds of data in certain special ways. These communalities apply most particularly when they are actually acting as accountants, but they share other off-the-job characteristics. As a group, accountants are more conservative than, say, motorcycle delivery boys. They are likely to be middle class, good credit and insurance risks, and so forth.

Positions may be classified into two groups: ascribed and achieved. Ascribed positions are those over which an individual has no control; for example sex and age. Achieved positions must be attained through some effort; for example accountant and club member. In the North American culture, social class (a prestige or status grouping) may be both. One has no control over the social class into which he is born, but may change it through education or marriage.

Roles as Learned Expectations. We have noted that the roles prescribed for various positions consist of standardized forms of behavior. We can also view them in terms of expectations. A person who is an accountant is expected to do whatever accountants do: keep financial records in an orderly and responsible way, be meticulous about figures, be prompt, diligent, and the like. The person who occupies the position of accountant, in turn, takes on society's expectations as his own. In effect, society's expectations are "mirrored" in the expectations he develops for himself. The mirroring of expectations holds true for roles prescribed for other positions as well.

Roles are learned sequences of behavior. As children, we learn first to behave the way our culture and our family expects children to behave. This learning carries over into our experiences outside the home, where behavior is likely to be differentiated according to the family's social status.

We also learn to take on behavior patterns characteristic of our sex. In all this, our attempts at expressing ourselves through various kinds of behavior are reinforced or not by others, in accordance with the extent to which we have satisfied their expectations. Behavior that is not reinforced in some way tends to drop out or become extinguished, and we find ourselves repeating sequences that are more likely to gain some degree of acceptance and approval. Along with these sequences of behavior, we learn the beliefs, values, and attitudes that provide the motivational background for the behavior we are learning. As boys, we learn not to play with dolls, because "dolls are for girls," no matter how attractive they might seem to us. As girls, we learn to display the kind of behavior that evokes the response "Isn't she sweet?", with all its attendant fringe benefits. As boys, we learn that climbing trees and bicycling is "fun," and playing house is "no fun." As girls, we learn that dressing up in mother's castoff clothes is "fun," and getting dirty when playing ball is "no fun." The values, attitudes, percepts, and roles attached to our positions as boys or girls become a part of us. They identify and define us and tell us and others "who we are."

"I wonder what it is in childhood that causes one guy to grow up a burglar and another guy a con man."

Drawing by D. Fradon; © 1966 The New Yorker Magazine, Inc.

Reciprocal Roles. As we become familiar with our own roles, we also become familiar with those of others. Roles are likely to be reciprocal. One cannot play the role of the mother without a child or a substitute for a child. One cannot play the role of a teacher without reference to a learner. Consciously or not, one of the first things we learn to do when we meet a stranger is to locate his position in some social structure, preferably our own. Once we do this, we know what his prescribed roles are and how they relate to the roles prescribed for our position. Then we know how to interact with him. Observe the reaction to a strange child who appears in a neighborhood play group. Immediately the questions start to fly: "What's your name? What does your father do? Where do you live? Where do you go to school?" These are only the first of a series of questions that will help the children define the position and probable role behaviors of the stranger and that will, in turn, enable them to determine how they should behave toward him.

A similar phenomenon occurs when a stranger, say, a tourist, appears in a remote Middle East village. Because he is not of the village or the area or even the country, he does not fit into the social structure. There is no position for him, no prescribed role, no way in which the villagers can interact with him. But he cannot be ignored. There he is, making noises in some strange foreign tongue, and obviously looking for something. A position must be found for him. The most obvious position is that of guest. Once this is decided, and it is usually decided almost instantaneously, there is great relief. One may not know how to respond to a tourist, but one knows how to respond to a guest, and whatever ritual is involved in greeting and treating guests now goes into operation. The tourist may be confused and mystified, but the villagers know exactly what to do. Indeed, their sense of honor *compels* them to behave in a hostlike manner.

Sex Roles

Social psychologists have conducted more research on behavior patterns related to sex differences than they have on other kinds of role-appropriate behavior. Every society differentiates between the roles performed by the two sexes. A relatively minor part of the behavior prescribed for each sex (e.g., the breast-feeding of infants) is due to obvious physical differences. Is the balance of the observed differences in behavior due, then, to less obvious biological factors—differences in hormonal balance, for example? Or do the differences result from social learning? Let us first look at the differences for clues to the relative importance of biology and of social learning.

Risk-Taking. In most cultures, men are expected to be more adventurous than women. These tendencies appear in childhood and seem to be quite consistent. Paul Slovic (1966) set up a game at a county fair to test sex differences in risk-taking. The game consisted of a panel of ten electric switches, nine of which were connected to an apparatus that would dispense a small amount of candy, and one that would sound a buzzer. Players were permitted to keep whatever candy they won, as long as they did not pull the buzzer switch. Inasmuch as all the switches looked alike, and the position of the buzzer switch varied with each trial and was unknown to the players, there was a strong element of risk in the game. The more switches a player pulled successfully, the greater the probability that the next switch would activate the buzzer, whereupon he would lose everything he had won.

Figure 9-1 shows Slovic's results. Between the ages of six and ten, there is little difference between boys and girls with respect to risk-taking, but after that age, girls tend to become more cautious and boys less so. There is little change in boys' risk-taking behavior from the age of eleven on. Although Slovic's game was open to all comers, more than twice as many boys as girls volunteered to participate (732 as against 312), which suggests that boys are also more interested than girls in engaging in new experiences and trying novel devices.

Aggressiveness. Males are also inclined to be more aggressive. One study tested the hypothesis that male college students would show more aggressiveness than women on a questionnaire designed to measure tendencies to express aggres-

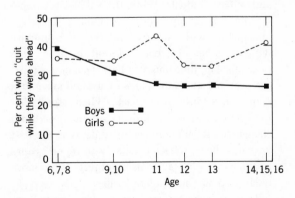

Figure 9-1. Percentages of children at various ages who stopped playing a game in order not to incur any further risk and lose all their winnings (Slovic, 1966).

sion. The male subjects not only indicated a greater willingness to commit aggressive acts, but also expressed less guilt about their aggressiveness. An interesting sidelight was the finding that women who were high academic achievers showed a low degree of aggression and a considerable degree of guilt about aggression, whereas the high achievers among men expressed a high degree of aggressiveness and a low degree of guilt. The results thus suggested that the highest achievers in each sex were those whose behavior and feelings corresponded with the pattern that is conventionally expected for their sex (Wyer, Weatherly, & Terrell, 1965). The tendency for sex-appropriate behavior to be associated with academic achievement evidently appears during the first years of school. Nicholas J. Anastasiow (1965) gave five- and six-year-old boys a choice of a variety of toys and found that those who selected toys appropriate to their sex role (soldier, fire engine, gun, blocks, or truck, in contrast to beads, doll, purse, dishes, or comb and brush) made higher scores in reading and were rated as more successful by their teachers.

Another study that demonstrates male preferences for aggressive behavior was conducted by Mary Moore (1966), who showed pairs of violent and nonviolent pictures to children, adolescents, and college students. While the subject was looking through an apparatus that enabled him to see one picture with one eye and the other picture with the other eye, two different pictures were presented simultaneously, a half second at a time, for example, the silhouettes of a mailman and a man with a knife in his back. When asked what they had seen, male subjects of all ages, from elementary school children to students in the first year of college, were more likely to report scenes of violence, whereas female subjects were more likely to report nonviolent scenes.

Interest in Social Interaction. The research we have cited tends to confirm everyday observation: males are more inclined to be adventurous, aggressive, and interested in violence, and females

are inclined to be more cautious, accepting, and passive. It would follow from this that females would have more interest and skill in behavior calculated to promote peace and mutual acceptance. It is important to note that such behavior can succeed only if one shows an interest in others. Indeed, it is difficult to determine which is cause and which is effect: are women more able to exercise skills consistent with peacemaking because they are more interested in people, or are they more interested in people because they want to develop peacemaking skills?

Women certainly seem to enjoy social interaction, perhaps for its own sake. Bernard Bass and George H. Dunteman (1963) studied the behavior of men and women assigned randomly to informal groups and found that men were more inclined to behave in task-oriented ways and women in interaction-oriented ways. In other words, men were more interested in using or helping the group solve problems, whereas women were more interested in talking and being with others.

The relationship between social interest and social behavior is shown by a number of studies. In one study subjects were interviewed singly by a graduate student who gazed steadily at them while asking either personal or innocuous questions. Subjects looked at the interviewer more often during the innocuous questions, and women subjects returned the gaze more often than men subjects, irrespective of the kind of questions that were directed at them, and irrespective of the interviewer's sex. During an informal discussion session that took place after each interview, women still made more "eye contact" than men did (Exline, Gray, & Schuette, 1965).

Eye contact is an important kind of social behavior because it signifies the willingness to initiate and establish personal relationships with another person. Unwillingness to meet another person's gaze may be due to any number of reasons, but it has the effect of maintaining a degree of social distance. Mutual eye contact is more common among social equals in our culture. Among unequals, the degree and kind of eye contact depends on the kind of relationship being established. Higher-status persons seek to establish eye contact with lower-status persons at times when the former are exerting their power by giving orders, making recommendations, or censuring. The willingness of the lower-status person to reciprocate eye contact is generally taken as symbolic of an agreement to obey, conform, or accept the censure. Lower-status persons may seek eye contact with higher-status persons if they are asking a favor or are trying to influence opinions. If the higher-status person does not reciprocate, this is taken as a sign that he does not wish to hear, understand, or be persuaded, whereas a willingness to reciprocate eye contact is generally taken to mean that the lower-status person's plea is being attended to and may be granted. Mutual eye contact, therefore, is perceived as acceptance and as having some positive social value in most social situations. Social situations charged with emotion, such as arguments, also are characterized by more eye contact. In such instances the intent seems to be that of facilitating communication by gaining the attention of the other. Eye contact also plays a significant role among infrahuman animals. In monkey groups, a low-status member cannot look directly at a high-status member without running the risk of attack (Delgado, 1963).

The greater willingness of women to look at others was found by Exline, Gray, and Schuette (1965) to be related to sex differences in attitudes toward people in general. On a questionnaire measure, female subjects were more likely than males to say that they wanted to be involved and to involve others in social interaction, and were more willing to give and receive affection.

It has been proposed that some of the differences in behavior between the sexes can be accounted for by the tendencies of women to be more people-oriented and men to be more thing-oriented. If this is so, one would expect that in a social situation, like a party, women would be more concerned with looking at others in the group and men would be more concerned with the details of the task at hand—namely eating or drinking. Specifically, women when drinking should gaze out into the room, and men should look at what they are drinking. The two photographs in Figure 9-2 suggest that the tendency does exist and that it begins in childhood. However, the sample is admittedly very limited ($N = 2$), and the reader is urged to observe for himself the next time he is in a situation where food and drink are consumed by both sexes.

The smiling response is another and perhaps more obvious way of indicating positive feelings toward others. If women are more interested in initiating and maintaining pleasant social rela-

Figure 9-2. Sex differences in drinking behavior (Lindgren).

tions with others, one would expect that they would do more smiling than men. In a study reported by Howard M. Rosenfeld (1966) in which assistants of the experimenter were instructed to seek approval from a naive subject, both men and women assistants used smiles to approximately the same extent—29 per cent of the time. When the assistants were asked to *avoid* the approval of subjects, however, the percentage of smiles dropped to 18 per cent for men, as contrasted with 25 per cent for women. The implication is that women were less able to bring themselves to stop smiling.

This interpretation is borne out in a comparison of the use of positive head nods. When the seeking-acceptance condition prevailed, men used positive nods 29 per cent of the time, whereas women used them 20 per cent. In the avoiding-acceptance condition, however, the percentage for positive nods dropped to 16 per cent for men, but *increased* to 24 per cent for women. The use of positive nods is particularly significant, because the naive subjects, when polled after the approval-avoidance experience (when they were still unaware of the purpose of the experiment), were more likely to express positive regard for the assistants who had used more positive nods. When the assistants were queried by the experimenters with respect to their reaction to the experiment, the women assistants were more likely to report that they had greater difficulty in behaving negatively or even neutrally toward the naive subject. As for the naive subjects, they expressed more positive regard for the women assistants than for the men assistants in the approval-avoidance situation. The results suggest that men reject others more willingly and more effectively, whereas women reject less willingly and less effectively, at least in situations where they have no self-initiated or spontaneous motive for expressing rejecting attitudes.

One would also expect that if women are more motivated toward social involvement than men, they would be more alert to various dimensions of social interaction in groups. Some research conducted by Ralph V. Exline (1957) on small groups of students bears this out: women subjects were more accurate than men in perceiving interpersonal relations in their groups. In another study concerned with social memory, women proved to be better than men at remembering names and faces of people, irrespective of whether they encountered them as photographs or in real-life situations (Witryol & Kaess, 1957).

To summarize the sex differences we have covered in this array of research findings, it appears that males tend to be more adventurous, aggressive, interested in violence, and task-oriented, whereas females tend to be more cautious, accepting, passive, interested in initiating and maintaining social contacts, unwilling to behave negatively or neutrally toward others, and inclined to evoke positive responses from others.

Instinct. None of these findings are very surprising, since they more or less confirm everyday observation. Not only are we aware that men are more aggressive, active, competitive, and that women are more passive, socially oriented, and accepting, but we also believe that they were "born that way." This is consistent with common sense and the conventional wisdom. In other words, common sense and the conventional wisdom would hold that behavioral differences between the sexes are due entirely to biologically inherited tendencies, or to put it more succinctly, to *instinct.*

Psychologists, and especially social psychologists, are inclined to be extremely suspicious of explanations based on instinct. We already touched on this in Chapter 2, when we pointed out that instinct theory does not explain enough. Evidence contrary to the instinct explanation of sex differences may also be drawn from everyday observation. For example, it is common to encounter men who are compliant and nurturant and not aggressive and women who are aggressive and domineering. Such behavior is of course counternorm, but there are enough cases to give us pause before accepting an instinct explanation for the usual sex differences in behavior.

The case for instinct could be made somewhat stronger if it could be shown that behavior identified with one sex or the other in our culture was similarly identified in other cultures as well. Values and norms are known to differ widely from culture to culture. If certain sex-oriented consistencies were found in spite of such variation, such a finding would provide some degree of support for instinct theories.

If men are biologically predetermined to be more dominant and aggressive than women, we would expect them to take more positions of leadership in various organizations both in the United States and elsewhere. At least one study shows that this does indeed occur. When samples of adults living in the United States, Great Britain, Germany, Italy, and Mexico were asked whether they had ever been officers of the organizations they belonged to, men were more likely than women to say "yes." As Table 9-1 shows, there were marked differences among the five countries, but in every instance but one, men were more likely to have held positions of leadership (Almond & Verba, 1963). The only exception is

Table **9-1.** Percentages of men and women in five nations who said they had been officers of organizations in which they held membership (Almond & Verba, 1963)

	Percentage of organization members who were officers					
	Total		Men		Women	
	%	N[a]	%	N[a]	%	N[a]
United States	46	(551)	41	(309)	52	(242)
Great Britain	29	(453)	32	(304)	22	(149)
Germany	16	(419)	18	(299)	9	(121)
Italy	23	(291)	24	(193)	19	(98)
Mexico	33	(242)	43	(146)	18	(96)

[a] Refers to the size of the sample on which the percentages were based.

the United States, but even here the overall number of men who were leaders was higher because more men were organization members. Thus the evidence does suggest that tendencies of men to lead transcend cultural boundaries and therefore may be to some extent biologically determined.

Culture. The thesis that sex differences in behavior are largely culturally determined appears in an anthropological study conducted by Margaret Mead (1935), who studied three primitive New Guinea tribes: the Arapesh, the Tchambuli, and the Mundugumor. She found that both men and women in the Arapesh culture behave in ways that are responsive to the needs and concerns of others and avoid aggressiveness and competition. The Arapesh of both sexes conform, in short, to behavior patterns that would be considered "feminine" in Western cultures. The behavior of men and women alike in the cannibalistic Mundugumor society is characterized by hostility, aggressiveness, violence, and lack of consideration for the rights and feelings of others—qualities we would consider "masculine." It was in the Tchambuli culture, however, that Mead found a real reversal. Tchambuli men are sensitive, carefully groomed, artistic, emotionally volatile, and given to bickering, whereas women are stable, practical, dominant, and aggressive in matters of sex. Mead's data strongly suggest that instinct is an insufficient basis for explaining sex differences in behavior, and that what we recognize as sex-appropriate behavior is the result of social learning, rather than of biological inheritance.

Further data in support of Mead's thesis are supplied by Ethel M. Albert (1963) an anthropologist who has studied social behavior in Central African tribes. Although Western societies assume that men, rather than women, are by nature of their skeletal and muscular build suited for heavy labor, most Africans believe the opposite. When Albert told some African women that men did the heavy work in her country, they expressed disapproval. Americans, they said, were making a mistake, because everyone knows that men drink too much and do not eat enough to keep up their strength. They are too tense and too inclined to wander about to develop the kinds of muscles and habits that are necessary for sustained agricultural labor. Men, they said, are not suited by nature for this kind of work.

Albert also noted other anthropological research data that indicate a lack of uniformity among different cultures with respect to what could be considered sex-appropriate behavior. Whereas Western societies expect men to be sexually aggressive and women to play passive or evasive roles, some African and American Indian societies, she reports, maintain that women are more driven by sex than men are. Among Zuñi Indians, it is the groom, not the bride, who looks forward to the wedding night with fear and apprehension. It is probably no coincidence that decisions in the Zuñi society are made by women.

Edward T. Hall (1959) notes that emotional and intellectual sex roles in Iran are approximately the reverse of what they would be in Western cultures. Men are not expected to conform to the strong, silent norm of the Western male, but are expected to show their emotions and even have tantrums. If they do not, other Iranians are likely to think that they lack vital human traits and are probably not dependable. Iranian men enjoy poetry and are supposed to be sensitive, intuitive, and not very logical. In Iran, it is the women who are supposed to be logical and practical.

In the light of reports like these, the belief that certain kinds of social behavior are biologically predetermined for men and others for women should be questioned and reexamined. The evidence as presented so far is, however, incomplete and may in fact be one-sided.

One dimension of behavior that has been overlooked in such reports is that of each sex's role in warfare. If sex differences in behavior are entirely learned, one would expect that women would carry the brunt of the fighting in some cultures, yet a survey of warfare practices shows

that fighting is almost entirely a masculine activity. In some cultures, as for example Russia and Israel, women are part of the fighting forces, but their role is essentially an auxiliary one. Even in the Tchambuli tribes the fighting is done by men. They are reluctant fighters, to be sure, but the point is that it is they who do it and not the women. The peaceful Arapesh also go to war, and the men do the fighting.

Biological Determinants. There is much research on aggressiveness among infrahuman animals. In brief, the findings show that aggressiveness tends to be a typically male characteristic. Among the primates, there is a great deal of variation in hostility and aggression, but males of any given species are more aggressive than females (Scott, 1958). Injection of male hormone also has the effect of increasing aggressiveness and dominance in animals that had previously not displayed such behavior (Clark & Birch, 1945, 1946; Guhl, 1949). Harry F. Harlow (1962) has presented some rather compelling evidence to support the instinctive position. Figure 9-3 shows the relative frequency with which male and female macaque monkeys observed by Harlow exhibited "threat responses" during the first year of life. Although female

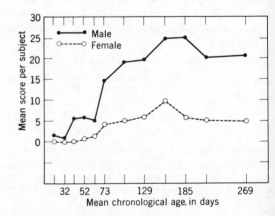

Figure **9-3.** Frequency of threat responses by male and female monkeys during the first year of life (Harlow, 1962).

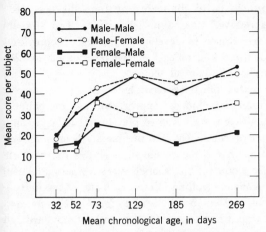

Figure **9-4.** Frequency with which male and female monkeys initiated play with members of their own and opposite sex (Harlow, 1962).

monkeys show some increase in aggressiveness during the period of development, there is no question that male monkeys are inclined to be far more hostile. Indeed, male monkeys show higher rates of both hostile and friendly aggressiveness. Figure 9-4 shows the frequency with which young monkeys initiated contact and interacted with one another in play situations. As the top graph lines show, male monkeys took the initiative in play more frequently. The two bottom lines show that female monkeys took considerably less initiative in play and also initiated it less often with male monkeys. Harlow's statistics on rough-and-tumble play are also impressive. Figure 9-5 shows that such aggressive and vigorous play is almost entirely a male pattern of behavior. If Harlow's female monkeys were learning anything, they were not learning how to rough-house. Figure 9-6 shows that they were, in fact, learning grooming. Caressing and stroking are not only feminine prerogatives in most human societies, but characteristic of female macaque monkeys as well.

Interaction between Social Learning and Biology. At this point, the evidence relating to instinctual and social-learning explanations of sex

role behavior must seem contradictory and confusing, and there may indeed be no clear answer as to what *really* is masculine and feminine or

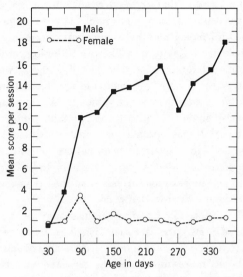

Figure **9-5.** Frequency of "rough-and-tumble" play for two male and two female monkeys during the first year of life (Harlow, 1962).

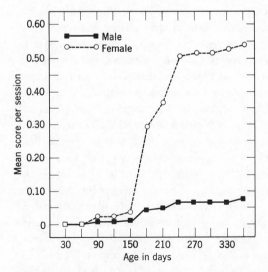

Figure **9-6.** Frequency of grooming behavior made by male and female monkeys during the first year of life (Harlow, 1962).

what the origin of what we recognize as masculine and feminine is likely to be. There may be a reasonable explanation, however, located somewhere between the two positions.

It does seem that aggressive, adventurous, and active behavior may be biologically predetermined for males, and that sympathetic, accepting, and passive behavior may likewise be biologically determined for females. The fact that these two contrasting patterns of behavior are consistent for the respective sexes among infrahuman animals suggests very strongly that similar biological forces operate for humans. Although there are wide variations from culture to culture in patterns of what is considered masculine or feminine, the sex-typed trends described do seem to be the ones most often encountered.

The differences between cultures may be accounted for by the fact that man is in many respects more flexible than the infrahuman animals. He learns more quickly, learns a greater variety of patterns, and is able to learn patterns of behavior that may drastically modify and even supplant some of the more biologically determined responses. As long as a form of behavior is physically possible, it can be learned by man. Men can learn to be motherly, and women can learn to be aggressive and competitive; men can learn to be graceful and socially sensitive, and women can learn to be blunt and insensitive; and so forth. The capacity of humans to learn and perpetuate patterns of learning can account for the variants observed by Mead, Albert, and Hall, noted earlier. The behavior of man thus appears to be *both* biologically *and* socially determined. This should give some reassurance to the champions for women's rights, who have been pointing out that inasmuch as work in an industrialized, urbanized, highly complex culture is less physically demanding than work in more primitive surroundings, there is less and less need for men to play dominant roles and greater opportunity for genuine equality between the sexes. The only remaining problems to be solved in achieving sexual equality

seem to be to eliminate war (and the need for aggressive, "masculine" behavior) and to get more women to develop an interest in complex, quantitative problems of the type posed by today's technological society.

Status. For the present, however, most cultures, Western included, appear to be masculine-dominated, with women playing secondary, supportive roles. This arrangement appears to be acceptable to most women, as shown by the fact that women who through stock ownership possess the controlling interest in many of the industrial and financial organizations in the nation have not rallied around the feminist standard in order to persuade the companies they control to change their policies regarding the hiring or promotion of women executives.

Further evidence for the acceptance by women of the status quo is shown by their willingness to grant more status to men. In a masculine-dominated culture, it would be expected that men would generally be more socially attractive than women. When girls say that attending college enables them to "meet interesting people," they are referring to men, not women. Indeed, women are much more likely than men are to say they are attending college in order to find a marriage partner (Binger, 1961). Even their dreams are revealing: women are more likely to dream about men than men are to dream about women (Hall & Dumhof, 1963).

The impact of the masculine emphasis in our culture appears quite early in life. A majority of girls in the primary grades in school expressed greater preference for masculine than for feminine things, and women are much more likely than men to have wished that they were of the opposite sex (Brown, 1958, 1962).

There is some evidence, however, that the differences between the sexes as to status and value are changing in the direction of greater equality, especially in the United States. Data in Table 9-1 show that the norms governing sex roles are more traditional in Great Britain, Germany, and Italy. For one thing, about twice as many men as women were members of voluntary organizations in those countries, as contrasted with about five women for every six men in the United States. Furthermore, only about 20 per cent of the women belonging to such organizations actually became officers in Great Britain, Italy, and Mexico, and only 9 per cent in Germany. This contrasts with 52 per cent for women in the United States, which is actually higher than the corresponding percentage for men. To state this in other terms, not only are American women twice as likely to join organizations as in the four other countries, but they are three times as likely to become officers.

As we noted in Chapter 8, there are great differences in the United States in the status of women at the various social levels. Members of the LC and the WC are more likely to function along traditional lines, with the men dominant and freer of responsibility and the women more likely to be tied to home and children. In MC homes, women achieve a much higher degree of equality, sharing in decisions regarding family policies, particularly in decisions that affect the spending of money. It is the LC man who is most likely to object to his wife's taking a job outside the home. Even when the money is sorely needed, as it usually is in LC homes, he is inclined to view a working wife as a threat to his status, as a public admission that he is incapable of supporting his family. A woman who works and earns money is a freer person than one who does not, because her contributions to the family income give her the implied right to share in decisions about how it should be budgeted. Furthermore, the fact that she has a job shows that she is able to support herself if the marriage should be dissolved.

Women's status is higher in the UC than in the MC. Since UC women are likely to outlive their husbands, they are also likely to control large fortunes. They also plan, direct, and manage the social affairs that determine who is associated with whom. Although MC women are quite active in community affairs, UC women are even more active and often play a leading part in politics at all levels—local, state, and federal.

As was previously stated, the North American core culture is essentially MC. The LC and WC members are continually reminded of MC values at every turn—through the mass media, the schools, contacts with governmental agencies, and the like. There is a tendency, therefore, for norms regarding the status and treatment of women to have some impact on LC and WC behavior. To use a social-learning approach to this phenomenon, the institutions in our society, being MC in character, reinforce MC patterns of behavior wherever they occur, with the result that the behavior of members of the other classes tends to drift in a MC direction. This process is also facilitated and expedited by the fact that sizable numbers of LC and WC young people become MC each year, usually by taking advantage of educational opportunities.

Changing Relationships between the Sexes. There have been few comparative studies of shifts in women's status over the years; hence it is difficult to find "hard data" that demonstrate this change. There is some evidence that American values are moving in a more "feminine" than "masculine" direction. The sharp declines in the number of lynchings and the number of persons executed for crimes since the beginning of the century are one indication of the feminine drift in American values. Peace movements have become stronger and more vocal, and patterns of behavior characterized by aggressiveness and hostility receive less public support with each decade. Note particularly the changes in police methods within the last twenty or thirty years.

Even attitudes of children and adolescents regarding members of the opposite sex are apparently changing. It has been traditional for there to be a degree of hostility and even some aggressiveness between boy and girl subcultures, particularly during the preadolescent period of development. Girls competed with boys academically, and boys found ways to tease girls and make fun of them. Traditionally, there were very few real friendships between boys and girls during this period. They had little in common (or thought they did), and boys caught playing or even walking with girls were subjected to much harassment by other boys. This hostility died out during middle and late adolescence, when boys found out that girls were interesting people to be with, on occasion. Middle-aged people have during the last few years been heard to comment that norms have changed considerably since they were in school, in that adolescents are dating earlier, "going steady" more frequently, and that there does not seem to be the intersex hostility that was characteristic of the preadolescent boy-girl relations.

A comparative study conducted by Raymond G. Kuhlen and Nancy B. Houlihan (1965) suggests that norms have indeed changed. Their study included data gathered in 1942, when one hundred students of each sex in grades 6, 9, and 12 were asked to indicate the names of fellow students they would like to have sit next to them in class or as companions for such activities as attending the movies, going skating, and studying. The same questions were asked of students in the same schools in 1963. As the data in Figure 9-7

show, students in 1963 were more willing to have members of the opposite sex as companions. The barriers that limit or inhibit interaction between the sexes had evidently been lowered or weakened during the intervening years.

Conflicts in Roles

Conflicts for Men. One problem that occurs with increasing frequency because of shifts in norms in sex-related behavior is that of role conflict. As men's values become less clearly masculine, in the traditional sense, and women's values correspondingly less feminine, the inevitable result is an increase in ambiguity. Role prescriptions in Mediterranean and Latin American cultures, which tend to be more traditional in their orientation, for example, are quite clear for each of the sexes. In Spanish-speaking areas the difference may even be accentuated by *machismo*, a set of values and attitudes that lead men to project an ultramasculine image through behavior characterized by arrogance, lack of self control, the sexual exploitation of women, and an enjoyment of violence. The general endorsement of this posture on the part of Latin-American men has made it difficult for other acceptable masculine patterns to make their appearance. In more industrialized and urbanized societies, as in North America, men may display traditional forms of masculine behavior, such as aggressiveness, adventurousness, and risk-taking, or they may display behavior that is considered "feminine" in traditional cultures and act in gentle, kind, understanding, and sympathetic ways. North American men may even play mothering roles, such as diapering, feeding, and comforting infants, without feeling that they are engaging in behavior that is inappropriate to their sex. There has even been some change in Mediterranean cultures. In Chapter 8 we reported a study by Prothro (1966), comparing Greek middle-class, working-class, and peasant norms in rearing young children. As the data reported in Table 8-1 showed, Greek middle-class fathers have become

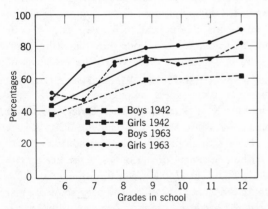

Figure **9-7.** Percentages of boys and girls at various school grades in 1942 and 1963 who chose companions of the opposite sex for various activities (Kuhlen & Houlihan, 1965).

more involved in the tasks of child care and are beginning to share decision making with their wives.

The fact that there are several somewhat contradictory roles available for men in urbanized cultures does make for role conflict, particularly at times when choices must be made between roles—whether to spend a Saturday at the office catching up on work, out playing golf with the gang, or with the family on a picnic at the beach. The more sharply defined sex-appropriate roles are, the less the role conflict.

Conflicts for Women. However difficult problems of role conflict are for men in our culture, they are even more difficult for women, particularly for those who attend college. Carl Binger (1961), a psychiatrist attached to Radcliffe College, notes that our educational system confronts college women with a choice between marriage, a career, or some combination of both. No matter how they resolve this choice, they are likely to feel guilty or somewhat less than fulfilled. The woman who drops out of college to marry is made to feel guilty by family, friends, and teachers, because "she could have made something of herself." The woman who continues college and goes on to graduate study and a career feels she has missed out on something because she did not marry. The woman who attempts to combine marriage with a career continually has the feeling that she is shortchanging either her marriage or her work and consequently is always in the position of feeling she is letting someone down. Men are much less likely to have such problems, because marriage and career are generally not perceived as different choices, or as especially incompatible with each other.

Binger notes that women often feel under considerable stress as a result of conflicting role prescriptions. If a college woman devotes her time and energy to study, she has fewer recreational contacts with men, and consequently is less likely to encounter a potential marriage partner. If she becomes socially active, her studies are likely to suffer, thus impairing her chance to prepare for a worthwhile career. The common reactions to this stress, according to Binger, are depression, exhaustion, and respiratory ailments.

Role conflict will occur in any situation in which two or more sets of expectations operate, and the usual result is some degree of tension and anxiety. In the situation we have just described, college women feel the need to follow the traditional injunction of displaying behavior that is traditionally feminine and thus attracting a potential mate, but at the same time parents, teachers, and friends expect them to go on and complete college in preparation for a career. The symptoms mentioned by Binger are side-effects of attempting to deal with the anxiety and tension resulting from the students' trying to determine "who they are."

Role Conflict in Organizations. Ambiguities in behavioral expectations for members of each sex are by no means the only source of role conflict in modern society. The stresses and strains of organizational life are also likely to create situations leading to conflicts in roles. This problem has been examined by Robert L. Kahn and others (1964), who studied the effects of role ambiguity and role conflict in industrial settings. Kahn and his associates conceived of roles in organizations as occurring in interlocking, interrelated networks, or "role sets." Individuals who perform certain roles respond to expectations of others involved in their role set, as well as to their own expectations. Role conflict is created when there is a difference between what others expect of one and what one expects of oneself. The presence of role conflict is revealed in low levels of satisfaction with the job, lack of confidence in the organization, decreased self-confidence, a sense of futility, and other work-related emotional problems.

The school superintendent's role was the subject of a study by Gross, Mason, and McEachern (1958). Individuals in this position find role conflict inevitable, inasmuch as they must cope with the contradictory expectations of teachers, parents, the governing board of the school, politicians, and the public at large, as well as the expectations they have for themselves. With so many demands to satisfy, no one is likely to be satisfied, and superintendents have learned to cope with role conflict by four major devices: yielding to pressure, sticking to professional standards, making compromises, or avoiding the responsibility of making relevant decisions.

Role Conflict for the "Hasher." An instance of role conflict within an organizational context that has been examined in some detail is that of the "hasher" in college sororities. At least two levels of role conflict are involved here. First, many of the tasks of a hasher—setting tables, washing and drying dishes, and mopping floors —are perceived by these male students as more feminine than masculine. Although adults of both sexes wait on tables in restaurants, serving food to large numbers of young women somehow seems more consistent with feminine than with masculine roles, as far as young men are concerned. Second, the work of the hasher is at best semiskilled and hence suitable for working class people rather than for young men whose very involvement in the processes of higher education makes them *ipso facto* middle class. The hasher also occupies a position at the very lowest level in the sorority, below that of house mother and the cooks. In addition, a hasher is expected to be neat, polite, and efficient; he is not allowed to address the girls while serving them (unless asked a question); and he is not allowed to date any of the girls during his off-duty hours. The position of hasher, in other words, carries with it expectations and implications of menial or "dirty" work, low prestige, and manifest subservience to and strict social distance from a group of college women (Zurcher, Sonenschein, & Metzner, 1966).

In one sense, there is no real conflict in role here. Hashers are not required or expected to display the role behavior of college students when they are waiting on tables or cleaning up kitchens. Nor are they expected to behave like hashers in the classroom. The chief problem occurs, as it does with the college women just discussed, when the individual is required to play roles incompatible with his self-concept. The problem of the women described by Binger is more acute: they are troubled with shifting self-concepts and have difficulty in deciding which "self" is more appropriate. As far as the hashers are concerned, their main role, and the one most consistent with their self-concept, is that of the college student, and it is only the need for funds that forces them to accept work as hashers. The role conflict, therefore, occurs in their having to behave as hashers according to expectations (role prescriptions) that are incompatible with the expectations emanating from their main role as college students.

The chief reaction to conflict of the hashers in the study just cited was one of resentment and hostility. Among their own group in the kitchen, they referred to the girls as "cows" or "pigs." They played practical jokes on them, such as dropping a marble or two into a gelatin grape salad mold. They appeared to get much satisfaction out of "getting the girls' goats" by spilling food, ignoring orders, answering criticism sharply, and the like. Another outlet for tension and hostility was horseplay in the kitchen: food throwing or water splashing, "in-group" jokes, and general zaniness. For example, the hashers created "bits," which were sequences of role-playing behavior, structured along certain lines. During the bit, everything in the work setting— hashers, cooks, sorority members, utensils, food —would be made a part of the dramatic scene, and hashers would adopt the appropriate terminology. For instance, the bit in one working session used the pretense that the kitchen and dining room were a "hell ship," with the hashers cast in the role of mutineers, the girls as "powdered pirates," and the cooks as "Ahab" and "Bligh." Knives became harpoons, meat became "salt hourse," going into the dining room was "walking the plank," and a bosomy sorority girl was nicknamed "the treasure chest." In another bit, the kitchen became the Third Reich, and the girls "Storm Troopers," while "bravery under fire" was rewarded by decoration with lettuce-leaf medals. Such dramatic bits served a useful purpose as a kind of psychodrama that enabled hashers to work off tensions and hostility and thus establish better control of role-conflict problems.

Compartmentalization. People usually deal with role conflicts of the type we have discussed by using a psychological defense mechanism termed "compartmentalization," whereby one actually becomes a different kind of person, at least on a superficial level, when engaging in the behavior that is most alien to the self-concept. Compartmentalization calls for a great deal of control, self-denial, and flexibility. Adults in a complex, industrialized, and urbanized society attempt to deal with this problem by arranging their lives so that role conflict is kept at a minimum and by taking on positions that are more consistent with their self-concept. Since each position always has a set of appropriate values and attitudes, a shift from one position to another requires that one take on the appropriate attitudes and values, along with the roles, and there is always the possibility that values learned in an unwanted position may develop a sort of permanent anchorage. The presence of incompatible values within a self-system leads to further tension and anxiety, and further attempts at compartmentalization.

Role conflict is also a common occurrence in formerly primitive societies now undergoing rapid change. Finding stable positions in such societies is not easy. In many instances, the individual finds himself disowned by traditional society but without a place in the new one. Even in such societies, however, social learning can take place at a rapid rate. In some of the new African nations, it is possible to find persons who function as traditional juju men (medicine men) and also as respectable civil servants or even Sunday

School teachers, without having any doubts or qualms about mutually incompatible aspects of their positions and roles. Others do not fare so well and break into raving fits when the tension becomes unbearable, whereupon they are likely to regress to more primitive patterns of behavior (Collomb, Zempleni, & Storper, 1965).

SUMMARY

Each position at various status levels in a social system carries with it certain rights and obligations, which set the norms specifying the kind of behavior appropriate to the satisfaction of said rights and obligations. Individuals perform certain roles to validate their right to occupy the positions they hold. The roles specified and prescribed by a society limit the behavior of its members in ways that are, in a broad and general way, supportive to the society and aid its functioning. Some roles become so identified with certain positions that they can be recognized whenever they appear, even out of their appropriate context. Police, judgmental, and parental roles are examples.

Positions in all societies fall into at least five types of groupings: age-sex, family-household, status, occupation, and friendship-common interest. Technologically advanced societies also include a sixth grouping: organizations. Positions in these groupings may be designated as ascribed or achieved. An individual has no control over positions that are ascribed to him, but must expend some effort to achieve the others.

The person who occupies a position is expected to behave in certain ways, and he tends to hold these expectations for himself and his own behavior. These expectations are acquired through the processes of social learning. In the same way we learn to recognize reciprocal clusters of roles and what to expect of those who occupy them. Once we know the positions occupied by others, we have a better idea of what to expect of them in the way of behavior.

A major source of the difference in the behavior of the two sexes can be found in the expectations that society has for the members of each sex and that they come to have for themselves. Researchers have expressed considerable interest in determining whether these sex-appropriate expectations and the resulting roles are acquired through biological inheritance or through learning. Research shows that males are more likely to become involved in behavior characterized by risk, aggressiveness, and task orientation, whereas females are more likely to prefer activities involving social interaction and ingratiation. Although these differences tend to occur in most cultures, they are not universal. Anthropologists have found a number of societies, most of them primitive, in which roles that Western culture considers "masculine" are played by women, and "feminine" roles are played by men. Studies of monkey colonies show that aggressive types of behavior are typically masculine, whereas the more passive types are feminine. These data suggest that aggressiveness in males and passiveness in females may be biologically determined for the human species, as well as for infrahuman animals. However, anthropological data also suggest that biologically determined trends in behavior can be channeled and redirected through social learning.

Most cultures, Western included, appear to be masculine-dominated, with women playing secondary, supportive roles. There have been changes, however. The status of women appears to be moving in the direction of greater equality, particularly at UC and MC levels, and society's values, such as those relating to the punishment of social deviants, seem to be moving in a "feminine" (less aggressive) direction.

The more masculine and feminine values and roles merge, the more role conflict is created for members of society. Women in college, for example, are often not sure whether they should train for careers in the masculine-dominated world of employment, or whether they should accept a more traditional sex role, or both. Role conflicts are also created when members of an organizational group develop different concepts of their positions than those held by others in the organization. Some positions, like that of the school superintendent, are particularly likely to generate role conflict, because different groups have such widely divergent expectations of what the position holder should or could do. The male college student who serves as a "hasher" in a sorority is an example of how mutually incompatible expectations can lead to role conflict, which in turn finds expression in various forms of aggressive behavior. Role conflict may also be resolved by "compartmentalization," whereby an individual shifts the more superficial aspects of his personality to conform with the demands of the situation.

SUGGESTED READINGS

Farber, S. M. & Wilson, R. H. L. (Eds.), *The potential of woman.* New York: McGraw-Hill, 1963 (Paperback).

Gross, N., McEachern, A. W., & Mason, W. S., *Explorations in role analysis: studies of the school superintendency role.* New York: Wiley, 1957.

Lieberman, S., The effects of changes in roles on the attitudes of role occupants. *Human relations,* 1956, **9**, 385-402.

Lindgren, H. C. (Ed.), *Contemporary research in social psychology.* New York: Wiley, 1969. See papers by Lieberman and Slovic in Section 7.

Mead, M., *Sex and temperament in three primitive societies.* New York: Morrow, 1935. (Reissued as a paperback by New American Library in 1950).

Merton, R. K., *Social theory and social structure* (rev. ed.). New York: Free Press, 1957.

CHAPTER TEN

Henry Clay Lindgren

St. Louis Post Dispatch, Black Star

Ken Heyman

Personality as a Social Phenomenon

Roles and Personality Formation. Personality, as Daniel Katz and Robert L. Kahn (1966) point out, is the product of social interaction. Inasmuch as social interaction takes place throughout the life span, an individual's personality undergoes a continual process of modification. This modification is likely to be slight in highly stable or sheltered environments, such as remote villages, where roles change but little and there are few changes in personnel. Conversely, modification is likely to take place at a more rapid rate when people are required to learn and play a variety of complex and at times unrelated roles in the context of groups whose membership is continually changing.

Our involvement in the roles we play is likely to have some kind of effect on the kinds of people we become, or, more accurately, are continually becoming. Although a role may be viewed as a kind of psychological garment that we put on and take off and that affects our appearance and behavior for the moment, the fact that this metaphor is appropriate does not necessarily mean that there is no residual effect when we are no longer playing the role in question. For one thing, the sequences of behavior that go to make up a role are learned, which means that they have been reinforced. Once they have been learned, they will reappear all the more readily, whenever situations are encountered that possess the potential for reinforcement. Furthermore, carrying out role-appropriate sequences of behavior requires that we learn certain perceptual styles—certain ways of looking at ourselves and our environment. These percepts enable us to determine what roles are called for in a given situation, how the roles are to be played, and even what kinds of feelings to have about the roles we play.

An example drawn from the classroom may help to illustrate this. Let us say that Miss Dale, a sixth grade teacher, has discovered that Dorothy is cheating on a geography quiz. Miss Dale's central role in this situation is that of a teacher. As long as she occupies this position, she is expected to follow the curriculum, assign homework, set quizzes and examinations, grade papers, and so forth. There are also an almost infinite number of subsidiary roles that relate to her position as a teacher. As the classroom situation changes during the teaching day, she will change from one subsidiary role to another. In this particular instance, her subsidiary role has become more that of a policeman, although some teachers might at this point play a psychotherapist's role, realizing that cheating is a problem of mental health as well as discipline. But Miss Dale is a fairly traditional teacher and she is going to play the role of the policeman or disciplinarian.

Miss Dale's decision to react as a disciplinarian was not a conscious one, in the sense that she did not stop to think of the various roles she might play in this situation and select that of the disciplinarian. Rather, it "came to her naturally"—she saw Dorothy cheating, and before she was even aware of what she was doing, she was moving in to apprehend the culprit. Although Miss Dale would probably deny it, her behavior was to some degree satisfying to her, in the sense that it seemed appropriate. She has learned that teachers are expected to act as disciplinarians at times and has come to expect the same kind of behavior from herself. She has probably also learned that authority figures, including teachers, are expected to take on disciplinary roles when they encounter wrongdoing.

Miss Dale's action in taking on the role of a disciplinarian is also reinforced by colleagues and students. She often hears about how this teacher caught a student red-handed or how that teacher lost control of her class because she neglected to play the disciplinary role or did not play it with enough conviction. Her pupils expect her to play this role as well. Little girls continually come to her with tales of wrongdoing, and when she comes upon a group of children who are doing something they should not, they eye her apprehensively, waiting for the blow to fall—figuratively speaking, of course, because Miss Dale has never been seen to strike a child.

Miss Dale has also learned the values that are basic to the disciplinarian, namely, an acceptance of the proposition that the norms of society must be upheld, that deviations from these norms must be noted and punished, that authority figures are the proper persons to enforce norms, and so forth.

Miss Dale has therefore learned a number of things with respect to her playing the role of the disciplinarian. She has learned that the role is part of the general role of being a teacher, she has learned that she should play it at times, she has learned how to play it, she has learned what kind of expectations to have for herself with respect to the role, what values and attitudes are appropriate, and how to feel as she carries out the duties of the role.

Miss Dale's way of dealing with Dorothy's cheating was to take the test paper from her, mark it with a big red "F," and place it in her class roll book. Dorothy put her head down on her desk and cried quietly for a while; the class returned to their quiz, somewhat shaken but at the same time somewhat reassured that crime does not pay and that retribution falls swiftly on anyone who believes otherwise. A few minutes later, the class started the arithmetic lesson for the day, and to all outward appearances the matter had been forgotten. Miss Dale was now playing the subsidiary role of the expositor and critic as she showed the class how to calculate the areas of squares and rectangles and called on the members of the class alphabetically to give answers to the questions in the textbook. She hesitated a little as she came to Dorothy's name, but Dorothy answered correctly without a pause. Everyone relaxed and the lesson went on.

It would appear that Miss Dale has been abl to change roles swiftly and easily and has n been in the slightest affected by the necessity t play the role of the disciplinarian. But has sh really? Being a disciplinarian involves playin a certain kind of role, to be sure, but it also mear taking on certain attitudes, values, and feeling Are attitudes, values, and feelings so easily p on and taken off? If one learns to feel and thir along certain lines in one situation, is there possibility that other situations will evoke sim lar thoughts and feelings? How will Miss Da feel, in other words, when she encounters wron; doing in situations in which she is not th teacher? If she sees a man taking a newspap from a display rack without paying for it, will sh ignore him? If her brother tells her about son ploy he uses to pad his expense account, will sh refrain from comment?

We would, of course, have to know a great de more about Miss Dale to predict with any degr of accuracy how she would behave in such situ tions, but it is reasonably safe to say that scho teachers who rather enjoy playing roles of di ciplinarians would be more likely to speak u under such circumstances than would, say, beau parlor operators or clerk typists. People who h bitually play certain roles are likely to find o portunities to play the roles outside of the usu contexts. One would expect, therefore, that lawyer might be unusually critical about th wording of statements, even when he is not fun tioning as a lawyer, or that physicians wou be inclined to be prescriptive about nonmedic matters.

What we are saying is that as we play roles, v learn ways of perceiving ourselves and the wor in general, and these ways of perceiving tend t become rather stable and persistent aspects the self. We also learn a repertory of roles th to a large extent identify and define "who v are." To put this into other words, the roles v learn constitute a significant dimension of o personality.

Personality Defined. The term "personality," as used by psychologists, refers to the total behavior of the individual, but particularly to those relatively enduring and consistent aspects that cause us to resemble others in some ways and to be totally different and unique in others. This is different from the term "personality" as used by laymen, which usually refers to the more superficial aspects of behavior—what psychologists sometimes call "stimulus value." "Personality," as used psychologically, refers to such concepts as "character" (the kind of behavior that is characteristic of an individual in crucial situations) and "temperament" (the basic trends in emotion and feeling that are characteristic of an individual). Both character and temperament are related to roles—the kind of roles we learn and particularly the way in which we play them. Roles, stimulus value, and character are learned patterns of behavior. Temperament is usually considered to be biologically determined by the kind of hormonal balance we inherit. As we pointed out in the foregoing chapter, the fact that men and women tend to have somewhat different kinds of temperament is due in part to differences in what they inherit biologically. However, note that we say "in part," because one of the major differences between man and the other animals is his capacity to learn an infinite range and variety of behavioral forms. Just as hyperactive Zuñi infants learn to be less active than Anglo infants, even so do women in some cultures learn behavior that in our culture would be considered masculine, whereas men may learn patterns that we consider to be essentially feminine. The kind of temperament we are born with may set some of the initial patterns of personality, but what we learn subsequently is even more important.

Birth Order as a Variable

Eagerness to Volunteer as a Personality Trait. Birth order is a good example of how the expectations, roles, values, and attitudes that are characteristic of certain positions produce recognizable personality patterns. Birth order has been a bothersome variable for research psychologists. Much of the work done with humans in the psychological laboratory depends on the cooperation of volunteers, and there is a consistent tendency for groups of volunteers to contain a higher percentage of individuals who were first-born in their families than those who were later-born (Suedfeld, 1964; Dember, 1964). To researchers, such a tendency means that they must screen volunteers to control any variables that might be due to birth order effects, because there is always the possibility that first-born individuals may differ from the general population in ways other than their tendency to volunteer. Furthermore, experimental findings are supposed to be based on samples drawn at random from the population; but the samples are *not* random, in that first-born individuals are overrepresented in them.

The eagerness of first-born individuals to volunteer may not in itself seem to be very significant, but psychologists have learned that behavioral tendencies that run counter to the expected trend are likely to be associated with other characteristics that deviate from the norm. We noted in Chapter 2 that first-born individuals tend to have an affinity for the company of others, particularly when placed in a stress situation (Wrightsman, 1960). They tend to express a strong need for affiliation (n Aff), which could perhaps be related to early experiences when they were the only child, and to later experiences when they were given charge of their siblings and experienced the semi-isolation from the group that almost every authority figure has learned as a part of his role. We will come back to this point, because it is an important theme in the personality patterns developed by oldest children. For the moment, however, let us consider other differences between first-borns and later-borns.

Success Differentials between First-borns and Others. Another difference between adults who were first-born and those born later appears in the greater intellectual, economic, and social success attained by the former. Harold E. Jones (1954) did a biographical study of eminent Englishmen, gifted children, persons listed in *American men of science,* and persons listed in *Who's who in America.* He found that the first-born were overrepresented in each of these groups, irrespective of the size of the families from which they came. Whereas one would expect, by chance, that 50 per cent of men from two-child families listed in *Who's who* would be first born, the percentage actually was 64. Thirty-three per cent of men from three-child families listed in *American men of science* would by chance be expected to be first born, but the actual percentage was 44, and so forth.

William D. Altus (1965) has found a similar phenomenon. As Figure 10-1 shows, a far greater percentage of first-borns, than would be expected by chance, make top scores on the National Merit Scholarship Qualifying Test. For example, although one would expect only 50 per cent of students from two-child families to have become "finalists," the actual figure was 66 per cent. Similar discrepancies exist for finalists from three- and four-child families.

These findings suggest that first-borns are likely to be more successful in competitions of this sort than are later-borns. First-borns, as Figure 10-1 also shows, are also more likely to enter universities. This overrepresentation of first-borns in university populations has been noted for many years—as far back as 1928. It is, in fact, a routine finding. Therefore, the common-sense explanation that the unusual number of first-born students in college populations today is due to high postwar birth rates can be dismissed. The national percentage of first births in 1945 was 35 per cent, whereas the overall percentage of first-borns entering Santa Barbara in 1963, eighteen years later, was 60 per cent. (Both figures include only children, as well as first-borns.)

Another common-sense explanation of the findings reported by Jones and Altus is the tradition of making the resources of the family available for the education of the first-born son. This should, of course, give him an advantage over his siblings. However, the fact that Altus' data apply to women as well as men points to the probability that first-borns enjoy some kind of a psychological advantage as well. The nature of

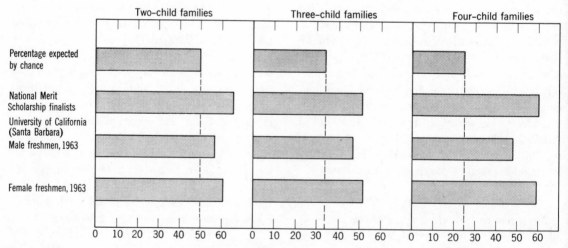

Figure **10-1.** Percentages of first-born, according to size of family, who became National Merit Scholarship Finalists or who entered the University of California at Santa Barbara in 1963 (Altus, 1965).

this advantage is suggested by a study by Edward E. Sampson and Francena T. Hancock (1967) of high school students in which first-born subjects, as contrasted with those who were second-born, scored higher on tests of the need to achieve (n Ach) and the need for autonomy. The results confirmed an earlier study by Sampson (1962), which showed higher n Ach for first-borns.

Birth Order and Social Acceptance. We noted earlier that tendencies to deviate from the group norm in one variable are generally associated with tendencies to deviate in other ways, and this is certainly true of first-borns. Prominence and success in intellectual activities apparently go with social success as well. C. Norman Alexander, Jr. (1966) conducted a study of the relationship between birth order and social acceptance for male seniors in thirty high schools and found that first-born students were more likely to be chosen by other students as friends. He found, furthermore, that first-borns were more likely to reciprocate friendship choices and to pick less popular students as friends than were later-born students. Somewhat contrary findings were reported by Stanley Schachter (1959, 1964), who found first-born fraternity members to be more dependent and less popular than later-born members. Alexander suggests that the difference between his results and those of Schachter may be due to selective factors, namely, the tendency of college fraternities to attract certain types of individuals but not others. He points out that his sample, which included 1410 students from thirty different high schools, is probably more representative of the general population. His findings are consistent with those of Schachter in the sense that both sets of results point to the importance of the need for affiliation (n Aff) in the motivational pattern of the first-born. Alexander points out, however, that the greater popularity enjoyed by his subjects is indicative of a higher degree of social sensitivity, rather than of the servility and overdependency hypothesized by Schachter. Indeed, the greater success and eminence attained by oldest children in a number of different fields would be more consistent with Alexander's than with Schachter's interpretations.

Relations to Authority Figures. In one study of birth order among university students, Edward S. Jones (1956) found that students who were first-born in two-child families were 20 per cent more likely to get A's and B's than were students who were second-born in such families. Students who were the oldest in families of three or more were 50 per cent more likely to get A's and B's than were students who were middle or younger children in families the same size. In a follow-up study twenty years after graduation, more of the first-born students achieved high levels of success in their chosen fields.

The ability to get good marks and to make progress in an occupational field suggests that first-borns are also able to get along with authority figures. Grade-getting is accomplished by task orientation (staying with a job and following through) and by being able to convince persons in authority (teachers, in this case) that one's work is worthy of a good grade. The grade-getter, then, is one who is able to identify with authority figures, take on some of their values, and use them as models for behavior. The first-born fits this pattern of behavior quite well. Some research by Robert D. Palmer (1966) shows that first-born individuals tend to have self-descriptions that are more similar to the self-descriptions of their parents than those of their siblings. First-borns appeared to be more willing to take on their parents' norms, especially with respect to matters relating to self-control and inhibition. In short, the first-born was found to be definitely more adult-oriented than the later-born siblings.

Psychologists, notably Schachter, have attempted to explain the kinds of tendencies exhibited by the first-born in terms of the fact that they enjoy a complete monopoly of their mothers' attention at first, a monopoly that is broken with the arrival of the next-born child. Even after this occurs, the first-born continues to have a certain priority, according to Schachter, for he is treated with greater concern, affection, and attention. Such an experience might logically produce an individual who is oriented favorably to adults and is interested in establishing a dependency type of relationship with them.

Birth-Order Positions and Roles. There is, however, a second kind of experience common to first-born children. More than any other child in the family, the first-born child has the experience of serving as a "junior parent." When the children go to the Saturday matinee it is the oldest who is given the money for the tickets and told to watch out for the others. If something goes wrong, it is he who is blamed. The roles of the oldest child are thus more precisely identified and defined than are those of the other children. As he carries out his tasks of serving as a guardian and a parental representative, he finds himself expressing the values and copying the behavioral patterns of his parents. Even though he is a minor authority figure, he takes on the values, attitudes, percepts, and expectations, and role behaviors that are characteristic of anyone who occupies a position of authority. It is hardly surprising that he relates better to adults than his siblings do. Nor is it surprising that other children tend to look up to him and value him for his leadership qualities.

A study by Reginald G. Smart (1965) of students at the University of Toronto shows that men who were first-born children were more likely to be involved in social and recreational clubs and to serve as elected officers.

First-borns also tend to be more supportive, which may account for their greater popularity. Robert L. Weiss (1966) had high school students listen to tape-recorded speeches and to try to "maintain rapport" with the speakers. They were asked to imagine that the speaker was talking to them individually, as if the two of them were alone. Whenever the listener wanted to indicate rapport or give support to what the speaker was saying, he was to press a button. Weiss found

that first-born and only children were inclined to do more button-pressing and were thus more supportive than were later-born children.

Tendencies of first-born children to identify with authority figures were demonstrated by an experiment conducted by Paul Lane Wuebben (1967), who asked participants in an experiment not to talk to others about what went on in the experiment. Every subject agreed not to do so, but when asked a week later whether they had spoken to others, 64 per cent admitted that they had spoken to at least one other person about the experiment. Significantly more of those who had cooperated with the experimenter by not talking to others were first-borns.

The evidence that we have presented shows that individuals who were first-born in their families are likely to behave somewhat differently from those who were later-born. The differences tend to be slight—they probably account for only about 5 per cent of the variation that could be observed in behavior—but the point is that the differences do tend to be consistent. We suggest that the differences we have noted occur in people who were first-born children more than in others, at least partly because these people had similar experiences and played similar roles. These experiences, in turn, tended to shape their behavior in certain consistent ways, and the roles they played as children led them to develop values, expectations, and personality traits that are in many ways similar to those of other first-born children, but different from those who were later-born, who had different experiences, and who played different roles when they were children.

The Self

Individuals who were first-born tend to behave in ways that are somewhat similar because they have somewhat similar self-concepts; that is, they tend to regard themselves and to think of themselves in similar ways. They are more likely to move to the forefront in social situations, not only because they are used to taking charge, but also because they have come to think of themselves as persons who take the initiative.

Self-concept and Self-image. When we say that first-borns have somewhat similar self-concepts we are referring to a rather general human tendency—the tendency to regard oneself as an object. The term "self-concept" is an abbreviated way of saying "attitudes toward and conceptions about one's self." Our worlds are populated by many people we observe but do not know, a moderate number we know casually, and a few we know quite well. The people we know well are distinguished from the less well known by the fact that we not only possess more information about them, but also have an interrelated and more or less integrated set of feelings and attitudes regarding them. Furthermore, we tend to think of them as occupying positions and playing roles in a miniature social system. At the center of that social system is the person we know best: ourself. This self represents an individual like the others we know, but differs from the others in the sense that it has greater value—for us.

George Herbert Mead (1934) pointed out that the self is a product of our interaction with others and that we can perceive ourselves only as a reflection in the eyes of another. C. H. Cooley (1902) noted our tendency to use others as a kind of looking glass in which we can view ourselves. "In imagination," he wrote, "we perceive in another's mind some thought of our appearance, manners, aims, deeds, character, friends, and so on, and are variously affected by it." The analogy to the looking glass, however, falls somewhat short of how we actually respond to the imagined percepts of others. The looking glass is a neutral and uncritical agent, whereas what others perceive in us is affected by the bias of what they are prepared to perceive, and what we think they perceive is further distorted by our own perceptual bias. "The thing that moves us to pride or shame is not the mere mechanical reflection of ourselves, but an imputed sentiment, the imagined effect of this reflection upon another's mind."

The self may thus be thought of as an "image" —the impression it makes on others, and the impression it makes on ourselves, as perceived in terms of the impression we think it makes on others. The self in this sense is referred to at times as the "self-image," a term which is sometimes used as synonymous with "self-concept." Strictly speaking, however, self-image refers more to the *impression* aspects of the self, whereas self-concept includes the idea of impression but also such other aspects as attitudes, values, motives, goals, expectations, and the like.

Field Theory and Self Theory. The ideas of Mead and Cooley serve as one basis for an approach to social psychology that is termed "field theory." Field theory, which is an attempt to express social-psychological events in terms borrowed from the physical sciences, was introduced into psychology by Kurt Lewin (1935). Lewin's system conceives of the behavior of the individual (designated as P in Figure 10-2) as governed by forces generated by the fields in which he is

located, as well as by systems of tension within himself. In Figure 10-2 the various boundary lines designate the limits of groups in which P holds membership. His nuclear family is UMC and Republican, but his extended family is divided in social class and political party. Second-generation Irish-Americans are more likely to be Democrats, and new arrivals from Ireland are mostly Democratic, although a few are Socialists (at least they were a generation ago, when this map was drawn). Only a few Elks are UMC, but all of them are Republicans. One of the advantages of topological mapping of social-psychological relationships is its economy in communicating rather complex relationships.

This method of representing social-psychological situations is termed "topology," a kind of geometry that is used to describe spatial rela-tionships without respect to quantitative mea-surement. Lewin used a variety of symbols and concepts to represent various aspects of the social-psychological field. Figure 10-2 is a .repre-sentation of "life space," which could also be drawn in such a way as to indicate the "space of free movement" P possesses. Another version of the drawing could show how tensions within P or forces generated by the social field propel him toward certain goals and how he is likely to en-counter certain barriers, some of which may be weak and some strong.

Some field theory ideas may be found in the work of Carl Rogers (1951) and Arthur W. Combs and Donald Snygg (1959), who postu-lated a self as existing in the center of a field of forces. "Self theory" is one term that has been applied to such concepts. The psychiatrist Harry

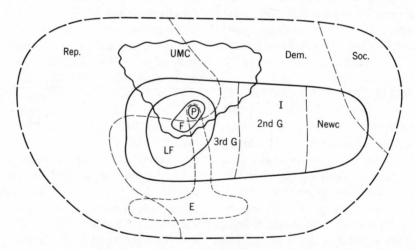

Figure 10-2. Topological map of the fields occupied by an adult male who is the head of a family, UMC, Republican third-generation Irish-American, and an Elk (after Lewin, 1948).

Key

P, person
F, family
LF, larger family
I, Irish-American
Newc., newcomers
2nd G, second generation in the USA

3rd G, third Generation in the USA
UMC, upper middle class
Rep., Republicans
Dem., Democrats
Soc., Socialists
E, Elks

Stack Sullivan (1947) also contributed to self theory in his writings about interpersonal attitudes and feelings. Although each proponent of a field, self, or interpersonal theory introduces elements that cause his theory to differ somewhat from the others, the theories do have much in common. For one thing, they all emphasize perception and all can be referred to as "cognitive theories." Lewin's field forces, for example, are the demands and stresses that are perceived or recognized by the individual. Interpersonal relations play a large part in all the theories; indeed Harry Stack Sullivan insists that personality exists only in terms of our interaction with others.

Psychoanalytic Theories of the Self. Although psychoanalytic theories tend to assign more importance to instinctual drives than does self theory, they have contributed to ideas relating to the nature of the self. For instance, some behavioral scientists use Sigmund Freud's term, "ego," to refer to the self. However, Freud uses the term "ego" in two somewhat different ways. The ego may refer to an entity or object. Freud is using the term in this sense when he refers to the ego being dominated by the id (instinctual processes) or by the superego (the moral standards of society as incorporated into the conscience). Freud also uses "ego" to refer to processes whereby the individual becomes aware of external reality and makes judgments or decisions about what actions are relevant and appropriate. The term "self" generally refers to *image*, the impression one has about one's behavior and one's impact on others, and to *identity*, the relationship between oneself and the surrounding social environment. Both ego and self are included in the more general concept of personality.

The ego is said to play a central and vital role in the organism's attempt to deal with instinctual and moral forces, as well as with external reality. If it is placed under too much pressure from any of these sources, it is likely to operate ineffectively. Certain distortions in perception are therefore invoked in order to "protect" the ego from injury. These distortions are what Freud calls "ego defenses." For example, repression enables the ego to deny or ignore certain kinds of forbidden motives; projection enables the ego to attribute the individual's own unworthy motives to others; sublimation enables the individual's unworthy motives to be expressed in socially acceptable ways without outraging the superego.

People who have a firm grasp on reality are said to have "ego strength," whereas the individual who is swayed from one extreme to another by conflicting demands from superego, id, and the social environment is said to have a "weak ego."

The "Ideal Self." Freud also referred to the "ego ideal," an aspect of the superego that serves as a reference point or standard in controlling behavior. Other psychologists refer to the "self-ideal" or the "ideal self," terms that have much the same meaning. The use of such terms assumes a difference between the self that one perceives as the "real self" and the self that one ought to have or ought to be. Carl Rogers (1951) theorized that the existence of a large gap between the perceived self and the self-ideal is generally an unhealthy state of affairs. Individuals whose behavior continually falls short of what they believe it should be are likely to be plagued by anxiety, self-hate, and feelings of inferiority. One of the objects of psychotherapy, according to Rogers, is to help individuals attain a greater and fuller degree of self-acceptance. Evidence for this point of view is provided by studies carried out at Rogers' clinic, which showed that discrepancies between patients' perceived selves and their self-ideals tended to diminish during the course of successful psychotherapy (Rogers & Dymond, 1954).

Other students of personality question whether the existence of a disparity between the perceived self and the self-ideal should necessarily be considered a sign of poor mental health. Phyllis Katz and Edward Zigler (1967) found that the disparity between the "real self" and the "ideal self" tends to increase between the ages of 11 and 17, with more intelligent children showing greater disparity than less intelligent ones. Their research suggests that as individuals become more mature and more aware of their potentialities, they develop higher and higher expectations of themselves. A certain degree of anxiety tends to accompany a perceived disparity between actual and potential accomplishment, but a moderate degree of anxiety appears to have positive value for optimum personal development. The problem lies in keeping anxiety within reasonable limits. Katz and Zigler note that as individuals progress to higher developmental levels, their increased capacity to deal with problems also enables them to find more problems or to create more problems for themselves. When anxiety reaches painful levels and begins to interfere with the ability to behave effectively and to enjoy life, it is time to consider Carl Rogers' writings and find ways to bring both the perceived self and the self-ideal back into a more comfortable relationship with each other.

Self-esteem. The amount of value we ascribe to the self is our "self-esteem." Like the other aspects of the self, this also is learned from others and becomes a reflection of how others regard us, or, more accurately, the value we think others attach to us as persons. One's behavior is likely to reflect his self-esteem, and this in turn has a reassuring effect on others. Thus there is a reciprocal interaction between one's self-esteem and the esteem expressed for one by others. This proposition was put to the test by S. Frank Miyamoto and Sanford M. Dornbusch (1956) who asked the members of ten groups (four fraternities and sororities and six college classes) to rate themselves and one another on four factors: intelligence, self-confidence, physical attractiveness, and likableness. They found that people with high self-ratings tended to be rated high by others and that the opposite was true of persons who had low self-ratings. They also asked their subjects to guess how others rated them and found that

again persons with high self-ratings tended to assume that others gave them good ratings. When they compared self-ratings with both assumed and actual ratings, they found that self-ratings were closer to assumed than actual ratings. In other words, persons were apparently more influenced by what they *thought* others felt about them than what others actually *did* feel.

Social Learning and the Self. To put this in a framework of social-learning theory, it would appear that as infants we learn, through processes of identification and reinforcement, to react to ourselves as objects possessing certain qualities or attributes. Will Campbell, aged two years and three months, is learning that sometimes he is "a bad boy." The particular occasion of this learning occurred when he tentatively introduced a cigarette into his mouth. This led to a slapping of the hands, a removal of the interesting object, and a scolding. A few days later, he was observed to reach toward a package of cigarettes that a guest had left lying on the coffee table, but before he could touch the package, he slapped his own hand and said, "Bad boy!"

Most examples of social learning are not as obvious as this one, but it does permit a glimpse of the kind of cognitive and affective processes involved in learning to regard oneself as an object possessing certain qualities. The way in which others react to us provides us with cues as to how we should regard ourselves. As we pick up these cues and express our reactions to ourselves in certain ways, some of these modes of behavior are reinforced and others are not. The closer our self-appraisals are to the opinions of others, the greater possibility that our behavior will be reinforced, whereas behavior that is inconsistent with the opinions of others will not be reinforced and may even be punished. The reinforcement may not necessarily be apparent to the observer; it may be expressed in subtle ways. Let us say that Will Campbell, now aged five, has been given charge over his younger brother, and that both are in the station wagon waiting for mother, who has gone into the supermarket for a bit of hurried shopping before lunch. If mother returns and finds that Will is talking to his brother in a friendly way, she may say nothing at all, but if she returns and finds the brother crying—for whatever reason—she will speak to Will in an irritated tone. Will thus learns that his mother's good will toward him depends on how his brother is behaving when she returns after a brief absence. He may then take on some of the behavior he has seen his parents use and engage his brother in some kind of interesting activity as a way of keeping his behavior on a positive level and at the same time maintaining good relations with his mother. His mother may even add further reinforcement by praising him or patting him on the head or by expressing positive regard in other ways. Thus Will simultaneously learns perceptions relating to his position (older brother), appropriate roles (being responsible for the welfare of the younger brother), attitudes toward himself (responsible, a *good* older brother), and attitudes his mother is likely to have toward him (someone she can depend on, a *good* older son).

Distortions in Self-perception. What we have been describing so far in our discussions of the self and its development as an entity is what happens if everything goes along normally and no difficult problems develop. Yet everyone knows individuals whose conceptions of themselves differ rather widely from those of others—the person, for example, who has strong potentialities and yet who is continually derogating himself and who will not make the effort to develop them. Everyone tells him he has talent, yet he steadfastly refuses to believe that he does. It is not our intention here to propose any general kind of theory to account for such distortion in self-perception; there probably are factors that are unique to each individual's experience that lead him to misperceive himself. It is important to note, however, that people are rarely successful in convincing such a person that he does indeed have the degree of talent that everyone says he

has. Indeed the misperception seems to be impervious to any evidence that would contradict it.

What we are describing here is a situation in which people appear to be resistive to social learning and which apparently contradicts what we have said about the power of others in shaping our attitudes and beliefs about ourselves. There are two aspects of this situation that deserve special attention. One is that we have learned certain attitudes about ourselves (which may or may not be valid, although that is not the point), and now others are trying to get us to *un*learn these attitudes. The second aspect is the fact that others, in praising or criticizing us, are trying to influence us by telling us that we are wrong in our self-appraisal. This attitude that they know us better than we do is likely to arouse a degree of defensiveness on our part. It threatens our feeling of security and shakes our belief that we are our own masters and are fully cognizant of what we are or are not.

What is being threatened, therefore, is not so much an isolated belief as it is part of a much larger system of perceptions, a system that derives strength and endurance from the fact that all elements are interrelated and integrated. The person who believes he has no talent, for example, cannot change that percept unless he also changes a great deal of what he believes about himself and the world. This is no easy task, and most people are exceedingly reluctant to undertake it, even though by any objective criterion they might have much to gain.

The Phenomenal Self. Arthur W. Combs and Donald Snygg (1959) conceive of the self-concept as the center of a system of percepts that they call the "phenomenal environment"—the environment as it is perceived by the individual (see Figure 10-3). The portion of the phenomenal environment that is perceived as being related or somehow involved with the self they term the "phenomenal self." Within this area are to be found objects and events that the individual sees as somehow important to him. The use of the

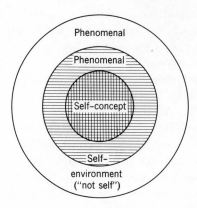

Figure **10-3.** A perceptual view of the self and its environment (Combs & Snygg, 1959).

modifier "my" may be considered as an indicator of what is included in the phenomenal self. "His car" or "cars in general" (as long as they can be perceived) may be within my phenomenal environment, but not within the boundaries of my phenomenal self. However, if I buy one of these cars, it becomes "my car" and becomes located somewhere within the phenomenal self. If the auto is a sports car, and I am a "hot engine" fancier, the chances are that it will lie closer to my self-concept than if it is a second-hand sedan that I use only to drive between home and work. But even a car in which there is little self-involvement can suddenly become psychologically very important. If I am standing near my office window and hear the crash of metal in collision, I may think only, "Some fool didn't watch where he was going." But when I go down stairs later to drive home and find that it was *my* car that was smashed, I suddenly feel very involved in the accident. I will probably think, feel, and act for the moment as though I myself had been hit. I will feel outraged, hostile, angry, and intent on securing punitive damages from the culprit. To any detached, objective observer, the car is definitely not me nor a part of me, yet I am acting as though it were a part of me. From a phenomenological point of view it is an extension of myself and hence may be considered as located within the boundaries of the phenomenal self.

If I behave in an outraged way because of the damage that my car has sustained, it is because I perceive that my phenomenal self is sustaining a "threat." Any event may become a threat, if the individual perceives it as bringing about some unwelcome change within his system of percepts —what might be called the "self-structure." Combs and Snygg state that the primary need of the organism is to enhance and maintain the phenomenal self. Anything that might interfere with our ability to enhance and maintain the phenomenal self is perceived as a threat. In the instance just cited, the damage to the car becomes a threat because someone has been able to damage an object with which the self is identified and has been able to escape with impunity. In the example of the individual who refuses to believe that he has any talent, the investment is in the *percept;* it is his way of perceiving himself that is being threatened, and he defends it by being rigid and dogmatic about evidence or opinions to the contrary.

The Self as a Source of Meaning. We organize our phenomenal worlds in ways that enable us to enhance and maintain our phenomenal selves. In other words, we sort things out, so to speak, in terms of whether they have a relationship to us and in terms of whether that relationship is positive, negative, or neutral. The resulting arrangement enables us to determine the degree to which we should concern ourselves with the events and objects we encounter and the kind of concern we should express.

Let us say that Lyle Morrow is very much interested in marine biology and wants to work for a Ph.D. in that field when he graduates. One day Lyle gets on a homeward-bound bus that is half full, and as he walks down the aisle, he notes that one of the passengers ahead of him is carrying a marine biology textbook. Lyle decides to sit down beside him and get acquainted.

Lyle had his choice of any number of empty

seats, yet he chose the one next to the person with the marine biology textbook. Why? A self-theory explanation would hold that Lyle's concept of himself as a marine biologist would be more enhanced by talking to another biologist than by sitting in just any seat.*

Our daily lives are full of instances in which we make choices, some of them major, but most of them minor, that have the purpose of strengthening and confirming our concepts of ourselves and the world as we see it. We perceive or do not perceive events in terms of whether they will enhance and maintain our phenomenal selves. We cannot perceive everything and hence tend to notice only those events that are somehow related to us, that is, have meaning for us. Structuring our environment in this way enables us to make predictions, to order our behavior, and to determine relationships between ourselves and past, present, or future events.

When the system we have created is put under stress—*threatened*, to use the term proposed by Combs and Snygg—we are likely to behave as though we personally are threatened. Charles Freed is a Democrat. This means that he not only tends to vote for candidates who are Democrats, but also identifies himself with the party: it lies to some extent within the boundaries of his phenomenal self. He also finds his identification with the party and its aims a convenient source of guidelines that can be used to order his thinking about social and political issues. We can understand, therefore, why he stalked out of the house in a rage when his father-in-law, Mr. Zack, said that he could not understand how any sensible person could have anything to do with a party that was being run by fools, cowards, and liars. After his wife and daughter scolded him for saying such a tactless thing, Mr. Zack tried unsuccess-

fully to smooth things over by saying that he didn't mean that Charles was any of those things —he was only referring to the candidates. But Charles remained angry and would not speak to his father-in-law for a month. In this instance, Charles felt threatened partly because his identity (his self-concept) was under attack, but also because his way of looking at things (as a Democrat) was attacked as well.

When the elections were held, most of the Republican candidates won. Mr. Zack, with rare self-restraint, refrained from expressing his jubilation. *His* phenomenal self had been enhanced by the event, whereas Charles' had been placed under additional stress. Charles felt depressed for some weeks. Not only did he feel personally defeated, but he wondered whether Democrats were really right after all. Up until the date of the election he had felt no need to change his way of looking at things, but now that the results showed conclusively that most people saw things the Republican way, Charles began to think that he should take a fresh look at the issues. When predictions turn out badly, we may question the system we have used for perceiving ourselves and our environment.

Field Independence and Dependence

Some people would say that if Charles changes his political affiliation from Democrat to Republican, as a result of his party's losing an election, he must be spineless, lacking in ego strength. Others would say that if he decides to change, it is because he is realistic and flexible, whereas a decision not to change would show that he is rigid and dogmatic. Either of these analyses might have a modicum of validity, but whether or not Charles changes parties is likely to be related to behavioral trends he has expressed in the past. Is he the kind of person who changes under pressure?

In Chapter 6 we explored some aspects of tendencies to yield to or resist social pressure in connection with authoritarian values and the need to achieve. All three of these variables were also

---

* Lyle's behavior could also be explained in terms of balance theory or attraction between persons possessing similar traits; however, this does not mean that the theories compete with one another, but rather that they represent somewhat different ways of looking at the same phenomenon.

found to have some relationship to social status. In this section we will examine behavior characterized by independence or dependence from another point of view: the extent to which people use themselves or their "field" as a basis for making judgments.

Tests of Field Dependence. The concept of field dependence as a factor in behavior was introduced largely through the work of H. A. Witkin and his associates (1954, 1962) at the State University College of Medicine in New York City. Witkin observed that people differed in the extent to which they used internal and external cues in making judgments about spatial relationships. In the rod-and-frame test (RFT), subjects were placed in a darkened room in which they could see only a rod suspended in a square frame located about six feet in front of them. Both rod and frame were tilted at angles that varied from the perpendicular. The subjects were then shown how to use controls to manipulate the rod and bring it to a true vertical position. The square, which could be manipulated only by the experimenter, was kept at an angle. The ordinary reaction is to use the square as a reference. We generally expect the sides of squares to be parallel or at right angles to the surface of the earth and seldom if ever have any occasion to use tilted squares as guides. Witkin found that some subjects were able to ignore the distraction of the tilted square and were able to bring the rod to a vertical position by relying on bodily cues, that is, they used their own upright position as a basis for determining when the rod was perpendicular. These people Witkin termed "field independent," inasmuch as they were able to make judgments independently of the field (in this case the tilted square) they were perceiving. Subjects at the other extreme tended to be greatly influenced by the tilted square and were less able to bring the rod to a true vertical position. These people he called "field dependent," because of their tendency to be influenced by the field as perceived by them.

Witkin measured the same tendencies through a variation of the RFT by tilting the chair in which the subject sat. In still another version, the body-adjustment test (BAT), he devised an instrument that would tilt *both* room *and* the subject's chair (see Figure 10-4). The subject's task in this situation was to operate controls to bring himself back to an upright position (the room remains tilted throughout the test). Field-dependent persons were of course more likely to be influenced by the position of the room and had greater difficulty in bringing themselves into a truly upright position. Another test used by Witkin and by other researchers in this area is the embedded-figures test (EFT), based on an earlier test by Kurt Gottschaldt (1926), which requires the subject to find a simpler figure within a larger complex figure. As in the other tests we have described, the field-dependent person tends to be more easily distracted by irrelevant details and is less able to perceive the figures he has been asked to find. Although the three types of tests tend to be positively correlated with one another, the EFT is the easiest to administer and is frequently used alone as a single estimate of field dependence.

Field Dependence as a Variable in Social Behavior. Witkin's work with field dependence would have little interest for social psychologists and students of personality unless it could be shown that being dependent on the physical field, rather than on oneself, was somehow related to rather generalized tendencies to base decisions on the dictates of the environment and not to use one's own experience as a guide. If people tend to be consistent, as we have maintained in this text, it may be predicted that those who use visual rather than kinesthetic cues in reporting their position in a tilted room would also tend to be more subject to social influences than would those able to maintain their independence of such distractions. Field-dependent persons, therefore, should resemble the yielders in the Asch experiments reported in Chapter 6.

Figure **10-4.** The tilted-room-tilted-chair test (Photography by David Linton).

The work of Witkin and his associates does indeed seem to point in that direction. They found that people scoring high in field dependence tended to show little initiative in challenging the status quo, were conventional in their attitudes and behavior, were submissive to authority, and liked to get into comfortable ruts. People scoring low on field dependence—that is, those who were field independent—were concerned about mastering the environment by striving to develop independence, leadership, special skills, and competencies. Unlike the field-dependent individuals, they were concerned with their inner life, with understanding motives for their own and others' behavior, and, when they had hostile feelings, were more inclined to express them with both directness and control. Field-dependent persons, however, tended to be pleasant and more likeable than those who were field independent, because the latter's resistance to being influenced was related to some degree of suspiciousness and ex-trapunitiveness—the tendency to blame or punish others for one's own difficulties.

The work of Witkin and his associates has been validated by other researchers, who have confirmed most of the group's findings. Persons scoring high in field dependence tend to be more readily influenced by the suggestions of a confederate of the experimenter in judging the movement of points of light in the autokinetic experiment (see pp. 95-96) (Linton, 1955); alcoholics score higher in field dependence than any psychiatric clinic group except patients with diffuse brain damage (Bailey, Hustmyer, & Kristofferson, 1959; Witkin, Karp, & Goodenough, 1959); and, contrary to expectations, persons scoring high in field dependence did not yield more in the Asch situation, but they did report that they were less sure of themselves in their judgments (Block, 1957). In a more recent study, Ludwig Immergluck (1966) found that field-dependent persons were more likely to be taken in by optical illusions, whereas field-independent persons were more likely to resist them.

Rogers Elliott (1961) also correlated the results of several measures of field dependence with scores on personality questionnaires and found that field dependence is characterized by tendencies to react in a confused fashion to situations marked by unusual degrees of novelty, incongruity, or lack of structure. This confusion tends to last until some system or order is imposed on the situation. Field-independent persons tend to find order within themselves, whereas field-dependent persons are unable to impose structure autonomously and must wait until it is suggested by someone or by the environment itself. Some of the differences between the behavior patterns of field-dependent and field-independent persons appear to be consistent with the ways in which they describe themselves. As Table 10-1 shows, field-dependent persons tend to stress socially desirable traits, whereas field-independent persons describe themselves as touchy, brooding, malcontent intellectuals. From the common-sense point of view, however, the latter would be expected to become unstable in the rod-and-frame or tilted-room situation; but instead these are the persons who are able to resist distraction and keep a firm grasp on reality. It is clear that we cannot count on a one-to-one relationship between self-reported personality characteristics and how people behave when faced by situations that require them to take some kind of action. Field-dependent persons probably do show self-insight when they report themselves to be more socially oriented. A number of studies show field-dependent individuals to be interested in others. One study reported that field-dependent subjects were better at identifying photographs of their acquaintances presented tachistoscopically (flashed on a screen for only a fraction of a second) than were field-independent subjects (Crutchfield, Woodworth, & Albrecht, 1958).

Field dependence and independence represent opposite ways of perceiving and reacting to the environment. As is the case with other behavior variables, the distribution is a normal one. Most people would score near the middle of the scale and would use both approaches in making decisions. The research that has just been reported, however, contrasts the behavior of individuals whose scores lie at one end or the other of the scale of field-dependent behavior. Although the research studies make use of extreme groups,

Table **10-1.** Perceptions of oneself found to be correlated with field dependence (Elliott, 1961)

Self-perceptions positively correlated with field dependence		Self-perceptions negatively correlated with field dependence[a]
Like being with others, sociable	vs.	Prefer solitary activities
Patient and reasonable with others	vs.	Impatient, demanding of others
Practical, commonsensical	vs.	Theoretical, intellectual
Conventional, proper	vs.	Unconventional, eccentric
Dependable, trustworthy	vs.	Irresponsible, forgetful
Quick, energetic	vs.	Slow in speech and movement
Ambitious	vs.	Lazy
Steady, even-tempered	vs.	Moody, temperamental
Seldom lose poise and composure in a social group	vs.	Easily confused and embarrassed except with close friends
Inclined to blame self when things go wrong	vs.	Inclined to blame others when things go wrong
Thorough, persevering	vs.	Undisciplined, distractible in work
Analytical, focused on points	vs.	Global, attend to wholes
Accept authority easily	vs.	Resistant to authority
Thoughtful, reflective, pensive	vs.	Active, matter-of-fact, unphilosophical
Friendly, attentive to others	vs.	Cool, aloof toward others
Bold, adventurous	vs.	Cautious, timid
Considerate, polite	vs.	Rude, insolent

[a] That is, correlated positively with field independence.

they do shed some light on how decision making is a function of personality structure and how the environment is perceived. Persons scoring toward the field-dependent end of the scale are more likely to regard the environment with a friendly, trusting eye. The boundaries between the phenomenal self and the not-self area of the phenomenal environment are weaker, more permeable, and less stable than they are for people who score toward the field-independent end of the scale. The latter are more inclined to be resistive and suspicious of their surroundings. People at both ends of the scale use their perceptions of the environment as cues for responses, but the field-independent persons are somewhat more likely to look at the cues with a skeptical eye and to use them as a basis for doing something else, whereas field-dependent persons are more inclined to accept them literally and uncritically.

Social Dependence and Independence

The work with field-dependent and field-independent people suggests that there is some relationship between field dependence and generalized tendencies to be dependent in a range of situations. Behavior, as we noted previously, tends to be consistent, and attitudes that lead to behavior characterized by dependency are likely to facilitate the learning of still other attitudes and forms of behavior.

Social Dependence and Social Learning. There is some evidence that people whose behavioral ratings place them at extremes of the dependent-independent continuum have different styles of social learning and that this difference manifests itself at a very early age. Dorothea Ross (1966) taught two groups of twenty-six nursery-school children to run a play post office. The groups had been selected out of 101 children in the school on the basis of the amount of dependent behavior they displayed, that is, on the extent to which the children asked for help in doing things, sought reassurance from adults, stayed close to adults, and displayed attention-getting behavior. The two

groups represented those children who showed the most and the fewest dependency symptoms. As the experimenter showed the children how to run the post office, she engaged in two kinds of behaviors. One set was relevant to operating the office (collecting money and giving change, stamping letters and mailing them in the proper slot, and the like), and the other set was irrelevant and nonfunctional (taking an indirect route to the mailbox, putting one foot on the chair while telephoning, and the like). Children who had been rated low in dependency learned more of the behavior relevant to running the post office, and the high-dependent children learned more of the irrelevant ones. Ross explained the difference in terms of the greater stress placed by parents of the less dependent children on achievement. The latter children were definitely more "task oriented." They paid close attention to the behaviors displayed by the model that were relevant to the job of running the post office, and tended to ignore the irrelevant ones. The high-dependent children, on the other hand, gave equal attention to all the model's behaviors. In actuality, the high-dependent children learned more than the low-dependent ones, for they learned both relevant and irrelevant behaviors. For such children, the fact that an authority figure was showing them something was the important thing, whereas for the low-dependent children the important thing was understanding the task and doing it correctly.

Dependence, Conformity, and Effectiveness. For a number of years psychologists at the Institute of Personality Assessment and Research at the University of California in Berkeley have been studying various components of personality, with special attention to conformity and independence. In one report of the research that has been thus far conducted, Donald W. MacKinnon (1962) compared the behavior of more successful and creative architects with less successful and less creative. Scores obtained on a number of different measures produced results that are consistent with much of the research on field dependence. For example, more creative architects were inclined to describe themselves as independent, individualistic, determined, industrious, and enthusiastic, whereas less creative architects described themselves as responsible, sincere, tolerant, reliable, dependable, and understanding. In other words, the less creative architects revealed a self-image more like that of the field-dependent persons, whereas the more creative architects seemed less concerned with social skills and personal attributes and stressed their independence and their preoccupation with their work—characteristics that would be more consistent with the field-independent person.

Similar findings resulted when Leonard V. Gordon (1966) compared scores made by samples taken from a general college population and those made by Peace Corps volunteers. His results, which are briefly reported in Table 10-2, show that most college students, when contrasted

Table **10-2.** Scales of the Survey of Interpersonal Values and Survey of Personal Values that discriminated between college students in general and Peace Corps volunteers (Gordon, 1966)

College students in general placed greater value on:	Peace Corps volunteers placed greater value on:
Support: being treated with kindness and understanding	Benevolence: doing things for other people
Conformity: conforming to rules and social conventions	Decisiveness: being definite and decisive
Recognition: being thought of as important	Leadership: being in a position of leadership or authority (women only)
Orderliness: being orderly and neat	Variety: having new and varied experiences
Economic Gain: economic or material gain	Achievement: accomplishing something important
	Independence: being free to do what one wants to do (women only)

with Peace Corpsmen, appear to be more concerned with achieving pleasant relations with others and with avoiding situations that might produce problems. They are also more inclined to look to their environment as a source of direction and support than are the Peace Corpsmen. Peace Corpsmen, on the other hand, are more interested in finding opportunities to challenge the environment and to change it. They appear to be more interested in confronting and solving problems. In short, the typical Peace Corps volunteer appears to be more independent than the average college student.

It may be worthwhile to utter a warning at this point with respect to the interpretation of research findings on conformity, dependence, and authoritarianism. It is easy to fall into the trap of assuming that independence is a totally "good thing" and that it consists mainly of defying and resisting authority, authority figures, and rules and regulations in general. In actuality, people who score high on independence, creativity, effectiveness, and task orientation do not necessarily have negative feelings about authority figures or regulations. As the research we have cited suggests, they are quite capable of learning from authority figures, but concentrate on the material related to the task at hand. Authority figures who insist on behavior irrelevant to the main task, however, quite naturally evoke feelings of irritation in independent people. The same holds true with rules and regulations: if they are functional and related to the task, task-oriented and independent people are likely to accept them. If they are not, they will find ways of circumventing them or, if there is no escape, are likely to accept them more or less philosophically.

It is important, however, to distinguish between the independent, task-oriented, and creative person and the one whose gestures of independence and defiance become an end in themselves. For such people, nonconformity becomes more important than "getting the job done."

Robert J. Smith (1967) conducted a study

showing that rebels and conformers differ from truly independent people and that both actually resemble each other. Smith devised a questionnaire to measure nonconformity and administered it to 162 male college students. Those who scored high on the test he termed the "rebels," because their responses indicated that they could be depended on to take an "anti" position on a wide range of socially approved types of behavior. Those who scored low, he called the "conformers," because they showed a readiness to accept socially approved behavior in a routine and unquestioning fashion. The middle-range scorers became the "independents," because they showed themselves as ambivalent about sociocultural norms: some were accepted and others not, but in any case, they neither categorically accepted nor rejected the norms merely because most people accepted them. The three groups were then studied as to their scores on other psychological measures. The independents scored significantly higher than both the rebels and the conformers on scales measuring positive self-regard, ego strength, or self-acceptance. They also scored higher than the other two groups on a scale measuring social responsibility and freedom from impulsiveness and self-centeredness. On both of these scales the rebels scored lower than the conformers, but the difference was not significant. In other words, rebels and conformers, as measured by these scales, were more like each other than they were like the independents. On a scale measuring the ability to make constructive use of conforming behavior to achieve and to accomplish desired goals, the independents scored higher than the other two groups, but the difference between them and the conformers was not significant.

Further differences appeared among the three groups when they played a two-person non-zero-sum game for cash rewards. In this game players find themselves tempted to make competitive responses aimed at exploiting or punishing their opponents. Such responses, however, make them vulnerable to attack and result in their losing more in the long run. Cooperative choices, on the other hand, are likely to result in higher mutual gains. The game, in other words, provides temptation to make unwise competitive moves but rewards the less tempting but wiser attempts to cooperate. Smith predicted that the conformers would be most cooperative and that the rebels would be least cooperative. However, results showed that it was the independents who played the game most successfully, whereas rebels, as predicted, made the poorest score. Rebels earned 57 cents on the average; conformists, 69 cents; and independents, 89 cents. Smith's research thus appears to confirm the everyday observation that the rewards in this life go primarily to the independents, with the conformers and the rebels following behind, in that order.

SUMMARY

As we play the more significant roles in our lives, we learn ways of perceiving ourselves and our environment. These perceptual styles tend to become rather stable and persisting aspects of our personality. The roles that we learn also identify and define "who we are" and constitute a major dimension of our personality.

The term "personality" refers to the relatively enduring and consistent aspects of our behavior that cause us to resemble others in some ways and to be unique in others. One aspect is stimulus value, which is close to the layman's concept of personality. Personality as conceived by the psychologist also includes the concepts of character and temperament. Although some aspects of personality, particularly those included under the heading of temperament, may be biologically determined, personality is for the most part composed of learned patterns of behavior.

Birth-order studies show how expectations, roles, values, and attitudes characteristic of certain positions lead to recognizable personality trends. Successful people, as indicated by listings in *American men of science* and *Who's who*, are more likely to have been first-born than later-born in their families. First-born individuals are also more likely to attend college, to make top scores on college entrance tests, to be socially accepted by their peers, score high in n Ach, and receive top marks in college. Some of their success is explained in terms of their generally good relations with authority figures. First-borns also are more likely to have played supervisory roles as parent substitutes for their younger siblings during childhood. Although the differences between first-born and later-born individuals are slight, they do tend to be consistent, and are explicable in terms of the different patterns of expectations and roles experienced during childhood.

The self-concept—attitudes toward and conceptions about one's self—is an important source of motivation. The self is the result of one's interactions with others and can be perceived only in terms of others' percepts of oneself. The self may be described as an element in a field of social forces, a concept developed by Lewin. Some of Lewin's ideas appear in theories developed by Rogers and by Snygg and Combs. The self in social psychology also includes psychoanalytic concepts of ego and the ego ideal. Although some psychologists believe that a gap between the self as perceived by the individual and his ideal self leads to poor mental health, some research shows that the gap between the perceived and the ideal self normally increases during adolescence and is greater in more intelligent children. There appears to be a positive relationship between the esteem others have for one and the esteem one has for oneself. Both realistic and unrealistic attitudes toward the self are learned in early childhood.

According to Combs and Snygg, portions of the phenomenal or perceived environment may be differentiated as the phenomenal self—those aspects of the environment in which the individual is involved. A portion of the phenomenal self is further differentiated as the self-concept. The self-concept of each individual therefore lies at the center of the phenomenal environment. We perceive and structure the phenomenal environment in ways that enable us to enhance and maintain the phenomenal self. When the structure we have created is put under stress (threatened) we are likely to behave as though we ourselves are threatened.

Personality may also be perceived in terms of the extent to which the individual depends on his external environment or his personal experiences. People whose judgments tend to be based primarily on cues in their external environment are termed "field-dependent," in contrast to field-independent people, whose judgments tend to be based on data from largely internal sources. One of a series of tests developed by Witkin requires the subject in a darkened room to operate a device bringing a rod to a vertical position within a luminous, tilted frame. Field-dependent individuals, in contrast with field-independent individuals, tend to show little initiative in challenging the status quo, to be conforming and submissive, and to be confused when faced by novel situations.

Children scoring high on social dependence tend to be less task oriented than those scoring low. Tests administered to architects show that the more successful ones tended to be more independent and less conforming in a number of ways than less successful ones were. A study comparing individuals characterized as independent, conforming, or rebellious, showed that the rebels were least accepting of social norms and the conformers were most accepting, with the independents occupying a medial position. When the subjects played a game calling for cooperation, the independents showed themselves most able to cooperate, and the rebels, least able.

SUGGESTED READINGS

Berg, I. A. & Bass, B. M. (Eds.), *Conformity and deviation.* New York: Harper, 1961.

Combs, A. H. & Snygg, D., *Individual behavior* (rev. ed.). New York: Harper, 1959.

Diggory, J C., *Self-evaluation: concepts and studies.* New York: Wiley, 1966.

Freud, A., *The ego and the mechanisms of defense.* New York: International Universities Press, 1946.

Lindgren, H. C. (Ed.), *Contemporary research in social psychology.* New York: Wiley, 1969. See papers by Katz & Ziegler, McDonald & Gynther, and Altus in Section 7.

MacKinnon, D. W., The nature and nurture of creative talent. *American psychologist,* 1962, **17**, 484-495.

McDonald, R. L. & Gynther, M. D., Relationship of self and ideal-self descriptions with sex, race, and class in Southern adolescents. *Journal of personality and social psychology,* 1965, **1**, 85-88.

Miyamoto, S. F. & Dornbusch, S. M., A test of interactionist hypotheses of self-conception. *American journal of sociology,* 1956, **61**, 399-403.

Palmer, R. D., Birth order and identification. *Journal of consulting psychology,* 1966, **30**, 129-135.

Witkin, H. A., et al., *Psychological differentiation.* New York: Wiley, 1962.

Worchel, P. & Byrne, D. (Eds.), *Personality change.* New York: Wiley, 1964.

CHAPTER ELEVEN

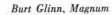

Society, Culture, and Personality

In Chapter 10 we presented some examples of how interpersonal experiences influence perceptual styles and self-regarding attitudes, which in turn influence social behavior—the interaction, in other words, between personality and the interpersonal environment. In the present chapter, we continue to give our attention to the interpersonal environment, but shall view it as part of a broader context: the culture.

A fish is not aware that he is in water, nor are we generally aware that we live in a culture. David French (1963), the anthropologist, notes that it is easy for us to "forget" our culture, even after we have become intellectually convinced that we have one. Our culture becomes for us "the way people do things," and it ordinarily comes as a shock when we step into another culture and find that people do things differently.

Culture consists of the overriding systems of values, beliefs, norms, artifacts, and symbols that have been developed by a society and are shared by its members. Each society develops ways of coping with its environment and making sense out of it. These approaches tend to become systematized and are transmitted to the following generations. Where environments are relatively stable, cultures may persist over long periods of time with relatively little change, but marked changes in the environment lead to changes in the cultures. When a plains society is forced to move to the high mountains, many of its practices are no longer appropriate and must be altered. If a hostile tribe settles nearby, the culture must adapt itself to that fact as well, if the society is to survive. Changes are also produced by the members themselves; just as cultural norms are strengthened when members conform, they are also weakened if enough members develop other patterns of behavior. There is therefore a constant interaction between members of a society and the culture they have inherited and transmit to their children.

Cultures function to reduce variability in the environment and make it more predictable and manageable. The effect of variations in the weather, for example, is reduced by clothing, housing, covered and insulated transportation, air conditioning, and central heating. The systems of artifacts thus developed become in turn part of the environment with which the society must cope.

The behavior patterns produced by a society also serve to reduce variations in human behavior. Social norms limit the way in which a society's members may express themselves and interact with one another, but the compensating reward for this loss of freedom is the ability to predict, anticipate, and cope with the behavior of others. These limitations are not restrictive in any complete or absolute sense, for every culture permits some areas of freedom for individual variation. It may prescribe religious rituals that must be very strictly adhered to, even to the point that any deviation requires that the ritual be started over again. But at the same time it may allow considerable freedom in the way in which social equals may interact with one another in informal situations. As a very general rule, the least variation in individual behavior is permitted by primitive cultures and the widest variation by industrialized and urbanized cultures. But even in the latter instances, variation is sufficiently restricted to the point that cultural differences can be recognized almost at a glance. We look at the way a gift is wrapped and say, "The Japanese do these things so well, don't they?" Or we are introduced to a stranger, listen to him talk for a minute, and then ask, "Aren't you from Texas?"

The restrictions or norms imposed by a society's culture are seldom viewed as objectionable by its members. As we noted earlier, they become so natural, so much a part of us, that we are oblivious of their existence, and it is only when we encounter others who behave according to a different set of norms that we are conscious of such a thing as "culture."

Such encounters can be disturbing or unsettling, or interesting and exciting, depending on the orientation of the individual. However, they can also serve as the basis for understanding the operation of forces that determine not only social behavior in different societies, but social behavior in general. As Muzafer Sherif (1963) notes, cross-cultural comparisons are necessary in the development of general laws and principles in social psychology.

Social Learning during the Early Developmental Years

Alex Inkeles (1963), a sociologist in the Department of Human Relations at Harvard, writes as follows about the role of cultural learning:

"Implicit in the idea that the members of a society share a system of action is the assumption that they have *learned* the appropriate responses to the cues given by others. The adults in a society are the end products of a long process of prior conditioning. They are thus equipped with a large repertory of standardized responses to meet the situations their sociocultural system will present. Societies experience a continuous turnover in personnel while maintaining relative stability in culture and social structure. The key to this continuity lies, in large measure, in the fact that successive generations learn their culture in all its complexity. They must also acquire a predisposition to accept, and an ability to act in accord with, the requirements of that part of the culture embedded in laws, art patterns, and a host of institutions. The key to this learning lies in the forms and content of childhood and later training."

Development during Infancy. Each individual represents, through his behavior, the culture into which he was born. As soon as the neonate (the newborn infant) makes its appearance, it begins to interact with its parents' culture. In effect, the culture immediately goes into action to give the neonate the treatment and the place or position reserved for it. Neonates have many things in common, irrespective of the culture into which they are born; they are helpless, they spend a great deal of time sleeping, they require a liquid diet, and so forth; but in spite of these basic similarities, each cultural group has a rather well-developed set of concepts about how infants should be treated and what can be expected of them. Infants in some Polish villages are tightly wrapped in swaddling clothes, because otherwise they might "thrash around and hurt themselves." In some cultures, the neonate becomes the center of attention and admiration; in others, he is relegated to the background and ignored.

The interaction between mother and infant is higher during the first few months of his life than it is at any other stage in his development, largely, of course, because he needs more attention during this period. Although there are great individual variations in the ways mothers in the same cultural context treat their infants, there are also some basic trends that are characteristic of certain cultures. Take the matter of soiling. All infants soil their clothing through urination and defecation and must be cleaned. The mother's reaction to the chore of cleaning provides her with opportunities to interact with the infant and transmit feelings and attitudes. Although filth has a high "nuisance value" in most cultures, some mothers will make little fuss over the cleaning, while others will act annoyed. Mothers in some cultures go about the task of cleaning the infant in a matter-of-fact manner, without comment. Some do it in a business-like manner, even brusquely or roughly. It is characteristic of mothers in other cultures to chide, "Oh you naughty boy, look what you've done to your nice clean clothes," and the like. Still other mothers look upon the task as an additional opportunity to interact with the infant, to fondle him, and to croon little phrases of love and affection.

It is impossible to say at what point the infant begins to grasp the essentials of his mother's attitude toward soiling. Very possibly he will get the message long before he is able to put it into words. But what is more important for his development as a person and as a member of a cultural group is that this soiling-and-cleaning sequence of behavior is one of several channels of interaction between him and the culture. The mother's behavior toward the child during this sequence gives her a chance to tell him who he is and what is expected of him, or, perhaps more precisely, what *will* be expected of him. And the more consistent her generalized attitudes and treatment, the clearer the message will be and the more readily he will grasp it when he has reached the stage of development in which he can become aware of who he is and how he feels about himself.

Contrast the attitudes of Rajput mothers in northern India, who believe that the future physique, temperament, and personal characteristics of infants are determined at birth by fate, with those of middle-class New England mothers, who believe that each infant represents a "bundle of potentialities," and that the kind of individual he becomes depends on the way in which parents, teachers, and peers mold these potentialities. It is hardly surprising that Rajput mothers take a rather passive attitude toward child rearing. After all, what difference does it make what mothers do, if what the child will become was determined at birth? New England mothers, on the other hand, work actively at the task of child rearing, reading books, consulting experts, and showing considerable anxiety in their attempt to do the "right things" in developing the child's potentialities to the utmost (Whiting & Whiting, 1960).

Later Influences during Childhood. The word "infant" means, literally, "a nontalking being," and it is the child's development of the ability to communicate that marks his emergence from infanthood into active participation with other members of the society into which he was born. When the child is able to talk, parents and other representatives of the culture go to work in earnest at the task of molding his behavior, values, attitudes, beliefs, and, inevitably, his personality.

The way in which middle-class children in America are taught self-reliance is one example. They are told:

"Smile and the world smiles with you,
Cry and you cry alone."

Not all middle-class Americans learn to be self-reliant, of course, but everyone is aware of it as an ideal and values himself and his behavior in accordance with the extent to which he has achieved this ideal. In traditional China, a man who became economically dependent on his adult children not only accepted this status, but boasted of it, telling everyone what good and dutiful children he had. An American parent in the same situation is likely to be ashamed of his dependency, to resent any reference to it, and to seek to reestablish his independence at the first possible opportunity (Hsu, 1961).

Self-sufficiency and independence are taught American children as much by the kind and quality of their parents' behavior toward them, as by what they are told. One of the best ways to observe this interaction is to watch children playing in a park. American children are generally granted a great deal of freedom when it comes to interacting with other children, getting dirty, running and shouting, and so forth. This permissiveness is consistent with the idea, expressed earlier, that children's potentialities must be developed. In other words, freedom to run, interact with others, and get dirty enable a child to find ways of developing his own potentialities. American parents also believe that such freedom enables children to learn how to cope with things, make their own decisions, solve their own problems, take responsibility for their own actions, and the like. American children are, generally speaking, expected to learn how to deal with their physical and social environment without the aid or intervention of adults, providing, of course, that the tasks are commensurate with their ability and that other tabus of the culture (such as harassing smaller children, expropriating the property of others, or being destructive) are not violated.

But French parents and their children behave quite differently. Maria Wolfenstein (1955) made a number of observations in Paris parks and noted that many children sit for long periods very quietly beside their parents and do not seem to need to run about as American children do. Children who shout are reproved by their parents. Although they are allowed to play in the sand, they are admonished not to get dirty. In fact, many children are brought to the parks in very elegant and unwashable clothes. A child playing in the sand very typically squats at his mother's feet, his bottom an inch off the ground but never touching. His hands but nothing else may get dirty, and he may frequently turn to his mother to have her wipe off his hands. Mothers and grandparents frequently express concern lest a given activity might prove to be too strenuous. A six-year-old boy was playing catch with an older brother. His return throws were a little wild, and he was told after every throw *"Doucement! Doucement!"* (Not so hard!), even though there was no danger of his hitting any bystanders. As children approach one another, the respective parents eye them mistrustfully, anticipating trouble. A mother called to her five-year-old son, who was going toward a three-year-old, *"Laisse le petit garçon!"* (Leave him alone!) It turned out that the older boy only wanted to play with the younger one, but his mother's anxious admonition indicated that she feared otherwise.

What parents are doing when they admonish, direct, encourage, or otherwise attempt to mold the behavior of their children is to project a constellation of images of how people should behave and what one should expect of others and of the world. The French child who is ordered not to go closer to the smaller boy is being told that it is best to stay away from unknown persons because there may be trouble, that is, the older boy may inadvertently injure the smaller boy, or the parents of the smaller child might object. Furthermore, the mother is presenting herself as someone who "knows best" and who should be consulted at every turn. When the French children observed by Wolfenstein encountered interference from other children, they turned to their mothers for help and protection. American children, on the contrary, are usually expected to take care of their own interpersonal difficulties, and not to come running to their mothers. Turning to authority figures for help is, according to the American view, something that is done only as a last resort and is taken as evidence that one has failed.

There are other qualities that appear in the interaction of these two groups of parents with their children. The American parents appear to be telling their children that people ought to be energetic and adventurous in their approach to life, that activity and restlessness are not only permissible, but quite normal, and perhaps even desirable. One's place in the world depends in part on what he has been able to affirm, maintain, and defend. Although the American child's future may be ambiguous and to some extent unpredictable, it can nevertheless be shaped by the energetic, adventurous person who is willing to meet problems head on. French parents, on the other hand, are saying that the world has dangers but is in charge of powerful, omniscient individuals, who have imposed a certain structure. Children should accept and respect this structure and not try to change it. Furthermore, if one behaves impulsively and heedlessly, persons in authority will take him in hand and will reprimand him for behaving in such an asocial manner.

There is a general feeling on the part of French parents that American children are *mal élevés*— badly brought up. According to European standards, American children are much too spontaneous, outspoken, and defiant of authority. European parents are inclined to believe that this behavior results from the fact that American parents subscribe to erroneous ideas about the effects of repression and discipline. What they overlook, of course, is that spontaneity, independence in judgment, and lack of reverence for authority are characteristic of the American value structure in general. This is demonstrated by the fact that American adolescents overseas regard European young people as overly inhibited, tattlers and talebearers, and tied to their mothers' apron strings. Accepting this judgment as a fact, without regard to differences in culture, is as erroneous as accusing American children of being *mal élevés* (Elkind, 1967).

The attitudes of French parents are but a reflection and an extension of a more generalized set of values that apply to all dimensions of French life. An examination of French business practices shows that there is much more concern with maintaining the status quo than there is in the American business world. The managers and directors of the typical American business are more concerned with increasing sales and efficiency and extending the field of their operations than are their opposite numbers in France. Indeed much of the current hostility expressed toward America by French businessmen and government officials is a direct or indirect result of the more or less successful invasion of the French economy by American business firms. Although the participation of Americans in the economic life of France has undoubtedly produced benefits and helped increase the per capita income of France, their presence is deeply resented. Every time an American firm buys into a French firm, there is consternation and at times even a degree of panic. The feeling is widespread that Americans do not *belong* in France, that they are poaching on private preserves and that their aggressiveness and venturesomeness are not in good taste. The point is that there is a relationship between the attitudes French people express in their child rearing and those that they express in their business behavior. Such attitudes and the consistency and the firmness with which they are expressed help give the French culture the qualities that make it uniquely French. There is also a corresponding degree of consistency in the attitudes that Americans express in *their* child rearing and business behavior. Furthermore, members of the two groups are in both instances quite sure that they are expressing and responding to the "way people are" (human nature) and the "way the world is" (reality).

Differences in Cultural Style

Independence and Individuality. Although French children are, according to American standards, suppressed, dominated, and bullied by their parents, they nevertheless turn out to be adults who have a well-earned reputation for being highly independent. Indeed, the inability of the French people to agree on government policy produced a marked instability in their national government during the decades before General de Gaulle came to power. There is also some psychological evidence that this reputation for stubborn independence has some basis in fact. Stanley Milgram (1961) conducted an experiment using a variant of the Asch situation, described in Chapter 6, in which subjects were made to believe that a majority of the in group supported an obviously incorrect judgment. In one of Milgram's experiments, French students sat in booths and listened to tones through earphones. They then heard what they thought were other subjects expressing judgments about the tones, whereupon they expressed their own judgment. In reality, what they heard were pretaped judgments made by the experimenter's confederates who had been coached to give the incorrect response on sixteen out of thirty trials. Similar experiments were conducted with Norwegian students.

Confirmation of the French reputation for independence was demonstrated when the Norwegian students proved to be more willing to agree with the false reports. When students were told that the study was very important, because results would be used in research dealing with aircraft safety, the amount of conformity to false norms dropped a little for both groups of students, but French students still conformed less than the Norwegians. The least amount of conformity to false norms was obtained when students were permitted to record their judgments privately, rather than announcing them aloud, while the greatest amount of conformity resulted when students heard criticism and abuse —"*Voulez-vous vous faire remarquer?*" or "*Skal du stikke deg ut?*" (Are you trying to show off?) —whenever their judgments differed from the false norm. In a final series of trials, students were permitted to press a bell to indicate that they wished to hear a pair of tones a second time. No comment was made when they asked for a replay of the tones, but they were criticized when they differed from the others. Under these conditions, Norwegians felt a little reassured, but

there was no difference on the part of the French students. Fourteen of the twenty French subjects asked for a replay of tones, whereas only five of the Norwegians did so.

The results, as depicted in Figure 11-1, show the variations in conformity under the various experimental conditions and also demonstrate the consistency with which French students resisted conformity. No matter how the data are analyzed, they point to the greater independence on the part of French students. Twelve per cent of the Norwegian students conformed to the false norms on all sixteen of the critical trials, as contrasted with only 1 per cent of the French. Forty-one per cent of the French students never yielded to the false norm, whereas only 25 per cent of the Norwegians were nonyielders.

One of the explanations for the difference in behavior between French and Norwegian students lies in the fact that the members of each national group tend to perceive and react to a given situation in a different fashion. Not only are Norwegians inclined to depend more on the judgment of others for the way in which they

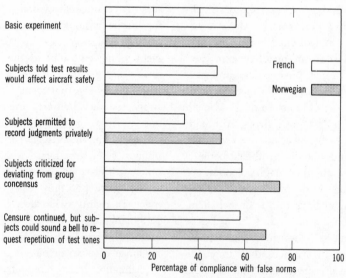

Figure 11-1. Differences in compliances on the part of French and Norwegian students under social pressure (Milgram, 1961).

judge reality, but they also appear to regard the judgment and approval of others in a more positive way. What cultures provide, therefore, is a particular way of looking at reality and the environment. It might even be said that the *meaning* of reality and experience differs from one culture to another. As one examines the behavior of individuals representing various cultures, these differences in perception or meaning occur repeatedly.

Discontinuities between Childhood Learning and Adult Behavior. One of the puzzling things about interpreting crosscultural data is that pieces which ought to fit together often do not appear to do so. The differences between the dependence and conformity learned by French children and their apparent independence and nonconformity when they become adults is a case in point. In this instance, however, the contradictions are more apparent than real.

In the first place, it is usual for cultures to have one set of norms for children and another set for adults. Although these two sets generally have much in common, they may have elements that are actually antithetical. It is also quite usual for children to be subjected to a great deal more restriction than adults. Adults are, after all, full-fledged members of the culture, and children are not. Hence if adults are permitted great latitude of freedom and independence by their culture, it does not necessarily follow that children will be allowed the same. Nor does it necessarily follow that children who have learned to be dependent cannot learn to be independent when they take on the roles of adulthood.

There is, however, a consistent thread that runs through both childhood and adulthood in France. French children learn to look to authority figures for cues as to how they should behave, and this tendency, albeit somewhat modified, persists in adolescence and adulthood. There is less of a tendency for French children and adults to pick up behavioral cues from their peers. Where norms are not specified by culture and

tradition, or persons in authority, the French individual may have a great deal of latitude to follow his personal inclinations. The kinds of stimulus situations presented by Milgram in his experiment may be considered examples of areas in which there are no guidelines. In such ambiguous situations, Norwegians, like Americans, evidently are more inclined to look to their peer group for indications of what to do.

The pattern of restriction and dependency in childhood, coupled with one of independence in adulthood, is one that rather generally characterizes Mediterranean cultures. Luigi Volpicelli,* Director of the Pedagogical Institute of the University of Rome, has pointed out that Italian teachers expect absolute conformity from their students. Each pupil has a notebook in which he writes his lessons; if the children's notebooks are exact replicas of one another, the teacher is considered to be doing a good job. According to Volpicelli, these rigidly conforming Italian children grow up to be adults who attempt to outdo one another in nonconformity and individuality. This individuality is more noticeable in some situations than in others: sitting behind the wheel of an automobile is said to bring it out in full force.

Cultural Differences in Perceptions of Interpersonal Events. Culturally determined perceptual styles learned in childhood are persistent and often resist attempts at change through training. The tendency to blame others for one's problems appears in all societies to some extent, but it is particularly marked in Mediterranean cultures. It is part of the training of psychiatrists to recognize such blame-avoidance as an underlying source of pathology in their patients and to treat it accordingly.

James C. Skinner (1966), an American psychiatrist who spent some time in Greece studying psychiatric education, reports that Greek psychiatrists, even those who had been trained abroad,

---

* Personal communication to the author.

seemed to be unable to perceive blame-avoidance as pathological. For example, when Greek patients told their psychiatrist that they did not feel responsible for interpersonal and other problems they were experiencing, an attitude that is typical among Greek men, he tended to accept it uncritically, even though his training had stressed the point that such problems could not be resolved until patients accepted some measure of personal responsibility. Both the psychiatrist and his patients believed it essential that the burden of personal guilt and responsibility must somehow be placed elsewhere.

This tendency to externalize problems, events, and impressions that in other cultures would be regarded as at least partly internal, seems to be an abiding Greek characteristic. In that connection, Skinner notes a general tendency for Greeks to think of interpersonal relations in grossly oversimplified ways. For example, any difficulty that arises in carrying out a plan or an activity is usually suspected to be the result of deliberate and conscious sabotage or interference on the part of some person.

Greeks also tend to externalize events that people in other cultures would consider essentially internal in nature. An example is the typical Greek reaction to dreams. Whereas most Europeans and Americans are likely to recognize that dreams are the result of inner tensions, unresolved problems, unfulfilled wishes and longings, and the like, Skinner states that Greeks tend to regard dreams as visitations by external beings. Greeks have a word to express the concept of "dreaming," but they prefer to talk about "seeing" a dream. This cultural tendency apparently has a long history. The ancient Greeks wrote of seeing dreams in which gods or their messengers appeared at bedside. Consistent with the exclusion of the dream from one's inner experience or responsibility is the tendency to regard the dream as a statement about the outside world or about external events that will shortly have some influence on the life of the dreamer.

Perceiving the Everyday World. Wayne Dennis (1957) is the author of another comparative study that reflects differences in the way in which American and Middle East children regard everyday objects. Dennis asked American, Lebanese, and Sudanese children to tell him "What is ——— for?" Some of Dennis' findings are reported in Table 11-1. The answers to this simple question not only showed differences in cultural attitudes, but also pointed to major differences in attitudes and values in the culture. Although children in all three cultural contexts tended to regard the *mouth* primarily as useful in eating, American children were more likely to mention its use in talking. This difference may reflect parental attitudes toward the participation of children in discussions. Traditional mores specify that "Children should be seen and not heard." Inasmuch as Lebanese customs are more traditional than American, and Sudanese are more traditional than Lebanese, it is not too surprising that these differences in traditionalism should be reflected in children's beliefs that the mouth is for talking. The appearance of "drinking" in the Sudanese replies was attributed by Dennis to the fact that the hot climate requires greater consumption of water. The use of *hands* also reflects local customs and the degree to which a culture has been Westernized. In the Sudan, eating without the use of cutlery is more common than it is in Lebanon, where, in turn, it is more common than it is in the United States. Reactions to *father* and *mother* reflect differences in roles, Westernization, and perceptions. Note that the response "nursing" to *mother* only appears among the Sudanese.

Boy and *girl* also evoke differential reactions. Girls are more likely to be perceived as "working, helping parents," and this type of response is also more common in the Middle East. "Playing" is a response that seems to be characteristically American. Children in all cultures play, but the American childhood years are more play centered than most. Play is seen by Americans as

Table 11-1. Differences in replies from American, Lebanese, and Sudanese children to the question: "What is —— for?" (Dennis, 1957)

Stimulus words and use-categories	Percentage of response frequencies		
	American	Lebanese	Sudanese
Mouth			
eating	61	74	71
talking	39	22	14
drinking	0	0	7
Hands			
eating	6	23	33
writing	11	10	16
working	12	12	12
playing	4	1	0
Mother			
providing food	16	51	7
providing care	62	44	41
nursing	0	0	19
Father			
working, earning money	55	76	10
buying food	1	16	7
providing care	12	6	16
assisting family	14	3	29
Boy			
going to school	16	37	7
working, helping parents	23	24	17
future reference	11	20	12
playing	34	9	0
Girl			
going to school	12	33	9
working, helping parents	28	45	34
future reference	12	11	0
playing	27	5	0
Dogs			
guarding, watching	16	66	62
barking, biting	9	19	0
hunting	4	8	7
pets, playing	49	4	3
Cats			
catching mice	16	63	53
meowing	6	13	2
pets, playing	52	6	7
Gold			
decorative	16	53	67
economic	61	26	2

very important for the proper development of children, and the child who does not or cannot play is viewed with some concern. *Dogs* and *cats* also figure in this play orientation. In America, they are included in many households to facilitate play experiences, whereas the Middle East household is more likely to include them for utilitarian purposes.

Gold also evokes a differential response, and one that is contrary to expectations based on common sense. One would expect that people in Lebanon and the Sudan, being less affluent than Americans, would be less likely to possess gold jewelry, yet the opposite is true. Most American women, even affluent ones, wear gold-colored "costume jewelry," whereas women in the Mediterranean area, irrespective of their economic level, would feel humiliated at having to wear any jewelry that was an imitation of gold. There is, of course, an economic aspect to this, in that gold jewelry can be pawned and hence has a degree of built-in economic security. But even more important is the feeling that the wearing of imitation gold means that one's husband is cheap, unappreciative, and has no pride. The American child sees very little gold and hence is inclined to think of it in abstract (economic) terms, whereas in the Middle East a child's mother is likely to go about her household chores loaded down with real gold jewelry.

Reaction to Catastrophe. The way in which the members of different ethnic groups respond to danger also suggests clues as to perceptual styles. At 1:05 A.M., on May 23, 1960, a great tsunami or "tidal wave," caused by an earthquake off the coast of Chile, destroyed some 500 dwellings in the city of Hilo, Hawaii. Sixty-one persons lost their lives in the wreckage. A 20-minute warning blast on a siren was sounded more than 4 hours before the tsunami hit the city, but only 40 per cent of the residents of the low-lying section of town evacuated the area. Ninety-five per cent of the persons interviewed later admitted that they had heard the siren, and 94 per cent of this group said they knew what it meant. The chief difference between those who left the area when the siren sounded and those who stayed turned out to be an ethnic one. As Table 11-2 shows, a majority of Filipinos, Japanese, and Portuguese did not leave, whereas a majority of Hawaiians did. The researchers suggested that the difference may have been due to the fact that Hawaiians have a rather elaborate mythology about the part Polynesian deities play in geophysical events and that such a belief facilitated adaptive reactions. In other words, belief in the gods enabled the Hawaiians to be more realistic about the impending danger (Lachman, Tatsuoka, & Bonk, 1961). Whatever the reason, the results of the survey made it clear that the Hawaiians perceived the situation quite differently than other ethnic groups and suggest that the reason for this difference may be found in the values and attitudes of the cultures involved.

The Culture as a Perceptual Filter. There is another interesting implication in the findings of the Hilo study. The Hawaiians are perhaps the least Westernized of the ethnic groups represented in the survey, yet they were the most responsive to the warning signal. Other data picked up by the research team show that level of edu-

Table **11-2.** Differences in the behavior of members of various ethnic groups in Hilo, Hawaii on hearing the warning siren in advance of the tidal wave of May 23, 1960 (Lachman, Tatsuoka, & Bonk, 1961)

Ethnic group	Behavior on hearing the warning siren			
	Left the area		Remained in the area	
	N	Per cent	N	Per cent
Filipino	10	30	23	69
Japanese	55	31	123	69
Portuguese	1	7	14	93
Hawaiian	51	69	23	31

cation was of negligible survival value: although persons with high school education were somewhat more likely to leave the area, college educated persons were as likely to remain as were persons with only a grade school education. Clues as to the possible meaning of these data may be found in the comments made by D. O. Hebb (1955b) as he reviewed some research conducted at McGill University dealing with reactions to isolation. The findings of these various studies are consistent with research we reviewed briefly in Chapter 2, namely, that exposure to stimulation, and particularly social stimulation, promotes general effectiveness, and isolation appears to prevent the development of effective responses to the environment. However, one set of studies reviewed by Hebb was concerned with the reactions of college students (presumably products of a normally stimulating environment) who were placed in isolation chambers for periods of up to several days. Every attempt was made to keep external stimulation at a minimum: subjects wore frosted goggles to make pattern vision impossible, rooms were soundproof, cardboard cuffs extended beyond their fingertips to prevent tactile sensations, and their heads were covered with soundproofed helmets in which speakers had been embedded. They were permitted to leave only to go to the toilet and to eat. During the stay in the cubicle, subjects showed dramatic losses in problem-solving ability. They complained that they were bored and looked forward to the mental arithmetic problems that were presented over the loudspeaker, but found themselves unable to concentrate and to put forth the necessary effort when problems were presented. Several of the subjects also reported vivid hallucinations during the period of sensory deprivation.

Hebb concluded that the studies showed that a certain amount of stimulation was necessary for normal functioning, even on the part of well-educated people who had been reared in a normally stimulating environment, and that people were actually quite vulnerable when it came to

breakdowns in functioning resulting from unusual experiences, such as sensory deprivation.
What ordinarily keeps us from being in a continual state of disruption and disturbance is the
protecting and mediating influence of the culture.
Civilization, said Hebb, eliminates sources of
acute fear, disgust, and anger to the point where
we often look with amused tolerance, for example, at the emotional behavior of primitive peoples who develop elaborate rituals and taboos to
deal with unsettling events, such as death. Our
feeling of superiority, according to Hebb, rests
on the fact that our culture arranges matters so
that we seldom if ever have to deal directly with
such crude matters. The whole process of socialization in civilized societies is contrived to ensure
that members of society will not act in ways that
provoke or become sources of strong emotional
disturbance, unless such behavior takes place
within the framework of highly ritualized circumstances. Football and basketball games, funerals,
boxing matches, and stage plays are examples of
such ritualized emotional outlets. In other respects we remain wrapped up in the insulating
cocoon of our culture and are thus permitted to
think of ourselves as less emotional than four-
year-olds (who are less culture bound than we
are) or members of primitive tribes.

To return to the Hilo study, it appears that the
less sophisticated Hawaiians were able to respond
in a more adaptive way to the imminent disaster
than the more sophisticated Japanese. Interviews
of those who did not evacuate the danger area in
advance of the tsunami shows that they really did
not think they were in danger. For example, they
thought there might be another warning or that
they were situated high enough to be safe. But if
Hebb's analysis of the way in which we insulate
ourselves against the perception of potentially
distressing events is valid, such replies may be
considered rationalizations. What we learn from
our culture is how to perceive our environment,
and if we are trying to attain a relatively calm
and stable way of life, we are inclined to misperceive or overlook events and elements that possess
a high potential for disturbance.

Core Values

American Core Values. One way to look at the
kinds of perceptions we learn from our culture is
to view them as being organized around core
values, that is, certain values that have a kind
of priority or precedence in determining other
values and attitudes. "Fair play" may be considered to be a core value in Anglo-American
cultures, because a whole complex of attitudes
and values is dependent on it—willingness to
abide by referees' decisions even when they are
disliked, the use of a light line in game fishing,
and so forth.

Walter Gruen (1964, 1966) has attempted a
kind of chart of American core values (see Table
11-3), using results of a questionnaire composed
of items that were found to be correlated with one
another when the questionnaire was submitted to
a sample of MC Americans. He found that WC
people agreed with the statements more than
LMC individuals, who in turn were more accepting of them than UMC persons. People 50 years
and older tended to agree with them more than
people 40 years and younger. High scorers among
college students tended to be more yielding,
when tested in the Asch conformity situation we
described earlier. High scorers also showed a
greater degree of conventionality, in that they
tended to prefer styles of dress, furniture, and
cars that were preferred by a majority of students. High scorers preferred to read *Life, Look,
Saturday Evening Post,* and the *Reader's Digest,*
and tended to avoid magazines like *Esquire, At-
lantic Monthly, Saturday Review,* and the *New
Yorker.* The questionnaire was also tested on
samples of German MC adults, Australian university students, and Northern Irish UMC adults.
Results from all three groups differed significantly
from comparable American groups, thus suggesting that the statements actually do reflect
American value patterns.

Table 11-3. American core values (after Gruen, 1966)

1. Vigorous pursuit of status change through upward social mobility.
    1.1 Success defined in terms of upward mobility and change in role (as contrasted with maintenance of stable role development).
    1.2 Gratification of wishes postponed to the future (as contrasted with immediate satisfaction of wishes).
    1.3 Optimism about the possibility of success resulting from one's own efforts.
2. Positive value attached to external and superficial qualities.
    2.1 Preference for extraversion as a basis for social interaction (e.g., many casual acquaintances, rather than a few close friends).
    2.2 Preference for superficial and stereotyped forms of expression (rather than unique, genuine, and more personalized kinds of self-expression).
    2.3 Positive valuing of youth and prettiness (as contrasted with a preference for qualities characterized by maturity, suspended judgment, and the "patina" of age).
    2.4 Lack of interest in reading and in books.
    2.5 Externalization of blame for one's fate (in contrast to internalization of blame—blaming oneself for one's problems).
3. Standardization of behavior.
    3.1 Insistence on conformity to community standards of behavior (as contrasted with a tolerance for individualistic or personalized standards).
    3.2 Preference for employment with stable, well-known organizations (in contrast with self-employment).
    3.3 Endorsement of traditional morality.

4. Impulse control and restriction.
    4.1 Tense, tight control of emotional expression (as opposed to free, relaxed, uninhibited expression of feelings).
    4.2 Preoccupation with schedules, regularity, and promptness (as contrasted with spontaneous and unstructured approach to daily routines).
    4.3 Extreme concern with cleanliness for its own sake (as contrasted with functional cleanliness).
    4.4 Preference for bland food, or food with little variety (in contrast to food of considerable variety, flavored with spices and sauces).
    4.5 Belief in romantic love (as opposed to love resulting from growth in mutual understanding and acceptance and the development of interests in common).
    4.6 Involvement in activity in order to avoid sensual experiences (as opposed to deliberate involvement in and enjoyment of sensual experiences).
    4.7 Emphasis on keeping busy (in contrast to the enjoyment of idle time and leisure for its own sake).
    4.8 Relaxation and recreation as health measures (rather than as enjoyable activities for their own sake).
    4.9 Faith in rationality (as contrasted with faith in intuition or in decisions that are based on or take cognizance of feelings and emotions).
5. Cult of freedom.
    5.1 Preference for small, autonomous families, without much personal involvement or interdependency (rather than close, interdependent ties with the extended family).
    5.2 Equality of birth (rather than limitations based on biological and social inheritance).
    5.3 Unlimited freedom for individuals (as against responsibility and commitment to others).

Earlier students of American values (e.g., Loeb, 1953) had reported that the LMC was most concerned with maintaining and affirming the key core values. However, Gruen's research suggests that concern for these values has shifted to the WC, and that the LMC, like the UMC, is becoming more pluralistic in the values it endorses. Some validity to this conclusion is lent by the fact that teachers told Gruen that they were somewhat inclined to encourage the development of counternorm values, whereas a generation ago teachers were considered to give a strong endorsement to the core culture.

There are two points that should be made before we leave this study. One is that the core values listed in Table 11-3 are somewhat inconsistent. There is forthright endorsement of individual liberty, for example, and equally forthright endorsement of conformity. Upward mobility creates changes and thrives in a changing, pluralistic social environment; this is incompatible with the traditionalism and longing for the security to be found in well-known, well-established organizations reflected in other values. However, the values are more consistent than inconsistent and are to a large extent interrelated.

The other point is that there is an overlap between these core values and the values characteristic of other cultures. Cultures do not exist as isolates in time and space. There is a great deal of borrowing and exchange among cultures, and cultures may develop similar values quite independently of each other. Gruen found that Australian students endorsed upward mobility, just as American students did, but favored tighter emotional control. As contrasted with American subjects, Germans were more likely to reject values related to extraversion, conformity, bland food, and the avoidance of sensuality, but gave an even stronger endorsement of statements relating to emotional control, romantic love, and punctuality. The Northern Irish subjects agreed very strongly with questionnaire items in a given value cluster but also disagreed strongly with others in the same area, thus suggesting that a different set of interlocking core values characterized their culture.

German-American Differences. The question of similarities and differences between value systems was explored by McClelland and others (1958) who studied the responses of American and German adolescent males to TAT cards selected to evoke imagery related to n Ach and n Aff. The American boys had more n Ach than their German counterparts, but there was no statistically significant difference in the n Aff scores of the two groups. There were, however, a number of qualitative differences in the way the two groups regarded their obligations to themselves and to society. The differences, revealed partly by the TAT stories and partly by a questionnaire administered in connection with the study, are summarized briefly in Table 11-4. Both American and German boys were inclined to endorse the idea of investing time and energy in accomplishing something, but for American boys the "something" was more likely to be related to their personal plans for self-development, whereas for the Germans the "something" was more likely to be related to their obligations to others. This does

Table **11-4.** Differences in the ways American and German youths perceive their obligations to themselves and to society (McClelland, Sturr, Knapp, & Wendt, 1958)

	Obligation to self
United States	High motivation to achieve (n Ach), coupled with an emphasis on individual accomplishment and self-development
Germany	High degree of "rational striving" (get the job done) greater emphasis on self-denial and self-restraint, greater participation in individualistic activities
	Obligation to society
United States	Active participation in a wide range of group activities, coupled with a greater sensitivity to the opinions and feelings of others
Germany	Greater concern over obligations to an idealistic code of decency (governing interpersonal behavior)

not mean that the Americans are unconcerned about others. On the contrary, they are much more inclined to be involved in a variety of group activities. The typical American youth in this study reported involvement in about five different group activities, whereas the typical German reported only one. The German is more concerned with the "idea" or the ideals of the group—the group in general, whereas the American tends to be interested in his interaction and social success with individuals in groups. The German student feels under strong obligation to the one or two groups in which he holds membership, whereas the American student is more broadly concerned, although concerned in a more limited way, with the several groups in which he holds membership. Americans are more likely to join groups in order to accomplish a particular purpose—to socialize, go swimming or hiking, carry out a particular task that is best done in a group context, and the like. The German, on the other hand, is looking for a place to invest his loyalty. Americans decide quickly and easily whether they want to join a group; for a German, this decision comes only after a considerable degree of soul searching. Whereas the American is more likely to take his recreation in group context, the German is more inclined to find modes of recreation (stamp collecting, reading, hiking) that can be done alone.

Bringing about Changes in Values. One question that often comes up when Americans discuss cultural values is: Can values be changed? This question has been raised with respect to both Japan and Germany, particularly with regard to the kinds of values underlying the behavior of their respective populations before and during World War II. Such problems are not readily amenable to social research, but some questionnaire studies, like the one just cited, shed some light on the structural aspects of the attitudes and values under consideration. The question has particularly interesting implications with respect to Japan, inasmuch as there has been a marked change in the formal aspects of government since the war. The question might be phrased: Has the introduction of democratic governmental forms in Japan had any effect on the attitudes and values of the Japanese people?

F. Kenneth Berrien (1965) has found that there is still a considerable degree of deference on the part of Japanese people in their interaction with people of higher status. For example, 54 per cent of Japanese blue-collar workers said that they would give up their seat if their immediate superior entered a crowded bus on which they were riding, whereas only 37 per cent of American blue-collar workers said they would offer their seat, since the fair rule is "First come, first served." When asked what they thought of their work, most Japanese employees maintained that it was a part of life comparable in importance to their life off the job, whereas most American workers were inclined to assign their work to a more subordinate place in their lives.

Berrien (1966) also administered the Edwards Personal Preference Schedule (EPPS), a questionnaire designed to measure the strength of fifteen psychological needs. American male students tended to score higher on needs for deference, as well as for achievement and dominance, whereas Japanese male students tended to score higher on needs for abasement, change, and endurance. American female students tended to score higher on needs for deference, achievement, affiliation, dominance, and nurturance, whereas Japanese female students tended to score higher on need for endurance. In analyzing the scores for Japanese men, Berrien concluded that, except for the unexpectedly lower scores on deference, the values reflected in the scores seemed to conform with the stereotype of the Japanese people, as revealed by their cultural and political history. The pattern of self-abasement, a reluctance to accept responsibility for leadership, a capacity for hard work, and a generally lower level of personal aspiration seemed to him to indicate that there had been not much change in these Japanese values since the period before World War II. He did note, however, that the low need for deference and the high need for change were both in marked contrast to the general direction of the values. He interpreted the EPPS scores for Japanese women students as indicating a desire to avoid becoming personally involved with others, and to maintain a high degree of insulation from community affairs.

After reviewing his own and other research, Berrien concluded that there was cause for both optimism and pessimism with respect to the growth of democratic values in Japan during the last twenty years. On the one hand, he noted the strong needs for self-abasement, and unwillingness to assume leadership, and the tendency to isolate oneself from the community that we have noted earlier. On the positive side, he noted that

Japanese students appear to be more concerned than American students about censorship, freedom of speech, and fair-employment practices. In these respects, the Japanese appeared to be more liberal than Americans. He felt that more data were needed, however, before one could decide whether these tendencies were indicative of a basic trend toward democratic attitudes and values or whether they were merely a temporary phase in Japanese thinking. In any event, Berrien questioned whether Japanese political and governmental operations, although outwardly democratic, were having any fundamental effect on attitudes and values of the Japanese people.

This gap between surface and subsurface aspects of behavior was explored by Stanley C. Plog (1963), who noted that there are many indications of cross-cultural exchanges between the United States and Germany. Americans drive Volkswagens, Porsches, and Mercedes, use German precision cameras, and consume large quantities of German beer. Germans, for their part, consume large quantities of Coca-Cola, shop at American-style supermarkets, and are very fond of American films. He found no evidence, however, that American and German personality trends were merging. He found that Germans and Americans were essentially much as Kurt Lewin (1936) described them a generation ago: Germans are stiff, formal, and self-inhibited with all but a few of their very close, intimate friends, whereas Americans tend to be affable, relaxed, and socially at ease even with strangers. Plog also found that Americans are much more willing than Germans to communicate information about themselves to a wide range of people, both strangers and intimates.

Acculturation and n Ach. Although Berrien's research suggests that the learning of some Western modes of behavior has been impeded in Japan by the hold of more traditional values, other research indicates that such values may aid the Japanese in other respects. Edward Norbeck and George DeVos (1961) have reviewed research relating to the adaptation of Japanese to American ways. The question has been asked why Japanese immigrants and their descendants have so readily adopted American attitudes and values, especially the motive to achieve, whereas other minority groups, some of them targets of less social discrimination, have resisted acculturation.

The success of the Japanese-Americans can apparently be explained, at least in part, by the fact that Japanese values of perseverance in pursuit of long-term goals, self-denial, obedience to authority, and a sense of obligation to parents are consistent with and reinforce American values that stress achievement and working for future goals. The drive to achieve is intensified by the desire of Japanese-Americans to honor their parents and to satisfy their obligations toward them by fulfilling the occupational goals that the latter have encouraged them to set.

These conclusions are supported to some degree by the finding that descendants of Japanese who settled in cultures which do not emphasize achievement values (e.g., Peru) show less achievement motivation than do Japanese-Americans.

SUMMARY

A culture consists of systems of values, beliefs, norms, artifacts, and symbols that have been developed by a society and that are shared by its members. Such systems exert a profound influence on the personality of the individual. The learning of appropriate patterns of behavior begins during infancy, with the parents serving as agents of the culture. This learning takes place as much by the way in which parents behave toward children as in what they tell them. An example is given of the differences in the interaction between American children and their parents in public parks and that of French children. American children are allowed a great deal more freedom to play in the dirt and to interact with other children than French children are. American children are thus learning about a world that should be explored and investigated independently, whereas French children are learning about a world that is potentially dangerous, but which is in charge of powerful, omniscient individuals, who have imposed a certain structure that should not be challenged or investigated. These two differences in world view lead to children's behavior that Americans see as normal, but that Europeans see as undisciplined. These values also appear in adult life, with French businessmen being more concerned than Americans with maintaining the status quo. This does not mean, however, that French adults are less independent in other ways. Some research shows that they are more resistive to influence from their peers than are, for example, Norwegians.

Other examples of differences in perceiving interpersonal events are drawn from observations of the behavior of Greek psychiatrists, who tend to go along with their patients' desires to place the blame for interpersonal problems on others. Blame-avoidant behavior is condoned by Greek culture, but not by the kind of psychotherapeutic training the psychiatrists had received in other countries.

The frames of reference provided by different cultures lead to differences in the way events of all types are perceived, whether the event is a dream, a household object, or even an impending disaster. The culture acts as a kind of filter that screens out stimuli that contradict or might disturb the individual's view of his environment. The way in which the environment is perceived is to a large extent determined by the core values prescribed by the culture. A study of American MC core values shows that they now are endorsed most strongly by WC members and that MC people have shifted to more pluralistic sets of values.

Studies of differences between American and German values shows that American boys scored higher in n Ach, but there were no differences in n Aff between the two groups. American boys are more involved with their peer groups, whereas German boys prefer individualistic activities. A study of Japanese values shows that changes take place slowly and that deference and self-abasement are still important cultural traits. On the other hand, the core values of the Japanese culture appeared to facilitate the progress and aculturation of Japanese emigrants in countries where achievement is considered highly desirable.

SUGGESTED READINGS

Benedict, R., *Patterns of culture.* Boston: Houghton Mifflin, 1934 (published in paperback by Penguin, New York, 1946).

Dennis, W., *Group values through children's drawings.* New York: Wiley, 1966.

Hebb, D. O., The mammal and his environment. *American journal of psychiatry,* 1955, **111**, 826-831.

Hsu, F. L. K., *Psychological anthropology: approaches to culture and personality.* Homewood, Ill.: Dorsey, 1961.

Kaplan, B. (Ed.), *Studying personality cross-culturally.* Evanston: Row, Peterson, 1961.

Kluckhohn, C., Murray, H. A., & Schneider, D. M. (Eds.), *Personality in nature, society, and culture* (Rev. ed.). New York: Knopf, 1953.

Lindgren, H. C. (Ed.), *Contemporary research in social psychology.* New York: Wiley, 1969. See papers by Peck and by Gallimore, Howard, & Jordan in Section 7.

Mead, M. and Wolfenstein, M. (Eds.), *Childhood in contemporary cultures.* Chicago: University of Chicago Press, 1955 (available in paperback).

Peck, R. F., A comparison of the value systems of Mexican and American youth. *Interamerican journal of psychology,* 1967, **1**, 41-50.

CHAPTER TWELVE

Ken Heyman

Henry Clay Lindgren

Suzanne Szasz

Communication

Communication as Perceived by Laymen and Psychologists. The layman's view of communication is likely to be relatively simple: everyone communicates or tries to; some understand; some do not. Laymen may also assume that people communicate because they have something to convey to others: information, feelings, demands, or arguments.

Although there is a great deal of validity to the layman's view, communication appears quite different to the behavioral scientist. For one thing, the behavioral scientist is likely to perceive complexities that laymen are inclined to overlook. For another, the layman's explanations of why people communicate leaves too much behavior unexplained. For example, why do people express so much misinformation and why do they communicate when they really have nothing to say? And why do they communicate in ways that disguise, rather than reveal, their feelings?

The complexities of communication are difficult to understand whether we are laymen or scientists, because we are continually engaged in it. We are always involved in sending, receiving, coding, or encoding messages: we exist in a psycho-social field that is rich and even overrich in communication. At times this can be very distracting, because so many different messages are being transmitted simultaneously. Seated at the breakfast table, we glance over the headlines. A dozen reporters' stories are clamoring for our attention. The kitchen radio is telling us to buy a new car, and our wife is admonishing the children. The telephone rings and the children compete with each other for the chance to answer it. The siren of an ambulance or perhaps a fire engine sounds in the distance, and someone down the street is blowing his horn to tell his car pool member that he is ready and impatient to get going. Another communication-rich day has begun.

Communication as a Tool. Most people would probably think of communication primarily as a tool. Communication in this sense is a process that enables us to send and receive messages carrying information and thus to attempt to exercise some control over our environment. To return to the breakfast table, we learn that the coffee is boiling hot, that our toast is ready, and that Ron's scout meeting is this evening. We say that we passed a restless night, feel irritable and edgy, will probably be a little late getting home from work, and please pass the butter. Information is exchanged, feelings are expressed, demands are made, and people are placed on notice that events will occur or may occur. As we use communication in this way, it is our servant, and we are its master.

This is an egocentric and essentially common-sense view of communication. It is valid up to a point, but fails to satisfy the behavioral scientist because it does not take into account a great many side effects that may at times be more significant than the intent and the more obvious informational burden of the messages being sent and received. Furthermore, it ignores a number of ways in which we use communication that are more than merely transmitting and receiving direct information.

It is easily understandable, however, why we should take a narrow view of communication. As we go about the tasks of everyday life, we are not likely to be concerned about the fine points, the details, and the nuances of communication behavior. It would be inconsistent with our roles as parent, student, secretary, or whatever, to become preoccupied with the kinds of communication phenomena that interest the behavioral scientist. Problems that interest him seem irrelevant at such times, just as the problems we experience in trying to communicate are generally of little interest to him.

Our usual problem in communication is likely to be that of finding ways to express ourselves adequately—finding the proper terms and phrases, avoiding statements that give others the wrong impression, trying to get others to talk about matters that interest *us*, and so forth. We are keenly aware of such problems when we struggle to find the right words to describe our complicated feelings, or when we hear friends and acquaintances express themselves so much more vividly than we can. We may even find ourselves somewhat jealous of our eloquent friends who always say things so well and who seem to have no trouble gaining the attention of the audience. At such times, our communication problem appears to be that of making a poorer representation of ourselves than we would like to make.

Raymond A. Bauer (1964), a specialist in communication at the Harvard School of Business, has pointed out that a major difference between the lay public and behavioral scientists is that the former tend to look upon communication as a situation in which a communicator manipulates or brings about changes in an audience. The communication of information, for example, is motivated by a belief that the audience will accept the information and will behave accordingly. The most obvious example of this concept

"What is it? WHAT IS IT? It's universal love expressed in paint, that's what it is . . . For Pete's sake, Ma, you should understand my work better than anyone . . . !"

Communication without transaction.

of communication can be found in advertising. The advertiser assumes that if his message reaches its intended audience, it will bring about some change in the audience's behavior: the audience will buy his product instead of another or will drop whatever it happens to be doing (sometimes the audience is instructed to do exactly that) and go out in search of the advertised product, money in hand.

Communication as Transaction. The behavioral scientist, according to Bauer, is more likely to think of communication as a transactional affair and to assume that communication has not taken place unless the audience has been involved in some more or less active way. Attending—that is, listening, watching, trying to understand—would be one example of involvement. Becoming engaged in a dialogue would be another example. However, there is no real transaction and hence no real communication unless both parties, communicator and audience, believe they have something to gain thereby.

Figure 12-1 presents a diagram of such a transaction. A state of tension builds up in the communicator to the point where he feels compelled to communicate some information that is directly or indirectly related to his feeling of tension. He selects a transmitter or medium for his communication. Ordinarily, the medium would be speech, but it also may be a gesture or a nudge. He could also communicate in writing, and he might also employ Morse code via short-wave radio. Whatever method he chooses, his information must be put in the form of a message, which in turn must be encoded in a form that is compatible with the information and the type of transmitter used. The actual transmission takes the form of a signal that is sent from the transmitter to the receiver via the channel. What communication specialists call "noise" may intervene to distort the signal. Technically speaking, any variability in the message received, which could not have been predicted at its source, is attributed to "noise." "Noise" can intervene at any point in the system; in Figure 12-1 we have shown it in the channel. When the signal has been received, the audience perceives it as being a message, decodes it, and interprets the message.

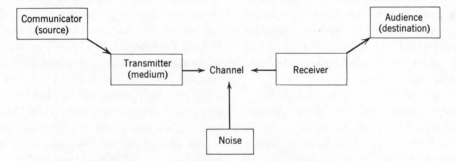

Figure **12-1.** Schematic representation of communication as a transaction.

Communication takes place as follows: 1. There is a build-up of tension in the communicator, which leads to the desire to communicate information. He thus becomes the source of a message. 2. A transmitter is selected. 3. The message is encoded in a way that is appropriate to the information and the type of transmitter used. 4. The encoded message is transmitted in the form of a signal. 5. As the signal passes through the communication channel, it may be subject to "noise" that will result in distortion. 6. The signal is received. 7. The audience perceives the signal as being a message. 8. The signal is decoded. 9. The resulting message is interpreted in order to determine its information content.

To put this into the framework of everyday experience, let us say that Linda sees Jim coming down the walk near the college library. Jim is deep in a book and is walking very slowly. Linda debates with herself as to whether she should disturb Jim, decides that social amenities should be observed, and says: "Hi!"

To review what has occurred up to this point, we note that a state of mild tension exists in Linda, one that is occasioned by Jim's appearance. This tension is a normal accompaniment to the realization that a friend is approaching. The uttering of a greeting not only reduces her tension somewhat, but also informs Jim that he has been recognized and is expected to respond. Linda could have put her message in the form of a friendly wave or a nod and a smile, but this type of signal would have been inappropriate because of Jim's involvement in the book.

If Jim is deeply engrossed in his book, however, he will not be aware that he has been signaled and will walk on. No communication has taken place. There is no transaction. Or he may pretend that he does not notice Linda and thus refuses to enter into a transaction. If, however, he does respond in kind, he goes through the same process of building up tension, encoding and uttering a signal, which is then perceived and decoded by Linda, who has now changed her role and has become an audience.

Communication and Social Relationships. Probably the most fundamental fact about communication, as far as the social psychologist is concerned, is that it serves as the basis for social relationships of all kinds. Communication is the cement, so to speak, that binds people together in social systems: groups, cultures, communities, or whatever. Daniel Katz and Robert L. Kahn (1966) state that social systems can be viewed as restricted communication networks—restricted in the sense that the flow of information from one unit to another in the system is focused and channeled in order to screen out irrelevant data —"noise"—that might interfere with the message being transmitted. Herbert A. Thelen (1960) points out that if there are sixty people milling about in a large room, the total number of potential channels of communication is $n(n-1)/2$ or 1770. However, if these sixty people are organized into a network of twelve combinations of five-man teams, with each person on a team having a clearly defined role dependent on the roles of the other four, the number of channels may be reduced in each work group to *ten*, if team members are mutually dependent, or *four* if they are arranged in a serial position. If the sixty people are organized in this way, each individual will be linked to the others by a theoretically noise-free channel and will be able to turn his attention, without risk of distraction, to the task at hand.

The fact that two people are able to communicate with each other implies not only that they occupy positions in some kind of social system but also that some kind of a relationship exists between them. The fact that they use a common language, or at least have access to a common set of symbols, means that they share some percepts and may even be members of the same cultural or ethnic group. Their communication makes them a two-person group, or dyad, albeit a temporary one that may dissolve in the next instant. But for the moment they have a relationship one to the other. The relationship may be of moderate intensity, such as that between two strangers on a bus who start talking politics and find that they share the same views. Or it may be fleeting and tenuous, as between a passerby who notices a mother helping her small son across the street and hears her say: "We must look both ways before we cross, to see whether any cars are coming." In the latter instance, the communication is not even intended for the ears of the passerby, but he does pick up the message, understands it, approves of it, identifies with the mother, and finds himself looking both ways with greater than usual care as *he* crosses the street.

A great deal more can be learned about the woman from her brief statement to her son, other than the fact that she knows one should be careful in crossing the street. Even if we did not observe her make this statement, but heard only a recording, we would probably assume that she was a mother (or perhaps a teacher) and that she was talking to a child. In other words, we would be able to make some reasonably accurate assumptions about her position, role, and status with respect to her audience (the child). We would learn something about her attitudes toward the child as well as toward herself. Some of this would of course be revealed by her tone of voice.

The information burden of any message, therefore, may be considered in terms of its implicit, as well as its explicit, aspects. The explicit information contained in the mother's admonition to her son concerns the desirability of looking both ways before crossing the street. The implicit information is that which may be deduced from the character of the message, the tone of voice in which it is delivered, the circumstances surrounding its delivery, and the like. The status, role, position, attitude, and mood of the sender of the message are implied, rather than explicit. A communication may thus convey a number of meanings in addition to those intended by the communicator and which may strengthen or even negate the information content of the message.

Communication and Identity. The communicator attends primarily to the explicit aspects of his message—the information he wishes to encode or the demand he wants to make. The audience may, however, have a high degree of interest in the *implicit* information in the message, particularly the information that reveals significant characteristics of the communicator—that says, in effect, who he is. This information is vital, because audiences generally give heed to communicators primarily in terms of who they are. Once the communicator's identity has been established, the audience will then give the message the kind of attention they believe is appropriate for such a person. The status of the communicator is understandably important. A high-status commu-

nicator will generally receive more attention from an audience, whereas a low-status communicator may not even get a hearing. To use the terminology we introduced in Figure 12-1, an audience is more likely to take steps on behalf of high-status communicators to reduce the noise in the channel by ignoring distractions, than it will for low-status communicators. To say that an individual has high status means that we have learned to attach more than the usual amount of value to his actions and beliefs, and this value also accrues to his utterances. Statements from presidents usually get more attention than statements from congressmen; statements from teachers get more attention than statements from children; and statements from people rating high in popularity get more attention than those who rate low. Although this is generally true, it is not always true. A two-year-old who makes a statement gets more attention than one made by his four-year-old brother, even though the latter's status may be higher. The fact that the two-year-old is making a statement at all is what draws attention. His statement becomes more noticeable because it is unexpected. The communicator's visibility is thus significant. High-status people receive more attention partly because their status makes them more visible, but low-status people may also achieve a degree of visibility under unusual circumstances.

We should also note that the audience's perception of the communicator's identity enables the audience to develop a kind of "set," that is, a certain predetermined sensitivity to the message it is receiving. A president may say something inane, but the audience, being set to hear something profound, may perceive it as profound. A child may say something profound, but if the parent is set to perceive something trivial, he may overlook the importance of what is being said.

The message therefore tends to reinforce whatever image the audience has of the communicator, but his image is derived from data that he previously revealed without being aware. We are referring here not only to what the communicator says and the way he says it, but also to the many other ways in which we communicate our identity —our choice of clothing, our grooming, the company we keep, our names, our gestures and expressions, and the like. Such communication works both ways, of course: the communicator reveals his identity to others and at the same time reaffirms it for himself.

An example drawn from an experience in the Middle East may help to illustrate this point. We were looking for the great Ummayad mosque in Damascus and were making our way down a passageway in the large covered market in the oldest part of the city, looking for all the world like tourists who were not sure where they were or where they were going. A passerby, who from his clothing was obviously a local person, stopped and asked in halting French if he could help us. We started to reply, when he interrupted and asked, hopefully, "¿Habla Usted español?" It was obvious that he was more comfortable in Spanish, so we switched over to that language. After he had told us how to find the mosque, we asked him how it happened that a citizen of Syria was so fluent in Spanish. His explanation was simple and almost obvious: "I am a Sephardic Jew. My people have spoken Spanish ever since we left Spain five hundred years ago."

After the defeat of the Arabs in Spain by Ferdinand and Isabella during the fifteenth century, non-Christians—Arabs and Jews alike —were subjected to considerable religious and economic harassment. They were, in effect, given the choice of leaving the country or of becoming Christians. Most of the Jews left to settle in lands controlled by Moslems in North Africa and the Middle East. They maintained their identity and their separateness from others through their religious practices, as reinforced by their common language, Spanish.* Although they became as fluent in Arabic or Turkish as any of the local

---

* Actually, *Ladino*, a medieval form of Spanish with some Hebrew words.

people, they conversed with one another in Spanish. Arabic or Turkish would have done as well, as far as a medium for communication was concerned, but Spanish had the advantage of being a "mother tongue." It is in our mother tongue that we feel most at home when trying to communicate complex feelings and attitudes. Somehow the language people speak as children seems more forceful and direct, more pungent and more intimate.

To return to the Sephardic Jews, Spanish served as a means that enabled them to establish strong and intimate bonds with one another. A Jewish merchant from Tunis, when visiting in Cairo, could use Spanish to identify himself to other Jews and thus gain special consideration, protection, help, or whatever he needed. The language helped to establish a bond between him and the other members of his ethnic group. Spanish similarly enabled Jews to establish and maintain a degree of difference between them and others: Jews were people who spoke Spanish, whereas non-Jews could not speak Spanish. Communicating in Spanish, then, became a social norm characteristic of Sephardic Jews.

Of all the forms of social interaction, the language people speak is the most compelling and enduring source of cultural identity. Cultural identities and differences tend to follow linguistic lines. Major differences in customs, values, attitudes, and rituals tend to be accompanied by differences in language, and similarities in language tend to reinforce similarities in social behavior. Americans feel closer to Canada and to England than to any other countries in the world because we share a common language, whereas countries that are divided along linguistic lines, like Belgium and Nigeria, encounter continual problems in maintaining national unity because linguistic differences reinforce and accentuate cultural differences. The unification of Italy in the nineteenth century was made possible because people in various parts of the country had finally, though in some cases reluctantly, agreed to use a common dialect for communication. In more recent times, the Catalans of northeast Spain have expressed their sense of being different from other Spanish citizens, as well as their resistance to the central government, by continuing to speak, write, and publish in Catalan. German-speaking Tyroleans living in Italy use their language as a way of maintaining identity with Austrian Tyroleans and resisting attempts to integrate them into the political, economic, and cultural life of Italy.

Educational level (and social class) may also be revealed by styles of expression. One can usually tell whether a speaker is middle class or lower class by his diction, word usage, pronunciation, grammar, and the like, although differences between middle and upper class are more difficult to determine, except in certain regions of the country. Stanley C. Plog (1966) used a literacy index to determine the status of persons writing letters to the editor of the Boston *Herald*. Letters were assigned scores on the basis of the quality of paper used, neatness, grammar and word usage, and maturity of handwriting. Estimates of the writers' probable educational levels were then made on the basis of composite scores. As Table 12-1 shows, Plog was able to predict educational level with approximately 75 per cent accuracy. Like other forms of communication, a letter therefore is a source not only of explicit information (what the writer intends to communicate), but also of implicit information. The letter writer tells his audience something about himself by the paper he choses, by his neatness, and so forth.

Social Distance and Communication. The importance of the style of language used by a communicator was also demonstrated by a study conducted by Triandis, Loh, and Levin (1966), who compared the relative effect of appearance and spoken English on the opinions of college students. The students listened to a tape-recorded statement that was spoken in either ungrammatical (low-status) or excellent (high-status) English. While they listened to the statement, a slide

Table **12-1.** Actual educational level of persons writing letters to the editor of the Boston *Herald*, as compared with predictions based on paper quality of letter, grammar, neatness, and graphic maturity (Plog, 1966)

Predicted education	Actual education		
	Grammar school	High school	College
Grammar school (Grades 1–8)	10	4	0
High school (Grades 9–12)	4	27	17
College (1–4 years)	1	8	62
N	15	39	79
Percentage of correct predictions	67%	69%	89%

of the man who was represented as the speaker was projected on a screen for them to watch. The man was either white or Negro and was either neatly dressed or poorly dressed. The students were then asked to indicate their willingness to admire the speaker, to welcome him as a neighbor or as a relative by marriage, and to accept him as a friend. When results were analyzed, dress was found to be of least significance in determining the reactions of students. The more prejudiced of the students were most influenced by race when it came to accepting the speaker as a neighbor, relative by marriage, or a friend; otherwise, the chief basis for reacting to the speaker was the quality of his English. In fact, the kind of English used by the speaker accounted for 80 per cent of the variance in deciding whether the speaker could be accepted as a friend, as far as politically liberal and moderate students were concerned.

Certain forms of communication behavior have a dual purpose, that is, they inform the audience simultaneously how the communicator perceives himself and how he perceives the audience. Frank N. Willis, Jr. (1966) had his students measure the distance between themselves and

Table **12-2.** Distances (in inches) at which conversations are initiated by persons occupying various social positions (Willis, 1966)

Position of person initiating conversation	Distance
Stranger	27.33
Acquaintance	23.80
Peer	23.87
Older person	26.67
Parent	26.00
Friends	19.50
Caucasian to Caucasian	22.00
Caucasian to Negro	28.00
Negro to Negro	24.00
Woman to woman	
Acquaintance	22.41
Friend	26.17
Close friend	17.75
Man to man	
Acquaintance	23.75
Friend	22.31
Close friend	23.08
Position of audience	
Woman	21.58
Man	24.46

persons who spoke to them in informal situations. Their findings, as reported in Table 12-2, show that there tends to be greater distance between a communicator and his audience if they are strangers, than if they are friends. A person who initiates a conversation when he is very close is saying, in effect: "I perceive that we are friends." The point at which he elects to start the conversation is thus a part of the communication. If he selects an inappropriate point—that is, if a stranger comes too close or a friend remains too distant—the general effect of the communication may be clouded or rendered ambiguous. Instead of paying careful attention to what the stranger is saying to us, we may be thinking such things as, "I don't like his oily, confidential manner," "Who does he think he is?," or "He certainly is presumptuous." Conversely, a friend who stands too far away is likely to evoke the feeling, "I wonder what is bothering him." In fact, the description "standoffish" is used to describe a person whose attitude is characterized by an undue amount of distance—physical or social.

Distances at which conversations are carried on also vary with cultures. Edward T. Hall, Jr. (1955) reports that distances of 8 to 13 inches between Latin American or Middle East men engaged in conversation are quite common, whereas in the United States such a distance would be considered very chummy or very aggressive. When North Americans converse with men from Latin America or the Middle East, they are likely to express some degree of discomfort at their conversation partner's aggressive familiarity. Since the natural reaction of the North American is to withdraw from such close contact, Latin Americans and Arabs are likely to describe North Americans as cold, distant, and haughty. North Americans design their automobiles with wide seats because they value "apartness," whereas Latin Americans do not know what to do with all the space in a typical American car, since they value closeness.

A British couple spoke with some irritation of their experiences in picnicking in the Lebanese countryside. They said that they liked to look for a pleasant nook in which to relax and enjoy their food in peace and solitude, but that whenever they stopped and started to unpack their picnic things, Lebanese driving down the road would also stop and set up their picnics nearby. In England, once a family had staked out a picnic spot, other Sunday drivers would recognize it as that family's territory and would seek picnic spots elsewhere. The English, like the Americans, value privacy and apartness, but Mediterranean peoples (including Latin Americans) prefer close, chummy sociability. The distance selected by the other means one thing to the English and North American, and something else to the Latin American and the Mediterranean person.

Language

Although we have described a number of non-verbal kinds of behavior used to transmit information, the most efficient and the most obvious mode of communication is language. Languages are normative systems of symbols or symbolic behavior which can be used to transmit or evoke shared meanings. Most languages are basically oral, but may be represented by conventions of written or printed signs. Scholars in literate societies have devoted much time and energy to analyzing the structure of written languages, and this has been paralleled by a tendency to use written language as the basis for instruction in foreign languages. In recent years, however, there has been a greater awareness of the importance of spoken language both as a basis for foreign language instruction and for studies in cognitive functioning.

Language and Thought. The idea that thought consists of "talking to oneself" has intrigued philosophers and scientists alike. Talking to oneself implies language, and language, as we noted above, consists of symbols. Symbols are abstractions; that is, they are sounds, signs, or gestures that represent events or objects—concepts, people, ideas, or whatever. All cognitive functioning is based on abstractions. It is very difficult and at best impractical to deal with events directly, for such an approach would severely limit one's scope of operations. For instance, if I were to go to the kitchen in the morning and try to scramble an egg for my breakfast without using symbols, I might very well spend the entire day at the task and then fail. Scrambling an egg involves getting one out of the refrigerator, finding a pan and butter, putting the pan on the stove, and so forth. If I could not function on a symbolic level, however, I could not even think of an egg or a pan unless I happened to see or feel one. Being without symbols would be like being in a foreign land where one knows not a single word of the local language and can find no one who understands either English or sign language. Such an experience would result in a desperate, panicky feeling of being trapped and helpless. Not being able to use any of the local symbols makes problem solving most difficult.

Under ordinary circumstances, however, the language we use supplies us with a rich fund of symbols that can be used to think about an infinite number of events and combinations of events. For most thought processes, we probably do not bother to recall the actual words to represent what we are thinking; thought generally moves faster than spoken language. But the events we think about are those that are represented for the most part by symbols. In fact, it is difficult to think of events for which we do not have any symbol. Somehow it is easy to manipulate an event symbolically if we have a symbol for it. It is as though we cannot know or think about something unless we know the symbol that represents it. We have all had the experience of having the learning of a new concept introduced by a new term.

Mr. Boria, a newcomer to the West Coast, was shopping for a Christmas tree. He said to the salesman, "I think I'd like a nice bushy spruce."

The salesman answered, "We don't have any spruce, but we have Douglas fir and white fir. I think you'd like the white fir; it's bushier."

"What's the difference between the two?" Mr. Boria wanted to know.

The salesman showed him.

"I'll take the white fir," Mr. Boria decided.

Douglas fir and white fir are terms or symbols used to represent two classes of events. Probably Mr. Boria would not have been able to respond to the two classes differently until he had the brief lesson from the sales clerk. But now he knows the difference and has learned symbols that enable him to attach labels or names to the difference. To be sure, he could learn that some conifers have flat, dark green needles, and others have gray green needles that are quite thick and curve upward from the stem. But his cognitive processes are facilitated immensely by knowing the proper terms to apply to the two kinds of tree.

Linguistic symbols thus have a very high degree of utility. Not only do they help us identify and define events, but we also become dependent on them to identify and define events that can be thought about. It thus appears possible that the way in which we think about events may to some degree be determined by the kind of language we use. This possibility is supported by the common finding in psychometrics that people who can think about complicated events in complicated ways know more symbols than people who can deal with relatively simple events in simple ways. The best single measure of intelligence (if one were to use only a single measure) is a vocabulary test. In other words, people who rate high on intelligence (i.e., who can deal with highly complex events efficiently and effectively) are likely to know more words than people who rate low on intelligence (who can process only simple classes of events and then only slowly and not very efficiently).

Language and Psychological Reality. Not only is the range of stimuli we can deal with limited by our repertory of symbols, but the kind of stimuli as well. Reality, as the self-theorists point out, is what we perceive, and what we perceive becomes reality for us. If the symbols we use determine what we perceive, then reality will be shaped by the symbols we use.

Benjamin L. Whorf (1950, 1956) arrived at conclusions along these lines when he encountered difficulties translating ideas into and from the languages of various American Indian tribes. Language, he said, is not so much a system for reproducing ideas as it is a shaper of ideas and a guide for the individual's mental activity. Whereas most people would say that language represents and is based on the way we perceive our environment, Whorf said the opposite: the way we perceive our environment is deter-

mined by the kind of language to which we are accustomed.

One study that appears to support the "Whorfian hypothesis," as Whorf's proposal has come to be called, consists of comparison of themes in stories told by bilinguals. Susan M. Ervin (1964) asked subjects who were fluent in both French and English to tell stories for standard Thematic Apperception Test (TAT) cards in both languages. She found that the stories women subjects told in English were more likely to be marked by achievement themes, and that stories told in French were more likely to portray verbal aggression and withdrawal as a way of coping with difficult interpersonal situations. Since the independent variables were the languages, it does appear that the kind of language employed by the subjects shaped their way of responding to the stimuli.

Another interpretation is in order, however. Ervin's knowledge of French and Anglo-American culture enabled her to predict the results she obtained. She predicted that women using English would produce a greater number of achievement themes, because Americans are more likely to encourage feminine achievement than the French are, and there is much greater sex-role differentiation in France. Ervin's prediction that stories in French would show more verbal aggression was based on the fact that the French tend to admire verbal prowess and emphasize skill in argumentation in their educational programs. She anticipated the greater use of withdrawal themes in the French stories because of her observation that French families tend to deal with disagreements not so much by compromise or by mutual avowals of a desire to cooperate as by both parties withdrawing from the situation and not speaking to each other. Inasmuch as Ervin's results could have been and indeed were predicted from behavioral trends in the two cultures, it appears that the culture, rather than the language, is the main source of the observed differences in the stories.

Our previous discussions have shown how such

diverse phenomena as sex roles, gestures, and values differ from one culture to another. Since the effects of culture are pervasive and extend to an almost infinite number of behavioral characteristics, it is likely that language structure is also affected. In other words, if culture may be considered as a "global" concept, it would appear that language, like other forms of interpersonal behavior, is only one aspect or dimension, albeit a very important one, of culture. As such, it implements and reflects culturally determined attitudes and values, and conversely helps to reinforce, sustain, and perpetuate them. Remember that Whorf came to propound his hypothesis because of difficulties encountered in translating from one language to another. This is an experience that every student of foreign languages has had. It is, for example, difficult to translate the English word "informal" into Italian. There is an Italian equivalent—*non formale*—but it does not communicate the positive values of relaxation and comfort that "informal" has in English, probably because Italian culture does not prize informality as we do, but places great stress on form. The Italian phrase *"fare la bella figura"* is equally untranslatable. We can try to translate it by saying, "cut a good figure," "keep your 'image' up," or "put a good face on things," but such attempts, though they possess some elements of *"fare la bella figura,"* do not really communicate the flavor of what Italians mean when they use the phrase. In both of these examples, the word or phrase is employed to communicate a value that is important in the culture. It is not so much that the words cannot be translated, but rather that the culture cannot be translated. Once out of context, the meanings of both the words and the idea are changed, because essential relationships are lacking and we tend to make associations that do not exist in the original language.

Psycholinguistics. The branch of psychology that is particularly concerned with language is psycholinguistics. Charles E. Osgood (1963) defines it as "the science of encoding and decoding processes in individual communicators." It includes the more specialized areas of *phonetics,* which is concerned with the terminal phases of encoding, and *psychoacoustics,* which is concerned with the initial phases of decoding. Psycholinguistics is, in turn, included in the broad field of *human communications,* which cuts across all the social sciences. Psycholinguistics itself cuts across a wide range of psychological fields, not only social psychology, but experimental psychology as well. One significant area of psycholinguistic study involves the application of learning theory to the use of language. A number of studies have shown, for example, that with a judicious use of reinforcement, subjects can be led to utter plural instead of single nouns, one type of pronoun instead of another, or one type of complex sentence in preference to other types. Problems of meaning, which we shall take up in the next section, constitute another area of major interest for psycholinguistic specialists.

These specialists may also work in the field of linguistics, a science concerned with describing the code of languages, that is, the rules that govern the distinctions between alternative messages. The elements that a linguistic specialist works with are *phonemes,* the sounds that are important in a given language; *morphemes,* the combinations of phonemes into meaningful units; and *syntax,* the rules governing the combination of morphemes into utterances.

Language learning is still another area of interest for the psycholinguist. Topics in this area include the learning of language by children, learning a second language, and bilingualism. Methods of study include observation, analysis of speech sounds by electronic devices, semantic analysis, and paper-and-pencil measures.

Samuel Fillenbaum (1966) notes that there has been a shift in psycholinguistics in recent years from an emphasis on the comparative study of languages, to a search for the linguistic universals which represent commonalities among all languages and which serve to define the nature of language. If such commonalities exist, there is a possibility that they may be biologically determined. Another problem of current interest to psycholinguistics is *productivity*, the combinatorial ability that enables people to understand and to utter what has never before been heard or said. Fillenbaum states that the fact that people are able to do this is a major principle leading to the concept of language as a form of rule-governed behavior. This is a matter of utmost importance to psycholinguists, because one of their major tasks is to identify and describe these rules.

Denotation and Connotation

Differences in Perception. A language, as we have said, consists of a system of symbols that possess meaning by common consent. From the common-sense point of view, symbols possess meaning because they "stand for something." *"Tavola," "Tisch,"* and *"mesa"* all stand for the class of objects we call "table" in English (and in French). This is all very simple and aboveboard, although it may be argued that each table is different from every other table in some way or other; that the characteristics of a given table change over a period of time, so that a table is not the same at one point of time as it was a moment before; and that each person's perception of a given table is different from every other person's perception (Hayakawa, 1950). There is generally little confusion about concrete objects like tables and chairs: one can point to the object in question, which usually clears up any doubt as to what the word means. In fact it is this aspect of meaning—the "pointing to" aspect—that is termed "denotative." The other class of meanings, those derived from the cognitive associations people are likely to make when they hear or use a word, are the ones that cause the most problems. These meanings are termed "connotative," because they are concerned not so much with the object that is specifically designated by a term, but what the term implies or suggests. The con-

notative meanings of a term often are more significant than the denotative ones. During the early days of the United States, captains of some ships were given "letters of marque" that permitted them to waylay merchant vessels sailing under enemy flags and to seize their cargo. These captains were called "privateers" by Americans, but the enemy probably called them "pirates" or worse. When the two words are applied to the same individuals, they may be said to be the same denotatively, but they certainly have different connotations. "Privateer" has legal and even heroic connotations, whereas "pirate" implies illegal and dastardly operations.

Real problems in meaning are encountered, however, when communication refers to abstractions, such as "peace," "socialism," and "education." The emotional charge carried by the words "peace" and "socialism" is so powerful that relatively little of their meaning is denotative. The words mean different things in different cultures and different things to different people. These are two examples of terms in which the connotative aspects of the words far exceed their denotative aspects. Even the fairly explicit word "education" creates problems. There is some agreement on the denotative aspects of the word, in that in all cultures it has something to do with teaching and learning, but in English it connotes "schooling," whereas in Latin countries it connotes "upbringing." The problem of meaning has become further confused because the English connotations of "education" are becoming familiar to government officials and scholars in Latin countries, with the result that the word is likely to mean somewhat different things to different people in the same culture.

What behavioral psychologists call the "frame of reference" is an important consideration in determining the meaning of a term. In the instance just cited, an Italian school administrator attending an international educational conference will use and react to *"educazione"* in its English sense, as referring to the result of schooling. But f he is discoursing with an Italian colleague, and reference is made to someone's *"educazione,"* he will understand that reference is being made to the person's manners and general deportment, which are the result, of course, of the kind of upbringing he has had. In the frame of reference used at an international conference, the word has one meaning, but in a more conventional frame of reference, it has another.

Empathy. One of the most crucial problems in interpersonal communication is that of determining what others are saying by using the words they choose—that is, the implicit, as well as the explicit, meaning of their messages. The term "empathy" is sometimes used to designate the ability to understand the feelings that another person is consciously or unconsciously communicating. The person who rates high in empathy is one who would be able to be aware of the connotations intended by the communicator. His task is simplified, of course, when he knows what frame of reference is being used. People who have had similar backgrounds of experience can understand one another better than people from other backgrounds, because they can empathize with one another more successfully. They share the same frame of reference, so that it is often unnecessary for them to say much in a given situation. Two men driving cars in parallel lanes down a crowded street come to a simultaneous stop, side by side, their progress having been blocked by a woman attempting to back a station wagon into a parking space that is obviously too small. The two men look at each other. One raises his eyebrows and looks skyward. The other nods his head. The grimace used by the first means: "What can you expect of a woman driver?" The two men share an attitude common in the American male subculture—that of having a low opinion of the skill of women drivers. Inasmuch as they share this attitude and inasmuch as both are caught in the same situation, all it takes is a single helpless gesture to achieve complete empathy.

In transactional terms, empathic communica-tion takes place through the reception of weak signals by way of channels in which the noise level is likely to be quite high. Often the communicator is not aware that he is communicating at all. A patient visits a physician for treatment of a mild throat infection. The physician notes that she seems to be under a great deal of stress. When he mentions this to the patient, she is surprised. She is going through the throes of a divorce, but was not aware that the tension she is feeling was so obvious.

When we say that the noise level in empathic communication is high, we are referring to the fact that the signals indicating the communicator's mood are often unnoticed. For one thing, they are slight: the way in which the individual holds his head, the tone of voice, and the like. For another, the audience may be concentrating primarily on the denotative content of the communicator's message and may miss the overtones that indicate feeling tones. Furthermore, the ability to decode signals indicating mood and feeling tone requires a heightened degree of arousal or awareness on the part of the audience.

Common sense would hold that it should be easier to empathize with a friend than with a stranger, and this supposition is supported by research, although only to a moderate degree. In a study of the accuracy of empathic judgments, Ronald Taft (1966) asked psychology students to predict how two fellow students would rate themselves on a list of adjectives. One of the target persons was a close acquaintance, and the other was known only casually. Students were able to predict friends' ratings somewhat more accurately than those of non-friends, but the difference, though statistically significant, was only slight. In 35 per cent of the students' attempts to predict, students were actually more accurate in predicting the responses of strangers than predicting the responses of their friends. Taft explained the ability of his subjects to score high in predicting the responses of strangers to their using a kind of stereotyped "modal personality" as a target in making their predictions. Inasmuch as such a stereotype was fairly accurate much of the time, students were able to be fairly successful in empathizing with strangers.

One of the reasons, of course, that they were able to be accurate is that they were drawn from the same subcultural group—a university student body—and consequently shared many attitudes and values, as well as common frames of reference, all of which facilitated the empathic process.

The Semantic Differential. We noted earlier that word meanings have denotative and connotative aspects, which is another way of saying that we have missed much of the informational content of a word if we are aware only of what it denotes. Osgood, Suci, and Tannenbaum (1957) have carried out factor analyses of the connotative or affective aspects of words and terms to find more precise ways of measuring variations in their informational content. They found that about 50 per cent of differences in meanings among words could be accounted for by three factors: evaluation, potency, and activity. These factors can, in turn, be measured by having subjects rate words

on a series of scales. The *evaluation* factor of an object or word can be measured on such scales as "good-bad," "clean-dirty," "beautiful-ugly," and the like. The *potency* factor can be measured by scales like these: "hard-soft," "rough-smooth," and "heavy-light." The *activity* factor can be measured by "fast-slow," "hot-cold," and "active-passive." Figure 12-2 represents the mean ratings of fifty-four psychology students from San Francisco State College, who were asked to rate France and the United States on nine scales. The first three scales represented the *evaluative* factor and showed that the respondents valued the two countries rather similarly, except that the United States had somewhat happier connotations for the raters than France. France is perceived as having connotations that are slightly, but not significantly, cleaner and fresher than the United States. The latter rates higher on the *potency* factor (the next three scales). There is no difference in "heaviness," but the United States carries connotations of strength and ruggedness to a greater extent than does France. Ratings on the last three scales show that the United States connotes more *activity* than France does for this group of subjects.

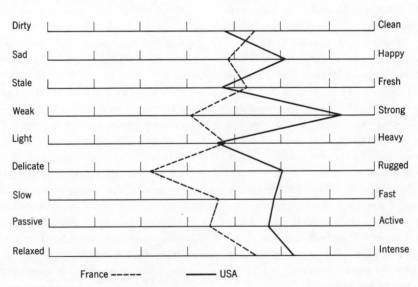

Figure **12-2.** College students' rating of "France" and "USA," using the semantic differential (Lindgren, 1966).

The semantic differential also has value in cross-cultural research. Malcolm M. Helper and Sol L. Garfield (1965) used it to study the process of acculturation in American Indian adolescents. The Indians, who were from various Plains tribes, were students in Flandreau School, a government boarding school serving some eighteen reservations. Students were asked to rate *Indian, White person, The future, Being on time, Planning ahead, Me, Me as I want to be, My mother, My father, Going home, Flandreau School, Quitting school, Drinking, Speaking English,* and *Getting mad.*

Responses were compared with those of white students attending a nearby high school. When ratings for each of the topics were ranked according to evaluation, potency, and activity, high-achieving Indian students were found to report connotations that were more similar to white students than those reported by low-achieving Indians. In general, white students tended to assign more value to *Planning ahead, Being on time,* and *The future* (boys only). High-achieving Indians, when contrasted with low-achieving Indians, were more likely to assign higher ratings to *Being on time, Planning ahead, Speaking English,* and *Me* (boys only). These results suggest that white students had higher levels of need for achievement than Indian students and that achieving Indian students were more likely to identify with whites and hence had more similar views on life.

The semantic differential has also been used by clinical psychologists to measure patients' attitudes toward various aspects of their lives. For example, a group of young people in Marseilles hospitalized for attempted suicide rated *Me* and *Father* as being less potent, and *Illness* and *Death* as having more value, than did a group of nonpatients their own age (Mouren, Tatossian, Blumen, & Guin, 1966). It appears that the suicidal patients were using these words in a somewhat different frame of reference than others are likely to do.

Word-Association Tests. Osgood and his coworkers measure connotation by asking respondents to rate words according to a standard list of bipolar terms. Still another way of measuring connotation is that of asking people to respond to a list of words with the first word that comes to mind: the word-association method. The most commonly used list of words is the one developed by Grace H. Kent and A. J. Rosanoff (1910) during the early part of this century. The responses to this list have been categorized and analyzed in terms of the responses of various groups. Educated people, for example, give fewer of the "popular" responses than do people of less education. The word-association method of measuring the connotative aspects of words is more difficult to deal with statistically than are approaches that make use of the semantic differential, but it has nevertheless produced some interesting results. Robert H. Koff (1965) administered the Kent-Rosanoff list in 1963 to children aged 8 to 12 and compared their responses with those given by children in 1916. He found that over the years there was a considerable degree of shifting in the kinds of primary (most popular) responses given. Whereas in 1916 children's responses were markedly different from those of adults, in 1963 they were no longer significantly different. As a result of his findings, Koff raised the question of whether children today were becoming socialized earlier than in 1916.

Mark R. Rosenzweig (1964) found a number of differences between French *lycée* and American college students and between students and workers, using the Kent-Rosanoff list. An analysis of primary responses of American students showed them to be more similar to American workmen, than French students were to French workers. In fact, French students' responses were closer to American students' responses than they were to the responses of French workmen. One interpretation of these differences is that the social gap between middle-class students and blue-collar workmen is considerably greater in France than it is in the United States. The fact that French workmen's use of language differs so markedly from that of students also suggests that the two groups have quite different ways of thinking and feeling about their environment. Another difference was the degree of commonality revealed by French and American responses. There was a much greater tendency for Americans, both students and workers, to use more of the same words, that is, there was less variance and fewer interpersonal differences among their responses. This finding is consistent with other reports of a high degree of individuality and independence among French people, as contrasted with people from other countries. The greater the degree of individuality, in other words, the greater the likelihood that word associations would be unique and idiosyncratic. The responses of American subjects, on the other hand, suggested that they were more closely identified with a common culture, and that they probably shared a greater number of common frames of reference. The higher degree of commonality also supports the observation that Americans are more socially sensitive, more involved with one another, and more "other-directed" than are the French.

Still another difference found by Rosenzweig concerned similarities and differences between stimulus words and responses with respect to parts of speech. Other research has shown that adults are more inclined to give a response that is the same part of speech as the stimulus word. When given the stimulus word "sky," for example, adults are more likely to respond with another noun, like "heaven," "clouds," or "earth." Children are more likely to respond with words other than nouns, like "blue," or "cloudy." Rosenzweig found that American students and workers and French students all tended to respond with words that were the same parts of speech as the stimulus words, as adults in other studies had done, but French workers tended to respond with words that were different parts of speech, more like children.

Stereotypes

The Usefulness of Stereotypes in Communication. All communication is based on a number of assumptions about the audience. In the absence of obviously contrary evidence, we are inclined to assume that the audience is like us, in that he, she, or they are likely to share the same frames of reference, to hold similar values, and to perceive things more or less as we do. Such an assumption is often erroneous, of course, but we make it because we have to make *some* assumptions about the audience, and our readiest and most obvious referent is ourself.

In most instances, however, we do have some information about the audience that enables us to outline our target somewhat more accurately and relieves us of the necessity to assume direct similarity to ourselves. If the speaker is a woman and the audience is a man, she is likely to assume that he does not want to talk about shopping for dresses, child care, or housekeeping problems. She will make this assumption because she has a cognitive map or mental picture of "what men are like," and this map does not include any marked degree of interest in these topics. Her cognitive map of men-in-general may also reflect other assumptions about men: perhaps an interest in baseball, a high sex drive, a tendency to become irritable over trifles, a tendency to drink too much on occasion, and the like, depending on what she has learned about men during her life. What we have been describing here is what is called a "stereotype," a tendency to perceive a certain class of events—usually people—in a certain way. Stereotypes involve a number of distortions in perception. For one thing, they assume that people of a certain class (men, women, teenagers, Negroes, Englishmen, or whatever) are alike in certain ways. The truth is, of course, that everyone is different, and the stereotype is a distortion because it ignores these differences.

Stereotypes are indispensable, however, in almost any kind of social interaction. It is impossible to know everything about everybody. A stereotype is a kind of shortcut, a way of abstracting a number of characteristics about another person or group of persons, organizing them into a pattern of expectations, and responding to the person or persons as though they were that pattern. It would be impossible to interact with or respond effectively to other people if we did not refer to stereotypes. When stereotypes are constructed realistically, they are based on what we have learned about how people behave in terms of their social positions, roles, classes, and so forth. When we use the telephone to call someone in a distant city, our stereotype of telephone operators tells us what to expect of them. Our stereotype in this instance is a fairly accurate guide, because a telephone operator's roles are highly structured and there is little variation in the way that different women play them. If we were to encounter a telephone operator off the job, however, we would have to resort to different stereotypes to determine what to expect of her. We would make some rapid judgments based on her manner of speech, the way she is dressed, the kind of person she is with, and what she happens to be doing at the moment. If she is in informal dress, wheeling a small child in a stroller, and shopping in a supermarket, we would call into operation the stereotypes we happen to have for mothers of young children.

When Stereotypes Mislead. Stereotypes interfere with our ability to function effectively with others when they lead us to make assumptions inconsistent with the kind of behavior usually exhibited by the target person. A student's stereotype of professors might include the assumption that they are not interested in talking to students. If the same student is also having difficulty in a course, he does not therefore regard the professor as a potential source of help, whereas in fact the professor might be quite willing to talk to the student and help clarify his problems. The student might be so convinced of the validity of his stereotype that he actually acts in ways that cause the professor to "prove" he is not interested in students. The student might, for example, approach the professor after class and say: "I am getting concerned about my grade in this course." This rather feeble remark is hardly the type that would awaken a sympathetic interest on the part of a professor. The professor looks up the grade, notes that it is about a "D" and replies, "Well, I think you *should* be concerned." The student waits for the professor to say, "Would you like to come in to my office to talk about it?", but the professor is waiting for the student to make the next move. Nothing further transpires, and they both go their separate ways, the student even further convinced of the validity of his assumption that professors are not interested in students.

This type of maneuver, as we have noted previously, is what is sometimes termed a "self-fulfilling prophecy," because the individual behaves in a way that evokes the kind of behavior he expects from the audience. Social learning takes place in such instances because the incorrect assumption has become reinforced by the fulfillment of the prophecy or expectation.

Incidentally, if the student had been more empathic, he would have said something like this to the professor: "I am having a problem with some of the concepts in this course. Could I talk to you about them?" Empathy in this instance would have told him that professors are usually interested in their subject and are hence eager to discuss it with students. A student who expresses concern about the grade he is receiving is also raising a question about whether he is being graded fairly and is thus questioning the professor's judgment.

As in the example we have described, stereotypes can be a kind of psychological defense against getting to know and understand others. Anxiety is an important factor in such instances. We commonly feel some degree of anxiety about interacting with people in positions of authority who are sitting in judgment on us, and we are also inclined to react defensively when anxious. The student finds it slightly reassuring that his stereotype of professors is correct. If he had been wrong, then he would have had to readjust his cognitive system in order to accommodate new information about professors. Some students could incorporate such data without much difficulty, but others would be troubled by the realization that they could reduce the social distance between themselves and professors and might even come to find them likable and helpful people. The insecure student prefers to maintain a considerable degree of social distance and not become involved with professors any more than is required. Thus anxiety serves to reinforce and sustain the stereotype and keeps the student from having to make any more adjustments (or accomplish any more learning) than he wishes. Unwittingly, of course, he contributes to a stereotype favored by professors, namely, that students really are not interested in learning—just in grades.

In brief, stereotypes are useful when they reduce the noise in a communication channel and thus enable us to receive the information the source is attempting to communicate, but they introduce noise into the channel when they are inappropriate and lead us to expect something other than the actual message.

Feedback

Feedback as an Orienting Mechanism. Stereotypes aid in communication if they are reasonably accurate and if they can be modified by new data. One way we can modify the stereotypes is by maintaining a state of active awareness about the effect our messages have on others. As we pointed out earlier, even the most useful stereotypes contain a high degree of error, in that we cannot anticipate everything about everybody and inevitably make some misjudgments about how statements will be received and interpreted. If maintaining stereotypes intact has a high value for us, we will be insensitive to signals indicating that we have erred, but if we are open and flexible about our stereotypes, we can modify them according to the data we receive from a process known as "feedback."

"Feedback" is a term that psychologists have borrowed from electronics. It is a process that occurs when data regarding the performance of a system (a machine or an organism, for example) is fed back into the system to permit correction and adjustment of the performance.* The automatic pilot on transport airplanes operates on feedback principles. If changes in air currents carry the plane off course, the automatic pilot steers the plane back on course. If, in doing so, there is a degree of overcompensation, information fed back into the mechanism enables it to correct for that as well. Examinations and quizzes provide feedback information for instructors and students alike. Students can discover deficiencies in their learning strategies, instructors can discover how successful their teaching has been, and presumably both can make the necessary corrections in their future behavior.

A great deal of social learning can be regarded as the result of feedback. The various modes of behavior that children use in attempting to fit themselves into their family and culture evoke responses from parents and peers, some positive and accepting, and some negative or neutral. These responses, in turn, provide information as to whether the behavior is appropriate or inappropriate. The appropriate behavior thus becomes reinforced and strengthened, and the inappropriate behavior drops out and is extinguished. This process goes on throughout life and forms the basis for our learning to adapt ourselves to the continually changing social situations in which we find ourselves. The more complex the situation, and the less sure we are of ourselves, the more we depend on feedback to keep us informed about what course of behavior to take. When learning a foreign language, for instance, we not only listen more carefully to what others

* The study of the regulation, control, and feedback of information in electrical circuits, machines, persons, and social groups is called *cybernetics* (Wiener, 1950).

say and how they pronounce their words, but we also scan their faces for clues to determine whether they have understood us and whether our pronunciation is acceptable. In speaking our own language in a comfortable social situation, we are much less concerned about feedback.

Feedback of Physiological Information. One especially ingenious study of the effect of feedback on attitudes was conducted by Stuart Valins (1966), who asked male psychology students to participate in an experiment described to them as a study of physiological reactions to sexually oriented stimuli. They were told that their reactions would be recorded while they viewed ten slides of seminude females (taken from *Playboy* magazine). Some of the groups of subjects were told that they would hear their heartbeats played back to them. What they actually heard was a recording. For one experimental group, the "heartbeats" were slowed down for certain slides, and for another group, speeded up. A control group heard the same sounds, but were told that they were hearing extraneous noise. The subjects who thought they were hearing changes in their heartbeats while they were looking at certain slides tended to rate those slides as more attractive or appealing than slides which were accompanied by a "normal heartbeat." In fact, the reinforcement had so powerful an effect that a follow-up survey without "heartbeats" taken three weeks after the experiment found the subjects still expressing a greater degree of preference for the "reinforced" slides than for the others they had seen.

When subjects were interviewed after the experiment, they reported that they had been surprised by certain slides, although they did not at first know why. The surprise sometimes took the form of an attack of coughing or sneezing, or that of noticing a resemblance to a former girl friend. They assumed that the surprise was due to something about the slide that was being shown to them and decided to examine it more closely. When they did so, they concluded that the girl pictured on the slide was indeed more attractive than the others and hence deserved a high rating.

What occurred can best be explained by cognitive dissonance theory. Dissonance was created for these students because they had not thought the girl pictured on the slide was any more attractive than the others, yet their "heartbeat" told them that they were responding differently to her. Dissonance was reduced by their decision that she was actually more attractive than they had thought at first. The fact that their decision to modify their rating of her made a significant impression on them is demonstrated by the finding that their preferences were still valid three weeks later.

Social Pressure in Feedback. Opinion changes were produced in this experiment because our perception of our heart rate is one source of information about our attitudes and feelings. For instance, a study by Robert Buckhout (1966) showed that when subjects were induced by verbal reinforcement to read statements aloud that were contrary to their previously expressed attitudes, their heart rate changed. However, other kinds of information fed back into the cognitive system are equally important. The studies of opinion changes induced by false norms discussed in Chapter 6 are another example. In such experiments, the subject who is about to announce his judgment of the length of lines or whatever is forced to compare it with the judgments of others, and the differences between what he observes and what he thinks they have observed forces him to reevaluate his opinion. In many social situations a mere awareness that one's opinion differs is enough to cause reconsideration. When the volume of feedback becomes more intense (say, when others make adverse comments), the amount of compliance is increased, as it was in the study of Norwegian and French subjects who found themselves in disagreement with judgments of other "group members" who were actually tape-recorded voices of the experimenter's accomplices (Milgram, 1961).

Empathy and Feedback. Empathy is obviously an important factor in feedback. Our skill in noting changes in feeling and attitude on the part of our audience enables us to determine whether our messages are getting through and what effect they are having. This information, once it has been fed back into our cognitive systems, further enables us to shift our approaches and to find more effective ways of communicating. The lecturer knows that he is losing the interest of the audience if he sees people talking to one another, shifting in their chairs, or showing other signs of restlessness. He can then change his pace in some way—by becoming more dramatic, stopping to tell a story, using more illustrations, or whatever. As the research we have just cited suggests, empathy also provides information that may lead us to change our minds as well as our communication techniques. Learning that others differ with what we are saying, and probably do not approve of us for saying it, may lead us to decide that we do not believe what we are saying and instead believe something else. It is this kind of feedback that, in the final analysis, shapes our opinions of ourselves, particularly in our earlier and more formative years.

Feedback of Direct Attempts to Influence. The fact that our self-concepts are so readily available to influences of this type does not mean that they can be directly manipulated. Actually, we tend to develop defenses against attempts at direct influence. This point is aptly demonstrated by a study in which high school students working singly were given the impression that they were collaborating with another student on a rating task. In one situation, the subject received a note from his fictitious partner saying, "I think we should both do. . .". In other situations, the "partner" wrote notes beginning with such phrases as, "I think I would like. . .", "I would prefer. . .", and the like. Subjects whose "partners" told them what choices to make were inclined to reject the suggestions, whereas those whose "partners"

merely stated a personal preference were inclined to go along with them (Brehm & Sensenig, 1966). The subjects obviously perceived association with a partner on an equal basis as a kind of a reward, whereas association at the price of some loss of freedom was perceived as a threat.

As we pointed out in Chapter 2, we are attracted to the stimulating effects of association with others as long as we can exercise control over the amount of stimulation to be derived. When the controls are out of our hands, however, the situation becomes less attractive. Thus the most effective way of exercising control is to seem to be (or actually to be) unconcerned with exercising control. The groups in the Asch false-norm situation were probably very effective because they made no *direct* attempts to influence the naive subjects, but promulgated their judgments on a take-it-or-leave-it basis. The Norwegian and French subjects in the Milgram (1961) experiment are a special case, because they were not *directed* to comply, but were ridiculed for not complying. We tend to be vulnerable to the peer group's indifference or its rejection, but its direct attempts to dominate us are more likely to meet with resistance.

SUMMARY

Behavioral scientists tend to see communication as a transactional process that involves both communicator and audience, whereas laymen tend to be preoccupied with the initial or message-sending phases of communication. Communication serves as the basis for social relationships of all kinds. A social system may be considered as a set of positions interconnected with communication channels. The kind of transaction identified as communication takes place through a series of actions in which communicators direct messages to audiences by way of transmitters, channels, and receivers. "Noise" may interevene at any point in the process to interfere with the transmission or reception of the message. The result is unanticipated variation in the message as received.

Communication takes place through messages, which may be explicit or implicit. Although the sender may be primarily concerned with the explicit information in a message, the audience will generally be interested in both the implicit and the explicit information that the message conveys. The implicit information will, for example, reveal something about the status and identity of the communicator, which in turn will have an effect on the receptivity of the audience and the amount of noise the message will encounter in the channel.

The kind of language used for communication is a major source of information with respect to cultural identity. Within a given culture, spoken language will also convey information as to the educational and social status of the communicator and will provide cues that may determine the acceptability of the speaker. The distance at which spoken communication is initiated is also related to the degree of acceptance that is anticipated by a speaker.

Languages are normative systems of symbols or symbolic behavior used to transmit or evoke shared meanings. Language bears an intimate relationship to thinking, a process that makes extensive use of linguistic symbols. The symbols of the language we use enable us to identify and define events that can be thought about, and the range of symbols that can be identified by an individual can be used as a measure of his cognitive ability or intelligence. Whorf suggested that the kind of language used by an individual sets the pattern of his thinking and perceiving. Research with bilinguals provides some support for Whorf's hypothesis, but findings can also be interpreted in terms of differences in the cultures for which the languages are appropriate.

Psycholinguistics is the science of encoding and decoding processes in individual communicators. This is a field that includes a wide range of fields in psychology, as well as linguistics, phonetics, and psychoacoustics. A basic problem in linguistics is the search for universals that apply to all types of language of whatever type, wherever they are used.

Symbols have both denotative (explicit) and connotative (implicit) aspects. The emotional charge of a symbol is its connotative aspect, and there are many words that carry a connotative loading in excess of their denotative information. The ability to understand the implicit and affective aspects of messages is termed empathy. Empathy is facilitated when senders and receivers of messages share common frames of reference. The noise level in empathic communication is likely to be high, because signals are weak and may go unnoticed. A paper-and-pencil device known as the semantic differential is used to measure the connotative aspects of symbols and other events, as well as differences in perceptual style, values, and attitudes. Associations that are usually made with respect to certain words can also be used as a measure of the latters' connotative aspects. Studies with word associations show that differences in association style between children and adults have decreased over the last fifty years or so and also that American college students are closer to American workmen, and to French students, than the latter are to French workmen.

The generalized assumptions that people have regarding other individuals and groups are termed stereotypes. The kind of stereotype that the communicator has regarding his audience determines the kind of message he initiates and how he sends it. The use of stereotypes is unavoidable, because it is impossible to know everything about everybody. For practicality and efficiency's sake one assumes that all the members of a given audience are similar, whereas in reality they are not. Stereotypes work much of the time because they are reasonably accurate (or not too inaccurate) with respect to relevant characteristics of the audience, but when they lead to false assumptions, they can cause difficulties. Stereotypes often serve as a kind of defense against getting to know others better.

Attempts at communication are guided and oriented by information that is fed back to the communicator through various channels, verbal and nonverbal. This type of information, termed "feedback," serves a variety of purposes. The more complex the social situation, the more we depend on feedback to determine what to do next. The extent to which opinions are based on feedback is shown by an experiment in which subjects were told that they would hear their heartbeat over electronic equipment while they looked at pictures of partially clad young women. Pictures viewed while the subjects heard a fictitious heartbeat that speeded up or slowed down were rated as more attractive. Such results can be explained through cognitive dissonance theory. Feedback also plays an important role in empathy, and information fed back to us in the form of group opinion can be influential, as long as attempts to control are not too obvious.

SUGGESTED READINGS

Brown, R., *Words and things*. Glencoe, Ill.: Free Press, 1958.

Carroll, J. B., *The study of language*. Cambridge: Harvard University Press, 1953.

Creelman, M. B., *The experimental investigation of meaning*. New York: Springer, 1966.

Hall, E. T., *The silent language*. New York: Doubleday, 1959. (Published as a paperback by Fawcett, New York, 1961)

Hoijer, H. (Ed.), *Language in culture*. Chicago: University of Chicago Press, 1954.

Lindgren, H. C. (Ed.), *Contemporary research in social psychology*. New York: Wiley, 1969. See papers in Section 8, "Communication."

Osgood, C. E., Suci, G. J., & Tannenbaum, P. H., *The measurement of meaning*. Urbana: University of Illinois Press, 1957.

CHAPTER THIRTEEN

Group Processes

What Makes a Group? Two or more persons engaged in any kind of a relationship with each other constitute a group. The members of a group may never meet: people who interact only through correspondence or who never interact directly may be considered members of groups under some conditions. The important characteristic is that there be a relationship. Two strangers, walking down the same street in San Francisco, side by side, are not a group as such, but when they are accosted simultaneously by a Girl Scout selling cookies, they become a group. The fact that she deals with them together makes them a group, and the fact that they are aware that they are sharing a common experience makes them a group. A poll taker who is interested in getting the opinions of San Franciscos residents on an issue might regard them as members of a fairly large group of people known as San Franciscans. He would thus perceive a relationship between them and would therefore treat them accordingly. He would go up to them individually and say that he is polling San Francisco residents. Such a statement would remind them for the moment that they are members of this larger group.

Most groups studied by social psychologists endure longer than that of the two strangers approached by the Girl Scout. Groups may survive only a few minutes, as in a problem-solving group set up for experimental purposes, or they may continue for the lifetime of all but a few of the members, as for example, national groups.

Most of our discussion so far in this book has been concerned with the effects of social interaction on *individual* behavior, with the ways in which individuals are attracted to one another, identify with others, define boundaries between themselves and others, are stimulated by others, and the like. Social psychologists are also interested in studying groups as such. Like individuals, groups also are entities that possess characteristics and properties which can be observed, measured, classified, and predicted. Just as it is possible to specify conditions that are likely to result in certain kinds of behavior on the part of individuals, it is also possible to determine conditions that will predetermine certain kinds of behavior on the part of groups. The term "group processes" is sometimes applied to the formulations of such tendencies. "Group dynamics," a term introduced by Kurt Lewin, is also used. Both terms carry the implication that groups are to be considered as entities characterized by change and on-going activity. This is not to deny that they have certain stable characteristics that may make them appear static at times, but the implication is that their special qualities can be observed and measured in terms of the activity that takes place within their boundaries.

Formation and Maintenance. Groups may be formed through accidental or fortuitous means beyond the immediate control of their members or they may be formed voluntarily, as a result of mutual attraction. The two strangers who became a group when the Girl Scout asked them to buy cookies are an example of the first type of group. The fact that they are both San Franciscans may or may not be an example of the second type—this would depend on the degree of choice they have as to their city of residence. An individual who has been sent by his Chicago firm to represent it in San Francisco presumably has less choice about his place of residence, although he could probably represent his employer equally well by maintaining an office in San Francisco and his home in one of the suburban areas. Hence he probably lives in San Francisco because he prefers to—that is, he is *attracted* to the city. In a free society, in which individuals may change employment and residence more or less at will, groups are somewhat more likely to be formed on the basis of mutual attraction.

Once groups have been formed, they tend to take on certain characteristics. They are likely to develop a *structure*, whereby members have positions that stand in relationship to one another. These positions, as we pointed out in Chapter 8, are defined by the expectations that the group has for the behavior of the persons occupying these positions and that are mirrored, in turn, by the expectations that the position holders have for their own behavior. We also noted that certain attitudes and ways of perceiving tend to be associated with certain positions and to be reflected in both the role behaviors and the self-concepts of persons occupying the positions.

In the two-person group, or dyad, composed of a poll taker and a respondent, the positions are the ones indicated: poll taker and respondent. The role of the poll taker is that of asking the questions assigned to him, and the role of the respondent is that of answering them. The role behaviors are reciprocal: the respondent expects the poll taker to ask him questions, and the poll taker expects the respondent to answer them. Although these are the normal roles for the two positions, not everyone in a group will accept them. Some people refuse to answer pollsters; others ramble, do not stick to the questions asked them, and use the opportunity to express their views on a variety of subjects. But most persons polled, at least in the American middle-class culture, follow the normal procedure. Reciprocal role patterns, positions, expectations, and certain predetermined attitudes and percepts constitute the structure that gives groups a degree of stability and predictibility.

Stability and Change. Even very informal groups have some of these qualities. A student sits down with a cup of coffee and a roll at a table in the college commons. He starts to read the college newspaper. Another student sits down with his roll and coffee. They say nothing. The first continues to read the paper; the second gazes off

into space while he sips his coffee. It can barely be said that they are a group. There is no interaction, yet the second student had his choice of tables. Most of the others were empty. It is a reasonable assumption that he passed by the others because he wanted some company while he ate his roll and drank his coffee. A third student arrives with coffee, toast, and a plate of scrambled eggs. He, too, was probably attracted by the existing nucleus of a group. As he begins to eat, his eye catches a headline on the back page of the paper being read by the first student. It mentions a *cause célèbre* on the campus, an instructor who is not being rehired for the forthcoming year because of lack of research activity. The third student turns to the second, gesturing at the headline with his fork, and says, "Isn't that a dirty shame? The only real teacher on the campus and they're letting him go."

The second student says, "Maybe, although I've heard that he isn't all that good."

A discussion then develops, with the third student maintaining that the instructor has been treated unjustly and that the college is losing one of its better, more dedicated teachers. The second student continues to express his doubts. The first student puts his paper down and enters the argument, agreeing with the third student that the dismissal is unjust.

The group has not been in existence more than 15 minutes, but during that period some structure develops. The first and third students attack the college administration and defend the faculty member; the second continues to express his doubts and moves gradually to a more pro-administration position. An objective observer would note that after the first 2 or 3 minutes of interaction it becomes possible to predict the general trend of the discussion; that is, he can expect with reasonable accuracy who will attack and who will defend the faculty member. The first and third students are more aggressive; the second, more subdued in his manner. A kind of norm develops in that the first and third interrupt the second and even each other; the second waits politely until the others are finished before making his points. Toward the end of the discussion, the third student is talking more than the first, who is talking more than the second. This development suggests that a kind of dominance hierarchy is developing.

A fourth student, carrying toast and coffee, passes by and catches the name of the instructor, lingers, and then sits down. He listens for a while, sipping his coffee and munching his toast. The newest member of any group is likely to be considered its junior, unless he displays some obvious trappings of status, in which case he may not stand on ceremony and may move into the conversation. Ordinarily this new arrival would be considered a peer, equal in status to the others, but for the moment he is the newest and most junior member of the group.

After he has waited for what seems like a respectable period of time—say 2 or 3 minutes—he says, "I've heard that the real reason why he is not being rehired is that he got mixed up with some New Left group."

This is new information, and, as the bearer of data hitherto unavailable to the others, the fourth student suddenly moves in status from the bottom to the top of the hierarchy. All are silent, waiting for him to continue. As he tells his story, however, the third student, who was the dominant member until the arrival of the fourth student, shows signs of impatience and finally interrupts, saying, "That's nothing new! And furthermore I don't think it has anything to do with the problem: not even the administration thinks that New Left groups are radical any more!"

The new member is thus put in his place and the status quo ante is maintained.

What we have tried to show in this chain of incidents is how purely informal and voluntary groups, though unstable in most respects, may develop some elements of structure in a relatively short time. The members of this group have created a status hierarchy of sorts, have occupied positions, and have developed a set of expectations for one another's behavior. The structure is a loose one, to be sure, yet it does endure for a number of minutes, maintaining itself through its flexibility.

Flexibility is not enough, however. The fourth student answers the third one: "Where have you been living? I know for a fact that three instructors in my major department didn't get promoted because they made speeches for New Left groups."

The third student asks, "How do you know there weren't other reasons?" and then says he has to go to class. He picks up his books and goes off. With his departure, nothing more is said, although the fourth student is clearly in the mood to continue talking. Within a couple of minutes, the other students have finished their breakfast and have gone off. Thus the group disintegrates, almost as rapidly as it formed.

Rewards, Costs, and Comparison Level. The willingness of people to remain with or to leave a group may also be perceived in terms of the rewards that are received and the costs that are incurred. The students who participated in the group we have just described joined and remained with the group in order to obtain certain rewards: the pleasant stimulation of being with others while eating, the joys attendant to self-expression, and the like. Costs of belonging to a group may also be monetary, as in the case of dues that are paid in order to maintain membership in clubs and other types of associations. Costs are, however, generally of a psychological nature. John W. Thibaut and Harold H. Kelley (1959) define *costs* in terms of anything that serves to interfere with or inhibit the performance of an action. The greater the effort that must be expended by an individual who wishes to affiliate with a group, the greater the cost of his participation. The costs may, for instance, be measured in terms of embarrassment, anxiety, irritation, or the necessity to cope with conflicting or competing needs. In the group just described, the costs of remaining in the group included willingness to listen to others and waiting one's turn to speak, refraining from angry insults, and the like. Toward the end of the life span of the group, its members had met their needs for self-expression and remembered commitments elsewhere. When costs of remaining exceed the potential rewards, the group breaks up.

Everyone has a standard or *comparison level,* to use the terminology of Thibaut and Kelley, against which he compares the costs expended and the rewards received as a result of his involvement in a group. This comparison level may be based on his observations of other members of his group or of other similar groups. For example, let us say that Harry Channing, a college graduate in business administration, is employed as an insurance salesman. Harry is one of two college graduates in the group, the remaining salesmen having completed high school or at best one or two years of college. The district sales manager, who chairs the weekly sales meeting that all salesmen must attend, gives most of his attention to the salesmen who he feels need the most help. Harry is usually ignored, because his sales record is satisfactory, while the other college-educated salesman, whose sales are lagging, gets much more attention. Harry is not aware of the sales manager's motives, however, and has become increasingly resentful of the treatment he is receiving. As a result, he is seriously considering leaving the company and finding some other line of work.

Harry's comparison level in this instance is based on his perception of the way in which his college-educated colleague is being treated. As far as Harry is concerned, their status is the same, yet he is the one who is ignored. His costs (irritation at being ignored, feeling of inadequacy at being rejected, and the like) have begun to exceed his rewards (satisfaction in being the member of a group, satisfaction in his sales record, and the like). The fact that Harry is considering leaving the company means that level of outcomes in this group has dropped for him to a point

where it is very close to the *comparison level for alternates*—the term that Thibaut and Kelley employ to designate the point of reference people use in deciding whether or not to remain with a group. The costs of seeking another position involve uncertainty and the actual work involved in canvassing available opportunities. After Harry considers these costs seriously, they may seem so high as to offer no particular advantage over his present situation, unpleasant as it is. As a result, the distance between the comparison level for his present group involvement and that of the comparison level for alternates will increase, and the present situation will appear relatively more attractive.

Developmental Stages in Group Participation

Infancy. Participating as a functioning member of a multi-person group may call for a fairly complex variety of skills. The basic rudiments of these skills are learned in our first groups—families—and they are developed gradually, as part of a process of social learning.

The earliest social interactions are of course dyadic—between mother and infant. Often both parents will interact simultaneously with the infant, but the latter can focus on only one at a time. During the first months, the nature of this interaction is rather primitive—more on a biological than a social level. It is not until the child begins to have some awareness of itself as a person that real social reciprocity begins. Even when children are age two or so, and they can talk a bit and interact on a largely nonverbal but nevertheless highly social way with another person, they often become confused when they must cope with two or more individuals at a time. A child may be playing happily with one parent when the other parent enters the room and says something either to the parent or the child. Often the child expresses a feeling of irritation, and not merely because of the interruption. The problem of trying to cope with the simultaneous presentation of two separate and different groups of stimuli is somewhat beyond the scope of the child's nervous system. Most children learn to deal with this problem within a few months or a year, although some accommodate themselves earlier than others.

Early Childhood. The classic study on the development of socializing is that done by M. L. Parten (1932) a generation ago. Parten observed the play patterns of preschool children and found that there was a definite progression by age through the sequence of solitary play, watching others play, parallel play (playing alone, but in the company of others), associative play (doing what others are doing, but not involved in a give-and-take type of activity), and cooperative play. Solitary play and parallel play were the norm between 2 and 3 years of age, with associative and cooperative play being more preferred from 3 years of age onward. As children mature they are able to accommodate more complex forms of interaction and also find complex forms more interesting. For the most part, however, preschool children are inclined to be individualistic and are little concerned about relating to multi-person groups as such. Very often they will pick one or two children as favored playmates, and may even play in groups of three or four, but generally they prefer more individualized activities. When children enter school they begin to learn social skills related to functioning in larger groups, such as sitting still and listening when others are talking.

The School Years. By the time children reach elementary school, their groups begin to show some of the characteristics of mature groups. Moses H. Goldberg and Eleanor E. Maccoby (1965) asked children to build a series of towers of blocks. Each group consisted of four second graders. Some groups, termed "stable groups," kept the same members for eight trials, whereupon members were shifted to other groups. Children in other groups, termed "changing groups," were changed from one group to another every second trial during the training period of eight trials and then were observed, as were those from the stable groups, for another set of eight trials. The effectiveness of the groups was measured by the number of blocks they were able to place in the towers they built. As Figure 13-1 shows, the stable groups were more effective, both during the training period and during the testing period.

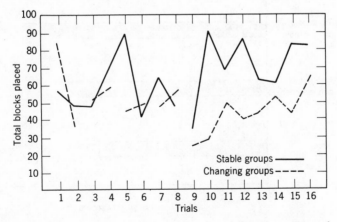

Figure **13-1.** Difference in performance between groups of second graders who were trained to build block towers in "stable groups" and "changing groups" (Goldberg & Maccoby, 1965).

What this study shows, among other things, is the importance of secure social relationships during this developmental stage. Children are still learning the rather complicated skills of co-operation—how to work as a team, how to keep out of the way of others, how to do things that are really helpful, and how to anticipate the moves of others.

The second thing that occurs when membership in groups is changed, and this applies to adult groups as well, is that the level of tension or anxiety rises. Each change in group composition represents a new situation for members to cope with. Mature persons can accommodate the greater amount of stress more easily than children can, but the productivity even of adults will often drop when a new member enters the group. Conversely, a skilled person who enters a new group will find himself operating at less than top efficiency until he becomes adjusted to the new situation.

By way of contrast, let us look at a study with adults in which changes in group composition were made from time to time. Small groups of college students were given the task of making judgments regarding the artistic merit of some drawings and estimating the number of dots on a projected slide. During this phase of the experiment the composition of some of the groups was changed by adding, removing, or replacing a single member. All groups were then given the task of writing captions for a cartoon. When the captions were judged according to the level of creativeness displayed, it was found that groups in which changes had been made were more creative than control groups in which no changes had been made (Figure 13-2). Evidently changes in membership had some kind of facilitative effect, as far as the production of creative responses was concerned (Ziller, Behringer, & Goodchilds, 1962). If changes in group structure result in increases in tension or anxiety, as we have pro-

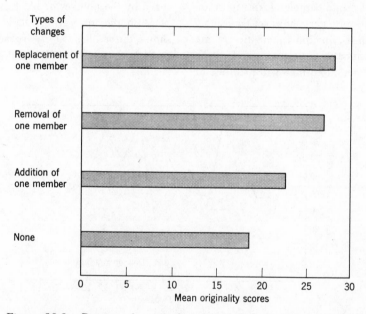

Figure 13-2. Degree of originality revealed by cartoon captions written by groups in which changes had been made during the training period, as contrasted with groups in which no changes had been made (Ziller, Behringer, & Goodchilds, 1962).

posed, the results of this study would be consistent with Hebb's (1955a) formulation of a curvilinear relationship between performance and the level of arousal, a concept presented in Chapter 2. For small children, the stress induced by changes in group composition is distracting and interferes with their effectiveness, whereas for adolescents and adults it can be a source of stimulation that results in heightened effectiveness.

Movement out of the Family Group. A number of observers of developmental patterns in children and adolescents have noticed how the focus of interest begins to shift during childhood from the family to the peer group. During the pre-school years, the norms, values, and attitudes of the child are those he has learned through interaction with members of his family, especially his parents. The positions that have the greatest psychological significance for him are those he occupies within the context of his family, that is, his position as a son or a daughter, as one who plays with and keeps an eye on baby brother, and the like. As he enters school, positions and roles in the social world outside the home begin to assume more importance, and his behavior is expected to conform to norms set by groups and agencies other than the family. The norms of the peer group grow in importance for him and ordinarily reach a maximum during the adolescent years. We say "ordinarily," because some young people are less influenced by peer norms, preferring to take their cues from their family or from the adult world, whereas others become virtual prisoners of peer group norms, and never really outgrow their psychological dependence on the peer group. As children and adolescents develop and mature, they also tend to become involved in an increasing variety of groups, in which they occupy different positions and encounter and are influenced by different kinds of norms.

What we have been describing, of course, is the general pattern of social development that takes place in the American culture. Children and adolescents in other cultures tend to be less affected by peer group norms and are also likely to be involved in a smaller number of groups.

Cohesiveness

The Nature of Cohesiveness. Groups may be formed voluntarily and spontaneously because of a felt need to socialize or to accomplish some practical aim, or they may be convened by some external authority, like a school board, a legislature, or the Secretary of Defense operating through a draft board. Once groups are formed, members will find themselves attracted to one another to a greater or lesser degree, as we noted in Chapter 12. The extent to which a group is found attractive by its members is termed its *cohesiveness.* Members of groups that rate high on cohesiveness find a high degree of satisfaction in being together, and little incentive is required to convene them. Groups that rate low on cohesiveness, on the other hand, must be maintained by some external pressure—penalties for nonattendance or nonparticipation, for example.

Nuclear families (families composed of parents and children) are likely to be highly cohesive, being held together by love, mutual dependence, a large number of shared experiences, and so forth. The nuclear family in America, however, tends to be less cohesive as children grow to adulthood and set up separate households. This is particularly true of males, who often keep in only tenuous touch with their parents and siblings. This occurs partly because American adult values stress independence rather than dependence on the family, and also because American families are geographically and socially mobile. European and particularly Mediterranean families are more close knit and highly cohesive, and this is even true of extended families, or larger families composed of nuclear families that are related by birth and marriage, and that live in close proximity. Americans tend to belong to many voluntary organizations and associations, whereas Europeans do not.

Groups composed of individuals who are also members of many other groups are likely to be less cohesive than those whose members have no competing interests. This is true of groups of friends, as well as families. Kurt Lewin (1948) has noted how the behavior of Americans toward strangers is characterized by an attitude of relaxed friendliness. It is easy to strike up an acquaintanceship with an American, and just as easy to terminate it. Germans, like other Europeans, find the acquaintanceship process more difficult, but once a friend has been made, he is a friend for life. These differences in friendship processes mean that Americans are likely to be involved in many groups of relatively low or easily terminated cohesiveness, whereas Europeans are likely to be involved in few groups of high cohesiveness.

Groups that are convened by an external authority are less likely to be cohesive, but they may become so, if members develop or already have a strong need for association. The members of a combat team are one example. They may have been selected more or less at random by the sergeant, but their mutual need to work together to accomplish their mission and protect themselves and one another makes cohesiveness imperative. The test of cohesiveness of such groups is the extent to which they stay together when they are away from their official assignment. Such groups often "go out on the town" together and have been known to "take on" the police and to fight one another's battles on leave, in much the same way that they did on the battlefield.

Similarly, groups that are formed spontaneously may turn out to be low in cohesiveness. The group described earlier that formed around coffee in the college cafeteria is an example of such a group. Generally speaking, however, groups formed by spontaneous mutual attraction have a better chance for survival, because they are likely to be composed of people who are brought together by some perceived similarity. They are likely to share values and frames of reference, which makes it easier for them to communicate and to function as a socially satisfying group.

Cohesiveness is based on a perceived similarity among persons. The more similar others appear, the easier it is to relate to them and the more socially attractive they are. Cohesiveness may also be expressed in terms of social distance. Members of highly cohesive groups feel close to one another and hence perceive little social distance separating them. People who are unwilling or unable to reduce social distance do not become members of highly cohesive groups. Rhoda Lee Fisher (1967) studied a group of elementary school boys 6 to 13 years of age who had been placed in a special class because of their inability to adjust to regular school demands. Each boy was given eight envelopes containing different sets of two or more paper cutouts of children and adults. The boys were told to place each set of figures on a sheet of paper. The boys' perception of social distance was scored by measuring the distance between the figures. When social distance scores for this group were compared with results of children from regular classes (who were presumably having no more than the usual problems in adjustment), it was found that the emotionally disturbed children tended to place the figures farther apart. The distance among the figures placed by the disturbed children was, in turn, positively correlated with the amount of hostility and aggressiveness expressed by their mothers. Results seem to indicate that parental hostility is reflected in children's inability to think in terms of cohesive relationships among people.

Research with Cohesiveness. In Chapter 3 we discussed a study by Festinger, Schachter, and Back (1950) which dealt with acquaintanceship patterns that emerged in a veterans' housing unit located at a major university, shortly after World War II. One finding of the study to which we gave particular attention was that of propinquity as a major determinant in social attraction. The study also dealt with group cohesion as the result of all forces that bind people together in groups. Sociometric attraction, which we discussed in Chapter 3, is one of those forces, but cohesiveness may result from other forces as well.

A study of cohesiveness by Kurt W. Back (1951) has become a classic in social psychology research. Back tested an idea that grew out of the 1950 study, namely, that no matter how created, group cohesion has similar properties and similar outcomes. Back observed the behavior of a number of subjects who first wrote a story based on a series of three photographs, then met together in two-person groups to discuss the story and improve on it, and finally worked alone in writing another version which was supposed to be an improvement on the first one. High and low conditions of cohesiveness were created for the two-person groups by the amount of emphasis placed on one of three conditions: *personal attraction* (the likability of the partner;) *task direction* (competition for a prize); and *group prestige* (serving as a model group). Results showed that participants in the high-cohesive groups under each of the three conditions were more involved in the work of the group, attempted to influence each other more, and were at the same time more accepting of influence. There were, however, some differences among the groups, according to the condition under which they worked. When cohesiveness was based on personal attraction, group members wanted to turn the discussion into a prolonged, pleasant conversation. When cohesiveness was based on the performance of a task, group members tended to be businesslike and to participate in the discussion only to the extent necessary to achieve the goal. Under group-prestige conditions, members acted cautiously, in order not to risk damage to their status. In this situation, one member of each pair tended to assume a dominant and influential role, and the other member, a submissive one. In low-cohesive groups, members tended to act independently and made little attempt to accommodate each other.

Cohesiveness in Work Groups. Because the need to socialize and to be with others is likely to pervade our lives and everyday activities, group activities that have practical or instrumental values are likely to develop emotional or affective values as well. That is, even though five or six individuals have been assigned a relatively distasteful task, they are likely to find some positive reward in the fact that they are working together on something. The fact that they are assigned to the same task gives them something in common, and, as they become involved in carrying out their duties, they develop common frames of reference and share common experiences. There may also be a degree of cognitive dissonance involved, and they may reason somewhat along these lines: "Inasmuch as we tend to associate with people that we like, the fact that we are associating with these people must mean that we like them."

Not every work group develops a high degree of cohesiveness. Sometimes resentment against the convening or supervising authority runs so high that it interferes with the development of positive regard for group members. The fact that the authority is resented, however, does not necessarily preclude the development of cohesiveness, because group members may find themselves united in their hatred of persons in authority. In some instances, however, hostility cannot be expressed directly or indirectly toward authority figures and becomes displaced instead on the task itself and on other group members. This is likely to occur when some group members accept the assignment more or less willingly and others do not. The result is a low degree of cohesiveness and an ineffective performance by the group.

Effects of Success and Failure. Psychologists have conducted a great many research studies of the relationship between cohesiveness and group effectiveness. H. Kölling (1962) observed groups of German apprentice mechanics during a contest. Successful groups tended to be more cohesive than unsuccessful ones. In this instance, the goal of each group was winning the contest, not merely socializing, and failure led to mutual rejection. In another type of study, Benjamin B. Wolman (1960) compared three types of groups with respect to their reaction to failure. One group was organized under conditions designed to promote mutual acceptance, in that they were told that all would share equally in rewards. A second group was instrumental in character; they were told that they would be rewarded individually, but could help one another if they wished. The third group was organized along altruistic lines; they were told that their efforts were for the benefit of science and that the research was very important. No rewards were promised this group. Cohesiveness, as indicated by the members' willingness to stay in the group was measured after the groups had encountered failure. Results showed that cohesiveness was least affected in the altruistic group and most seriously affected in the instrumental group. It appears that members of the instrumental group tended to blame one another for their failure, and very possibly held them responsible for the negative self-regard that generally results when failure occurs. In the other two groups, where mutuality was more of a factor, members felt that they had gained something from the association with others even though they had failed at the task. The fact that their social needs were satisfied to some extent enabled them to regard other members more positively, and this attitude contributed to the attractiveness (i.e., the cohesiveness) of the group.

In another type of study, girls were organized into high- and low-unity groups and given group tasks to perform. Half the groups were informed that they had succeeded at their tasks, and the other half were informed that they had failed. In the second phase of the experiment, subjects were given tasks to perform individually. Those who had been in high-unity groups that had "succeeded" in their assignments approached the new tasks with more confidence and gave themselves high self-evaluations. Girls who had been in high-

unity groups that had "failed" were less confident and rated themselves correspondingly lower. Girls in the low-unity groups were the least affected by the reported performance of their groups (Zander, Stotland, & Wolfe, 1960). The point is that a high degree of cohesiveness in a group enables and encourages members to identify themselves with the group and to become involved in the group's tasks to the point that the group's success or failure becomes their own.

Compatibility and Cohesiveness. The ability of people to develop harmonious relationships with one another—compatibility—is obviously related to cohesiveness: the more compatible group members are with one another, the more attractive the group will be. One study comparing the performance of groups composed of highly compatible members with that of groups composed of members possessing less compatibility found that the compatible group made fewer errors in solving problems. They also took less time, but the difference was not statistically significant (Moos & Speisman, 1962).

Compatibility is not always a boon, however, for tasks that involve competition. Joseph E. McGrath (1962) formed three-man ROTC rifle teams of students who had given favorable ratings to one another and compared their performance in a series of marksmanship contests with the performance of teams composed of students who had not rated one another favorably. The latter teams had significantly better marksmanship scores and also made more improvement during the contest. In analyzing the results, McGrath suggested that the difference in performance might be due to the fact that the first teams were more concerned with interpersonal success, whereas the second teams were less concerned and thus could become more task oriented. Inasmuch as members of the second teams did not care particularly for one another, they were less likely to be preoccupied with the problem of maintaining friendly relations and were able to concentrate on the task of improving their marksmanship. In effect, cohesiveness in the self-chosen teams was sustained at the expense of group effectiveness, because the drive to maintain positive group feeling worked at cross purposes to the drive to improve marksmanship.

Adherence to Group Norms. The study by Back (1951) mentioned previously showed that increased pressures for uniformity resulted in highly cohesive groups. Conversely, the cohesiveness of a group is reflected in the extent to which members adhere to uniform patterns of behavior, or group norms. Conformity to norms is both a cause and an effect of group cohesiveness. Individuals' need to become a group and to develop relationships with one another leads them to develop shared behavior patterns or norms, and their acceptance of these norms gives them a sense of unity. Members who deviate from the group norms are a threat to its cohesiveness. Some research by Stanley Schachter (1951) shows that the greater the degree of cohesiveness in a group, the less tolerant members are of deviants. Members who deviate in cohesive groups also become the targets of much more communication than is directed at other members. Deviant behavior is a threat to cohesive groups; it arouses tension and anxiety, and members feel moved to "do something about it." It is only natural that they would attempt to reduce some of their tension by trying to persuade deviant members to "go along with the group" and to mend their deviating ways. It does not seem to matter whether the deviating behavior poses a genuine threat to the official goals of the group or not. As this is written, "hippies" in the Haight-Ashbury district in San Francisco are attracting a great deal of attention, far out of proportion to the number of their members. A great deal of "communication" is directed toward them in the form of reports in the public press, spectators' comments, harassment by police and various city inspectors. One can theorize that this blast of "communication" was initiated by the fact that "hippies" are middle-class "dropouts." If they were upper or lower class, they would not attract as much attention.

Seen in another context, the behavior of young people who have become "hippies" is not exceptional. Young middle-class people often rebel against the middle-class establishment. Only the form differs from one context and one generation to another. The "Bohemianism" of Paris students a century ago is one example; the espousal of Communist causes by Latin American university students is another. Counternorm behavior patterns are, however, difficult to sustain over an extended period of time. As one University of California official put it a few years ago, when Free Speech Movement students conducted a "sit-in" strike in the university administration building: "Ten years from now these young people will be wondering what they were doing in Sproul Hall."

Morale

The willingness of group members to work together is affected partly by the attractiveness of the group—cohesiveness—and partly by their confidence that their joint efforts will make some positive contribution toward their goal. This feeling of confidence and optimism with respect to problems or tasks is termed *morale*. Group morale is the composite of the morale of individual members. It is largely a function of cohesiveness; if a group is not attractive, its goals, its members, or both will be rejected. Morale may also be engendered by a sense of responsibility to the group, as well as to society in general.

Commitment and Responsibility. Leonard Berkowitz and Louise R. Daniels (1963) studied the performance of individuals asked to carry out various tasks in situations in which others depended on them. Subjects worked under the direction of a supervisor. Under one experimental condition, they were told that the supervisor would receive a rating based on their productivity. Other subjects were told that the supervisor's rating would *not* depend on their productivity.

When some of the latter subjects were told that their supervisor would shortly learn of their performance, they worked harder than those who were told that he would not find out about their productivity until much later. The work of the first group of subjects, on the other hand, was little affected by the immediacy of the supervisor's review. The point is that the first group knew that the supervisor was depending on their doing a good job and hence did not need any special incentives to work harder. The second group felt little responsibility to the supervisor, and it was only when they were told that he would be checking up on them shortly that they became more productive. If willingness to work hard is one indicator of morale, it would appear that the first group had a higher degree of morale than the second.

The Irrelevancy of External Factors. Inasmuch as optimism and morale are positively related, we often assume that any kind of frustration or difficult problem will lead to lower morale. Research in this area suggests that on-the-job difficulties are more likely to interfere with morale than are problems encountered off the job. In 1942, Daniel Katz and Herman Hyman (1947) studied working and living conditions for employees in two New England shipyards producing ships needed in the war effort. One yard took an average of 76 days to produce a ship, whereas the other yard took 207 days. Workers in both yards had to cope with difficult living conditions: temporary and uncomfortable housing, long commutes, bitter winter weather, inadequate recreational facilities, and resentment expressed toward the newcomers by long-time residents. An analysis of off-the-job problems showed no essential difference between the two groups of workers, but morale was significantly higher in the more efficient yard. A survey showed, for example, that only 38 per cent of the workers in the more efficient yard had considered quitting, as contrasted with 56 per cent in the other. Only 20 per cent of the workers in the second yard expressed confidence in the

yard's management, compared with 67 per cent in the first. Employee dissatisfaction ran higher in the less efficient yard on almost every criterion: production, use of workers' skills, satisfaction with use of workers' time, promotional policy, and so forth. The researchers' findings pointed to a circular causal relationship between production and morale, with good production giving workers a feeling of accomplishment, which in turn leads to increased effort, whereas low production reduces motivation and in turn leads to reduced productivity. Findings also showed that workers can deal with difficult problems off the job, as long as satisfactions at work enable them to maintain high morale. There are, of course, sound humanitarian reasons why workers' off-the-job problems should be alleviated, but we should not fall into the trap of assuming that correcting such deficiencies will solve morale problems at work.

Social Climate

Both morale and cohesiveness are related to a third dimension of group life: its emotional or social *climate*. We sometimes speak of the emotional "atmosphere" that prevails during an encounter, and may characterize it as warm or cold, accepting or hostile, tense or relaxed, or whatever. If a certain kind of atmosphere is characteristic of a certain group over an extended period of time, one can say that a certain kind of climate exists.

Perceptual Set. Ralph V. Exline (1957) asked groups of subjects to pretend they were vocational counselors discussing what action to take on a counselee's case. Subjects took a personality test beforehand. Half of the subjects were told that they tested high on congeniality and were being assigned to groups in which other members rated equally high on that variable. The other half were told that they rated low on congeniality and probably would not find their group very congenial. When the discussion sessions were over, subjects were asked to rate the behavior of the other members of their group. Subjects in "congenial" groups were more inclined to perceive behavior that was related to the solution of the task at hand, whereas subjects in "less congenial" groups showed a slight but not significant inclination to see their partners' behavior as more concerned with personal relationships within the group. Evidently, being placed in a noncongenial group makes the task somewhat less interesting than it would be in a congenial group.

The Leader's Effect on Climate. Exline manipulated the atmosphere of his groups by providing each with a perceptual set; that is, the members were set to anticipate a greater or lesser degree of congeniality in the group to which they were assigned. In the classic study of group climate, however, the atmosphere was determined by the leader. Kurt Lewin, Ronald Lippitt, and Ralph K. White (1939) trained leaders of boys' hobby clubs to play three different kinds of roles, which were termed "autocratic," "democratic," and "laissez-faire." When leaders were behaving autocratically, they were to plan, direct, and scrutinize the work of the boys. Communication was to take place primarily between the leader and the boys, and interaction among the boys was to be discouraged. When leaders were playing laissez-faire roles, they were to do the opposite. They were not to supervise the boys or do any planning, and were to offer opinions and help only when asked. In their democratic roles, leaders were to help the boys plan, but not to plan for them. They were to participate on an equal basis as much as possible, and to encourage communication among the boys.

Results showed that behavior patterns in the groups varied in accordance with the kind of climate the leader created. Autocratic climates produced a great deal of work-oriented behavior, but there was a low degree of personal involvement on the part of members, because when the leader left the room, the boys tended to abandon their tasks and to become involved in horse-play and other kinds of behavior that were not task-oriented. They also became more dependent on the leader, less able to make decisions for themselves, less able to work together cooperatively, more easily discouraged, and more inclined to behave aggressively toward weaker members of the group.

Under democratic conditions, the boys did not work quite so hard, but they showed a higher degree of involvement in their tasks. When the leader left the room, for example, they were more likely to continue with it and to resist attempts to distract them. The democratic climate also appeared to encourage a greater degree of communication and cooperation among the boys, and there was no appearance of the tendency to victimize weaker members that characterized the autocratic conditions.

Under laissez-faire leadership, morale and group output were both low, and irresponsibility ran high. However, laissez-faire groups were somewhat less distractible when the leader was out of the room, because tasks had been initiated by the boys themselves.

As well as showing how the climate of a group may have a marked effect on the behavior of the members, the findings of Lewin and his associates have a number of important implications for the kinds of influence leaders may have on the groups they supervise. We shall discuss this subject at greater length in the next chapter.

Roles and Expectations. Climate is the result as well as the cause of the behavior of group members, and how members play the roles that are expected of them is an important determining factor. Ewart E. Smith (1957) organized five-member problem-solving groups, each consisting of three naive subjects and two confederates who had been instructed to remain silent. In some groups the nonparticipating confederates announced that their role would be that of "listener"; in other groups no such announcement was made and the other members had no prior expectation that the confederates would remain silent. The latter groups were much less effective in problem solving. The roles played by the confederates remained ambiguous throughout the experiment, and the other members of the group did not know how to accommodate them in their problem-solving activities. Members also felt ill at ease in these groups and expressed more defensiveness than they did in groups in which confederates announced that they were going to be listeners. In control groups, in which there were no silent confederates, satisfaction with the group's activities ran higher, and there was less defensiveness. Evidently the presence of a nonparticipant has an unsettling effect on small-group activities, even when members know that he is not going to participate. It should be noted that nonparticipation is counternorm behavior in a group that is expected to solve problems. Furthermore, it is very difficult to deal with the behavior of a member who deviates from the norm and who does not even respond to communications directed to him.

Types of Groups

The behavior of group members will also be affected by the types of groups in which they function. Space limitations do not permit a discussion of the full range of group types, and we shall comment instead on a few that appear to have a more significant effect on behavior.

Primary and Secondary Groups. The more deeply involved we are in a group, the greater effect it is likely to have on our attitudes and behavior. Our greatest degree of personal involvement is not likely to occur in *secondary groups,* but in *primary groups,* to use the terminology developed by Charles H. Cooley (1909). Primary groups are those in which interpersonal relationships take place on a face-to-face basis and with great frequency (e.g., daily). Such relationships are likely to be on a more intimate level than relationships in groups in which there is less personal contact. Families are the most obvious example of primary groups. Others include children's play groups, combat teams, and work groups. Secondary groups are those in which rela-

tionships are on a more impersonal basis, more abstract, and more distant, socially and geographically speaking. Political parties, professions, and national groups are examples of this type. Primary groups demand and receive more personal involvement, and they are likely to permit wider swings in emotional tone. Love, disappointment, depression, rage, and elation are more likely to be expressed within the context of primary groups, whereas expressions of emotion to members of secondary groups are likely to be more restrained and perhaps suppressed altogether. To put this in other words, primary groups enable us to experience our major satisfactions and dissatisfactions. Primary groups are likely to be more cohesive than secondary groups, because it is within the context of such groups that our most pressing social needs—needs for love and attention, for example—are satisfied.

Formal and Informal Groups. Primary groups are likely to be informal, whereas formality is more often a characteristic of secondary groups. A secondary group may require a fairly complex degree of structure in order to maintain itself and to achieve its objectives, whereas too much complexity gets in the way of the functioning of small groups. Many groups that are low in structure, however, are likely to be not very stable, that is, they are likely to develop and disappear spontaneously, like the coffee-drinking group of students we described earlier in this chapter. Their membership is inclined to be less rigidly determined, and may undergo more radical changes. Structure helps make a group more stable and enables it to resist drastic changes. The formal structures of many secondary groups, like religious organizations and nations, have enabled them to survive for centuries.

Exclusive and Inclusive Groups. Exclusive groups are those that limit membership to certain classes of individuals. Associations of engineers that admit only persons with certain kinds of professional preparation and experience are one kind of exclusive group; faculties in which membership is on an invitational basis (i.e., through being hired) are another type. Still another kind of exclusive group are the neighborhood associations that make it difficult or impossible for persons with certain ethnic characteristics (non-whites or Jews, for example) to live in the area. Exclusiveness in the first two kinds of groups is more likely to be on a functional basis: associations of engineers exist for the purpose of enabling engineers to communicate with one another, to engage in cooperative enterprises primarily of interest to engineers, and to enforce standards of training and professional practice, among other things. It would be inappropriate for persons qualified, say, only as plumbers or sea captains to secure membership in such an organization. Faculties are composed of people who have the kind of qualifications that are consistent with scholarly undertakings. The manager of a beauty parlor might yearn for a faculty post, but a college could not fulfill its educational and scientific goals unless it limited its hiring to people with academic qualifications.

As was pointed out in previous discussions of social attraction, we tend to be attracted to people whom we perceive as similar to us. Engineers like to interact with other engineers not only because they can work better on common problems, but also because they find it easier and more satisfying to relate to other engineers than to people in other professions. One way to maintain this high degree of perceived similarity in such a group is by excluding nonengineers. Neighborhood associations are also trying to maintain a degree of psychologically comfortable similarity among residents by excluding persons from the "wrong" ethnic groups, but such criteria are less functional than those imposed by professional organizations and faculties. The right to become a member of a professional organization or a faculty can be earned, whereas the right to reside in an exclusive neighborhood cannot be earned, at least it cannot as long as society condones the exercise of "restrictive covenants,"

whereby residents agree not to sell or rent to "undesirable persons."

Restrictive covenants are based on the idea that some people are better or more worthwhile than others, although this intent is usually denied by participants in such agreements, who claim that they are merely exercising the right to determine the people with whom they wish to associate. The point often overlooked is that such decisions are made on the basis of characteristics related to social status and caste, rather than on the social behavior and the personal values of the persons excluded. A basic question, however, is whether such exclusion is consistent with the values of the society in which it occurs. Traditional societies are likely to tolerate aristocratic values—that is, they accept the premise that some people are better than other people by reasons of being born into one family rather than another. Social behavior is irrelevant to such a frame of reference, for prestige is inherited, rather than earned, in such societies. If, on the other hand, a society is governed by equalitarian values—values that base prestige and other forms of acceptability on social behavior—attempts to promulgate aristocratic values will be seen as inappropriate. It can be argued, of course, that people in a free society should be permitted to operate according to aristocratic values if they wish, but when the individuals concerned are already at or near the top of the power structure, they exercise influence far in excess of their proportionate representation in the community and are thus in a position to block or otherwise modify the processes whereby an equalitarian society maintains and perpetuates itself.

Inclusive groups are encountered with greater frequency within the context of equalitarian societies. These are groups that open their doors to all comers and may, in fact, actively solicit memberships. Political parties, hobby clubs, and civic betterment groups are examples of inclusive groups. Unlike exclusive groups, they set no special qualifications for membership other than a sharing of interests with other members, although it is generally assumed that members accept the goals and the operating rules of the organization. The proliferation of such groups is especially noticeable in the United States. A comparative survey of samples of respondents in the United States, Great Britain, Germany, Italy, and Mexico showed that the typical North American was much more inclined to be a member of an organization than were residents of other countries sampled (see Figure 13-3). In the United States, the majority of the organizations are those likely to be considered inclusive; the percentage is lower in the other countries. The degree to which North Americans are involved in their organizations is also revealed by the percentage who become officers. As Figure 13-3 shows, this percentage is higher in the United States than elsewhere (Almond & Verba, 1963).

In-Groups and Out-Groups. Any discussion of exclusiveness in groups inevitably leads to the question of in-groups. In-groups are sometimes called "we-groups," in contradistinction to out-groups or "they-groups." In-groups are characterized by a strong sense of mutual identification, to the point where members feel isolated and out of place when out of the context of the group. Membership and participation in such groups is likely to evoke strong feelings of loyalty, sympathy, and devotion. Citizens of countries in which there is a strong sense of nationality are likely to think of the relationship between themselves and people in other countries as "we" and "they." This feeling is less marked in some of the newer countries, where "we" is likely to represent the tribe or community of which one is a member, and "they" to consist of everyone else.

In recent years, "in-group" has come to be used with respect to groups that have a greater amount of power in a society. One example of such an in-group would be the families listed in the *Social Register.* A small, closely knit group or clique that controls the policy of a larger group, like a political party, a church, or a corporation, may be termed an in-group in that sense. White Anglo-Saxon Protestants are a very large in-group in

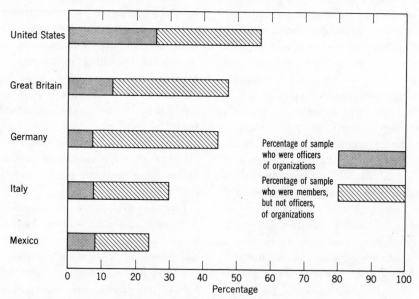

Figure 13-3. Percentages of samples from various countries who were members and officers of organizations (Almond & Verba, 1963).

"I'm sorry, but this is a quintet."

American economic life. There is a tendency for in-groups to attempt to perpetuate themselves and to resist efforts of out-group members to get them to share their power. One way in which in-groups cope with the real or fancied encroachment on their rights and privileges is to increase the social distance between themselves and out-group members. This can be done by arranging matters so that in-group members seldom if ever come in contact with out-group members. In the past this was done by restrictive covenants governing housing. If out-group members are forced to live outside of one's neighborhood, the amount of possible interaction is thereby reduced. Under such conditions, out-group members can be admitted into the houses of in-group members in the role of servants, because differences in status implied by the positions of employer and servant are sufficient to keep interaction within the limits of a highly structured relationship that implies and maintains much social distance. Keeping out-group members out of certain kinds of employment also reduces the degree of social interaction, as does employing them only in subordinate positions.

There is a danger, of course, that the exclusiveness of in-groups will lead to their own undoing, and histories of ruling cliques and oligarchies are full of such examples. If groups are concerned about productivity, creativity, and general effectiveness, it would seem that the research by Ziller, Behringer, and Goodchilds (1962), that we cited earlier in this chapter, contains an important lesson, because their results imply that groups permitting changes in their membership are more effective than those whose membership is stable. A study by Robert Lee Hoffman and Norman R. F. Maier (1961) also points in this direction. These psychologists studied the problem-solving behavior of two kinds of groups, one composed of individuals who had similar patterns of personality, as measured by the Guilford-Zimmerman Temperament Survey, and those whose personality traits varied. After observing the work of the groups for a period of two semesters, they concluded that the heterogeneous group produced higher-quality solutions. Exclusiveness tends toward homogeneity and static complacency, whereas heterogeneity seems to stimulate greater effectiveness.

Membership Groups and Reference Groups. It is obvious that groups in which we hold membership will have some effect on our behavior. Our membership in a given group is more or less contingent on our willingness to accept its norms and values. We do not have to be a member of a group in order for it to affect our behavior. As we pointed out in Chapter 4, any group that has a normative effect on our behavior is a reference group, because we "refer" our behavior to its standards. T. M. Newcomb's (1943) study of the effect of faculty values on the values of Bennington College students is a classic study of the effect of reference groups on behavior. In this study, Newcomb found that the liberal values of the faculty influenced students' values, as was shown by the latter's movement in a liberal direction. Similar results were found by Irvin J. Lehmann (1963), who studied the class of 1962 at Michigan State University from their freshman year onward. He found that students not only became more liberal, but also became more proficient in solving verbal problems, more receptive to new ideas, and more rational, scientific, and less stereotyped in their beliefs. The assumption is, of course, that they

used the members of the faculty as a reference group in making these changes in their behavior.

The Measurement and Analysis of Group Interaction. In Chapter 3 we described sociometric techniques: the way in which patterns of intermember attraction can be measured. A sociogram depicts the vectors of attraction and repulsion as they exist or existed at a certain point in time. Interactional analyses, however, are concerned with the on-going processes of group behavior. One method that has had a considerable amount of use is the *Interaction Process Analysis* developed by Robert Freed Bales (1965), a technique that can be employed to measure the extent to which participants in a discussion group play roles related to the group's task or to its social functioning. The scoring categories in Bales' system, as listed in Figure 13-4, can be used as a basis for recording all interactions, verbal and

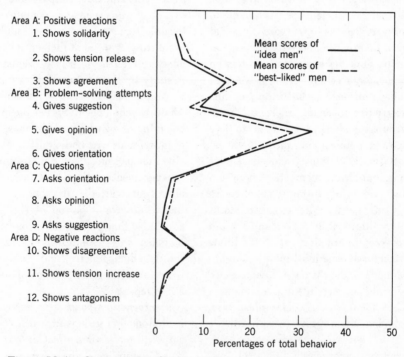

Figure **13-4.** Composite profiles, according to Bales' scheme of analysis, of 44 top men on ideas and 44 best-liked men in their discussion groups (Slater, 1955).

nonverbal, that take place within a group setting. The following is a sample discussion, with scoring categories indicated:

Chairman: There isn't enough money left in the operating fund for supplies to carry us to the end of the fiscal year. (*Gives information*) Do any of you have any suggestions as to how we might handle this? (*Asks for opinion*)

Member A: Seems to me we ought to start the meeting by reading the minutes. (*Gives opinion* and *shows antagonism*)

Chairman: The secretary isn't here yet, (*Gives information*) and I thought we might get some discussion going on the shortage. (*Gives opinion*)

Member B: I agree. (*Gives opinion* and *shows agreement*) Besides the minutes were mailed to us, and we've all seen them. (*Gives information*)

Member A: I didn't get my copy. (*Shows disagreement*)

As each individual makes a scorable remark, a tally is made by the observers in the appropriate column on his sheet. It is thus possible to get a record of the extent to which he participates and the kind of participation that is characteristic of him. The amount of participation is an index of his *activity* in the group. The number of tallies in Areas B and C are an indication of the extent to which the member is *task-oriented*, whereas Areas A and D provide indices to his *sociability*.

Figure 13-4 shows the composite profiles of men who were the top idea men in their groups, but who were not the best liked, as contrasted with those who were the best liked, but who were not top idea men. The groups met together for forty-four sessions. As the graph lines show, men who were best liked tended to show more positive reactions (Area A) and to ask more questions (Area C), whereas idea men tended to make more problem-solving attempts (Area B) (Slater, 1955).

Bales states that he originally assumed that people in discussion groups scoring high on likability would also score high on activity and task ability (ideas), but his research has shown that task-oriented members tend to be the most active, and that liked members tend to be only moderately active. Furthermore, task-oriented members are not always the best-liked people. Indeed, task ability and likability appear to have a low correlation and even seem to be somewhat incompatible. This was particularly true of groups that met together for an extended number of sessions. On the first meeting of the groups studied by Bales, about 56 per cent of the members rated highest on ideas also rated highest on likability, but by the fourth meeting, top idea rankers were rated the most likable only 8 per cent of the time. This low correlation may be due to the fact that idea men are inclined to talk a great deal and to dominate conversation. This tendency often comes to be resented by other members of the group. Bales found that about one-third of the group members he observed talked a great deal and were nonetheless liked. These were individuals who initiated a lot of interaction, that is, their talking led others to respond. The talkers who ranked lower in being liked were those who evoked a much lower degree of response.

Bales found that his groups tended to operate under a system of "dual leadership," in which one leader would play the role of the "task specialist," and another would play the role of the "social specialist." The first type of leader sees to it that the group does its job, whereas the second facilitates the attainment of the kind of social rewards that most people expect from interaction with others. The member who rates high on ideas, likability, and activity is a relatively rare person, according to Bales, and corresponds to the traditional conception of the "good leader" or "great man." Unfortunately, the opposite type—the individual who rates low in ideas, likability, and activity—is much more common.

SUMMARY

A group consists of two or more persons engaged in any kind of relationship with each other.

Even informal, short-lived groups develop some elements of structure, in the sense that members occupy positions, develop status relationships, and play reciprocal roles. The rewards of participating in a group must be reckoned against its costs. The relationship between rewards and costs that a member expects for a given group serves as his comparison level, which may also be referred to his comparison level for alternates—the reward-cost ratio he would expect in other situations available to him.

During infancy and early childhood, most group relations are dyadic, but as development proceeds, children become involved in larger, more complex groups and for longer periods of time. During early years in school, children begin to learn to use groups for cooperative action. Some degree of group stability is important at this age, and if frequent changes are made in group composition, completion of group tasks becomes less effective. However, changes in composition of adult groups may have a facilitative effect on performance. During the middle years of childhood, the focus of interest begins to shift from the family to the peer group, with the influence of the latter generally reaching its maximum during adolescence.

The attractiveness a group develops for its members is termed its cohesiveness. In contrast to Americans, Europeans tend to belong to fewer and more cohesive groups. Perceived similarity among members, shared values, willingness to reduce social distance, and shared frames of reference help to increase group cohesiveness. No matter how it is created, group cohesion has similar properties and similar outcomes. Work groups may become cohesive if members are able to satisfy affective needs, or if members have a common enemy, such as a supervisor. Failure can be destructive to cohesiveness in a task-oriented group, but less so in groups that are more socially oriented. Compatibility generally facilitates cohesiveness, but cohesiveness and compatibility are not necessarily conducive to group effectiveness in

some kinds of tasks (e.g., under competitive conditions). Members who deviate from group norms in cohesive groups may be subject to considerable attention and even harassment on the part of group members, because deviation threatens the security of the group.

The morale of a group is reflected in the optimism and confidence with which its members approach their task. A feeling of responsibility to the job facilitates morale. There is a circular relationship between production and morale, in that high morale leads to high levels of production, which in turn result in good group feeling and optimism. Morale and cohesiveness are also related to the kind of climate that prevails in a group. The classic study conducted by Lewin, Lippitt, and White showed that the behavior of members of a group was significantly affected by changes in group climate as induced by changes in leadership style. Climate can adversely be affected if the roles played by members are ambiguous.

Small, intimate, face-to-face groups—primary groups—are the ones that demand and receive the highest degree of personal involvement. Our relationships with secondary groups are likely to be more impersonal and diffuse. Interpersonal relations in primary groups tend to be on an informal basis. Groups may also be exclusive or inclusive, depending on their functions and goals. Exclusivity in task groups may result from the need to have only properly qualified people as members. In socially oriented groups, exclusivity may be caused by a desire to include only people with similar interests or backgrounds. In traditional societies, exclusiveness is more likely to be based on social status than in more equalitarian societies. In the latter type of society, a relatively larger number of groups are likely to be inclusive. Exclusiveness may also foster sharp divisions between in-groups (or we-groups) and out-groups (or they-groups). The existence of such divisions reduces the opportunity for equal-status contact between members of different groups. It is not necessary to be a member of a group for it to have an effect on one's behavior. Any group whose norms are used as a reference point for behavior or the formation of attitudes and values is a reference group.

Interaction among members of face-to-face groups may be observed, recorded, and measured by Bales' interaction process analysis. Such behavior may be classified under such headings as posi-tive or negative, problem solving, or questioning. This method of scoring makes it possible to pro-duce profiles for each group member, showing the kind of contribution he is making to the group. Studies indicate that leadership in groups tends to center on idea men, or task specialists, and social specialists. Task groups need people in both kinds of roles, and it is relatively unusual to find an individual who can do well in both.

SUGGESTED READINGS

Cartwright, D. and Zander, A. (Eds.), *Group dynamics: research and theory* (2nd Ed.). New York: Harper and Row, 1960.

Homans, G. C., *The human group.* New York: Harcourt, 1950.

Lindgren, H. C. (Ed.), *Contemporary research in social psychology.* New York: Wiley, 1969. See papers by Maccoby and Goldberg and by Smith in Section 9.

Shepard, C. R., *Small groups: some sociological perspectives.* San Francisco: Chandler, 1964. (Paperback)

CHAPTER FOURTEEN

Wayne Miller, Magnum

Gerry Cranham, Rapho-Guillumette

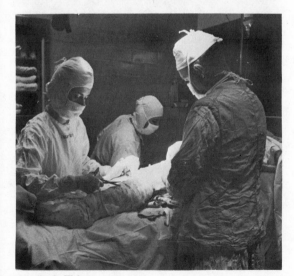

Elizabeth Wilcox

Group Task Performance:
Problem Solving, Cooperation,
and Competition

Groups vs. Individuals in Problem Solving. We begin our discussion in this chapter by asking whether groups actually are more efficient than individuals in getting things done. Groups are obviously better equipped to accomplish some things, particularly those that require teamwork and cooperation, but many other kinds of tasks are done better by individuals, because others would simply get in the way. There are some tasks, however, that can be done by either individuals or groups, and that are a potential source of controversy. These tasks consist of problems whose solution requires analysis, recourse to sources of information, and experience in problem solving in various contexts.

In Chapter 3 we discussed some experiments in which subjects' ability to solve problems calling for a degree of creativity or ingenuity was tested under group-discussion (brainstorming) conditions and under conditions of working alone. These studies, taken as a whole, showed that performance was superior when subjects worked alone, but that participation in brainstorming tended to facilitate subsequent individual performance (Taylor, Berry, & Block, 1958; Dunnette, Campbell, & Jaastad, 1963; Lindgren & Lindgren, 1965a, 1965b). All these studies concerned tasks involving what J. P. Guilford (1959) has termed "divergent thinking," in that the subject is given a problem situation and is expected to create as many different solutions as possible. Another type of problem calls for "convergent thinking." Such problems have a limited number (usually only one) of appropriate solutions, and the subject is expected to examine the elements in the problem situation, discard some and use others, and thus "converge" on the correct solution. Convergent problems lend themselves more readily to experimental situations, because it is easier to measure performance and to evaluate results.

The question of whether groups or individuals are superior in problem solving was studied by an experiment conducted by Jacob Tuckman and Irving Lorge (1962), who asked Air Force Reserve Officers Training Corps cadets at Columbia College and Manhattan College to work on a task known as the "Mined Road Problem." This problem is one of a number developed by the Office of Stategic Services (1948) for use in selecting special agents during World War II and involves a complicated series of tasks which would be hazardous if carried out in a real-life situation. The cadets were directed to solve it with paper and pencil. Briefly, the problem is that of five men trying to escape from enemy territory, who have to cross a road that has been mined with supersensitive mines that cannot be neutralized, detonated, or dug up. The most elegant solution consists of their using various items lying around, building a bridge over the road, and removing traces of their escape route. The poorest solutions consist of actions that in real life would have led to the death or capture of members of the team.

Tuckman and Lorge set up two different conditions for the experiment. In the experimental condition, individuals worked alone in studying the problem and in writing up what they considered to be the best solution. The following day, the same subjects were organized randomly into five-man groups, given the same problem, and asked to solve the problem again as a group. Under the control condition, groups of five cadets were given the same problem and asked to solve it as a group, without their having seen or worked on it beforehand.

The individuals working alone produced solutions that were inferior to those produced by the groups, and there was little difference in the quality of the solutions produced by the experimental or the control groups. Comparison of the performance of the experimental groups with that of the individual members who had worked alone the previous day showed that the groups producing the best solutions were composed of members whose previous (individual) performance was quite good. In fact there was a Pearsonian correlation of .54 between the solutions of groups and the previous solutions of their best single members. The investigators concluded that the superiority of the group was due to the greater probability of finding adequate solutions. In other words, five sources of solutions were found to be better than one. They also noted that although the groups were more efficient than individuals working separately, the groups as a whole were actually rather inefficient. They tended to form cliques or subgroups that worked independently, with one clique attempting to convince the other of the soundness of its approach. At least one individual in most groups did not participate at all, and in several groups the discussion was dominated by a single member, who tried to coerce the other members into accepting his solution.

Improving the Functioning of Groups through Democratic Leadership. The observations of Tuckman and Lorge suggest that the groups would have been more effective if the efforts of members had been coordinated by proper leadership. The effect of using trained leaders was studied by Norman R. F. Maier (1950), who compared the performance of problem-solving groups led by individuals trained in democratic proce-

dures with that of groups led by untrained individuals. The problem contained some distracting features that led the majority of the subjects to give an incorrect answer. As in the Tuckman and Lorge study, subjects first worked on the problem alone and then discussed it in groups. Results showed that groups headed by trained leaders were more likely to produce correct solutions. Maier explained these results in terms of his observation that leaders trained in democratic processes saw to it that everyone in the group had a chance to make a contribution. Since the members who had arrived at the right answer were in the minority, it was important that this minority be heard if the group was to be helped to find the right answer. Nontrained leaders were less likely to recognize and protect the rights of minorities in their groups, whereas trained leaders restrained the more aggressive and domineering members and saw to it that minorities had a proper hearing.

Improving the Functioning of Groups through Structure. The functioning of groups can also be facilitated when positions and roles are well defined. Groups cannot function effectively without some kind of structure, and *ad hoc* groups, like those created for the Tuckman and Lorge experiment, have difficulties in proceeding with their task until they have achieved some understanding of who will lead and who will follow. Structure is even more important in groups that must not only solve problems, but must also carry out their decisions.

The importance of structure in such groups is indicated by a study conducted by William T. Smelser (1961), who made use of an ingenious type of problem involving the operation of a model railroad, a technique that had been developed by Edwin E. Ghiselli and Thomas Martin Lodahl (1958). Smelser assigned teams of two subjects the task of running two trains in opposite directions around a circular single track. Each subject had a control panel that he could use to regulate the speed and direction of his train and to shunt it onto sidings to let the other train pass. The performance of the team was measured by the number of round trips made by both trains during 3-minute trials.

The subjects in this experiment consisted of students who had scored either very high or very low on a test measuring personality characteristics associated with tendencies to be socially dominant. Subjects were assigned to two-person groups organized according to different patterns or structures. In Type A groups, for example, a subject scoring high on the test (high dominant) would be assigned the task of dispatcher—that of making the final decisions in running the railroad —and a subject scoring low (low dominant) would be given the subordinate role. Type B groups consisted of a high-dominant and a low-dominant subject, but there were no instructions as to who would be the dispatcher. In another type of group, a low-dominant subject would be assigned the role of dispatcher, and a high-dominant subject would be given the subordinate role. There were in all seven different types of group patterns, with varying combinations of position assignments and personality types.

Smelser's results showed that assigning one person a dominant role and the other a subordinate tended to produce superior results, as long as the personality patterns of both subjects were not inconsistent with their roles. The best performance was turned out by the groups in which high-dominant individuals were placed in dominant roles, and low-dominant individuals in subordinate roles. Groups composed of low-dominant people in dominant roles and high-dominant people in subordinate roles did the poorest. Holding the latter group apart as a special case, the results showed that the assignment of roles did aid the functioning of the groups, since such groups did better than those in which no assignments were made. Experience also facilitated the performance of groups. Each group ran through six 3-minute trials. The greatest differences among the types of groups appeared during the first trial, but five

trials later, all groups had improved, and there was little difference between the best and the poorest group. In other words, even those groups composed of individuals whose personality traits were incompatible with their assigned roles were capable of learning how to use the structure imposed on them.

The model-railroad method was also employed by Edwin E. Ghiselli (1966), who assigned the same task used by Smelser to teams of three and four subjects. Inasmuch as such a task calls for skillful timing, the ability to learn a complex set of electrical relays, and the capacity to anticipate fast-moving events, common sense might lead one to predict that the more intelligent the team, the better its score. Results showed that the more intelligent teams did indeed perform more effectively during the early trials, but intelligence had negligible effect during the middle phase and appeared to be actually detrimental during the final phase.

One might assume also that people who like to work in groups (as contrasted with those preferring to work alone) would be more likely to contribute to the success of such teams, but Ghiselli found that this dimension of personality interfered with success during the early trials and was a negligible factor thereafter.

The best predictor of performance during the second and third phases of the experiment was what Ghiselli called "skewness" on a Decision-Making Scale, a test measuring personality characteristics related to decision making. This scale consisted of pairs of adjectives that top-management and middle-management personnel tended to react to differently when asked to select adjectives that best described them. A high score on the scale is typical of individuals who resemble top-management people in terms of their attitude toward decision making—that is, they tend to perceive themselves as active, self-reliant, confident in social relations, straightforward, and dignified. Middle-management people tend to see themselves as careful planners, thoughtful, seldom making rash decisions, and avoiding the appearance of being controversial persons or of exhibiting self-centered behavior. Teams composed entirely of members who scored high on this scale however, were actually somewhat less effective in running the railroad than teams scoring low. The teams with *one person* who scored significantly higher on the Decision-Making Scale than the other members of the team, however, were the ones who did the best during the second and third phases of the experiment. The greater the similarity of the team members on the Decision-Making variable, the less effective the team. In other words, groups with a single member who was uncontested as a self-confident decision maker did the best, after the initial learning stages.

It seems to be a reasonable assumption that personality traits associated with decision making are also associated with dominance. If so, some of Smelser's results appear to be consistent with those of Ghiselli. In both studies, unstructured groups containing one person scoring high on these traits turned in superior performances during early trials. In such instances, the high-dominant (or decision-making) individual very likely took over the management of the operation, structured the group, and assigned subordinate roles to the rest of the team. Ghiselli's results also seem consistent with those of Tuckman and Lorge, in that in both instances a preliminary measure of ability was positively correlated with performance. In the Tuckman-Lorge study the preliminary measure was the score made on the problem solution written alone, which was found to correlate positively with group performance; in the Ghiselli study the measure was a test of intelligence, which was found to correlate positively with performance during the first or learning stage of the experiment. Inasmuch as the Tuckman-Lorge study consisted of only a single group problem-solving session, and did not go into additional phases, we have no basis for comparing the two studies beyond that point.

Centralized and Decentralized Group Structure

The research discussed up to this point suggests that there are at least two factors related to the effectiveness of groups concerned with problem solving: (1) the structure of the group (the appropriateness of the participants' roles and the clarity with which they are perceived) and (2) the characteristics of the members (intelligence, analytical ability, personality traits). We now turn our attention to another group of studies also concerned with the structure of problem-solving groups, but with particular emphasis on the effect that channels of communication have on performance.

As noted in Chapter 12, any social system can be perceived as a restricted communication network—restricted in the sense that communication is not diffuse and random, but is channeled between specified positions in the network. These restrictions limit individual freedom, but at the same time they reduce interference ("noise" in the channel) and enable the system to function efficiently. The way in which communication is channeled may affect the efficiency of the organization, as well as the kinds of satisfactions that people will receive as a result of their participation.

Alexander Bavelas (1950) and Harold J. Leavitt (1951) conducted a series of experiments using various arrangements of communication channels with problem-solving groups, each composed of five subjects. Figure 14-1 depicts the three main types of communication networks used in their research. The circles represent positions in the communication nets and the lines represent the open channels. Subjects placed in the positions indicated could communicate only in writing and only to the persons to whom they were connected by channels. The "wheel" type of arrangement, with its central, coordinating position, was found to be the most efficient. It rated high in speed and accuracy and produced

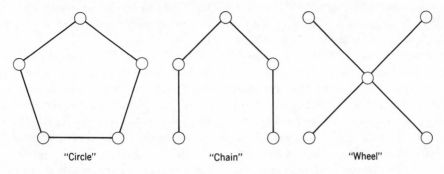

"Circle"   "Chain"   "Wheel"

Ratings

Characteristic	Circle	Chain	Wheel
Speed	Slow	Fast	Very fast
Accuracy	Poor	Good	Very good
Organization	No stable form	Slowly emerging but stable	Almost immediate and stable
Emergence of leader	None	Marked	Very pronounced
Adaptation to sudden changes in task	Very good	Poor	Poor
Morale	Good	Poor	Very poor

Figure 14-1. Characteristics of three kinds of five-man, problem-solving groups (after Bavelas & Barrett, 1951).

a stable organization almost immediately. Participants had little doubt who the leader was: he was the individual occupying the central position. The wheel formation, therefore, represents the traditional, autocratic or authoritarian type of organization. The leader is in complete control, members can communicate only to him, and he can communicate to anyone he pleases. He is free, but they are not. Only he can make decisions, because he has all the information.

The "chain" arrangement is basically the "wheel" modified into an organization containing three hierarchies instead of two. Like the "wheel," it is an autocratic structure. The leader is obviously the person in the center, but the subjects at each end have no contact with him and do not know what his powers are. They communicate only with the persons between them and the center, who may be the leaders, as far as they know. These intermediate leaders know that the center man is the leader, and he knows it, too. In some ways this arrangement represents a pyramidal feudal hierarchy, with each person swearing fealty and owing allegiance to his next highest superior. This network was relatively efficient for solving problems; the organization emerged slowly, but was stable.

The "circle" arrangement is the most "democratic" of the three types. Each position is equal in power, and any leadership that emerges comes by virtue of other qualities than the position occupied. This network was the least efficient. It developed no stable organizational form, and members could not agree who the leader was.

When it came to flexibility, however, the circle was markedly superior. It could adapt itself to changes in task more readily than could the other two types. This finding is reminiscent of the results of the classic experiment conducted by Lewin, Lippitt, and White (1939) using experimental social climates in boys' clubs. In that experiment (discussed in Chapter 11), the autocratic climate was found to be slightly more efficient, but the democratic and laissez-faire groups continued work when the leader was out of the room and were better able to resist distraction and criticism when a "janitor" entered the room, presumably to fix the lights. The autocratic groups, on the other hand, were more likely to "fall apart" and to engage in horseplay.

The other significant finding in the research by Bavelas and Leavitt concerns morale. Persons occupying central positions in the "wheel" and "chain" nets reported themselves as being satisfied with the groups' activities, but those on the periphery were dissatisfied. Persons in the "circle," however, were uniformly satisfied.

Further research with small groups raises some questions on the extent to which the findings of Bavelas and Leavitt regarding group efficiency can be generalized. Marvin E. Shaw (1964) reviewed a number of such studies, including some of his own (1954), and concluded that whereas centralized groups, like the wheel, are more efficient with simpler problems, decentralized groups, like the circle, are more efficient with complex problems. Individuals in key positions in centralized groups have a considerable degree of autonomy and are relatively independent. This leaves them free to solve simple problems quickly and to coordinate the flow of limited amounts of information. With complex problems, however, the amount of information is greatly increased and the person in the central position becomes saturated with data. Coordinating the communication of information and making the necessary decisions becomes much more involved. Individuals occupying positions in the circle, although they send and receive many more messages than do individuals on the periphery of the wheel, are less likely to become saturated with information and better able to deal with whatever data they have or receive.

Shaw's results have been challenged by Mauk Mulder (1960), who conducted experiments using complex problems with four-man circle and wheel groups. Although circles were more effective during the first two out of five problems, wheels surpassed the performance of circles during the last three problems. Mulder interpreted these results as indicating that centralized group structures are better than decentralized ones in decision making, irrespective of whether problems are simple or complex. The fact that decentralized groups appear to have an advantage with complex problems during early trials merely indicates, according to Mulder, that it takes longer for a structure of working relationships and roles to emerge in centralized groups. Although Shaw and Mulder are using similar data, they come to contradictory conclusions, and more research is obviously needed to resolve their differences.

One study that shows results consistent with Shaw's interpretations was conducted by Roby, Nicol, and Farrell (1963), who studied the speed of problem solving of four-man teams of airmen. Half the teams were organized according to a *centralized* structure, with responsibility centered in one team member. The other half were organized according to a *distributed* structure, with responsibility shared equally by all members. The centralized groups were more efficient with problems calling for coordination of action among group members, but the groups with distributed structure were more efficient with problems requiring members to deal with environmental changes. Their findings thus suggest that decentralized groups are more flexible and readily adaptable to novel situations.

Cooperation and Competition

Formalized Cooperation. Much of what we accomplish as individuals and as groups depends on our ability to get others to work with us on common tasks and for mutually acceptable goals. This is true at all levels of group functioning, irrespective of whether the groups are centralized or decentralized, or whether they are working on simple or complex problems. What we are referring to the process known as *cooperation*—working together for mutually acceptable goals. The goals of the cooperators need not be identical, but achieving them must result in satisfaction for all parties concerned. Cooperation may involve merely our participation in a set of reciprocal role behaviors. We enter the post office to mail a package. We hand the package to the postal clerk who weighs it, computes the postage, and tells us how much it will be. We hand him some money; he affixes the postage and gives us back our change.

What we have just described is a series of cooperative actions, each one initiating and being initiated by the role behaviors of the persons occupying the positions of post office patron and postal clerk. Handing the parcel to the clerk was the signal for him to begin an appropriate sequence of role behaviors. His completion of this sequence led us to give him some money, which started him on another segment of behavior. We are satisfied because we were able to send the package off by mail, and he is satisfied because he performed the service for which he was employed. In this instance, his satisfaction is a reflection of our satisfaction.

This interaction between us and the postal clerk represents, as we said, cooperation on a rather simple level. The mutual expectations and the resulting behaviors are all spelled out by custom and culture. In such instances, no one has to do anything creative, ingenious, imaginative, or out of the ordinary in any way.

The kind of cooperation that takes place between individuals occupying positions of unequal power and status actually amounts to obedience or compliance. It is similar to the cooperative interaction we have just described because it depends heavily on the roles prescribed for the participants. The role of the supervisor calls for him to order, demand, or request compliance, and the role of the subordinate calls for him to obey. Some argue that such an arrangement is not really cooperation, because cooperation implies a relationship between people who are relatively equal in status, or who are equal as far as a particular situation is concerned. In the post-office incident, it really does not matter who the patron *really* is (who he is when he is not playing the role of the patron); to all intents and purposes, patron and postal clerk are equal and are mutually dependent. In a situation where there is an authority figure and a subordinate, the former may *talk* about getting cooperation, but he may mean obedience and compliance. To be sure, there are many kinds of arrangements between the supervisor and the supervised in which the power of the former is severely limited, either by the way in which the situation is formulated or by the existence of a democratic atmosphere, in which event the demands of the supervisor are made in the form of requests and are treated as such. In more authoritarian settings, however, there is no doubt that obedience and compliance are what pass for "cooperation."

Cooperation in Problem-Solving Groups. Cooperation at a more advanced level may take place in problem-solving situations—situations that have a relatively high degree of ambiguity and a low degree of structure or predictibility. Under such conditions, conventional roles and status levels are of little value and may actually interfere with the problem-solving processes. Most of the research conducted by psychologists into the nature of cooperative processes deals with situations of this type and takes place among subjects who are equal in status.

Many of these studies contrast cooperative with competitive behavior. Cooperation, as we have said, involves mutual goals, but competition is concerned with personal goals. In competition, individuals try to secure a greater-than-equal share of the rewards available to members of the group. In the usual type of experiment, this gain can be made only at the expense of others, although in everyday situations this is not always true. For example, Robert, usually a high-B student, feels challenged and even somewhat irritated by Elsa, a straight-A student who is in the same seminar with him. To compete with her, he does extra reading, writes and delivers an especially good paper, and consequently gets an A. Elsa also gets her A, and the other students in the seminar get their usual grades, so nobody loses. There is always the risk, of course, of encountering a professor who grades "strictly on the curve," but such is not usual in seminars, student folklore to the contrary notwithstanding.

Common-sense attitudes toward competition are based on the traditional idea that there is only a fixed quantity available for use or distribution of the "good things in life"—economic advantages, comfort, fame, happiness, and the like. This idea leads to the further assumption that individual betterment and progress can come only at the expense of others. Your success, in other words, automatically means loss and deprivation for me. This concept plays an important part in the value and belief systems of peasant cultures throughout the world, as the anthropologist George M. Foster (1967) points out, but it also has a strong appeal to many in urbanized, industrial societies, particularly to members of the lower classes. Modern economic theory, however, looks upon wealth as an entity that may be expanded by an investment of time, money, and energy in productive activity. Societies in which n Ach tends to run high are likely to be both economically productive and competitive, although government controls are often found necessary to keep competition within reasonable limits, on the one hand, and to ensure that enough competition does in fact take place, on the other. Antimonopoly legislation is an example of the latter type of control.

One of the classic studies of competition was conducted by Alexander Mintz (1951) who introduced groups of fifteen to twenty-one subjects

to a glass jar that contained a number of paper cones. Any one of the cones could be removed from the jar by pulling on a string that was tied to its peak and thus drawing string and cone through the opening at the top of the jar. It was not possible to remove more than one cone at a time, because they jammed in the neck of the jar (see Figure 14-2). After a few tries, the subjects were able to remove all the cones from the jar by taking turns and not getting in one another's way —in other words, by cooperating. The bottom of the jar was connected to a source of water which gradually filled the bottle, thus adding a note of stress—it was imperative to remove the cones before they came in contact with the water. The subjects who had learned to cooperate, however, learned to perform their tasks efficiently, in spite of this distraction. When Mintz changed the rules and offered any subject a cash reward if he could get his cone out of the bottle before it got wet, subjects who had previously encountered little difficulty in getting their cones out of the jar dry now encountered great problems. In twelve out of sixteen trials under reward conditions, "traffic

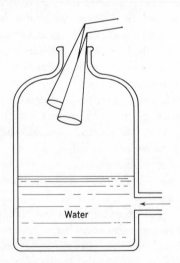

Figure 14-2. Cross-section of a glass jar used in the cooperation-competition experiment, showing two cones in a "traffic jam" at the neck of the cone (Mintz, 1951).

jams" developed in the neck of the bottle. In three of the remaining trials in which participants succeeded, they refused the rewards, thus suggesting that they had not really regarded the situation as a competitive one.

Mintz conducted this series of experiments because of his interest in the behavior of crowds in panic situations, as, for example, a fire in a theater. Loss of life in such situations can be avoided if people behave cooperatively, but instead a sense of panic sweeps over the crowd and people become preoccupied with their own survival. Mintz considered his competitive situation to be analogous to panic conditions, because participants were concerned only about their own welfare to the exclusion of any consideration for others. Under such conditions, cooperative behavior was not perceived by the subjects as rewarding. The fact that they had learned to function cooperatively in previous trials now became irrelevant,

and their intense preoccupation with their own welfare prevented their adopting the self-disciplines basic to cooperative endeavor.

A number of other researchers have found that competition leads to a higher level of performance than does cooperation. For example, Richard deCharms (1957) tested groups of subjects under conditions in which they were either rewarded equally (cooperative) or according to their achievement (competitive). Although he introduced a number of other variables not relevant to our present discussion, the results showed that the performance of each of the competitive groups exceeded that of each of the cooperative groups. One of the differences, however, between the deCharms study and that of Mintz, is that the former consisted of individual tasks that were merely divided among the group members, whereas the efforts of the groups in the Mintz study were interdependent.

"They say the department is riddled with dissension."

© LOOK Magazine, 1967.

When individual needs are permitted to predominate in situations calling for interdependent action, confusion may result.

An attempt to resolve some of the contradictions in the results of various studies of cooperation and competition was made by L. Keith Miller and Robert L. Hamblin (1963), who reviewed the literature on this subject and conducted a study of their own. They examined twenty-four different studies and noted that systems of differential rewards (which lead to competition) generally had a detrimental effect on performance in studies where interdependence among group members was essential to the completion of the task. This was true, for example, of the Mintz (1951) study. In studies where there was low task interdependence, however, like that of deCharms, differential rewards usually led to a heightened degree of group productivity.

To test the generality of this finding, the researchers set up a series of problems to be solved by three subjects each working in an isolated booth connected to other booths by an electrical system of lights and switches. The task was to determine which one of thirteen numbers the experimenter had selected. Each participant had a different set of four numbers that the experimenter had *not* selected; hence a pooling of the data revealed the correct answer. In the high-interdependence situation, guessing was not permitted, and subjects were forced to cooperate to solve the problem. In the low-interdependence situation, there was no restriction on guessing, and cooperation was hence less valuable. In the two differential reward conditions, rewards were determined by the rank order in which the group members solved the problem, with the speediest member receiving more points than the other members. In the equally rewarded situation, the members got the same reward, irrespective of individual differences in their speed in solving the problem.

The results, as depicted in Figure 14-3, supported one of the hypotheses derived from their analysis of the research literature. Under the high-interdependence condition, rewarding individual members on the basis of their performance interfered with the productivity of the group. However, differential rewards under conditions of low interdependence had little effect on performance.

The fact that Miller and Hamblin were unable to show a relationship between facilitated performance and productivity does not necessarily contradict the results of deCharms' study; the two studies used different tasks and cannot be considered as comparable. The Miller and Hamblin study does demonstrate, however, that competition intereferes with performance when the roles of members working on a task are interdependent. The question of whether competition aids or deters the productivity of groups working on other types of tasks remains open.

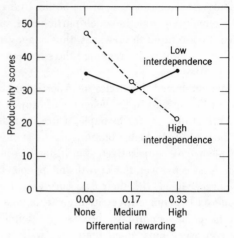

Figure **14-3.** Differences in group productivity* resulting from various degrees of individual differences in rewarding under low- and high-interdependence conditions (Miller & Hamblin, 1963).

* Productivity scores represent 90 less the average time in seconds per solution under each of the conditions. The productivity curves show that, under conditions in which group members are highly dependent on one another, the greater the difference in individual rewards, the poorer the performance. Where team members are only minimally dependent on one another (low interdependence condition), individual differences in rewarding have little effect.

Cooperation, Competition, and Group Feeling. Productivity is not the only measure of group effectiveness. Inasmuch as people are attracted to groups in order to satisfy social needs, how members feel about the groups in which they participate is an important consideration.

One study of such feelings was conducted by Robert E. Dunn and Morton Goldman (1966), who asked subjects to work on problems that could be solved through group-discussion methods. Some of the groups were told that the members would be rewarded individually; others were told that they would be rewarded as a total group. Some of the groups were in competition with other groups; others were not. Results showed that members found the experience more satisfying when rewards were shared equally. Furthermore, members of noncompetitive groups expressed more liking for one another than did members of competitive groups. The authors took issue with the common assumption that introducing competition among groups induces cohesiveness and "good in-group feeling," and interpreted their study as suggesting that such rivalry may not only be unnecessary but may also do social harm through arousing intergroup tensions.

The results of Dunn and Goldman's study appear to be contradicted by the findings of Julian, Bishop, and Fiedler (1966), who studied the morale of Army combat engineering squads. Nine squads were involved in intergroup competition in the conduct of their training and garrison duties; eighteen squads were not. Questionnaire measures of interpersonal relations and personal adjustment were administered before and after the three months' period of experimentation. Results showed that the competing soldiers showed gains in self-esteem, emotional adjustment, and adjustment to Army life, in contrast to the other soldiers, most of whom showed some deterioration on these variables. The members of competing squads also made significantly lower scores on a measure of anxiety and were more accepting of one another as work partners. The researchers concluded that under some conditions, intergroup competition could have a quasitherapeutic effect on the participants.

It may well be that the difference in results reported in the studies by Dunn and Goldman and by Julian et al. is due to the kind of task involved. Dunn and Goldman were observing the behavior of college students working for brief periods in an unfamiliar situation on the solution of problems, an activity that is likely to have a high degree of intrinsic interest value, whereas Julian, Bishop, and Fiedler were studying the behavior of military personnel working over an extended period of time on tasks that probably could be characterized as repetitive, monotonous, and boring. It is quite possible that competition made the tasks more interesting for the service personnel and hence improved their morale, but that it interfered with the performance of the college students who were trying to cope with a novel situation. Thus the differences between the two types of results may be another instance of the inverted-U relationship between stress and performance (Hebb, 1955a).

Some support for this idea may be found in a study that showed that subjects working in discussion groups under competitive conditions reported more satisfaction with their tasks, even though problems were solved more efficiently under cooperative conditions. The experimenter, Marvin E. Shaw (1958), concluded that competitive situations arouse stronger motivation to achieve (n Ach) than do cooperative situations, but that this stronger motivation may actually interfere with performance on certain tasks and thus result in poorer scores. Such results suggest that if motivation is a factor in getting people to work on tasks, it may be worthwhile to introduce competition to get people "involved," even at the risk of some loss of efficiency. If production is an important goal, an unmotivated, cooperative group would be less effective than a more highly motivated, competitive group.

In real-life situations, however, employees are

likely to be well aware of the motivating power of competition and often set up defenses in the form of group sanctions against members who permit themselves to become involved in competition. "Gold-bricking" and "goofing off" are terms applied to normative behavior aimed at resisting the efforts of management to get workers involved in competition, and those workers who do compete in spite of group norms are called "rate breakers" or "rate busters" by their fellow employees. We have noted this phenomenon previously and will discuss it further in Chapter 16.

One reason why workers resist the introduction of competitive measures is that under such conditions they are likely to become ego-involved in their work, because each individual realizes that he is "on trial" as an individual and others will judge him by his performance. And, what is probably even more important, he will be led to judge himself accordingly.

Traditional societies are likely to be less competitive than urban, industrial societies. Behavior in such societies tends to be more formalized according to position and status, whereas the members of urban, industrial societies, oriented as they are toward middle-class values, must earn the positions and status they occupy. Life in urbanized societies offers many opportunities, large and small, to prove oneself competitively. Interestingly enough, such societies also offer greater number of opportunities to function co-operatively in nonprescribed situations—for example, in group problem solving. Life in urban, industrial societies is full of ambiguous problems without clear and easy answers, whereas life in traditional societies presents relatively fewer problems and provides answers for all or most of them. There is thus a greater need in urbanized societies for a democratic type of problem solving in which all participants have equal status— the kind of problem situation that psychologists use as a basis for their experimentation.

Today we are much concerned about involving people throughout the world in large-scale prob-

lem solving. The problems of the world—health, education, peace and war, air and water pollution, population control, and the like—cannot be solved by individual people or individual nations. They can only be solved by cooperation and collaboration.

It is interesting, if perhaps ironic, that the most competitive societies also generate the most equal-status cooperation.

Cooperation and Competition in Two-Person Games

Nonzero-sum Games. The most recent attempts by psychologists to study cooperation and competition have made use of what are termed "non-zero-sum games." Such games are differentiated from "zero-sum games," which are the typical parlor games, like casino or dominoes, where one player wins whatever the other person loses. The only sensible approach to zero-sum games is to play them competitively, since that is the only way to win.

Nonzero-sum games (mentioned briefly at the end of Chapter 10) are more complex. In general, mutual cooperation will lead to modest gains for both players, mutual competition will lead to losses for both, and attempts to cooperate on the part of one player, when coupled with a competitive move by the other player, will lead to a major gain by the competitive player and a minor gain (or a loss) by the cooperative one.

In a typical game, players sit in different rooms and press buttons to signal their choices, with results announced to them after both have chosen. Figure 14-4 depicts a pay-off matrix for such a game. It can be seen that it is in the best long-range interest of both A and B to choose the left alternative, because they both will win 6¢. However, A will be tempted to choose the right-hand alternative, because he stands a chance of winning 7¢ and causing his opponent to win only 4¢. This will work, however, only if B has chosen the left alternative, because if B has chosen the right-hand alternative, they both lose 1¢. Choosing the and B chooses

	Left		Right	
Left	A wins 6¢	B wins 6¢	A wins 4¢	B wins 7¢
Right	A wins 7¢	B wins 4¢	A loses 1¢	B loses 1¢

If A chooses

Figure 14-4. Pay-off matrix for two person game designed to test cooperative and competitive strategies (Minas, Scodel, Marlowe, & Rawson, 1960).

left alternative is a cooperative choice, because it enables both sides to win a modest amount, but if one opponent makes this cooperative gesture and the other has simultaneously made a competitive one, the would-be cooperator comes off second best and the exploitive competitor wins.

The pay-off matrix depicted in Figure 14-4 is one that calls for cooperative behavior if participants are to make any headway. However, research using this payoff matrix shows that participants cooperate only about 50 per cent of the time. Even with other matrices that make cooperative behavior more rewarding, participants are unable to engage in cooperative responses more than 53 per cent of the time. When subjects were playing with a simulated player who cooperated 100 per cent of the time, their responses were cooperative only 38 per cent of the time (Minas, Scodel, Marlowe, & Rawson, 1960). Such results would seem to raise a question about the common assumption that cooperation breeds cooperation. However, another study by Bixenstine and Wilson (1963) showed that when the simulated partner's choices changed from a less cooperative to a more cooperative strategy in the middle of a series of games, there was a tendency for players to increase their percentage of cooperative responses as well. Even in such instances, the cooperativeness of players did not exceed 60 per cent, although the simulated opponent was making 95 per cent cooperative responses.

The player who makes a left (cooperative) choice in a game which has a pay-off matrix like Figure 14-4 is by definition trusting, because he is assuming that his opponent will not take advantage of him by making a right-hand (competitive) choice. Martin Deutsch (1960) conducted an experiment in which subjects made the first move (player A) in such a game and then made the second move (player B) in a second game in which the other player had already made a trusting (cooperative) choice. Persons who made trusting first moves were likely to make trustworthy second moves, whereas those who made suspicious (competitive) first moves were likely to take advantage of the other player during the second move by making an untrustworthy (competitive) choice. Furthermore, persons making suspicious and untrustworthy choices tended to score higher in authoritarianism on the F scale than did those making trusting and trustworthy responses.

Lawrence S. Wrightsman (1966) conducted a similar experiment and found that it made no difference in the results whether play money or real money was used. About 30 per cent of the subjects were "trusting" in both conditions. Like Deutsch, he found that "trusting" subjects scored lower on the F scale than "distrusting" ones. Wrightsman also found some differences between trusting and distrusting subjects on a personality test measuring philosophies of human nature. Trusting subjects scored higher on scales attempting to measure positiveness or general favorability, trustworthiness, altruism, and independence.

The "Trucking Game." Another type of two-person game involving the use of electronic equipment has been devised by Martin Deutsch and Robert M. Krauss (1960). Players are told that they are the owners of two trucking firms, Acme and Bolt. Each must send a truck in opposite directions along the same one-lane road. They also have alternate, circuitous routes to their goals. If trucks from both firms are blocked, face-to-face, in the middle of the one-lane stretch, they both lose money, because the pay-off is determined by the amount of time need to complete the trip. If Acme is able to send its truck down the road, thanks to Bolt's using the long, alternate route, then Acme makes more than Bolt, who may even lose money. It is obviously to their mutual advantage to take turns at going through the one-lane stretch. Players may be given bargaining power in terms of a "threat"—a gate which each can close at his end of the one-lane road, thus forcing the other player to proceed by the alternate, circuitous, money-losing route. Deutsch and Krauss found that players were more likely to find ways to cooperate and to maximize mutual gains under conditions in which they had no gates (no threats). They concluded that when players possessed potential threats, they tended to use them, thus increasing hostility and competitiveness and making cooperation more difficult. Shomer, Davis, and Kelley (1966) experiment with a variation of Deutsch and Krauss's approach and gave their players gates, but no alternate routes. They found that the availability of threat actually encouraged communication between the players and facilitated their working out cooperative arrangements. Krauss and Deutsch (1966) trained some of their players in bargaining methods and found that they earned higher pay-offs (because they were more cooperative) than players who had not had this kind of training.

The results obtained so far with such research suggest that anxiety may be a factor in the degree to which people are willing to make cooperative or competitive moves. The greater the degree of threat they perceive, the more likely they are to make choices that lead to short-range, low-reward goals, goals that will be detrimental in the long run. People who are characteristically suspicious seem to be more readily panicked into choosing short-range goals—at least Wrightsman's (1966) study suggests this is so—whereas people who are generally trusting are more willing to expose themselves and make themselves vulnerable in the hope of bringing about cooperative solutions.

Both the trucking game and nonzero-sum games are attempts to simulate, admittedly on a small scale, the kinds of situations in which individuals and groups find themselves when trying to achieve goals that involve the cooperation and potential competition of others. Such games call forth mixed motives (Schelling, 1960), because players must determine whether their decisions will be based on cupidity or altruism. The elements of such games are found in any human situation which evokes mixed motives, be it deciding whose turn it is to do the dishes tonight, or determining what move will immobilize a hostile nation without bringing on a war.

Games research so far does not permit us to draw any firm conclusions that apply to the solution of such dilemmas. The results seem to be highly specific to the experimental situations being devised and do not readily permit generalizations. On the positive side, however, the general approach used in these studies appears to be promising, because they are able to encompass within a small scope the significant variables in conflicts that are basic to human progress and survival.

SUMMARY

Studies comparing group with individual performance on problems calling for *divergent* thinking (many good solutions) show that individuals working alone are more productive, particularly after they have participated in group brainstorming. Results of studies comparing group and individual performance on tasks calling for *convergent* thinking (one best solution) show that groups are superior. An experiment by Tuckman and Lorge showed that groups were more effective than individuals working alone, because members of groups collectively could provide more possible solutions than any single member working alone. Maier showed that qualities of group solutions of complex problems could be improved if group leaders were trained to permit minority opinion to be heard. Performance of groups can also be improved if the structure is clear—that is, if members know who is the leader and particularly if the personal qualities of members are appropriate to their assigned positions. The most efficient groups in one study were those who included one member who had scored noticeably higher than the other members on a personality test measuring traits associated with decision making.

Early experiments with various structural arrangements in small problem-solving groups showed that groups with a highly centralized structure (wheel) tended to be more efficient, but that groups with decentralized structured (circle) tended to be more satisfying to group members and more flexible as well. Later research showed that decentralized groups were superior on complex problems, whereas centralized groups were not. Still another study showed that centralized groups were also efficient with complex problems, provided they were given sufficient time to develop the kind of structure needed.

A great deal of cooperation takes place in informal ways when people perform interlocking and reciprocal roles. When supervisors talk about getting cooperation from their subordinates, they usually mean compliance and obedience. In laboratory task groups, a concern for individual goals at the expense of group goals leads to competition and interferes with performance in situations in which members must function interdependently. Where there is low task interdependence, competition may help stimulate a higher level of achievement and make the task more interesting. On the affective outcomes of group interaction, research presents mixed results. One study with members of discussion groups found that members were better satisfied and liked one another better when rewards were shared equally (conducive to cooperation) than when rewards were given out individually (conducive to competition). However, another study with Army combat engineering squads in training showed that morale and psychological adjustment were improved when competition was introduced. These contradictory results can perhaps be explained in terms of the kind of task assigned and differences in the populations from which the subjects were drawn. In real-life situations where production is a factor, employees often resent attempts to introduce competition into the work situation and will harass workers who do so. Urbanized societies tend to be more competitive than traditional ones, yet they also generate situations that can be solved only by cooperation on an equal-status basis.

Research with two-person nonzero-sum games, in which cooperation results in modest gains for the players whereas mutually competitive tactics usually result in losses, shows that participants cooperate only about 50 per cent of the time. Even 100 per cent cooperation on the part of one player was able to evoke only 38 per cent cooperation on the part of the other players. There are some differences among players with respect to personality patterns, with those who are generally trusting making more cooperative responses than those who are not. In a similar type of two-person game, involving the operation of imaginary trucking firms, it was found that players could cooperate better if they were unable to enforce threats. Players who were taught to bargain were also more successful in playing the game. Although results from such studies are probably specific to the experimental settings in which they occur, they are able to create situations that are to some extent highly realistic, in the sense that they evoke mixed motives of cupidity and altruism on the part of participants.

SUGGESTED READINGS

Collins, B. E. & Guetzkow, H., *A social psychology of group processes for decision-making.* New York: Wiley, 1964.

Deutsch, M., Cooperation and trust: some theoretical notes. In M. R. Jones (Ed.), *Nebraska symposium on motivation.* Lincoln: University of Nebraska Press, 1962.

Lindgren, H. C. (Ed.), *Contemporary research in social psychology*. New York: Wiley, 1969. See papers 9.3 to 9.7, inclusive.

McClintock, C. G., Gallo, P., & Harrison, A. A., Some effects of variations in other strategy upon game behavior. *Journal of personality and social psychology*, 1965, 1, 319-325.

Rapoport, A. and Chammah, A. M., *Prisoner's dilemma*. Ann Arbor: University of Michigan Press, 1965.

Thelen, H. A., *Dynamics of groups at work*. Chicago: University of Chicago Press, 1954. Available also as paperback)

Thibaut, J. W. and Kelley, H. H., *The social psychology of groups*. New York: Wiley, 1959.

CHAPTER FIFTEEN

Group Task Performance: Leaders and Leadership

As we have noted previously, people come together in groups to satisfy both task and social needs. Their ability to satisfy these needs depends on a number of factors, not the least of which is the behavior of their leaders. Some of the research covered in Chapter 14 made the point that the effectiveness of groups depends largely on their ability to find a workable kind of structure, particularly a structure that makes it clear who shall dominate, direct, and influence, and who shall occupy subordinate positions. The research by Smelser (1961) that we discussed also indicated that such structural arrangements function better if key positions are occupied by people who are suited for them by reason of certain personal characteristics.

The research by Lewin, Lippitt, and White (1939), described in Chapter 13, also showed how persons in leadership positions can markedly influence the group climate, which in turn has a significant effect on the behavior and productivity of group members. In the present chapter we shall explore in greater detail some of the ways in which leaders behave, the kinds of characteristics they are likely to display, and the behavior that results on the part of the members of the groups they lead.

Functions of Leaders

Definitions of Leadership. Leadership, as Bernard M. Bass (1960) points out, is a kind of interaction between or among people. Any group member's attempt to change the behavior (including attitudes, values, and feelings) of one or more members of a group is an attempt at leadership. However, leadership does not consist merely of the attempt; the degree to which it has occurred is indicated by the extent to which the intended change takes place.

This definition of leadership means that any member of a group can play leadership roles at some time or other. Indeed, it is possible to measure any group member's leadership behavior on a scale ranging from considerable down to very little or none. Even in groups that have autocratic leaders and a relatively high degree of structure, members who are low in status and prestige may at times display behavior that influences others—even leaders. An analysis of such groups, however, would show that leaders are more likely to influence and that nonleaders are less likely to do so. Although anyone who successfully influences can be said to be exercising some kind of leadership, this type of influence most usually occurs within the structure of a social system. If the behavior persists, it is likely to contribute to the development of a system that has stability and endures over a period of time.

Daniel Katz and Robert L. Kahn (1966) maintain that the term "leadership," as it is used in social science literature, has three major meanings: the attribute of a position, the characteristics of a person, and a category of behavior. In most discussions, the three meanings are employed simultaneously, that is, they are used to refer to a person who possesses certain qualities, who occupies a certain position, and who behaves in certain ways. The three meanings are in no sense mutually exclusive; they are ways of recognizing that the influence potential of leaders may be related to different qualities or characteristics. A lieutenant will be obeyed by a company of soldiers if he gives a certain order, irrespective of whether he is the kind of person whom they would ordinarily look to for leadership or whether the kind of behavior he displays is very leaderlike according to the usual norms. In this instance, his position alone makes him a leader. When Hatshepsut made herself pharoah of Egypt toward the end of the second millenium B.C., her decrees were obeyed like those of the kings who preceded and followed her, even though there had never been a female pharoah before.

Leadership and the Power to Influence. The position occupied by an official or unofficial leader gives him a greater leverage when it comes to power and influence than does the position of any other member of a group. We usually expect leaders to try to influence our behavior, and their attempts to influence constitute some of the role behaviors attached to the position of leader. We expect, in turn, that we shall be influenced, because such expectations are consistent with the position of follower or subordinate.

A study by L. Richard Hoffman and Norman R. F. Maier (1967) demonstrates rather clearly that an individual who is put into a leadership position will try to influence the group and that the group, in turn, will permit itself to be influenced. The researchers assigned a problem involving human relations in an industrial setting* to groups of three and four college sophomores and directed them to discuss it with a view to producing the best solution possible. One member of each group was selected at random to serve as group leader. Before the discussion session, the leaders were privately promised a reward of $1.50 if they would achieve the goal set for them. Half were told that the goal was the highest-quality solution to the problem, and half were told that the goal was the group's satisfaction with the solution. An analysis of the solutions showed that even when the leaders' goal was the satisfaction of the group, they still exercised more influence on the solution the group adopted than did the other members of the group. Not only did the

---

* This particular problem was selected largely because previous experience had shown that discussion groups of college students resolved it in a number of different ways, thus making it possible to detect the influence of various group members.

leaders tend to dominate and control discussion, but their domination and control was accepted by the group. When we recollect that these leaders were selected randomly from the group, and not because of any indication of interest or ability in leadership, the results of this study are clear evidence that the position of leader tends to endow whoever the holder happens to be with considerable power and influence.

Leaders also perform other roles than that of influencing the members of their group. For example, a leader may communicate with other groups on his group's behalf. He may serve as a channel of information. He may help meet some of the dependency needs of group members who are looking for a parent figure or a source of reassurance. Behavior of his that is irrelevant to the goals of the group may also be imitated by other group members: they may, for example, start using his brand of cigarettes or some of his favorite expressions.

Some leaders will not ordinarily be visible as such, even though they exercise a considerable degree of influence. The secretary to an executive may be such a person. She is in a key position to control the flow of communication to and from her boss and may often serve as an interpreter of his wishes to subordinates. She may also, in various ways, influence his opinions on various matters and communicate ideas to subordinates that are more hers than his. If she plays her roles subtly enough, few people will be aware that she is actually leading. Other secretaries are less subtle; their influence is both resented and feared, but this does not necessarily interfere with their ability to exert influence.

Leaders may thus be official and unofficial. Official leaders generally have the advantage, because they are more visible, and group behavior becomes almost automatically referred to their attitudes and attempts to influence. Unofficial leaders are more likely to gain power when official leadership is unavailable and a power vacuum develops. This may occur when the leader is physically absent, or it may occur when the group rejects or ignores the leader. In the example of the secretary who comes to wield considerable influence, it is possible that her boss is preoccupied with other problems, that his responsibilities are too extensive for him to handle easily, or that he finds it more efficient to use his secretary as a kind of junior partner in his attempts to lead. In democratically oriented groups, leaders often play their roles in such a way to encourage the development of junior-grade leadership among the other members of the group, as a way of improving group effectiveness and morale and increasing involvement.

Official leaders go by many titles: president, chairman, captain, manager, mayor, legislator, and chief are some of them, but teachers, consultants, lawyers, physicians, and policemen also serve as leaders much of the time.

Power and Prestige. The extent to which leaders can influence the behavior of others is termed *power.* Power varies with the *prestige* of the leader: the degree to which his actions are regarded as significant, relevant, and important by others. Prestige may be attached to a position; even positions of intermediate status have a greater or lesser degree of built-in prestige to the end that anyone who occupies them is able to exercise some degree of influence, irrespective of who he is. Individuals also have a greater or lesser degree of prestige, based partly on the positions they occupy in other contexts and partly on the way in which their behavior is perceived by others. A television celebrity is given special consideration when he appears at a social gathering, for he is listened to more carefully and is permitted to "upstage" local leaders. Celebrities possess *salience,* the quality of being highly visible and standing out against a background. In political contests, this quality alone may on occasion attract enough attention to cause voters to elect those who possess it to high political offices. Prestige is also related to an individual's claims to status on the basis of the position or positions held in other contexts or to the social class of which he is a member.

The Transferability of Leadership. What this means is that there is a tendency for individuals who play leadership roles in one context to play them in others as well. This tendency is stronger when situations are similar, of course, but the carryover effect does persist even when situations are dissimilar (Carter, Haythorn, & Howell, 1950). In effect, the perceptions, attitudes, values, and ways of thinking that these individuals have learned in various group settings become a part of their general pattern or style of behavior. When they enter a new group, they begin playing roles that are familiar to them. They interact with others in a leaderlike way, and this behavior, in turn, tends to evoke followerlike behavior from the other group members. A chain of behavior is set into operation whereby their perception of themselves as leaders helps others to perceive them in the same way.

This phenomenon appeared in a study of two Parent-Teacher Association groups each of which met together for three sessions to look at and discuss mental health films. The post-film discussions were tape recorded, and experimenters kept notes in order to identify the initiator and target of every comment that was made. Experimentors also collected biographical data on the participants and administered sociometric instruments. At the third and final meeting of the groups, members were asked to indicate whom they would like to have as president and vice president of their group, if it were to continue. Data from these various sources enabled researchers to determine three kinds of status for each participant: interaction, friendship, and leadership.

Results showed that all three kinds of status measures were positively intercorrelated, but that leadership status accounted for most of the variance. The researchers also concluded that discussion in small groups of this type, where people are already acquainted, is largely confined to those members of the group who enjoy superior status in other contexts by virtue of their education and profession. Not only were these higher-status individuals more active in their participation, but they also addressed most of their comments to one another. Members who ranked low in leadership status tended to address their remarks toward high-status persons, instead of to other low-status members. Although the leaders of the group also ranked high on the friendship choices made by other members, an analysis of scores showed that it was leadership and not friendship that determined the amount of participation in the discussion (Lana, Vaughan, & McGinnies, 1960).

Types of Leaders and Categories of Leadership

There are many ways in which individuals can influence others, although some roles and activities are more conducive to influence than others. Indeed, any action in which an individual contributes to group goals in a way that is significantly different from other members can be considered as a kind of leadership. Almost any typology that applies to a given role or position will be deficient in the sense that each behavior category runs the risk of including too much or too little of the relevant activities performed. Yet some kind of descriptive analysis appears to be in order if only to suggest what leaders actually do in influencing others. As we proceed through this rather extensive list, it is important to keep in mind that many of the categories overlap, and that the activities of a given leader will put him into several, if not most, of these categories.*

The Administrator. This broad, general term covers a wide variety of activities: planning, coordinating, managing, directing, and organizing. Administrators are people who see that things get

---

* Concepts embodied in this typology are drawn from a number of sources, including Bass (1960); Krech, Crutchfield, and Ballachey (1962); and Lindgren (1954).

done. They occupy key positions in organizations or groups that have been created to accomplish a specific end or goal, usually that of producing goods or providing services. The administrator's two main tasks are to direct the maintenance of organizational processes and to carry out the organization's policies.

Administration may also include policy making, although many experts see policy making as separate from administration, maintaining that the two functions call for separate skills and generally are carried out by separate individuals and groups. In the United States, for instance, the Congress is supposed to make policy, and the President, as the chief executive and chief administrative officer, is supposed to carry it out. In reality, however, the administrator's control of personnel and resources, and his access to information, not only puts him in a position to make policy, but also a series of unexpected events may create emergencies calling for prompt, on-the-spot decisions that only he is in a position to make. The attempt to maintain administration and policy making as separate functions usually results in an uneasy balance of power between administrators and policy makers, with administrators having the initial advantage, but with policy-making groups having the final say and possessing a veto power.

The Bureaucrat. This term is usually applied to individuals who hold positions in the intermediate and lower levels of the administrative hierarchy in an organization and who have more or less specialized duties in directing and supervising organizational processes. Any large organization must divide up its functions into special areas, each of which is assigned to a separate branch, irrespective of whether the organization is governmental, military, religious, or business in character. Whatever power the bureaucratic leader may possess derives from the structure of the organization and the formalized regulations that prescribe, define, and limit his roles and functions. Organizations that have existed over a period of time are likely to develop structures with a high degree of flexibility and durability. The Roman Empire, for example, is said to have been able to withstand the debilitating effects of decades of misrule by incompetent emperors, some of them merely adventurers and opportunists, by virtue of a strong bureaucracy that carried on the business of the Empire in spite of what was going on at the top levels.

The Policy Maker. The policy maker may also be an administrator; he is less likely to be a bureaucrat, although even lesser bureaucrats may at times make policy by the way they carry out their duties. In large organizations, policy makers are likely to be members of boards of directors or legislators. The administrator generally serves as the chief consultant to bodies of policy makers and, when policy has been formulated, carries it out.

The Expert. The expert generally works in a consultant capacity to policy makers and administrators. He is a specialist in some field of information that is of value to the organizational leaders. He may participate in the formulating of policy and in planning, but his role is generally that of a commentator, critic, and special resource person.

The first three types of leaders described are what is termed "line." They are charged with the responsibility of formulating objectives and/or carrying them out. The expert is "staff," because he bears no direct responsibility for the results that obtain as a result of the efforts of line personnel. Medical specialists, personnel managers, industrial psychologists, and public relations officers are all "staff" in a manufacturing organization, whereas foremen, superintendents, production managers, and salesmen are all "line." In a school system, the superintendent, teachers, and principals would be "line" personnel, whereas the school psychologists, counselors, and school nurses would all be "staff."

The Ideologist. Like the expert, the ideologist is a specialist, but he is a specialist in ideas and beliefs, rather than in some technical field. The ideologist is concerned with the basic theories that are implied by various forms of social behavior. Saint Augustine, Luther, Galileo, Mohammed, Karl Marx, and Theodore Herzl are examples of highly influential ideologists whose teachings have altered the lives of millions. Most leaders are ideologists to some extent; that is, their attempts to lead reflect some pattern of beliefs as to what the goals of the group should be and how they should be attained.

The Charismatic Leader. "Charisma" is a Greek term used to designate a favor or a gift granted by God that enables the recipient to have some special power with respect to his fellow men—the ability to heal or to perform miracles, for example. The term was introduced into social science by Max Weber (1947), who applied it to leaders with strong emotional appeal. When this is coupled with an ideology, as it was with such diverse individuals as Luther, Mohammed, St. Francis, and Adolf Hitler, the combination can be very attractive, particularly for the dissatisfied. Yesterday's charismatic leaders were likely to be religious; today's are likely to be political. The difference, however, may be largely superficial, because the charismatic political leader of today is able to imbue his followers with a zeal that goes beyond mere politics and is, in the final analysis, built largely on unquestioning faith in his miraculous powers. Eric Hoffer (1951) calls the followers of charismatic leaders "true believers," and makes the point that their blind faith is based on a belief in their own worthlessness and inadequacy. It is only through identifying with a "movement" and a superleader, he says, that they are able to gain a sense of selfhood and personal adequacy.

We have used the term "charismatic leader" to apply to leaders whose appeal is largely emotional. Most leaders who are successful succeed in part because they have qualities that enable their followers to identify with them. Social attractiveness, as we have noted, is based largely on perceived similarity, and however different from his followers a leader may appear to an observer, he still is similar enough to them in order for them to find ways to identify with him. Franco would not be attractive to the Spanish if he were Italian and if he did not represent values that many Spanish people feel are important and essentially Spanish. Katz and Kahn (1966) point out that in the presidential elections of 1952 and 1956, Adlai Stevenson had charisma for American intellectuals, but not for the rank and file. Dwight Eisenhower, on the other hand, talked and acted like the man in the street, for all his military and academic honors, and therefore had more charisma for the average voter.

The Political Leader. The political leader embodies something of most of the leader types we have discussed so far. He is a policy maker, is often an ideologist, and must have at least a touch of charisma in order to be elected. Although he operates within an organization—a government —he often functions like an entrepreneur or independent trader. Politicians achieve goals for themselves, their friends, and the people who elect them by elaborate systems of bargaining and favor trading. Nonpoliticians are disturbed by this practice whenever they learn of it; it smacks of chicanery, double-dealing, and graft. There is no doubt that politicians have used these methods to further their own ends, but the fact remains that negotiation and compromise are necessary in any problem-solving situation involving the interests of multiples of groups and individuals. No one can have his own way all the time, and political arrangements are needed to ensure a more or less equitable sharing of benefits and rewards. And so political agreements are made: "I'll support your bill to increase the number of circuit judges. I'll agree that there is a tremendous backlog of cases and that the judgeships are needed. But I'll expect your support for my bill to increase minimum salaries for teachers when it comes up."

What nonpoliticians do not realize is that their voting for a legislator is in effect a political agreement of much the same nature: the electorate agrees to support the prospective legislator in exchange for his willingness to support their political goals.

The Symbolic Leader. An important dimension of a leader's role is his ability not only to represent and speak for his group, but also to represent his group symbolically. The Ambassador from Thailand is treated with respect because he represents (i.e., stands for) the people of Thailand. In a manner of speaking, he "is" Thailand in this country. In a meeting of heads of state, of course, the King of Thailand will "be" Thailand and will be treated with respect as though he embodied all the Thai people in his person. On several occasions, vice presidents of the United States have been pelted with eggs by left-wing elements in the countries they were visiting. It is possible that the animosity so expressed was personal, but it is more likely that they were so treated because they were perceived as representing the United States. In other words, the egg throwers thought of themselves as insulting a country they despised. The official apologies of the host country after the incident were a way of recognizing that the insults were directed toward the United States and of expressing embarrassment at not being able to control this group of dissidents.

Symbolic leaders also have a high degree of ritual value. Relations between groups of people, like nations, take place between symbolic leaders interacting in a very formal, ritualistic way, that is, in ways that have been prescribed by custom and precedent. Although such ritual is often criticized as being "empty" or "meaningless," it appears to provide a necessary channel for communication and interaction.

There are many other instances, of course, in which leaders or authority figures act out symbolic and ritualistic roles. The general manager presides over a dinner at the best restaurant in town to celebrate the retirement of a timekeeper who has been with the company for forty years. On behalf of the management he presents him with a check and on behalf of the employees he presents him with a gold watch. It is all very symbolic and has little utilitarian value, but the ceremony does provide everyone with an opportunity to wish the old timekeeper well. Such rituals can also have a positive effect on the cohesiveness of the total group, because their purpose is to show solidarity and personal appreciation and not to achieve production. The general manager is the logical person to perform the ritual, because he, more than anyone else, represents the total group.

An analogous example is the action of the father giving the bride away at a wedding. Everyone knows that in our society the bride is a free agent and needs no one to give her to her husband, but important occasions seem to require something both special and traditional in the way of a show—a ritual—to express the degree of importance we attach to them. The father, in this instance, is an authority figure who represents the family and is the logical person to play this role.

The Parent Figure. The earliest group that most of us experience is the family, and the first leaders with whom we become acquainted are our parents. As we go on to school, teachers take on parental roles, and the school has by law a relationship with us that is *in loco parentis*—in place of a parent. There is a tendency, particularly during childhood and adolescence, for us to regard all authority figures in somewhat the same way we regard our own parents. This tendency may even linger throughout life, with the result that leaders and other persons in authority often take on certain parental characteristics. Leaders' roles, furthermore, often resemble those of parents: they reward, punish, admonish, chide, encourage, direct, and so forth. These are all part of the role traditionally assigned to parents and particularly to fathers.

There are two main types of parental leaders. One is the dominating, forbidding, punishing, demanding, authoritarian leader—the so-called "father figure." The other is the nourishing, sheltering, understanding, supportive, reassuring leader—the "mother figure." Most leaders, irrespective of their sex, represent a combination of these two types. They are reflected, for example, in the leadership styles termed "structure initiation" and "consideration," which we discuss later in this chapter. Some leaders emphasize one more than the other, of course. A counselor or psychiatrist is more likely to emphasize the "mother" qualities, whereas a policeman or an assembly-line foreman is more likely to represent the "father" qualities, with many individual exceptions in each case, of course.

The Leader as a Target for Hostility. It is quite common for people to feel a degree of ambivalence, resentment, or even hostility toward authority figures. This appears in the relatively large number of cartoons that satirize the problems of business executives, professors, psychiatrists, political leaders, and the like. This hostility may stem from a wish that we might be free of leaders —free, that is, to speak and act for ourselves without any interference or unwanted help. Perhaps we resent the fact that leaders are perceived as being more important—more visible—than the rank and file—us. When we see the mayor of our city driving around town in a chauffeur-driven Cadillac, we may think: "That's only right. After all, we are proud of our city, and we wouldn't want the mayor to greet important people in an ordinary car." But we may also think: "Who does the mayor think he is, anyway? He's no better a person than I, and he could get along just as well in a Volkswagen, instead of driving around in that fancy rig at my expense!" There is, in other words, a tendency to want to elevate leaders and at the same time to bring them down to our own level.

One of the functions of leaders is that of taking on a high degree of responsibility for the operation of the groups they head. If members are not satisfied with results, they are likely to look for someone to blame, and the logical target for blame is the person in charge.

Table **15-1.** Stems and completions in a Sentence Completion Test designed to measure attitudes toward authority figures (from data supplied by Lindgren and Lindgren, 1960)

Stem	Sentence completion	Attitude expressed
College presidents generally	are men of wide cultural background.	Acceptance
	impress me as rather stiff and un-approachable.	Hostility
	are awesome.	Anxiety
Most employers	are satisfied with my work.	Acceptance
	should take a course in personal relations.	Hostility
	upset me.	Anxiety
When I have dealings with businessmen	I like to trust them.	Acceptance
	I am struck with their materialism.	Hostility
	I usually feel somewhat inferior, out of my element.	Anxiety
When I was in grade school, the teachers	I had were good.	Acceptance
	did not impress me.	Hostility
	were frightening.	Anxiety

Americans are inclined to express hostile feelings toward leaders somewhat more openly than people in more traditional cultures, a tendency perhaps suggesting that Americans rate high in hostility toward leaders. Another possible interpretation may be that hostile feelings toward leaders may be submerged—suppressed or repressed—in other cultures. In one set of studies, American, Canadian, and Arab subjects were asked to take a sentence-completion test,* in which the "stems" (beginnings of sentences) all referred to authority figures. Completions were classified as "accepting," "hostile," or "anxious." Table 15-1 lists some of the stems used in the studies and gives examples as to how completions were classi-

* The sentence-completion test is a type of semistructured projective test. Like other projective tests, it attempts to tap motives and attitudes that lie beyond ordinary awareness.

fied. Overall results showed that Arabs and Canadians gave more hostile responses than Americans. Americans tended to show more acceptance of authority figures than Canadians, who in turn showed more acceptance than Arabs. An item-by-item analysis showed, however, that Canadians tended to be more accepting than Americans of prestigious figures ("famous people," "judges," "naval officers"), whereas Arabs tended to be more accepting of people in authority with whom they came into direct personal contact ("When I have a difference of opinion with an instructor," "Being reprimanded and criticized"), but were more hostile toward governmental authority figures ("policemen," "government ministers," "army officers") (Lindgren & Lindgren, 1960; Sallery & Lindgren, 1966).

Some of the resentment felt toward leaders may be due to a belief that they receive more than their share of the rewards. Solidarity and cohesiveness are reinforced, as we noted in Chapter 14, when rewards are shared equally by groups. In one study of small group behavior in which problems of the "twenty-questions" type were solved, the groups who shared equally in rewards and who functioned without leaders made higher scores and expressed more satisfaction than did groups whose leaders received an extra reward (Goldman, Bolen, & Martin, 1961).

It is quite possible, of course, that a group's ability to express hostility toward its leader may have some positive effects on its performance. Some psychologists maintain that the expression of negative feelings has a cathartic or cleansing effect and enables the individual to focus his energies on creativity, production, and cooperation, and other forms of positive behavior (Dollard et al., 1939; Menninger, 1948; Baruch, 1949). Other psychologists find contrary evidence (Bandura & Walters, 1963). It is quite possible that the free expression of hostility helps in some situations and hinders in others. The problem at this moment seems to be that of finding out what the characteristics of those situations are. In any event, the most valid conclusion seems to be that all groups tend to have both positive and negative feelings about leaders, but that the extent to which negative feelings are freely expressed varies from culture to culture. Although evidence is scanty, it seems likely that free expression of hostility and resentment is more common in cultures characterized by more democratic values and attitudes and more inhibited in cultures characterized by more authoritarianism.

Characteristics of Leaders

Salience. Whatever personal qualities leaders possess, they do have this characteristic in common: they stand out from the rest of the group. This quality of salience is achieved in some instances solely because of the position occupied. Many individuals appointed to leadership positions are the kind of people who would blend into the group if they had not been elevated to positions of authority. Once they occupy leadership positions, however, they achieve a degree of salience that no other group member possesses.

Intelligence. Common sense would suggest that persons appointed, elected, or otherwise perceived as leaders rate higher in intelligence than the rank and file, and research appears to bear out this supposition. Ralph J. Kiessling and Richard A. Kalish (1961) made use of an assessment procedure known as the "leaderless group discussion" technique, a method whereby applicants for positions requiring the exercise of leadership qualities are assembled in small discussion groups. No leader is assigned or appointed, and group members are "on their own." Judges then observe the group through a one-way screen and score the performance of individuals in terms of the extent to which they display behavior that aids or facilitates the functioning of the group. The process can therefore be used as a method for rating potential for "natural" leadership. In the study conducted by Kiessling and Kalish, a significant and positive correlation (.35) was found between leadership ratings and scores made on standard intelligence tests. Similar results—a correlation of .28—were reported by Morris Showel (1960), who investigated the relationship between leadership ratings of Army trainees and their scores on the Army General Classification Test. Showel also found that trainees rating high on leadership tended to possess more interpersonal information about other trainees.

Adjustment. The roles that leaders play are probably more demanding than those played by members of the groups they lead. If this is so, it would then appear that neurotic tendencies would interfere with leaders' effectiveness. As we have shown, persons who are perceived as leaders tend to rate higher on intelligence than persons not so perceived. It is very likely that our perception of an individual's adjustment also helps determine our willingness to perceive him as a leader.

The relationship between adjustment and leadership was studied by Stephen J. Fitzsimmons and F. L. Marcuse (1961), who administered a sentence-completion test to fifty university students who had been presidents of their fraternities and a matched group of fifty fraternity members who had held neither fraternity nor nonfraternity positions of leadership. This procedure enabled the researchers to study two sharply contrasting groups, the elected leaders and the nonleaders, thus eliminating those who had held minor positions of leadership. When the sentence-completion responses were scored on twelve different adjustment categories, leaders had higher (better adjusted) scores on eleven. Although there was some overlap between the two groups, results indicated that leaders had fewer neurotic traits than did nonleaders. The researchers concluded that leadership tends to operate most effectively in the absence of negative personality traits that might interfere with their performance.

Some studies by David O. Moberg (1953a,b) also confirm the positive relationship between leadership and adjustment. Moberg found that people who had played leadership roles in their churches tended to be better adjusted in old age than those who had not. He found no difference in adjustment between old people who had been church members and those who had not; leadership was the only significantly relevant variable.

Deviancy. The findings we have reported so far are consistent with common sense: most people would not be surprised to learn that leaders tend to be more intelligent and less neurotic than the average person. The idea, however, that leaders deviate more from the norms than others do may come as a surprise. Somehow, deviancy seems to imply psychopathology, which would of course be inconsistent with the notion that leaders are well adjusted.

There are a number of studies that suggest that leaders tend to be freer of normative pressures than most people. One investigation of yielding and nonyielding behavior of members of cliques showed that the leaders and the members with the lowest status tended to conform the least, whereas middle-status members conformed the most (Harvey & Consalvi, 1960). Ronald S. Wilson (1960) obtained much the same results when he polled high, low, and intermediate status members of groups about their personal beliefs.

These results suggest that leaders and low-status members both are relatively independent of group pressures. Very probably, because leaders are less neurotic they are able to use their ability to think independently in the service of the group, whereas low-ranking members are not. High-ranking group members, furthermore, are evidently able to express deviant views in ways that are less likely to upset other group members, whereas lower-status members either have not learned this technique or are not interested in doing so. Leaders tend to be more concerned about group solidarity than most people. In one study of small group interaction, they agreed with others more and made more attempts to reduce tension than did other members of the groups (McClintock, 1963). It is possible that leaders tend to be people who are able to keep a reasonable balance between maintaining the cohesiveness of the group and expressing nonconforming ideas and behavior. Inasmuch as the solidarity of the group is an important goal for them, they are less likely to compromise it by indulging in the free expression of ideas and feelings that deviate too markedly from those of most of the group members.

Social Distance. The fact that leaders prize solidarity and cohesiveness in the groups for which they are responsible does not necessarily mean that they also favor closeness and intimacy with group members. A number of studies show that the most effective leaders, as measured by the performance of their groups, are those who are able to maintain a degree of social or psychological distance between themselves and the other members of the group they supervise. This is especially true of work groups.

Fred E. Fiedler (1958) made a study of the effectiveness of a variety of task groups and compared successful and unsuccessful high school basketball teams, surveying teams, Air Force bomber crews, Army tank crews, open-hearth shops in steel mills, and farm supply cooperatives, and found that psychological distance between supervisors and the supervised was positively correlated with various success measures. He concluded that the person who leads a work or task group should be an individual who is able to maintain a degree of psychological distance between himself and the other members of the group. He theorized that this type of relationship enables the person in authority to be more objective, which in turn prevents his becoming emotionally involved in or overly attached to his subordinates and permits the establishment of better discipline and businesslike working conditions. He made it clear, however, that these conclusions apply only to work groups, and that other types of tasks, such as heading policy-making groups, probably demand leaders with different attitudes toward their subordinates. Sheer social distance, however, is insufficient in and of itself as a predictor of group success, for the leader must also be accepted by the other members of the group. This, in turn, implies a high degree of task-orientation on the part of the members, because they would probably be unwilling to submit to a leader's attempts to enforce discipline, unless they were committed to the successful completion of the tasks assigned them.

Structure Initiation vs. Consideration in Leaders

The results of Fiedler's research seem to support the traditional idea that a supervisor should command, direct, discipline, and reward in order to be effective. This model, however, has been subjected to a considerable degree of criticism by psychologists, as well as by other experts in the field of employee relations, who have maintained that it is the more democratic, permissive, considerate, and person-oriented type of leader who

gets the best results. This latter school of thought has taken its cues from work done during the late 1920's and early 1930's at the Hawthorne plant of the Western Electric Company, located near Chicago (Homans, 1965; Roethlisberger & Dickson, 1939).

The Hawthorne Study. Research at the Hawthorne plant consisted of three major activities: (1) interviews and inquiries aimed at learning something about the attitudes employees have toward their work; (2) observation of work habits and interpersonal relations among teams of workers; and (3) study of the work behavior, interpersonal relations, and production of a group of five women engaged in putting together small electrical relays.

Research findings showed, among other things, that there was a considerable gap between the ideas of management and staff about employee attitudes toward work and the attitudes that employees actually had. Management assumed, for example, that the employees' primary motivation was economic, and had therefore arranged pay schedules in such a way that increased production would be reflected in increased earnings. Workers, however, tacitly agreed among themselves as to what a "fair day's work" should be and limited their production accordingly. Group solidarity and cohesiveness were more important goals to them than was individual accomplishment, a possibility that was overlooked by management in the latter's structuring of the work situation. Like managers in other plants, managers at Hawthorne thought they could influence the behavior of workers by controlling the factor of reward: wages. Workers, on the other hand, were able to elude control much of the time by finding rewards (group solidarity) that were outside management's perceptual field.

The relative unimportance of material rewards was also demonstrated by a series of experiments with the small team of women working on relay assemblies. The working conditions of this group were manipulated by the researchers in a number of different ways during the four and one half years they were observed. The results of the experimentation were puzzling: production rose irrespective of whether working conditions were improved (by increasing the number and length of rest periods, for example) or worsened (eliminating rest periods, for example). When the women were asked about the reasons for their higher production, they reported themselves somewhat at a loss to explain it. They knew they were more productive, yet somehow it was easier to produce more in the experimental situation than it was to produce less in the regular work situation. They reported that it was "more fun" to work in the special group, and they also liked being away from the surveillance of their usual supervisors.

There were, in addition, some other differences that appeared to contribute to the increased production. For one thing, they were consulted by the top supervisor before any change was put into effect. For another, they were able to talk freely among themselves, something they had been unable to do in their regular work situation. They were also taken off piecework and were paid a flat wage, no matter how much or how little they produced. What seemed to be most important to the researchers, however, was the fact that the women realized that they were taking part in an important experiment. This increased their interest in their job. They received a great deal of attention and, as we noted in Chapter 2, the need for attention is a strong motivating force.

The differences between the former working conditions of these women and those of the experimental situation can be summed up in a word: consideration. These women were receiving more consideration of their needs and interests as individuals than they were in their former work situation. The experimenters had unconsciously arranged a situation that met more of the workers' psychological and social needs than had the situation in which they usually worked.

During the years that followed the Hawthorne study, and particularly during World War II, the interest in developing employer-employee relations based on a "human relations" approach grew, particularly among psychologists and sociologists concerned with industrial situations. We shall have more to say in Chapter 16 about some of this research and the techniques that have been developed to implement its findings, but for the present we will direct our attention to the controversy that has emerged between the proponents of the "consideration" approach, based on the Hawthorne study and similar research, and the proponents of "structure initiation."

The International Harvester Study. One of the organizations that made use of "human relations" training programs for its supervisory personnel was the International Harvester Company. The program at International Harvester was focused on foremen, because it was felt that the attitudes and behavior of supervisors at this level would have maximum impact on morale, worker satisfaction, and, of course, production.

During the time that this training program was under way, the Personnel Research Board of the Ohio State University was engaged in studying supervisory effectiveness at International Harvester. Psychologists employed by the Board were interested in two patterns of supervisory leadership, one termed "consideration" and the other "structure initiation." Consideration patterns of behavior are consistent with democratic, permissive, considerate, and person-oriented attitudes, whereas behavior concerned with the initiation of structure tends to be consistent with organizing, planning, directing, and criticizing attitudes. The leader who is oriented toward consideration is concerned primarily with meeting the psychological and emotional needs of the members of the group, whereas the leader who is primarily oriented toward structure initiation is concerned with getting the job done. Although the two dimensions appear to be opposites, they are in fact independent, correlating $-.01$. This means that they are not mutually exclusive and that a leader can display attitudes that are strongly oriented toward consideration, strongly oriented toward structure initiation, or neither, or both (Stogdill & Coons, 1957).

The Personnel Research Board undertook an evaluation of the special training that International Harvester foremen were receiving. Their findings were not very reassuring for those who had hoped that special courses of this nature would bring about real changes in the values and behavior of supervisory personnel. The researchers, Fleishman, Harris, and Burtt (1955), administered attitude questionnaires before and after the special two-week training period, with a follow-up two to ten months later. They found that attitudes did in fact move in the direction of "consideration" and away from "structure initiation" during the training period, but that the effect did not last. After a few months back on the job, the foremen rated *lower* in consideration and higher in structure initiation than they had before the special training. This effect, furthermore, was confirmed by reports of the foremen's behavior, as given anonymously by their subordinates. Some of the foremen also were given a one-week "refresher" course in human relations some time after they had been back at the plant. As far as the researchers could determine, this had little effect on their attitudes, and their behavior, if anything, moved in the direction of more structure initiation.

As the researchers probed more deeply into the problem, they found that foremen worked in basically two kinds of situations. Foremen on production lines, where they were required to meet schedules, tended to be more oriented toward structure initiation and to work under supervisors who also favored structure initiation. Furthermore, production foremen who received highest ratings from their supervisors tended to score high on structure initiation and low on consideration. Foremen in jobs that were not concerned with production (stores, inspection, and maintenance) tended to score high on consideration and

low on structure initiation and worked under supervisors who scored in the same direction. Workers, as might be expected, tended to prefer foremen who rated high in consideration and low in structure initiation. Furthermore, there was more absenteeism and a higher number of grievances filed in the departments headed by foremen who scored high in structure initiation.

The researchers concluded that human relations training has little effect, if trainees go back to work for supervisors who are more concerned with production than with human relations; hence any real change in attitudes in an organization must start with the top people. They also concluded, however, that the leader who is preoccupied with morale (consideration) may be less efficient than one who is preoccupied with production. If production and morale are *both* important considerations, it appears as though leaders must initiate structure and be considerate at the same time. The effectiveness of a combination of consideration and structure initiation has since been confirmed by Michael Beer (1966), who conducted a survey of some fifteen thousand employees of a large insurance company and found that a supervisor who was perceived as considerate by his subordinates could effectively increase their initiative by initiating more structure in his dealings with them.

Leaders' Attitudes toward their "Least Preferred Co-worker." Fiedler's research showing that more efficient groups are characterized by some degree of social distance between leaders and the people they supervise tends to support the idea that structure initiation is necessary if production groups are to function efficiently. Psychological or social distance is an important factor in structuring groups, and the leader who takes steps to initiate a structure that maintains a considerable degree of distance is evidently the type employers prefer as a production line foreman.

Fiedler (1965) has refined his methods of measuring psychological distance by reducing them to two statistics: (1) a measure of the difference the leader perceives between his most and his least preferred co-worker in the group; and (2) the degree to which he regards his least preferred co-worker favorably. The two measures are virtually interchangeable. In general, a leader who is primarily consideration oriented tends to perceive his least preferred co-worker in a favorable light, and perceives little difference between his most and his least preferred co-workers. A leader primarily oriented to structure initiation, on the other hand, tends to have negative feelings about his least preferred co-worker and perceives great differences between him and his most preferred co-worker. The leader's evaluation of the least preferred group member is represented in Fiedler's research by the LPC score, which of course would be high for leaders oriented primarily to-

ward consideration and low for those oriented primarily to structure initiation.

Fiedler studied the performance of some 800 different task groups and found that leaders who have low LPC scores generally turn out to be more effective. He also found, however, that it is important to take into account the leader's relations with group members, the degree to which the task is structured or made highly specific, and the amount of power possessed by the leader. Fiedler has broken down these three conditions into nine different arrangements, which he has ranked in terms of the extent to which they work out to the advantage of the leader. The most favorable situation is one in which the leader has good relations with his group, has been assigned a highly structured problem, and has a high de-

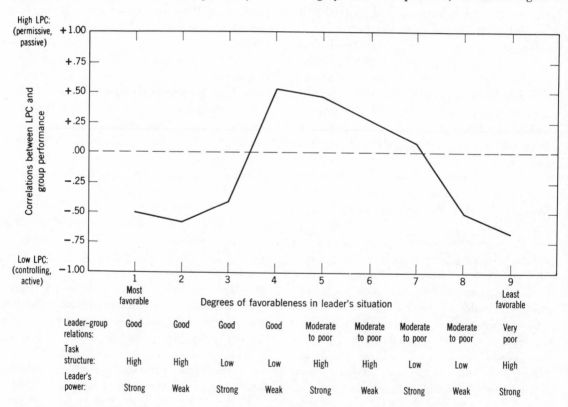

	1 Most favorable	2	3	4	5	6	7	8	9 Least favorable
Leader-group relations:	Good	Good	Good	Good	Moderate to poor	Moderate to poor	Moderate to poor	Moderate to poor	Very poor
Task structure:	High	High	Low	Low	High	High	Low	Low	High
Leader's power:	Strong	Weak	Strong	Weak	Strong	Weak	Strong	Weak	Strong

Figure **15-1.** Medians of correlations between leaders' LPC scores and the performance of their groups, classified according to the conditions prevailing in the groups (Fiedler, 1965).

gree of power. Although he has everything his way in such a situation, his chances for success can be compromised if he has a high LPC score, as Figure 15-1 shows. The graph shows that leaders low in LPC—that is, who were controlling, active, and oriented to structure initiation—tended to be more effective in most kinds of work situations. Leaders high in LPC—that is, who were permissive or passive—tended to be more effective under only two conditions, one in which leader-group relations were good, task structure low, and the leader's power weak, and the other in which the leader's power was moderate to poor, the task structure high, and the leader's power strong. The relationship was approximately zero between the leader's LPC and group effectiveness in situations in which leader-group relations were moderate to poor, the task structure low, and the leader's power strong.

Fiedler's findings were subjected to cross-validation by John A. Sample and Thurlow R. Wilson (1965), who devised an ingenious method for putting them to the test. Fourteen teams composed of undergraduate students taking a course in experimental psychology were formed, six of them headed by student leaders who rated low in LPC and eight by leaders who rated high. Teams were assigned ten problems in operant conditioning of rats which they were to complete over a two-month period. Grades were assigned to team members in accordance with the performance of their teams. The eighth assignment in the series was given under stress conditions, in that the 90 minutes allowed was 15 minutes less than the time allowed for routine assignments. Furthermore, this assignment was given extra weight in determining final marks for the course. Groups headed by the low LPC leaders did slightly better work during the routine assignments, but the difference was not statistically significant. On the stress assignment, however, the difference in favor of the low LPC leaders was significant. Sample and Wilson broke each team's task into three phases. The chief difference between high and low LPC

leaders appeared during the initial or planning phase, in which LPC leaders gave more direction and stimulated more task-oriented discussion among their subordinates than did high LPC leaders. The high LPC leaders, on the other hand, spent a higher percentage of time during the planning phase in positive socioemotional behavior, that is, making and eliciting comments that were supportive, reassuring, and group building. During the next phase of the problem, when the rat was actually being conditioned, the amount of direction given by low LPC leaders was actually less than that given by high LPC leaders, whereas their positive socioemotional responses were higher. During the third or paperwork phase of the problem, the number of suggestions given by low LPC leaders continued to decrease, whereas those of high LPC leaders tended to increase (see Figure 15-2).

The general behavior pattern of the two types of leaders was therefore reversed. The low LPC leader tended to concentrate more of his direction and control of the group during the planning

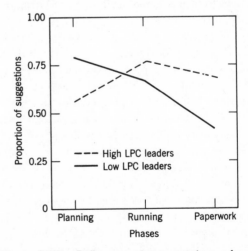

Figure **15-2.** Differences in proportions of suggestions given by high LPC (considerate, permissive) leaders and low LPC (structuring, dominative) leaders during three phases of a laboratory assignment conducted under stress conditions (Sample & Wilson, 1965).

phase and was more relaxed and even jovial, during the running of the experiment and the subsequent preparing of the report, whereas the high LPC leader tended to spend the planning phase in building good group feeling. As a result, the experiment was not as well planned and he was forced to do more directing and organizing during the latter two phases of the experiment. The two types of leaders obviously perceived the task differently: the low LPC leader correctly perceived the task as one demanding careful planning and therefore concentrated on this phase of the work. Once the job had been properly planned, he was able to relax and be more sociable. The high LPC leader tended to see the task as an opportunity to socialize and used much of his planning time accordingly. When the time came to run the experiment, the group was less well prepared and somewhat disorganized. These different styles of perception and group functioning made little difference during routine assignments, because stress was minimal and there was enough time to make the necessary adjustment and corrections to turn out an acceptable job. During the stress problem, however, the superior planning of the low LPC leader made itself evident, whereas the relatively poor planning of the high LPC leader resulted in a poor performance. Still another problem encountered by the high LPC leaders was control of the group during the paperwork phase of the problem. Each group member had a separate assignment during this phase, and, when the paperwork was done in a large classroom, the team members moved apart in order to work on their chores. During the stress problem, however, team members were forced to work in close proximity in a small room. Under such conditions, members of groups led by leaders high in LPC had more difficulty in refraining from socializing than did those led by low LPC leaders.

The results of Sample and Wilson's experiment support Fiedler's findings and are consistent with those of the International Harvester study. Actually, they are not inconsistent with the Haw-

thorne study. All three studies seem to show that consideration and high LPC did not interfere with group performance of routine tasks, and the latter two studies indicate that morale is higher if the leader is considerate. Under such conditions, work requires a minimum amount of attention, and socialization not only does not interfere, but makes the task situation more enjoyable. Thus the employer gains in terms of production and the employee gains in terms of social rewards. It is primarily under stress situations that the difficulty occurs. When time is short and the demands for production are high, as on the assembly line in a tractor factory or in an experiment that has to be completed in 15 minutes less than the usual time, socialization must be put aside and the entire group must become task-oriented. It is at such times that the high LPC leader has difficulty in shifting into a new set of roles. Furthermore, the group that has been strongly oriented toward socialization also has difficulty in reorienting its goals. Presumably a leader who rates high on both structure initiation and consideration has less difficulty under both routine and stress conditions. Group members are more willing to take their cues from such a leader and accept his restructuring of the situation during stress conditions. High LPC leaders evidently tend to be people who are unable to anticipate the nature of stress situations and to organize their groups accordingly. They have a more limited repertory of roles and may feel awkward and ill-at-ease in actively directing their groups. Very likely some of this uneasiness communicates itself to group members and adds to the confusion.

It should be noted that the leaders of groups studied by Sample and Wilson were psychology students who were used to operating in permissive situations, such as those that prevail in academic environments. The low LPC leaders, being aware of norms that emphasize benign attitudes on the part of authority figures and sanction punitive ones, were perhaps not as likely to express negative behavior as are, say, foremen of tractor assembly lines. They were, furthermore, working with teams of peers, and their power was low. Very likely the situation corresponded to the second degree of favorableness for leaders, according to Fiedler's scheme, as illustrated in Figure 15-1—that is, a situation characterized by good leader-group relations, high task structure, and weak leader power. The results tended to confirm Fiedler's thesis that such an arrangement would be more favorable to low LPC leaders than to high ones.

An analysis of group feeling conducted by Sample and Wilson showed that there was little difference in the way that high and low LPC leaders were regarded by team members. Low LPC leaders were perceived as stimulating more ideas than high LPC leaders, but there was no difference in the way members perceived the two kinds of leaders in terms of the latters' attempts to increase cooperation and criticize constructively were concerned. Contrary to what might be supposed, there was no difference in the total amount of positive socioemotional behavior displayed by the two types of leaders. Both types of leaders were friendly to their group members, but expressed this friendliness at different times during the assigned tasks. It was not the occurrence of positive behavior that distinguished between the two kinds of leaders, but rather their timing of such behavior.

The importance of considerate behavior on the part of the leader should not, therefore, be minimized. The leader's ability to structure the task and to direct the work of his subordinates may be the prime factor in group success in most problem situations, but low cohesiveness and morale can be destructive to the efforts of even the best leaders. Fiedler and W. A. T. Meuwese (1963) studied the behavior of Army tank crews, B-20 bomber crews, antiaircraft artillery crews, and creative discussion groups to determine the relationship between intelligence and group performance. They found that the leader's intelligence was positively correlated with performance in cohesive,

but not in uncohesive groups. In Army tank crews, furthermore, the intelligence of all the members of the task group was correlated positively with proficiency in cohesive, but not in uncohesive, groups.

In concluding this portion of our discussion of structure initiation, consideration, and LPC, it is worth noting that the findings are consistent with the two basic leadership functions that Bales (1965) found in his group studies, namely, task-orientation and social-emotional support. Both types of leadership are needed for effective group functioning. In groups that are functioning adequately, one of two types of situations is likely to occur: (1) the social-emotional needs of the groups are met by their acceptance of a task-oriented leader, or (2) another type of leader in the group—what Bales calls a "social specialist" —is helping the group meet its social-emotional needs.

Leaders as Facilitators of Social Learning

A leader, as we have noted, is someone who influences behavior. This proposition can be restated as: a leader is someone who induces learning. Inasmuch as changes in the individual's behavior induced or initiated by changes in the environment constitute a major type of learning, and inasmuch as the leader is an agent of the social environment, the leader's role is that of organizer or director of learning: a teacher. Even the leader's task in establishing himself as a source of influence is a problem in inducing learning, because he must get his subordinates to develop (learn) a set whereby they will respond to his cues.

The leader's overall, global role as an instigator of learning may be subdivided or classified into a number of subroles, which we shall discuss separately.

The Leader as a Model. In Chapter 4 we discussed how learners make use of the behavior of other members of the group as a model for their own. This form of learning is particularly important for the development of social norms and is, as Bandura and Walters (1962) point out, the chief way in which behavior that has not been in the repertory of the learner is acquired. Leaders play a key role in such learning, partly because they are the most visible members of their groups and partly because their concern with group goals leads them to make special efforts to see that members, particularly new ones, learn the behavioral norms that contribute to the group effort. Leaders are able to bring about this kind of learning because group members have permitted them to become influential, because they have endowed them, in effect, with prestige.

The special advantage enjoyed by leaders in playing modeling roles has been studied by Robert N. Vidulich and Gerald A. Bayley (1966), who asked a confederate to serve as an experimenter and to sit near a subject in a casual social setting (a university coffee shop, a lounging room in the university field house, or a bench in front of the university library). After the experimenter introduced himself as "Dr. Johnson of the English Department" (high status) or "Bob Johnson, a graduate student in English," (low status) he produced a book of cartoons which he showed one at a time to the subject. The first five cartoons were used to determine the naive subject's general reactivity to cartoons. During the second phase, the experimenter laughed loudly at each of five cartoons. The reaction of subjects was rated on an "Amusement Rating Scale," with scores ranging from "1" (no reaction or negative reaction) to "7" (high-intensity laugh) by a group of judges who observed the experimenter and the subject from a short distance. The results in two sets of similar experiments showed that subjects were significantly more responsive to the laughter cues of the experimenter when he represented himself as having high status than when he represented himself as having low status.

In another experiment involving the use of confederates, members of college sorority pledge classes participated in operant conditioning trials together with two members who had been previously instructed to give certain kinds of responses. In half the groups, the confederates were officers of the sorority (high status) and in the other half, they were chosen at random from the members of the group (low status). Subjects were tested in groups of ten, consisting of eight naive subjects and two confederates, and were told that each was to utter a single word, any word, when her turn came. The confederates uttered "animal" words in some block of trials and "human" words in others. Results showed that the naive subjects learned the critical responses more quickly when the confederates were officers than when the confederates were members without special status (Knapp & Knapp, 1966).

The Leader as a Participant. A leader's ability to influence group members is subject to a number of conditions and qualifications. In our discussion of LPC we noted that both group cohesiveness and the clarity and structure of tasks are important. A leader may exert influence merely because he is known to have status and prestige with other groups, but if his position is perceived as relevant to the group in question, his attempt to influence will have more meaning. To put this in other terms, a leader who is an outsider will, in general, have less influence than a leader who is perceived as a functioning member of the group.

This point is brought out in an experiment in which psychologists compared the performance of groups headed by leaders who participated with those whose leaders did not do so. Malcolm G. Preston and Roy K. Heintz (1949) organized discussion groups composed of four and five college students and asked each group to elect a leader. Half the leaders were instructed to participate with their groups in problem solving and the other half were instructed to supervise their groups, but not to participate in the problem-solving process. Participatory leaders were more effective in getting group consensus than were nonparticipatory leaders, and were also more able to bring about changes in the attitudes of group members, changes that paved the way for the solution of the assigned problems. Furthermore, members of groups led by participatory leaders were more pleased with their work, more inclined to find the assigned task interesting, and more likely to regard themselves as effective workers.

The Leader's Effect on Self-regarding Attitudes. We noted in Chapter 10 how membership in a group leads individuals to take on certain patterns of thinking, feeling, and acting, which may eventually assume a certain degree of permanence and stability to the point where they may be considered as personality traits. Leaders, too, may bring about such changes, partly because they are highly visible as models, and partly because their statements and representations have the general effect of group pronouncements—that is, an opinion stated by a leader is often given a weight approaching that of the entire group membership, inasmuch as the leader is taken to represent the group. The leader, as we have pointed out, symbolizes and epitomizes the group and may frequently serve as their agent.

In Chapter 4 we discussed research by Ellis Batten Page (1958) which showed that the amount of attention given by an authority figure —a teacher—had a significant effect on the work of students. The more extensive and personal the comment written by the teacher on the quiz paper of the student, the more responsive the student. Teachers' comments, like those of other persons in authority, generally have a high reward value.

This point was also demonstrated by a study conducted by Harold I. Haas and Martin H. Maehr (1965), who asked eighth grade boys to rate themselves on a questionnaire dealing with coordination and motor skill. The boys were then observed by a group of adult judges as they went through their paces in a "physical development test," first as a group, and then individually. The judges, who had been introduced as "physical

development" experts, then expressed disapproval or praise about one aspect of each boy's performance. When the boys filled out the questionnaire a second time, the comments of the judges tended to be reflected in the scale or part of the questionnaire appropriate to the skill that had been praised or criticized, and there was an additional effect on related scales. This effect tended to persist, as shown by measures administered to the boys one day, six days, and six weeks after the experimental treatment, as Figure 15-3 shows.

Effect of the Group on the Leader. One of the chief differences between more democratic cultures and those that have more traditional values is the belief that almost anyone can learn the skills of leadership. This attitude, which appeared in Europe during the late medieval period, is in contradistinction to older ideas that leadership skills are instinctive or can only be inherited. "As part of their conflict with the feudal nobility, the bourgeoisie supported a conception of leadership as learnable behavior which, through thought, discussion, and rational organization, could master the social process. In this sense, then, leadership was accessible to all men of will and intellect . . ." (Gouldner, 1951). The assumption that leadership is the result of a learned process is also basic to the work of modern social scientists.

The learning of leadership is to a large extent a matter of learning the roles, values, attitudes, and perceptions that go with the position of leader in the group. In this chapter we have dealt with these topics largely from the standpoint of the leader, who exhibits certain kinds of behavior in order to influence others. We should also note, however, that there is a reciprocal effect: groups influence leaders, just as leaders influence groups. The leader learns the techniques and behavior style of leadership through being reinforced by his success in influencing others. This process takes place through the data that are fed back to the leader through whatever channels are available. Leaders have perhaps a common tendency to reduce the amount of this feedback and to re-

LEADERS AND LEADERSHIP

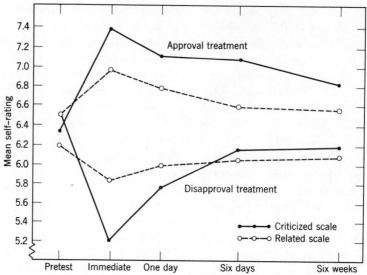

Figure **15-3.** Effect of praise or disapproval by "physical development experts" on the self-ratings of eighth grade boys, with respect to specific and related types of skills commented upon by the judges (Haas & Maehr, 1965).

gard it as distracting or even irrelevant, and this tendency suggests that leaders are as reluctant to be influenced (to learn) as anyone else. Learning, as we have noted elsewhere, involves changes that may have an effect on the self-structure, and we ordinarily prefer to remain as we are.

There are other reasons why leaders avoid being evaluated. Evaluating subordinates is consistent with the role of leaders, but subordinates are not ordinarily expected to evaluate leaders, except very indirectly or among themselves and not publicly. Open criticism of leaders is generally considered detrimental to cohesiveness and is usually indulged in only when a dissident segment of the group has decided that it is necessary to change leaders in order to attain or to change the goals of the group. Such behavior may, of course, differ with respect to the climate prevailing in a group: the more democratic the group, the more criticism of the leader is likely to be tolerated, and the more traditional and authoritarian the group, the more it is likely to be suppressed. The

study of American, Canadian, and Arab attitudes toward authority figures we discussed earlier supports this observation. Americans are more openly critical of authority figures than Canadians are. A college professor in Canada, for example, is generally treated with more deference than one in an American college. And Arabs are considerably more deferential and less publicly critical of authority figures than are Canadians. The more private beliefs as expressed on sentence-completion tests were, as we pointed out, in essentially negative relationship to the public behavior we have just described, with Americans' responses being the most accepting, and Arabs' responses being the least accepting, of persons in authority (Lindgren & Lindgren, 1960; Sallery & Lindgren, 1966). The differences in behavior toward leaders are, of course, differences of degree, rather than of kind. Leaders may be treated with less deference in face-to-face situations in the United States, in contrast to the treatment they get in Canada or the Middle East, but even in the

United States they usually receive more deference than is accorded other group members. The picture is somewhat complicated by the fact that there are channels existing in all these countries whereby criticism can be directed against leaders. The public press offers one such channel of communication. Members of some labor unions, professional societies, and college faculties also feel freer than most members of society to criticize their leaders openly.

In spite of these occasional outbursts of criticism, there is, nevertheless, a rather general tendency for group members to exercise some restraint in criticizing leaders. This attitude may arise from a fear of incurring the ill will either of the leader himself or his supporters, or it may derive at times from a desire to protect the leader from unpleasant experiences. Such attitudes are of course more widespread in groups characterized by an authoritarian structure. This situation is often decried by democratically oriented leaders, who state publicly that they would like to improve their leadership skills and would encourage open discussion and even criticism in order to effect that end. True, it is often difficult to get group members to respond to such pleas, for they are naturally wary of promises not to take retributive action, and leaders have been known to behave defensively when their invitation to criticize has been accepted. The only device that seems to provide the maximum information and the maximum protection for the communicator is the anonymous questionnaire. Some business firms maintain "suggestion boxes" in order to provide a channel for such communication; others employ consultants to conduct "morale studies" in order to pick up deficiencies in leadership and other problems. Little is known, however, about the effectiveness of such methods. They are obviously a way whereby the group can influence the behavior of their leaders, but are the leaders teachable?

One study that suggests that persons in authority can be influenced by feedback from their sub-ordinates is an experiment conducted by Gage, Runkel, and Chatterjee (1963), in which approximately 3900 sixth graders rated their teachers, as well as an "ideal teacher," on a twelve-item scale. To insure anonymity, their replies were sent directly to the Bureau of Educational Research at the University of Illinois. Each teacher was also asked to fill out a questionnaire describing herself, using the same twelve categories, and also describing how she thought the average student would describe her. A few weeks later, half the teachers received a report summarizing the ratings of their students; the other half of the teachers served as a control group and received their reports only when the term was over. Approximately five weeks after the first group of teachers had received the feedback report, the researchers asked both groups of the students, those in the control and experimental groups alike, to rate their teachers again.

Results showed that teachers in the experimental group had improved in ten out of the twelve categories of behavior rated. The most significant changes were in willingness to praise students for something said in a class discussion, in explaining arithmetic more clearly, in using examples drawn from pupils' experience, and in asking the class what they thought of something that had been said (a device used to encourage group participation in discussion).

The authors of the study concluded that teacher behavior could be influenced by feedback and that its susceptibility to such influence could be explained in terms of consonance theory. In other words, a teacher who believes that her pupils would perceive her behavior as fairly close to ideal, and who then discovers through the feedback process that they do not, is faced by the need to make some kind of adjustment in order to bring her perceptions of her pupils, her behavior, and herself back into balance. If she feels that they have misjudged her, she will try to convince them of their error; if she feels that they are correct, then she will have to think less of herself.

The most practical way of reducing the strain is to change her behavior in a direction that will come closer to their ideal and that will thus enable her to be more accepting of her own behavior.

SUMMARY

Leadership is a kind of interaction among or between people whereby individuals influence the behavior or motivation of others. This type of influence usually occurs within the structure of a social system and tends to contribute to its stability. Leadership refers to the attributes of a position in the social structure, the characteristics of a person, and a category of behavior. The significance of the position of a leader is shown by a study demonstrating that individuals who are assigned to leadership positions on a random basis will try to influence groups, and that groups will tend to let themselves be influenced. Some leaders are not officially identified, yet must be considered such because of their influence.

The influence of a leader is his power, and the amount of power he has depends in part on his prestige. There is a tendency for people who play leadership roles in one context to play them in others as well. The greater the similarity between such situations, the greater the likelihood of their playing such roles.

Types of leaders include the administrator (planning, coordinating, managing, directing, organizing), the bureaucrat (maintenance and supervision of organizational operations), the policy maker, the expert (commentator, critic, special resources), the ideologist (theories, beliefs), the charismatic leader (emotional appeal), the political leader, the symbolic leader, and the parent figure. The leader can also serve as a target for the group's resentment and hostility, and blame. Americans tend to be more open in their expression of hostility toward leaders than do people in more traditional cultures, but some studies using projective tests suggest that Americans may actually be more genuinely accepting of leaders.

Leaders tend to have the quality of salience— the tendency to be more visible and to stand out from the rest of the group—and are likely to rate higher in intelligence and psychological adjustment than nonleaders. They also tend to be freer of the normative pressures of the group than is the average member.

There is a controversy between two schools of thought in leadership research. One approach emphasizes consideration, and the other emphasizes task orientation, structure initiation, and social distance. Data from the Hawthorne study conducted some forty years ago tend to support the consideration position; however, a more recent set of studies conducted at the International Harvester Company shows that the style of leadership is likely to depend in part on the demands of the situation. Supervisors in production work tend to emphasize structure initiation, whereas supervisors in nonproduction work tended to be characterized by consideration in their dealings with subordinates. More recent work by Fiedler shows that leaders who are task oriented, and who maintain some degree of psychological distance between themselves and their subordinates, are better able to see differences between their most- and least-preferred co-workers, whereas leaders who are consideration-oriented see little difference. An analysis of a wide number of work situations showing varying degrees of structure and leader power shows that leaders who are psychologically distant and task oriented are generally more effective. Fiedler's research has been cross-validated with a study involving teams of students conducting experiments in a psychological laboratory. In general, research on these two dimensions adds up to the conclusion that task groups need task-oriented leaders, but that group members must also have some way of obtaining social-emotional rewards from their work if morale is not to suffer.

The leader's task in influencing behavior may be conceived as that of inducing learning. Leaders are able to carry out this function by serving as models for behavior and by participating in the activities of the group. Leaders may also have a significant influence on the way in which group members regard themselves. There is a tendency for leaders not to encourage evaluation of their own behavior on the part of their subordinates, and the general practice is for group members to withhold criticism—at least on a face-to-face basis. Some research shows, however, that the behavior of leaders can be influenced by such evaluation, once the channels of communication have been opened.

SUGGESTED READINGS

Anderson, L. R., Leader behavior, member attitudes, and task performance of intercultural discussion groups. *Journal of social psychology*, 1966, **69**, 305-319.

Bass, B., *Leadership, psychology, and organizational behavior*. New York: Harper, 1960.

Beer, M., *Leadership, employee needs, and motivation*. Columbus: Bureau of Business Research, Ohio State University, 1966 (paperback).

Dubin, R., Homans, G. C., Mann, F. C., & Miller, D. C., *Leadership and productivity*. San Francisco: Chandler, 1965 (paperback).

Fiedler, F., *Theory of leadership effectiveness*. New York: McGraw-Hill, 1967.

Gordon, L. W. & Medland, F. F., The cross-group stability of peer ratings of leadership potential. *Personnel psychology*, 1965, **18**, 173-177.

Gordon, T. *Group-centered leadership*. Boston: Houghton Mifflin, 1955.

Lindgren, H. C. (Ed.), *Contemporary research in social psychology*. New York: Wiley, 1969. See papers on leadership in Section 10.

Petrullo, L. & Bass, B. M. (Eds.), *Leadership and interpersonal behavior*. New York: Holt, Rinehart, and Winston, 1961.

CHAPTER SIXTEEN

Ken Heyman

Marilyn Silverstone, Magnum

Ken Heyman

Social Processes in Organizations

Organizational Structure

Characteristics of Organizations. The relationship between organizations and leaders is circular and reciprocal: leaders develop organizations and organizations develop leaders. Leaders play organizing roles in social systems to satisfy their own personal needs as well as the expectations of their followers, and when people come together to form groups for this or that purpose, they are likely to find or create the leadership they require. The result of this interaction among people, the need to accomplish something, and leadership is an organization.

Organizations, according to Daniel Katz and Robert L. Kahn (1966), are social devices for accomplishing some stated purpose efficiently through group means. Organizations are perceived by them as open systems, a concept psychologists have borrowed from biology. Any organism can be considered as an energy system which has inputs, transformation processes, and outputs. Inputs in an organization consist of the raw material that is processed and turned into products of some kind. The raw material for the adjustment section of an insurance company would consist of insurance claims; the output would consist of claims that had been settled. The transformation processes would consist of the use of the application of specialized information and talents, legal processes, negotiations—whatever would be needed to satisfy a claimant and still conform to the limits and restrictions imposed by law and by company policy. The input for a university would be students, teaching materials, books, money and so forth. The transformation process would consist of lectures, assignments, study, research, discussion, counseling, and the like; and the output would be educated individuals.

Katz and Kahn also view organizations in terms of interlocking systems of social roles or as clusters of activities expected of individuals occupying certain positions in a system. These roles or activities are mutually interdependent. If the work of the organization is to be accomplished, not only do we expect people to perform the tasks that have been assigned to them, but they in turn also expect that others will reciprocate. In the organizations we call colleges, we expect instructors to teach, but their willingness to teach is ineffective unless students learn. The teaching of instructors and the learning of students are thus mutually dependent one on the other. To make sure that transformation processes occur in an orderly fashion, organizations develop rules and regulations, which are backed up by rewards and penalties and thus constitute the authority system for the organization. Unless participants agree that there must be rules and that they are to be observed, organizations cannot function.

Bureaucracies. Authority in modern social organizations is based on rational and legal considerations, which are in turn based on practical social experience. The organization that is most likely to embody the system of interlocking roles, reinforced by what Max Weber (1947) terms "rational legal authority" is the bureaucracy. Bureaucracies are inevitable and also absolutely necessary to the functioning of a complex, industrialized, and urbanized society. Nevertheless, they attract a great deal of adverse criticism from a variety of sources. Some criticize bureaucracies because they are not efficient enough: output is too small, transformation processes take too much time, and backlogs of input are too high. Katz and Kahn are sympathetic to this complaint, and they suggest a number of ways in which organizations, including bureaucracies, may change in order to become more efficient. We shall discuss some of these changes in a separate section

315

farther along in this chapter. Others criticize bureaucracies because they are too impersonal and thus dehumanize both the participants and the persons served. Such criticism is likely to be expressed by those who long for the kind of simplicity in interpersonal and intergroup relations that is to be found in more primitive societies, but who are unwilling to put up with the disadvantages and the monotony found in such societies. Katz and Kahn point out that bureaucratic roles do not, as popularly assumed, demand all of an individual's personality. Organizations do not generally require that the individual be married to the subsystem in which he is located, and he therefore has a considerable degree of choice in patterning his life as he chooses. Furthermore, a person occupying a given position in a bureaucratic structure typically plays a number of different roles on and off the job. Almost everyone in an urbanized culture like ours functions in a number of different organizations, some of which are bureaucracies, and some of which are less formally organized.

The problem of modern man is not that bureaucracies keep him from being human, but that he can become human in so many different ways. It is the availability of so many different choices that creates dilemmas for man in an urbanized society, rather than the lack of choices. The freedom to choose among several options may at times create feelings of anxiety and panic, to the point where the individual comes to believe that he is trapped in a choiceless situation. What this usually means, however, is that the individual is trying to cope with his anxiety by distorting the reality of the situation and is unable to perceive the options that actually are available to him.

Types of Organizations. A description of the kinds of organizations that are likely to emerge in a complex society may be helpful here, if only to illustrate the importance of the functions they fulfill. Katz and Kahn recognize four major types: productive (or economic), maintenance, adaptive, and managerial or political.

Productive or economic organizations are the kind that most obviously fit the open system model. These are the organizations that manufacture goods, provide services to the general public or a segment thereof, and create wealth. They carry on activities like farming and mining, manufacturing and processing, and communication and services. Their output supplies needs for food, shelter, clothing, and recreation, and provides the rewards and incentives that lead people to behave in ways that keep the social order functioning.

Maintenance organizations do not maintain society's equipment, but its members instead. They are devoted to the socialization of people. Schools and churches are maintenance organizations that perform the functions of education, indoctrination, and training. So do publishing houses and the mass media, although their primary role places them among the productive or economic organizations. A second group of organizations cares for the restorative function and provide health and welfare activities, as well as reform and rehabilitation.

Adaptive functions are filled by social structures that create knowledge, develop and test theories, and apply information to existing problems. In this class we find research institutes and universities, as well as organizations devoted to encouraging the arts and thus help create new concepts of experience.

Managerial or political functions are those concerned primarily with maintaining the social structure, rather than with the individual members of society. The state, as the major authority structure of society, is the key organization here. It mobilizes society against internal and external threats and provides the legal framework necessary to determine rights and responsibilities, and to protect individuals and other legal entities from one another. Included in this category are various subsystems of government, as well as political parties, pressure groups, labor unions, and organizations of professional people.

An organization may of course perform functions in several of these categories. A prison may produce school furniture and thus come under the heading of productive or economic organization. It may be considered as an institution devoted to rehabilitation by some, and by others as devoted to protecting society from its enemies. And it may also be the locale for programs that use prisoners as volunteers in medical research. Its chief function, however, falls in the managerial-political category, although most social scientists would argue that it would attain its goals more successfully if it would function more definitely as an institution of reform and rehabilitation.

Psychological Needs Met through Organizations

Satisfaction in Employment. People may become involved in the work of an organization because they are interested in its objectives. A physicist may, for example, join a research institute because he is interested in doing research, and a youth may go to work for a railroad because he aspires to the job of a locomotive engineer. But people rarely do things for simple reasons; any action or decision is likely to be the result of a number of different forces that are brought to bear on an individual. We commented on one of these forces in the second chapter, when we discussed the universal need for meaning that leads us to find both identity and definition in our affiliation with others. Economic forces are also involved: the right to participate or even survive in most complex societies is one that must be paid for, and work is for most people the chief means of gaining the necessary economic power.

Employment within some kind of organizational structure can thus be seen as a way of satisfying a number of needs. Some people find work more satisfying than others. A survey of a nationwide sample of American men showed that 83 per cent of professional and technical workers and 80 per cent of managers and proprietors reported themselves as satisfied with their work, as contrasted with 64 per cent of clerical and sales workers and 65 per cent of unskilled workers. The first two groups were more likely to mention "ego satisfactions" in connection with their work— that is, satisfactions resulting from personal involvement, opportunities for self-expression, amount of responsibility, and the like. "Extrinsic satisfactions"—pay, working conditions, and job security—were more likely to be mentioned by clerical and blue-collar workers (Gurin, Veroff, & Feld, 1960). The problem of finding satisfactions within the context of an organization is thus more readily resolved by people with higher social status than it is by people with lower status.

It may be that the greater satisfaction of higher-status people is due in part to the fact that their jobs enable them to make decisions. Nancy Morse (1953) found, in a survey of a sample of white-collar workers, that only 24 per cent were satisfied with the amount of decision making they were doing, and 76 per cent wished to make more.

Managerial Satisfactions. Even among high-status people with more than the usual amount of freedom to make decisions, there are dissatisfactions. Haire, Ghiselli, and Porter (1966) studied the extent to which managers of business organizations in a number of different countries found satisfactions in their work. As a framework for their analysis, they used a fivefold classification of psychological needs, based on the writings of Abraham Maslow (1954) (see Chapter 5). The first two needs are largely concerned with extrinsic rewards; the last three with intrinsic rewards. The needs they studied were defined as follows:

Security: includes both psychological and economic security—the confidence a manager has in being able to keep his job.

Social: opportunities to help others and to develop close friendships. (This would correspond closely to n Aff.)

Esteem: self-esteem, as well as the prestige enjoyed inside and outside the company. (Keep in mind that prestige is a factor in the ability to influence others.)

Autonomy: authority exercised by the manager, together with his opportunity for independent thought and action.

Self-actualization: opportunity for personal growth and development, feeling of self-fulfillment, and feeling of worthwhile accomplishment.

This hierarchy of motives is ranked from the most elementary, the need for security, to the most advanced or complex, the need to actualize oneself. People who are preoccupied with lower-level needs are not likely to accomplish higher-level ones; indeed higher-level needs may not be very strong for such people. Conversely, people who are concerned about higher-level needs are relatively unconcerned about lower-level ones, either assuming that they will be taken care of automatically as higher-level needs are satisfied, or feeling that they are of a lesser degree of importance in the total scheme of things.

It comes as no surprise to learn that the motive most likely to be unfulfilled for these managers was self-actualization. As the most "advanced" need on the hierarchy, it is the most difficult to satisfy. Some may even argue that the very nature of man makes it impossible for him to satisfy this need. It can also be argued that such a need is likely to go unfulfilled within the context of a business organization—perhaps within *any* organization. It is also possible that the highly individualized nature of self-actualization is such that a person's resources and successes outside an organization are more significant than what happens within the organizational structure.

The researchers found a number of interesting differences between countries as to the percepts and experiences of the managers they surveyed. As Table 16-1 shows, the most satisfied managers were found in the Scandinavian countries (Germany also rated quite high, but appears only twice in the table), whereas the least satisfied managers were in Italy and India. There are many variables that do not appear in this report,

Table **16-1.** Degree to which managers in various countries perceive their psychological needs as being fulfilled by their work (Haire, Ghiselli, & Porter, 1966)

Psychological needs	Highest countries	Lowest countries
Security	India (+21)[a]	France (−29)
	Sweden (+14)	Italy (−16)
Social	USA (+30)	Germany (−37)
	Japan (+29)	Italy (−33)
Esteem	Argentina (+38)	India (−35)
	Sweden (+28)	USA (−26)
Autonomy	Sweden (+49)	India (−49)
	Germany (+35)	Italy (−44)
	Norway (+35)	
Self-actualization	Denmark (+34)	Italy (−59)
	Sweden (+30)	India (−35)
Total (all needs)	Sweden (+29)	Italy (−33)
	Norway (+17)	India (−23)

[a] Scores are standard scores with a mean of 0 for each need. A plus score means that managers in that country tend to agree that their work satisfies the need in question to a higher degree than managers do in other countries sampled, whereas a minus score means the opposite—namely, that managers in that country tend to agree that their work satisfies the need in question to a lesser degree than do managers in other countries sampled.

of course, not the least of which are the expectations that managers bring to a job. It may be, for example, that managers in Italy and India have higher expectations with respect to their work than do managers from the Scandinavian countries, and consequently are more vulnerable when it comes to disappointment. Some other data gathered by the researchers show that this may be so: Indian managers felt that *all* the needs were important to them, whereas Scandinavian managers tended to downgrade their importance. Italian managers also downgraded the importance of needs, with the exception of Esteem.

Cultural differences also affected managers' beliefs as to what extent democracy should characterize the behavior of individuals at various levels within the structure of organizations. Managers in Italy and Spain were more likely to associate the functions of deciding, creating, cooperating, persuading, directing, and reprimanding with higher-status positions. Managers in Germany, Argentina, and India made similar associations, but did not make them so strongly. In other words, the latter were more able to see that lower-status individuals might also occasionally exercise these functions. Making mistakes was generally associated by the managers with low-status positions, but managers in the United States and England associated this with high-status positions, thus suggesting a greater willingness to hold higher-status people responsible for mistakes. One would expect, in organizations run along authoritarian lines, that the highest degree of satisfaction would be expressed by older managers and the lowest degree by younger. Data showed, however, that this condition was most likely to prevail in France, Denmark, and the United States.

Styles of Orientation toward Group Life. The needs that people seek to meet within the context of organizations are to a large extent related to their general orientation to groups. Some research done by Bernard M. Bass and George Dunteman (1963) shows that how an individual functions in a group setting may be classified according to three different styles or orientations: task orientation, interaction orientation, and self orientation.

Task-oriented persons describe themselves as self-sufficient, resourceful, with good control, aloof, introvertive, not sociable, aggressive, competitive, and independent. Such individuals tend to have above-average intelligence and are scholastic "overachievers." Persons rating high in task orientation are more likely to be men than women, and among men, engineers tend to rate high in this factor. In leadership behavior, task orientation would seem to be more closely related to structure initiation than to consideration. It is also more consistent with n Ach than with n Aff.

Interaction orientation is more characteristic of women than men. Persons scoring high on this trait are likely to describe themselves as unaggressive, with low needs for autonomy and achieve-

ment. They also said that they would rather work in a group or volunteer for discussions than work on problems alone. Interaction-oriented people in positions of leadership probably rate high on consideration and low on structure initiation.

Persons scoring high on self-orientation describe themselves as disagreeable, dogmatic, aggressive, competitive, sensitive, effeminate, introvertive, suspicious, jealous, tense and excitable, anxious, lacking in control, fearing failure, and feeling insecure. They prefer to work alone on tasks rather than with a group. When there is a call for volunteers for psychological experiments, self-oriented individuals are more likely to hang back unless pay is offered, whereas task-oriented individuals volunteer readily even for unpaid tasks.

The reaction of groups to individuals displaying these three styles of behavior was studied by Bass and Dunteman by analyzing interpersonal ratings of members of discussion groups who met in ten "leaderless group discussion" sessions over a period of two weeks. One set of groups consisted of supervisors of management training from a firm of industrial consultants, and the other set were women secretaries. Group members who scored high on task orientation were perceived as being the most valuable members of the group. They were also most likely to perform the following functions:

Helping members express ideas.
Helping groups stay on target.
Helping to get to the meat of issues.
Giving good suggestions on how to proceed.
Providing good summaries when needed.
Encouraging group to a high level of production.
Taking the lead in selecting topics.
Working hard.
Offering original ideas.
Sensing when to talk and when to listen.
Influencing successfully.
Concerned about the group's completing its job successfully.
Not running away when faced with problems.

Task-oriented members of supervisors' groups were also seen as providing helpful and objective feedback to members and as being easy to understand. Although task-oriented individuals were seen as being helpful in secretaries' groups, they were also perceived as making unjustified assumptions, blocking the group, dominating, imposing their will on the group, annoying others, and continuing to push a point even after being blocked repeatedly. The secretaries agreed, however, that the removal of task-oriented members from their groups would be a loss. It appears that women who play the structure-initiating roles that are typical of task-oriented people are perceived by other women as very helpful, but such behavior is at the same time less consistent with the culturally determined expectations we have for women, and their aggressive efficiency is more likely to be resented.

Interaction-oriented members were perceived as less helpful by their groups. They were not concerned about aiding the group to complete jobs successfully, did not provide good summaries when needed, did not take the lead in selecting topics, did not help the group stay on target, and did not encourage the group to a high level of production. At the same time, they did not dominate or impose their will on groups, and interaction-oriented secretaries were seen as making others feel at ease.

There was very little consistency among self-oriented people as to the group roles they played, although there was a tendency to rate them low on helping others to feel at ease.

If task-orientation is, as we have suggested, positively correlated with structure initiation, the findings of Bass and Dunteman appear to be consistent with those of the Ohio State University group and of Fiedler (1965) that we discussed in Chapter 15. Group members may feel more at ease with interaction-oriented people, but task-oriented individuals are perceived as being more helpful in aiding groups to attain their goals.

Bass and Dunteman got some further interesting results when they assigned members of supervisors' and secretaries' groups to new groups that were homogeneous with respect to the orientation of the members—that is, all persons scoring high in task-orientation were assigned to one set of groups, all persons scoring high in interaction orientation to another set, and so forth. The new grouping evoked the most positive reaction from interaction members, who were now free to interact without any task-oriented person urging them to work on significant problems. The task-oriented members, conversely, felt more negative about their groups: it is difficult to lead in a group composed entirely of leaders. Their experience is somewhat reminiscent of the findings of Ghiselli (1966), discussed in Chapter 14, who reported that the most effective teams of toy railroad operators were those who had one person only who was outstanding on a significant trait. When leaders are in oversupply, they evidently get in one another's way. The self-oriented group also tended to have negative feelings about their experience and reported a high degree of conflict. This group apparently felt the lack of a task-oriented leader to pull them together and thus resolve interpersonal tensions.

Bass and Dunteman also believed that the results tended to confirm the common observation that leaders are likely to rate higher than other group members on traits valued by the group. Where physical prowess is valued, leaders tend to be above average in strength and skill; where group members are hostile and resentful, leaders are likely to rate above average in vocal aggressiveness; and so forth. In two of the homogeneous groups, those composed of task-oriented and of interaction-oriented individuals, the leaders rated higher than the other members on the trait concerned, but the opposite was true of the self-oriented groups, where the leader was next to the lowest in self-orientation. It appears that self-orientation is of little value in group interaction, and members of such groups are inclined to select as their leader someone who rates lower in this orientation and who presumably rates higher on either or both of the other two orientations.

Organizations as Systems of Communication

Communication as a Function of Status. The communication needs of a large organization present a number of complex, difficult problems that are not likely to be readily resolved. The higher an individual's position in the status hierarchy, the freer he feels to initiate communication. Unfortunately, we cannot say that freedom to initiate communication is correlated with receptivity to communication, particularly communication that emanates from below. Nor can we say that low-status persons are necessarily more responsive to communication. A low-status person generally must be receptive to messages from above, but there are practical limits to how much information a person can absorb without reacting to it in ways that are neither intended nor antici-

"You've got to try to get along with people, Hennessey. You're not the boss around here yet!"

© *Wall Street Journal*, 1959.

pated by the organizational authorities. As noted in Chapter 12, effective communication requires the participation of both the initiator and the receiver in order to be effective. Unless a genuine transaction has taken place, communication is not likely to influence behavior.

There are a number of ways in which low-status people characteristically react when they are unwilling or unable to respond to messages. When orders and directions are very specific, they may sabotage the whole operation by following through meticulously and refusing to do anything that is not required of them. A nurse being treated as a "cog in the machinery" by an autocratic physician may, for example, withhold vital information about a patient's condition on the grounds that the doctor did not request her comments on the case and hence was obviously not interested in hearing them.

Another common reaction is apathy toward the job. There is almost a universal tendency for people to equate their personal worth with the work they do. When people are not free to communicate upward, they realize that their status is low and that their job is unimportant. They are therefore likely to find other activities in which to become involved—perhaps recreational activities on or off the job. If their attitudes have been task oriented, they will tend to shift to interaction-oriented or self-oriented modes, or they will try to move to positions in which they have more autonomy.

Persons who find themselves at the receiving end of a one-way communication channel may also release pent-up feelings by displacing them on a scapegoat—an individual who has become the common target for group hostility. Rate-busters or ratebreakers are, as we have pointed out in other contexts, rejected by groups and thus readily qualify for the role of scapegoat. Rate-busters characteristically are highly task-oriented and unquestioningly loyal to the management of the organization. Since the norm of workers who have been isolated from communicative contact with higher status levels is likely to be that of minimum compliance, the higher output of the ratebuster is perceived by them as a deviant pattern of behavior and one that calls for punishment or harassment. Alert managements often save ratebusters from their fate by promoting them and making them foremen or straw bosses. Such a move may satisfy the ratebuster's need for achievement and at the same time officially recognize his isolation from the group.

Communication and Organization Size. A number of studies of different types of business organizations have shown that the size of the organization is negatively correlated with job satisfaction and productivity, and positively correlated with absenteeism, employee turnover, accident rates, and labor disputes. In other words, the larger the organization, the lower the degree of productivity and worker satisfaction, and the higher the absenteeism, the employee turnover, the accident rate, and the number of labor disputes (Porter & Lawler, 1965). It is very likely that communication is a factor here. The larger the organization, the greater the potential number of channels of communication, and the greater the possibility for confusion. Furthermore, the larger the organization, the larger the size of work groups and the more difficult it becomes for employees to relate to one another in small groups. Since it is within the context of small, primary groups that we find our deepest satisfactions and most effective communication, one solution to the problem of efficiency and morale in large organizations would seem to be that of structuring the work in such a way that it could be performed by small groups linked together by open, two-way channels of communication. Such a reform is of course likely to be resisted by organizations dominated by authoritarian management, for whom centralized control has become more vital than effectiveness and productivity. Chris Argyris (1964) observes that the policies of such organizations are likely to lead lower-status members to develop informal procedures and subsystems in order to do their jobs and at the same time find personal satisfactions. These informal structures must of course always be concealed from management at the next higher level. The energy used for maintaining and hiding such structures is therefore unavailable for the productive effort of the organization as a whole. As a consequence, the organization operates at a less-than-desirable level of efficiency and is unable to adapt itself to the social environment of today's world, an environment that daily becomes more complex, more unpredictable, and more unstable.

Communication and Influence. The whole problem of organizational communication appears to revolve around the factor of influence. A low-status position is low not only because it is hooked onto the end of a one-way communication channel, but also because persons in higher-status positions are able to influence its occupant more readily than he can influence them. The ability to communicate therefore implies the ability to influence. Organizational leaders probably provide one-way channels of communication not so much because they want to deprive lower-status members of the opportunity for self-expression as much as they want to shield themselves from that source of influence, as we noted in Chapter 13. The less influence to which leaders are exposed, the freer they are to make decisions, and the freedom to make decisions, as we have indicated, is one of life's deeper and richer satisfactions.

What organization officials may have lost in blocking this source of influence, however, is some of the power to influence their subordinates. In one study of the relationships between 656 salesman and thirty-six branch-office managers, researchers found that the degree of control a manager was able to exercise over his salesmen was positively related to the amount of control they were able to exercise over him. Furthermore, the more control that managers and salesmen exercised over each other the better the salesmen's performance and the greater their satisfaction with their manager (Bachman, Smith, & Slesinger,

1966). If the findings of this study can be extrapolated to other situations, it would seem that organization officials have more to gain than to lose by permitting feedback communication and thus opening up the possibility of being influenced from below. The results also suggest that the supervisor who tries to exert great influence over the behavior of his subordinates, without making it possible for them to influence him, is thereby reducing the amount of actual control he has over them. Although he governs the rewards and penalties, it is they who hold the trump cards. In the final analysis, it is their cooperation or non-cooperation that will determine whether the whole organizational effort will succeed. They can, as we noted earlier, find ways to comply with his directives without becoming productive or efficient, and many an organization has foundered because top officials were unwilling to admit or were unaware of how dependent they were on the cooperation of persons occupying low-status positions.

Integrating Subgroups into the Organization. One of the tasks of the leadership in an organization is that of finding some way to integrate the smaller subgroups in the organization into the larger organizational structure. People are more likely to find their social-emotional needs met in smaller, face-to-face groups than they are in a large organization. Very often these smaller work groups, such as one would find in a shop or an office, are highly cohesive and have an intense peer loyalty. This loyalty can work for an organization, if group members perceive a correlation between their goals and the goals of the organization. As Rensis Likert (1961) points out, if the behavior and attitudes of supervisors lead lower-status members to reject the organization's objectives and to work instead at cross purposes with top management, the result can be a drop in productivity and an increase in wastage.

The people in what is known as "middle management" play a crucial role in integrating the subgroups of organization into the main structure. They are, so to speak, the "link pins" between organizational levels. The individual at this level must be aware that he is in the middle between his subordinates and top management and must be able to relate in both directions. On the one hand he must be able to identify with top management and their desire for production and efficiency, but on the other, he must be able to identify with employees and their desires for security, identity, and other social-emotional goals. He must therefore be as effective and persuasive in representing his subordinates' views to top management as he is in representing top management's interests to his subordinates.

According to Likert, the style of leadership throughout the organization is even more important than employees' attitudes toward the company and their interest in their work. He maintains that the most effective organizational leaders are those who are as concerned with human values as they are with efficiency, economy, and the effective use of technology. Likert maintains that the development of such leadership requires new patterns of management, particularly patterns that are genuinely "participative." Without such participation, top management, middle management, and work groups are likely to become isolated, one from the other, and thus unable to communicate and work together effectively toward common goals.

Autonomy, Productivity, and Job Satisfaction. Some of Likert's ideas find support in a study conducted by Nancy C. Morse and Everett Reimer (1956), who compared the effect of centralizing and decentralizing the decision-making process in an industrial organization that had four parallel divisions engaged in routine clerical work. Two divisions were included in the Hierarchical experimental condition, in which upper-management personnel were given a more active role in making decisions. The other two divisions were included in the Autonomy program, which was designed to give the rank-and-file employees a more active role in the making of decisions. Mea-

sures administered before and after the inaugura-
tion of the programs were used to determine the
effect of the experimental treatments. Results
showed that satisfaction with the job with supervisors, and with the company in general increased
for employees involved in the Autonomy program,
but not for those in the Hierarchical program,
whose satisfaction indexes showed a general decline. Productivity, as measured by comparing
clerical costs with company standards, increased
for both types of treatment, with the Hierarchy
treatment showing the greater gain. This increase
was achieved in the Hierarchical treatment by
management's reducing the number of employees
assigned to various tasks. In the Autonomy treatment, the number of employees was reduced by
normal attrition, and the employees themselves
voluntarily redistributed the work load and thus
obviated the need of replacing employees who
had left. In any event, the results do not support
the researchers' hypothesis that the Autonomy
treatment would result in greater productivity,
although it is possible that a different measure of
productivity would have showed different results.
The results strongly supported their hypothesis
that employee satisfaction would be greater in the
Autonomy condition.

Organizational Change

The Persistence of Traditional Patterns. The
problem of getting organizations to function was
in former times perceived as that of placing people
who were legitimate leaders (by reason of noble
birth, for example) in charge of a task and giving
them sufficient power in the form of money, facilities, and personnel to accomplish it. As technology
developed, it became apparent that leaders needed
expertise, as well as prestige. During the middle-
class revolution that began with the demise of
feudalism, the world learned that organizational
leaders did not need any special claim on legitimacy, and that the necessary expertise could be
learned. We now know that technical expertise
is not enough, either, and that the effective leader

of today must also understand human motivation
and group processes if the organizational undertaking is to succeed. Workers in the past had little
choice about serving industrial organizations—
the choice was literally that of working or starv-
ing. Workers today, however, have more options.
The hazards of not working are not as severe as
they once were, and a worker who has any degree
of skill is likely to have a choice of work opportunities. Once he is employed, he is in a position
to control, through his union or through other
means, the degree to which he commits himself
to the job. He may go into business for himself,
or join the Army or go to school to prepare for a
different type of work. The greater range of
options that workers have today quite understandably makes organizational management a more
highly complex task than it was in former times.

Organizational efficiency is also hampered by
the fact that we have inherited a number of beliefs
and behavior patterns from bygone and simpler
days. These modes of thought and action lead
managers to do things that work at cross purposes
to the main goals and objectives of the organizations they head. The delegation of power, influence, and control *down* a pyramidal power
structure (but never up) is one of them; the idea
that subordinates will perform more efficiently
and make fewer mistakes if their duties are made
highly specific is another. The belief that the main
motivators of employee productivity are economic
and extrinsic is still another. Many managers
today are psychologically sophisticated and are
searching for ways to bring about changes that
will make their organizations more effective, and
the use of novel techniques on a trial-and-evalua-
tion basis is increasing. In this section we discuss
some of the newer techniques that are currently
being used to bring about changes in organizations in the hope of making them more effective.

Improvement in Human Relations. The study
conducted at the Hawthorne plant of the Western
Electric Company, discussed in Chapter 15, provided insights that led to some of the first attempts

at change. The Hawthorne study showed that workers' motivational patterns were quite different from those traditionally hypothesized by management, that the social relations among the workers themselves were an important factor in their behavior, and that communication between workers and management had an important bearing on morale and production.

A number of programs implementing these principles were put into operation during the years that followed the publication of results from the study during the middle 1930's. These programs received special impetus during World War II, when a number of firms instituted human relations training for supervisors to keep morale at high levels, reduce absenteeism and turnover, and improve efficiency and production. Most of these programs were never evaluated in any kind of controlled study, and it is thus difficult to determine whether they had any real effect. The International Harvester study discussed in Chapter 15 raised some questions as to whether the typical "human relations program" is only a gesture on the part of top management or whether it is a sincere effort to modify the organizational structure. The fact that top administrators and policy makers are exempt from so many of these programs also poses a question as to whether they are sincere. As we pointed out in Chapter 15, foremen who spend time undergoing special training in human relations, and who then return to work situations in which their supervisors are functioning in ways contrary to what has been taught in the courses they have just completed, are understandably cynical about using the considerate patterns of behavior they have learned.

Not all the programs have failed, however. One evaluation study compared companies that had done a great deal to improve communication between management and employees with those firms that had made much less effort. Differences between the two groups of companies are suggested by the fact that 72 per cent of the companies in the first group were making use of group discussion meetings and planned to make even greater use in the future, whereas only 49 per cent of the second group were using this method and only 37 per cent planned to expand the use of this method. The practical value of the more enlightened policy was shown by the fact that companies in the first group were much less likely to have had a major or a minor strike in the two years preceding the survey and were also more optimistic about their ability to get along with unions (Opinion Research Corp., 1952).

The United Steelworkers of America and steel companies instituted a Human Relations Committee as a way of improving communication and reducing tension in contract negotiations. The Committee was composed of representatives of both labor and management and was given the task of resolving problems before official bargaining and contract negotiation began. Meetings were designed to permit free exchange of information and opinion, facilitated with rules like this one: any member of the committee could change his mind on any subject at any time, and no statement made by a member could be brought up later to embarrass him when formal bargaining actually began. As a result of improved communication and understanding, the Committee was able to eliminate much of the tension and hostility surrounding issues that had been repeated sources of dissension in previous years (Jones, 1963).

Group Decision Method. Many of the methods of improving communication and morale make use of some version of group decision. A number of studies have shown that people are more likely to follow through on decisions that they have made as part of a group discussion than they are to follow the suggestions and exhortations of authority figures. Kurt Lewin (1965), for example, reported on studies concerned with such problems as getting housewives to use cheaper cuts of meat during the shortages of World War II, to give their children more milk, and to supplement children's diet with orange juice and Vitamin D additives. Housewives who listened to lectures by experts, or who were given individual personal instruction by an expert, were less likely to follow the prescribed behavior than were housewives who had participated in 25-minute group discussions dealing with the problem. Similar results were reported by Betty Wells Bond (1956) in getting women to follow certain practices with respect to early detection of cancer, and by Jacob Levine and John Butler (1952) in getting supervisors to change their standards of rating employees.

The influence of group decision, as contrasted with that of being told, evidently derives from a number of factors generated through group interaction. One factor is the persistence of the effect of group norms even after an individual has left the physical context of the group. This phenomenon was reported by Muzafer Sherif (1936) in his study of the autokinetic effect we discussed earlier and has also appeared in a number of other studies we reported. Another factor is that of active, as opposed to passive, participation in decision making. In the study of the effects of antismoking propaganda, it was shown that the person who played the role of the propagandist was much more likely to be affected by the propaganda than was his audience (Elms, 1966). It is quite possible that participation in a decision making group has a somewhat similar effect on participants.

A number of studies have explored the reasons why people are more likely to change their minds (and their behavior) after group discussion. Any proposed change in behavior carries a psychological risk or threat, because the possibility of change raises anxieties and tensions. This threat potential is often sufficient to discourage the person who is trying to decide whether he will make the change. Discussion may enable people to reduce this anxiety somewhat by spreading or diffusing the risk or responsibility for the change (Wallach, Kogan, & Bem, 1964). Salomon Rettig's (1966) research suggests that discussion helps make the change more legitimate. A person who changes

runs the risk of deviating from group norms, whereas if the group produces a new norm that incorporates the change, he avoids that risk and may actually reinforce his acceptance by the group by following the new norm.

Cognitive dissonance may also be a factor. A person who finds himself going along with the trend in a group discussion would be likely to experience dissonance if he did not change his behavior to conform to the new direction, even though the new pattern of behavior is inconsistent with what he has done in the past. On the other hand, there is little dissonance if he merely sits and listens to an authority figure tell him how he should behave. Any dissonance that might be created by that experience can be easily resolved by explanations of why he has not followed the recommended technique in the past and will be unable to do it in the future. Such explanations may be voiced openly, or they may take the form of "excuses to oneself."

In spite of its considerable power, the group-decision method has not been used to any great extent by organizations interested in changing the attitudes and behavior of lower-echelon personnel, perhaps because of certain natural limitations in the method. If it is used in its "pure" Lewinian form, the official convening the group discussion commits himself to abide by the members' decisions. Few organizations wish to take the risk of standing by any decision that groups of low-status members are likely to make. A college instructor, for example, turned over to the students the task of assigning final grades in a seminar and then was shocked when they decided that every class member had earned an "A." Not only was this not her evaluation of the work of the group, but it seemed to her that they had abdicated their responsibility to make valid judgments. She therefore rejected their decision and assigned the grades she thought they had earned. The class was outraged and appealed to the administration. The administration upheld the instructor, but the students still felt that the instructor had acted in bad faith. As word of the incident spread among the other students majoring in the field, the feeling grew that faculty members could not be trusted, and this in turn interfered with the relations between students and faculty.

This example is drawn from academic life, but similar outcomes have resulted when persons in authority have tried to use the group-decision method with their subordinates without genuine awareness of what they were getting involved in.

A second weakness of the group-decision method is the requirement that the group be small enough to enable members to become personally involved. This presents no problem for a work group of four to twelve persons, but as numbers exceed twelve or so, the possibility of a group decision involving all members is thereby diminished. Larger numbers can be involved through representation, of course, but this will only work when there is good communication between elected leaders and the rank and file. A number of nationwide strikes have been "settled" at the top level, only to have the settlements rejected by local unions who felt that their leadership had "sold them out." In such instances the social distance had become so great that the rank and file no longer felt identified with their leadership.

In spite of these shortcomings, group-decision technique is a powerful agent for organizational change, and one whose real potentialities are barely exploited as yet.

T-Groups, Sensitivity Training, and Therapy Groups. The years since World War II have seen a rapid increase in the number of organizations in the business, governmental, and educational world that have made use of what are called T-groups ("T" stands for training). The T-group is a kind of extension of the group-decision approach and makes use of another of Lewin's concepts: group dynamics. T-groups had their real start in 1947, when the National Training Laboratories started holding summer training sessions at Bethel, Maine, for people interested in improving their effectiveness in groups. T-groups consist of from ten to sixteen people, plus one or two trainers, who meet together for an hour and a half to two hours, every day for two or three weeks. They have no agenda, structure, tasks, or procedural rules, but instead improvise as they go along. The purposes of T-groups as they have now evolved are that of helping members become aware of the effect others' behavior has on them and that their behavior has on others, learning to understand and to respond to the behavior and attempts at communication of others, and, above all, to increase the empathy of the participants. Inasmuch as empathy consists of the ability to be aware of the feelings and attitudes of other people, such learning depends a great deal on the sensitivity one has developed toward others.

As T-group members meet and experience a group situation that totally lacks structure and direction, they struggle and flounder in a series of attempts to create structure and meaning. As this process continues, the trainers comment from time to time on the way in which members interact with one another, on the extent to which they are communicating freely or not, on attempts to dominate or escape from the group, and the like.

Persons who have participated in sensitivity training maintain this experience has enabled them to learn more effective ways of relating to others. They point out that it has taught them to understand better what others are trying to say, how and when feelings are hurt, why others annoy them, and so forth. Presumably this experience and this understanding helps them to be more effective as participants in an organization composed of other human beings. The difficulty— and Katz and Kahn (1966) point this out—is that T-group members go back into organizational environments that have not changed and that tend to reshape them in the old molds. T-groups, therefore, seem more likely to help individuals than organizations.

This problem has been approached by the method of having all the members of work teams, often including people from levels of power and authority, participate in sensitivity training. Although such adjustments in the method might theoretically focus the power of the T-group as a change agent on the structure and procedures of an organization, evidence is lacking as to its success, unless one wishes to accept as evidence the growing willingness of management to become involved in such training. For example, one high-ranking State Department official said, after participating in a one-week program of sensitivity training: "It was the most valuable experience of my career in the State Department" (Marrow, 1966). However, if such methods are to facilitate the development of morale and productivity, they must inevitably involve top management, because it is there that the policies are made and the characteristics of an organization's social climate are set. The effectiveness of many hours of sensitivity training can be seriously impaired, if top management is not affected and continues to behave in ways that are antithetical to the spirit of T-group work or are totally unrelated to it.

T-groups are also being introduced in other countries. They have, for example, been introduced experimentally in Eastern Nigeria, under the auspices of the Ford Foundation, and in Japan as well. One study evaluating the effect of T-groups on Japanese businessmen shows that in spite of Japanese restraints, sensitivity training nevertheless had positive effect. One of the objectives of such training is the attainment of "openness"—an uninhibited, natural willingness to reveal one's feelings. Pretraining measures showed that Japanese, as might be expected, are considerably less "open" than Americans are with their wives and with others when it comes to personal problems, job success, positive feelings, and negative feelings. After sensitivity training, however, Japanese subjects had made more progress toward openness than a comparable group of Americans had (Massarik, 1965).

Recent years have also seen a rapid growth in the number of "encounter groups" of various types, which have a more frankly therapeutic aim than sensitivity training. Such groups function in ways similar to T-groups, except that they are more ambitious. Merely becoming sensitive to others and their needs is not enough; they also attempt to promote a greater degree of self-understanding, self-integration, and "authenticity," to use one word that members of such groups frequently employ to describe their objectives.

Such therapy groups are similar in some ways to T-groups, but they are concerned with more fundamental aspects of individual adjustment, rather than with the individual's interaction with others. They have been used to help reorient groups of co-workers within organizational frameworks, as for example an engineering and metals concern in England, whose therapy groups were supervised by consultants from the Tavistock Institute in London (Jacques, 1951). Unless therapy can be integrated with the problems and structure of entire organizations, however, it seems to be of limited value in bringing about organizational change. A number of management consultant firms have attempted to facilitate the process of change by providing counseling services for top management personnel and then working down the power structure, gradually involving people at each succeeding level in therapeutic "encounter" groups. Although this approach has promise, there is a lack of evidence as to whether the method has any long-range effects.

As of the present writing, research from a number of different studies suggests that organizations can be strengthened and made more effective if ways can be found to involve people in decisions that affect them and to open up two-way channels of communication. The devices that have been tried so far seem largely piecemeal. It is possible that if starts are made at the top of the organizational power structure to introduce new approaches to human relations, the organizational climate can be changed in such a way as to make therapeutic and sensitivity training endeavors worthwhile. Organizations, even large ones, possess the power to serve society and provide satisfactions for those who work within their structure, but much must be done to humanize them if they are to reach the fullest extent of that potential.

SUMMARY

Organizations are social devices for accomplishing some stated purpose efficiently through group means and are the result of interaction among people, the need to accomplish something, and leadership. Organizations may also be conceived as open systems having inputs, transformation processes, and outputs. Still another concept is that of organizations as systems of interdependent social roles or clusters of activities. One type of organization is the bureaucracy, a much-criticized type of institution, but one that is essential in a complex society. The major types of organizations are productive or economic, maintenance, adaptive, and managerial or political. Factories, farms, and mines are examples of productive-economic organizations; schools, churches, and hospitals, of maintenance organizations; research institutes and universities, of adaptive organizations; and political parties, labor unions, professional societies, and the state itself, of managerial-political organizations. Some organizations perform functions in several of these categories.

If organizations are to be effective, they must satisfy the psychological needs of their members and employees, as well as accomplish the purposes for which they were organized. Managers, proprietors, technical workers, and professional workers are generally better able to obtain satisfactions from their employment than are clerical, sales, and unskilled workers. The former type of organization member or employee is more likely to mention ego satisfactions (personal involvement, self-expression, responsibility) in connection with the job, whereas the latter type of employee is more likely to mention extrinsic satisfactions (pay, working conditions, and job security). Even high-status employees have dis-

satisfactions, however. One survey of managers in a number of different countries shows that the need most likely to go unsatisfied is the need for self-actualization (opportunity for personal growth, self-fulfillment, and accomplishment). The most satisfied managers are in Scandinavia and Germany, and the least satisfied managers are in Italy and India.

The way in which individuals function in group settings may be classified according to three different styles or orientations: task orientation, interaction orientation, or self orientation. Men tend to rate higher than women on task orientation, and engineers rate particularly high. Women tend to rate high in interaction orientation. Self-oriented people prefer to work alone, rather than with groups. Task-oriented individuals tend to be most often preferred as group leaders.

The higher the status of a member of an organization, the freer he feels to initiate communication; however, such freedom does not imply a corresponding degree of receptivity. Low-status people who are denied the right to communicate with higher-status people may react by sabotaging the organization's operations in subtle or obvious ways; becoming engaged in interesting activities unrelated to their tasks; or displacing hostility on scapegoats. Overachievers in industrial organizations often become scapegoats.

The larger the organization, the more complex are its communication problems, and the lower its productive efficiency and worker satisfaction. Large size is also associated with high rates of absenteeism, employee turnover, labor disputes, and accidents. One study shows that a sales manager's success in influencing his salesmen is positively correlated with their ability to influence him. A major problem in organizations is that of integrating subgroups into the larger organizational group. Individuals occupying positions at the middle-management level play crucial roles in this linkage and are successful to the extent that they can represent the interests of subgroups to top management and the interests of management to subgroup members. A comparative study of hierarchical (centralized) and autonomous (decentralized) structures in a large organization showed no difference in economy of operation over an eighteen-month trial period, but employee satisfaction declined in the hierarchical condition and increased in the autonomous condition.

Workers today have more options and hence more freedom than they used to. This has increased the complexity of the task faced by organizations and calls for changes in attitudes and new techniques of management. The Western Electric study led to the widespread introduction of programs of human relations training, but the International Harvester study raised questions as to whether limiting such programs to middle-management has any real effect on employee relations or production. Efforts made to improve communication throughout the organization have produced positive results, according to one survey. Getting people involved in a group decision process may be a useful way of bringing about organizational change, because such decisions are

more likely to be carried out by participants than decisions made by top management and communicated to subordinates. One problem with group decisions is that management may not wish to abide by the group's decision. Another is that decision-making groups must be small enough to permit the involvement of members. A type of group that has attracted wide-spread attention is the T-group, which sets itself the task of helping members find more effective ways of working and interacting with others, with particular emphasis on the affective aspects of interpersonal relationships. One difficulty with such approaches has been the fact that members go back into organizational environments that tend to reshape them in the old molds. If top management can be involved in such training, however, there is a chance that the psychological climate of the entire organization may be changed for the better. Therapy groups are similar in methodology to T-groups, but they are more ambitious and attempt to bring about fundamental changes in the emotional life of participants.

SUGGESTED READINGS

Argyris, C., *Integrating the individual and the organization.* New York, Wiley, 1964.

Katz, D. & Kahn, R. L., *The social psychology of organizations.* New York: Wiley, 1966.

Kornhauser, A., *Mental health of the industrial worker.* New York: Wiley, 1965.

Likert, R., *New patterns of management.* New York: McGraw-Hill, 1961.

Lindgren, H. C. (Ed.), *Contemporary research in social psychology.* New York: Wiley, 1969. See papers on organization in Section 10.

Maier, N. R. F. & Hayes, J. J., *Creative management.* New York: Wiley, 1962.

CHAPTER SEVENTEEN

Gerry Cranham, Rapho-Guillumette

Les Barry, D. P. I.

Henry Clay Lindgren

Aggression and Its Management

Movement toward, away from, or against Others. There are, as Karen Horney (1945) once pointed out, three basic ways in which we can relate to others: we can move toward them, away from them, or against them. Horney was writing about modes of dealing with interpersonal disturbances, but the scheme works equally as well for any kind of human relationship. We have tended to stress the "toward" type of movement in this book so far—the kind of behavior which is based on social attraction and the need for affiliation (n Aff) and which expresses itself in such phenomena as interaction orientation, cohesiveness, cooperation, and consideration, because this is the primary direction in social behavior. The need to move away from others and the maintenance of social distance and privacy is also important and appears in behavior characterized by independence, exclusiveness, as well as in task orientation, autonomy, and the need to achieve or n Ach. The drive to achieve status may also be considered as moving away from others, if the prime motive is to maintain social distance, but it also may be an expression of the need to move against others, if the basic motive is to exploit and dominate others. Moving against others also takes the more obvious form of hostile and aggressive behavior.

Social systems are held together by people's desires to move toward one another, and movements away from or against others are perceived as potential threats to the social order. We have noted how competition and other forms of self-oriented behavior are perceived as deviant by groups with any degree of cohesiveness. The rate-buster or achiever is, as we have mentioned, harassed by his colleagues in an attempt to get him to maintain group cohesiveness by conforming to production norms that are more characteristic of the group. Movement against others is likely to call for more severe measures, because it poses an even greater threat to the group. Another reason why groups are threatened by movements away from or against others is the possibility that such behavior may be contagious and may start a trend that will eventually destroy the group. A high degree of self-centeredness on the part of group members may even lead to panic in stress situations, as has been shown in a number of catastrophes, such as the fire in the Cocoanut Grove Night Club in Boston during World War II. Hostile, aggressive behavior may also become contagious, if not checked.

There are times, of course, when movement against others may contribute to the cohesiveness of a group. Competition that pits one group against another may, as we have noted, increase cohesiveness within the context of the groups themselves, and the heightened morale that appears during the early stages of a war is sometimes perceived as so desirable that many a shaky government has become involved in armed conflict as a way of drumming up popular support.

Movements toward, away from, and against others may also be perceived as reactions to danger, imminent injury or destruction, meaninglessness, discontinuities between expectation and reality—situations that psychologists refer to collectively as "threat." Indeed, most negative emotions may be characterized in terms of the kind of behavior that individuals believe is appropriate in the face of the threat. A person who perceives his course of action as that of moving *away* from the source of the threat may be said to be afraid, anxious, or panicky, whereas a person who perceives his course of action as that of moving *against* the source of the threat may be said to be angry, enraged, or irritated. Movement *toward* the source of the threat would in effect be a denial that the threat is actually a threat.

333

Hostility and Aggression. Movement against others is, as we have pointed out previously, generally discouraged by members of social systems, unless it is directed against sources of threat to the group itself. Such behavior is commonly described as "hostile" or "aggressive." The term "hostile" is generally used to characterize the attitudinal background of the behavior, whereas the term "aggressive" usually refers to the act of moving against another person or object. Arnold H. Buss (1961), in his review of theory and research dealing with aggression, defines "aggression" as *"a response that delivers noxious stimuli to another organism,"* and "hostility" as "an attitudinal response that endures: *an implicit verbal response involving negative feelings (ill will) and negative evaluations of people and events."*

Aggression, according to the theory developed by John Dollard and others (1939), is the result of frustration. More specifically, "an interference with the occurrence of an instigated goal-response at its proper time in the behavior sequence" (frustration) leads to a "sequence of behavior, the goal-response to which is the injury of the person toward whom it is directed," (aggression). The Dollard theory has stimulated much research in hostility and aggression (Berkowitz, 1958). Although it is widely accepted by psychologists as a theoretical framework, it has also been criticized as being too limited. For one thing, as Buss points out, it conceives of aggression as occurring only in the presence of anger and thus neglects a whole class of aggressive responses. For another, aggressive actions might well be directed toward and reinforced by the acquisition of some reward (such as money) and not toward injuring the victim.

In a later review, Leonard Berkowitz (1965) states that the frustration-aggression hypothesis should be altered in at least three ways. First, the emotion that results from frustration (anger), does not necessarily result in aggression, but creates only a *readiness* for aggressive acts. Second, even with this readiness to act aggressively, aggression will not occur unless there are suitable cues available, as, for instance, stimuli that are associated with the present or previous instigators of anger. Third, instead of postulating that all aggression "presupposes the existence of frustration," we now know instead that appropriate cues may lead to aggressive behavior when previously learned aggressive habits are aroused. These habits can be learned without the learner necessarily being frustrated. The work of Bandura and Walters (1963), for example, shows that subjects can acquire aggressive habits merely by observing the behavior of an aggressive model.

In spite of these shortcomings of the frustration-aggression model, no competing theory of aggression with a comparable following among psychologists has appeared. One of the problems in developing an adequate theory lies in the fact that aggression appears in so many different contexts and with a variety of motives. The symptoms of aggression may seem similar, but the causes appear to be diverse, as we shall see from the discussion in this chapter.

Hostility and Outsiders. The term "hostile" has an interesting etymological history, and one that has a degree of psychological importance. Its root "hos," appears in words like "hospice," "hostage," "host," "hospitality," and "hotel" and is even related in a roundabout way to the word "guest." What these words have in common is that they are all concerned with the treatment of outgroup members: strangers. As the various forms of the word have been borrowed back and forth from culture to culture, they have developed both positive and negative meanings, some related to the stranger himself (the guest) and others related to the person who deals with the stranger (the host). Our treatment of the stranger depends on how we perceive him: if we see him as a threat, we are hostile, but if not, we greet him with hospitality.

Biological Bases of Aggression. It is a matter of some controversy among behavioral scientists as to whether we are biologically organized to behave in hostile or in accepting ways toward others. Ashley Montagu (1955), an anthropologist, claims that the basic drives in man, as well as in the lower animals, are positive and accepting, leading to patterns of affiliation and cooperation. Konrad Lorenz (1966) tends to follow the direction indicated by Sigmund Freud's (1955) "death wish," and proposes not only that man and the other mammals have aggressive instincts, but that aggression has a certain utilitarian value. Some clinical psychologists are inclined to favor the Freudian position that both destructive and creative instincts motivate man's behavior, whereas others prefer an orthogenic point of view, namely, that basic drives are positive and that organisms will develop in healthy, positive ways, unless prevented from doing so by severe environmental stress (Rogers, 1951; Combs & Snygg, 1959). Inasmuch as persuasive evidence can be marshalled to support each one of these positions, the question of whether hostile-aggressive motives are "natural" (instinctive) or learned remains open.

The position we have taken in this book is that the major trends in human social behavior are learned and not instinctive. This does not rule out the possibility that man may be biologically predisposed to behave in certain ways. As we noted in Chapter 9, aggressiveness and venturesomeness appear to be more characteristic of male primates, and socializing, of female primates. However, man's high degree of responsiveness to reinforcement leads him to develop a wide variety of patterns. Inasmuch as aggression, whether biologically or socially induced, can become a primary threat to the structure and goals of society, it becomes important to note what steps society takes or may take to induce the kind of learning that weakens or rechannels aggressive motives.

The Perception of Threat. The evidence shows that the tendency to perceive threat appears at a very early stage in human development. H. R. Schaffer (1966) conducted a longitudinal study of thirty-six infants and found that the average infant in the sample began to show fear of strangers at about 36 weeks. Females in this sample showed the usual pattern of being more responsive to social situations than males, for they reached this developmental milestone at about 35 weeks, whereas the mean for males was 37 weeks. The possibility that social learning is involved in the development of the fear reaction is shown by the fact that the more siblings there were in the family, the later the appearance of the fear reaction. Furthermore, the more people who came in contact with the infant, the later the reaction developed. There was no relationship between the delay of the reaction's appearance, however, and the amount of contact the infant had with its mother.

Interest in aggression appears almost as soon as children can talk. Louise Bates Ames (1966) conducted an exploratory study of stories told by preschool children at the Gesell Institute Guidance Nursery School in New Haven, Conn., and found that themes of violence predominated for all ages (two to five years) and for both sexes. Inasmuch as most of these children were from upper-middle-class families, it cannot be said that their lives had been marked by exposure to an unusual number of grim and shocking events. Some of Ames' data, reported in Figure 17-1, show that themes of violence predominate and follow a curvilinear trend, starting at 64 percent at age 2 and ending the preschool period with 78 percent at age 5. Boys are more likely to express violent themes in their stories from 3 years of age onward. The proportion of kind or friendly themes drops during the age span covered by the report, with boys reporting consistently fewer of these themes than girls, although the difference between the sexes diminishes toward the end of the period. Themes involving death tend to increase during the period, with girls reporting more of such themes at first, and boys surpassing them toward the end of the period. In general, boys' themes tended to be more violent and less friendly than those of girls. This was particularly true

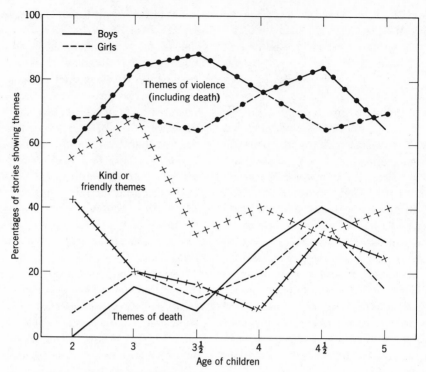

Figure **17-1.** Percentages* of various themes in stories told by preschool children at various ages (Ames, 1966).

during the later stages of the developmental period.

The Stimulus Value of Violence and Aggression. Although one could engage in a great deal of interesting speculation as to whether Ames' findings support an instinctual or a learning approach to the appearance of hostile-aggressive tendencies, there is one strong possibility why violent themes crowd out friendly ones in children's stories or, for that matter, in adult fiction as well, and that is: stimulus value. There is no doubt that violence and aggression are more stimulating or tension-arousing than their opposites. Man, as we pointed out in Chapter 2, has an overriding need to be

stimulated. Association with others is more stimulating than being alone, and observing, planning, coping with, or actually participating in violence or aggression is more stimulating than merely being with others. We should keep in mind, of course, that the relationship is curvilinear, and that too much stimulation can be as dysfunctional as too little, but under ordinary circumstances more stimulation is more attractive than less.

There are many everyday examples of the ability of violence to attract attention. Stormy seas breaking against a coast are more interesting than a quiet sea. Observe how quickly people gather around the scene of an accident, or how they drop everything to go to a fire. We often complain that newspapers print only bad news and seldom print the good things that happen to

*The percentages at any given age may add up to more than 100 per cent, because a given story could show more than one theme—that is, it could contain a theme of violence and a kind or friendly theme as well.

people; this merely confirms the fact that readers find bad news more attractive. And murder mysteries and shoot-'em-up Westerns outsell love stories and poetry many times over.

The Effect of the Culture on Hostility and Aggression. This generalized interest in violence does not mean that learning is not a factor in the kinds of preferred hostile-aggressive behavior. Members of lower-class groups express more direct physical aggression than do middle-class people. Middle-class members, on the other hand, are more likely to engage in more abstract forms of competitive behavior and to approach violence in a symbolic way (e.g., through reading). Still another factor, of course, is that the educational and economic level of middle-class people makes a wider range of stimulating activities available to them. It is highly probable that differences in attitudes toward hostility and aggression are learned and that the learning process begins very early.

One study of traditional, largely preliterate societies shows that there is a relationship between patterns of crime and patterns of child rearing. Theft, which is primarily a crime against property, and crimes against persons, such as assault, rape, and murder, were the two types of crime that were studied. Societies that are indulgent toward children tend to have low rates of theft, whereas societies that stress responsibility, self-reliance, achievement, and obedience, to the extent that children are likely to develop anxieties about behavior in these areas, tend to have high rates of theft. Societies that arouse anxieties in children for failing to behave in dependent ways tend to have high rates of crimes against persons. Child-rearing patterns are of course related to other factors in a given culture. The three factors listed in Table 17-1 under the heading of "Socioeconomic factors" provide clues to the complexity of the societies being studied. In general, it appears that the greater the complexity of the society, the higher the rate of theft.

Adult attitudes are related to child-rearing patterns as well. In societies where the sense of property is highly developed, and where there is widespread mistrust about property, the incidence of thefts is likely to be high. The researchers find three possible interpretations for these statistics: (1) the greater the importance of property, the greater the variety of acts that will be classified as crimes against property; (2) a high frequency of theft leads to an emphasis on property; or (3) the greater the importance of property, the more effectively does theft serve personal needs to which property seems to be related (Bacon, Child, & Barry, 1963).

Although the societies studied by the researchers are primitive and, for the most part, preliterate, some of the characteristics appear to apply to more advanced societies as well. Urbanized, industrialized societies are likely to develop anxieties in children about responsibility, self-reliance, achievement, and obedience. This is particularly true at the lower-middle-class levels of such societies. These societies are also likely to be highly complex and to stress property rights. One would expect that crimes against property would run high in such societies, as indeed they do. The Federal Bureau of Investigation report for 1965 shows, for example, that 238,978 out of a total of 2,780,015 offenses, or less than 10 per cent, were for murder, negligent manslaughter, forcible rape, and aggravated assault, and the balance were for robbery, burglary, larceny, and auto theft—crimes against property. Industrialized societies appear to have created the kind of social climate that encourages stealing, but discourages crimes against persons. It may be that there is a relationship between the complexity of a society and the extent to which violence is tolerated. If so, it would be expected that industrialized, urbanized societies would have higher rates of crime against property, whereas less developed societies would have higher rates of crimes against persons, which are generally more violent than crimes against property. Although comparable figures are not readily available, there are some data to

Table **17-1.** Factors in forty-eight societies (largely preliterate) that are related to the frequency during adulthood of theft and crimes against persons (Bacon, Child, & Barry, 1963)

	Correlations	
Factors	Theft	Crimes against persons
Child-rearing patterns		
Childhood indulgence	high negative	n.s.[a]
Responsibility socialization		
anxiety	high positive	n.s.
Self-reliance socialization anxiety	positive	low positive
Achievement socialization anxiety	positive	n.s.
Obedience socialization anxiety	positive	n.s.
Dependence socialization anxiety	n.s.	high positive
Socioeconomic factors		
Social stratification	positive	n.s.
Level of political integration	positive	n.s.
Degree of elaboration of social		
control	high positive	n.s.
Adult attitudes		
Sense of property	high positive	low positive
Trust about property	negative	low negative
General trustfulness	low negative	high negative
Environmental kindness in folk tales	negative	low negative
Environmental hostility in folk tales	low positive	high positive

[a] Not statistically significant.

show that countries that are less developed economically have higher murder rates than do highly developed countries (United Nations, 1965).

Within our own culture, differences in child-rearing methods may also lead to different attitudes toward aggression. We have noted that lower-class members learn to be more tolerant of aggression than middle-class members, but even within the middle class there is a considerable degree of variation. One study using male college students, all presumably middle class, took place under conditions in which the subjects were led to expect punishment (electric shock) for failures, reward (cash payment) for successes, or information (being told whether a response was "right" or "wrong") for successes or failures. The task

they would be tested on, they were told, would involve their memorizing vocabulary words in an artificial language, Esperanto. Before the experiment began, however, they were asked to fill out a questionnaire rating the instructor who was to give them the test and who would presumably shock them, reward them, or inform them of their failures or successes, depending on the experimental condition that would prevail for the subjects in question. They also filled out questionnaires asking for ratings of themselves and of "typical" university students. At this point, the experiment terminated.

When the questionnaire replies of the subjects were scored, it appeared that students who described their parents' child-rearing methods as democratic tended to identify with their instructor best under the reward-and-information conditions, whereas those whose parents were more restrictive and authoritarian identified best under the punishment condition. The experimenters concluded that their results supported the idea that individuals reared in an authoritarian atmosphere would, as adults, be more inclined to identify with aggressors, whereas those who had been reared in democratic environments would be more inclined to identify with authority figures who were supportive and benign (Baxter, Lerner, & Miller, 1965).

Institutionalized and Personalized Forms of Aggression. It would be well, at this point, to note that there are at least two major varieties of interpersonal and intergroup aggression. One type is institutionalized aggression, aggression that has the sanction of the group or society, usually, but not always, because the target is perceived as some kind of a threat. Under this heading would be included the punishment of lawbreakers. Punishment may cover everything from death and torture to public reprimand, and its severity will depend on the norms and values of the society on whose behalf the penalty is exacted. The point is that any such penalty is a form of socially legitimized aggression. This is not to raise any questions regarding the effectiveness or the morality of punishment, but merely to note that it is a form of aggression.

Some forms of institutionalized aggression are legitimate only in a limited way. Looting and burning may appear to be an appropriate form of aggression to bands of irregulars in the jungles and mountains of underdeveloped countries. For them it is institutionalized and legitimate. The majority of the population however, probably denies the legitimacy of the institution the irregulars represent, as well as the actions they perform. The shooting of looters during a riot by policemen is seen as illegitimate and unwarranted aggression by the looters, who reject society and its institutions, but the society on whose behalf the police are acting may view such action as a legiti-

mate, appropriate, and proper defense of its institutions.

Warfare is another example of institutionalized aggression. The people of a country that attacks or invades another, harasses its nationals, or destroys its property generally believe that it is acting legitimately in defense of its institutions. The other country is likely to believe otherwise. Fortunately, most international aggression does not reach the drastic level of warfare. Instead, countries resort to such watered-down and institutionalized forms of aggression as angry speeches by heads of state, economic sanctions, treaties with other nations, protective tariffs, and the like.

The second type of aggression is personalized. It ranges from murder and mayhem to angry words. The more severe forms are forbidden by law, but some rather vigorous forms, like boxing and wrestling, are permitted and even encouraged in our culture.

The chief difference between institutionalized and personalized forms of aggression, as far as the more severe forms are concerned, lies in the attitudes and feelings of members of society. The individual who commits an aggressive act that has been legitimized by society may be praised and rewarded, may feel no guilt at all, and may even feel virtuous. His behavior is perceived as that of defending society and its institutions and is thus consistent with society's norms. The individual who engages in an equally violent form of aggression for personal reasons will, on the other hand, be regarded as an enemy of society. His behavior has not been legitimized and is perceived as counternorm, deviant, and reprehensible. The difference is a perceptual one, but the perception takes place within the frame of reference and the mores of the society concerned.

Prejudice and Intergroup Hostility

The Nature of Prejudice. The norms a society develops determine not only how much hostility can be openly expressed, but also what forms it can take. The more complex the society, the more likely it is to insist that hostility be expressed symbolically, rather than directly. In our society, hostility may be "sublimated," to use the Freudian term, by being worked off in competitive sports and games, hard physical work, problem-solving endeavor, or competitive enterprise. Latent hostility is often expressed toward certain groups in the form of prejudiced actions. For example, a society may use the police to harass groups of teenagers whose choice of dress or leisure-time activities is at variance with the norms of the adult culture.

There are several general principles that appear to operate in prejudiced and hostile forms of behavior:

1. Society, some segment of society, or its agents designates some readily identifiable group as an appropriate target and as a suitable object for hostility and/or aggression.
2. The target group should be different in some way that the prejudiced group believes to be significant and inferior: poor, young, nonwhite, female, members of an unpopular religious faith, homosexual, foreign, or whatever.
3. Members of the target group should collectively or individually appear vulnerable in some way.
4. Stereotyped beliefs which support the negative attitudes toward members of the target group are learned, usually during childhood.
5. Hostile attitudes and/or behavior assume a degree of legitimacy and constitute an institutionalized form of aggression, thus freeing the individual from the need to feel guilty.
6. Society generally provides some kind of channel in the form of more-or-less sanctioned behavior that facilitates the expression of hostility toward the target persons. Depending on the norms of the society and the situation involved, modes of expressing prejudice may range from merely ignoring target persons to lynching or exterminating them.

In recent years, prejudiced treatment of nonwhites has attracted a great deal of attention on the part of behavioral scientists and lay people alike. Nonwhite members of society readily fit in with the foregoing criteria, because they are visibly different from the dominant white group, and, because they are usually poor and uneducated, they ordinarily lack the means to secure legal protection against exploitation and harassment. Society also provides ways of expressing prejudice, such as pejorative language ("nigger," "greaser," "spick," etc.) or exclusion from employment and housing. People who are chronically bitter or suspicious tend to express more prejudice toward nonwhites than do people whose generalized hostility lies closer to the norm (Bettelheim & Janowitz, 1950). It is not necessary for people to be seriously maladjusted to be prejudiced. The willingness of normal, everyday people to maintain racially segregated housing and to exclude nonwhites from equal participation in the rewards of society is evidence that visible difference, perceived vulnerability, and learned patterns of behavior, are sufficient to evoke prejudiced responses.

Perceived Difference as the Basis for Prejudice. Milton Rokeach (1965) makes the point that a perceived difference in belief systems is the most significant basis for prejudice. The interpretation has been criticized by Harry C. Triandis (1961) on the grounds that Negroes are excluded from certain neighborhoods because they are Negroes, not for their beliefs. Evidence that supports Rokeach's position, however, has been supplied by the study by Donn Byrne and Terry J. Wong (1962), we mentioned in Chapter 3. Byrne and Wong found that similarity in attitudes led to positive ratings of a fictitious stranger, irrespective of his race, and irrespective of the degree of measured prejudice of the rater. This problem has been further explored in a study of ninth-grade white students, who were asked to evaluate four "typical teenagers." Each subject was given questionnaires that had presumably been filled out by four other teenagers, two white and two Negro. A "white" and a "Negro" questionnaire were answered with responses like those the subject himself had given two months earlier, when he had filled out a questionnaire of teenage attitudes, and the other two "white" and "Negro" questionnaires were filled out with responses that differed considerably from those he had given. Results gave some support to Triandis' contention, in that the average acceptance score for the two fictitious whites was somewhat higher than the mean score for the two fictitious Negroes. A further analysis of the scores showed, however, that the teenagers were reacting primarily in terms of similarity of beliefs and only secondarily in terms of race. Fictitious Negroes, for whom similar attitudes were reported, were for instance, accorded considerably more acceptance than fictitious whites with dissimilar attitudes (Stein, Hardyck, & Smith, 1965).

The results of this study also suggest that a great deal of prejudiced behavior results from the fact that people have no prior knowledge of the attitudes and values of the target individuals and hence make their decisions on the basis of stereotyped beliefs about the minority group in question. A correlational analysis of the data in the foregoing study showed that the teenagers responded to a fictitious Negro who had been represented as unlike them in values in much the same way that they had responded earlier to an otherwise unspecified Negro teenager about whom they had no information. In other words, "Negro" to them meant "someone who has values unlike mine." Inasmuch as the target person in this instance is assumed to have values that do not resemble those of the dominant group and that may actually be in opposition, people in the dominant group tend to maintain a high degree of social distance by seeing to it that he is isolated from the rest of society. Exclusion from neighborhoods, schools, and job opportunities are among the methods most commonly used to maintain social distance. The maintenance of social distance has a circular or reciprocating effect on the stereotyped belief that serves as the basis for isolation, because it helps perpetuate and reinforce the prejudiced behavior. If we arrange matters so that we have little or no contact with people who are the targets of our prejudice, we will never find out whether they have similar values or not. Indeed the authors of the study cited earlier stated that the results constitute a strong argument in favor of more interaction on an equal-status basis between members of dominant and minority groups.

Vulnerability as the Basis for Aggression. Considerable research in recent years has demonstrated the appropriateness of the second, third, and fifth criteria or preconditions for the expression of prejudiced behavior—namely, the perception of the target group as different and as vulnerable and the consequent sanctioning of aggressive behavior by society. Stanley Milgram (1963) designed a classic experiment making use of simulated electric shock that suggests some of the lengths to which people will go, once an individual has been designated as a worthy target for aggression.

Subjects in Milgram's study were led to believe that they were involved in an attempt to measure the effect of punishment on learning. As each subject appeared at the laboratory, he met a second subject (actually an accomplice of the experimenter). The two then drew lots to see who would be the "learner" and the "teacher" in the experiment. The drawing was rigged so that the accomplice would always be the "learner." The "learner" was then strapped into a realistic-appearing electric chair type of apparatus, and the naive subject was taken to an adjoining room, where he was shown how to operate a switchboard that purportedly administered shocks to the "learner." There was a series of thirty switches that could be used to deliver shocks ranging from 15 volts (labeled as "slight shock") to 300 volts ("intense shock"), 360 volts ("extreme intensity shock"), 420 volts ("danger: severe shock"), and even 450 volts ("XXX"). The subject was told to read lists of words with multiple-choice options over a microphone, and that the "learner" would respond by pressing the button for one of four lights to indicate his reply. The "teacher" was instructed to press a lever that would presumably shock the "learner" every time the latter made an error. Each shock was to be of a higher intensity than the previous one. As the "learning" session progressed, a number of the teacher-subjects became anxious or even upset, particularly when the shock level reached 300 volts ("intense shock") and the "learner" pounded on the wall between the rooms. When this occurred, the subjects usually looked to the experimenter for guidance, only to be told that they had no choice but to go on with the experiment. From this point on, nothing further was heard from the learner, and he did not even respond to the "teacher's" questions. Subjects were then told that a failure to reply must be counted as a wrong answer and that they were to give the "learner" the next higher shock on the scale and go on with the list of words, continuing to increase the shock with each failure to respond.

When a sampling of senior psychology majors was asked to predict what proportion of naive subjects would go through to the end of the experiment and administer what the subjects thought was a 450-volt shock, they guessed that not more than 2 or 3 per cent would do so. Even Milgram's colleagues doubted that many subjects would administer shock above the 240-volt level. What actually happened, however, was that no subject refused until the 300-volt level was reached (when the "victim" pounds on the wall) and at that point only five out of the forty subjects withdrew from the situation. An additional nine subjects dropped out at the next succeeding shock levels, and twenty-six (65 per cent) actually continued until the last switch (450 volts) had been pulled. At that point, or at whatever point the subject withdrew, the experiment was explained to the subject, and the "victim" appeared and assured the subject that he had not been shocked.

The subjects were without exception relieved to learn that the shocks had only been simulated. Some of the subjects were exceedingly upset by the experience. Milgram writes:

"I observed a mature and initially poised businessman enter the laboratory smiling and confident. Within 20 minutes he was reduced to a twitching, stuttering wreck, who was rapidly approaching a point of nervous collapse. He constantly pulled on his earlobe, and twisted his hands. At one point he pushed his fist into his forehead and muttered: 'Oh God, let's stop it.' And yet he continued to respond to every word of the experimenter, and obeyed to the end."

Milgram (1964) conducted a variation of his initial experiment in which the "shocks" were administered to the "learner" by three "teachers": a naive subject and two confederates of the experimenter. In this experiment, the "teachers" received instructions that they were to recommend the shock level to be administered whenever the "learner" failed a test item. The two "teachers" who were confederates made their recommendations first, thus implicitly putting social pressure on the naive subject to go along with them. However, the "teachers" were also told that the shock that would be administered by the third (naive) teacher would be at the lowest level suggested. Hence the naive "teacher" was free to call for and administer a shock level of only 15 volts if he wished. The experimental situation was thus similar to the Asch (1956) and IPAR experiments we described in Chapter 4, except that some kind of action (punishment) was taken as a result of the decision of the naive subject.

The unanimous recommendations of the stooges followed a uniformly increasing trend, starting with 15 volts on the first error or "critical trial," and increasing with 15-volt increments for each of the succeeding trials until a maximum of 450 volts had been recommended for the thirtieth critical trial.

Whereas the "learner" in Milgram's first experiment had protested only once by kicking the wall at the 300-volt level, the "learner" in this experiment began to complain at 75-volts. The complaints had all been prerecorded on magnetic tape, which was activated when the lever for the appropriate shock level was pulled. At 75 volts to 105 volts, the learner was heard to grunt slightly. At 120 volts he shouted that the shocks were becoming painful. Painful groans were heard at the 135-volt level, and at 150 volts, the "learner" cried that he wanted to be released because of a heart disturbance. Cries of this type were repeated with each succeeding higher level until 180 volts, the "learner" cried out: "I can't stand the pain," and by 285 volts his response to the shock was an agonized scream. At 300 volts he shouted that he would no longer provide answers to the test. The two confederates appeared to remain indifferent to the "learner's" complaints throughout the experiment.

The results, as depicted in Figure 17-2, show that there was a marked tendency for the naive subjects to go along at least part way with the stooges' recommendations. The subjects in the control group who worked alone and who, like the experimental subjects, were free to administer any shock they wished, tended to administer shocks at the 50-volt level, on the average. There was a considerable degree of variation in the shocks administered by the forty experimental subjects. Three never gave over 30 volts, but ten reached the 405-volt level and seven actually went along with the two stooges' recommendations all the way to 450 volts.

An analysis of the background of the experimental subjects showed the usual social-class effects, with persons having high school education or less complying with the stooges' suggestions to a greater extent than subjects with some college education.

The conditions prevailing in Milgram's two experiments are, as we noted, consistent with the conditions listed earlier for prejudiced and hostile behavior. The "victim" shows himself to be inferior by making mistakes and hence is perceived as having "deserved" or "earned" his

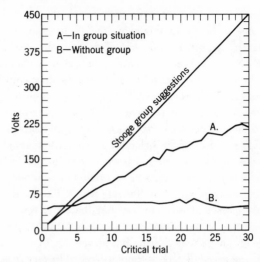

Figure 17-2. The effect of social pressure on the willingness of a naive subject to administer electric shock (Milgram, 1964).

In the situation represented by Curve "A," the two stooges recommend that the naive subject shock the "learner" for every error on a gradient that increases steadily from 15 volts on the first critical trial to 450 volts on the thirtieth trial. The subjects in the experimental situation tended to go along with their recommendations, and by the thirtieth trial were shocking the "learner" at about 225 volts, on the average. Curve "B" represents the performance of the control subjects, who worked alone, without social pressure. They tended to shock the "learner" at about 50 volts.

punishment. Society, as represented in the first experiment by the experimenter and in the second by the two stooges, designates the channel—administration of electric shock by the naive subject —whereby its hostility and rejection may be expressed. In effect, the naive subject becomes the agent whereby society aggresses against the individual who has been "prejudged" and is thus made the target of prejudice. In the second experiment, the naive subject actually collaborates with society in determining the level of aggressiveness with which prejudice is to be expressed.

The first experiment produced, as we have

noted, a high degree of distress on the part of some subjects. In this experiment, subjects were given to understand that they had no choice about administering even higher levels of shock, whereas in the second they were told they could decide for themselves. The apparent choicelessless in the first experiment probably contributed to their distress by making them feel helpless. In this situation their behavior is somewhat analogous to that of the apartment house owner who tells the Negro couple in an obviously apologetic and embarrassed tone that he would like to rent an apartment to them but that the other tenants (or the community) would object. This may or may not be true, but he has never put his belief to the test and acts as though it were in fact true. The first experiment's subjects and the apologetic apartment-house owner regard themselves as the instruments of society who are charged with administering sanctions that they do not agree with. Hence their distress.

The Prejudice of the Passive Observer. What occurs, however, when the subject is a bystander who watches the victim punished? Although in this instance the subject is not the instrument whereby society vents its hostility on the target person, he nevertheless cannot avoid the feeling of being involved. Watching punishment ordinarily creates tension on the part of the observer, tension that is presumably increased if the observer identifies and empathizes with the punished individual. The effects of such an experience on observers were studied by Melvin J. Lerner and Carolyn H. Simmons (1966) by means of an experiment in which a naive subject watched what she thought was another student being shocked for errors made while learning a list of nonsense syllables. The other student was of course a confederate who was not shocked at all, but who gave a realistic performance. The subjects then filled out a questionnaire designed to measure the impression the other student made on them. Under one of the experimental conditions, the subjects were informed that the experi

ment was now over; under another condition, they were told that they would see her shocked a second time. Results showed that subjects expressed more rejection for the "victim" when they believed that she would be shocked again and that they were powerless to help her. Whereas the subjects in Milgram's first experiment expressed their concurrence with society's evaluation of the victim by administering more electric shock when ordered to do so, these subjects expressed their concurrence by rejecting and devaluing the victim. Any other option would have increased cognitive dissonance for them. If they believed that she was a worthy person, a person like them, they would feel guilty for not having taken some steps (perhaps volunteered in her place or raised an objection) to keep her from being shocked. Since they had taken no such steps, the easiest way to avoid responsibility or guilt feelings (which would have led to an increase in cognitive dissonance) was by deciding that she probably deserved the treatment she received.

Lerner and Simmons encountered an interesting result with one of their experimental conditions, in which the victim protests that she does not want to be shocked, but is persuaded by the experimenter on the grounds that participating as a subject in an experiment is a course requirement, and the other student will not get the credit if she does not go through with the experiment as planned. The victim then generously agrees to participate. In this situation, the victim appears in the role of a martyr who agrees to suffer if it will benefit the group. The victim then leaves and the rest of the experiment proceeds as in the other conditions. The ratings of the victim made by subjects under the "martyr" conditions are the lowest of all the experimental conditions, thus indicating the maximum rejection. The experimenters suggest that these perplexing findings show that people have a strong need to feel that this is a good and just world and that the martyr's suffering threatens this need more than the suffer ing of less nobly motivated people. It is also likely that the willingness of the martyr to suffer on behalf of the subjects created even more cognitive dissonance for them than did the standard experimental condition and that they had to go even further in rejecting her in order to reduce the dissonance.

Prejudice, Hostility, and Aggression as "Normal" Behavior. Everyday life is full of examples of how people become the targets of society's hostility. The willingness of society to punish the deviant is a function of both the degree of deviancy and the status of the deviant. Generally speaking, an unimportant or slight deviancy from the social norms on the part of a low-status person is enough to evoke the use of sanctions, whereas a high-status person is treated more leniently. The situation is somewhat complicated by the fact that socially prescribed role behaviors differ at various status levels, but the trend is nevertheless a pervasive one. A judge's son and a bank president's daughter are permitted more latitude in their behavior at school than are the children of laborers. Murderers with higher social status are much more likely to escape the electric chair or the gas chamber than are murderers with lower status. The implications are rather obvious to anyone who wants to take the trouble to analyze the data, but few are so motivated.

The studies we have cited also suggest that almost anyone may commit hostile, aggressive, and prejudiced acts without feeling guilty about them, providing such behavior takes place within the context of established social norms and is thus legitimized. It is actually possible to feel virtuous and responsible as a result of such actions. The problem thus appears to be twofold—that of being willing to recognize that one is capable of hostility, aggression, and prejudice, and that of being able to recognize these trends in oneself and one's fellow group members when such actions are being carried out. These problems are difficult because the possibility of exhibiting behavior

motivated by prejudice is generally inconsistent with the self-image. Furthermore, cohesiveness and norm-following are so strong that the examination of the group's motives itself becomes a kind of deviant behavior that is perceived as highly threatening to the group's morale or even to its existence.

Intergroup Conflict

The Perception of External Threat. A good example of the operation of these principles is the way in which people behave when an intergroup conflict is in preparation or is actually in progress. Interracial tensions, political campaigns, strikes, and wars are examples of intergroup conflicts. At such times any suggestion that the motives of one's group may be suspect are treated as a form of treason. Whenever the group perceives itself as being threatened by an outside source, morale and cohesiveness are valued even more highly than usual, and norms become highly specific and rigidly defined. Everything becomes organized in terms of defensive and offensive strategies, and activity that does not contribute to group goals may be regarded as suspect. Self-sacrifice and commitment are the order of the day, and group members outdo one another to prove their loyalty and dedication.

This problem is especially aggravated when groups are in the process of coping with a "real threat." The term "real threat" is one used by Douglas T. Campbell (1965) in describing situations in which the interests of groups (nations, for example) are in conflict with one another. The more the conflicting parties have to gain by victory, the more intense the threat is likely to become. Threat may also be aggravated by a history of past group conflict, as well as by the presence of hostile, threatening, and competitive out-group neighbors. Campbell points out that the perception of "real threat" causes hostility toward the source of the threat and that this hostility is bolstered by ingroup solidarity, a greater awareness of in-group identity on the part of the members of the threatened group, and a sharper definition or "tightness" of the in-group's boundaries. Much of this comes under the heading of "ethnocentrism." Real threat also reduces defection from the group and increases tendencies to punish and reject defectors. However, once Campbell has made his points about the effects of "real threat," he goes on to say that the false perception of threat from out-groups (seeing threat where none actually exists) leads to much the same results.

Research into the Dynamics of Intergroup Conflicts. The social scientist has a difficult task during times of stress, partly because group members are especially unresponsive to social research whose findings may threaten the basis for the coordinated functioning of the total group, and partly because the scientist, as a member of the group involved in the conflict, generally cannot avoid identifying with one side or the other. Group tension, in other words, has a polarizing effect on group members and nonmembers alike, and even though the scientist would like to maintain the kind of detachment and objectivity that the scientific method calls for, he is after all, only human and is likely to be drawn by personal sympathies to one side or the other. Maintaining objectivity and detachment is actually hazardous, because identity and definition become crucial during times of tension: "Either you're for us or you're against us—there's no middle ground."

In spite of the polarizing effect of the forces of group cohesion, it is nevertheless possible to study the factors and conditions that aggravate or reduce intergroup hostility with the view of promoting the understanding of human behavior or of developing a fund of information that may have practical value for peacemakers and others interested in human survival. Such research can best be carried on during times when tensions are relatively low, recognizing, of course, that there will always be members in any group who will be outraged at any attempt to study hostility and prejudice scientifically. Research may also be

carried on under group-conflict conditions by third parties who work under the auspices of outside, disinterested agencies, although persons operating under such conditions have problems in avoiding involvement or being labeled as favoring one side or the other.

In the light of these various considerations, social research conducted in the laboratory has a number of obvious advantages. It provides the means whereby the scientist's involvement in issues can be controlled and operations can be sheltered from an overactive public scrutiny. Most laboratory research is concerned with the formulating and testing examples of general principles, and this aspect of behavior is generally of less interest to the general public, whose concerns tend to be topical and immediate, rather than theoretical. Thus it is possible to conduct research into hostility, aggression, morale, and other motivational dimensions of group conflict, including war, without having to become involved in the rightness or wrongness of one side or another in an ongoing war or even in the war itself. This does not imply that psychologists tend to be personally neutral about war, for the great majority strongly oppose it. Indeed, it is the general antipathy to war that has led to much research dealing with hostility and social conflict. But when a scientist is involved in conducting research into various aspects of the basic, underlying emotion—hostility—he can function adequately and scientifically only if he plays a completely neutral and detached role.

With these considerations in mind, let us turn to research, largely taking place in the laboratory, that deals with the stimulation and control of hostility and aggression.

Coping with Hostility through Catharsis. One principle attractive to researchers is the idea that hostility can be dissipated harmlessly if it can be expressed in some nonviolent way. This approach is consistent with the frustration-aggression hypothesis (Dollard et al., 1939) we discussed earlier and assumes a kind of mechanical model in which a charge of hostility becomes built up and must find some kind of outlet. Presumably, unless the pent-up hostility finds a harmless outlet, it will explode in some aggressive act. This principle finds its expression in clinical counseling, whereby the client or patient is permitted and encouraged to "blow off steam" and thus relieve some of the pressure to "do something" about his anger and resentment. Common experience also shows that people who have been offended or insulted feel less hostile after they have had a chance to tell someone about it.

Seymour Feshbach (1955) conducted what has become a classical study of this approach to hostility reduction. He arranged for a colleague to insult a number of college classes by making derogatory remarks about their limited intellectual interests and their maturity. Other subjects were treated in a friendly manner. One of the insulted groups took a series of aptitude tests; the other wrote stories for four cards selected from the Thematic Apperception Test (TAT). The first two groups thus served as control groups, whereas the third received the experimental treatment. The hypothesis that the hostility in the second group would remain high, but that it would be lowered in the third group (because of the opportunity to express hostility through fantasy), was supported by the results.

Some field research with "hard-core delinquents" also supports the idea that catharsis is an effective reducer of hostility. In this research, delinquents were paid to talk into tape recorders with the understanding that they were providing data for researchers who were interested in finding out what it was like to be a delinquent. After about a dozen sessions, the boastful mood of the subjects became subdued and there was a general improvement in their behavior (Schwitzgebel & Schwitzgebel, 1961).

There are, however, two sides to catharsis. Although everyday experience shows that it is possible to reduce aggressive tendencies through talk, it is also possible to "talk oneself into a rage."

Michael Kahn (1966) found that Harvard freshmen who were insulted and angered by a laboratory technician disliked their annoyer more after having had a chance to tell the latter's supervisor about their mistreatment, whereas those who remained quiet for 20 minutes and who had no opportunity to express themselves had a more favorable opinion. It may be that the fact that subjects had an opportunity to talk to a high-status person may have had something to do with the difference between Kahn's results and those of the other two studies we have cited.

Leonard Berkowitz (1962) delineates three types of difficulties with catharsis as a theoretical construct:

1. Acts of hostility may be followed by weaker or less frequent aggressive responses not because hostility has been relieved by catharsis but because of guilt or anxiety on the part of the attacker brought on by his initial hostile actions.
2. The attacker may be frustrated further or may stimulate himself to continued aggression.
3. Hostility may be dissipated if the original anger-inciting frustration has been eliminated.

Research performed in recent years presents mixed results with respect to the question of whether the opportunity to aggress reduces hostility. One group of studies has found that the opportunity to express aggression directly to a frustrator was followed by a reduction in tension as measured by physiological indicators of tension (Hokanson, Burgess, & Cohen, 1963; Berkowitz, 1962). Another study using similar methods, however, showed that subjects who were not permitted to aggress reduced their physiological arousal level more than those who were allowed to do so (Holmes, 1966). Some of the differences in results may be accounted for by the fact that the latter study used only female subjects, whereas the other studies used mixed-sex groups. But the lack of agreement does raise questions about the value of catharsis as an easy and obvious means of controlling aggressive tendencies and suggests that other means be explored as well.

"Tell him off, Henry. Don't keep things bottled up inside you."

Reprinted with permission from *The Saturday Evening Post*

© 1959, The Curtis Publishing Co.

Coping with Hostility through Social Learning. One approach that appears to have possibilities is social learning. There is considerable evidence to show that the readiness to aggress, like other complex patterns or behavior, results from or at least can be controlled by learning. Like differences in authoritarianism, to which it is related, aggressiveness differs among cultures and according to various child-rearing patterns. Ralph Epstein and S. S. Komorita (1966) showed lower-middle-class children in grades three to five slides of a group of people they called "Piraneans" and asked the typical social distance questions, such as, "Would you want these people to visit your country?" The slides depicted a variety of children, one at a time, who were clearly white, Negro, Oriental, middle-class, and lower-class. As expected, the children expressed a desire to maintain more social distance between themselves and the lower-class children who were depicted on the slides than between themselves and middle-class children. More social distance was also preferred with respect to Negroes, in contrast with white and Oriental children. When the researchers asked children to indicate how they thought their parents would rate the children on the slides, the reported ethnocentrism (prejudice) of the parents was significantly related to that of the children (see Figure 17-3). In all likelihood, the parents played a part in their children's learning to be prejudiced. Figure 17-3 also shows that the degree of punitivity of the parents (as reported by the children) may have been a factor, although the relationships are not clear cut. At the extremes of the scale of ethnocentrism, however, the graph shows that there is a slight tendency for a higher degree of parental punitivity to be related to children's prejudice, with the typical least-

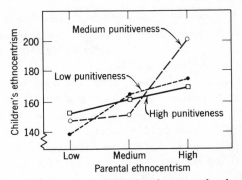

Figure **17-3.** The relationship between the degree of ethnocentrism or prejudice expressed by children and the amount of parental ethnocentrism and punitiveness (Epstein & Komorita, 1966).

prejudiced child being one who has as his behavioral models parents who are low in both prejudice and in punitivity. The importance of having the right kind of model is also shown by the finding that parents' prejudice is more closely related to a child's prejudice than is the severity with which they administer punishment.

This does not mean that punishment has no effect on aggressive tendencies. One study of men who had been convicted of crimes characterized by a high degree of violence showed that they were more likely to have been punished severely by their parents than were men who had grown up in the same depressed residential area but who did not have criminal records (McCord, McCord, & Howard, 1963). If we follow the line of reasoning developed by Bandura and Walters (1963), it would appear that the aggressive behavior of the parents, as expressed through their punitivity, served as a model for their sons' behavior. It is not surprising that men who were unable to exercise control over their antisocial impulses had parents who also were unable to control their anger and expressed it through severe physical punishment. Children cannot learn self-control if adequate models are not available.

We have noted elsewhere that males tend to be more aggressive than females. The fact that this difference can be found in most cultures suggests

that a genetic factor may be involved, but the wide differences in the degree of hostility and aggressiveness characteristically displayed by males who are members of different cultures suggest that learning is probably a major component in whatever pattern eventuates. Some hostility and aggression is universal in the human species, and men may be more hostile and aggressive than women, but the evidence that degrees and modes of hostility are modifiable through learning is available in such quantity as to be a source of encouragement to those who are interested in controlling and reducing it.

The research dealing with the reduction of hostility and aggression through symbolic means as a kind of catharsis has produced mixed results, as we have noted. Observation and comparison, however, will show that aggressive behavior tends to be restrained in societies that have norms which reduce and restrict the overt expression of hostility and that encourage its expression symbolically, rather than directly.

Social Norms and the Control of Aggression. The term "norms" provides one of the keys to the greater success of urbanized societies in this respect. Social norms, as we have shown, hold groups together and enable them to develop cohesiveness. Some norms in urbanized societies become codified in the form of laws, governmental procedure, and organizational structure. Irrespective of the amount of good will and altruism that the members of a society have learned to express, conflicts of interest are bound to occur. The fact that car owners carry insurance takes care of situations in which drivers' interests conflict and accidents result. Laws regarding individual liberties take care of situations in which the individual's and society's interests are in conflict, for they specify what is fair and equitable for all concerned. A householder may not play his hi-fi at top volume until 3 A.M., but the law may not interfere with his buying and listening to a recording of Earl Browder reading Karl Marx if he wants to.

There is always an area of instability and vagueness when it comes to individual rights that run counter to society's mores, and in any society that has a norm of being genuinely concerned about the rights of individuals, this area is under continual review and redefinition. The point is, however, that much aggression is averted or thwarted because it *is* counter-norm. The problem in a community and a nation appears to be partly that of developing statements of norms (laws and customs) which are mutually and internally consistent, and which protect both society and the individual from acts of aggression, and partly that of enabling people to become participants in a cohesive society. If people feel that they are genuine participants, they will have less difficulty accepting society's norms as guidelines for their behavior.

Norms for International Behavior. It is very likely that the same principles would work on the international level, as well as on the community and national level. Groups of nations are less cohesive than are groups comprising a nation that has a high degree of self-identity. Similarly, some of the new, emerging nations lack internal cohesiveness and have not as yet developed norms that are generally accepted by the subgroups they comprise. The presence or absence of strong norms is both a cause and an effect of the amount of cohesiveness present. The development of norms of international behavior grows in part out of necessity. Regulations governing maritime and aviation transportation are one example of norms that have a high degree of acceptance among nations. Radio transmission, the passage of mails, and regulations governing sports are examples of international norms that have somewhat less influence but are in process of development, and there are many others. Participation in the United Nations is a kind of norm that has different meaning for different countries. International trade and the need to exchange information of a technical nature also contribute to the development of international norms.

The opening up of channels of communication actually precedes the development of norms, because a nation must be informed about other nations before it can become interested in cooperating. It follows also that channels of communication expand and extend themselves in support of norms, because norms that exist on a fairly abstract level, as international norms do, require a great deal of communication.

If nations continue to expand their base of interaction, they will inevitably develop stronger, more extensive, and more complex communication and norm networks. Such a development will not, of course, proceed without setbacks and complications. Some nations may deliberately isolate themselves from participation in such networks, preferring not to benefit from them. Other nations will isolate themselves in a selective way, as the Arab countries have from Israel, and as Albania has from the rest of Europe. Some nations, such as Sweden, will participate more actively in the development of norms, whereas others, such as Paraguay or Yemen, will participate only marginally.

One possible side effect of the strengthening of norms and channels of communication will be an eventual reduction in international aggression or war. The rapidity with which this reduction can take place depends on the extent to which nations are willing to commit themselves to norm building. Nations that are less committed constitute more of a threat to international cohesiveness than the more committed nations, and if small-group research can be extrapolated to the international level, one would predict that nations that isolate themselves from others, or that behave in counternorm ways, will eventually become subject to more pressure than will nations that are participating in the development of norms. Some of this pressure may take the form of military action, as for example the presence of United Nations troops in Cyprus and in the former Belgian Congo. If patterns of international cooperation are strong enough, these actions should be of relatively short duration. The events of the past few years suggest, however, that the will to cooperate and to participate in international norm building is still quite weak.

To put this into slightly different terms, the ability of man to avoid destructive wars depends on his willingness to participate in the development of an international organization—of a structure, that is, composed of norms, channels of communication, regulations, and so forth, just like an organization composed of people. If such an organization is to be successful, it should derive its main impetus from the needs of the nations and people that compose it. It will be more functional if it is based on positive motives—such as the need of people for freer, richer, and more stimulating patterns of living—than on negative ones, such as the need to eliminate war or a war-maker. Defensive motives may mobilize energy more rapidly, but they are also likely to burn themselves out quickly, whereas group-building motives, although they are less dramatic and often become subordinated in times of stress, have more staying power. Group-building needs are, as we pointed out early in the book, basic and fundamental to human behavior. To us the words of Katz and Kahn (1966), implementing such needs and creating the necessary organizations emphasize "an ethic from below based on social experience." The actions that become legitimate in the developing of organizations therefore take on "the pragmatic meaning of observing traffic rules rather than obeying a moral imperative."

SUMMARY

Three basic ways we can relate to others are through moving toward them, away from them, and against them. Social systems are maintained primarily by movement toward others, and movement against others is generally considered to be a threat to the group. At times, however, movement against others may contribute to cohesiveness. This is likely to occur during intergroup competi-

tion or when the movement is directed against those considered to be threats to the group.

Movement against others is aggression, a form of behavior which is usually motivated by hostility. According to one widely accepted theory, aggression is the result of frustration. The frustration-aggression theory, however, does not take into account aggression that occurs in the absence of anger, the fact that frustration may only lead to a readiness to aggress, the need for appropriate cues, and learned habits that lead to aggression in the presence of appropriate cues even when there is no frustration.

There is a controversy among behavioral scientists about whether aggressive behavior is "natural" (instinctive) or learned. Research with infants and young children shows that tendencies to perceive and react to threat appear quite early. Children actually seem to be more interested in aggressive, violent themes than in friendly ones. One possible explanation may be that such violent themes are more stimulating, hence are more interesting. Some cultures are inclined to encourage aggressive behavior. In contrast to primitive societies, urbanized, industrialized societies appear to encourage more crimes against property and fewer crimes against persons. Within our own society, lower-class members are more likely to engage in aggressive behavior than are middle-class members.

Aggression may be institutionalized or personalized. Institutionalized aggression may take the form of punishment of lawbreakers, warfare, or organized violence. Institutionalized aggression appears legitimate to the society on whose behalf it occurs, whereas personalized aggression does not. Persons who engage in severe forms of personalized aggression are likely to be considered enemies of society, and dealt with accordingly.

Intergroup hostility may take the form of prejudice, whenever society or a cultural group has designated some readily identifiable group as a suitable target for stereotyped, negative attitudes. In most instances the target group is different from the dominant group in a way that is felt to be significant and also appears vulnerable. Prejudiced attitudes are perceived as legitimate and are supported by stereotyped beliefs which are learned, usually during childhood. Furthermore, society generally provides some channel for the expression of hostility toward target persons. Some studies show that differences in belief systems provide the most important basis for prejudice, and that similarity in beliefs may counteract prejudice. However, the fact that dominant groups evaluate targets of prejudice in terms of a stereotyped set of beliefs, and interact with the target individuals as little as possible, makes it difficult for dominant groups to be aware of the similarities that do exist.

Milgram has designed an experiment that shows the lengths to which people will go in expressing aggression, once a suitable target has been identified and a channel has been designated. Subjects were told to shock a "learner" (actually a stooge) at increasingly higher levels for failure to learn a list of words. Most of the subjects followed the instructions of the experimenter, even using shock levels indicated as dangerous. Similar results were obtained when subjects were put in a group with two other "teachers" who suggested continually higher shock levels. Although subjects had the right of veto, most of them tended to go along with the suggestions, although the supposed victim was heard to complain loudly and bitterly about the pain he was suffering. These experimental situations are analogous to that of social prejudice in that the "victim" is perceived as different and inadequate because he has failed. Furthermore, society, in the form of the experimenter of the two stooges, has designated the "victim" as a suitable target for aggression and has indicated the means (electric shock) whereby he will suffer institutionalized and legitimized aggression. In another experiment, subjects watched what they thought was another student being shocked for making mistakes. When told they were powerless to help her, they tended to have

negative attitudes toward the "victim," thus indicating a degree of concurrence with the treatment she was getting.

When groups are threatened by one another, they may engage in active forms of aggressiveness. At such times it becomes difficult for the social scientist to maintain objectivity, particularly if he is identified with one side or another. Social research conducted in the laboratory has obvious advantages at such time, because hostility and aggression can be studied in isolation from the real conflict. Some early research with hostility has shown that it can be reduced by catharsis, that is, through finding some way of expressing it, rather than suppressing or repressing it. More recent research has raised questions about the value of catharsis.

Children learn prejudice from parental attitudes. Parents who punish severely may also encourage antisocial tendencies on the part of their children. Severe punishment results in part from poor impulse control on the part of parents, and children cannot learn to control their aggressive impulses if they do not have adequate models. Although hostility and aggression may be universal, evidence shows that they can be controlled through learning, and that those societies which are best able to reduce the incidence of aggressive behavior are the ones that provide symbolic and indirect ways of expressing it. Social norms in such societies also provide ways through which problems that might otherwise lead to interpersonal aggression are resolved.

One of the difficulties in controlling aggression on the international level through appropriate norms is that groups of nations tend to be less cohesive than national groups. However, some international norms are developing out of nations' need to have some kind of control over their interaction with one another. The opening of channels of communication also has positive effects. Reduction in international aggression will take place to the extent that nations are willing to commit themselves to norm building as a part of developing an organization of nations. This task is likely to be more successful if it is based on positive motives, like the desire for the good life, rather than on negative ones, like the elimination of war or war-makers. These organizations work best when based on such practical motives as the need to have and to observe traffic rules, rather than on obeying moral imperatives.

SUGGESTED READINGS

Allport, G., *The nature of prejudice.* Boston: Beacon, 1954.

Bandura, A. & Walters, R. H., *Social learning and personality development.* New York: Holt, Rinehart, and Winston, 1963.

Berkowitz, L., *Aggression: a social psychological analysis.* New York: McGraw-Hill, 1962.

Buss, A. H., *The psychology of aggression.* New York: Wiley, 1961.

Dollard, J., Doob, L. W., Miller, N. E., & Sears, R. R., *Frustration and aggression.* New Haven: Yale University Press, 1939.

Lindgren, H. C. (Ed.), *Contemporary research in social psychology.* New York: Wiley, 1969. See Section 11, "Aggression and its management."

Stagner, R., *The psychology of industrial conflict.* New York: Wiley, 1956.

Yates, A. J., *Frustration and conflict.* New York: Wiley, 1962.

References and Author Index

Works cited in this book are listed alphabetically by author and year of publication. Numbers in boldface type following each citation refer to the text pages on which the works are cited.

Abegglen, J. C., *see* Warner and Abegglen.

Abrahams, Darcy, *see* Walster et al.

Adems, J. S., Toward an understanding of inequity. *J. abnorm. soc. Psychol.*, 1963, **67**, 422-436. **129**

Ader, R., & Tatum, R., Free-operant avoidance conditioning in individual and paired human subjects. *J. exp. anal. Behavior*, 1963, **6**, 357-359. **93**

Adorno, T. W., Frenkel-Brunswik, Else, Levinson, D. H., & Sanford, R. N., *The authoritarian personality*. N.Y.: Harper, 1950. **77, 89**

Albert, Ethel M., The roles of women: a question of values. In Farber & Wilson, Eds., *The potential of woman*. N.Y.: McGraw-Hill, 1963. **169**

Albrecht, R. B., *see* Crutchfield et al.

Alexander, C. N., Jr., Ordinal position and sociometric status. *Sociometry*, 1966, **29**, 41-51. **185**

Allen, V. L., Effect of knowledge of deception on conformity. *J. soc. Psychol.*, 1966, **69**, 101-106. **100**

Allport, G., *The nature of prejudice*. Boston: Beacon, 1954. **353**

Almond, G. A., & Verba, S., *The civic culture: political attitudes in five nations*. Princeton: Princeton U. Press, 1963. **169, 262**

Altus, W. D., Birth order and academic primogeniture. *J. pers. soc. Psychol.*, 1965, **2**, 872-876. **184**

Ames, E. W., *see* Brennan et al.

Ames, Louise B., Children's stories. *Genet. Psychol. Monogr.*, 1966, **73**, 337-396. **335-336**

Anastasiow, N. J., Success in school and boys' sex-role patterns. *Child Developmt.*, 1965, **36**, 1053-1066. **166**

Anderson, L. R., Leader behavior, member studies, and task performance of intercultural discussion groups. *J. soc. Psychol.*, 1966, **69**, 305-319. **311**

Andrews, J. D. W., The achievement motives and advancement in two types of organizations. *J. pers. soc. Psychol.*, 1967, **6**, 163-168. **85-86**

Argyris, C., *Integrating the individual and the organization*. N.Y.: Wiley, 1964. **322, 330**

Aronson, E., & Mills, J., The effect of severity of initiation on liking for a group. *J. abnorm. soc. Psychol.*, 1959, **59**, 177-181. **14-16, 121**

Aronson, Vera, *see* Walster et al.

Asch, S. A., *Social psychology*. Englewood Cliffs, N.J.: Prentice-Hall, 1952. **112**

Asch, S. A., Studies of independence and conformity. A minority of one against a unanimous majority. *Psychol. Monogr.*, 1956, **70**, No. 9 (Whole No. 416). **97-99, 342**

Asch, S. A., Effects of group pressure upon the modification and distortion of judgments. In Maccoby, Newcomb, and Hartley, eds., *Readings in social psychology*, 3rd ed. N.Y.: Holt, 1958. **98**

Atkinson, J. W., & Feather, N. T., *A theory of achievement motivation*. N.Y.: Wiley, 1966. **89**

Atkinson, J. W., *see also* McClelland & Atkinson, and McClelland et al.

Bachman, J. G., Smith, C. G., & Slesinger, J. A., Control, performance, and satisfaction: an analysis of structural and individual effects. *J. pers. soc. Psychol.*, 1966, **4**, 127-136. **322**

Back, K. W., Influence through social communication. *J. abnorm. soc. Psychol.*, 1951, **46**, 9-23. **255, 257**

Back, K. W., *see also* Festinger et al., 1950.

Bacon, Margaret K., Child, I. L., & Barry, H., III, A cross-cultural study of correlates of crime. *J. abnorm. soc. Psychol.*, 1963, **66**, 291-300. **337-338**

Bagby, J. W., A cross-cultural study of perceptual predominance in binocular rivalry. *J. abnorm. soc. Psychol.*, 1957, **54**, 331-334. **34**

Bailey, W., Hustmyer, F. E. & Kristofferson, A. B., Visual perception of the vertical by alcoholics. *Amer. Psychologist*, 1959, **14**, 394. (Abstract) **195**

Bales, R. F., Task roles and social roles in problem-solving groups. In Steiner & Fishbein, Eds., *Current studies in social psychology*. N.Y.: Holt, Rinehart, & Winston, 1965. **264, 305**

Ballachey, E. L., *see* Krech et al.

Bandura, A., & McDonald, F. J., Influence of social reinforcement and the behavior of models in shaping children's moral judgments. *J. abnorm. soc. Psychol.*, 1963, **67**, 274-281. **59-60**

Bandura, A., & Walters, R. H., *Social learning and personality development.* N.Y.: Holt, Rinehart, & Winston, 1963. **58, 61, 63, 67, 297, 306, 334, 349**

Banta, T. J., & Hetherington, Mavis, Relations between needs of friends and fiances, *J. abnorm. soc. Psychol.,* 1963, **66**, 401-404. **47**

Barclay, J., *see* Kelman and Barclay.

Barrett, D., *see* Bavelas & Barrett.

Barron, F., *Creativity and psychological health.* Princeton: Van Nostrand, 1963. **112**

Barry, H., III, *see* Bacon et al.

Bartlett, F. C., *Remembering.* Cambridge: Cambridge U. Press, 1932. **32**

Baruch, Dorothy, *New ways in discipline.* N.Y.: McGraw-Hill, 1949. **297**

Bass, B., Authoritarianism or acquiescence? *J. abnorm. soc. Psychol.,* 1955, **51**, 616-623. **79**

Bass, B. M., *Leadership, psychology, and organizational behavior.* N.Y.: Harper, 1960. **289, 292**

Bass, B. & Dunteman, G. H., Behavior in groups as a function of self-, interaction, and task orientation, *J. abnorm. soc. Psychol.,* 1963, **66**, 419-428. **166, 319-320**

Bass, B. M., *see also* Petrullo & Bass and Berg & Bass.

Bateson, N., *see* Schopler & Bateson.

Bauer, R. A., The obstinate audience: the influence process from the point of view of social communication. *Amer. Psychologist,* 1964, **19**, 319-328. **224-225**

Bavelas, A., Communication patterns in task-oriented groups. *J. Acoust. Soc. Amer.,* 1950, **22**, 725-730. **274-276**

Bavelas, A., & Barrett, D., An experimental approach to organizational communication. *Personnel,* 1951, **27**, 366-371. **275**

Baxter, J. C., Lerner, M. J., & Miller, J. S., Identification as a function of the reinforcing quality of the model and the socialization background of the subject. *J. pers. soc. Psychol.,* 1965, **2**, 692-697. **338-339**

Bayley, G. A., *see* Vidulich & Bayley.

Bechtel, R. B., & Rosenfeld, H. M., Expectations of social acceptance and compatibility as related to status discrepancy and social motive. *J. pers. soc. Psychol.,* 1966, **3**, 344-349. **89**

Beer, M., *Leadership, employee needs, and motivation.* Ohio State U., Bureau of Business Research. Monogr. No. 129, 1966. **301, 311**

Behringer, R. D., *see* Ziller et al.

Beisser, P. T., et al., *Classification of disorganized families for use in family oriented diagnosis and treatment.* N.Y.: Community Research Assoc., 1953. **47**

Bem, D. J., *see* Wallach et al.

Benedict, Ruth, *Patterns of culture.* Boston: Houghton Mifflin, 1934. **13, 62**

Bennett, E. L., Diamond, M. C., Krech, D., & Rosenzweig, M. R., Chemical and anatomical plasticity of brain. *Science,* 1964, **146**, 610-619. **25-26**

Berg, I. A. & Bass, B. M. (Eds.), *Conformity and deviation.* N.Y.: Harper, 1961. **201**

Bergum, B. O., & Lehr, D. J., Effects of authoritarianism on vigilance performance. *J. appl. Psychol.,* 1963, **47**, 75-77. **93**

Berkowitz, L., The expression and reduction of hostility. *Psychol. Bull.,* 1958. **55**, 257- 283, **334**

Berkowitz, L., *Aggression: a social psychological analysis.* N.Y.: McGraw-Hill, 1962. **347, 353**

Berkowitz, L., The concept of aggressive drive: some additional considerations. In L. Berkowitz, Ed., *Advances in experimental social psychology.* N.Y.: Academic, 1965. **334**

Berkowitz, L., & Daniels, Louise R., Responsibility and dependency. *J. abnorm. soc. Psychol.,* 1963, **66**, 429-436. **257**

Berlyne, D. E., *Conflict, arousal, and curiosity.* N.Y.: McGraw-Hill, 1960. **38**

Berlyne, D. E., Curiosity and exploration, *Science,* 1966, **153**, 25-33. **25**

Berrien, F. K., Japanese vs. American values, *J. soc. Psychol.,* 1965, **65**, 181-191. **218**

Berrien, F. K., Japanese values and the democratic process. *J. soc. Psychol.,* 1966, **68**, 129-138. **218**

Berry, P. C., *see* Taylor et al.

Bettelheim, B. & Janowitz, M., *Dynamics of prejudice.* N.Y.: Harper, 1950. **340**

Binger, C. A. L., Emotional disturbances among college women. In Blaine & McArthur, Eds., *Emotional problems of the student.* N.Y.: Appleton-Century-Crofts, 1961. **172, 175**

Birch, H. G., *see* Clark & Birch.

Bishop, D. W., *see* Julian et al.

Bixenstine, V. E. & Wilson, K. V., Effects of level of cooperative choice by the other player on choices in a prisoner's dilemma game. Part II. *J. abnorm. soc. Psychol.,* 1963, **67**, 139-148. **283**

Block, C. H., *see* Taylor et al.

Block, J. A., A study of affective responses in a lie-detection situation. *J. abnorm. soc. Psychol.,* 1957, **55**, 11-15. **195**

Blumen, G., *see* Mouren et al.

Bolen, M. E., *see* Goldman et al.

Bond, Betty W., Group discussion-decision: an appraisal of its use in health education. Minneapolis: Minnesota Dept. of Health, 1956. **326**

Bonk, W. J., *see* Lachman et al.

Borum, Elizabeth A., & Livson, N., Mental test score changes at kindergarten entry, *J. exper. Educ.,* 1965, **34**, 89-91. **26**

Bradburn, N. M., N achievement and father dominance in Turkey, *J. abnorm. soc. Psychol.*, 1963, **67**, 464-468. **85**

Breed, W., Suicide, migration, and race: a study of cases in New Orleans. *J. soc. Issues*, 1966, **22**(1), 30-43. **16-17**

Breedlove, J., *see* Levinger & Breedlove.

Brehm, J. W., Motivational effects of cognitive dissonance. In M. R. Jones, Ed., *Nebraska symposium on motivation*. Lincoln: U. of Nebraska Press, 1962. **119-120**

Brehm, J. W. & Cohen, A. R., *Explorations in cognitive dissonance*. N.Y.: Wiley, 1962. **116, 117, 128, 129**

Brehm, J. W. & Cole, Ann H., Effect of a favor that reduces freedom. *J. pers. soc. Psychol.*, 1966, **3**, 420-426. **105**

Brehm, J. W., & Sensenig, J., Social influence as a function of attempted and implied usurpation of choice. *J. pers. soc. Psychol.*, 1966, **4**, 703-707. **242**

Brennan, W. M., Ames, E. W., & Moore, R. W., Age differences in infants' attention to patterns of different complexities. *Science*, 1966, **151**, 354-356. **25-26**

Bronfenbrenner, U., Socialization and social class through time and space. In Maccoby, Newcomb, & Hartley, Eds., *Readings in social psychology*, 3rd ed. N.Y.: Holt, 1958. **143-144**

Brooks, J., *The great leap: from the Old World of 1939 to the New Era*. N.Y.: Harper & Row, 1966. **142**

Broughton, A., *see* Efran & Broughton.

Brown, D. G., Sex-role development in a changing culture. *Psychol. Bull.*, 1958, **54**, 232-242. **172**

Brown, D. G., Sex-role preference in children: methodological problems. *Psychol. Rep.*, 1962, **11**, 477-478. **172**

Brown, R., A determinant of the relationship between rigidity and authoritarianism. *J. abnorm. soc. Psychol.*, 1953, **48**, 469-476. **80**

Brown, R., *Words and things*. Glencoe, Ill.: Free Press, 1958. **244**

Brownfield, C. A., *Isolation: clinical and experimental approaches*. N.Y.: Random House, 1965. **29, 38**

Buckhout, R., Changes in heart rate accompanying attitude change. *J. pers. soc. Psychol.*, 1966, **4**, 695-699. **241**

Burgess, M., *see* Hokanson et al.

Burtt, H. E., *see* Fleishman et al.

Buss, A. H., *The psychology of aggression*. N.Y.: Wiley, 1961. **334**

Butler, J., *see* Levine & Butler.

Byrne, D., Parental antecedents of authoritarianism. *J. pers. soc. Psychol.*, 1965, **1**, 369-373. **80**

Byrne, D., & Clore, G. L., Jr., Effectance arousal and attraction. *J. pers. soc. Psychol.*, 1967, **6**, No. 4, Part 2 (monogr.). **51**

Byrne, D. & Griffitt, W., A developmental investigation of the law of attraction. *J. pers. soc. Psychol.*, 1966, **4**, 699-702. **45-46**

Byrne, D., & McGraw, C., Interpersonal attraction toward Negroes. *Hum. Relat.*, 1964, **17**, 201-213. **46**

Byrne, D. & Wong, T. J., Racial prejudice, interpersonal attraction, and assumed similarity of attitudes. *J. abnorm. soc. Psychol.*, 1962, **65**, 246-253. **6, 46, 340**

Byrne, D., *see also* Worchel & Byrne.

Calvin, A. D., Social reinforcement, *J. soc. Psychol.*, 1962, **66**, 15-19. **56, 58**

Campbell, D. T., Social attitudes and other acquired behavioral dispositions. In S. Koch, Ed., *Psychology: a study of a science. Vol. 6. Investigations of man as a socius.* N.Y.: McGraw-Hill, 1963. **71-72**

Campbell, D. T., Ethnocentrism and other altruistic motives. In D. Levine, Ed., *Nebraska symposium on motivation*. Lincoln: U. of Nebraska Press, 1965. **345-346**

Campbell, D. T., *see also* N. Miller et al.

Campbell, J., *see* Dunnette et al.

Cantril, H., *The "why" of man's experience*. N.Y.: Macmillan, 1950. **32**

Carlsmith, J. M., Collins, B. E., & Helmreich, R. K., Studies in forced compliance: I. The effect of pressure for compliance on attitude change produced by face-to-face role playing and anonymous essay writing. *J. pers. soc. Psychol.*, 1966, **5**, 1-13. **116-117**

Carlsmith, J. M., *see also* Festinger & Carlsmith.

Carroll, Eleanor E., *see* Kohn & Carroll.

Carroll, J. B., *The study of language*. Cambridge: Harvard U. Press, 1953. **244**

Carter, L. F., Haythorn, W. & Howell, M. A., A further investigation of the criteria of leadership. *J. abnorm. soc. Psychol.*, 1950, **45**, 350-358. **291**

Cartwright, A. & Zander, A. (Eds.) *Group dynamics: research and theory*, 2nd ed. N.Y.: Harper & Row, 1960. **267**

Centers, R., *The psychology of the social classes*. Princeton: Princeton U. Press, 1949. **136, 137**

Centers, R., *see also* MacKinnon & Centers.

Chammah, A. M., *see* Rapoport & Chammah.

Chance, M. R. A. & Mead, A. P., Competition between feeding and investigation in the rat. *Behaviour*, 1955, **8**, 174-182. **25**

Chapanis, Natalia P. & Chapanis, A. C., Cognitive dissonance: five years later. *Psychol. Bull.*, 1964, **61**, 1-22. **129**

Chatterjee, B. B., *see* Gage et al.

Chave, E. J., *see* Thurstone & Chave.

Chiaravallo, G., *see* Wells et al.

Child, I. L., *see* Bacon et al.

Christie, R., Eysenck's treatment of the personality of Communists. Psychol. Bull., 1956, **53**, 439-451. **78**

Christie, R. & Jahoda, Marie (Eds.) *Studies in the scope and method of "The authoritarian personality."* Glencoe, Ill.: Free Press, 1954. **89**

Christie, R., *see also* Klineberg & Christie.

Church, C., *see* Coopersmith et al.

Clark, G. & Birch, H. G., Hormonal modification of social behavior. *Psychosom. Med.*, 1946, **8**, 320-331. **170**

Clark, R. A., *see* McClelland et al.

Clore, G. L., Jr., *see* Byrne & Clore.

Cohen, A. R., *see* Brehm & Cohen and Zimbardo et al.

Cohen, J., *see* Riessman et al.

Cohen, M. F., *see* Hokanson et al.

Cole, Ann H., *see* Brehm & Cole.

Collins, B. E. & Guetzkow, H., *A social psychology of group processes for decision-making.* N.Y.: Wiley, 1964. **285**

Collins, B. E., *see also* Carlsmith et al., and Helmreich & Collins.

Collomb, H., Zempleni, A. & Storper, D., Some considerations on role, status and human relations in Black Africa. Unpublished paper read at Amer. Psychol. Assn. convention at Philadelphia, September, 1965. **177**

Combs, A. W. & Snygg, D., *Individual behavior*, rev. ed. N.Y.: Harper, 1959. **188, 191-192, 335**

Consalvi, C., *see* Harvey & Consalvi.

Cooley, C. H., *Human nature and the social order.* N.Y.: Scribners, 1902. (Reprinted by Free Press, New York, 1956) **29, 187**

Cooley, C. H., *Social organization.* N.Y.: Scribner, 1909. **260**

Coombs, R. H. & Kenkel, W. F., Sex differences in dating aspirations and satisfaction with computer-selected partners. *J. Marriage Faml.*, 1966, **28**, 62-66. **43**

Coons, A. E., *see* Stogdill & Coons.

Cooper, J., *see* Linder et al.

Coopersmith, S., Church, C. & Markowitz, J., Creativity and social class. Unpubl. paper read at April 1960 meeting of Eastern Psychol. Assn. **148**

Couch, A. & Keniston, K., Yeasayers and naysayers: agreeing response set as a personality variable. *J. abnorm. soc. Psychol.*, 1960, **60**, 151-174. **79**

Creelman, Marjorie B., *The experimental investigation of meaning.* N.Y.: Springer, 1966. **244**

Crutchfield, R. S., Conformity and character. *Amer. Psychologist*, 1955, **10**, 191-198. **99-100, 101, 102**

Crutchfield, R. S., Woodworth, D. G., & Albrecht, R. B., USAF WADC Tech. Rep., 1958, No. 58-60. (ASTIA Document No. AD 151 039). **196**

Crutchfield, R. S., *see also* Krech & Crutchfield and Krech et al.

Culbertson, Frances M., Modification of an emotionally held attitude through role playing. *J. abnorm. soc. Psychol.*, 1957, **54**, 230-233. **118**

Dabbs, J. M., Jr. & Leventhal, H., Effects of varying the recommendations in a fear-arousing communication. *J. pers. soc. Psychol.*, 1966, **4**, 525-531. **108**

D'Andrade, R. G., *see* Rosen & D'Andrade.

Danziger, K., Independence training and social class in Java, Indonesia. *J. soc. Psychol.*, 1960a, **51**, 65-74. **146**

Danziger, K., Parental demands and social class in Java, Indonesia. *J. soc. Psychol.*, 1960b, **51**, 75-86. **146**

Davis, A. H., *see* Shomer et al.

deCharms, R., Affiliation motivation and productivity in small groups. *J. abnorm. soc. Psychol.*, 1957, **55**, 222-226. **279**

Delgado, J. R., Cerebral heterostimulation in a monkey colony. *Science*, 1963, **141**, 161-163. **167**

Dember, W. N., Birth order and need affiliation. *J. abnorm. soc. Psychol.*, 1964, **68**, 555-557. **183**

Dennis, W., Uses of common objects as indicators of cultural orientations. *J. abnorm. soc. Psychol.*, 1957, **55**, 21-28. **212-213**

Dennis, W., *Group values through children's drawings.* N.Y.: Wiley, 1966. **220**

Dennis, W., The mental growth of certain foundlings before and after adoption. Unpublished paper, 1967. **27-28**

DeSoto, C., Kuethe, J. L. & Wunderlich, R., Social perception and the self-perception of high and low authoritarians. *J. soc. Psychol.*, 1960, **52**, 149-155. **80**

Deutsch, M., Trust, trustworthiness, and the F scale. *J. abnorm. soc. Psychol.*, 1960, **61**, 138-140. **283**

Deutsch, M., Cooperation and trust: some theoretical notes. In M. R. Jones (Ed.), *Nebraska symposium on motivation.* Lincoln: U. of Nebraska Press, 1962. **285**

Deutsch, M., *see also* Krauss & Deutsch.

Deutsch, M. & Krauss, R. M., The effect of threat upon interpersonal bargaining. *J. abnorm. soc. Psychol.*, 1960, **61**, 181-189. **283-284**

Deutsch, M. & Krauss, R. M., *Theories in social psychology.* N.Y.: Basic Books, 1965. **20**

De Vos, G., *see* Norbeck & De Vos.

Diamond, M. C., *see* Bennett et al.

Dickson, W. J., *see* Roethlisberger & Dickson.

Diggory, J. C., *Self-evaluation: concepts and studies.* N.Y.: Wiley, 1966. **201**

Dodson, J. D., *see* Yerkes & Dodson.

Dollard, J., Doob, L. W., Miller, N. E., Mowrer, O. H. & Sears, R. R., *Frustration and aggression.* New Haven: Yale U. Press, 1939. **297, 334, 346**

Domhoff, B., *see* Hall & Domhoff.

Doob, L. W., *see* Dollard et al.

Dornbusch, S. M., *see* Miyamoto & Dornbusch.

Dowart, W., Ezerman, R., Lewis, M. & Rosenhan, D., The effect of brief social deprivation on social and nonsocial reinforcement. *J. pers. soc. Psychol.*, 1965, **2**, 111-115. **57-58**

Dubin, R., Homans, G. C., Mann, F. C., & Miller, D. C., *Leadership and productivity.* San Francisco: Chandler, 1965. **311**

Dunn, R. E. & Goldman, M., Competition and noncompetition in relationship to satisfaction and feelings toward own-group and nongroup members. *J. soc. Psychol.*, 1966, **68**, 299-311. **281**

Dunnette, M. D., Campbell, J. & Jaastad, K., The effect of group participation on brainstorming effectiveness for two industrial samples. *J. appl. Psychol.*, 1963, **47**, 30-37. **94, 271**

Dunteman, G. H., *see* Bass & Dunteman.

Eells, K., *see* Warner et al.

Efran, J. S. & Broughton, A., Effect of expectancies for social approval on visual behavior. *J. pers. soc. Psychol.*, 1966, **4**, 103-107. **102**

Eisenman, R., Scapegoating and social control. *J. Psychol.*, 1965, **61**, 203-209. **110**

Elkind, D., Review of B. Reymond-Rivier, *Le developpment social de l'enfant et de l'adolescent. Contemp. Psychol.*, 1967, **12**, 8-9. **209**

Elliott, R., Interrelationships among measures of field dependence, ability and personal traits. *J. abnorm. soc. Psychol.*, 1961, **63**, 27-36. **196**

Elms, A. C., Influence of fantasy ability on attitude change through role playing. *J. pers. soc. Psychol.*, 1966, **4**, 36-43. **106-107, 117-118, 326**

Empey, L-M. T. & Erickson, M. L., Hidden delinquency and social status. *Soc. Forces*, 1966, **44**, 546-554. **157**

Endler, N., Conformity as a function of different reinforcement schedules. *J. pers. soc. Psychol.*, 1966, **4**, 175-180. **100-101**

Epstein, R., Authoritarianism, displaced aggression, and social status of the target. *J. pers. soc. Psychol.*, 1965, **2**, 585-589. **80**

Epstein, R., Aggression toward outgroups as a function of aggressive models. *J. pers. soc. Psychol.*, 1966, **3**, 574-579. **80**

Epstein, R. & Komorita, S. S., Prejudice among Negro children as related to parental ethnocentrism and punitiveness. *J. pers. soc. Psychol.*, 1966, **4**, 643-647. **348-349**

Erickson, M. L., *see* Empey & Erickson.

Ervin, Susan M., Language and TAT content in bilinguals. *J. abnorm. soc. Psychol.*, 1964, **68**, 500-507. **232**

Exline, R. V., Group climate as a factor in the relevance and accuracy of social perception. *J. abnorm. soc. Psychol.*, 1957, **55**, 382-388. **258, 168**

Exline, R., Gray, D., & Schuette, D., Visual behavior in a dyad as affected by interview content and sex of respondent. *J. pers. soc. Psychol.*, 1965, **1**, 201-209. **166**

Ezerman, R., *see* Dowart et al.

Farber, S. M. & Wilson, R. H. L. Eds., *The potential of woman.* N.Y.: McGraw-Hill, 1963. **178**

Farrell, F. M., *see* Roby et al.

Feather, N. T., *see* Atkinson & Feather.

Feld, Sheila, *see* Gurin et al.

Ferson, Jean E., *see* Kelly et al.

Feshbach, S., The drive-reducing function of fantasy behavior. *J. abnorm. soc. Psychol.*, 1955, **50**, 3-11. **347**

Feshbach, S., *see also* Janis & Feshbach.

Festinger, L., *A theory of cognitive dissonance.* Evanston, Ill.: Row, Peterson, 1957. **14, 115-116, 128, 129**

Festinger, L., The psychological effects of insufficient rewards. *Amer. Psychologist*, 1961, **16**, 1-11. **121**

Festinger, L., *Conflict, decision, and dissonance.* Stanford: Stanford U. Press, 1964. **129**

Festinger, L. & Carlsmith, J. M., Cognitive consequences of forced compliance. *J. abnorm. soc. Psychol.*, 1959, **58**, 203-210. **116, 117, 119**

Festinger, L., Schachter, S. & Back, K. W., *Social pressure in informal groups.* N.Y.: Harper, 1950. **48, 51, 254**

Fiedler, F. E., Interpersonal perception and group effectiveness. In Tagiuri & Petrullo, Eds., *Person perception and interpersonal behavior.* Stanford: Stanford U. Press, 1958. **298-299**

Fiedler, F. E., The contingency model: a theory of leadership effectiveness. In Proshansky & Seidenberg, Eds., *Basic studies in social psychology.* N.Y.: Holt, Rinehart, & Winston, 1965. **301-303, 305, 320**

Fiedler, F. E., *Theory of leadership effectiveness.* N.Y.: McGraw-Hill, 1967. **311**

Fiedler, F. E. & Meuwese, W. A. T., Leader's contribution to task performance in cohesive and uncohesive groups. *J. abnorm. soc. Psychol.*, 1963, **67**, 83-87. **305**

Fiedler, F. E., *see also* Julian et al.

Fillenbaum, S., Review of Sheldon Rosenberg, Ed., *Directions in psycholinguistics. Contemp. Psychol.*, 1966, **11**, 243-244. **233-234**

Firestone, I., *see* Zimbardo et al.

Fisher, Rhoda L., Social schema of normal and disturbed school children. *J. educ. Psychol.*, 1967, **58**, 88-92. **254**

Fitzsimmons, S. J. & Marcuse, F. L., Adjustment in leaders and non-leaders as measured by the sentence completion projective technique. *J. clin. Psychol.*, 1961, **17**, 380-381. **298**

Fleishman, E. A., Harris, E. F. & Burtt, H. E., *Leadership and supervision in industry: an evaluation of a supervisory training program.* Ohio State U., Bureau of Business Research. Monogr. No. 33, 1955. **301**

Foster, G. M., *Tzintzuntzan: Mexican peasants in a changing world.* Boston: Little Brown, 1967. **278**

Fraser, S. C., *see* Freedman & Fraser.

Freedman, J. L. & Fraser, S. C., Compliance without pressure: the foot-in-the-door technique. *J. pers. soc. Psychol.*, 1966, **4**, 195-202. **106**

French, D., The relationship of anthropology to studies in perception and cognition. In S. Koch, *Psychology: a study of a science. Vol. 6. Investigations of man as a socius.* N.Y.: McGraw-Hill, 1963. **205**

Frenkel-Brunswik, Else, *see* Adorno et al.

Freud, Anna, *The ego and mechanisms of defense.* N.Y.: International Universities Press, 1946. **201**

Freud, S., *Beyond the pleasure principle.* London: Hogarth, 1955. **335**

Gage, N. L., Runkel, P. J. & Chatterjee, B. B., Changing teacher behavior through feedback from pupils: an application of equilibrium theory. In Charters & Gage, Eds., *Readings in the social psychology of education.* Boston: Allyn & Bacon, 1963. **309**

Galbraith, J. K., *The affluent society.* Boston: Houghton Mifflin, 1958. **4-5**

Gallo, P., *see* McClintock et al.

Garfield, S. L. & Helper, M. M., Parental attitudes and socio-economic status. *J. clin. Psychol.*, 1962, **18**, 171-175. **148**

Garfield, S. L., *see* Helper & Garfield.

Getzels, J. W. & Jackson, P. W., *Creativity and intelligence.* N.Y.: Wiley, 1963. **112**

Ghiselli, E. E., Psychological properties of groups and group learning. *Psychol. Rep.*, 1966, **19**, 17-18. **273, 320**

Ghiselli, E. E. & Lodahl, T. M., Patterns of managerial traits and group effectiveness, *J. abnorm. soc. Psychol.*, 1958, **57**, 61-66. **272-273**

Ghiselli, E. E., *see also* Haire et al.

Glueck, S. & Eleanor, *Unravelling juvenile delinquency.* N.Y. Commonwealth Fund, 1950. **152-153**

Goldberg, M. H. & Maccoby, Eleanor E., Children's acquisition of skill in performing a group task under two conditions of group formation. *J. pers. soc. Psychol.*, 1965, **2**, 898-902. **251**

Goldman, M., Bolen, M. E. & Martin, R. B., Some conditions under which groups operate and how this affects their performance. *J. soc. Psychol.*, 1961, **54**, 47-56. **297**

Goldman, M., *see* Dunn & Goldman.

Goldman, S., *see* Wells et al.

Gollin, E. S., Organizational characteristics of social judgment: a developmental investigation. *J. Pers.*, 1958, **26**, 139-154. **147**

Goodchilds, J. D., *see* Ziller et al.

Goodenough, D. R., *see* Witkin et al. 1959.

Gordon L. V., Values of the Peace Corps volunteer, *Psychol. Rep.*, 1966, **18**, 328. **198**

Gordon, L. W. & Medland, F. F., The cross-group stability of peer ratings of leadership potential. *Personnel Psychol.*, 1965, **18**, 173-177. **311**

Gordon, T., *Group-centered leadership.* Boston: Houghton Mifflin, 1955. **311**

Gottschaldt, K. Ueber den Enfluss der Erfahrung auf die Wahrnehmung von Figuren, I: Ueber den Einfluss gehäufter Einprägung von Figuren auf ihre Sichtbarkeit in umfassenden Konfigurationen. *Psychol. Forschung.*, 1926, **8**, 261-317. **194**

Gouldner, A. W., Ed., *Studies in leadership.* N.Y.: Harper, 1951. **307**

Gray, D., *see* Exline et al.

Green, R. L., After school integration—what? Problems in school learning. *Personnel Guid. J.*, 1966, **44**, 704-710. **150**

Griffitt, W., *see* Byrne & Griffitt.

Grinder, R. E., & McMichael, R. E., Cultural influences on conscience development: resistance to temptation and guilt among Samoans and American Caucasians. *J. abnorm. soc. Psychol.*, 1963, **66**, 503-507. **109-110**

Gross, N., Mason, W. S., & McEachern, A. W., *Explorations in role analysis: studies of the school superintendency role.* N.Y.: Wiley, 1958. **175, 178**

Gruen, W., Composition and some correlates of the American core culture. Mimeographed publication by the author, 1964. **215-216**

Gruen, W., Composition and some correlates of the American core culture. *Psychol. Rep.*, 1966, **18**, 483-486. **215**

Grusec, Joan, & Mischel, W., Model's characteristics as determinants of social learning. *J. pers. soc. Psychol.*, 1966, **4**, 211-215. **66**

Guetzkow, H., *see* Collins & Guetzkow.

Guhl, A. M., Heterosexual dominance and mating behavior in chickens. *Behaviour*, 1949, **2**, 106-120. **170**

Guilford, J. P., *Personality.* N.Y.: McGraw-Hill, 1959. **271**

Guin, P., *see* Mouren et al.

Gurin, G., Veroff J. & Feld, Sheila, *Americans view their mental health.* N.Y.: Basic Books, 1960. **317**

Guttman, L., The basis for scalogram analysis. In Stouffer et al., Eds., *Measurement and prediction.* Princeton: Princeton U. Press, 1950. **76**

Gynther, M. D., *see* McDonald & Gynther.

Haas, H. I. & Maehr, M. L., Two experiments on the concept of self and the reaction of others. *J. pers. soc. Psychol.*, 1965, **1**, 100-105. **307-308**

Haggard, E. A., Isolation and personality. In Worchel & Byrne, Eds., *Personality change.* N.Y.: Wiley, 1964. **38**

Haire, M., Ghiselli, E. E., & Porter, L. W., *Managerial thinking: an international study.* N.Y.: Wiley, 1966. **317-318**

Hall, C. & Domhoff, B., A ubiquitous sex difference in dreams. *J. abnorm. soc. Psychol.*, 1963, **66**, 278-280. **172**

Hall, E. T., Jr., The anthropology of manners. *Sci. Amer.*, 1955, **192**(4), 84-90. **230**

Hall, E. T., Jr., *The silent language.* N.Y.: Doubleday, 1959. **170**

Hamblin, R. L., *see* Miller & Hamblin.

Hancock, Francena T., *see* Sampson & Hancock.

Hardyke, Jane A., *see* Stein et al.

Harlow, H. F., The heterosexual affectional system in monkeys. *Amer. Psychologist*, 1962, **17**, 1-9. **170-171**

Harris, E. F., *see* Fleishman et al.

Harrison, A. A., *see* McClintock et al.

Harvey, O. J. & Consalvi, C., Status and conformity to pressures in informal groups. *J. abnorm. soc. Psychol.*, 1960, **60**, 182-187. **298**

Hayakawa, S. I., *Language in thought and action.* N.Y.: Harcourt, Brace, 1950. **234**

Haythorn, W., *see* Carter et al.

Hebb, D. O., Drives and C.N.S. (conceptual nervous system). *Psychol. Rev.*, 1955a, **62**, 243-254. **30, 38, 108, 253, 281**

Hebb, D. O., The mammal and his environment. *Amer. J. Psychiat.*, 1955b, **111**, 826-831. **38, 214**

Heider, F., Attitudes and cognitive organization. *J. Psychol.*, 1946, **21**, 107-112. **121-122**

Heider, F., *The psychology of interpersonal relations.* N.Y.: Wiley, 1958. **121-122, 129**

Heintz, R. K., *see* Preston & Heintz.

Helmreich, R. L., & Collins, B. E., Situational determinants of affiliation preference under stress. *J. pers. soc. Psychol.*, 1967, **6**, 79-85. **36**

Helmreich, R. L., *see* Carlsmith et al.

Helper, M. M. & Garfield, S. L., Use of the semantic differential to study acculturation in American Indian adolescents. *J. pers. soc. Psychol.*, 1965, **2**, 817-822. **237**

Helper, M. M., *see* Garfield & Helper.

Hereford, C. F., Selz, N., Stenning, W., & Natalicio, L., A cross-cultural comparison of the active-passive dimension of social attitudes. *Interamer. J. Psychol.*, 1967, **1**, 33-39. **62**

Hess, R. D., Educability and rehabilitation: the future of the welfare class. *J. Marriage Faml.*, 1964, **26**, 422-429. **144**

Hetherington, Mavis, *see* Banta & Hetherington.

Hitchcock, J. T., *see* Minturn & Hitchcock.

Hoffer, E., *The true believer.* N.Y.: Harper, 1951. **35, 293**

Hoffman, L. R. & Maier, N. R. F. Quality and acceptance of problem solutions by members of homogeneous and heterogeneous groups. *J. abnorm. soc. Psychol.*, 1961, **62**, 401-407. **263**

Hoffman, L. R., & Maier, N. R. F. Valence in the adoption of solutions by problem-solving groups: II. Quality and acceptance as goals of leaders and members. *J. pers. soc. Psychol.*, 1967, **6**, 175-182. **290**

Hoijer, H. Ed., *Language in culture.* Chicago: U. of Chicago Press, 1954. **244**

Hokanson, J., Burgess, M., & Cohen, M. F. Effects of displaced aggression on systolic blood pressure. *J. abnorm. soc. Psychol.*, 1963, **67**, 214-218. **347**

Hollingshead, A. B., *Elmtown's youth.* N.Y.: Wiley, 1949. **136, 139, 141, 148**

Hollingshead, A. B., & Redlich, F. C., *Social class and mental illness.* N.Y.: Wiley, 1958. **148**

Holmes, Alice, Sociometric study of neighborhood play group. San Francisco State College, unpublished, 1963. **50**

Holmes, D. S., Effects of overt aggression on level of physiological arousal. *J. pers. soc. Psychol.*, 1966, **4**, 189-194. **347**

Holt, R. R., Forcible indoctrination and personality change. In Worchel & Byrne, Eds., *Personality change.* N.Y.: Wiley, 1964. **112**

Holtzman, W. H., *see* Kelly et al.

Homans, G. C., The human group. N.Y.: Harcourt Brace, 1950. **48, 267**

Homans, G. C., Group factors in worker productivity. In Proshansky & Seidenberg, Eds., *Basic studies in social psychology.* N.Y.: Holt, Rinehart, & Winston, 1965. **299-300**

Homans, G. C., *see also* Dublin et al.

Horney, K., *Our inner conflicts.* N.Y.: Norton, 1945. **333**

Houlihan, Nancy, *see* Kuhlen & Houlihan.

Howard, A., *see* McCord et al.

Howell, M. A., *see* Carter et al.

Hsu, F. L. K., American core value and national character. In F. L. K. Hsu, Ed., *Psychological anthropology: approaches to culture and personality.* Homewood, Ill.: Dorsey, 1961. **207**

Hustmyer, F. E., *see* Bailey et al.

Hyman, H., *see* Katz & Hyman.

Immergluck, L., Resistance to an optical illusion, figural after effects, and field dependence. *Psychonom. Sci.*, 1966, **6**, 281-282. **195**

Inkeles, A., Sociology and psychology. In S. Koch, Ed., *Psychology a study of a science. Vol. 6. Investigations of man as a socius.* N.Y.: McGraw-Hill, 1963. **206**

Izard, C. E., Personality similarity and friendship. *J. abnorm. soc. Psychol.*, 1960, **61**, 47-51. **47**

Izard, C. E., Personality similarity and friendship: a follow-up study. *J. abnorm. soc. Psychol.*, 1963, **66**, 598-600. **47**

Jaastad, K., *see* Dunnette et al.

Jackson, J., *see* Rosenfeld & Jackson.

Jackson, P. W., *see* Getzels & Jackson.

Jacques, E., *The changing culture of a factory.* London: Tavistock, 1951. **328**

Jahoda, Marie, *see* Christie & Jahoda.

Janis, I. L., & Feshbach, S., Effects of fear-arousing communications. *J. abnorm. soc. Psychol.*, 1953, **48**, 78-92. **107-108**

Janis, I. L., & Terwilliger, R., An experimental study of psychological resistance to fear-arousing communications. *J. abnorm. soc. Psychol.*, 1962, **65**, 403-410. **108**

Janowitz, M., *see* Bettelheim & Janowitz.

Jenkins, J. G., Nominating technique as a way of evaluating air group morale. *J. Aviat. Med.*, 1948, **19**, 12-19. **50-51**

Jenkins, W. O., & Stanley, J. C., Partial reinforcement: a review and critique. *Psychol. Bull.*, 1950, **47**, 193-234. **23**

Jennings, Helen H., *Leadership and isolation.* N.Y.: Longmans Green, 1950. **51**

Jessor, R., *see* Roberts & Jessor.

Jolly, A., Lemur social behavior and primate intelligence. *Science*, 1966, **153**, 501-506. **24**

Jones, D. R., Steel pioneers method of solving hot issues before real bargaining. *Wall Street J.*, Feb. 15, 1963, **58** (No. 33). **325**

Jones, E. E., Conformity as a tactic of ingratiation. *Science*, 1965, **149**, 144-150. **103-105**

Jones, E. E., *see also* Linder et al.

Jones, E. S., College graduates and their later success. U. of Buffalo Studies, 1956, **22**, No. 4. **185**

Jones, H. E., The environment and mental development. In L. Carmichael, Ed., *Manual of child psychology,* 2nd ed. N.Y.: Wiley, 1954. **184**

Julian, J. W., Bishop, D. W., & Fiedler, F. E., Quasi-therapeutic effects of intergroup competition. *J. pers. soc. Psychol.*, 1966, **3**, 321-327. **281**

Kaess, W. A., *see* Witryol & Kaess.

Kahn, M., The physiology of catharsis. *J. pers. soc. Psychol.*, 1966, **3**, 278-286. **347**

Kahn, R. L., Wolfe, D. M., Quinn, R. P., Snoek, J. D., & Rosenthal, R. A., *Organizational stress: studies in role conflict.* N.Y.: Wiley, 1964. **175**

Kahn, R. L., *see also* Katz & Kahn.

Kalish, R. A., *see* Kiessling & Kalish.

Kaplan, B., Ed., *Studying personality cross-culturally.* Evanston: Row, Peterson, 1961. **220**

Karp, S. A., *see* Witkin et al., 1959.

Katz, D., & Hyman, H., Morale in war industries. In Newcomb & Hartley, Eds., *Readings in social psychology.* N.Y.: Holt, 1947. **258**

Katz, D., & Kahn, R. L., *The social psychology of organizations.* N.Y.: Wiley, 1966. **181, 226, 289 294, 327, 315-316, 351**

Katz, D., & Stotland, E., A preliminary statement to a theory of attitude structure and change. In S. Koch, Ed., *Psychology: a study of a science. Vol. 3. Formulations of the person and the social context.* N.Y.: McGraw-Hill, 1959. **71**

Katz, F. M., The meaning of success: some differences in value systems of social classes. *J. soc. Psychol.*, 1964, **62**, 141-148. **157**

Katz, Phyllis, & Zigler, E., Self-image disparity. *J. pers. soc. Psychol.*, 1967, **5**, 186-195. **189-190**

Kavanau, J. L., Behavior of captive white-footed mice. *Science*, 1967, **155**, 1623-1639. **24**

Kelley, H. H., *see* Thibaut & Kelley, and Shomer et al.

Kelley, J. G., Ferson, Jean E., & Holtzman, W. H., The measurement of attitudes toward the Negro in the South. *J. soc. Psychol.*, 1958, **48**, 305-317. **75**

Kelman, H. C., & Barclay, J., The F scale as a measure of breadth of perspective. *J. abnorm. soc. Psychol.*, 1963, **67**, 608-615. **80**

Keniston, K., *see* Couch & Keniston.

Kenkel, W. F., *see* Coombs & Kenkel.

Kent, Grace H., & Rosanoff, A. J., A study of association in insanity. I. Association in normal subjects. *Amer. J. Insanity*, 1910, **67**, 37-96, 317-390. **237**

Kiessling, R. J., & Kalish, R. A., Correlates of success in leaderless group discussion. *J. soc. Psychol.*, 1961, **54**, 359-365. **297**

Kipnis, Dorothy M., Changes in self concepts in relation to perceptions of others. *J. Pers.*, 1961, **29**, 449-465. **120-121**

Klineberg, O., & Christie, R., Eds., *Perspectives in social psychology.* N.Y.: Holt, Rinehart, & Winston, 1965. **20**

Kluckhohn, C., *Mirror for man.* N.Y.: McGraw-Hill, 1949. **62**

Kluckhohn, C., Murray, H. A., & Schneider, D. M., Eds., *Personality in nature, society, and culture,* rev. ed. N.Y.: Knopf, 1953. **9**

Knapp, Deanne E., & Knapp, D., Effect of position on group verbal conditioning. *J. soc. Psychol.,* 1966, **69,** 95-99. **306**

Knapp, R. N., see McClelland et al., 1958.

Koff, R. H., Systematic changes in children's word-association norms, 1916-1963. *Child Developmt.,* 1965, **36,** 299-305. **237**

Kogan, N., *see* Wallach et al.

Kohn, M. L., Social class and the exercise of parental authority. *Amer. sociol. Rev.,* 1959, **24,** 352-366. **144-145**

Kohn, M. L., Social class and parent-child relationships: an interpretation. *Amer. J. Sociol.,* 1963, **68,** 471-480. **144-145, 157**

Kohn, M. L., & Carroll, Eleanor E., Social class and the allocation of parental responsibility. *Sociometry,* 1960, **23,** 372-392. **145**

Kölling, H., Gruppen in Wettwerb. *Z. Psychol.,* 1962, **166,** 119-128. **255**

Komorita, S. S., *see* Epstein & Komorita.

Kornhauser, A., *Mental health of the industrial worker.* N.Y.: Wiley, 1965, **330**

Krauss, R. M., & Deutsch, M., Communication in interpersonal bargaining. *J. pers. soc. Psychol.,* 1966, **4,** 572-577. **284**

Krauss, R. M., *see also* Deutsch & Krauss.

Krech, D., & Crutchfield, R. S., Theory and problems of social psychology. N.Y.: McGraw-Hill, 1948. **32**

Krech, D., Crutchfield, R. S., & Ballachey, E. L., *Individual in society.* N.Y.: McGraw-Hill, 1962. **100, 292**

Krech, D., *see also* Bennett et al.

Kristofferson, A. B., *see* Bailey et al.

Kuethe, J. L., *see* DeSoto et al.

Kuhlen, R. G., & Houlihan, Nancy., Adolescent heterosexual interest in 1942 and 1963. *Child Developmt.,* 1965, **36,** 1049-1052. **174**

Lachman, R., Tatsuoka, M., & Bonk, W. J., Human behavior during the tsunami of May. *Science,* 1960, **133,** 1405-1409. **213-215**

Lana, R., Vaughan, W., & McGinnies, E., Leadership and friendship status as factors in discussion group interaction. *J. soc. Psychol.,* 1960, **52,** 127-134. **291-292**

Langer, Elinor., Science in the mountains: NRAO astronomers to leave for city. *Science,* 1965, **150,** 722-724. **6**

LaPiere, R. T., Attitudes and actions. *Social Forces,* 1934, **13,** 230-237. **73**

Lawler, E. E., III, *see* Porter & Lawler.

Leavitt, H. J., Some effects of certain communication patterns on group performance. *J. abnorm. soc. Psychol.,* 1951, **46,** 38-50. **274-276**

Lehmann, I. J., Autobiography of a freshman class. *Measurement in education, yearbook of the National Council on Measurement in Education,* 1963, **20,** 115-123, **264**

Lehr, D. J., *see* Bergum & Lehr.

Lerner, M. J., *see* Baxter et al.

Lerner, M. J., & Simmons, Carolyn H., Observer's reaction to the "innocent victim": compassion or rejection. *J. pers. soc. Psychol.,* 1966, **4,** 203-210. **344**

Leventhal, H., & Niles, Patricia., A field experiment on fear arousal with data on the validity of questionnaire measures. *J. Pers.,* 1964, **32,** 459-479. **108**

Leventhal, H., & Watts, Jean C., Sources of resistance to fear-arousing communications on smoking and lung cancer. *J. Pers.,* 1966, **34,** 155-175. **108**

Leventhal, H., *see also* Dabbs & Leventhal.

Levin, L. A., *see* Triandis et al.

Levine, J., & Butler, J., Lecture vs. group decision in changing behavior. *J. appl. Psychol.,* 1952, **36,** 29-33. **326**

Levinger, G., & Breedlove, J., Interpersonal attraction and agreement: a study of marriage partners. *J. pers. soc. Psychol.,* 1966, **3,** 367-372. **121**

Levinson, D. H., *see* Adorno et al.

Lewin, K., *A dynamic theory of personality.* N.Y.: McGraw-Hill, 1935. **187**

Lewin, K., *Resolving social conflicts.* N.Y.: Harper, 1948. **188, 254**

Lewin, K., Group decision and social change. In Proshansky & Seidenberg, Eds., *Basic studies in social psychology.* N.Y.: Holt, Rinehart, & Winston, 1965. **325-326**

Lewin, K., Lippitt, R., & White, R. K., Patterns of aggression behavior in experimentally created "social climates." *J. soc. Psychol.,* 1939, **10,** 271-299. **12, 259, 276, 289**

Lewis, M., *see* Dowart et al.

Lieberman, S., The effects of changes in roles on the attitudes of role occupants. *Hum. Relat.,* 1956, **9,** 385-402. **178**

Likert, R., A technique for the measurement of attitudes. *Arch. Psychol.* (NY), 1932, **28,** No. 194. **75**

Likert, R., *New patterns of management.* N.Y.: McGraw-Hill, 1961. **323**

Linder, D. E., Cooper, J., & Jones, E. E., Decision freedom as a determinant of the role of incentive magnitude in attitude change. *J. pers. soc. Psychol.,* 1967, **6,** 245-254. **117**

Lindgren, H. C., *Effective leadership in human relations.* N.Y.: Hermitage, 1954. **292**

Lindgren, H. C., The semantic differential as a measure of perceptual set toward various countries. San Francisco State College, unpublished research, 1966. **236**

Lindgren, H. C., Brainstorming and the facilitation of creativity expressed in drawing. *Percept. Mot. Skills*, 1967, **24**, 350. **95**

Lindgren, H. C., & Lindgren, Fredrica, Expressed attitudes of American and Canadian teachers toward authority. *Psychol. Rep.*, 1960, **7**, 51-54. **296, 308**

Lindgren, H. C., & Lindgren, Fredrica, Brainstorming and orneriness as facilitators of creativity. *Psychol. Rep.*, 1965a, **16**, 577-583. **94, 271**

Lindgren, H. C., & Lindgren, Fredrica, Creativity, brainstorming, and orneriness: a cross-cultural study. *J. soc. Psychol.*, 1965b, **67**, 23-30. **94-95, 271**

Lindgren, H. C., & Mello, Maria Jorgiza, Emotional problems of over- and underachieving children in a Brazilian elementary school. *J. genet. Psychol.*, 1965, **106**, 59-65. **152**

Lindgren, H. C., *see also* Sallery & Lindgren.

Linton, H. B., Dependence on external influence: correlates in perception, attitudes, and judgment. *J. abnorm. soc. Psychol.*, 1955, **51**, 502-507. **195**

Linton, R., *The study of man*. N.Y.: Appleton-Century-Crofts, 1936. **161**

Linton, R., *The cultural background of personality*. N.Y.: Appleton-Century-Crofts, 1945. **13, 162**

Lippitt, R., *see* Lewin et al.

Lipset, S. M., Democracy and working-class authoritarianism. *Amer. sociol. Rev.*, 1959, **24**, 482-501. **153-154, 157**

Littig, L. W., & Yeracaris, C. A., Achievement motivation and intergenerational occupational mobility. *J. pers. soc. Psychol.*, 1965, **1**, 386-389. **84**

Litwin, G. H., *see* Meyer et al.

Livson, N., *see* Borum & Livson.

Lodahl, T. M., *see* Ghiselli & Lodahl.

Loeb, M. B., Implications of status differentiation for personal and social development. *Harvard educ. Rev.*, 1953, **23**, 160-174. **216**

Loh, W. D., *see* Triandis et al.

Lorenz, K., *On aggression*. (Trans. by Marjorie Kerr Wilson) N.Y.: Harcourt, Brace, & World, 1966. **335**

Lorge, I., *see* Tuckman & Lorge.

Lowell, E. L., *see* McClelland et al.

Maccoby, Eleanor E., *see* Goldberg & Maccoby.

MacKinnon, D. W., The nature and nurture of creative talent. *Amer. Psychologist*, 1962, **17**, 484-495. **197-198, 201**

MacKinnon, W. J., & Centers, R., Authoritarianism and urban stratification. *Amer. J. Sociol.*, 1956, **61**, 610-620. **153**

Maehr, M. H., *see* Haas & Maehr.

Maier, N. R. F., The quality of group decisions as influenced by the discussion leader. *Hum. Relat.*, 1950, **3**, 155-174. **272**

Maier, N. R. F., & Hayes, J. J., *Creative management*. N.Y.: Wiley, 1962. **330**

Maier, N. R. F., *see* Hoffman & Maier.

Malinowski, B., *The sexual life of savages in Northwestern Melanesia*. N.Y.: Eugenics, 1929. **13**

Mann, F. C., *see* Dubin et al.

Marcuse, F. L., *see* Fitzsimmons & Marcuse.

Markowitz, J., *see* Coopersmith et al.

Marlowe, D., *see* Minas et al.

Marrow, A. J., Managerial revolution in the State Department. *Personnel*, 1966, **43**(6), 2-12. **328**

Martin, R. B., *see* Goldman et al.

Maslow, A., *Motivation and personality*. N.Y.: Harper, 1954. **31, 80, 317-318**

Mason, W. S., *see* Gross et al.

Massarik, F., "Saying what you feel": reflections on personal openness in Japan. *International Understanding*, 1965, **2**(1). **328**

McCandless, B., *Children and adolescents*. N.Y.: Holt, Rinehart, & Winston, 1961. **148**

McClelland, D. C., *The achieving society*. Princeton: Van Nostrand, 1961. **83, 86-87, 89**

McClelland, D. C., N. achievement and entrepreneurship: a longitudinal study. *J. pers. soc. Psychol.*, 1965, **1**, 389-392. **84-85**

McClelland, D. C., & Atkinson, J. W., The projective expression of needs. I. The effect of different intensities of the hunger drive on perception. *J. Psychol.*, 1948, **25**, 205-222. **82**

McClelland, D. C., Atkinson, J. W., Clark, R. A., & Lowell, E. L., Eds., *The achievement motive*. N.Y.: Appleton-Century-Crofts, 1953. **82, 89**

McClelland, D. C., Sturr, J. F., Knapp, R. N., & Wendt, W. H., Obligations to self and society in the United States and Germany. *J. abnorm. soc. Psychol.*, 1958, **56**, 245-255. **217**

McClintock, C. G., Group support and the behavior of leaders and nonleaders. *J. abnorm. soc. Psychol.*, 1963, **67**, 105-113. **298**

McClintock, C. G., Gallo, P., & Harrison, A. A., Some effects of variations in other strategy upon game behavior. *J. pers. soc. Psychol.*, 1965, **1**, 319-325. **286**

McCord, Joan, McCord, W., & Howard A., Family interaction as antecedent to the direction of male aggressiveness. *J. abnorm. soc. Psychol.*, 1963, **66**, 239-242. **349**

McCormick, B. L. *see* Worchel & McCormick.

McDonald, F. J., *see* Bandura & McDonald.

McDonald, R. L., & Gynther, M. D., Relationship of

self and ideal-self descriptions with sex, race, and class in Southern adolescents. *J. pers. soc. Psychol.*, 1965, **1**, 85-88. **201**

McEachern, A. W., *see* Gross et al.

McGinnies, E., *see* Lana et al.

McGrath, J. E., The influence of positive interpersonal relations on adjustment and effectiveness in rifle teams. *J. abnorm. soc. Psychol.*, 1962, **65**, 365-375. **256**

McGraw, C., *see* Byrne & McGraw.

McGuire, W. J., Attitudes and opinions. In Farnsworth, McNemar, & McNemar, Eds., *Annual review of psychology*. Palo Alto: Annual Reviews, 1966. **108-109, 121**

McMichael, R. E., *see* Grinder & McMichael.

McReynolds, P., A restricted conceptualization of human anxiety and motivation. *Psychol. Rep.*, 1956, **2**, 293-312. **29-30**

Mead, A. P., *see* Chance & Mead.

Mead, G. H., *Mind, self, and society*. Chicago: U. of Chicago Press, 1934. **187**

Mead, Margaret, *Growing up in New Guinea*. N.Y.: Morrow, 1930. **13**

Mead, Margaret, *Coming of age in Samoa*. N.Y.: Morrow, 1934. **13**

Mead, Margaret, *Sex and temperament in three primitive societies*. N.Y.: Morrow, 1935. **169, 178**

Mead, Margaret, *Male and female: a study of the sexes in a changing world*. N.Y.: Morrow, 1949. **13**

Mead, Margaret, & Wolfenstein, Martha, Eds., *Childhood in contemporary cultures*. Chicago: U. of Chicago Press, 1955. **220**

Meade, R. D., Achievement motivation, achievement, and psychological time. *J. abnorm. soc. Psychol.*, 1966, **4**, 577-580. **85**

Medlund, F. F., *see* Gordon & Medlund.

Meeker, M., *see* Warner et al.

Meer, S. J., Authoritarian attitudes and dreams. *J. abnorm. soc. Psychol.*, 1955, **51**, 74-78. **80**

Mello, Maria Jorgiza, *see* Lindgren & Mello.

Menninger, W. C., Recreation and mental health. *Recreation*, 1948, **42**, 340-346. **297**

Meresko, R., Rubin, M., Shontz, F. C., & Morrow, W. R., Rigidity of attitudes regarding personal habits and its ideological correlates. *J. abnorm. soc. Psychol.*, 1954, **49**, 89-93. **80**

Merton, R. K., *Social theory and social structure*. N.Y.: Free Press, 1957. **13, 178**

Metzner, E. L., *see* Zurcher et al.

Meuwese, W. A. T., *see* Fiedler & Meuwese.

Meyer, H. H., Walker, N. B., & Litwin, G. H., Motive patterns and risk preferences associated with entrepreneurship. *J. abnorm. soc. Psychol.*, 1961, **63**, 570-574. **84**

Milgram, S., Nationality and conformity. *Scient. Amer.*, 1961, **205**(6), 45-52. **209-210, 211, 241, 242**

Milgram, S., Behavioral study of obedience. *J. abnorm. soc. Psychol.*, 1963, **67**, 371-378. **341-342**

Milgram, S., Group pressure and action against a person. *J. abnorm. soc. Psychol.*, 1964, **69**, 137-143. **342-343**

Miller, D. C., *see* Dubin et al.

Miller, D. R., The study of social relationships: situation, identity, and social interaction. In S. Koch, Ed., *Psychology: a study of a science. Vol. 5. The process areas, the person, and some applied fields: their place in psychology and in science*. N.Y.: McGraw-Hill, 1963. **34, 47, 133, 161**

Miller, L. K., & Hamblin, R. L., Interdependence, differential rewarding, and productivity. *Amer. sociol. Rev.*, 1963, **28**, 768-778. **280**

Miller, N., Campbell, D. T., Twedt, Helen, & O'Connell, E. J., Similarity, contrast, and complementarity in friendship choices. *J. pers. soc. Psychol.*, 1966, **3**, 3-12. **51**

Miller, N. E., *see* Dollard et al.

Mills, J., *see* Aronson & Mills.

Minas, J. S., Scodel, A., Marlowe, D., & Rawson, H., Some descriptive aspects of two-person, non-zero-sum games. Part II. *J. Conflict Resolut.*, 1960, **4**, 193-197. **283**

Minturn, L., & Hitchcock, J. T., The Rajputs of Khalapur, India. In B. B. Whiting, Ed., *Six cultures: studies of child rearing*. N.Y.: Wiley, 1963. **63**

Mintz, A., Non-adaptive group behavior. *J. abnorm. soc. Psychol.*, 1951, **46**, 150-159. **278-280**

Mischel, W., Delay of gratification, need for achievement, and acquiescence in another culture. *J. abnorm. soc. Psychol.*, 1962, **62**, 543-552. **85**

Mischel, W., *see also* Grusec & Mischel.

Miyamoto, S. F., & Dornbusch, S. M., A test of interactionist hypotheses of self-conception. *Amer. J. Sociol.*, 1956, **61**, 399-403. **190**

Moberg, D. O., Church membership and personal adjustment in old age. *J. Geront.*, 1953a, **8**, 207-211. **298**

Moberg, D. O., Leadership in the church and personal adjustment in old age. *Sociol. Soc. Res.*, 1953b, **37**, 312-316. **298**

Montagu, M. F. A., *The direction of human development*. N.Y.: Harper, 1955. **335**

Moore, Mary, Aggression themes in a binocular rivalry situation. *J. pers. soc. Psychol.*, 1966, **3**, 685-688. **166**

Moore, R. W., *see* Brennan et al.

Moos, R. H., & Speisman, J. C., Group compatibility and productivity. *J. abnorm. soc. Psychol.*, 1962, **65**, 190-196. **256**

Moreno, J. L., *Who shall survive?* 2nd ed. Beacon, N.Y.: Beacon House, 1953. **49, 51**

Morrow, W. R., *see* Meresko et al.

Morse, Nancy, *Satisfactions in the white-collar job.* Ann Arbor: Survey Res. Center, 1953. **317**

Morse, Nancy C., & Reimer, E., The experimental change of a major organizational variable. *J. abnorm. soc. Psychol.,* 1956, **52,** 120-129. **323-324**

Moskos, C. C., Jr., Racial intergration in the armed forces. *Amer. J. Sociol.,* 1966, **72,** 132-148. **135**

Moulton, R. W., Effects of success and failure on levels of aspiration as related to achievement motives. *J. pers. soc. Psychol.,* 1965, **1,** 399-406. **89**

Mouren, P., Tatossian, A., Blumen, G., & Guin, P., La tentative de suicide du sujet jeune. *Annales médico-psychologiques,* 1966, **124**(1), 1-16. **237**

Mowrer, O. H., *see* Dollard et al.

Mulder, M., Communication structure, decision structure, and group performance. *Sociometry,* 1960, **23,** 1-14. **276**

Murray, H. A., et al., *Explorations in personality.* N.Y.: Oxford U. Press, 1938. **81**

Murray, H. A., *see also* Kluckhohn et al.

Natalicio, L., *see* Hereford et al.

Newcomb, T. M., *Personality and social change.* N.Y.: Dryden, 1943. **264**

Newcomb, T. M., *Social psychology.* N.Y.: Dryden, 1950. **32**

Newcomb, T. M., An approach to the study of communicative acts. *Psychol. Rev.,* 1953, **60,** 393-404. **122**

Newcomb, T. M., The prediction of interpersonal attraction. *Amer. Psychologist,* 1956, **11,** 575-586. **44**

Newcomb, T. M., *The acquaintanceship process.* N.Y.: Holt, Rinehart, & Winston, 1961. **18, 44, 51, 122, 123, 129**

Newcomb, T. M., Stabilities underlying changes in interpersonal attraction. *J. abnorm. soc. Psychol.,* 1963, **66,** 376-386. **44, 126-127**

Newcomb, T. M., *see also* Price et al.

Nicol, Elizabeth, *see* Roby et al.

Niles, Patricia, *see* Leventhal & Niles.

Norbeck, E., & De Vos, G., Japan. In F. L. K. Hsu. Ed., *Psychological anthropology: approaches to culture and personality.* Homewood, Ill.: Dorsey, 1961. **219**

O'Connell, E. J., *see* Miller et al.

Office of Strategic Services (OSS), *Assessment of men.* N.Y.: Rinehart, 1948. **271**

Opinion Research Corp., Industrial relations, policy, and action. *Opinion Index for Industry,* 1952, **10**(10), October. **325**

Osborn, A. F., *Applied imagination,* rev. ed. N.Y.: Scribner, 1957. **94**

Osgood, C. E., Psycholinguistics. In S. Koch, Ed., *Psychology: a study of a science. Vol. 6. Investigations of man as a socius.* N.Y.: McGraw-Hill, 1963. **233**

Osgood, C. E., Suci, G. J., & Tannenbaum, P. H., *The measurement of meaning.* Urbana: U. of Illinois Press, 1957. **236**

Page, E. B., Teacher comments and student performance: a seventy-four classroom experiment in social motivation. *J. educ. Psychol.,* 1958, **49,** 173-181. **55-56, 307**

Palmer, R. D., Birth order and identification. *J. consult. Psychol.,* 1966, **30,** 129-135. **185, 201**

Parsons, T., & Shils, E., Eds., *Toward a general theory of action.* Cambridge: Harvard U. Press, 1951. **13**

Parten, M. L., Social participation among preschool children. *J. abnorm. soc. Psychol.,* 1932, **27,** 243-269. **251**

Pearl, A., *see* Riessman et al.

Peck, R. F., A comparison of the value systems of Mexican and American youth. *Interamer. J. Psychol.,* 1967, **1,** 41-50. **220**

Peristiany, J. G., Ed., *Honour and shame: the values of Mediterranean society.* Chicago: U. of Chicago Press, 1966. **112**

Petrullo, L., & Bass, B. M., Eds., *Leadership and interpersonal behavior.* N.Y.: Holt, Rinehart, & Winston, 1961. **311**

Piaget, J., *The moral judgment of the child.* Glencoe, Ill.: The Free Press, 1948. **59**

Piers, G., & Singer, M., Shame and guilt: a psychoanalytic and a cultural study. Springfield, Ill.: Thomas, 1963. **109**

Plog, S. C., The disclosure of self in the United States and Germany. Unpublished paper read at annual convention of American Psychological Assn., Philadelphia, 1963. **219**

Plog, S. C., A literacy index for the mailbag. *J. appl. Psychol.,* 1966, **50,** 86-91. **229**

Porter, L. W., & Lawler, E. E., III., Properties of organization structure in relation to job attitudes and job behavior. *Psychol. Bull.,* 1965, **64,** 23-51. **322**

Porter, L. W., *see also* Haire et al.

Preston, M. G., & Heintz, R. K., Effects of participatory versus supervisory leadership on group judgment. *J. abnorm. soc. Psychol.,* 1949, **44,** 345-355. **306**

Price, K. O., Harburg, E., & Newcomb, T. M., Psychological balance in situations of negative interpersonal attitudes. *J. pers. soc. Psychol.,* 1966, **3,** 265-270. **126, 127**

Priest, R., & Sawyer, J., Proximity and peership: changing bases of interpersonal attraction. Unpublished paper read at annual convention, American Psychological Assn., Chicago, 1965. **49**

Prothro, E. T., Socialization and social class in a transitional society. *Child Developmt.*, 1966, **37**, 219-228. **145-146, 174**

Quinn, R. P., *see* Kahn et al.

Rapoport, A., & Chammah, A. M., *Prisoner's dilemma.* Ann Arbor: U. of Michigan Press, 1965. **286**

Rawson, H., *see* Minas et al.

Redlich, F. C., *see* Hollingshead & Redlich.

Reimer, E., *see* Morse & Reimer.

Reiss, I. L., Social class and campus dating. *Soc. Probl.*, 1965, **13**, 193-205. **44-45**

Retting, S., Group decision and predicted ethical risk taking. *J. pers. soc. Psychol.*, 1966, **3**, 629-633. **326**

Riessman, F., *The culturally deprived child.* N.Y.: Harper, 1962. **148**

Riessman, F., Cohen, J., & Pearl, A., Eds., *Mental health of the poor.* N.Y.: Free Press, 1964. **157**

Roberts, A. H., & Jessor, R., Authoritarianism, punitiveness, and perceived social status, *J. abnorm. soc. Psychol.*, 1958, **56**, 311-314. **80**

Roby, T. B., Nicol, Elizabeth, & Farrell, F. M., Group problem solving under two types of executive structure. *J. abnorm. soc. Psychol.*, 1963, **67**, 550-556. **276**

Roethlisberger, F. J., & Dickson, W. J., *Management and the worker.* Cambridge: Harvard U. Press, 1939. **299-300**

Rogers, C. R., *Client-centered therapy.* Boston: Houghton Mifflin, 1951. **188, 335**

Rogers, C. R., & Dymond, Rosalind, F., Eds., *Psychotherapy and personality change.* Chicago: U. of Chicago Press, 1954. **189**

Rokeach, M., *The open and closed mind.* N.Y.: Basic Books, 1960. **340-341**

Rosanoff, A. J., *see* Kent & Rosanoff.

Rosen, B. C., Race, ethnicity, and the achievement syndrome. *Amer. Sociol. Rev.*, 1959, **24**, 47-60. **152**

Rosen, B. C., & D'Andrade, R. G., The psychological origins of achievement motivation. *Sociometry*, 1959, **22**, 185-217. **85**

Rosenfeld, H. M., Approval-seeking and approval-inducing functions of verbal and nonverbal responses in the dyad. *J. pers. soc. Psychol.*, 1966, **4**, 597-605. **168**

Rosenfeld, H. M., *see also* Bechtel & Rosenfeld.

Rosenfeld, H. M., & Jackson, J., Temporal meditation of the similarity-attraction hypothesis. *J. Pers.*, 1965, **33**, 649-656. **47**

Rosenhan, D., *see* Dowart et al.

Rosenthal, R. A., *see* Kahn et al.

Rosenzweig, M. R., Word associations of French workmen: comparisons with associations of French students and American workmen and students. *J. verbal Learn. verbal. Behav.*, 1964, **3**, 57-69. **237-238**

Rosenzweig, M. R., *see also* Bennett et al.

Ross, Dorothea, Relationship between dependency, intentional learning, and incidental learning in preschool children. *J. pers. soc. Psychol.*, 1966, **4**, 374-381. **197**

Rottmann, L., *see* Walsten et al.

Rubel, M., *see* Wells et al.

Rubin, M., *see* Meresko et al.

Runkel, P. J., *see* Gage et al.

Russell, P. N., *see* Wilson & Russell.

Sallery, R. D. H., & Lindgren, H. C., Arab attitudes toward authority: a cross-cultural study. *J. soc. Psychol.*, 1966, **69**, 27-31. **296, 308**

Saltz, E., & Wickey, J., Resolutions of the liberal dilemma in the assassination of President Kennedy. *J. Pers.*, 1965, **33**, 636-648. **125**

Sample, J. A. & Wilson, T. R., Leader behavior, group productivity, and rating of least-preferred co-worker. *J. pers. soc. Psychol.*, 1965, **1**, 266-270. **303-305**

Sampson, E. E., Birth order, need achievement, and conformity. *J. abnorm. soc. Psychol.*, 1962, **64**, 155-159. **185**

Sampson, E. E., & Hancock, Francena, T., An examination of the relationship between ordinal position, personality, and conformity: an extension, replication, and partial verification. *J. pers. soc. Psychol.*, 1967, **5**, 398-407. **185**

Sanford, F. H., The use of a projective technique in attitude surveying. *Publ. Opin. Quart.*, 1951, **14**, 697-709. **76**

Sanford, R. N., *see* Adorno et al.

Sawyer, J., *see* Priest & Sawyer.

Schachter, S., Deviation, rejection, and communication. *J. abnorm. soc. Psychol.*, 1951, **46**, 190-207. **257**

Schachter, S., *The psychology of affiliation.* Stanford: Stanford U. Press, 1959. **36, 38, 44, 185**

Schachter, S., Birth order and sociometric choice. *J. abnorm. soc. Psychol.*, 1964, **68**, 453-456. **185**

Schachter, S., *see also* Festinger et al.

Schaffer, H. R., The onset of fear of strangers and the incongruity hypothesis. *J. child Psychol. Psychiat.*, 1966, **7**, 95-106. **335**

Schelling, T. C., *The strategy of conflict.* Cambridge: Harvard U. Press, 1960. **284**

Schneider, D. M., *see* Kluckhohn et al.

Schopler, J., & Bateson, N., A dependence interpretation of the effects of a severe initiation. *J. Pers.*, 1962, **30**, 633-649. **16**

Schuette, D., *see* Exline et al.

Schwitzgebel, R., & Schwitzgebel, R., Reduction of adolescent crime by a research method. *J. soc. Therapy*, 1961, **7**, 212-215. **347**

Scodel, A., *see* Minas et al.

Scott, J. P., *Aggression*. Chicago: U. of Chicago Press, 1958. **170**

Scott, W. A., Attitude change through reward of verbal behavior. *J. abnorm. soc. Psychol.*, 1957, **55**, 72-75. **56**

Sears, R. R., *see* Dollard et al.

Selz, N., *see* Hereford et al.

Sensenig, J., *see* Brehm & Sensenig.

Shaw, M. E., Some effects of problem complexity upon problem solution efficiency in different communication nets. *J. exper. Psychol.*, 1954, **48**, 211-217. **276**

Shaw, M. E., Communication networks. In L. Berkowitz, Ed., *Advances in experimental social psychology*, vol. 1. N.Y.: Academic, 1964. **276**

Shepard, C. R., *Small groups: some sociological perspectives*. San Francisco: Chandler, 1964. **267**

Sherif, M., A study of some social factors in perception. *Arch. Psychol.*, **1935**, No. 187. **12**

Sherif, M., *The psychology of social norms*. N.Y.: Harper, 1936. **95-96, 326**

Sherif, M., Social psychology: problems and trends in interdisciplinary relationships. In S. Koch, Ed., *Psychology a study of a science. Vol. 6. Investigations of man as a socius*. N.Y.: McGraw-Hill, 1963. **17, 64, 206**

Sherif, M., & Sherif, Carolyn W., *Groups in harmony and tension*. N.Y.: Harper, 1953. **17**

Sherif, M., et al., *Intergroup conflict and cooperation: the Robbers Cave Experiments*. Norman, Okla.: Institute of Group Relations, 1961. **17**

Shils, E., *see* Parsons & Shils.

Shomer, R. W., Davis, A. H., & Kelley, H. H., Threats and the development of coordination: further studies of the Deutsch and Krauss trucking game. *J. abnorm. soc. Psychol.*, 1966, **4**, 119-126. **284**

Shontz, F. C., *see* Meresko et al.

Showel, M., Interpersonal knowledge and rated leader potential. *J. abnorm. soc. Psychol.*, 1960, **61**, 87-92. **297**

Shuval, Judith T., Self-rejection among North African immigrants to Israel. *Israel Ann. Psychiat. relat. Discipl.*, 1966, **4**, 101-110. **155**

Simmons, Carolyn H., *see* Lerner & Simmons.

Singer, M., *see* Piers & Singer.

Singer, R. P., *The effects of fear-arousing communications on attitude change and behavior*. Unpublished PhD dissertation, U. of Connecticut, 1965. **108-109**

Skinner, B. H., *Science and human behavior*. N.Y.: Macmillan, 1953. **58**

Skinner, B. H., Operant behavior. *Amer. Psychologist*, 1963, **18**, 503-515. **57-58**

Skinner, J. C., Symptom and defense in contemporary Greece: a cross-cultural inquiry. *J. nerv. ment. Dis.*, 1966, **141**, 478-489. **211-212**

Slater, P. E., Role differentiation in small groups. *Amer. sociol. Rev.*, 1955, **20**, 300-310. **264**

Slesinger, J. A., *see* Bachman et al.

Slovic, P., Risk-taking in children: age and sex differences. *Child Developmt.*, 1966, **37**, 169-176. **165**

Smart, R. G., Social-group membership, leadership, and birth order. *J. soc. Psychol.*, 1965, **67**, 221-225. **186**

Smelser, W. T., Dominance as a factor in achievement and perception in cooperative problem solving interactions. *J. abnorm. soc. Psychol.*, 1961, **62**, 535-542. **272, 289**

Smith, C. G., *see* Bachman et al.

Smith, E. E., The effects of clear and unclear role expectations on group productivity. *J. abnorm. soc. Psychol.*, 1957, **55**, 213-217. **259**

Smith, E. E., The power of dissonance techniques to change attitudes. *Publ. Opin. Quart.*, 1961, **25**, 626-639. **5**

Smith, M. B., *see* Stein et al.

Smith, R. J., Explorations in nonconformity. *J. soc. Psychol.*, 1967, **71**, 133-150. **198-199**

Snoek, J. D., *see* Kahn et al.

Snygg, D., *see* Combs & Snygg.

Solomon, P., et al., Eds., *Sensory deprivation*. Cambridge: Harvard U. Press, 1961. **38**

Sonenschein, D. W., *see* Zurcher et al.

Speisman, J. C., *see* Moos & Speisman.

Spelt, D. K., The conditioning of the human fetus *in utero*. *J. exper. Psychol.*, 1948, **38**, 338-346. **61**

Spiro, M., Social systems, personality, and functional analysis. In B. Kaplan, Ed., *Studying personality cross-culturally*. Evanston: Row, Peterson, 1961. **109**

Spock, B., *Baby and child care*. N.Y.: Pocket Books, 1957. **144**

Stagner, R., *The psychology of industrial conflict*. N.Y.: Wiley, 1956. **353**

Stein, D. D., Hardyke, Jane A., & Smith, M. B., Race and belief: an open and shut case. *J. pers. soc. Psychol.*, 1965, **1**, 281-289. **341**

Stenning, W., *see* Hereford et al.

Stogdill, R. M., & Coons, A. E., *Leader behavior: its description and measurement*. Ohio State U., Bureau of Business Research Monogr. No. 88, 1957. **300-301**

Stotland, E., *see* Katz & Stotland, and Zander et al.

Sturr, J. F., *see* McClelland et al., 1958.

Suci, G. J., *see* Osgood et al.

Suedfeld, P., Birth order and volunteers for sensory deprivation. *J. abnorm. soc. Psychol.*, 1964, **68**, 195-196. **183**

Taft, R., Accuracy of empathic judgments of acquaintances and strangers. *J. pers. soc. Psychol.*, 1966, **3**, 600-604. **235**

Tannenbaum, P. H., Mediated generalization of attitude change via the principle of congruity. *J. pers. soc. Psychol.*, 1966, **3**, 493-499. **129**

Tannenbaum, P. H., *see also* Osgood et al.

Tatossian, A., *see* Mouren et al.

Tatsuoka, M., *see* Lachman et al.

Tatum, R., *see* Ader & Tatum.

Taylor, D. W., Berry, P. C., & Block, C. H., Does group participation when using brainstorming facilitate or inhibit creative thinking? *Admin. Sci. Quart.*, 1958, **3**, 23-47. **94, 271**

Tenenbaum, S., The teacher, the middle class, the lower class. *Phi Delta Kappan*, 1963, **45**, 82-86. **143, 148**

Terrell, G., *see* Wyer et al.

Terwilliger, R., *see* Janis & Terwilliger.

Thelen, H. A., *Dynamics of groups at work*. Chicago: U. of Chicago Press, 1954. **286**

Thelen, H. A., Exploration of a growth model for psychic, biological, and social systems. Unpublished paper, 1960. (As cited by Katz & Kahn, 1966) **226**

Thibaut, J. W., & Kelley, H. H., *The social psychology of groups*. N.Y.: Wiley, 1959. **249-250**

Thurstone, L. L., & Chave, E. J., *The measurement of attitudes*. Chicago: U. of Chicago Press, 1929. **75**

Thurstone, L. L., The influence of motion pictures on children's attitudes. *J. soc. Psychol.*, 1931, **2**, 291-305. **75**

Triandis, H. C., A note on Rokeach's theory of prejudice. *J. abnorm. soc. Psychol.*, 1961, **62**, 184-186. **340-341**

Triandis, H. C., Loh, W. D., & Levin, L. A., Race, status, quality of spoken English, and opinions about civil rights as determinants of interpersonal attitudes. *J. pers. soc. Psychol.*, 1966, **3**, 468-472. **229**

Tuckman, J., & Lorge, I., Individual ability as a determinant of group superiority. *Hum. Relat.*, 1962, **15**, 45-51. **271-272, 274**

Twedt, Helen, *see* Miller et al.

Ulibarri, H., Social and attitudinal characteristics of Spanish-speaking migrant and ex-migrant workers in the Southwest. *Sociol. soc. Res.*, 1966, **50**, 361-370. **154**

United Nations, *Demographic yearbook*. N.Y.: United Nations, 1965. **337-338**

Valins, S., Cognitive effects of false heart rate feedback. *J. pers. soc. Psychol.*, 1966, **4**, 400-408. **241**

Vaughan, W., *see* Lana et al.

Verba, S., *see* Almond & Verba.

Veroff, J., *see* Gurin et al.

Vidulich, R. N., & Bayley, G. A., A general field experimental technique for studying social influence. *J. soc. Psychol.*, 1966, **69**, 253-263. **306**

Walker, N. B., *see* Meyer et al.

Wallace, J., Role reward and dissonance reduction. *J. pers. soc. Psychol.*, 1966, **3**, 305-312. **118**

Wallach, M. A., Kogan, N., & Bem, D. J., Diffusion of responsibility and level of risk taking in groups. *J. abnorm. soc. Psychol.*, 1964, **68**, 263-274. **326**

Walster, Elaine, Aronson, Vera, Abrahams, Darcy, & Rottmann, L., Importance of physical attractiveness in dating behavior. *J. pers. soc. Psychol.*, 1966, **4**, 508-516. **42-43**

Warner, W. L., & Abegglen, J. C., *Big business leaders in America*. N.Y.: Harper, 1955. **135**

Warner, W. L., & Lunt, P. S., *The social life of a modern community*. New Haven: Yale U. Press, 1941. **13, 16, 136, 138, 141**

Warner, W. L., Meeker, M., & Eells, K., *Social class in America*. Chicago: Science Research Assoc., 1949. **13**

Watts, Jean C., *see* Leventhal & Watts.

Weatherly, D. A., *see* Wyer et al.

Weber, M., *The theory of social and economic organization*. (Trans. by A. M. Henderson and T. Parsons). T. Parsons, Ed., N.Y.: Free Press, 1947. **293, 315**

Weiner, B., Need achievement and the resumption of incompleted tasks. *J. pers. soc. Psychol.*, 1965, **1**, 165-168. **85**

Weinert, G., *see* Wells et al.

Weisenberg, M., *see* Zimbardo et al.

Weiss, R. L., Some determinants of emitted reinforcing behavior: listener reinforcement and birth order. *J. pers. soc. Psychol.*, 1966, **3**, 489-492. **186**

Wells, W. D., Chiaravallo, G., & Goldman, S., Brothers under the skin: a validity test of the F scale. *J. soc. Psychol.*, 1957, **45**, 35-40. **80**

Wells, W. D., Weinert, G., & Rubel, M., Conformity pressure and authoritarian personality. *J. Psychol.*, 1956, **42**, 133-136. **101**

Wendt, W. H., *see* McClelland et al., 1958.

Westby-Gibson, Dorothy, *Social perspectives on education*. N.Y.: Wiley, 1965. **148**

White, R. K., *see* Lewin et al.

Whiting, Beatrice B., Ed., *Six cultures: studies of child rearing*. N.Y.: Wiley, 1963. **67**

Whiting, J. W. M., & Whiting, Beatrice B., Contributions of anthropology to the methods of studying child rearing. In P. H. Mussen, Ed., *Handbook of research methods in child development*. N.Y.: Wiley, 1960. **207**

Whorf, B. L., *Four articles on metalinguistics*. Washington: Foreign Service Institute, 1950. **232**

Whorf, B. L., *Language, thought, and reality*. (J. B. Carroll, Ed.) Cambridge, Mass.: Technology Press, 1956. **232**

Whyte, W. H., Jr., *The organization man.* N.Y.: Simon & Schuster, 1956. **48**

Wiener, N., *The human use of human beings: cybernetics and society.* Boston: Houghton Mifflin, 1950. **240**

Wilensky, H. L., Class, class consciousness and American workers. In W. Haber, Ed., *Labor in a changing America.* N.Y.: Basic Books, 1966. **141-142, 157**

Willis, F. N. Jr., Initial speaking distance as a function of the speaker's relationship. *Psychonomic Science,* 1966, **5**, 221-222. **229-230**

Wilson, K. V., *see* Bixenstine & Wilson.

Wilson, P. R., & Russell, P. N., Modification of psychophysical judgments as a method of reducing dissonance. *J. pers. soc. Psychol.,* 1966, **3**, 710-712. **118**

Wilson, R. H. L., *see* Farber & Wilson.

Wilson, R. S., Personality patterns, source attractiveness, and conformity. *J. Pers.,* 1960, **28**, 186-199. **298**

Wilson, T. R., *see* Sample & Wilson.

Winch, R. F., *Mate-selection: a study of complementary needs.* N.Y.: Harper, 1958. **47, 51**

Witkin, H. A., Karp, S. A., & Goodenough, D. R., Dependence in alcoholics. *Quart. J. Stud. Alcohol,* 1959, **20**, 493-504. **195**

Witkin, H. A., et al. *Personality through perception.* N.Y.: Harper, 1954. **194-195**

Witkin, H. A., et al., *Psychological differentiation.* N.Y.: Wiley, 1962. **194-195**

Witryol, S. L., & Kaess, W. A., Sex differences in social memory tasks. *J. abnorm. soc. Psychol.,* 1957, **54**, 343-346. **168**

Wolfe, D. M., *see* Kahn et al., and Zander et al.

Wolfenstein, Martha, French parents take their children to the park. In Mead & Wolfenstein, Eds., *Childhood in contemporary cultures.* Chicago: U. of Chicago Press, 1955. **208**

Wolfenstein, Martha, *see also* Mead & Wolfenstein.

Wolman, B. B., Impact of failure on group cohesiveness. *J. soc. Psychol.,* 1960, **51**, 409-418. **256**

Wong, T. J., *see* Byrne & Wong.

Woodworth, D. G., *see* Crutchfield et al.

Worchel, P., & Byrne, D., Eds., *Personality change.* N.Y.: Wiley, 1964. **201**

Worchel, P., & McCormick, B. L., Self-concept and dissonance reduction. *J. Pers.,* 1963, **31**, 588-599. **44**

Wrightsman, L. S., Jr., Effects of waiting with others on changes in levels of felt anxiety. *J. abnorm. soc. Psychol.,* 1960, **61**, 216-222. **36, 183**

Wrightsman, L. S., Jr., Personality and attitudinal correlates of trusting and trustworthy behaviors in a two-person game. *J. pers. soc. Psychol.,* 1966, **4**, 328-332. **283, 284**

Wuebben, P. L., Honesty of subjects and birth order. *J. pers. soc. Psychol.,* 1967, **5**, 350-352. **186**

Wunderlich, R., *see* De Soto et al.

Wyer, R. S., Jr., Effects of incentive to perform well, group attraction, and group acceptance on conformity in a judgmental task. *J. pers. soc. Psychol.,* 1966, **4**, 21-26. **101**

Wyer, R. S., Weatherly, D. A., & Terrell, G., Social role, aggression, and academic achievement. *J. abnorm. soc. Psychol.,* 1965, **1**, 645-649. **166**

Yates, A. J., *Frustration and conflict.* N.Y.: Wiley, 1962. **353**

Yeraceris, C. A., *see* Littig & Yeraceris.

Yerkes, R. M., & Dodson, J. D., The relation of strength of stimulus to rapidity of habit-formation. *J. comp. Neurol. Psychol.,* 1908, **18**, 459-482. **30**

Zajonc, R. B., *Social facilitation. Science,* 1965, **149**, 269-274. **60, 93-94**

Zajonc, R. B., *Social psychology: an experimental approach.* Belmont, Calif.: Wadsworth, 1966. **7**

Zander, A., Stotland, E., & Wolfe, D., Unity of groups, identification with group, and self-esteem of members. *J. Pers.,* 1960, **28**, 463-478. **256**

Zander, A., *see also* Cartwright & Zander.

Zempleni, A., *see* Collomb et al.

Zigler, E., *see* Katz & Zigler.

Ziller, R. C., Behringer, R. D., & Goodchilds, J. D., Group creativity under conditions of success or failure and variation in group stability. *J. appl. Psychol.,* 1962, **46**, 43-49. **252**

Zimbardo, P. G., Cohen, A. R., Weisenberg, M., & Firestone, I., Control of pain motivation by cognitive dissonance. *Science,* 1966, **151**, 217-219. **119**

Zurcher, L. A., Jr., Sonenschein, D. W., & Metzner, E. L., The hasher: a study in role conflict. *Social Forces,* 1966, **44**, 505-514. **176-177**

Subject Index